PUSHKIN
ON
LITERATURE

————◆◆◆◆◆————

ω

PUSHKIN
ON
LITERATURE

selected, translated and edited by
TATIANA WOLFF

Revised Edition
with an Introductory Essay by
JOHN BAYLEY

THE ATHLONE PRESS

LONDON

Revised edition first published in Great Britain 1986 by
The Athlone Press, 1 Park Drive, London NW11 7SG
Reprinted 1998

© 1971, 1986 Tatiana Wolff
© 1986 John Bayley, 'In Search of Pushkin'

ISBN 0-485-12135-2 pb

Printed in the United States of America

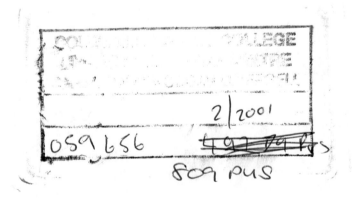

To my father
in memory of my mother

————◆◆◆◆◆————

CONTENTS

ILLUSTRATIONS

2 and 17 are reproduced by courtesy of the British Library

PREFACE

What the hammer? What the chain?
In what furnace was the brain?
What the anvil? What dread grasp
Dare its deadly terrors clasp?

William Blake

It is a privilege to be invited into an artist's workshop, to find oneself surrounded by his rough drafts, his sketches, his work in progress. It affords a rare opportunity to observe the processes of art, to see how new forms are created and new ideas expressed. The aim of this book is to open the door for English readers into Pushkin's workshop, so as to show with what fusing passion he gathered into himself the literary experiences of many cultures and then achieved in his own work something entirely original, which combines the Renaissance spirit of expansion and exploration with classical control and sense of proportion, the individualism of Romanticism with the social realism of the nineteenth century. In his work Russian literature caught up with the rest of Europe and Russian as a language became a tool of the finest flexibility.

Pushkin's position in Russia is supreme, a fact that still represents an enigma to English readers. A wide gulf is fixed between his reputation in Russia and abroad. Pushkin's poetry and plays translate badly; his prose is out of scale when set beside that of later Russian novelists. For years, outside Russia he was reduced to little more than a librettist for Russian nineteenth-century composers and 'based on the work of Alexander Pushkin' in numberless opera programmes seemed his chief claim to fame. *Ruslan and Lyudmila, Evgeny Onegin, Boris Godunov, The Queen of Spades, The Golden Cockerel*, meant Glinka, Tchaikovsky, Mussorgsky and Rimsky-Korsakov, rather than Pushkin. With the rise of interest in comparative literature a new niche was found for him: 'Russia's Byron'. Had this been said at the beginning of the nineteenth century, when Byron blazed like a sun in European eyes, it would have been understandable; but it was said when Byron himself had been allotted a modest position in the English poetic hierarchy, only just holding his own as a major poet. Pushkin had passed with second-class honours. This label is misleading and inadequate, and the problem remains. Russians speak about him with one voice: from Tolstoy to Pasternak, from Blok to Anna Akhmatova, old and young, emigré and Soviet, they read him and they quote him and they write about him tirelessly; and the rest, unless they know Russian, mostly remain un-convinced and pay polite lip-service.

This book attempts to look at Pushkin in a different way. It tries to catch the man as he works, to follow him through his life, listening in as he talks and criticizes and shouts with joy or frustration, accepts one thing with passionate enthusiasm and rejects another with impatient dismissal. A book very similar in plan to this was published in Russia by N. N. Bogoslovsky in 1950 called *Pushkin – Critic* and in 1962 it was reissued with a new title: *A. S. Pushkin on Literature*. The change of title was important and right, for it avoids creating a false impression and consequent dissatisfaction. Pushkin was never a systematic critic of literature; he was not detached enough for the role. All he wrote reflects his own needs as a writer, and his comments are no less valuable for that. However, if one is led to expect something from him which is scholarly, accurate, rounded-off, one may well be disappointed; for he was volatile in judgement, casual about detail, and rarely bothered to draw his articles to a conclusion. The finished products are his own works; these comments are the sparks that flew off in the process of creation.

Pushkin very rarely published replies to his critics, but he often dashed them off for his own satisfaction and when he embarked on a new form – a 'Shakespearian' tragedy or a novel in verse – he used to define his aims and clarify his thoughts by drafting prefaces. All these contain nuggets. Though they have often been quoted from they have never been fully translated before; yet the personality of the man emerges only when all these pieces are put together, the brilliant and perceptive with the hasty and wayward.

For the same reason – to get as near as possible to the full man – these articles, prefaces and notes have to be set side by side with what Pushkin wrote of literature in his letters. The circumstances of his life were such that a great deal of what he normally would have said to friends and fellow writers had to be written to them. However he rarely gave a whole letter over to thoughts on literature: these jostle among

xiv

the gossip and small talk of day-to-day affairs and have to be extracted from a thicket of proper names and highly improper allusions, sometimes of such outspoken coarseness that Russian editors resort to rows of dots.

Here again English readers, brought up on Keats and Coleridge, face disappointment. Reviewing the English edition of Pushkin's letters Ted Hughes wrote:

> we inevitably come for confidences and a tour of the poetic works, as we do to Keats. Pushkin gives nothing away. He is always visiting you on brisk business. Or if you visit him, he's always somehow showing you the door, in a delightful manner. Frank and direct, not meandering but seizing one thing after another and laying it cleanly open, yet playful. But brief; and nothing much has been said. (*The Listener*, 1 October 1964.)

It is the 'nothing much' that is relative; and even while he voices his disappointment Ted Hughes has touched on the important point that Pushkin lays whatever he seizes upon 'cleanly open'. The acute penetration is very rewarding and compensates for the lack of extended analysis.

Ted Hughes's reactions to Pushkin are important for they are a poet's response. For the same reason Pushkin's reactions to all the writers he wrote about are important. Speaking of the many possible approaches to the study of Shakespeare, Una Ellis-Fermor stressed the particular value of that of fellow poets: 'Keats or Pushkin making an imaginative exploration with passion, wonder and awe, may in the fullest sense of the word be said to "study" Shakespeare, every resource of intellect and imagination, such as only another poet can bring, dedicated to the re-examining of his seemingly limitless imaginative experience.' (*The Study of Shakespeare*, 1948.) There is another quality which deserves attention: the total commitment to literature which one feels in all that Pushkin wrote. However agitated his life was, when he was writing no social or political pressures were allowed to intrude. This sort of dedication is both valuable and rare. Virginia Woolf has described it in an essay on the critic Walter Raleigh (1926):

> When we read the letters of Keats, the diary of the Goncourts, the letters of Lamb, the casual remarks of that unfashionable poet Tennyson, we feel that, waking or sleeping, these men never stopped thinking about literature. It is kneaded into the stuff of their brains. Their fingers are dyed in it. Whatever they touch is stained by it. Whatever they are doing their minds fill up involuntarily with some aspect of the absorbing question.

Taste in literature changes – Tennyson is no longer 'unfashionable' –
but the basic truth remains, that there are some men who are of the
very stuff of literature, and Pushkin is undoubtedly of their company.

Comparative literature is a branch of study which can easily become
parasitic. A student of literature writing on Pushkin writing on Chateaubriand's translation of Milton's *Paradise Lost* sounds like poetry at third
remove; and when that student of literature comes in his turn to be
criticized, poetry itself will probably have flown out of the window.
But the breaking down of boundaries between national literatures can
be productive and life-giving, and Pushkin's defence of Milton against
the misrepresentation of him by French Romantic writers is a valuable
reminder that poetic empathy transcends differences of time and place
(see pages 452-61 and 486). Victor Zhirmunsky, a leading Soviet scholar
of comparative literature, has pointed out the similarity between Goethe
and Pushkin in the sustenance they drew from the literature of many
countries. It was a 'creative assimilation of classical, oriental, Western
European and Slavonic literatures and folklores, which he recreated
(much as Goethe did) in new poetical compositions which were both
highly personal and national in character' ('On the Study of Comparative Literature', 1967).

The plan of this book is chronological, in order that Pushkin's
literary development should stand out clearly. The selection is comprehensive: only those articles and notes have been left out which deal
with Russian authors little known in England or which involve the
verbal analysis of poems, the point of which would be lost in translation. The articles which Pushkin wrote for his review *Sovremennik*, when
at long last he was allowed to publish it, are nearly all given in full –
even the unwieldy one on John Tanner; they show how chance con-
tingencies controlled his choice of theme at the one period of his life
when he wrote regular literary criticism for a public. A mixed bag of
books presented themselves for review, but in writing of them he nearly
always managed to touch on some fundamental issue or to include
some wryly ironic aside, which illuminates his view of the human condition. Many of Pushkin's comments on his conflicts with the censorship
have also been included, for these show only too clearly the difficult
conditions under which Russian writers have always worked.

I have made no attempt to assess the quality of Pushkin's criticism.
This would require a range of literary knowledge comparable to his.

In an article published in *Shakespeare Survey V* (1952) I attempted to
assess the importance of Shakespeare in Pushkin's development, but I
am in no position to do the same for all the other authors of which he
wrote. I have also made no attempt to write a full life of Pushkin or
a study of his creative work. However, biographical introductions to
each section are included so as to give a frame of reference to the
extracts, and all that is mentioned in them is relevant to these extracts.
A Field Marshal's dress uniform is provided with a discreet row of
hooks on which to hang his medals: these introductions are the hooks,
the medals are Pushkin's.

My chief aim has been to let Pushkin speak for himself in the intimacy of his study; to try to catch the relaxed, casual tone of his letters
and notebooks. Translation presented some difficulties. Russian men
use endearments to each other which sound affected in English; other
nuances, such as exist, for instance, between the use of 'you' and 'thou',
are inevitably lost; it is difficult to steer a course between Regency
pastiche (Byron again) and modern colloquialisms, which fall oddly
from Pushkin's lips, while, on the other hand, to render his writing too
formally would be to spoil its life and flavour.

Alexander Blok chose 'gaiety' as Pushkin's outstanding quality
when he spoke on the 84th anniversary of his death in 1921, when
Russia was in post-Revolutionary travail. On the same day, in one of
the last poems he wrote, he called on Pushkin to sustain his country
with his joy in time of tempest, as he had always done. Pushkin's spirit
never fail to sustain.

ACKNOWLEDGEMENTS

This book has been a long time in the making and there are many debts of gratitude to pay, stretching over the years. It was begun in the summer of 1947 on the suggestion of the late Professor Una Ellis-Fermor and the late Professor Vivian da Sola Pinto, who both urged me to translate this material, much of which was not available in any language other than Russian. At that early stage I was also much helped by the encouragement of the late Mr Alexander Halpern and by Sir Maurice Bowra. It was then, too, when I was first planning the edition, that I met Professor Henry Gifford, who was working in the same field and who generously changed his own plans to fit in with mine, and he has remained a valued friend and ally ever since.

I would like to acknowledge a debt to the Editors of the USSR Academy of Sciences editions of Pushkin, which I have used as a basis for all my work; to N. N. Bogoslovsky, the plan of whose book *Pushkin – Critic* (Moscow, 1950) has influenced that of mine; and to Professor Ernest J. Simmons, Monsieur Henri Troyat and Dr J. Thomas Shaw, to whose works on Pushkin I have also constantly referred.

I would like to thank the Director of the All-Union A. S. Pushkin Museum in Leningrad, Marina N. Petai, and her Staff, particularly Mr S. Landa who helped with the selection of photographs, for their generosity in supplying me with practically all the illustrations for this volume. I would also like to express my appreciation for all the help I have received from the staff of the North Library of the British Museum and for the shelf-room I was afforded there over a long period.

It is impossible to name all the friends who have contributed many valuable suggestions but I would like particularly to thank Mrs Elizabeth Obolensky, who read many of the translations in the early stages of the work, Dr John Bayley and Mr David Castillejo, who both read extensive sections of the manuscript, and Mrs Irene Andrews, who has been a tireless and encouraging typist.

There is one further acknowledgement to make and that is to my father. He has been involved from the book's inception to its final word. For his unflagging help and enthusiasm, I offer my thanks and my love.

1971

Revised edition

It is with the greatest pleasure and gratitude that I welcome the addition of John Bayley's Introductory essay 'In Search of Pushkin' to this revised edition of *Pushkin on Literature*. His Comparative Commentary, *Pushkin*, came out at the same time as the first edition and we were brought together in many reviews. It is therefore a particularly happy circumstance to be 'on board' together this time.

1986   T.W.

EDITOR'S NOTE

The dating throughout the correspondence follows the Julian calendar used in Russia up to the Revolution, which in the nineteenth century was twelve days in arrear of the Gregorian calendar.

The transliteration of Russian names and titles follows the scheme recommended by the British Academy, with some minor modifications. Certain names which have become familiar in a form that is not consistent with this scheme have been kept in their familiar form: for example, Alexander, Evgeny and Tatiana have been used in preference to Aleksandr, Yevgeny and Tatyana. The names of monarchs and of capital cities have been anglicized. In formal contexts, as in letter-headings, the full name St Petersburg is used, but when referred to in letters it appears as Petersburg. All Russian reviews are referred to by their Russian names. A list of these names with their English equivalents follows below.

Ateney	Athenaeum
Aziatsky Vestnik	Asiatic Messenger
Biblioteka dlya Chteniya	Library for Reading
Blagonamerenny	Well-Intentioned
Damsky Zhurnal	Ladies' Journal
Dennitsa	Dawn
Detskaya Biblioteka	Children's Library
Evropeets	European
Literaturnaya Gazeta	Literary Newspaper
Literaturny Muzey	Literary Museum
Literaturnye Listki	Literary Pages
Mnemozina	Mnemosyne
Moskovskie Vedomosti	Moscow News
Moskovsky Nablyudatel	Moscow Observer
Moskovsky Telegraph	Moscow Telegraph
Moskovsky Vestnik	Moscow Messenger
Nevsky Almanakh	Nevsky Almanac
Nevsky Zritel	Nevsky Viewer
Novosti Literatury	Literary News
Polyarnaya Zvezda	Polar Star
Russkaya Starina	Russian Antiquity

Russkaya Talia	Russian Thalia
Russky Arkhiv	Russian Archive
Russky Invalid	Russian Invalid
Severnaya Lira	Northern Lyre
Severnaya Pchela	Northern Bee
Severny Arkhiv	Northern Archive
Severny Merkuri	Northern Mercury
Severnye Tsvety	Northern Flowers
Sibirsky Vestnik	Siberian Messenger
Sovremennik	Contemporary
Syn Otechestva	Son of the Fatherland
Talia (see Russkaya Talia)	Thalia (see Russian Thalia)
Teleskop	Telescope
Tiflisskie Vedomosti	Tiflis News
Trudy Volnovo Obshchestva	Publications of the Free
Rossyskoy Slovesnosti	Society of Russian
	Literature
Uraniya	Urania
Vestnik Evropy	Messenger of Europe

BIBLIOGRAPHY – THE BICENTENNIAL EDITION

ENGLISH TRANSLATIONS OF SELECTIONS AND OF INDIVIDUAL WORKS

PUSHKIN, A. S. *Alexander Pushkin*. Selected and edited by A. D. P. Briggs. Everyman Paperbacks, 1997.
—— *Alexander Pushkin. Collected Narrative and Lyrical Poetry*. Translated in the Prosodic Forms of the Original by Walter Arndt. Ann Arbor, 1984
—— *Eugene Onegin*. Translated by James E. Falen. World's Classics series, O.U.P., 1995.

COLLECTIONS OF ARTICLES AND WORKS OF REFERENCE

The Complete Working Notebooks of Alexander Pushkin, in 8 volumes. Published by the Institute of Russian Literature (Pushkinskii Dom) of the Russian Academy of Sciences and the St Petersburg Partnership Consortium, 1995.
'Mir Pushkina', Pisma O. S. Pavlishchevoy k muzhu i ottsu 1831–1837. St Petersburg, 1994.
TSYAVLOVSKII, M. A. *Letopis zhizni i tvorchestva A.S. Pushkina 1799–1826*. Izdanie 2-oe, Leningrad 1991.
VATSURO, V. E. *Pushkin i kniga*. Moscow, 1982.
—— *Zapiski Komentatora*. St Petersburg, 1994.
VOLKOV, PAVEL (REDAKTOR) *Boldino. Osen 1830 Photoliteraturnaya kompositsiya*. Moscow, 1989.

WOLFF, TATIANA *Pushkin and English Literature : A Creative Response*. First Pushkin Lecture, delivered at Queen's University, Belfast on 10 October 1990.

BOOKS ON PUSHKIN, BOTH LIFE AND WORKS

ABRAMOVICH, S. *Poslednii god*. Khronika. Moscow, 1991.
—— *Pushkin v 1833 godu*. Khronika. Moscow, 1994.

BETHEA, DAVID M. (Ed.) *Pushkin Today*. Indiana University Press, 1993.

BRIGGS, A. D. P. *Eugene Onegin*. C.U.P., Landmarks of World Literature Series, 1992.

CLAYTON, J. DOUGLAS *Ice and Flame*. Aleksandr Pushkin's *Eugene Onegin*. University of Toronto Press, 1985.

CORNWELL, NEIL *Pushkin's The Queen of Spades*. Bristol Critical Studies in Russian Literature, 1993.

DALTON-BROWN, S. *Pushkin's Evgenii Onegin*. Bristol Critical Studies in Russian Literature, 1997.

DEBRECZENY, P. *Social Functions of Literature. Alexander Pushkin and Russian Culture*. Stanford, 1997.

EDMONDS, ROBIN *Pushkin. The Man and His Age*. London, 1994.

EIDELMAN, N. YA. *Pushkin. Iz biografii i tvorchestva 1826–1837*. Moscow, 1987.

FOMICHEV, S. A. *A.S. Pushkin Boris Godunov*. Kommentarii U. M. Lotman i S. A. Fomichev. St Petersburg, 1996.

GREENLEAF, MONIKA *Pushkin and Romantic Fashion*. Fragment, Elegy, Orient, Irony. Stanford University Press, 1994.

HOISINGTON, SONA STEPHAN (Trans. and ed. with introduction and notes) *Russian Views of Pushkin's* Eugene Onegin (Verse passages translated by Walter Arndt). Indiana University Press, 1988.

IEZUITIVA, R. V. & LEVKOVICH, YA. A. *Pushkin v Peterburge*. Leningrad, 1991.

KERTSELLI, LARISA *Mir Pushkina v evo Risunkakh*. Moscow, 1988.

KUNINA, V. V. *Poslednii god zhizni Pushkina*. Perepiska. Vospominaniya. Dnevniki. Moscow, 1990.

LOTMAN, U. M. *Pushkin. Biografiya pisatelya*. Stati i Zametki 1960–1990. *Evgenii Onegin* Kommentarii. St Petersburg, 1995.

PETRUNINA, N. N. *Proza Pushkina*. Leningrad, 1987.

SHAW, J. THOMAS *Pushkin. Poet and Man of Letters and his Prose*, Collected Works, Volume 1. Los Angeles, 1995.
—— *Pushkin Poems and Other Studies*, Collected Works, Volume 2. Los Angeles, 1996.

TODD, WILLIAM MILLS III *Fiction and Society in the Age of Pushkin*. Ideology, Institutions, and Narrative. Harvard University Press, 1986.

VAN SAMBEEK-WEIDELI, BEATRICE *Evgenii Onegin*. A. S. Pushkina Bibliografiya. Peter Lang, Bern, Frankfurt am Main, New York, Paris, 1990.

IN SEARCH OF PUSHKIN

'Perhaps I am elegant and dignified in my writing,' Pushkin once wrote to a young female admirer, 'but my heart is that of a completely common fellow.' The more one thinks about it the more one feels what an arresting comment that is. Of course Pushkin is making a joke – a joke about himself – and a characteristic one. But is it possible to imagine any other poet of the time – even Byron – saying such a thing? From Schiller and Wordsworth to Keats and Chateaubriand the romantic writers took it for granted that their hearts, their feelings, their souls and sensibilities, were all at one in what they wrote. And that is an assumption – a convention perhaps one should call it – which is still with us today. 'One life – one writing,' claims the poet Robert Lowell, identifying himself with his work in an American romantic tradition of which Walt Whitman had been the great spokesman. But Pushkin, at the height of the romantic era, casually suggests something quite different: that the artist and the man are, in his case, divided. And this in turn indicates another division: that the artist is both creator of literature and objective critic of it.

That flippant remark in a letter to an adoring young female contains, in fact, an important clue to the reason why Pushkin was such a good critic, as well as being a great poet. And it may well be the best thing to approach him first *as* a critic, rather than as a great poet. It is notoriously difficult for a reader who does not read Russian, even if he is a lover of poetry, to see why Pushkin's poetry is so good. But where Pushkin on literature is concerned there is no such problem. Even in translation, his sense of it is dazzling, unmistakable. He knows at once and by instinct what good writing is and why, and he has an unerring feeling for what makes a really great genius in the business. He puts his finger at once, for example, on the reason why Shakespeare's characters are much more interesting than Molière's, even though he knew very little English and depended on reading Shakespeare in a French translation. I shall return to that in a moment.

If the reader can become familiar with Pushkin's personality as a critic and commentator on literature, he is in the best position to understand why he is a great poet. For Pushkin the artist is as detached and objective about a work of art – his own or another's – as is Pushkin the critic. By taking us through his development as a reader, as a *consciousness* of literature, Tatiana Wolff helps to give us the best insight on him as a writer. Her invaluable book brings together all the scattered evidence – letters, essays, diaries, notes and casual remarks – which together add up to a unique portrait of Pushkin as a literary man.

But what exactly did Pushkin mean by his heart being 'quite common'? Not, I think, that as a writer he pretended to be one thing, and was himself, as a man, quite different. Inconsistency is common enough among writers, even great writers; with some great novelists it is almost an occupational disease. Tolstoy's inconsistency is monumental, as has been long and variously recognised, and so is that of D. H. Lawrence. It is true of many novelists that most of their best work is autobiography in fictional form. And the self that they present in their novels is very different from the self that their wives actually had to live with. One of the most poignant outbursts in the diary of the Countess Tolstoy is to the effect that her days would be so much more tolerable if her husband showed in his dealings with her, and his family, and with life in general, even the merest fraction of the perception and insight which so wonderfully illuminate his novels. No doubt Frieda Lawrence might have said the same, although in Lawrence's case inconsistency is more mercurial, even playful, as if he were flaunting the contradictions in his attitudes before the public and defying them to object.

Of course one cannot accuse either writer of hypocrisy. Their inconsistency is part of the dynamism of their genius. Tolstoy knew that he was worldly, sensual, egocentric, an aristocrat to the bone, and with a mind that cut ruthlessly through every kind of shallowness, or disguise, or the commonplace in other people. He knew it, and it was anguish to him, for he longed to be simple and virtuous and celibate and humble. One of his most telling self-portraits is in *Father Sergius*, his story of an aristocratic soldier who becomes a monk, but who can never quite rid himself of his appetites, or of his fundamental arrogance. Whatever his wife may have thought, Tolstoy as an artist was fully aware of the way that he functioned, and this was why he came to abhor the whole idea of his own art, as it is manifested in his great novels. Lawrence might almost have been thinking of Tolstoy when he observed that the great strength of the novel, as art, was that it was so 'incapable of the absolute'. Tolstoy yearned for 'the absolute', but he knew in his heart of hearts that he could never get it. Lawrence, too, hankered unceasingly to be the presiding genius of an ideal society, a beautiful commune where sex would be harmonious, and men and women would do their own separate things in primitive dignity and simplicity. And he knew too, and his art does, that this was just a dream: that human life cannot be founded upon any 'absolute', and so neither can any novel.

Inconsistency on this scale parodies, but also reveals, the contradictions that are at the root of all human nature. The work of Tolstoy and Lawrence is true in the most vital sense to what we are; and by being themselves on such a scale in their art they seem to make life and art, as it were, into one. Shestov, the Russo-Jewish philosopher and critic, observes that Tolstoy, Dostoevsky and Chekhov – three great Russian writers – all share a remarkable power of concealing one subject and one attitude to life under another (he maintains, for example, that Tolstoy's real hero in *War and Peace* is not the seeker and thinker Pierre but the normally decent and conventional landowner Rostov) and that this capacity for contradiction is an essential part of their peculiar genius. Shestov also suggests that their reverence for Pushkin – shared too by all other Russian writers – is because of the poet's primal directness and simplicity: that he is, as it were, the clear fountain from whose original source flow all the deep, disturbed and turbid waters that make up the great Russian novel.

However that may be, it is clear that Pushkin's sardonic contrast between his 'elegant' writings and his 'common' self means something quite different from, say, the contrast between Tolstoy the artist and Tolstoy the man. Pushkin seems in his own way to be pointing out something familiar to the classic idea of literature, the idea embodied in the art of Horace, or Dante, or Shakespeare, or Mozart, the idea that the artist is a perfectly ordinary man, with normal commonplace instincts and habits, who happens to have been given a divine gift, a gift from the Muse. With this he has the power to create not only what W. H. Auden called 'the halcyon structures' of art, but to reflect in it all human and worldly life, event, character, situation – himself remaining essentially passive and uninvolved. That is why Pushkin could comment on his own work almost as if it had been written by someone else, or criticise other writers and forms of art with the same detachment.

But of course Pushkin is not as ordinary as he pretends – if he were he would not be the brilliant and intelligent critic of his own and other men's work that he is. The gift of the Muses may be bestowed on a quite ordinary person, but not on one so ordinary that he could not evaluate what he himself had written, and know whether it was good or bad! None the less

Pushkin loved in his own art to stylise the distinction between the fullness of the poet inspired and the emptiness of the poet when inspiration leaves him. In his poem 'The Echo' he compares the poet's nature to the echo which responds 'should a beast roar in the dense forest, a horn sound, thunder peal, a maiden sing beyond the hill . . .' Only the echo itself has no voice to answer it, and nor has the poet who has sung whatever tune inspiration has brought from the world. In his 'little tragedy' *Mozart and Salieri*, one of a series which he thought of calling 'dramatic investigations', he contrasts the insouciant figure of Mozart, and the earnest, painstaking Salieri, who cannot bear the thought that music should lose its arduous dignity in the hands of this playboy of genius. Salieri is not jealous of Mozart; he is jealous for the reputation of music. Better that Mozart should die than that music should be dragged in the gutter by him, whatever marvels this blasphemous god – 'not worthy of himself' – should produce on the way.

Pushkin's attitude to his art is made most fully explicit in *Egyptian Nights*, a tale that combines both verse and prose, seriousness and comedy. Charsky, a Petersburg aristocrat, is also a secret poet. Most of the time he leads the life of a man about town, gambling and dining out, but once a year the fit comes on him to get rid of what he calls the 'rubbish' in his head, and he shuts himself up and scribbles from morning to night. This was precisely Pushkin's own practice. During the famous 'Boldino autumns', spent alone at his little estate in the country, he produced most of his prose and poetry, working with extraordinary speed, and throwing out sketches and ideas as described in his magical poem 'Autumn'. The other figure in *Egyptian Nights* is equally significant. It is that of a poor Italian 'improviser', who makes his living by producing extempore verses at a public performance on any subject an audience may give him. The theme of 'Cleopatra and her lovers' has been drawn from the vase by a young Petersburg miss in long gloves. The improviser looks embarrassed and confused. Humbly and uncertainly he asks what was intended – 'because the great queen had so many of them'. General laughter and the young ladies blush. But at the moment when the artist seems most at the mercy of a philistine society 'he felt the approach of the god', and the dazzling verse – Pushkin's own incomparable tetrameters – streams from his lips, leaving the audience mute with admiration.

The scene is brilliantly funny and moving too, but it is also Pushkin having a laugh at himself. He affected to despise the crowd, the vulgar and the fashionable, but here is the poet bowing to its demands and producing all the finer poetry in consequence. When Charsky first tested the improviser's powers he asked him to declaim on the theme of 'inspiration', and the Italian made a magnificent defence of the poet's freedom to scorn the crowd and choose any subject he wishes, including one that is trivial and unelevated, 'as the great eagle sails past tower and crag to perch on a withered stump'. Pushkin is having a laugh all round, and the joke is continued by the fact that the improviser on the gala night breaks off at the climax of his lurid tale: the moment when the great queen has offered herself to all takers, the price of a night of her favours being death, and three have accepted – an old soldier, a philosopher, and a handsome youth on whom Cleopatra bestows a quick glance of regret. The couch is spread; the poem ends.

I must return in a moment to Pushkin's fascinating and characteristic habit of breaking off a story at or before the climax, but the point I would emphasise now is his lack of 'seriousness' – in the modern sense. His poet figure (for clearly Charsky and the improviser are two sides of Pushkin's own artistic self) throws off a masterpiece without caring what it means or what impression it makes. As his observations on his own works and their reception show – those on the epic poem *Poltava* for instance – he was quite prepared to defend what he had written and the way he had written it, but his comments are always extremely practical and down to earth. So Shakespeare might have commented on the stage details in *Hamlet*; but Pushkin would no more have talked about the 'meaning' of one of his works, or what he was 'trying to do' in it, than we can imagine Shakespeare discussing the meaning of *Hamlet*.

From an early romantic narrative poem like *The Fountain of Bakhchisārai* to his novel in verse *Evgeny Onegin*, the historical novel *The Captain's Daughter*, that terse melodrama *The Queen of Spades*, and the climactic poem *The Bronze Horseman*, everything that Pushkin wrote is indeed 'elegant and dignified', in the sense that it is an aesthetic masterpiece, a work whose subject seems exactly adjusted to its form. That may sound cold. The notion of 'perfection' is not one an experienced reader cares for very greatly, and the idea of the maker as detached from his creation, aloof and paring his finger-nails, as James Joyce put it, is not one to which most of us respond, and certainly not one to which Russians instinctively respond. Dostoevsky used to speak of Pushkin's 'secret', as if there were indeed some enigma or mystery behind the 'elegance', in the way he did things and what he meant by them, which it was the task of future generations to understand.

But indeed there is no secret and no mystery, only an engaging paradox which Pushkin himself summed up in his comment to that young admirer.

Pushkin's secret is a very homely one, and it is that his attitude to art was entirely unexpected and unfashionable at the time he was writing. Goethe would have, and indeed did, spend hours discussing the meaning of *Faust* with critics and admirers who crowded reverently round him. So would European and Russian poets during and up to the end of the century. Blok and Rilke (a great admirer of Pushkin and of Russian culture) have indeed a kind of open secret which is immanent in all their poetry, which is its 'soul', so to speak, and intimate with all their interior life. Something similar is true of T. S. Eliot, and perhaps of all modernists, as it was once true too of the romantics. Pushkin is outside all this. He could borrow from and use anything from European literature in his time except its *zeitgeist*, the spirit of literature in his time. That spirit he saw from outside. It belonged, we might say, to Evgeny Onegin and to Lensky, the youthful poet who is killed in a duel by Evgeny Onegin. The pair represent two aspects of their age. Pushkin is neither Evgeny nor Lensky, nor even a mixture of both, but his awareness of the two, and their relationship, is vital to the novel.

Vital, too, to the fact that his heart, as he put it, was completely common. One is tempted to say that of all great writers he most epitomises common sense, and that what Pushkin spoke of as wholly down to earth is not far from the attitude of Cervantes's Sancho Panza. And yet of course he was proud – extremely proud – of his ancient family, just as he was of being descended on the side of his mother, a Gannibal, from the little Ethiopian boy who had been given to Peter the Great and became a general in his service.

But his very inconsistencies – not agonised like Tolstoy's nor paranoiac like Lawrence's (though Pushkin would have got on with Lawrence and enjoyed his sense of fun) – have the common touch. He is good-natured in them, as when he remarked that of course he despised his country from head to toe, but he wasn't going to hear any damn foreigner do the same. He never sought, as an artist and writer, to impose any ideas or philosophy of his own. However exigent as an artist – and like many great artists he took far greater pains than he sometimes pretended – he never imposed as a literary 'character' or personality. Wittgenstein remarked that one could talk, rightly, about the 'great heart' of Beethoven, but that the great heart of Shakespeare (or Mozart he might have added) was in some way not a possible concept. In making this point Wittgenstein certainly implied the spiritual superiority of Beethoven, and a case in general for 'the spirit' familiar to us in European culture since Hegel's time. Pushkin fills the bill here as little as Shakespeare. But Schiller's famous dictum about the difference between the naive and reflective in literature does not fit the case with him either. Pushkin 'calls things for the first time by their Russian names', yet he is in no sense a naive artist. On the other hand his intelligence is never on display, never makes weighty statements: it is always well below the elegant and animated surface.

And it is in its own way a basic intelligence. Pushkin has a disconcerting habit of showing up more profound and more 'serious' writers, playing the deadpan critic in what he writes as an artist. A remarkable example is his 'Scene from Faust', modelled on Goethe's great poem and purporting to be an episode from it. Published in 1828 under the mischievous title 'A New Scene between Faust and Mephistopheles', it takes place by implication in the limbo after the end of *Faust* Part I (the massive *Faust* Part II, of the existence of which Pushkin was ignorant, was only completed in 1832, a few months before Goethe's death). Pushkin's penetrating common sense shows itself in the way in which his brilliant verses, composed in the same trochaic metre as Goethe's, expose the artistic weakness behind the touching idealism of the relation between Goethe's Faust and Margaret. Though Goethe's Faust has betrayed and deserted her, their love was none the less tender and pure, and Faust at the climax is determined to rescue her from the prison in which she is held for killing their love child. Gretchen's pregnancy and madness, abandoned by her lover, is conveyed by Goethe not only with great emotional force but with a realism remarkable for its time and subject. But Pushkin concentrates on the blankness left by Goethe in the feelings of Faust himself. Remorselessly Pushkin's Mephisto points out that even while the pair were enjoying their love together Faust could not but be aware of the simplicity of Gretchen's tender ardour, could not but be aware of the difference between her love and his own. At the most happy and thoughtless moments Faust could not help thinking of the contrast between his 'obedient lamb' and himself, and unconsciously despising her for it.

Pushkin's Faust is furious at Mephisto's perception, which none the less he cannot deny. And the author himself, writing in verse as swift and dazzling as Mozart's music in *The Marriage of Figaro*, is not insistent and knowing like his Mephisto but light-hearted and good-natured. None the less the point has been made. Goethe's Faust is ideal man: Pushkin's, the average man as he really is, disillusioned by the present and compelled to feed on illusions about the past. The psychological insight looks forward to that of the quiet and equally good-natured Chekhov, in his stories and plays.

However conventional and romantic their subjects, all Pushkin's narrative poems exhibit this same down to earth awareness of the way human beings really feel and behave. This does not mean that their griefs, loves and passions are inauthentic, no more than their capacity for fidelity and goodness. But life is as it is, and his poetry never forgets the fact. In *The Prisoner of the Caucasus*, one of his early works, the young hero is rescued by a Circassian girl who has fallen in love with him. But naturally he thinks of nothing but getting away, and in her grief at his going she throws herself into a mountain torrent. He hears and sees, but he does nothing. A friend afterwards chided Pushkin for allowing his hero this ungallant behaviour, and the poet retorted that he knew from experience what the rivers of Georgia were like, and that his hero would have been very ill-advised to attempt a rescue. In the most remarkable of his early narrative poems, *The Gipsies*, the hero Aleko, like a step-child of Rousseau, is convinced that he will find the simple, free and virtuous life with a Gipsy tribe and in the love of a Gipsy girl; but the girl turns out promiscuous, and Aleko, forgetting all the high-minded precepts he is supposed to have imbibed from primitive nature, kills her and her lover in a fit of murderous jealousy.

It is part of Pushkin's aesthetic never to labour a point, but to break off at the moment when meaning seems to have harmonised most economically with poetic skill. His 'Little Tragedies' are brief because he sees no point in proceeding, act by act, from exposition to denouement: his poetry can do the job more quickly, uniting economy with perfect grace. His art never deflates the subject that it treats: it makes it more compelling and more magical even while, in a sense, it 'deromanticises' it. *The Stone Guest*, the 'little tragedy' which tells Pushkin's version of the Don Juan story, makes Don Juan an ordinary human being rather than a fabulous seducer. Instead of being coldly and cheerfully intent on adding to his score, Pushkin's Don Juan falls genuinely in love with the attractive girls he encounters, because he is fascinated by the difference between one and another of them! Laura is as gaily amoral as he is; Inez, a girl whose seductiveness lies in her sadness and lack of vitality; while Donna Anna, the Commander's wife, has something cold, placid and tranquil about her which Juan finds the most irresistible combination of all. The hidden irony of the piece is that Juan is destroyed at the moment when he has fallen most deeply in love.

The 'Little Tragedies', it could be said, investigate without coming to conclusions. They are also the closest Pushkin came in his art to revealing the secrets of his own natural heart. We have seen how the sardonic contrast of Mozart and Salieri reveals Pushkin's awareness of the kind of artist he was himself. The idea of fate in *The Stone Guest*, and of unexpectedly 'meeting one's fate' in love, is very close to his vision of his own personal life. It could almost be said that *The Stone Guest* came true for him, for his beautiful young wife Natalia seems to have appealed to him by her coldness and her physical reserve – after his experience of so many hot-blooded young ladies – and it was she who was the direct cause of his death in a duel with the French officer he suspected of seducing her.

'The Little Tragedies' show most clearly Pushkin's strikingly cosmopolitan and international outlook, and how he constructed a perfect and detached work of art out of odds and ends of European anecdote, culture and tradition, together with an acute instinct for the psychological, and an amused sense of himself. The actual models for them were the Dramatic Scenes written by Barry Cornwall, a very minor English writer who had achieved some success with these highly-coloured little romantic episodes, themselves based on Shakespeare. It was indeed the new vogue for Shakespeare in France and in the rest of Europe which had introduced Pushkin to them, as usual in a French translation. Pushkin admired Barry Cornwall (the pen name of Bryan Procter, a friend and contemporary of Keats, Byron and Leigh Hunt) and found them more useful than Byron's plays. Just before he drove out in the snow for his fatal duel Pushkin had been writing a letter to a lady correspondent of *Sovremennik*, the magazine he edited, suggesting she do a translation of Cornwall's work into Russian. It is by the way a curious coincidence, which may be more than a coincidence, that one of Cornwall's more spirited pieces, entitled *Juan*, is about a Don Juan who has killed the old husband of one of his female conquests, is now *married* to her, and so intensely jealous that he stabs her from a mistaken conviction that she has been unfaithful.

The Stone Guest perfects the genre which Pushkin had adapted from Cornwall, and was the climax of the three weeks he spent at Boldino in 1830 – to have composed the three little tragedies in so short a time was an extraordinary feat even by Pushkin's standards. Later he returned to the poetic drama form with a remarkable fragment called *Rusalka*, based on material which he had characteristically picked up not from a Russian source (though all Soviet critics are insistent on his use of Russian folklore) but from an operatic piece in German. It tells the story of an undine or water nymph – 'rusalka' is the Russian equivalent and the venue has been changed from the Danube to the Dnieper – a miller's daughter, who had drowned herself after being abandoned by a noble seducer, who in her new being as 'a cold powerful rusalka' is determined to take revenge on her former lover. As in the case of *Egyptian Nights*, and as so often with Pushkin, the story appears rather banal, as if it were a challenge to the poet's verbal skill as well as to his hidden intelligence. Certainly it is among the most packed and haunting pieces that he wrote, and enigmatic as well, for it is impossible to tell whether Pushkin broke it off deliberately or simply abandoned it. I incline to think the former, because his interest in form made him attentive to the contemporary Romantic concept of the fragment, and he produces his own inimitable versions of it. Many of his shorter poems break off in this way, and even the novel in verse, *Evgeny Onegin*, could in one sense be said to be incomplete, or at least uncompleted.

Rusalka is in its way a return to the Faust scene. As Pushkin's poetry silently points out that Faust never felt the same about Gretchen as she did about him, so in *Rusalka* it calmly but inflexibly discloses the ease, the relief even, with which the Prince withdraws from his beloved, on the grounds that he must make a suitably grand marriage, and the anguish of love and remorse which then comes over him after she has drowned herself. Pushkin's verse manages to convey not only how much she loved him, as it also makes us feel how Tatiana loved Onegin, but – more subtly still – how much it is that image of her in love with him that afterwards haunts the Prince. Pushkin's instant grasp of, and delineation of, character makes us aware that the same passion for him, which he now vainly recalls, could also make her become quite a different sort of woman from the one he fondly remembers. Hence the symbolism – as it virtually is – of the 'cold powerful rusalka', and the revenge she is about to take when the dramatic poem breaks off.

Poetry – in this case Pushkin's pellucid and incomparable blank verse – is of course an essential part of the effect, just as the wonderfully intricate stanzas of *Evgeny Onegin* create its whole tone and structure as a novel. Each of his short tragedies has lines which haunt the work's whole being, and as it were represent its atmosphere. The key line from *Rusalka* is – as so often – untranslatable, because in another language it sounds rather flat ('But he is flat, your poet!' said Flaubert to Turgenev, who was trying to convince him of Pushkin's greatness). It merely conveys the information that the Prince, after the girl's death, takes to spending most of his time 'alone in the forest on the Dnieper's banks'. The line in Russian has a heavy and chilling poignancy and weight which sounds through the whole story.

In his last years Pushkin became convinced that he could do without poetry, that prose was the thing to go for; and in addition to his delightful serio-comic *Tales of Belkin* he began several experimental novels or stories, which seem to depend on the psychological exploration of some affair or goings-on in society. Unlike the poems these are genuine fragments, in the sense that the author did clearly intend to continue, but was either prevented by haste or business from doing so, or decided that he could not after all handle the situation at story or novel length. Some of them are fascinating, and show that Pushkin had it in him to become a great novelist in the modern manner, a prose novelist whose work would have been not only elegant and gripping but extremely down to earth. Most readers of Tolstoy's novels know that the germ of *Anna Karenina* was a fragmentary beginning of a novel of Pushkin's that begins with the words 'The guests were arriving at the dacha.' Tolstoy said that this was just how a novel should open. But his debt to Pushkin in *Anna Karenina* goes far beyond this opening sentence. Pushkin's novel, or perhaps *nouvelle*, would have centred, so it seems, on a headstrong, odd, fascinating girl, who moves in the best Petersburg society. She married for advantage, is dissatisfied with her life without knowing why, takes a lover, and goes to live in a little house – 'in the corner of a little square' is how an alternative fragment of the *nouvelle* opens – where her lover comes to visit her. What clearly intrigued Pushkin as a subject is the actual oppression of the girl in what she feels to be an ideally 'free' situation. Madame Bovary is lurking in the wings, for this situation has always been of interest to novelists since Flaubert, and never more so than today. Her lover does not feel free either:

> He had never meant to tie himself down with such bonds. He hated boredom, feared obligation, and valued his egotistical independence above all else. But it was a *fait accompli*. Zinaida remained on his hands. He pretended to be grateful, but in fact he faced the pain of his liaison as if performing an official duty.

Zinaida, or Volskaia as she is called in the alternative manuscript, finds herself very much in the position of Anna Karenina, cut off from her friends, locked into a relationship which offers no prospect of natural development. And the real feelings of her lover might almost have been described and analysed by Tolstoy, writing of Vronsky in the latter stages of his relationship with Anna. Indeed it may strike us that Tolstoy, almost as if he were under Pushkin's spell, takes what is really a very down to earth view of the 'great lovers' in his massive novel. Behind all the build-up, the characterisation, the contrasting love and life of the Levin family, the spiritual anguish and regret, there remains at the bottom of *Anna Karenina* a hard nugget of tough Pushkinian common sense. He got tired of her: and she was in the self-destructive position of a woman whom her lover would abandon if he could. Anna's fears and jealousy know that their sexual passion was what really counted, and now it has grown cold.

Critics have often remarked, and sometimes disapproved of, the fact that Tolstoy involves us in Anna's situation without any preliminary discourse about her background and state of mind. That too may have unconsciously come from the way he followed up Pushkin's opening. Pushkin was a master of instant characterisation, as is shown by the contrast in *Rusalka* between the passionately loving and ultimately formidable miller's daughter and the gentle pathetic Princess, who finds that the Prince neglects her and is always away from home. The portraits have a curious independence, free from, and outside of, the melodramatic events of the story.

The way Pushkin does this, particularly in a dramatic context, reveals his deep appreciation of the characters in Shakespeare's plays, and, what is more remarkable, the natural talent he discovered for creating the same kind of characters himself. What might be called Pushkin's Law is founded on his observation of Shakespeare's practice: that the people in his plays never behave 'in character', that they are never, as he puts it, 'compromised by their situation'. He objects to Byron's plays on the ground that in them 'a conspirator says "Give me a drink" conspiratorially – and that's ridiculous'. From this comes 'self-consciousness of dialogue'. But in Shakespeare the characters speak and think outside what is dramatically required of them. Shylock, writes Pushkin, unlike Molière's miser, is not just miserliness personified: he is witty, child-loving, with dignity even in his resentments, petty at one moment and at the next proudly conscious of his race. Pushkin was particularly fascinated by this type of person in Shakespeare's *Measure for Measure*, which he altered and adapted into a dramatic poem called 'Angelo'. Angelo is not a hypocrite, though the play requires him to behave like one.

In the context of European literature Pushkin must be said to play a vital and remarkable role in the transition from flat characters based on the old drama (Sir Walter Scott is full of them) to the complex characterisation and psychology of the modern novel. As I remarked when writing a critical study about him (*Pushkin: A Comparative Commentary*) it is only ignorance of the language and of his work which have prevented him being recognised in the west as one of the great pioneers and experimenters of modern literature. That is why *Pushkin on Literature* performs such an important service in showing the range and diversity of his perceptions, and the ways in which he thought about the problems involved.

'Pushkin's Law' of characterisation applies in almost everything that he wrote. Even though his historical novel *The Captain's Daughter* is closely based on Scott's *Waverley* the characters are far more alive than in Scott, far less subdued to the conventional requirements of the genre. In *The Queen of Spades* much of the interest derives less from the excitements of the gambling yarn, and its young 'hero of the will', Hermann, than from the portrait of the old Countess and her ward Liza, portraits drawn with as much depth and sympathy as economical skill. The same goes for the minor characters, as well as the major ones, in *Evgeny Onegin*, characters like the old nurse and Olga, sister of the heroine Tatiana. In his witty and elaborate commentary on the verse novel, Vladimir Nabokov observes that Olga is perhaps not quite the simple flirtatious fair-haired young *ingénue* she appears to be. After Lensky's death in the duel she mourns him appropriately, but is soon cheered by a handsome young officer, and we leave her standing at the altar, that eternal smile on her lips and her eyes modestly cast down. 'Is there something of a cunning young demon about Olga?' wonders Nabokov. 'What does that smile imply?' Whatever it does, it is significant that we can speculate about Pushkin's characters in the same way that we do about the persons in Shakespeare's plays, or in Jane Austen's or Henry James's novels.

Nabokov even goes on to wonder whether Tatiana was quite so steadfast in her decision to reject Onegin's final advances at the end of the poem. Well, we may wonder about that too, for Pushkin is adept at raising the vulgar world of gossip to the level of high art. Certainly the novel is open-ended, in his usual fashion, and nothing comes to anything in it – just like life we might say. Pushkin called it 'a free novel', one that did not conform to the rules of any genre, but was 'a collection of parti-coloured chapters, half-funny, half-sad, poetical, but vulgar too.' The Russian formalist critic Shklovsky has decided that Pushkin intended to give us not the story of his couple, but 'a game with this story', in which the pattern goes that she falls for him, and nothing comes of it, and then he falls for her, and nothing comes of that either.

This view of the book as a graceful and artificial dance, a 'spirited and elegant' affair, is in keeping with the supreme poetic mastery of the stanzas, and the play of wit and personal references which Pushkin had also found in a translation of *Tristram Shandy*, a piece of fictional sport which he much admired. The stanza form of *Evgeny Onegin*, and the rhymes that it requires, have been the despair even of experts who have tried to put it into English: Nabokov decided that the only way to make an accurate version was to leave out the rhymes. But the recent rhymed version by Charles Johnston shows that it can be done, and he has managed to convey a great deal of Pushkin's worldly wit and spirit. He has also managed admirable versions of other poems by Pushkin, including *The Bronze*

Horseman. Walter Arndt has also given us a fine and vigorous version of this great poem, among many others included in his recent volume – *Pushkin, Collected Narrative and Lyrical Poetry.* However vexed the question of translating Pushkin may be, we do at least now have the whole of his work rendered into either good prose or competent verse. Admirable plain prose versions are supplied by John Fennell in his Penguin selection of the poetry, and by Dimitri Obolensky in his *Penguin Book of Russian Verse.* The latest addition, which fills all the remaining gaps, is Paul Debreczeny's *Complete Prose Fiction*, translated and annotated, which includes all the prose fragments and unfinished stories not previously available in English.

But to return in conclusion to *Evgeny Onegin*, the work by which Pushkin is most familiar to western readers. The formalist view of it as a kind of witty and beautiful game is in one sense a perfectly true and justified one. But ordinary Russian readers have never seen it like that, any more than English admirers read Jane Austen's novels just for sparkling and witty drawing-room comedy. As it happens Pushkin had never heard of Jane Austen, whose work was done a decade or so before he began to write, but we may be sure he would have appreciated her 'sharp tongue and warm heart', her appreciation of love and virtue together with her total lack of sentimentality. The characters in *Evgeny Onegin* are even more familiar to Russian readers than are Jane Austen's to English ones, and for generations of the Russian intelligentsia (including Dostoevsky) they have been a subject of discussion and endless debate.

That in itself may show how much they are 'alive', and not just puppets manipulated in a game of wit and language. Compared with the almost wholly cerebral and ingenious formalistic novels to which we are accustomed today (the names of John Fowles and Italo Calvino come to mind) *Evgeny Onegin* is a 'free novel' in a very popular sense. Pushkin refuses to be 'serious', and in refusing to be so he also opts out of the in-built seriousness of the formalistic game and returns to the simple and spontaneous reactions and emotions of the heart. But about these he will not be solemn and intense either. He would not let Tatiana and Onegin die tragically like Richardson's Clarissa and Lovelace. He wrote 'Rubbish!' in his copy of Constant's *Adolphe*, at the point where the distraught French hero throws himself on the ground and wishes it would swallow him up. The death of Constant's heroine, Ellénore, when she is deserted, struck him as equally *voulu*. He detected a lack of spontaneity in these love stories, so artfully crammed with sensibility; and though his own heroine Tatiana is a great reader and has filled her head with dreams and fancies 'from Richardson and from Rousseau', it is Pushkin's triumph to show that she falls in love absolutely and overwhelmingly, in the most touchingly direct way. No contemporary European love story had anything as moving and direct as the scene in which Tatiana, unable to sleep, confides to her old nurse what it feels like to have fallen in love. And in the same way Pushkin persuades us completely that when Onegin, who has patronised the love that young Tatiana artlessly poured out to him in the vegetable garden, sees her later as a beautiful married woman in Petersburg he himself really does fall helplessly in love with her. The formal comedy pattern is also a matter of strong, hopeless and spontaneous emotion.

But, as Pushkin says, Onegin did not run mad, or die of grief, or even become a poet. And nor did Tatiana, who no doubt went on resolutely living for a husband and family. Pushkin's sense of the humdrum nature of life, which art must both transform and remain faithful to, never deserts him. Even in his most conventional work, the tragedy *Boris Godunov*, he ended on a note of anti-climax, giving the impression that history has no time for dramatic confrontations and resolutions, but just goes lumbering clumsily and unsatisfactorily on. (Pushkin's old enemy Bulgarin complained that 'nothing in this play is complete'.) Nor is it in *Evgeny Onegin*; or rather we might say that the game, the pattern, is complete, but that the story, with all its real feelings and emotions and events, is not.

But those are for the reader to continue with, since they seem to become – as with *War and Peace* or *Crime and Punishment* – a part of his own life and experience. Pushkin found the same paradox was true of his own creative process. He tells us that when Onegin and young Tatiana first appeared to him, 'through the mist that dreams arise on', he did not know how their story was going to end, the

> free romance's far horizon,
> still dim, through crystal's magic glass.
> (trans. C. Johnston)

And indeed after the present ending he continued to write on for a while, producing some stanzas about Onegin going on a journey, but he soon came to see that the poem was over. His free novel had proclaimed its own kind of inevitability, leaving us with what is on the one hand a happy game in art, and on the other a moving exploration of the nature of life and what Necker, father of Madame de Staël, and quoted by Pushkin in one of his chapter epigraphs, called 'the morality that is in the nature of things'.

Pushkin's achievement here seems to me still underrated, at least in the context of western novels. There is an odd sympathetic link between his idea of a 'free novel' and the spontaneous way in which his hero and heroine fall – though at different times – in love with each other. In other famous love stories of the nineteenth century – *Adolphe, Le Rouge et le Noir, Madame Bovary* – the will of the characters to fall in love seems to correspond in artificiality to the will exercised by their creators that they should do so. Pushkin has all the French incisiveness and powers of analysis, and yet is free from the blinkers of French cultural tradition – and in particular the tradition of *amour.* Cultivated sensibility meant nothing to him, and he was irritated by the higher sentimentality. But the ordinary vulgar kind simply amused him; indeed he found it congenial, as is shown by his indulgence to two gushing young ladies who were quite saddened and cast down by the plot and ending of *Evgeny Onegin.* One of them wanted the poet Lensky, killed by Onegin in the fatal duel, to have been only wounded, 'then Olga could have looked after him and they would have grown even fonder of each other.' The other would have had Onegin wounded, 'so that Tatiana could have looked after him and he could have learnt to love and value her.'

What a nice idea! Art however has its own reasons, which seldom correspond to the wishes of the heart. And Pushkin was a rigorous artist. He knew that great art loved the common touch, but that it could never tolerate what was merely facile, in either a highbrow or a lowbrow form.

JOHN BAYLEY

Section I

CHILDHOOD, BOYHOOD AND YOUTH

... At the election of the Romanovs? The ungrateful
ones! Six Pushkins signed the Electoral Charter! And two
more had to put their marks, not being able to write!
And I, their literate descendant, what am I? Where am I?
Letter to Baron A. A. Delvig, June 1825

THE Pushkins who made their mark on the Electoral Charter of
the first Romanov to the throne of Russia did so as boyars, as
members of an established nobility. They traced their descent from
Grigory Pushka who lived at the beginning of the fifteenth century
and who, in his turn, traced his line back to Ratsha who had settled
in Russia in the thirteenth century, finding service at the court of St
Alexander Nevsky.

Pushkin was very consciously an aristocrat with a 'six-hundred-year-
old name' and often expressed his resentment at having to toady for
favour at the hands of the 'upstart' Romanovs. But the Pushkins, though
undoubtedly of ancient stock, were as a family lacking in lustre and
over the centuries lived in obscurity from which they occasionally burst
out in acts of violence: Pushkin's great-grandfather murdered his wife,
while his grandfather was rumoured – according to Pushkin – to
have hanged a French tutor whom he suspected of being his wife's
lover.

More interest has always been centred on Pushkin's maternal great-
grandfather – the Ethiopian, Ibrahim Hannibal. Born of allegedly
noble stock, he appears to have been bought by a Frenchman collecting
gifts, both human and animal, for Louis XIV; but in Cairo his path
was intercepted by Turkish officials and, instead of being taken to
Paris, he was shipped to Istanbul where he was placed in the Sultan's
seraglio. From there he was purchased by Peter the Great's envoy and
sent to the Russian court, arriving in 1706. In the following year he
was baptized into the Orthodox church at Vilna, with Peter standing
as godfather and the Queen of Poland as godmother.

True to his eminently practical nature Peter did not conceive of his
Ethiopian's courtly functions as being purely decorative. In 1717 he
sent him to Paris to study fortification and military mining. This sojourn
in France was to have long-range repercussions on the education of
his great-grandson, for when Ibrahim returned to Russia he brought

3

back with him a small library, which was to form the nucleus of that extensive French library in which Pushkin later so avidly browsed.

Ibrahim's second wife, Christine Schöberg, was the daughter of an army captain, a Lutheran of Swedish-German descent. They had eleven children of which the third son, Osip, was Pushkin's maternal grandfather.

In 1742, for various services Ibrahim had rendered, ranging from expert advice on fortifications to the planning of the Royal Firework displays, the Tsarina Elizabeth, Peter the Great's daughter, raised him to the rank of Major-General and gave him the country estate of Mikhailovskoe in the province of Pskov – a gift which was to be of great significance to Pushkin. Major-General Ibrahim Hannibal died in 1781, only eighteen years before Pushkin was born.

The matrimonial affairs of Pushkin's maternal grandfather were almost as tempestuous as those on his father's side of the family and ended in bigamy. Of his two wives the first was a Pushkin by birth and her daughter, Nadezhda, married a distant cousin, Sergey Lvovich Pushkin. These two were Pushkin's parents.

Sergey Lvovich and Nadezhda Osipovna were a well-matched couple. Both were worldly and enthusiastically sociable, displaying charm and wit in the drawing-room which, once the guests had gone, frequently gave way to irascibility. Enjoying literary salon society they lived for most of the year in their town house in Moscow, in a state of constant disarray and mounting debts, and neglected their country estate. They paid scant attention to their three children.

Alexander was born in Moscow in 1799. His sister Olga was two years older and his brother Lev six years younger. Up to the age of nine Alexander was phlegmatic and morose, then he became precociously well read and increasingly refractory. When only a year old he had had his first encounter with a Tsar, which proved characteristic. He was out for a walk with his nurse when they chanced to encounter the Emperor Paul I. Pushkin's nurse omitted to remove her charge's bonnet in the Imperial presence and was sternly rebuked. This was not to be the last time that Pushkin's cap was not doffed to his sovereign's will.

His parents' general adherence to the principle that children should be seen and not heard had its advantages for Pushkin. He was allowed to sit in on the literary gatherings which frequently took place at the Pushkin house, which numbered such men as Karamzin, Zhukovsky, Dmitriev, Batyushkov and A. I. Turgenev among the guests. More important still, he was given free access to his father's extensive French library. His brother remembered how, as a child, he used to spend whole nights reading in his father's study. This reading was unsupervised and unselective. He absorbed French literature wholesale, as well as many of the Greek and Latin classics in French translation. He read both philosophical and political authors and erotic novels, marking out early in life the extensive range of his future interests.

The series of governesses and tutors – French, German and English – to whose charge the Pushkin children were entrusted did not find a biddable pupil in Alexander. In a plan for an autobiography drawn up years later, Pushkin noted that his first troubles stemmed from his governesses; and in a semi-autobiographical fragment – 'A Russian Pelham' – with an obvious eye to himself, he summed up, 'not one of my tutors could cope with such an intolerable boy'. Writing in 1826 of the state of private education in Russia he remarked bitterly,

> In Russia private education is most inadequate and most immoral: the child is surrounded exclusively by servants, sees only the basest examples, grows either self-willed or servile, does not receive any notion of justice, of reciprocal human relationships, of true honour. His education is confined to two or three foreign languages and to an elementary knowledge of all the sciences, taught by some hired teacher. . . . There is no time for hesitation: private education must be abolished at all costs.

Fortunately his own education did not end in the family schoolroom.

But Pushkin's domestic entourage was not confined to his casual parents and his exasperated tutors. An understanding grandmother – Maria Alexeevna Hannibal – who, in a household given over to French, encouraged Pushkin to speak and write in Russian; a cheerful uncle – Vasily Lvovich Pushkin – with a flair for writing light verse and a first-hand knowledge of the French literary scene; and a loving nurse – all contributed to Pushkin's well-being as a child. Of these influences the nurse was the most remarkable. Arina Rodionovna was a serf of Pushkin's maternal grandparents and had been freed by his grandmother in 1805 on the sale of the estate of Kobrino to which she had belonged. She did not leave her mistress, however, but moved with her and became the Pushkins' nurse on the birth of the younger son, Lev. She had an inexhaustible store of Russian folk-tales and legends, songs and proverbs, from which Pushkin never ceased to draw inspiration. This was the balancing factor to the classical and French influences to which Pushkin was subject in his early reading and in his formal education and provided the impetus he needed to establish Russian as a literary language, himself becoming, in the fullest sense of the words, Russia's poet. Pushkin expressed his gratitude to Arina Rodionovna many times in his poetry and lovingly drew her portrait as Tatiana's nurse in *Evgeny Onegin*.

When Pushkin was twelve his further education was considered. The first plan was to send him to a school run by Jesuits but then a much more tempting possibility presented itself. The Emperor Alexander I, inspired by French and English examples, decided to found a Lycée in a wing of his palace at Tsarskoe Selo. There, carefully selected scions of the best families would be trained for the most responsible posts in the state service. The education would be free of charge and the boys would be in residence for six years, during which time, it was later decreed, they would not be allowed to leave the confines of the Lycée. The Pushkins immediately began to pull appropriate strings. Alexander was brought to St Petersburg by his Uncle Vasily and, sponsored by A. I. Turgenev, attended the entrance examination. He was passed fourteenth out of the thirty accepted, and thus became one of the Lycée's foundation-pupils. I. I. Pushchin, who was to be Pushkin's first and one of his closest friends at the Lycée, remembered him at this examination: 'a lively boy, with curly hair and quick, darting eyes, looking a little embarrassed.'

The Lycée officially opened on 19 October 1811. The curriculum was extensive and the masters as well as the pupils were hand-picked; the accommodation and grounds were, literally, palatial; corporal punishment was forbidden. Planted in this royal greenhouse Pushkin throve turbulently. Though not widely popular because of his touchiness and quick temper, he was soon at the hub of literary activities at the Lycée. Nicknamed 'the Frenchman' because of his astonishing knowledge of French literature and thought, he continued to extend this knowledge throughout his schooling, with the result that a classical taste for clarity and precision remained a controlling element in his later Romanticism. However there were many subjects in which he was far from industrious, and he won few golden opinions from his masters. He took eager part in pranks: first in nocturnal egg-flip parties, later in adventures of an amorous nature, finally in escapades with the guards officers stationed at Tsarskoe.

Pushkin's report after his first year at the Lycée shows a consistent picture:

Russian and Latin: more understanding and taste than industry but has competitive spirit. Fairly good progress. *French*: has become more industrious and makes constant progress. The second in the class. *German*: in spite of his quick wits and memory he makes no progress whatsoever. *German and French Literature*: bad progress, showing no aptitude, no application, and no will to learn; spoilt by upbringing. *Logic and Ethics*: very intelligent, ingenious and witty, but lacks application and makes insignificant progress. *Mathematics*: sharp wits used only for idle chatter, very lazy and bumptious in class. Indifferent progress. *Geography and History*: more talent than application, does not concentrate. Fairly good progress. *Drawing*: excellent gifts but hasty and careless. No noticeable progress. *Handwriting*: gifted and industrious. *Fencing*: fairly good. *Morals*: little consistency and firmness, loquacious, witty, noticeably good-natured but very irascible and flippant.

The qualities which were to characterize all Pushkin's letters and critical notebooks are already clearly marked: intelligence and wit; a warm heart and a quick temper; a mind at once alert and flippant. The one constant factor in his progress was that he was writing more and more poetry. Pushchin remembers how from the very start Pushkin's poems were in a different class from those of his fellows. He became the Lycée Poet Laureate.

The Lycée was an enclave at the heart of the Empire. Its routine, however, remained comparatively unruffled as soldiers rode past its gates on the way to fight Napoleon in 1812, though there were plans for its evacuation to the north as the French armies advanced deeper into Russia. Moscow burnt. The boys' sense of community was heightened by their isolation at such a critical period and very close friendships were established. Pushkin's Lycée friends became his correspondents for life; of them Pushchin, Küchelbecker and Delvig were particularly important.

Ivan Ivanovich Pushchin (1798-1859) was the son of a general. He and his cousin had been sponsored for admission to the Lycée by their grandfather, Admiral Peter Ivanovich Pushchin. Pushchin's attention was caught when Pushkin's name was called, perhaps because of the similarity in their names; the boys were introduced and immediately became friends. At the Lycée they had adjacent bedrooms and Pushchin, who was a cheerful, gregarious boy, often soothed Pushkin's ruffled spirits and acted as a mediator between him and the other boys.

7

Pushchin did not write poetry himself but he was one of the first to marvel at Pushkin's gift. Ironically in a school established to breed higher civil servants, what did in fact spread were liberal and even revolutionary ideas. Pushchin was early involved in a secret political society but though he knew that Pushkin's political opinions were in line with his own he was afraid to tell him of this, fearing his indiscreet and impulsive, fiery nature. This political activity eventually led Pushchin on to the Senate Square on 14 December 1825, and thence to life-long exile in Siberia.

Another future Decembrist among Pushkin's friends at the Lycée was Wilhelm Karlovich Küchelbecker (1797-1846). His father, a German, had attended the University of Leipzig at the same time as Goethe, but in the 1770s had settled in Russia, and Wilhelm was born in St Petersburg. The Küchelbeckers were neither wealthy nor influential people but they had influential friends, including General Barclay de Tolly, and it was they who sponsored Küchelbecker's application to the Lycée.

Küchelbecker was an odd-looking, ungainly boy, and he was much teased by his fellows. He studied eagerly and mastered several European languages as well as Greek and Latin. He was a 'walking dictionary' in Pushkin's respectful estimation. While at the Lycée Küchelbecker belonged to the same secret political society as Pushchin, and after he left school, when travelling in western Europe, thought of sailing to Greece to take part in the War of Independence. However, on account of a series of public lectures on Russian language and literature in which he expressed views hostile to autocracy, he was summoned back to Russia and continued to be under surveillance until he too rallied to the Senate Square on 14 December 1825 – an ardent revolutionary. His fate was the same as Pushchin's – a life spent in solitary confinement and then in Siberia.

Of all his school-friends it was Delvig who was closest to Pushkin. He was a fellow poet and 'man of letters'. They worked together in a series of Lycée magazines and anthologies. They read together and, under Küchelbecker's guidance, began to lace their classical and French favourites with the first heady draughts of German Romanticism. They laid their future plans. Years later, Pushkin still remembered how Delvig had outlined his 'Russian Idyll' to him in the hall of the Lycée 'after a dull mathematics lesson'.

Baron Anton Antonovich Delvig (1798-1831), whose father was a member of the military staff at the Moscow Kremlin, was among the

8

original intake of boys into the Lycée who met at the entrance examination in 1811. Pushkin remembered him at school as being phenomenally lazy and extremely imaginative, spinning fantastic yarns to which the other boys listened round-eyed and open-mouthed. Like Pushchin and Küchelbecker, as a schoolboy Delvig belonged to the secret society – the Sacred Association (*Svyashchennaya Artel*), whose members later transferred to the first of the Decembrist societies, the Union of Salvation. But unlike the other two, Delvig was not drawn into serious revolutionary commitments although he always remained closely associated with Decembrist circles. After leaving the Lycée he was soon at the centre of literary activity in St Petersburg, a friend and publisher of that brilliant group of young poets who came to be known as Pushkin's Pleiad. They were all to be stunned with grief at his sudden, early death.

Throughout his schooldays Pushkin wrote poetry, much of which appeared in the Lycée anthologies. In July 1814, the first of his poems to be published – 'To my friend, a poet' – appeared in the *Vestnik Evropy*. In January 1815, an incident at the public examination at the Lycée set the seal on his reputation as the rising light of Russian poetry. The examination was attended by the doyen of Russian poets, Derzhavin. Pushkin himself has described vividly how Derzhavin, having slumbered through a large part of the proceedings, was galvanized into attention when he began to recite his poem 'Recollections in Tsarskoe Selo'. Repin has painted the scene (see plate 2): Pushkin in school uniform stands, with head thrown back and arm flung out, in the full flow of recitation, while Derzhavin, half risen from his chair, leans forward to hear him better. 'I live on . . . He is the one who will replace Derzhavin' was the old poet's subsequent verdict. The mantle had fallen.

Various marks of recognition followed. He was commissioned to write poems for one or two state occasions; Zhukovsky, a poet of established reputation, sent him a copy of his latest book prior to publication; he earned the good opinion of the historian Karamzin, who came to the Lycée with Pushkin's uncle and heard him recite; he was invited to participate in the activities of the celebrated literary society, the Arzamas. He could now meet on a new footing the writers he had seen at his father's literary soirées. Zhukovsky, A. I. Turgenev, Batyushkov, Vyazemsky (later his closest friend and constant correspondent): he was one of them now – on nickname terms.

The Arzamas was a spearhead of advance in Russian letters, waging a war of styles against the conservative Discussion Society of Lovers of the Russian Word. Following the lead given by Karamzin, the members opened up for literature the rich, as yet untapped resources of the Russian language; and attacked the restrictions imposed by outworn conventions of poetic diction. In subject-matter too, the wider possibilities of Romanticism and realism lay ahead.

Towards the end of his schooldays the rules restricting the boys' exeats were relaxed and Pushkin made frequent forays outside the confines of the Lycée in search of new company. He had the entrée to Karamzin's house and – for less sober parties – frequented the barracks of the Hussar regiment stationed at Tsarskoe. One of the Hussar officers whom he first met at Karamzin's was Peter Chaadaev, a remarkable man who became his close friend. Chaadaev was six years older than Pushkin. He had fought in the wars against Napoleon and had been with the Russian army in Paris. A fluent linguist, he was very drawn to western European culture; and after resigning his commission in 1821 was to spend several years travelling extensively in Europe. On returning to Russia in a critical frame of mind, his views, boldly expressed in a 'Philosophical Letter', proved unacceptable to Nicholas I and he was declared to be insane. Chaadaev combined the style and panache of a guards officer with a serious religious and philosophic bent and a social conscience. He interested Pushkin in philosophy and made him want to enlist in the Hussars: both these enthusiasms were short-lived but their friendship survived.

On 9 June 1817 Pushkin graduated from the Lycée; he was eighteen years old. He was graded ninth in the final examinations and received an average diploma, the only subjects in which he shone being Russian and French literature and fencing. Though towards the end of his time at the Lycée he had grown very restless, he had enjoyed his schooldays and he left with several firmly established friendships, a store of pleasant memories, and a notebook in which he had copied out thirty-six of his poems, very carefully selected. 19 October, the day on which the founder-pupils of the Lycée held their reunions, was several times marked by Pushkin by poems addressed to his friends, the most eloquent and moving of which he wrote in 1825 when confined to his estate in Mikhailovskoe. In the years of exile which followed, scattering his friends, their days together discussing poetry while strolling under the lime trees of Tsarskoe had the afterglow of a golden age.

On graduation Pushkin was given a post as Junior Secretary at the Ministry of Foreign Affairs. He took his duties very lightly. He lived the life of a dandy on a shoe-string, affected boredom and long finger-nails, involved himself in a series of duels and undermined his health in a series of amatory adventures. In the first chapter of *Evgeny Onegin* Pushkin later described the social whirligig on which he himself had once swept round and round – from dinner to ballet, from ball to bed, and on again on the morrow.

The members of the Arzamas welcomed Pushkin ('The Cricket', as they called him) on his arrival in St Petersburg, and though the society itself was soon disbanded continued to watch his progress with tender solicitude. When Pushkin, in the midst of all his distractions, at last finished his first long poem, *Ruslan and Lyudmila*, which he began at the Lycée, Zhukovsky was delighted. As Derzhavin had done, he gave Pushkin pride of place among Russian poets, sending him a portrait of himself (see plate 8) with the dedication: 'To the victorious pupil from the defeated master, on that most solemn day on which he completed his poem *Ruslan and Lyudmila*, 1820, 26 March, Good Friday.'

Soon after coming to St Petersburg Pushkin and Delvig had joined the Society of the Green Lamp. The members, many of them Guards officers, forgathered in a room in which a green lamp hung as a symbol of hope, and combined literary pursuits with political discussions of liberal tendency, with the attendant pleasures of women and wine. There were other, more serious, political gatherings being held in St Petersburg at the time, but from these Pushkin was excluded. Even at the Lycée Pushkin's friends, although they knew that he sympa-thized with their ideas, had feared to include him in their subversive political activities in view of his indiscretion and impulsiveness; and this remained true. Nevertheless Pushkin contrived to cock a snook at the government in his own fashion, in biting lampoons and in poems – notably his ode 'Freedom' and 'The Village' – in which he expressed his hatred of autocracy and his hopes for the end of serfdom. He was treading dangerously near the Emperor's toes.

Pushkin's poems were soon on everyone's lips. 'There was not at that time a literate ensign in the army who did not know them by heart. Generally speaking Pushkin was the voice of his generation . . . a truly national poet, such as Russia had never had,' wrote the Decem-brist Ivan Yakushkin. Finally the Emperor moved. One day, on meeting the Director of the Lycée in the palace grounds at Tsarskoe, the Emperor asked him to walk along with him and then said: 'Pushkin will have to be exiled to Siberia: he has flooded Russia with scandalous verses; all the young men know them by heart.' Influential friends intervened and, instead of Siberia, Pushkin was sent to Ekaterinoslav

in the south of Russia to work under General Inzov. He was equipped
with a thousand roubles for travelling expenses and a letter of introduction from the Minister of Foreign Affairs, in which both his gifts and
his failings were brought to the General's attention: '. . . Il n'y a pas
d'excès auquel ce malheureux jeune homme ne se soit livré – comme il
n'y a pas de perfection à laquelle il ne puisse atteindre par la supériorité
transcendante de ses talents . . .'

Byron and Ovid were now to be his tutelary geniuses.

1815

————◆••◆————

DIARY

I.

28 November. Zhukovsky gives me his poems.[1]

10 December. Yesterday I wrote the third chapter of 'Fatam or human reason: the Natural Law'.[2] . . . In the morning I read 'The Life of Voltaire'.[3]

I have started on a comedy – I don't know if I shall finish it.[4] The day before yesterday I wanted to start on a heroic poem 'Igor and Olga'.[5]

[1] This was obviously a red-letter day for Pushkin. Zhukovsky gave him a pre-publication copy of the first part of his *Poems*, which came out *circa* 7 December 1815.

[2] This work does not survive.

[3] Probably *Vie de Voltaire* by the Marquis de Condorcet (1787).

[4] One of Pushkin's friends at the Lycée, A. D. Illichevsky, wrote of this comedy on 16 January 1816:

> . . . [Pushkin] is now writing a comedy in five acts, in verse, called 'The Philosopher'. The plan is fairly good, and so is the beginning: that is the first act – all that is written at present – promises well – the verses, it goes without saying, [are good] and there are as many witty remarks as one could wish for! God give him patience and resolution – this is the first big 'ouvrage' begun by him – an 'ouvrage' with which he wants to open his career on leaving the Lycée. . . . (K. Y. Grot, *Pushkinsky Litsey, 1811-1817*, p. 60.)

The comedy did not survive. Pushkin did not embark on drama again till 1825 when he wrote *Boris Godunov*.

[5] It has been suggested that Zhukovsky encouraged Pushkin to write on a heroic theme, for he himself was at that time planning a poem, 'Olga', in imitation of Scott's *Lady of the Lake* (K. Bartenev, *A. S. Pushkin, Materialy dlya evo biografii*, 1855, pt. 2, p. 27). European literature was at this time steeped in Gothic romance and heroic balladry and Zhukovsky, particularly through his translations from English and German, was largely responsible for their popularity in Russia. Pushkin wrote several poems on Russian heroic themes but not one on Igor and Olga.

1816

————◄••••►————

LETTER

2. To Prince P. A. Vyazemsky[1]   *27 March 1816*
                                                        Tsarskoe Selo

I must admit that only the hope of receiving from Moscow some poems by the Chapelle and Boileau[2] of Russia could overcome my blissful indolence. So be it! But don't blame me if my letter causes Your Poetic Grace to yawn; it's your own fault. Why did you tease the unfortunate anchorite of Tsarskoe Selo, who was already tormented by the furious demon of scribbling. . . .

What shall I tell you of our secluded life? Never has the Lycée . . . seemed to me so unbearable as it does now. I assure you that living the life of a recluse is in fact quite senseless, in spite of all the philosophers and poets who pretend to have lived in the country and to love silence and quiet. . . .

It is true that the end of our time at the Lycée draws near. One year left. But another whole year of pluses, minuses, laws, taxes, the sublime, the beautiful! . . . that is awful. . . . It's damnable to keep a young man locked up and not allow him to take part even in such innocent pleasures as interring the defunct Academy and the Discussion Society of the murderers of the Russian word.[3] But nothing can be done about it.

Out of boredom I often write boring verse (at times very boring) and often read poems that are no better. . . .

[1] Prince Peter Andreevich Vyazemsky (1792-1878) was one of Pushkin's closest friends and most faithful correspondents. He was himself a poet and a critic. He was on a visit to St Petersburg to attend meetings of the Arzamas (see pages 9-10), and had only recently met Pushkin. This is Pushkin's first surviving letter to him.

[2] Vyazemsky's poetic style was formed under the influence of French classicism. He had written poems in the vein of Chapelle and Boileau.

[3] Pushkin longed to join in the literary fray, between the Arzamas on the one side and the Russian Academy and the Discussion Society of Lovers of the Russian Word on the other, concerning the kind of diction considered suitable for literature. At meetings of the Arzamas new members pronounced mock funeral orations on members of the rival faction.

1819

DRAFT LETTER

3. Draft letter to N. I. Krivtsov[1]

*Second half of July/
beginning of August 1819
Mikhailovskoe*

Living in the freedom of England do you remember that there exists
in the world the district of Pskov . . . and that the lazybones whom you
probably remember and with whom you are probably angry also misses
you every day? I do not like writing letters – the tongue and the voice
are barely capable of expressing our thoughts – and the pen is so stupid
and so slow – a letter cannot take the place of a conversation. All the
same I am at fault, knowing that a letter from me could remind you
for a moment of our Russia, of evenings at Turgenev's[2] and Karamzin's.[3]

[1] Nikolai Ivanovich Krivtsov (1791-1843) had been wounded in the war
against Napoleon, had travelled widely in Europe and was at this time in
the diplomatic service, posted in London. He had first met Pushkin at
the Turgenevs' in June 1817. When he was leaving for London Pushkin
gave him an inscribed copy of one of his favourite books, Voltaire's *La
Pucelle d'Orléans*. In August 1818, Krivtsov sent Pushkin some blasphemous
verses from London, which upset Turgenev. This draft letter may be
Pushkin's tardy acknowledgement.

[2] Alexander Ivanovich Turgenev (1784-1846), a historian and archivist, was
one of the leaders of intellectual society in St Petersburg and a member
of the Arzamas. He was a close friend of the whole Pushkin family.

[3] Nikolai Mikhailovich Karamzin (1766-1826), the eminent Russian historian and novelist, welcomed Pushkin to his house and admired his talent,
but he did not approve of either his liberal political opinions or his dissipated way of life.

1820

NOTE

4. My comments on the Russian theatre[1]

. . . The public moulds dramatic talent. Who forms our public? Before the curtain goes up on opera, tragedy or ballet the young man about town strolls through all ten rows of the stalls, treading on everyone's feet, chatting to one and all, whether he knows them or not.

'Who have you come from?' – 'From Semenova, from Sosnitskaya, from Kolosova, from Istomina.'[2] – 'How favoured you are!' – 'She is singing, she is acting, she is dancing today – let's applaud her – let's call her out! She is so charming! She has such eyes! Such a foot! Such talent!' . . . The curtain goes up. The young man and his friends, moving from place to place, are in raptures and applaud. Far be it from me to censure ardent, heedless youth; I know it calls for indulgence. But can one rely on the opinions of such critics?

A tragic actor thunders more loudly, more vigorously than his wont; the Gods are transported with ecstasy, applause lifts the roof. . . .

A futher comment. The majority of those who fill the stalls are too concerned with the fate of Europe and of their fatherland, are too worn out by work, are too serious-minded, too important, too cautious in expressing soul-stirring emotions to feel any concern for the quality of dramatic art (Russian at that). And if at half-past six the same faces appear from the barracks and the council chamber to fill up the front rows of reserved stalls, it is for them a matter of agreed etiquette rather than a pleasant relaxation. On no account can one expect any sound views and judgements to be born of their cold vacuity, and, even less, any signs of feeling. Consequently they serve but as respectable decoration for the Bolshoy Kamenny theatre,[3] and in no way belong either to the crowd of enthusiasts or to the company of enlightened or impassioned critics.

One further comment. These great men of our day, bearing on their faces the monotonous stamp of boredom, hauteur, worry and stupidity, inseparable from the pattern of their lives, these regular occupants of the front row, frowning at comedies, yawning at tragedies, dozing at operas, attentive perhaps only at ballets, must they not perforce dampen

16

the performance of our most ardent actors and induce a state of indolence and languor in their souls, that is, if nature has endowed them with souls? . . .

1 Written in January 1820, not published in Pushkin's lifetime. Pushkin was a keen theatre-goer and often took part in discussions on theatrical topics at meetings of the Green Lamp. These notes might well have been prepared for one such discussion. Pushkin gave them to the actress Semenova, whom he currently worshipped, who later passed them on to Gnedich. The picture Pushkin drew here of the St Petersburg theatre audience later formed the basis for the vivid stanzas in the first chapter of *Evgeny Onegin* (xx-xxii) in which Onegin's visit to the ballet is described, and all the glitter and applause, the enthusiasm and the boredom, are subjected to the roving scrutiny of the young dandy.
2 Semenova and Sosnitskaya were actresses; E. I. Kolosova was a ballet-dancer and her daughter, Alexandra, an actress much admired by Pushkin; Istomina was the ballet-dancer described in the stanzas in *Evgeny Onegin* mentioned above.
3 The Bolshoy Kamenny theatre (the big stone theatre) was the chief theatre in St Petersburg at the beginning of the nineteenth century. The Conservatoire now stands on its site.

LETTERS

5. To Prince P. A. Vyazemsky
28 March 1820
St Petersburg

. . . My poem is drawing to an end1 – I think of finishing the last canto one of these days. I am tired of it – and so am not sending you excerpts.

1 *Ruslan and Lyudmila*, completed in draft on 26 March 1820. On the same day Zhukovsky gave Pushkin his portrait with the inscription conceding him pride of place as a poet (see page 11).
Ruslan and Lyudmila contained everything called for in heroic romance: mounted combats and wizardry; an enchanted princess and a helpful hermit; a wealth of magical properties – sword, beard, vanishing cap. A very long poem, it flows mellifluously on, describing fantastic adventures in a lightly ironic, mocking tone, cutting across all the classical canons of propriety and decorum. It was both hailed and condemned as an example of the new 'Romantic' school and the influences of Ariosto and Wieland were detected. The public was delighted by its novelty, while the critics were appalled by its 'barbarous' subject-matter and simple unpretentious diction. It inaugurated a new era in Russian poetry. Pushkin had spun his tale too elaborately and towards the end he was flagging. He later came to see its faults and described it as frigid (see no. 175, page 252). He wrote the Epilogue in July 1820 when already in exile in the south and in it struck

17

a Byronic note of expended youth. The completed poem was published the same summer, extracts from Cantos I and III having appeared in the spring in the periodicals *Nevsky Zritel* and *Syn Otechestva*. The magical fairy-tale prologue – the best-known part of the whole poem – was not written till 1825-26 in Mikhailovskoe and was added to the second edition (1826).

6. To Prince P. A. Vyazemsky   *About 21 April 1820*
                                                      St Petersburg

He [Katenin][1] was born too late – and both in character and outlook belongs entirely to the eighteenth century. He is as vain of being an author and is as involved in literary gossip and intrigue as he would have been in the celebrated age of Philosophy. Then all Europe was fascinated by the quarrel of Fréron and Voltaire,[2] nowadays it would astonish nobody; whatever one may say, ours is not an age for poets – maybe that is nothing to grieve about – and yet it is a pity. The circle of poets grows narrower hour by hour: soon we will be obliged, because of the shortage of listeners, to whisper our verses to each other and be grateful for that. In the meantime send us your poems – they are delightful and soul-restoring. 'The First Snow'[3] is delightful; 'Melancholy' even more so. Have you read the latest works of Zhukovsky, who rests with God?[4] Have you heard his 'Voice from the other World'[5] and what do you think of it? Petersburg is oppressive for a poet. I am longing for foreign lands; perchance the air of the south would revive my spirit.[6] I have finished my poem;[7] and only the last, i.e. the concluding verse has given me real pleasure. You will read extracts in the reviews and will get a copy once it is published – I am so sick of it that I cannot bring myself to copy out some excerpts for you. My letter is dull, because from the day that I became a noteworthy figure for the gossips of St Petersburg[8] I grow stupider and older not week by week but hour by hour. Forgive me. Answer my letter,[9] please – I am very glad that I embarked on correspondence.

[1] Pavel Alexandrovich Katenin (1792-1853), poet, dramatist and critic. He served as an officer in the Preobrazhensky Guards regiment, and fought in the Napoleonic wars; but in 1820 he was forced to retire for political reasons, and two years later was exiled from St Petersburg to the country. Pushkin had met Katenin in 1818. At first their mutual interest in widening the scope of language considered suitable for poetry by drawing in elements of popular speech and in the promotion of realism both in diction and subject-matter brought them together; but their literary tastes proved

to be very different and they drifted apart. Katenin's chief interest lay in the theatre and his tastes in drama were enthusiastically neo-classical; also he disliked the pre-Romantic fantasies and melancholy reveries of Zhukovsky and his followers, and attacked them passionately. When in 1832 he published his collected poems and verse translations Pushkin wrote a sympathetic review (see no. 256). Having for a spell rejoined the army and seen service in the Caucasus, Katenin finally retired with the rank of major-general in 1838 and from then on lived in seclusion on his estate.

[2] Élie Fréron (1719-76) attacked the heretical opinions of Voltaire and the Encyclopedists in his periodicals, *Lettres sur quelques écrits de ce temps* and *Année Littéraire*. He drew fire. Voltaire retaliated in epigrams, in the satire *Le Pauvre Diable* and in the mock-heroic poem *La Pucelle*, which Pushkin much admired at this time, and in the comedy *L'Écossaise*, in which he referred to Fréron's journal as 'L'Âne Littéraire'.

[3] Pushkin was to use a line of this poem as an epigraph for the first book of *Evgeny Onegin* and to recall its beauties in *Evgeny Onegin* ch. 5 stanza 3.

[4] Pushkin spoke of Zhukovsky as of one deceased because he was disappointed that he was at that time writing so little poetry.

[5] A free version of Schiller's poem 'Thekla. Eine Geisterstimme', written in 1815 and published in 1818.

[6] Pushkin was never to be allowed to go abroad. He was, however, soon to be sent to breathe 'the air of the south'.

[7] *Ruslan and Lyudmila*, see pages 17-18.

[8] Trouble was brewing for Pushkin at this time, see p. 11.

[9] In his reply to this letter, written from Warsaw on 30 April, Vyazèmsky criticized Katenin for failing to appreciate Zhukovsky's poetry and – in his turn – said he saw no merit in Katenin's verses. He was sorry that in his letter Pushkin had spent time on Katenin instead of writing about himself.

FROM DRAFT OF THE ABOVE LETTER

... Most of us have grown accustomed to regard poetry as a favoured mistress on whom we occasionally drop in, in order to spin a yarn or sow our wild oats, without forming any heartfelt attachment and having little respect for her dangerous charms. Katenin, on the other hand, comes to her in pumps and freshly powdered and settles down for life with her on a platonic basis, regarding her with a combination of reverence and pomposity. Whatever one may say, ours is not a poetic age, our minds are not poetically inclined; and nowadays Voltaire's rhymed couplets could not have the effect that they used to produce – there does not seem to be any reason to regret this, and yet it is a pity. ...

Section II

SOUTH—WITH BYRON

WITHIN a month of his arrival in Ekaterinoslav Pushkin was off again, on a journey that was to influence his poetic development profoundly. All happened with extreme promptness: he reported to General Inzov, caught a fever, languished for a few days on a diet of lemonade, was found on his sick-bed by General Raevsky and, given leave of absence, was borne away to the mineral springs of the Caucasus to convalesce. From there he was to proceed, with the Raevskys, to the Crimea.

General Nikolai Raevsky was a hero of the 1812 war, in Napoleon's words 'of the stuff that marshals are made of'. He had a large family: four daughters and two sons, of whom Pushkin had met the younger, Nikolai, when he was stationed in the guards at Tsarskoe Selo. In the weeks that followed in their company, Pushkin experienced the dual impact of Caucasian scenery and Byron's poetry. The mountains, the cataracting rivers and the sea provided the setting. The Raevsky sisters gave ample scope for the play of tender passion. The cynical, worldly-wise Alexander Raevsky filled the role of saturnine 'hero'. A Byronic phase was inevitable.

From the day in 1812 'when waltzing and Lord Byron came into fashion', when Byron awoke to find himself famous and *Childe Harold* on every table, he had dominated the European literary scene for over a decade. Apotheosis came at his death in the war of Greek independence. He had caught the mood of his generation – melancholy, ironic, eager to experience with intensity passions uncurbed by social pressures and restraints, drawn to the exotic, the primitive, the remote. Bulwer-Lytton wrote in 1833 of the first two cantos of *Childe Harold*,

> they touched the most sensitive chord in the public heart – they expressed what everyone felt. The position of the author, once attracting curiosity, was found singularly correspondent with the sentiment he embodied. His rank, his supposed melancholy, even his reputed beauty added a natural interest to his genius. He became the Type, the Ideal of the state of mind he represented. . . .

The rocky promontories and ruined cloisters of Romantic poetry were seen peopled with disillusioned, freedom-loving Byronic heroes, their faces marked by past experience, men who had seen their finest hour by the time they were twenty. Themselves showing exceptional powers of endurance, they inspired the love and loyalty of beautiful and brave women. The stress throughout was on the exceptional and 'larger-than-life'. In character as in setting it was the unusual that interested the public: the customs of isolated tribes and the experience of exceptional people. What the Byronic movement did not take over from its master was Byron's humour and satiric wit, his impatience with pretence and hypocrisy, the realism with which he described his varied and vivid experience. It was the Byron of the Eastern tales and not the Byron of *Don Juan* that fathered such a progeny throughout Europe.

Pushkin wrote his first Byronic poem ('Day's lamp has gone out') on the sea-crossing to Gurzuf in the Crimea. Marked with love's wounds, he was sailing away from the sweet sorrows of youth in search of fresh experience. He intended to head his poem with the epigraph ' "Goodnight my native land." Byron'. In fact Byron's spirit was to hover over the whole holiday. The Raevsky girls were devotees of Byron and embarked on teaching Pushkin English – a language he had so far neglected – using his poems as a textbook. Their elder brother, Alexander, whom Pushkin had not previously met, made a strong impression. A good deal older than Pushkin, he was an arch-cynic, a spirit of negation, denying the validity of any positive feelings: a Byronic character *à outrance*. It was widely believed by Pushkin's contemporaries that Pushkin had him in mind when, in his poem 'The Demon' written in 1824, he spoke of an evil genius who had poured poison into his young, ardent soul, who despised inspiration, did not believe in the existence of love and freedom, and refused to bless any living creature. Pushkin publicly denied this identification (see no. 80), but be this as it may, to the younger man Alexander Raevsky must have seemed like a character straight out of Byron's Eastern tales.

For the first time Pushkin saw the kind of scenery that Byron admired. He came in contact with primitive tribes who, in their austere, un-complicated lives, displayed exceptional loyalty and bravery. Interest in local 'colour' and customs was an adjunct of Romanticism. The value of the regional and the remote was asserted in the face of excessive neo-classic standardization. The virtues of the unspoiled peasant were contrasted with the vices of over-civilized urbanity. Having been shed by St Petersburg, Pushkin threw himself enthusiastically into studying the *mores* of the Circassians and gipsies; but right from the start this interest led him towards realism, and the true quality of his poetry lies in the extraordinarily sharp definition of his descriptions. He amassed information, both ethnographic and historical, not to use as picturesque appliqué but in order to ground his poems in reality. In fact Pushkin had more in common with the Byron who admired the wit and precision of Pope, and who observed and zestfully rendered the multifarious detail of life, than with the Byron of *Le Byronisme* and *Byronismus*.

Byron's poetry provided Pushkin with a bridge. Under its influence he moved forward towards increasing realism both in subject-matter and style, with an accompanying interest in every detail of character and of the texture of daily life. Eventually it led him to the writing of history and historical fiction, inspired by the further example of Scott. When he became dissatisfied with the strongly marked blacks and whites of routine heroes and villains, he turned to the finely shaded nuances of a 'psychological' novel. It is precisely because Byron's influence on Pushkin was a bridge rather than a terminus that it is incorrect to write of him, as has often been done, as the Byron of Russia.

Pushkin's first long Byronic poem – *The Prisoner of the Caucasus* – was begun on this holiday. In spite of Byron's ritual prefatory denial of autobiographic intention, it had become customary to identify him with his heroes, to see him as Conrad or Lara or the Giaour, not to mention Childe Harold. By writing *The Prisoner of the Caucasus* in the first person Pushkin seemed to be courting the same sort of identification, but in his comments on his poem he said that he did not fit the role of a Romantic hero.

The story of the self-sacrificing, unrequited love of the Circassian girl for the Russian prisoner whom she frees is economically told. Her love breaks against his drained emotional passivity and she drowns herself when she has filed through his chains and given him his freedom. He looks back but does not dive in to rescue her. What is most memorable in this poem is the crystalline description of the snowy peaks of the Caucasus, dominated by Elbruz, gleaming majestically against an azure sky; and the thumbnail sketches of the Circassians, bristling with weapons, who were making a last stand in defence of their mountain fastnesses against the encroaching Cossacks. The setting rather than the hero dominated this poem; he is dwarfed by the scale of the natural scene around him and his emotional condition is similarly reduced in importance by its comparison with the fight for survival of the tribes among which he finds himself. The epilogue of the poem, which with

25

measured grandeur of rhythm celebrates Russia's final victory over the turbulent Circassians, was written in Odessa several months later than the rest of the poem. The exalted note which Pushkin sounded in it shocked and saddened Vyazemsky; he felt Pushkin had stained his poem with the blood of conquest (see page 63).

On returning to General Inzov, Pushkin found that the headquarters had been moved from Ekaterinoslav to Kishinev, and he was given quarters in the General's house. The General reported to St Petersburg that he was keeping Pushkin busy translating into Russian Moldavian laws that had been drawn up in French. He also asked that Pushkin should be paid a salary, for his parents sent him no money and he was running out of clothes. In every respect Inzov kept an avuncular eye on Pushkin's activities and after escapades used to confine him to his room, having first confiscated his shoes. Pushkin was often to be found sitting at home in this sad predicament.

It was not long after his return from the Caucasus that Pushkin set off on another prolonged visit, this time to the Davydovs at Kamenka. The Davydovs were half-brothers of General Raevsky. Alexander, the elder of the two brothers, was later to be memorably described by Pushkin as a living embodiment of Falstaff (see pages 464-5). The younger brother, Vasily, was a member of the Southern secret society and their house was frequented by notable future Decembrists, such as Yakushkin and General Orlov. Here Pushkin again found himself caught up in the undercurrent of revolutionary politics – and he was again sadly aware that he was not admitted to the inner councils of the men most deeply involved.

During his stay at Kamenka he was given the billiard-room as a study and it was here that he completed *The Prisoner of the Caucasus* in February 1821, lying extended on the billiard table. In March he returned to Kishinev.

His return coincided with the outbreak of the Greek insurrection. Alexander Ypsilanti had just crossed the Pruth and had issued his appeal to revolt from Jassy. Pushkin's first reaction was enthusiastic. He joined a Masonic lodge – Ovid No. 25 – in order to plan support for the Greeks; but no sooner had he done so than his activities were reported back to St Petersburg and were made the subject of official enquiry. Nevertheless for Pushkin these were months of political involvement. He met Pestel, the most zealous and energetic of the revolutionaries. He wrote a splendid short poem – 'The Dagger' – in which he warned of the Nemesis that waits for tyrants and celebrated the liberating assassinations of history, ending with those of Marat and Kotzebue. This poem, though it was not published in Pushkin's life-time, was widely circulated in manuscript. The French writer Ancelot wrote home to France five years later:

> Quand une langue n'est pas fixée . . . il est difficile et glorieux de l'écrire avec une mélodieuse pureté: cette gloire, que peut reven-diquer M. Joukowski, appartient également au jeune auteur de la pièce de vers que je transcris ici. Je te dirai son nom quand je te reverrai, mais je ne dois pas le confier au papier, confident souvent indiscret en Russie.

[Ancelot's translation of 'The Dagger' follows.]

> Je m'estime heureux, mon ami, d'avoir pu te faire connaître ce morceau qu'il est difficile de se procurer ici, car l'auteur ne l'a point publié, et je n'ai pas besoin d'en indiquer le motif. Le fanatisme républicain qui respire dans ces vers, l'énergie sauvage des senti-ments qui les ont inspirés, annoncent quelles idées font germer dans les esprits d'une classe nombreuse de jeunes Moscovites, l'éducation qui leur est donnée et les communications devenues plus fréquentes entre eux et les différentes nations de l'Europe . . . Ces idées n'ont point encore filtré dans le peuple; mais elles ont envahi tout ce que la Russie compte de jeunes gens instruits que leurs études ont mis en contact avec les mœurs nouvelles et les modernes institutions.
>
> Je ne m'étendrai pas davantage sur les sentiments qui ont dicté cette pièce de vers, coupable panégyrique de l'assassinat; et sans doute il est inutile que je te fasse remarquer la vigueur, la rapidité, l'éner-gique concision qui la distinguent; la dernière pensée surtout me paraît admirable: le tribunal des francs-juges attachait le nom de la victime à l'instrument de sa vengeance; mais ici *le poignard est sans inscription*, il menace tous les tyrans, quels qu'ils soient!

It is little wonder that in 1826 Ancelot did not dare name Pushkin as the author of this poem in those darker months which followed the crushing of the Decembrist revolution.

In 1821, however, Pushkin's political ardour was short-lived. He was disillusioned by the Greeks he saw in Kishinev and by the quarrelling that had broken out between the leaders of the insurrection. He settled back to poetry – and women. Among the women was Calypso Polikh-roni, the daughter of a Greek fortune-teller, to whom he dedicated a poem in 1822. She was reputed to have been kissed by Byron: the connection was tenuous but exciting.

Politically, Byron gave a lead to his generation but Pushkin was not disposed to follow it. Byron's early poverty and his ostracism from conventional society on account of his private life – 'mad, bad and dangerous to know' – combined with a feeling of innate superiority as an aristocrat, led him to identify himself time and again with the under-privileged and the politically oppressed. He spoke in the House of Lords for the Chartists; he sympathized with the cause of freedom in Italy; he laughed to scorn the established order in Europe; he went to fight for Greece. Whether he was writing of the dying gladiator in the Colosseum or of the prisoner of Chillon, there is never any doubt where Byron's sympathies lay. Because of his position as an outcast from English respectability and because of his European reputation as an English lord and an 'homme fatal', Byron felt and was free to speak his mind; and he did.

Pushkin too was a poor aristocrat, with the same inborn sense of social superiority. He too had a highly developed sense of social justice and was outraged by the tyranny and brutality that political power gives rise to. But by temperament Pushkin was ill suited to serious political activity. He stood on the edge of the political arena and concentrated his creative attention on the private concerns of individuals. The anguish of Tatiana, the guilty conscience of Boris Godunov, the grief of an old gipsy or of a demented clerk, these were his first concern. On public themes he steered an independent course. He glorified Peter the Great in *Poltava* and expressed compassion for victims of his auto-cratic rule in *The Bronze Horseman*. Particularly after the tragic events of 1825 Pushkin never felt himself free to speak his mind fully on anything that might be interpreted as reflecting on the power of the Tsar and, particularly in prose, often wrote impatiently on political questions, as if angry that he should be expected always to hold liberal opinions. Into this category fall his remarks on Greece and on Radishchev's celebrated indictment of autocracy, *The Journey from St Petersburg to Moscow*. On the other hand, however embittered his private troubles made him, he remained absolutely devoted to his first concern: the launching of Russian literature – poetry, prose and drama – into the mainstream of European culture. Artistic integrity was not to be sacrificed for any considerations. He was confined to Russia and could not, like Byron, shake the dust of an unsympathetic motherland off his feet. To have made a political stand under Nicholas I would have been tantamount to suicide. It is fortunate for Russian literature that he did not choose to make it. His life was to be difficult and short enough.

On 8 May 1821, Napoleon died on St Helena. He was fifty-two. In the few years which separated the Master of Europe from the exile on the rock in mid-Atlantic a transformation had taken place in the emotions which the name 'Napoleon' aroused. The ogre – 'Boney' – had almost taken on the likeness of a god. The young Romantic poets of Europe honoured in his passing the grandeur which an exceptionally gifted man can attain. They celebrated the scope of his conquests at the same time as deploring the extent of the carnage for which he was responsible:

> Qu'à son nom, du Volga, du Tibre, de la Seine,
> Des murs de l'Alhambra, des fossés de Vincenne,
> De Jaffa, du Kremlin qu'il brûla sans remords,
> Des plaines du carnage et des champs de victoire,
> Tonne, comme un écho de sa fatale gloire,
> La malédiction des morts!
>
> Victor Hugo, 'Ode Sixième, Les Deux Îles'

They recorded the tremors which his death sent through the countries he had dominated:

> Ei fu. Siccome immobile,
> Dato il mortal sospiro,
> Stette la spoglia immemore
> Orba di tanto spiro,
> Cosi percossa, attonita
> La terra a nunzio sta,
> Muta pensando all'ultima
> Ora dell'uom fatale.
>
> Manzoni, 'Il Cinque Maggio'

Both the ageing Goethe, who had always admired Napoleon – he measured up to Olympian standards – and the nascent Heine paid their tributes. So had Byron, in words laced with irony. His attitude to Napoleon had changed from the scorn for the fallen idol, which he had expressed in the 'Ode to Napoleon Buonaparte' written in 1814, to a point of equilibrium between admiration and sympathy on the one hand and withering condemnation on the other, for the man

> Whose game was Empire, and whose stakes were thrones;
> Whose table Earth – whose dice were human bones.
>
> *Age of Bronze*

This Janus-like view of Napoleon was expressed in the *Age of Bronze* and in the meditations which followed the celebrated description of Waterloo in *Childe Harold*, Book III. Byron was saddened by the humiliation suffered by this eagle among men, but he felt Napoleon had missed his opportunity of becoming a great liberator like Washington, electing instead to be just another Caesar on a grand scale. Byron was at this time filled with hope by the revolutionary stirrings in Spain, in America, and in Greece. Soon he himself would be mourned throughout Europe.

Pushkin's 'Ode to Napoleon' also looked at him from two angles. He began by stressing the tyranny Europe had to endure and ended on a note of compassion for the man who died alone, far from his native land and his son. It is a poem of great dignity written in sonorous, measured tones. It was the first of Pushkin's poems that Tolstoy learned by heart and it remained one of his favourites.

In December 1821 Pushkin went on a few days' journey through Bessarabia. Although his visit was a short one it provided the impetus for his next poems. Pushkin was intrigued by the various nomadic communities he saw living in the steppe, including gipsies and bands of outlaws. He collected impressions for *The Robber Brothers* and *The Gipsies*. This journey also emphasized a connection he liked to romanticize between himself and Ovid, both victims of imperial oppression, both exiled to the shores of the Black Sea. He wrote an ode to Ovid in which, speaking with passionate sympathy of his Bessarabian exile, he drew obvious parallels with himself. The poem clearly channelled his own emotions and for this reason Pushkin did not expect it to be passed by the censorship. He assured Ovid how fresh and green his memory was in the country in which he had died, and took pleasure in the thought that, although he did not share Ovid's genius, at least he shared his fate. This poem was published anonymously in the *Polyarnaya Zvezda*. Pushkin later wrote of Ovid again briefly, but memorably, in *The Gipsies*.

Back in Kishinev, Pushkin wrote *The Robber Brothers* which was based on an incident which he had witnessed in Ekaterinoslav. Two brothers, shackled together, have made a bid for freedom, swimming under fire across a fast-flowing river, and one of them tells of the other's subsequent death and of his own escape. In this narrative are clearly heard echoes of *The Prisoner of Chillon*, which Zhukovsky had just translated into Russian with remarkable success.

Another long poem that Pushkin was writing at this time was *The*

Fountain of Bakhchisarai. The starting point for it was a visit that Pushkin had made with Nikolai Raevsky to a ruined harem. Both its Eastern setting and its story of the jealous passion of a Circassian concubine neglected by the Khan for his Polish captive, whose fair beauty had unwittingly stolen his affection – a Rowena set beside a Rebecca – made it an ideal subject for Romantic poetry and Pushkin handled it with Byronic fluency and assurance. *The Fountain of Bakhchisarai* was published in 1823 with an introduction by Vyazemsky, in which he placed Pushkin at the forefront of Russian poets. The poem was a tremendous success; at last Pushkin had earned a substantial sum of money. *The Prisoner of the Caucasus* had brought him only 500 roubles; for *The Fountain* he received 3,000. This was a great help, for he had been in desperate straits and had been sounding an increasingly bitter note in his letters: 'I sang . . . for money, for money, for money – such I am in my naked cynicism.' (See page 82.) Besides, he now had a very wide public and would soon be in the position to earn his living by writing alone.

When Pushkin wrote of his calling as a poet he did not write of afflatus; on the contrary, he always wrote of himself as a craftsman. The Muse was his gossip and mistress, with whom he did not have to be on the best behaviour – powdered and in pumps. And yet he knew that his work had exceptional quality and staying-power.

It was at this time that Pushkin's voluminous correspondence on literary matters got under way. It was of vital importance to him. During the years he was away from the centres of literary activity it was to be his life-line, his sole means of keeping in touch with what was being written and what was being said on literary matters. He wrote almost daily, most often to Vyazemsky, but also to his brother, to Delvig, to Bestuzhev, to Pletnev, and so on. The letters came in spate, full of comments on the books he had read, requests for more books, praise, blame, vituperation, enthusiasm. He questioned, argued and swore, and continually urged his friends to take up arms in the 'battle of the books' on behalf of the emerging Romantic writers against the establishment critics of the neo-classical school and, of course, against the censors. Pushkin did not always agree with his friends on what was most worthwhile in the new school of Romantic poetry. He was opposed to the old rules and restrictions on subject-matter and diction, but he also disapproved of Karamzin's sentimentality and of Zhukovsky's Gothic fantasies. There was a note of increasing urgency in Pushkin's determination to replace the influence French literature had on Russian with that of German and English literature. He stressed this time and again, laying the emphasis more and more strongly on the need to learn from Shakespeare.

In moments of financial pressure he would be prepared to compromise with the censor provided his works were passed for publication quickly. Though the tone of even such letters is light and self-depreciatory one can imagine how much it cost Pushkin, with his personal pride and severe standard of verbal precision and economy, to expose his works in this way to the black pencil of the censorship.

With one of his letters to Vyazemsky (1 September 1822), he sent his latest poem – the blasphemous *Gavriiliada*, in which both the story of the temptation of Eve and that of the Annunciation are handled with sustained ribaldry. The closing lines now read with bitter irony. In them, Pushkin prays to God, the defender and protector of cuckolds, to grant him security, humility and continuing patience, tranquil sleep, a faithful wife, peace within his family, and love for his neighbour. It was the same year as saw the publication of Byron's *Vision of Judgement* but Pushkin's poem had been written in the April of the previous year. The poem could not see print till after the 1917 Revolution. Pushkin used to deny having written it; but the sparkling lightness of touch was unmistakable, the long-standing enthusiasm for *La Pucelle* had borne fruit. Vyazemsky must have treated the manuscript with the caution with which one handles powder-kegs. 'Pushkin has sent me one of his splendid frivolities,' he wrote to A. I. Turgenev on 10 December 1822. The poem later circulated in manuscript and Pushkin had to answer for it, but on 31 December 1828 the Tsar declared 'I am fully acquainted with the facts of this case and it is absolutely closed.' *The Gavriliada* temporarily drew off Pushkin's spleen against the establishment, which included the Church, and he never again resorted to a blasphemous subject, though there was to be a bit of trouble over lessons in 'pure atheism' from an Englishman called Hutchinson (see page 88).

The night of 28 May 1823 was to be a literary landmark in Pushkin's career. On it he began work on *Evgeny Onegin* – his masterpiece. He was to work on it for seven years.

In July 1823, he left the service of the kindly General Inzov and moved to Odessa. Inzov was most distressed at parting with him and feared the reception Pushkin would meet with from Count Vorontsov, the Anglophile Governor-General of Novorossia. Voronstov was a haughty and punctilious man and would have little patience with the unconventional fire-cracker he was getting on his staff, however brilliant he might be as a poet. On his part Pushkin, who was the world's worst sycophant, would strongly resent the deference expected by Milord Vorontsov.

One of the attractions of being in Odessa was the presence there of the Italian Opera. Pushkin had always enjoyed theatre-going and now he looked forward to some Rossini, but he gave short shrift to Vyazemsky who was at the time collaborating with Griboedov on a one-act comic opera: 'What put it into your head to write an opera, making the poet subservient to the musician? . . . I wouldn't lift a finger, even for Rossini.' (See page 71.) What would he have thought of the situation that obtained in England for years when 'words by Pushkin' in the programmes of the great operas by Mussorgsky, Tchaikovsky, Glinka and Rimsky-Korsakov were his chief claims to fame?

A few months after settling in Odessa, Pushkin's difficulties with his new superior, Count Vorontsov, were intensified by the fact that he fell passionately in love with his wife, Countess Elizabeth Vorontsov, and began to pay her open court. This electric situation was further complicated by a rival in love, his old 'demonic' friend Alexander Raevsky. Vorontsov, perpetually irritated by Pushkin's presence, tried several times to get him posted elsewhere. He wrote on 27 March 1824 to the Minister of Foreign Affairs complaining of this feeble imitator 'of a disreputable eccentric called Lord Byron'. Nothing happened. On 2 May he wrote again, 'I repeat my request; please rid me of Pushkin. He is perhaps a fine young man and a good poet, but I want no more of him, either in Odessa or Kishinev.' Three weeks later he sent Pushkin to the Kherson district to gather information on a plague of locusts.

Pushkin was perfectly aware of the motives behind the posting and he considered it an insulting assignment for a celebrated poet. However, he performed his task, waded waist-deep through locusts and then wrote his reports – the only one to survive is in rhyme:

> The locusts flew on and flew on, then alighted
> To stay,
> They sat and they sat and ate everything up, then
> Were off and away.
>
> (trans. R. T. Weaver)

He then resigned his post.

Creatively Pushkin's activities at this time were far from the futility of his official functions. He had begun *The Gipsies*, one of his finest poems, in which he moves away from the flowing mellifluousness which had marked his Byronic period to a terser, more dramatic style, with scenes in dialogue to mark the significant moments of the action. Belinsky dated the growth of Russian realism from the description of the gipsy camp in this poem, which has the quality of Shakespeare's description in *Henry V* of the encamped armies on the eve of Agincourt. Pushkin used for this poem the material he had gathered on his travels in the Moldavian countryside; but he was not painting a romantic back-cloth against which to set a towering hero, but instead took the opportunity to comment wrily on the 'civilized' man's inability to measure up to and understand the moral standards of more primitive people. Aleko's revengeful jealousy brings havoc to the family into which he has strayed and earns the dignified reproof of the old gipsy. His desire for freedom was a selfish one and it did not allow for the freedom of others. Aleko was not fit to live in a community and the gipsies abandoned him on the steppe.

In this poem Ovid's exiled spirit – a friendly *genius loci* – hovers over Pushkin's poetry for the last time. Pushkin did not complete *The Gipsies* by the Black Sea but took it with him on the next stage of his exile, to his parents' country estate at Mikhailovskoe.

On 19 April 1824, Byron died in Missolonghi. It was a shattering loss. Jane Welsh wrote to Thomas Carlyle: 'My God, if they had said that the sun or moon was gone out of the heavens, it could not have struck me with the idea of a more awful and dreary blank in creation than the words "Byron is dead!" '; Matthew Arnold wrote:

> When Byron's eyes were shut in death,
> We bow'd our head and held our breath.
> He taught us little: but our soul
> Had *felt* him like the thunders roll.

John Cam Hobhouse, a close friend of Byron, was not alone when he read the news 'in an agony of grief'. The Greeks ordered the suspension of Easter festivities. All shops in Greece closed for three days and general mourning was observed for twenty. At sunrise on 20 April, thirty-seven minute guns fired their salute, one for each year of his life. Almost 150 years later, Patrick Leigh Fermor describes the effect on Greece of Byron's death as follows:

> The news of his death, as it spread through the dismal lanes of Missolonghi in that rainy and thundery dusk, scattered consternation;

his name, famous already, soared like a sky rocket into the Greek firmament and lodged there as a fixed star whose radiance grows brighter as the years pass. '*O Vyron*', '*Lordos Vyronos*' or, more sophisticatedly, '*O Mpaïron*', is Greek property now. Thousands of children are baptized by his name, and his face is as familiar as any hero's in ancient or modern Greece. Every English traveller, however humble or unimpressive, and whether he knows or deserves or wants it or not, is the beneficiary of some reflected fragment of this glory. (*Roumeli*, p. 172.)

Byron's death was an event of European significance and its tremor was felt throughout the continent. But Pushkin refused to rise to the occasion and to write an elegy. Vyazemsky's wife, Princess Vera, wrote to her husband in great distress on 27 June 1824: 'Pushkin absolutely refuses to write on Byron's death. I think that he is too busy, and above all too involved to work on anything apart from his Onegin. . . .' But there was more to it than that. Pushkin writing to Vyazemsky himself a few days earlier had acknowledged that the event called for something on the scale of a fifth canto for *Childe Harold*, but he did not feel himself capable of writing it. For one thing the cause of Greek independence had lost its lustre for him (see page 92 and notes). Uncharacteristically for both men, Pushkin asked for a mass to be said for the peace of the soul of Boyar George.

Pushkin was at this time very preoccupied with his own troubles. Vorontsov was still determined to get rid of him and he now had new evidence to be used against him. The police had intercepted a letter Pushkin had written in April or the early part of May in which he had said:

reading Shakespeare and the Bible, though the Holy Ghost sometimes appeals to me, I prefer Goethe and Shakespeare. You ask what I am doing: I am writing colourful stanzas of a romantic poem – and am taking lessons in pure Atheism. There is an Englishman here, a deaf Philosopher, the only intelligent Atheist I have yet met. He has covered about a thousand pages to prove qu'il ne peut exister d'être intelligent Créateur et régulateur, destroying in passing the feeble proofs for the immortality of the soul. This system, though not as comforting as is usually thought, is unfortunately the most likely to be true.

The Englishman, Dr Hutchinson – who may have been physician to the Vorontsovs, was to end his life as an Anglican clergyman – but this dangerous association gave the authorities the necessary handle to have Pushkin sent out of Odessa. The Emperor too, whose feelings towards Pushkin had mellowed on reading *The Prisoner of the Caucasus*, was displeased by this new proof of iconoclasm. Pushkin was given 389 roubles as travelling expenses. He then packed his draft of *The Gipsies* and of the first three chapters of *Evgeny Onegin* and set off to Mikhailovskoe, where he was ordered to live under police supervision.

On arriving at Mikhailovskoe he completed his poem 'To the Sea'. It was a farewell to the Black Sea, on which he had not been allowed to embark, and to Byron. In a few noble stanzas Pushkin paid his tribute to his master:

> Another genius has left us,
> Another master of our thoughts.
> He vanished, mourned by freedom,
> Leaving the world his laurel-wreath . . .
> The earth has emptied . . .

The romantic beauties, the demonic companion, the crags and cliffs, were all left behind. Pushkin now settled to a life of rural seclusion and turned from Byron to an intensive study of Shakespeare.

1820

―――――◆▶◆―――――

LETTERS

7. To L. S. Pushkin[1]

24 September 1820
Kishinev

. . . From here [Kefa][2] we went by sea past the southern shores of Tavrida to *Yurzuf*, where the Raevsky family was staying. At night on the boat I wrote an Elegy[3] which I'm sending you; forward it, unsigned, to *Grech*.[4] The ship sailed past mountains covered with poplars, vines, laurels and cypresses, with Tatar villages flickering by everywhere, and anchored off Yurzuf. . . . Thank you for the poems; but I would have thanked you more for prose. For God's sake regard poetry as a kind, wise granny, on whom one can sometimes drop in to forget for a moment all the gossip, the newspapers and the bustle of life, and to be entertained by her charming chit-chat and fairy tales; but it is rash to fall in love with her. . . . I need money very badly!

[1] This is Pushkin's first letter from his southern exile. He was at this time on good terms with his younger brother, Lev, and while in exile entrusted him with various literary commissions. He also took it on himself to give him brotherly advice on the ways of the world. Lev, in his turn, knew many of Pushkin's poems by heart and quoted them at length, acting as a walking edition of his poetry.
[2] Now called Feodosiya.
[3] See page 24. Published by Grech in the same year, unsigned, in the *Syn Otechestva*.
[4] Nikolai Ivanovich Grech (1787-1867), literary critic and publisher of the review *Syn Otechestva* and later of *Severnaya Pchela*. Grech was quick to recognize Pushkin's talent but their relationship deteriorated when Grech became associated with the reactionary critic Bulgarin.

8. To N. I. Gnedich[1]

4 December 1820
Kamenka

. . . A few Nos. of the *Syn Otechestva* have been reaching me. I saw the excellent translation of *Andromaque*,[2] which you read to me in your Epicurean study. . . . I read in the papers that *Ruslan*, published in order to relieve pleasurably moments of boredom, is being sold with a beautiful illustration.[3] Whom should I thank for that?

[1] Nikolai Ivanovich Gnedich (1784-1835), poet and translator, notably of the *Iliad*. He was responsible for getting Pushkin's *Ruslan and Lyudmila* through the press.

[2] Excerpts from Racine's tragedy translated by Gnedich were published in the *Syn Otechestva*.

[3] Sketch by A. N. Olenin, the President of the Academy of Arts, depicting several of the chief episodes in the poem.

NOTE

9. Note to *The Prisoner of the Caucasus*

The benign climate of Georgia does not compensate this splendid country for all the tribulations which it continually has had to endure. The songs of Georgia are pleasant and in large measure mournful. They celebrate the fleeting successes of Caucasian arms, the deaths of our heroes – Bakunin[1] and Tsitsianov,[2] acts of treachery, murders, occasionally love and felicity.

[1] Lieutenant-Colonel Bakunin was in command of a battalion of *chasseurs* and Cossacks, which was ambushed and slaughtered on the Caucasian front in 1796.

[2] Prince Pavel Dimitrievich Tsitsianov (1754-1806), Russian General. In 1802 appointed Commander-in-Chief on the Caucasian front. Killed by the Persians while attempting to extend Russia's dominions to the shores of the Caspian, south of the Caucasian range.

1821

DIARY

10.

2 April. Spent the evening at N.G.'s[1] – a charming Greek girl. Speaks of A. Ypsilanti;[2] in the company of five Greeks I alone spoke like a Greek, they were all despairing of the Hetairia[3] being successful in its enterprise. I am absolutely sure that Greece will triumph, and the 25,000,000 Turks[4] will leave the flourishing country of Hellas to the lawful heirs of Homer and Themistocles.

9 April. I spent the morning with Pestel,[5] an intelligent man in the full sense of the word. He says, 'Mon cœur est matérialiste mais ma raison s'y refuse'. We had a metaphysical–political–moral, etc., conversation. He has one of the most original minds I know.

I got a letter from Chaadaev.[6] 'Your reproaches, my friend, are harsh and unfair: I will never forget you. Your friendship took the place of happiness – my frigid soul can love no one but you.' I am sorry that he did not get my letters; they would have pleased him. I must see him.

4 May. I was enrolled as a Mason.[7]

[1] No record remains of who she was.

[2] Alexander Ypsilanti (1792-1828). In 1820 he was elected president of the Philike Hetairia (see below) and on 6 March 1821 led a rebel force across the Pruth into Moldavia and issued a call to arms against the Turks. In June he was defeated and fled to Austria.

[3] The Philike Hetairia, a secret society dedicated to the cause of Greek Independence, founded in Odessa in 1814.

[4] An inflated number, presumably a slip of the pen.

[5] Pavel Ivanovich Pestel (1793-1826), a leading Decembrist, head of the Southern branch of the secret Union of Salvation. He had been sent to Bessarabia to collect information on the Greek rising.

[6] See page 10. In April 1821, Pushkin twice wrote of Chaadaev in his poetry. In a poem written on 11 April to his inkwell, he bequeathed it to Chaadaev – 'his favourite of bygone years'; while on 6 April he had addressed a poem to him (published in *Syn Otechestva*, No. 35 (1824)) in which he wrote of how much he had always valued Chaadaev's friendship, des-

cribed him as 'the foe of the inhibiting fetters of convention' and looked forward eagerly to the day when they could again 'argue, read and re-read, judge, criticize and revive their freedom-loving hopes'. This last line with its mention of 'freedom-loving' hopes – used by Pushkin as Russian equivalent of *libéral* – was deleted by the censor. See letter to Grech (no. 13).

[7] Pushkin joined the Lodge 'Ovid No. 25', which was closed down on 9 December 1821. General Inzov was questioned on Pushkin's Masonic activities but denied any knowledge of them. When the lodge was closed Pushkin appropriated all the ledgers of the Order and from 1823 used them as rough notebooks.

LETTERS

11. To Baron A. A. Delvig[1] *23 March 1821*
Kishinev

. . . In your absence you were ever present in my heart, while the reviews[2] kept me in touch with your muse. You remain the same, with a splendid but indolent talent. How much longer will you frivol away your time; how much longer barter your genius for silver tanners? Write some glorious poem, only not on the four quarters of the day or the four seasons of the year;[3] write *your own Monk*.[4] Sombre, heroic, forceful, Byronic poetry – that is your true sphere. Kill the old Adam in yourself, but do not slay the inspired poet. As for myself, my dear, let me tell you that I have finished a new poem – *The Prisoner of the Caucasus*,[5] which I hope to send you shortly. You won't be altogether pleased with it, and you will be right. What is more, I have other poems brewing in my mind, but I am not writing anything at the moment. I am assimilating my memories, and am hoping soon to collect some new ones. What have we to live by, my dear Delvig, grown old in our youth, save memories?

[1] See pages 8-9.

[2] In 1820 and in the early part of 1821 Delvig's poems were published in the *Works of the Free Society of Lovers of Russian Literature* (*Trudy Volnovo Obshchestva Lyubiteley Rossyskoy Slovesnosti*) and in the *Nevsky Zritel*.

[3] A reference to the popularity of such works as *Il Giorno* by Giuseppe Parini and James Thomson's *Seasons*.

[4] Another favoured subject at the time. Delvig, however, never settled to it.

[5] Pushkin had completed his poem while staying at Kamenka (see page 26).

12. To N. I. Gnedich   *24 March 1821*
                                                            Kishinev

. . . The vesture designed by you[1] for *Ruslan and Lyudmila* is splendid;
and it is now the fourth day that I am getting childish pleasure from
the printed text, the vignette and the binding. And I warmly thank
the much respected [Olenin]; these strokes are the sweet proof of his
courteous goodwill. It will be a long time before I see you again; circumstances here reek of a long, long separation! I pray to Phoebus and
Our Lady of Kazan[2] that I may return to you while still young, with
memories and with another new poem; the one I have just finished is
called *The Prisoner of the Caucasus*. It is evident from your letter that you
expect a great deal – you will find little – very little. From Beshtu's
cloud-capped, snowless heights I could only glimpse in the distance the
icy peaks of Kazbek and Elbruz. The setting of my poem should have
been the shores of the roaring Terek, on the borders of Georgia, in the
desolate gorges of the Caucasus – yet I set down my hero on the monotonous plains, where I myself spent two months, where four mountains
– the last spur of the Caucasus – rise, far apart from each other. The
whole poem has no more than 700 lines. I shall send it to you soon so
that you can do what you like with it.

Give my regards to all those acquaintances who have not yet forgotten me and embrace my friends – I am waiting impatiently for the
appearance of the ninth volume of the History of Russia.[3] What is
N. M. [Karamzin] doing? Are he and his wife and children well? I
miss that worthy family terribly.

[1] Gnedich had supervised the publication of *Ruslan and Lyudmila* which – in
Pushkin's absence – had been left in the charge of his young brother and
Lev's friend, S. A. Sobolevsky.
[2] Our Lady of Kazan, a famous icon.
[3] *The History of the Russian State* by N. M. Karamzin, published in twelve
volumes (the twelfth remained incomplete at Karamzin's death and was
published posthumously) between 1816 and 1829. Pushkin greatly admired Karamzin's History and used it as a source book for *Boris Godunov*
(see page 158). Volume VIII had appeared in 1818.

13. To N. I. Grech   *21 September 1821*
                                                            Kishinev

. . . Yesterday I saw in the *Syn Otechestva* my epistle 'To Chaadaev';[1]
that's censorship for you! I am sorry that the word *freedom-loving*[2] proved

unpalatable: it expresses so well the current usage of *libéral* and is absolutely Russian. . . .

I would like to send you an excerpt from my *Prisoner of the Caucasus* but feel too lazy to copy it out. Would you like me to sell you a whole slice of the poem? It's 800 lines long and each line contains four feet; it's divided into two cantos. I will sell cheaply so that the goods should not have time to grow stale. Vale.

[1] On Pushkin's friendship with Chaadaev see page 10.
[2] The censorship deleted the line containing the word 'freedom-loving'. See no. 10, note 6.

1822

―――――――◆◆◆◆◆――――――

DRAFT ARTICLES AND NOTES

14. On Prose[1]

D'Alembert once said to La Harpe: do not speak of Buffon to me. Buffon writes, 'The noblest of all man's conquests was this proud, fiery, etc., animal.' Why not simply say – the horse?[2] Laharpe was astonished by the philosopher's dry reasoning. But d'Alembert was a very intelligent man – and, I must admit, I almost agree with him.

I mention in passing that they were discussing Buffon – a great master at describing nature. His style, in full flower and in its amplitude, will always remain a model for descriptive prose. But what are we to say of our writers who, deeming it too low to write plainly of ordinary things, think to liven up their childish prose with embellishments and faded metaphors! These people will never say 'friendship' without adding 'that holy sentiment, of which the noble flame, etc.' They want to say 'early in the morning', and they write 'hardly had the first rays of the rising sun irradiated the eastern edge of the azure sky'. How new and fresh all this is! Is it better simply for being longer?

I read an account by some lover of the theatre, 'this young foster-child of Thalia and Melpomene, bountifully endowed by Apollo . . .'. My God, put 'this good young actress' and continue, for you can be sure that nobody will notice your locutions or will thank you for them.

'The despised "Zoïlus", whose sleepless envy spills its soporific poison on the laurels of Russia's Parnassus, whose tiresome obtuseness is equalled only by his tireless venom.' For Heaven's sake, why not call a spade a spade? Is it not shorter to say 'Mr X, the editor of such and such review'?

Voltaire provides the best example of reasonable diction. In *Le Micromégas* he satirized the preciosity of Fontenelle's refined expressions, for which the latter could never forgive him.

Precision and brevity – these are the two virtues of prose.[3] It demands matter and more matter – without it brilliant expressions serve no purpose. In this it differs from poetry. (But actually it would not harm our poets to have a considerably larger stock of ideas than it is usual to find among them. Our literature will not go far on memories of departed youth.)

43

To the question 'Whose prose is the best in our literature?' the answer is, Karamzin's. But that, as yet, is no great praise.

[1] Draft for an article. The draft remained unfinished and was not published in Pushkin's lifetime.

[2] This comment of the Encyclopedist d'Alembert, quoted in the biographical note on Buffon by Baron Cuvier in the *Œuvres complètes de Buffon*, published by H. R. Duthillœul, 12 vols. (Paris, 1822), was in fact made to Comte de Rivarol and not to La Harpe. A slip of memory on Pushkin's part.

[3] Throughout his life these virtues were the hallmarks of Pushkin's own prose.

15. Notes on eighteenth-century Russian history[1]

. . . Only a fearful cataclysm could destroy the deep-rooted slavery which exists in Russia; and nowadays our political freedom is inseparable from the emancipation of the peasants; all classes and conditions are united against the general evil in the hope of betterment and a firm, peaceful unanimity could soon place us on a par with the enlightened peoples of Europe. . . .

The reign of Catherine II had a powerful influence on the political and moral state of Russia. Raised to the throne by the conspiracy of a few rebels, she enriched them at the people's expense and degraded our restless nobility. If to reign means knowing the weakness of the human spirit and taking advantage of this knowledge, then in this respect Catherine deserves the wondering admiration of posterity. Her splendour blinded, her affability attracted, her generosity forged bonds. The very voluptuousness of this cunning woman consolidated her rule. Provoking only feeble murmurs among the people, grown accustomed to respect the sins of its rulers, she aroused odious rivalry in the higher ranks of society, as one needed neither brains, nor merits, nor talents, to attain second place in the kingdom. Many were called and many were chosen; but in the long list of her lovers, doomed to be despised by posterity, the name of the strange Potemkin[2] will be marked out by the hand of history. He shared with Catherine part of her military glory, as it is to him that we are obliged for the Black Sea and for the brilliant though futile victories in Northern Turkey.

The humiliation of Sweden and the destruction of Poland, these are Catherine's claims to the gratitude of the Russian people. But in time history will come to a true assessment of the influence of her reign on manners, will reveal the cruel practices of her despotism beneath the personal meekness and tolerance – the people oppressed by her deputies, the treasury plundered by her lovers – will uncover the serious mistakes in her political economy, her insignificance as a legislator, the sickening buffoonery of her relations with contemporary philosophers[3] – and then the voice of the captivated Voltaire will not be able to shield her glorious memory from the curse of Russia.

Catherine abolished the status (or, more accurately, the nomenclature[4]) of slavery, but gave away about a million government peasants (that is free husbandmen) as gifts, and imposed serfdom in free Malorossia and the Polish provinces. Catherine abolished torture but the secret police flourished under her patriarchal rule; Catherine loved enlightenment, but Novikov,[5] who was the first to spread its rays, passed through the hands of Sheshkovsky (the timid Catherine's domestic hangman) to prison, where he remained till her death. Radishchev[6] was exiled to Siberia; Knyazhnin[7] was flogged to death; and Fonvizin,[8] whom she feared, would not have escaped a similar fate had he not been so famous.

Contemporary foreign writers showered excessive praise on Catherine: it was very natural, they knew her only by her correspondence with Voltaire and by the reports of those whom she allowed to travel. The farce of our deputies,[9] so indecorously played out, had its influence in Europe; her 'Instructions'[10] were read everywhere and in all languages. This was cause enough to place her on a level with the Tituses and Trajans [of history]; but reading over these hypocritical Instructions, it is impossible to restrain one's feelings of righteous indignation. It was pardonable for the philosopher of Ferney to extol the virtues of a Tartuffe in skirts and a crown; he did not, could not, know the truth. But the baseness of Russian writers is beyond my comprehension.

    Paul's reign proves one thing: that Caligulas can be born even in an enlightened age. Russian defenders of autocracy do not agree with this, and make of Madame de Staël's famous jest[11] a basis for our constitution. En Russie le gouvernement est un despotisme mitigé par la strangulation.[12]

---

[1] These notes are dated 2 August 1822 and were written in Kishinev. Although they concern Pushkin's historical rather than his literary opinions, they contain some strongly worded comments on Catherine II's relations with writers.

² Grigory Alexandrovich Potemkin (1739-91), Field-Marshal, one of Catherine the Great's favourites. It was under his aegis that the Russian Empire was extended to the Black Sea. He annexed the Crimea and fought a long campaign against Turkey.

³ Catherine was an ardent admirer of the Encyclopedists, particularly of Voltaire, and corresponded with him and with d'Alembert and Diderot. She also corresponded with Baron F. M. von Grimm, whose letters to a number of princes spread the ideas of the Encyclopedists through the courts of Europe.

⁴ In a decree of 15 February 1786, Catherine forbade her subjects from signing themselves her 'slave' when addressing her in writing. They had to use the phrase 'most loyal subject' instead.

⁵ Nikolai Ivanovich Novikov (1744-1818), writer, satirist, journalist, educationalist and publisher. Novikov devoted his life to the struggle against serfdom. All his many activities were devoted to this end. In a series of satirical magazines he attacked the landowning class, extolled the peasantry and undermined Catherine II's conception of herself as an 'enlightened' despot. He felt that the best hope of progress lay in the spread of education and, setting up a press, published textbooks on a wide variety of subjects. In 1792 he was arrested on Catherine's orders and confined for fifteen years to the fortress of Schlüsselberg. He was freed by Paul I, but was not allowed to continue his activities, either in Paul's reign or in that of Alexander I.

S. I. Sheshkovsky was Catherine's secret service investigator, notorious for his use of the whip. He handled Radishchev's case as well as Novikov's.

⁶ Alexander Nikolaievich Radishchev (1749-1802) is best known for his book *Journey from St Petersburg to Moscow*, in which he attacked serfdom and absolutism. It was published in 1790 and in the same year Radishchev was exiled to Siberia. See Pushkin's article on Radishchev (no. 296, page 385).

⁷ Yakov Borisovich Knyazhnin (1742-91), neo-classical dramatist, poet and translator. In his work he borrowed extensively from French authors. In 1789 he wrote a tragedy – *Vadim of Novgorod* – of which the hero was a freedom-loving republican who rebelled against a tyrannical ruler. He was aware of the delicate nature of his subject-matter in the prevailing political climate and withheld publication. He died of a fever; Pushkin's idea that he was flogged to death was apocryphal. After his death, the Countess Dashkov – at that time on bad terms with Catherine – arranged for the publication of *Vadim of Novgorod* (1793), whereupon it was promptly burnt by order of the Senate.

⁸ Denis Ivanovich Fonvizin (1744-92), satirist and dramatist. He exposed the hypocrisy of official panegyrics of monarchs and wrote against Catherine's despotic rule and against her favourites. In his comedy *The Adolescent*, he attacked the abuses of serfdom. Though the style of his writing was neo-classical, the content of his work was realistic; and he strongly influenced the development of Russian realistic drama, in the work of such dramatists as Griboedov, Gogol, and Ostrovsky.

[9] To a legislative commission set up by Catherine II to advise her on domestic reforms. Little came of the project.

[10] Drawn up by Catherine in 1766 for her commission on domestic reform, they show the influence of Montesquieu's ideas.

[11] In chapter XVII of Part II of *Dix Années d'exil* (1818), Madame de Staël quotes herself as saying to Alexander I: 'Sire . . . votre caractère est une constitution pour votre empire, et votre conscience en est la garantie.'

[12] In this sentence Pushkin appears to be paraphrasing the following comments by Madame de Staël in *Dix Années d'exil*: '. . . Ces gouvernements despotiques, dont la seule limite est l'assassinat du despote, bouleversent les principes de l'honneur et du devoir dans la tête des hommes.' (Part II, Ch. XIV) and '. . . Et cependant que deviendrait un pays gouverné despotiquement, si un tyran au-dessus de toutes les lois n'avait rien à craindre des poignards? Horrible alternative, et qui suffit pour montrer ce que c'est que des institutions où il faut compter le crime comme balance des pouvoirs.' (Part II, Ch. XIX.)

See also Pushkin's article on Madame de Staël (no. 76).

16. Note[1]

Only a revolutionary like M. Orlov or Pestel can love Russia, in the same way as only a writer can love language. Everything must be created in this Russia and in this Russian language.

[1] The names in this note, first published in 1884, were abbreviated so that their identification is a matter of supposition. Mikhail Fedorovich Orlov and Pavel Ivanovich Pestel were both revolutionaries, whom Pushkin met at the time of writing (see page 26).

Pushkin here associates his own task – which he was so brilliantly to accomplish – of putting the full resources of the Russian language to use in literature, with that of the revolutionaries engaged in planning a new system of government.

17. On French Literature[1]

Of all literatures it had the greatest influence on ours. . . . Of what does French literature consist? Troubadours. Malherbe survives on account of four lines of an ode to du Périer[2] and some lines by Boileau.[3] Maynard is pure but weak. Racan, Voiture – rubbish. Boileau, Racine, Molière, La Fontaine, J. B. Rousseau, Voltaire. Boileau kills French literature, his strange judgements, Voltaire's envy – French literature is perverted – the Russians are beginning to imitate it – Dmitriev. How can one imitate it? Its stupid versification – timid, pale language – always on leading strings. Rousseau is a fool in his odes[4] – Derzhavin.

I cannot decide what other literature I prefer, but we have our own language – we must be bolder! – national customs, history, songs and folk-tales, etc.[5]

What have the two in common?

[1] See also Pushkin's article on classical and Romantic poetry (no. 79).

Pushkin's rejection of French literary influence was sharpened by the fact that the Russians tended to imitate the second-rate French writers of the eighteenth century. He soon decided that it was the English and the Germans that had to be read (see page 68).

[2] The four memorable lines in Malherbe's ode to du Périer, 'Consolation à Monsieur du Périer':

> Mais elle étoit du monde, où les plus belles choses
> Ont le pire destin;
> Et rose elle a vécu ce que vivent les roses,
> L'espace d'un matin.

[3] Boileau, *L'Art poétique*, I, lines 131-42, 'Enfin Malherbe vint, etc.'
[4] Compare Pushkin's letter to Vyazemsky, no. 84. He preferred Jean-Baptiste Rousseau's epigrams to his odes.
[5] Pushkin always set a very high value on Russian folk literature as an exceptionally rich poetic source. See his letter to his brother, no. 67, and his letter to Pletnev, no. 222.

LETTERS

18. To Prince P. A. Vyazemsky   *2 January 1822*
                                                     Kishinev

. . . Zhukovsky drives me mad – what does he see in Moore, that prim imitator of disgusting oriental imagination? The whole of *Lalla Rookh* is not worth ten lines of *Tristram Shandy*;[1] it is high time he used his own imagination and took his subjects from domestic sources. But what about Baratynsky?[2] Admit that he will surpass Parny and Batyushkov,[3] if he continues to stride ahead as he has done up to the present. For the lucky man is only 23![4] Let us leave the field of eroticism to him and rush off, each in his own direction, for otherwise there is no help for us. My *Prisoner of the Caucasus* is finished. I want to publish it but am too lazy and have too little money – and the financial success of my enchanting Lyudmila curbs my inclination to go into print[5] . . .

[1] Zhukovsky published a translation of 'Paradise and the Peri' from *Lalla Rookh* – 'The Peri and the Angel' – in 1821 in *Syn Otechestva*. Thomas Moore's poem retained its popularity throughout the nineteenth century,

going into countless editions in many languages. (It was the favourite poem of Rosamond Vincy, a young lady of refined tastes of the 1830s, *Middlemarch*, ch. XVI.)

Pushkin possessed Sterne's *Tristram Shandy* in a French translation (Paris, 1818).

See Pushkin's letter to Vyazemsky no. 94.

[2] Evgeny Abramovich Baratynsky (1800-44) was the leading poet of the group that came to be known as 'Pushkin's Pleiad'. Pushkin had met him in St Petersburg in 1818, where he was serving in a Guards' regiment, and right from the start set a high store on his talent, particularly as an elegiac poet (see his articles on Baratynsky, nos. 138, 153, 180). Pushkin thought that the lack of appreciation shown for Baratynsky's poetry was indicative of the lamentable state of Russian literary criticism. At this time Baratynsky was stationed in Finland. Pushkin corresponded with him but his letters to him have not survived, though some of Baratynsky's replies have been published. See Pushkin's letter to Vyazemsky, no. 24 (page 56).

[3] Konstantin Nikolaievich Batyushkov (1787-1855) had settled in St Petersburg in 1802 and had been drawn into the literary circle headed by Derzhavin, Krylov and Karamzin. He fought in the Napoleonic Wars and was wounded, but later was in Paris with the Russian army as adjutant to General N. N. Raevsky. Between his spells of active service he had written many poems and had translated some by Parny. He became a member of the Arzamas and in 1817 attended its meetings. Pushkin had admired both Batyushkov and Parny while at the Lycée and had addressed two poems to Batyushkov, 'our Russian Parny'. Batyushkov, in his turn, had been quick to recognize Pushkin's talent but wrote to A. I. Turgenev in 1818 that he should be sent to Göttingen for a three-year diet of milk-soup and logic.

Batyushkov's own life proved very unhappy and he was increasingly subject to mental breakdowns. From 1818-22 he lived in Italy for reasons of health but his condition deteriorated and he returned to Russia. He died in 1855 of typhus but his creative life had ended in 1821.

[4] So was Pushkin at the time of writing!

[5] *The Prisoner of the Caucasus* was bought outright for 500 roubles by N. I. Gnedich, who then published it at his own expense and sent Pushkin only one copy. *Ruslan and Lyudmila* brought in even less. The edition was bought up by a bookseller, I. V. Slenin, but he only made Pushkin occasional payments, sending him books in place of cash.

19. To N. I. Gnedich

29 April 1822
Kishinev

Parve (nec invideo) sine me, liber, ibis in urbem,
Heu mihi! quo domino non licet ire tuo.

I should add, not out of false modesty, vade, sed incultus, qualem decet exulis esse![1] The shortcomings of this tale, poem, or what you will, are so obvious that for a long time I could not bring myself to publish it. I submit my *Prisoner of the Caucasus* to you, an exalted poet and enlightened judge of poets, as a reward for sending me your lovely Idyll[2] (of which we will talk at leisure), and, having been spoilt by your friendship, endow you with the dull cares of its publication. Call it A Story, A Tale, A Poem, or do not give it any sub-title; publish it either in two cantos or in one, with or without an introduction. I leave it entirely in your charge.[3] Vale.

[1] A slightly inaccurate quotation of Ovid's *Tristia*, Book I, 1st Elegy, ll. 1-3. Pushkin liked to draw parallels between his exile and Ovid's.

[2] 'The Fishermen' published in the *Syn Otechestva*, No. 8 (1822), and as a separate edition in the same year.

[3] See note 5 to the letter no. 18 above. Pushkin was very disappointed by the financial outcome of this arrangement. This edition of *The Prisoner of the Caucasus* had as frontispiece E. Heitman's engraving of Pushkin as a youth (see plate 4) with the following comment in the notes: 'The publishers attach a portrait of the author, drawn when he was young. They consider that it is pleasant to preserve the youthful features of a poet whose first books are marked with extraordinary talent.'

FROM DRAFT OF THE ABOVE LETTER

. . . The shortcomings of this tale, poem, or what you will, are so obvious that for a long time I could not decide whether to publish it. The simplicity of the plan almost approaches poverty of invention; the description of the customs of the Circassians is not connected to any of the incidents and is nothing more than a geographical article or a traveller's report. The chief character (and there are only two) is better suited to a novel than to a poem – and then what sort of a character is he? Who will be interested in the description of a young man who has lost all sensibility through calamities unknown to the reader? His idleness and indifference to the barbaric cruelty of the mountain race and to the charms of the Circassian girl may be very natural, but where lies their power to touch? It would have been easy to enliven the story with events arising out of the subject. The Circassian who captured my Russian could have been the lover of my [Circassian girl] who rescued him; her mother, her father, and her brother, could each have had their own parts to play, their own personalities. I neglected all these possibilities, in the first place from laziness and secondly because these sensible ideas came to me when both parts of my Prisoner were already finished, and I lacked the spirit to start again.

Those who scolded me for not giving my Finn[1] a name will not find one *proper name* here, and will certainly consider it an unpardonable impertinence; though it is true that the greater part of my readers do not ask for any names, and I stand in no fear of there being any confusion in the tale.

The local colour is accurate, but will it prove pleasing to readers pampered
by the poetic panoramas of Byron and Walter Scott? I am even afraid of
bringing them to mind by my pale, feeble sketches – the comparison will
prove fatal to me.[2] Fortunately our Aristarchuses[3] are in no position to
demolish me with any thoroughness; their grave criticism worries me very
little, they are as harmless as they are obtuse. . . .

You will observe that I am not blinded by parental tenderness with
regard to the P. of the C. but I must admit that I love it, I don't know myself
for what. There are heartfelt lines in it – my Circassian girl pleases me, my
soul is touched by her love. The beautiful myth of Pygmalion embracing
the cold marble pleased Rousseau's flaming imagination.[4]. . . I have another
fragment of 200 lines,[5] shall I send it to you for the censor?

[1] A character in *Ruslan and Lyudmila*.

[2] Pushkin was very attracted by the poetic vistas which were opened up to him by the descriptions of unfrequented and exotic landscapes and peoples in the poetry of both Byron and
Scott, and he followed in their footsteps in his Southern Tales.

[3] Literary critics.

[4] Jean-Jacques Rousseau wrote a short sketch in prose on the Pygmalion story (published
in Brussels, 1772), which was later versified by A. Berquin. Pushkin at first also referred
to Schiller at this point but later crossed his name through. Pushkin himself remembered
the Pygmalion story again in the stanzas on women which should have opened the first
chapter of *Evgeny Onegin* but were published separately in the *Moskovsky Vestnik* in October
1827.

[5] Part of *The Robber Brothers*, which Pushkin had completed in 1821. Pushkin was dissatisfied
with this poem and burnt most of it. A section which remained with N. N. Raevsky was
published in *Polyarnaya Zvezda* in 1825 and then as a separate edition in 1827. Ekaterina
Orlov (*née* Raevsky) wrote to her brother, A. N. Raevsky, on 8 December 1821 of *The
Robber Brothers*, 'Pushkin has sent Nikolai a section of a poem which he does not mean
either to publish or complete. It has a strange theme which, it seems to me, harks back
to the reading of Byron.'

20. To A. A. Bestuzhev[1]   *21 June 1822*
Kishinev

. . . I am sending you my Bessarabian ramblings[2] and hope that they
will be of use to you. Pay my respects to my age-old friend the Censorship;[3] it seems the dear creature has grown even more intelligent. I
cannot understand what in my elegiac fragments could have troubled
her chastity – still we must stand firm, even if simply as a point of honour.
I leave them entirely at your disposal. I foresee obstacles to the printing
of the verses to Ovid, but the old lady can and must be duped, for she
is extremely stupid; it seems that my name has been used to scare her.
Don't mention me by name but hand her my poems under whatever
name you like (for instance the obliging Pletnev's[4] or of some sentimental
traveller who is wandering through the Tauride[5]); I repeat, she is

terribly silly, but is nevertheless fairly tractable. The main thing is that my name should not reach her and then everything will be arranged.

It was with the keenest pleasure that I noticed in your letter a few lines from K. F. Ryleev,[6] which are a pledge to me of his friendship and of his having remembered me. Embrace him for me, dear Alexander Alexandrovich, as I shall embrace you when we meet.

[1] Alexander Alexandrovich Bestuzhev (1797-1837) was a Guards' officer and a man of letters. He collaborated with his friend, K. F. Ryleev, in publishing three issues of an almanac, *Polyarnaya Zvezda*, to which Pushkin contributed. He took part in the Decembrist rising and was exiled, first to Siberia and then to the Caucasus. It was then that he won literary fame for his highly romantic adventurous tales of Caucasian life, written under the pseudonym of Marlinsky. His stories of warfare written from experience in the field pointed the way to Tolstoy's *Tales of Army Life*. He was killed in the Caucasus in a skirmish with the local inhabitants.

[2] Among the poems thus described was the epistle 'To Ovid', which Pushkin had completed the previous December. It was passed by the censorship and Bestuzhev published it, without signature, in *Polyarnaya Zvezda* in 1823.

[3] The word 'censorship' in Russian is in the feminine gender. Pushkin continually refers to it as a hag, bitch, etc.

[4] Peter Alexandrovich Pletnev (1792-1865) met Pushkin in 1817 at Zhukovsky's and became his friend and literary agent. The epithet 'obliging' was very apt as he was always anxious to help people in any way he could. When Pushkin died, Pletnev said of their relationship: 'I had the happiness for twenty years to enjoy the friendship of our famous poet. As I did not once leave Petersburg during that time, I was everything to him: his kinsman, his friend, his publisher, his cashier.' He added that Pushkin sometimes sent him his manuscripts with alternative versions still in place, leaving it to him to decide which to print. Pletnev himself was a poet and literary critic. He taught the Tsar's children literature and later became Professor of Russian Literature at St Petersburg University and then Rector of the University.

[5] The Crimea.

[6] Kondraty Fedorovich Ryleev (1795-1826), poet and revolutionary, was a deeply committed man. He had seen active service in the Napoleonic war and had been to Paris with the Russian army. On his return he retired from the army and settled in St Petersburg, holding various legal and commercial posts while getting drawn deeper and deeper into the revolutionary movement. He was a passionate admirer of Byron, particularly for his championship of revolutionary causes, and in his own poetry concentrated on social themes, using medieval Russian heroes as mouthpieces for Decembrist sentiments. 'I am a Citizen not a Poet', he wrote to his closest friend, Alexander Bestuzhev, with whom he collaborated in writing revolutionary songs as well as in publishing the almanac *Polyarnaya Zvezda*. In 1823 he joined the Northern secret society and soon became its leader.

On 14 December 1825 he blazed with activity and on the 15th was arrested. On 13 July 1826 he was hanged.

21. To N. I. Gnedich   *27 June 1822*
                                                          Kishinev

. . . You have saved me a lot of trouble by assuring the future of *The Prisoner of the Caucasus*.[1] Your comments on its shortcomings are perfectly just, and too indulgent; but the deed is done. Pity me – I live among Getae and Sarmatae;[2] nobody understands me. I have no enlightened Aristarchus by my side; I write just as it comes, hearing no inspiriting advice, neither praise nor blame. But what think you of our censorship? I must admit that I never expected it to show such outstanding progress in aesthetics. Its criticism confers honour on its taste. I am forced to agree with it on all points. . . .

In all humility I am enclosing these verses for the censors to examine – in the meantime congratulate it for me. Of course some will say that aesthetics are not its concern, that it must render unto Caesar the things that are Caesar's, and unto Gnedich the things that are Gnedich's; but who cares what they say.

. . . I am waiting impatiently for *The Prisoner of Chillon*;[3] there can be no comparison between it and *The Peri*, and it is worthy of a translator of the calibre of the bard who wrote Gromoboy[4] and The Old Woman. But actually I am sorry that he is engaged on translation, and of fragments at that. Tasso, Ariosto and Homer are one thing; Matthisson's[5] songs and Moore's ugly tales are quite another. He once spoke to me of Southey's poem *Roderick*;[6] ask him from me to leave it alone, despite the request of a certain charming lady. English literature begins to have an influence on the Russian. I think that it will be more beneficial than the influence of the timid and over-refined poetry of France. Then several men will fall, and we shall see where I. I. Dmitriev[7] will stand, with his *feelings* and *thoughts* culled from Florian and Legouvé.[8] . . .

[1] See no. 19.
[2] i.e. primitive and unlettered people. Pushkin may have picked on these particular tribes because Ovid had written of the Getae, as he had of the Greek grammarian and critic Aristarchus.
[3] *The Prisoner of Chillon* was translated by Zhukovsky in 1822. *The Peri and the Angel* from Moore's *Lalla Rookh* was also translated by Zhukovsky (see no. 18), and so was Southey's 'Ballad, shewing how an old woman rode

double, and who rode before her'. Zhukovsky translated this ballad in October 1814 but it was not published till 1831, for the censorship refused to pass a poem in which the Devil is described as entering a church. The verse Zhukovsky had to alter was

> And in He came with eyes of flame,
> The Devil to fetch the dead,
> And all the church with his presence glow'd
> Like a fiery furnace red.

In his version the Devil waits outside the shattered church door.
[4] The first part of a long ballad-poem – 'The Twelve Sleeping Maidens' – by Zhukovsky, first published separately in *Vestnik Evropy* in 1811.
[5] Friedrich von Matthisson (1761-1831), German lyric poet.
[6] Pushkin possessed a French translation of Southey's *Roderick, the Last of the Goths*, published in Paris in 1820.
[7] Ivan Ivanovich Dmitriev (1760-1837) began his career in the army but in the latter part of his life became a Senator and Minister of Justice. His life spanned the growth of Russian literature from Fonvizin to Gogol, but his own poetic activity was concentrated in the last decade of the eighteenth century. He wrote fables, translating and adapting those of La Fontaine and Florian, and satires, choosing as one of his main targets the fashion for writing odes in the style of Lomonosov and Derzhavin. By thus undermining the dominance of the ode and by writing poetry in a language free of archaisms and poetic diction, Dmitriev helped to pave the way for Pushkin and his school, doing for poetry what Karamzin was at the same time doing for prose. He was quick to appreciate Pushkin's poetic gifts and wrote of him enthusiastically to A. I. Turgenev in 1818; but, though he still found much that was brilliant in *Ruslan and Lyudmila*, his appreciation of it was tempered with criticism, which accounts for Pushkin's piqued attitude to him at this time.
[8] Jean-Pierre Claris de Florian and Gabriel-Marie Legouvé, minor French didactic writers of the second half of the eighteenth century.

22. To P. A. Katenin

19 July 1822
Kishinev

. . . You have translated *Le Cid*;[1] I congratulate you and dear old Corneille. I think *Le Cid* is the best of his tragedies. Tell me, did you have the praiseworthy courage to retain the gallant slap on the face[2] on the fastidious stage of the nineteenth century? I heard it called indecent, ludicrous, *ridicule*.[3] *Ridicule!* A Spanish knight slapping the face of a warrior grown grey in harness! *Ridicule!* My God, it should inspire more horror than Atreus's goblet.[4] Anyway, I hope to see this tragedy in the winter; at least I shall try to. I am pleased, for I foresee that the slap will land on the cheek of either Tolchenov or Bryansky.[5]

[1] Katenin's translation of *Le Cid* was both published and performed in St Petersburg in 1822.
[2] The incident in which le Comte de Gormas slaps the face of the aged Don Diègue (Act I, scene iii).
[3] Pushkin uses the French word throughout the passage.
[4] The scene in Crébillon's tragedy *Atrée et Thyeste* (1707), in which Atrée gave his brother his children's blood to drink, horrified Crébillon's contemporaries.
[5] Both actors whom Pushkin disliked.

23. To L. S. Pushkin[1]

21 July 1822
Kishinev

... Write and tell me the literary news: how is my *Ruslan*? Is it not selling? Has the censorship banned it? Let me know. If Slenin has bought it then where is the money? I need it. How is Bestuzhev's publication[2] getting on? Have you read the poems I sent him? How is the Prisoner?[3] ... They write to me that Batyushkov has gone mad: impossible. Stop this rumour.[4] How is Zhukovsky and why doesn't he write to me? Do you see Karamzin? Answer all my questions if you can – and quickly. Also ask Delvig and Baratynsky to write. What about Wilhelm?[5] Is there any news of him?

[1] The hectic way in which Pushkin asks for news of his friends in this letter is indicative of his sense of isolation.
[2] The almanac *Polyarnaya Zvezda*.
[3] *The Prisoner of the Caucasus* was through the censorship and in the press. It came out in August.
[4] Unfortunately it was true that Batyushkov had begun to show symptoms of insanity.
[5] Küchelbecker.

24. To Prince P. A. Vyazemsky

1 September 1822
Kishinev

You can judge for yourself how delighted I was to see your familiar scrawl. For almost three years I have only heard unreliable news of you at second hand – and here I don't hear a single European word spoken. Forgive me if I talk to you of Tolstoy,[1] for I value your opinion.

You say that my verse is no good. I know, but my intention was [not] to embark on a literary battle of wits but to repay by a sharply worded insult the secret injuries inflicted by a man with whom I parted on terms of friendship and whom I hotly defended at every opportunity. He found it amusing to make an enemy of me and to entertain Prince Shakhovskoy's garret with epistles at my expense. I learnt of all this when already in exile and, believing revenge to be among the first Christian virtues, in my impotent rage bespattered Tolstoy from afar with journalistic mud. You say that a criminal indictment does not come within the province of poetry; I don't agree. Where the sword of justice does not reach, the whip-lash of satire scourges. Horatian satire, which is subtle, light and gay, will not stand up to the grim fury of a loaded lampoon. Voltaire himself realized this.

... I am sorry that you do not fully appreciate Baratynsky's delightful talent. He is more than an imitator of imitators, he is full of truly elegiac poetry. I have not yet read *The Prisoner of Chillon*. What I have seen of it in the *Syn Otechestva* is delightful ...

> He, too, was struck and day by day
> Was wither'd on the stalk away.[2]

You distressed me very much by your assumption that your living poetry had departed this life. If that is true, it lived long enough to acquire fame but not long enough for our fatherland. Fortunately, though I understand you, I don't entirely believe you. Age inclines one to take up prose,[3] and if you take it up seriously European Russia is to be congratulated. But then what are you waiting for? Surely you are not tempted by Pradt's[4] monthly fame? Take up regular work, write in the quiet of independence, create our metaphysical language[5] already germinating in your letters – and then God's will be done. People who can read and write will soon be needed in Russia, then I hope to be in closer touch with you; meanwhile I embrace you from the soul.

P.

I am sending you a poem in a mystic vein[6] – I have become a courtier.[7]

---

[1] Count Fedor Ivanovich Tolstoy (1782-1846) was nicknamed 'The American' because he had visited the Aleutian islands (at that time Russian settlements) and often dressed in Aleutian costume. Tolstoy had read an epigram on Pushkin, whom he called Chushkin (chush = nonsense), to the members of Prince A. A. Shakhovskoy's literary salon, which Pushkin here refers to as his garret. Pushkin parried by writing of Tolstoy in a

poem addressed to Chaadaev as 'the philosopher who in previous years had astonished the four quarters of the globe by his depravity, but on growing enlightened, smoothed over his disgrace, gave up wine and became a cheat at cards'.

Although Tolstoy had a bad reputation as a quarrelsome debauchee, he was an intelligent man and was on friendly terms with most of the leading writers of the day. Vyazemsky, who was on good terms with him, had asked Pushkin to tone down what he had written. Pushkin later made up his quarrel with Tolstoy and they became friends.

[2] Pushkin quotes, slightly inaccurately, two lines of Zhukovsky's translation of *The Prisoner of Chillon*, verse viii.

[3] Cf. *Evgeny Onegin*, VI, xliii:

> The years, to rigorous prose inciting,
> Are frolic rhyme away affrighting . . .
> (trans. Oliver Elton)

[4] Dominique de Pradt (1759-1837), Archbishop, diplomat and publicist. De Pradt was an indefatigable writer of pamphlets on political themes, the interest of which was ephemeral.

[5] Pushkin frequently commented on the fact that Russian was not yet equipped to deal with abstract thought. He hoped Vyazemsky would remedy this situation.

[6] *The Gavriiliada* (see page 32).

[7] A mocking reference to the growing mysticism of Alexander I and of some of his entourage. Throughout this letter Pushkin is in a belligerently anti-Christian mood.

25. To L. S. Pushkin

4 September 1822
Kishinev

. . . By the way, talking of poetry, what I have read of *The Prisoner of Chillon* is delightful. I am waiting impatiently for the success of the . . . of Orleans.[1] But the actors! the actors! Blank verse pentameters demand a completely new declamatory style. Even now I can hear the tragic and portentous thunder of Glukho-rev.[2] They will act the tragedy in the style of The Death of Rolla.[3] What will the splendid Semenova do, surrounded as she is? God preserve and bless her – but I fear the worst. Don't forget to let me know about it; take a ticket in my name from Zhukovsky for the first night. I have been reading Küchelbecker's poetry and prose. What an odd fellow! Only he could have got into his head the Jewish idea of singing the praises of Greece – glorious, classical, poetic Greece, Greece where everything breathes of mythology and heroism – in archaic Russian verses lifted wholesale from Jeremiah.[4]

What would Homer and Pindar have said? What do Delvig and Baratynsky say?

... Actually I feel that prose suits Pletnev better than poetry – he has no feeling, no life [in his poetry] – his style is as pale as a corpse.[5] Remember me to him (i.e. to Pletnev, not to his style) and assure him that he is our Goethe.

[1] Schiller's *Die Jungfrau von Orleans*, translated by Zhukovsky in 1821. It was not passed for the stage because of the temptation it offered of showing a vision of the Virgin Mary, nor was it published in a separate edition. Pushkin has punned on the title.

[2] Pushkin is here punning on the name of the actor Glukharev (meaning a dull roar).

[3] Kotzebue's *Die Spanier in Peru, oder Rolla's Tod*, first produced in Russia on 27 August 1822.

[4] Pushkin is here referring to Küchelbecker's poem 'The Prophecy', beginning 'The voice of the Lord came unto me'.

[5] Having commented on a few more poems by Küchelbecker, Pushkin then goes on to speak of Pletnev, one of whose poems had riled Batyushkov. Owing to Lev's indiscretion, Pletnev got to hear of Pushkin's views on his poetry. He wrote a long and moving verse epistle to Pushkin, in which he started by saying that, far from being angry at his biting criticism, he felt spurred on by it to fresh efforts and that he preferred Pushkin's proud anger to the cold smile of a hypocrite.

Pushkin was very upset by this incident and wrote a letter of explanation and apology to Pletnev (see no. 29). The close bond between the two men was in fact strengthened by this exchange.

26. To N. I. Gnedich

27 September 1822
Kishinev

The Prisoners[1] have arrived for which I am heartily grateful to you, dear Nikolai Ivanovich. The changes demanded by the censorship were to my advantage; I must admit that I expected to see the marks of its fatal claws in other places, and felt anxious. ... The lithograph of Alexander Pushkin[2] is masterly, but I don't know if it's a good likeness; the publishers' note is very flattering – I don't know if it's justified. Zhukovsky's translation est un tour de force. The devil! A man of extraordinary strength in combating difficulties![3] One has to be a Byron to describe with such terrifying truth the first signs of madness, and a Zhukovsky to re-express them. I think that Zhukovsky's style has greatly matured of late, though it has lost its initial charm. He will never write another

Svetlana or Lyudmila or such delightful elegies as the first part of The Twelve Sleeping Maidens.[4] Pray God he may start creating.[5]

Prince Alexander Lobanov offers to print my trifles in Paris.[6] Save me, for Christ's sake; restrain him at least till I come back – and I'll dive out and come and see you. Katenin has written to me, I don't know if he got my reply. How stupid your Petersburg has grown! Yet one ought to go there for a spell. My guts ache for the theatre. . . .

[1] Pushkin's *Prisoner of the Caucasus* and Zhukovsky's translation of *The Prisoner of Chillon*.

[2] Pushkin's portrait was engraved, not lithographed.

[3] 'A man of extraordinary strength in the combating of difficulties' is a line taken from Vyazemsky's epistle 'To V. A. Zhukovsky' published in *Syn Otechestva* in 1821. Pushkin again quoted this line in writing of Zhukovsky to Vyazemsky in 1825.

[4] 'Svetlana' (1812), 'Lyudmila' (1808), 'The Twelve Sleeping Maidens' (1809-17), all ballads by Zhukovsky.

[5] Pushkin wanted Zhukovsky to stop translating for a time and to do some original work.

[6] Prince Alexander Lobanov-Rostovsky had offered to print in Paris a collection of early poems by Pushkin, which Pushkin had gambled away to Vsevolozhsky in 1820. Pushkin was anxious that no collection should be published without his having a chance to exclude some poems and correct and rearrange others. He had very decided views on the composition and format of collections of his verse (see no. 91).

27. To L. S. Pushkin   *October 1822*
                                                        Kishinev

If you were at hand, my precious, I would box your ears. Why did you show my letter to Pletnev? In a friendly exchange I indulge in harsh and ill-considered judgements; they should remain between us – all my quarrel with Tolstoy springs from the indiscretion of Prince Shakhovskoy.[1] Incidentally, Pletnev's epistle is possibly the first piece he has written under the pressure of intense feelings. It shines with true beauty. He proved able to take advantage of his favourable position vis-à-vis myself; the note he strikes is bold and honourable.[2] I will reply to him by the next post.

Tell me, my dear, is my Prisoner creating a stir? As Orlov[3] asks, *A-t-il produit du scandale? Voilà l'essentiel.* I hope that the critics won't let the Prisoner's character rest; he is created for them, my dear boy. I don't get the reviews, so please make an effort and write and tell me what they say – not in order to reform me, but to humble my vanity.

[1] See no. 24 and notes.
[2] See no. 25, note 5.
[3] Major-General M. F. Orlov.

28. To V. P. Gorchakov[1] *October/November 1822*
Kishinev

Your comments,[2] my dear, are very just – even too lenient. Why didn't my prisoner throw himself into the water after the Circassian girl? As a man he acted with great common sense, but it is not prudence that is required of a poem's hero. The character of the Prisoner is not a success; this proves that I am not fit to be a hero of a Romantic poem.[3] I wanted to exemplify in him that indifference to life and its pleasures, that premature ageing of the soul, which have become characteristic of nineteenth-century youth. Of course it would have been better to have called the poem *The Circassian Girl* – I didn't think of that.

The Circassians, their customs and manners, take up the larger and better part of my narrative; but that part is not connected to any other, and in fact serves as an *hors d'œuvre*. Altogether I am very displeased with my poem, and consider it to be greatly inferior to *Ruslan* – although its verse is more mature.

[1] Vladimir Petrovich Gorchakov (1800-67), a friend and admirer of Push-kin's in Kishinev. He was a Lieutenant in the infantry division stationed there, under the command of Major-General Orlov. In May 1822 he was sent on a survey of Bessarabia.
[2] Gorchakov's comments do not survive.
[3] Pushkin is playfully referring to the practice of identifying the heroes of Romantic poems with their authors. This was particularly true of Byron's heroes, see no. 142.

29. Draft letter to P. A. Pletnev[1] *November/December 1822*
Kishinev

I did not reply to you for a long time, my dear Pletnev;[2] I intended to answer in verse, worthy of yours, but put off the attempt as you are in too favourable a position vis-à-vis myself and were only too well able to use this to good advantage. If the opening line of your epistle is written as sincerely as the rest, then I no longer repent of my momentary unfairness – it produced an unexpected ornament for literature. If, on the other hand, you are angry with me then your verses, however charming they are, will never console me. You would, without doubt, forgive my thoughtless lines if you knew how often I am a prey to what they call the spleen.[3] At such times I am angry with the whole world, and no poetry has the power to move my heart. Do not think, however, that I am incapable of appreciating your indisputed talent. A feeling for the graceful is not entirely blunted in me – and when I am in my right mind the harmony, poetic precision, nobility of utterance, beauty of structure, and purity in formal finish charm me in your verses as in the poetry of those I love most. . . .

Forgive my candour, it is a pledge of my respect for you. Sine ira, dear bard, let us strike hands and farewell.

I see from my brother's letters that you and he are friends. I envy you both.

[1] Only the draft of this letter survives.
[2] See no. 25 and note 5, and no. 27.
[3] Spleen was an occupational disease of young Romantics. In a long note on its literary history in the eighteenth and early nineteenth centuries, V. Nabokov quotes James Boswell, *The London Magazine*, October 1777: 'I flatter myself that *The Hypochondriack* may be agreeably received as a periodical essayist in England, where the malady known by the denomination of melancholy, hypochondria, spleen, or vapours, has been long supposed almost universal.' (Commentary on *Evgeny Onegin*, vol. II, pp. 150-6.)

1823

———◆◆◆◆◆———

LETTERS

30. To Prince P. A. Vyazemsky

You should be ashamed of yourself for not sending me your address; I should have written to you a long time ago. Thank you, dear Vyazemsky! May God console you for consoling me. You cannot imagine how pleasant it is to read what an intelligent man has to say about oneself.[1] ... All you say about Romantic poetry is delightful, you did well to be the first to raise a voice in its favour – the malady of France would have killed our adolescent literature. We have no drama, Ozerov's attempts[2] are stamped with poetic style which is, furthermore, imprecise and stale; besides, when did he not follow the mannered rules of the French stage? I know what makes you regard him as a Romantic poet: Fingal's reverie[3] ... but the whole tragedy is written according to all the rules of Parnassian orthodoxy; while the Romantic dramatist accepts no rules but inspiration. Confess: all this is only stubbornness. Thank you for the fillip aimed at the censor, but he deserves even more: it is shameful that members of the noblest class of society, who are – after all – the intellectuals, should be subjected to the arbitrary dictates of a cowardly fool. We laugh, whereas it seems it would be better to tackle the Birukovs[4] seriously; it is high time we gave weight to our opinion and forced the government to respect our voice – the contempt felt for Russian writers is intolerable; think this over at leisure, then we'll join forces. Let's have a strict censorship, I agree, but not a pointless one. Have you read my Epistle to Birukov?[5] If not, get it from my brother or from Gnedich. I read your poems in *Polyarnaya Zvezda*; they are all delightful – but for Christ's sake, don't neglect prose: you and Karamzin are the only ones who can write it. 'Glinka knows the language of the heart.'[6] ... What is that? Bestuzhev's article on our brotherhood is very immature – but here in holy Russia every printed word produces an effect; therefore we must lose no opportunities and must publish sympathetic comments on any article – be it political or literary – which has even a modicum of sense. Who better than you could take on himself the tedious but useful function of supervising our writers. My poems are searching for you all over Russia – I waited for you in Odessa in the autumn and would come to you, but everything goes against me. I don't know if I'll see you this year. Write to me in the meantime, if by post – then more cautiously, if *by hand* – whatever you like; and can't you send me some of your poems? I am desperate for some. . . . Do you ever see Chaadaev? He berated me for the Prisoner,[7] for he thinks he is not sufficiently *blasé*; unfortunately Chaadaev is a specialist in these matters; revive his marvellous soul, Poet! for you must surely love him – I can't imagine him any different from what he was like before. One word more about *The Prisoner of the Caucasus*: you say, my dear, that he's a son of a bitch for not mourning the Circassian girl – but what could he have said? *He understood everything* expresses it all; the thought of her should have taken possession of his soul and permeated all his thoughts – that is obvious, it could not have been otherwise; there is no need to put everything into words – that is the secret of being fascinating. Others are disappointed that the prisoner did not plunge into the river to drag out my Circassian girl[8] – well you just try; I have swum in Caucasian rivers – one can drown there sooner than find a soul; my prisoner is an intelligent man, and reasonable, he is not in love with the Circassian girl – he was right not to have drowned himself.[9] Goodbye, my dear Vyazemsky.

[1] Vyazemsky's glowing article on *The Prisoner of the Caucasus* was published in *Syn Otechestva* (1822). Apart from praising the poem, Vyazemsky listed a few criticisms concerning the hero's character, the poem's inconclusiveness, etc. More significantly, at the same time as writing his article, Vyazemsky wrote the following to A. I. Turgenev (27 September 1822, Ostafyevo):

> I am sorry that Pushkin stained the concluding verses of his tale with blood. What sort of heroes are Kotlyarevsky and Yermolov? What is good about the fact that he
>
> > 'Destroyed and annihilated the tribes
> > Like a black plague'?
>
> The blood freezes in one's veins and one's hair stands on end at such glory. If we educated the tribes, then there would be something to celebrate in song. Poetry is not the ally of executioners; politically they may be necessary and then it's for the court of history to judge whether they can be justified or not, but a poet's hymns should never glorify slaughter. I am grieved by Pushkin: such exultation is a real anachronism. It is also a pity that, obviously, I will not be able to drop even a hint of this in my article. My humane and moral sentiment would appear as a seditious move and devilish counsel in the eyes of our Christ-loving censors.

Vyazemsky's letter to Pushkin, to which he is here replying, did survive but it is clear that he did not raise these objections to him, for Pushkin's delight with Vyazemsky's article is unclouded.

2 Vladislav Alexandrovich Ozerov (1769-1816), a dramatist popular in the early nineteenth century. His plays were neo-classic in form but in feeling were tinged with the sentimentalism of Karamzin's school. Pushkin thought little of them and he and Vyazemsky often argued about their merits. In his article on *The Prisoner of the Caucasus* Vyazemsky had spoken of Ozerov's 'excellent talent'.

3 Act I, scene ii of *Fingal*, a tragedy in three acts, 'in verse, with choruses and pantomimic ballets' by Ozerov (1805), based on Macpherson's epic poem of the same name. A characteristic choice of subject at a time when Ossianic melancholy was ubiquitous.

4 Alexander Stepanovich Birukov, one of the censors.

5 Pushkin's 'Epistle to the Censor' (1822) was not published in his lifetime but was widely circulated in manuscript. In it Pushkin began by accepting the need for a censorship, 'what is right for London is premature in Moscow', and commiserated with censors on the tedium of their task, forced as they are to read all the trash that is written. He then mounted a full-scale attack on 'the fool and coward' Birukov, 'a tiresome Eunuch astray among the Muses'.

6 Fedor Nikolaievich Glinka (1786-1880), a minor poet. Pushkin is here quoting from an article by A. A. Bestuzhev, 'A Glance at old and new literature in Russia', *Polyarnaya Zvezda* (1823). Bestuzhev wrote that Glinka had a command of the language of feelings as Vyazemsky had of the language of thoughts. The article contained a glowing tribute to Pushkin, whom Bestuzhev hailed as a new Prometheus.

7 Chaadaev's letter on *The Prisoner of the Caucasus* has not survived.

8 See page 60.

9 Pushkin often spoke of his characters in this detached way, as if they had a life of their own for which he was not responsible.

31. To Prince P. A. Vyazemsky   *March 1823*
                                                     Kishinev

Thank you for your letter but not for the poem: I did not need it. I had already read 'The First Snow' in 1820 and know it by heart. Haven't you written anything new? For God's sake send it or Pletnev and Ryleev will wean me of poetry. Do me a favour, write to me in more detail of your dispute with the censors.[1] This concerns the whole orthodox fraternity. Your suggestion that we should join together to complain against the Birukovs may have unfortunate consequences. According to military regulations if more than two officers present a report simultaneously the action constitutes a revolt. I don't know if

writers can be subjected to a court martial but a joint complaint on
our part could put us under dire suspicion and cause a lot of trouble. . . .
To combine in secret while appearing to act independently would seem
the safer course. In such a case one should regard poetry, if you will
allow me to say so, as a craft. Rousseau lies, not for the first time, when
he says *que c'est le plus vil des métiers*.[2] Pas plus vil qu'un autre. Aristocratic
prejudices suit you, but not me – I look on a completed poem as a cob-
bler on a pair of boots he has made: I sell it for profit.[3] The Master
of the guild considers my jackboots are the wrong shape and cuts them
down, spoiling the goods; I stand to lose by it; I complain to the district
police; all that is as it should be. I hope soon to take issue with Birukov
and will harry him on this point – but it is difficult to tweak him by the
nose at two thousand versts' remove. I am wallowing in Moldavian
mud, the devil only knows when I'll scramble out. . . . You could do
some wallowing in our native mud with the thought:

Even the mud of our fatherland is sweet and pleasing to us.[4]

Cricket[5]

Here are a few obscenities for you.[6]

[1] Vyazemsky had made a formal complaint to the censor because one of his
articles had been almost rewritten.
[2] Jean-Jacques Rousseau, *Émile*, vol. I, book 3: 'J'aime mieux qu'il soit
cordonnier que poète.'
[3] Cf. no. 48 and note 3.
[4] Pushkin is parodying a famous line by Derzhavin in his poem 'The Harp',
in which he said that even the smoke of one's fatherland is sweet and
pleasing.
[5] Pushkin's Arzamas nickname.
[6] Pushkin enclosed five epigrams with this letter.

32. To Prince P. A. Vyazemsky   *5 April 1823*
Kishinev

My hopes did not materialize: I will not be able to come either to
Moscow or to Petersburg this year. If you go to Odessa in the summer,
couldn't you make a detour to Kishinev? I shall introduce you to the
heroes of Skulyany and Seku, Iordaki's brothers-in-arms,[1] and to the
Greek girl who was kissed by Byron.[2]

Is it true what they say of Katenin?[3] Nobody writes to me of anything – Moscow, Petersburg, and the Arzamas have forgotten me completely. . . . They say Chaadaev is going abroad[4] – it is high time; but

I regret it out of selfishness – to travel with him was my fondest hope – now God knows when we shall meet. . . .

Some poems, for God's sake send some poems, fresh ones.

[1] In 1821, battles between Greeks and Turks were fought at Skulyany on the Pruth and at the monastery of Seku. Georgaki of Olympus was surrounded and blew himself and all his men up rather than fall into Turkish hands. This marked the end of the Hellenic rising in the north.

[2] Calypso Polykhroni.

[3] Katenin was sent out of St Petersburg for hissing Semenova at the theatre. He remained in the country for ten years, not returning to St Petersburg till 1832.

[4] Chaadaev remained abroad till 1825, visiting England, France, Switzerland, Italy and Germany.

33. To N. I. Gnedich

13 May 1823
Kishinev

. . . If one can embark on the second edition of *Ruslan* and *The Prisoner*,[1] then the simplest course for me is to rely on your friendship, experience and care; but your suggestions make me hesitate for a number of reasons. (1) Are you sure that the censors, having perforce passed *Ruslan* the first time, won't now come to their senses and bar the way to its second coming? I have neither the strength nor the intention to replace the old version with a new one in order to oblige. (2) I agree with you that the Introduction is rather boring verbiage, but I can on no account agree to the edition of any new ramblings on my part. I have promised them to Ya. Tolstoy[2] and they have to appear separately. It is true I have a poetic trifle ready,[3] but NB the censors.

Tout bien vu wouldn't it be better to round it off with an introduction. Let me try, with luck it won't prove boring. I seem to be in favour with the Russian public.

> . . . je n'ai pas mérité
> Ni cet excès d'honneur, ni cette indignité.[4]

Come what may, I will grasp my *opportunity* to impart to it some blunt, but possibly useful, home truths. I know the measure of this public's understanding, taste and education very well. We have people who stand out above the public, these the public is unworthy to appreciate; others are on its level, those it loves and esteems. . . .

What are you doing, whose talents and work are far above the childish public? How is Homer getting on?[5] I haven't read anything splendid for a long time. Küchelbecker writes to me in tetrameters[6] that he has been to Germany, to Paris, to the Caucasus, and that he fell off his horse – all this apropos *The Prisoner of the Caucasus*. I have had no news from my brother for a long time, nor of Delvig and Baratynsky – but I love them, lazy as they are. Vale, sed delenda est censura.

PS I haven't got a portrait of myself – and why the devil should I?

[1] The second editions of these two poems came out in 1828.
[2] Pushkin had been corresponding with Yakov Nikolaievich Tolstoy at the time of Prince Lobanov-Rostovsky's offer to publish Pushkin's juvenilia in Paris, see no. 26 and note 6. No collection was in fact published.
[3] At this time Pushkin had written both *The Robber Brothers* and *The Fountain of Bakhchisarai*. As in his letter to Bestuzhev written a month later Pushkin says that he has burnt *The Robber Brothers*, he is probably here referring to *The Fountain of Bakhchisarai*.
[4] Racine, *Britannicus*, Act II, scene iii.
[5] Gnedich was engaged on a translation of the *Iliad*, which he began in 1807 and published in 1829, see no. 161.
[6] Küchelbecker's epistle to Pushkin was occasioned by the appearance of *The Prisoner of the Caucasus* by which he was much moved, seeing in it parallels to his own fate.

34. To A. A. Bestuzhev

13 June 1823
Kishinev

Let me be the first to step across the bounds of propriety and thank *thee*[1] heartily for *Polyarnaya Zvezda*,[2] for your letter, for your article on literature, for *Olga*, and especially for the 'Evening in the Bivouac'. All this is stamped with your seal, i.e. your wit and splendid liveliness. Of your 'Glance' we could argue at leisure; I must admit that there is no one I want to argue with more than with you and Vyazemsky[3] – only the two of you can rouse me. For the present I must complain to you on one score: how can one omit to mention Radishchev[4] in an article on Russian literature? Whom then are we to mention? This silence is unforgiveable both on your part and on Grech's[5] – and I did not expect it of you. . . .

On the subject of 1824,[6] I will try to send you my Bessarabian ramblings;[7] but can't we again besiege the censorship and at the second assault gain possession of my anthology? I have burnt the Robbers – which is what they deserved. One fragment survived with Nikolai Raevsky;[8] publish it if such native words as tavern, whip and gaol will not afright the gentle ears of *Polyarnaya Zvezda*'s female readers. But then why be afraid of female readers? 'There are none, nor will there be any, in the land of Russia'[9] and that is nothing to grieve about either.[10]

[1] Pushkin here crossed the threshold from *you* to *thou* – an irreversible move, and a mark of warm affection and intimacy. Using the second person singular in English produces quite the wrong impression, so for the rest of the letter 'you' has been restored.

[2] In *Polyarnaya Zvezda* for 1823, Bestuzhev had published a short story set in medieval Novgorod – 'Roman and Olga' – another set in the Napoleonic war – 'An Evening in the Bivouac' – and an article – 'A Glance at old and new literature in Russia'.

[3] Vyazemsky commented on this remark in his autobiography, saying that his arguments with Pushkin were mainly on literary matters, as on politics they more or less agreed.

[4] On Radishchev see no. 296.

[5] Radishchev is not mentioned in N. I. Grech's *Short History of Russian Literature* (1822).

[6] The 1824 issue of *Polyarnaya Zvezda*.

[7] Pushkin sent a part of *The Prisoner of the Caucasus* and nine short poems.

[8] See note 5 to Draft of no. 19, page 51.

[9] Quoted from Ryleev's 'Ivan Susanin'. Ryleev was referring to traitors.

[10] For Pushkin's views on female readers see his Notes published in *Severnye Tsvety*, 1828 (page 210) and in *Evgeny Onegin*, III, xxvii.

35. To Prince P. A. Vyazemsky

19 August 1823
Odessa

I am bored, dear Asmodaeus,[1] I am ill, I want to write – but somehow I don't feel my usual self. There is something I would like you to do: Gnedich wants to buy the second edition of *Ruslan* and *The Prisoner of the Caucasus* from me – but timeo Danaos, i.e. I am afraid that he will deal with me as he did before.[2] I have promised a foreword – but the thought of prose makes me sick. Get in touch with him – take on this second edition yourself and sanctify it with your own prose, the only one in our prosaic land.[3] Don't praise me, but scold Russia and the Russian public – stand up for the Germans and the English – destroy those aristocrats of classical poetry.[4] One more request: if you undertake the edition – be frank with me, get from me the full cost – don't give me presents – my dear Aristocrat, this is the very reason why I have had no business dealings with you till now. Reply by hand![5]

I owe my brother a letter. What sort of a man is he? They say he is a good fellow and a Moscow dandy – is that true? . . .

¹ Vyazemsky's nickname in the Arzamas.
² Pushkin was not satisfied with the financial returns of *Ruslan and Lyudmila* and *The Prisoner of the Caucasus*, see note 5 to no. 18.
³ Vyazemsky took on himself the second editions of *Ruslan and Lyudmila* and *The Prisoner of the Caucasus*, both of which appeared in 1828. The second edition of *Ruslan* contained Pushkin's famous introductory lines, which he wrote in Mikhailovskoe in 1825-6, and a foreword in which he replied to criticism which had been levelled at the poem.
⁴ The French writers Pushkin was at this time reacting against.
⁵ It was safer to do so.

36. To L. S. Pushkin   *25 August 1823*
                                         Odessa

. . . for a long time my health has called for sea-water baths and I forced Inzov round to the point of allowing me to go to Odessa.¹ I left my Moldavia and made an entry into Europe. The restaurants and the Italian opera reminded me of old times and, by God, renewed my spirit. . . . I still cannot get used to the European way of life – though incidentally I go nowhere except to the theatre. . . . I read [Tumansky²] excerpts from the Fountain of Bakhchisarai (my new poem), having said that I would not want it published as many places refer to one woman, with whom I was for a very long time very stupidly in love, and Petrarch's role does not appeal to me. . . .

Explain to my father that I cannot live without his financial assistance.³ With the censorship in its present state I cannot live by my pen; I did not learn carpentry, nor can I become a teacher although I know my catechism and the first four rules of arithmetic – but I am employed and not of my own free will – and it is impossible to resign. I am cheated by everything and everyone – so clearly whom am I to rely on if not on my nearest and dearest. . . . Farewell, my dear boy – I have got the spleen – and writing this letter has not cheered me up.

PS So be it, I'll send Vyazemsky *The Fountain* – leaving out the delirious ravings of love⁴ – but it's a pity!

¹ See pages 32-3.
² Vasily Ivanovich Tumansky (1800-60), poet serving in Vorontsov's chancellery.
³ Pushkin's salary at this time was 700 roubles a year. His father was notoriously mean.
⁴ The last ten lines of the poem, probably addressed to Maria Nikolaievna Raevsky, later Princess Volkonsky.

37. To Prince P. A. Vyazemsky   *14 October 1823*
Odessa

On your advice, dear Asmodaeus, I have let Gnedich know that I
am entrusting the edition of *Ruslan* and *The Prisoner* to you,[1] and so the
matter is settled. I don't remember whether I asked you to write an
introduction, a foreword, etc., but thank you very much for your
promise. Your prose will assure the fortunes of my verses.[2] What
changes has Raich[3] spoken to you about? I have never been able to
improve on anything once I have written it. *Ruslan* only needs the
addition of an epilogue[4] and a few verses for canto VI, which I sent to
Zhukovsky too late. . . .

Your comments on my Robbers are unfair; that as a story c'est un
tour de force is no praise – on the contrary; but as far as style is concerned I have written nothing better.[5] Between ourselves the Fountain
of Bakhchisarai is rotten, but its epigraph is delightful.[6]

[1] The second editions, see no. 35.
[2] *The Fountain of Bakhchisarai* was published in Moscow in 1824 with an
introduction by Vyazemsky. This took the form of a conversation between
the publisher and a classicist, with the publisher defending Pushkin's poem
and the new Romantic school of poetry against the carping criticism of his
opponent.
[3] Simeon Egorovich Raich (1792-1855), a teacher – the poet Tyutchev was
one of his pupils, and a translator from Latin and Italian.
[4] See no. 5.
[5] Vyazemsky's comments did not survive. Pushkin himself was dissatisfied
with much of *The Robber Brothers* and burnt most of it.
[6] For the epigraph, Pushkin adapted a line from the Persian poet Sadi,
quoted in Moore's *Lalla Rookh* in the introductory section to 'Paradise
and the Peri': '. . . a fountain, on which some hand had rudely traced
those well-known words from the Gardens of Sadi – "Many, like me, have
viewed this fountain, but they are gone, and their eyes are closed for ever!" '
  It was because he used this epigraph that Pushkin changed the title of
his poem from 'The Harem' to 'The Fountain of Bakhchisarai'.

38. To Prince P. A. Vyazemsky   *4 November 1823*
Odessa

Here, my dear and worthy Asmodaeus, is my latest poem[1] for you. I
have thrown out what the censors would have thrown out for me, and
also what I did not wish to expose before the public. If these disconnected fragments strike you as being worth printing then have them

published; but do me a favour, don't give in to that bitch of a censorship, bare your teeth over every verse and, should it prove possible, tear her to pieces for my sake. Except for you I have no protector *there*. One further request: write a foreword or a postscript to Bakhchisarai ... I am enclosing a police report as source material,[2] glean some facts from it (but obviously don't mention the source). Also look up the article on Bakhchisarai in Apostol-Muraviev's Travels[3] and copy out the more tolerable passages – and then cast the spell of your prose over it all, the richly endowed heiress of your delightful poetry, for whom I am in mourning. Will she really not be resurrected. . . .

What put it into your head to write an opera, making the poet subservient to the musician?[4] Give honour where it is due. I would not lift a finger even for Rossini.[5] As for my work, I am now writing not a novel but a novel in verse, the devil of a difference. Something like *Don Juan*[6] – it is useless even to think of publication; I am writing quite casually. Our censorship is so arbitrary that it's impossible to assess one's permitted range. It's better to forget about it – 'if really you're to take, then take your fill, or where's the use to smirch your bill?'[7]

PS ... Would you believe it, I haven't yet read the article of yours with which you seduced the censorship. That is what living the life of an Asiatic means – one doesn't read the reviews. Odessa is a European town – so there are no Russian books here.[8]

---

[1] *The Fountain of Bakhchisarai.*
[2] The police report does not survive.
[3] *A Journey through the Tauris* by Ivan Matveyevich Muraviev-Apostol (St Petersburg, 1823). It contained a description of the Khan's palace at Bakhchisarai and mentioned the legend surrounding the beautiful Polish Countess Pototsky, who was said to be buried there. In his poem, Pushkin calls her Princess Maria.
[4] See page 33. Vyazemsky and Griboedov collaborated on the libretto for a one-act comic opera called *Which is the brother, which the sister; or, One deception follows another*, with music by A. N. Verstovsky, which was performed on 24 January 1824. Vyazemsky wrote to A. I. Turgenev on 18 November 1823 that he was up to his eyes in vaudevilles, and that 'Odessian Pushkin' had sent him *The Fountain of Bakhchisarai*, asking him to write a foreword. Turgenev replied on 29 November, 'Yesterday I again wrote to Count Vorontsov on Pushkin's behalf. Although he finds life gayer in Odessa it's harder to live there, as everything is expensive and board and lodging is not provided as it was at Inzov's.'
[5] Pushkin was at this time enjoying Rossini's operas in Odessa.
[6] This was the first mention in Pushkin's letters of *Evgeny Onegin*. Cf. his later comments on the relationship of *Evgeny Onegin* to *Don Juan*, no. 92.

[7] Two lines from Krylov's fable, 'The Raven Chick', translated by Sir Bernard Pares.

[8] Written in answer to two articles published in the *Vestnik Evropy*. Vyazemsky's article was not passed by the censorship and was not published till his collected works appeared in 1878.

DRAFT OF THE ABOVE LETTER[1]

. . . Re-reading your letters makes me want to argue. You write somewhere, discussing Romanticism, that from the time of the revolution[2] even poetry has changed in style – and mention A. Chénier.[3] Nobody respects and loves this poet more than I, but he is a true Greek, a classic among classics. C'est un imitateur savant. . . . He exhales the air of Theocritus and the Anthology. He is free of Italian concetti and of French antithèses – but as yet he hasn't a drop of Romanticism in him – Lamartine's first *Méditations*[4] are, of their kind, no better than Ryleev's Thoughts;[5] I have read the latter recently and haven't yet come to my senses – how suddenly he has matured – Parny[6] is just as usual – Millevoye[7] is neither one thing nor the other but is good only in elegiac trifles. La Vigne[8] is a pupil of Voltaire – and struggles in Aristotle's old nets – France has as yet no Romanticism – and it is Romanticism which will regenerate poetry, which is at present dead. Mark my word – the first poetic Genius in the fatherland of Boileau will get smitten with such a frenzy for liberty that your Germans will be as nought. At the moment there are fewer poets in France than here. . . .

Much good is there in our civilization! It makes me sad to see the direction in which everything is moving here – you alone could bring them to heel both from left and right, shake up old reputations, discipline new ones, and show us our true path . . . and you have given us poetry, that I cannot stomach. What put it into your head to write an opera, making poetry the slave of music? Give honour where it is due – I would not lift a finger, even for Rossini. As for my work, I am now writing not a novel but a novel in verse, the devil of a difference – something like *Don Juan*. The first canto or chapter is finished – I will send it to you. I am writing with rapturous absorption, which has not happened to me for a long time.

[1] Pushkin expanded some of the ideas expressed in this draft, which were not incorporated in the letter of 4 November, in two other letters to Vyazemsky – 8 March and 5 July 1824 (nos. 50 and 60).
[2] The French Revolution.
[3] Pushkin possessed the 1819 edition of André Chénier's poems and had inscribed on the fly-leaf the following lyric, not included in this edition, which he later – very successfully – translated:

> Près des bords où Venise est reine de la mer,
> Le gondolier nocturne, au retour de Vesper,
> D'un aviron léger bat la vague aplanie,
> Chantant Renaud, Tancrède et la belle Erminie.
> Il aime les chansons, il chante. Sans désir,
> Sans gloire, sans projets, sans craindre l'avenir,
> Il chante, et, cheminant sur le liquide abîme,
> Sait égayer ainsi sa route maritime.

... Comme lui je me plais à chanter.
Les rustiques chansons que j'aime à répéter
Adoucissent pour moi la route de la vie,
Route amère et souvent de naufrages suivie.

As his poem addressed to Chénier – which he wrote in 1826 – shows, Pushkin deeply sympathized with Chénier's doomed stand against the tyranny of the guillotine during the Reign of Terror. Pushkin's poem was heavily cut by the censorship and the forbidden verses were then passed round in manuscript with the tagged-on title 'On 14 December'. This led to trouble for Pushkin – interrogation and renewed surveillance by the secret police. Pushkin referred to Chénier several times in his letters. As can be seen in the above draft, he saw him as the last of the French classical writers rather than as the first of the Romantics, an opinion later upheld by Anatole France in opposition to Sainte-Beuve.

4 Lamartine's *Méditations poétiques*, vol. I published in 1820, vol. II in 1823. Pushkin found Lamartine's poetry mellifluous but repetitive, see no. 178.

5 Ryleev's *Dumy*, published in St Petersburg in 1825, were narrative poems on episodes in Russian history, of which the struggle for liberty was the unifying theme.

6 Évariste-Désiré Desforges, vicomte de Parny (1755-1814). His light, erotic verse influenced Pushkin in the Lycée period.

7 Charles-Hubert Millevoye (1782-1816), French poet of Romantic melancholy; among his best known poems – with characteristic titles – are 'Le poète mourant' and 'La chute des feuilles'. Pushkin had the 1823 edition of his collected works in his library.

8 Casimir Delavigne (1793-1843), French poet and playwright. He wrote elegies on current political themes such as the tribulations of Greece and of post-Napoleonic France, which were popular in his day. In his tragedies he relaxed some of the classical conventions but did not claim as much freedom as the Romantic dramatists.

39. To Prince P. A. Vyazemsky   *11 November 1823*
                                                    Odessa

And here are the Robbers[1] for you. I was inspired to write this fragment by a true incident. In 1820, during my stay in Ekaterinoslav, two robbers, chained together, swam across the Dnieper to safety. I didn't make up either their stay on the island or the drowning of one of the guards. Some of the lines are reminiscent of the translation of *The Prisoner of the Chillon*. That is unfortunate for me. I tally with Zhukovsky by accident, my fragment was written at the end of 1821.

1 Pushkin sent Vyazemsky what he thought was worth preserving of his poem *The Robbers*, and this was published in *Polyarnaya Zvezda* for 1825. Zhukovsky's translation of *The Prisoner of Chillon* appeared in 1822.

40. To Baron A. A. Delvig   *16 November 1823*
                                                    Odessa

... You write too little, my dear, or at any rate you publish too little. But then I live as an Asiatic and don't read your reviews. The other day your lovely sonnets came my way – I read them avidly, with delight and gratitude for the inspiring memory of our friendship. I share your hopes concerning Yazykov and your long-established love of Baratynsky's pure Muse.[1] I am waiting impatiently for the publication of your verses; as soon as I receive them I shall kill the fatted calf and praise the Lord – and will deck my hut with garlands – even if Birukov[2] finds all this too voluptuous . . . I am sorry that my elegies are written against religion and the government: I am a semi-Khvostov, I like writing poems (but not copying them out) and do not like sending them to be published (though I like to see them in print).[3] You ask for The Fountain of Bakhchisarai – I sent it the other day to Vyazemsky. It is a series of disconnected fragments for which you will reprove me, but praise me none the less. I am now writing a new poem, in which I babble on to excess.[4] Birukov will not see it because he is a naughty and capricious boy. God only knows when we shall read it together – I am bored, my dear fellow! That is my life's refrain. If my brother Lev would at least gallop over to see me in Odessa! Where is he, what is he doing? I don't know a thing. Friends, friends, it is time I changed the distinction of exile for the joy of reunion. Is it true that Rossini and the Italian opera are coming to us? My God! They are the envoys of Paradise. I shall die of dejection and envy.

PS Order a copy of the German version of *The Prisoner* to be sent to me.[5]

---

[1] In one of his sonnets, which he dedicated to Yazykov, Delvig forecast a splendid poetic future for him. Delvig thanked the gods for having given him the possibility in his earliest years to recognize and encourage such outstanding poets as Pushkin and Baratynsky. Their fame was his reward.

Nikolai Mikhailovich Yazykov (1803-46) had begun publishing his poems in 1819. Pushkin was also quick to recognize his talent and wrote of him to his brother Lev as 'our Byron'. They first met in Trigorskoe in 1826. Yazykov reacted against the sentimental melancholy of the early Romantics and in his poetry struck a more high-spirited note. He wrote melodiously and extended the range of Russian poetic vocabulary.

Pushkin always praised Baratynsky's poetry, see *passim*.

[2] The censor. Delvig's poems were published in 1829.

[3] As an epigraph to a collection of his verse epistles (1814), Count D. I. Khvostov had used the line 'I love writing verses and having them published'.

[4] *Evgeny Onegin.*

[5] *The Prisoner of the Caucasus*, translated into German by A. E. Wulfert, published in 1823: *Der Berggefangene von Alexander Puschkin*. For this translation Wulfert received a gold repeater watch from the Russian Empress.

74

41. To A. I. Turgenev   *1 December 1823*
Odessa

... One has to spend three years in stuffy Asiatic confinement, as I have, in order to appreciate the true value of the air of Europe, lacking in freedom though it be. .... Talking of poetry: you wanted to see the ode on the death of Napoleon. It isn't good, here are the most tolerable stanzas. .... This [the concluding, 15th] stanza is now meaningless, but it was written at the beginning of 1821 – it is the last delirious expression of my liberalism.[1] I have renounced it and the other day wrote an imitation of a parable by that moderate Democrat J.C. (a sower went out to sow his seed) ...[2]

Shame on Zhukovsky; in what way am I inferior to Princess Charlotta? Why hasn't he written me a line in the course of three years? Is it true that he is translating *The Giaour*?[3] In the meantime I am writing a new poem at my leisure, *Evgeny Onegin*, in which I choke in gall. Two cantos are already completed.

[1] Pushkin quoted stanzas 4-6 and the concluding stanza (15) of his ode 'To Napoleon', written in July 1821 and published in 1826 in an expurgated version. The very stanzas Pushkin here selected as the best (4-6) were excluded by order of the censor. See pages 29-30 for the poetic repercussions of Napoleon's death.

    In the last stanza Pushkin declared that Napoleon had pointed out their great destiny to the Russian people and had, from the darkness of his exile, bequeathed freedom to the world.

[2] Pushkin here quotes a short poem beginning 'A sower of freedom in the wilderness...'

[3] Princess Charlotta, daughter of the Duke of Würtemburg, married the Grand Duke Michael of Russia. Zhukovsky greatly admired her and wrote for her the poem 'The Angel and the Singer', when she came on a visit to Russia in October 1823.

    Zhukovsky did not translate *The Giaour*.

42. To Prince P. A. Vyazemsky   *1-8 December 1823*
Odessa

... I would like to preserve in the Russian language a certain biblical obscenity. I do not like to see traces of European affectation and French refinement in our primitive language. Coarseness and simplicity suit it better. I preach from an inner conviction, but out of habit write otherwise.

    ... What is Griboedov? I was told that he has written a comedy about Chaadaev; which, in the present circumstances, is exceedingly noble of him.[1]

I am sending the Robbers.

[1] Alexander Sergeevich Griboedov (1795-1829) wrote his celebrated satiric comedy, *Woe from Wit*, of which scores of lines were to become proverbial, in 1823-4, and it was circulated in manuscript. It was not published till 1833. Many of Griboedov's contemporaries thought that the hero, Chatsky, newly returned from travels in Western Europe, was a portrait of Chaadaev, who was at the time abroad, having been forced to resign his commission after political disturbances in his regiment. Pushkin did not read Griboedov's comedy till 1825 (see page 132). Griboedov was murdered in Teheran in 1829, while acting as Minister-plenipotentiary. See pages 383-4 for Pushkin's strange encounter with his coffin, as it was being trundled back to Russia from Persia in a bullock-cart.

Pushkin obviously considered there was a certain amount of risk involved in making a hero of Chaadaev.

1824

MISCELLANEOUS NOTES

43. Letter to the Publisher of the *Syn Otechestva*[1]   *April 1824*
                                                                Odessa

It has been my lot in the course of the last four years to be the subject of comments in the press. Often unfair, often improper, some did not merit any attention, others it was impossible to answer at a distance. The self-justification of an author whose vanity has been touched could not have interested the public; it was my intention to correct without comment in the new edition shortcomings which had been brought to my notice in various ways, and reading with lively gratitude the occasional flattering compliments and expressions of approval, I felt that it was not the rather faint merit of my poems alone that gave rise to such gracious expressions of indulgence and friendship.

I now find myself obliged to break silence. Prince P. A. Vyazemsky, having undertaken as an act of friendship the editing of 'The Fountain of Bakhchisarai', added to it a Conversation between the Publisher and an Anti-Romantic, a conversation which he had probably invented for, if among our publishing classicists there are many who resemble the Classicist of the Viborg side in the force of their opinions, there is, I think, not one among them who expresses himself with such point and urbane politeness.

One of our literary judges did not like this Conversation. He published, in the fifth number of the *Vestnik Evropy*, a second Conversation between the Publisher and the Classicist, in which among other things I read the following:

Publisher: And so you don't like my Conversation?
Classicist: I confess I think it is a pity that you published it with the excellent poem by Pushkin, I think the author himself will regret it.

The author is very pleased that he has the opportunity of thanking Prince Vyazemsky for his splendid gift. The 'Conversation between the Publisher and a Classicist from the Viborg side or from Vasilievsky Island'[2] is written for Europe in general rather than exclusively for

77

Russia, where the opponents of Romanticism are too weak and insignificant and are unworthy of such a brilliant retort.

I neither wish, nor have the right, to complain on any other count, and accept the praise of the anonymous critic with sincere humility.

Alexander Pushkin

[1] Published in *Syn Otechestva*, No. 18 (3 May 1824). Vyazemsky's introduction to *The Fountain of Bakhchisarai* had provoked a riposte from the 'classical' side, published anonymously in *Vestnik Evropy*. Pushkin now joined in.

[2] Districts of St Petersburg, on the other side of the Neva from the centre of the city.

44. Note [1]

The causes slowing down our literature's progress are usually taken to be: (i) the widespread use of French and neglect of Russian.[2] All our writers complain of this – but who is to blame if not themselves? Excluding those whose concern is poetry, there is no one for whom the Russian language can hold sufficient attraction – we have as yet neither literature nor books; from childhood we have gleaned all our knowledge, all our ideas from foreign books, we have grown used to thinking in a foreign language (we have no such thing as a metaphysical language[3]); the enlightenment of the age demands serious subjects for reflection, as food for minds that can no longer be satisfied by the brilliant play of imagination and harmony alone; but learning, politics and philosophy have not yet found expression in Russian; our prose is as yet so little formed, that even in ordinary correspondence we are obliged to *create* turns of phrase for the expression of the most common ideas; and in our indolence we prefer to express ourselves in a foreign language, whose mechanical forms have long been in existence and are known to everyone.

But, I will be told, Russian poetry has reached a highly civilized level. I agree that a few of Derzhavin's odes – despite the uneven quality of the style and the incorrectness of the language, are full of flashes of true genius; that in Bogdanovich's *Dushenka*[4] one comes on verses, even whole pages, worthy of La Fontaine; that Krylov has surpassed all fabulists known to us, with the possible exception of the above-mentioned La Fontaine; that Batyushkov, Lomonosov's fortunate successor, did for the Russian language what Petrarch did for Italian; that Zhukovsky would have been translated into all languages, had he himself translated less.

[1] Draft comment on Bestuzhev's article published in *Polyarnaya Zvezda*,

1824, 'A Glance at Russian literature in 1823', found in Pushkin's papers dated 1824, not published in his lifetime.

² In *Evgeny Onegin*, III, xxvi, Pushkin wrote:

> Another problem looms: I'd better,
> Indeed I must, beyond dispute,
> Translate for you Tatiana's letter,
> To save my country's good repute.
> In Russian she was poorly grounded;
> She never read our journals; found it
> Too great a toil to speak her mind
> In her own language; was inclined,
> Therefore, to write in French. Despairing
> Again I ask you, what to do?
> Our ladies have not, hitherto,
> Their loves in Russian been declaring.
> Our lordly tongue cannot compose
> As yet, epistolary prose.
>   (trans. Oliver Elton)

And in his unfinished story 'Roslavlev' written in 1831, first published anonymously as a translation 'from the French' in *Sovremennik*, No. 3 (1836), and then posthumously in *Sovremennik*, No. 7 (1837), he wrote on the same theme again:

> Here I will allow myself a short digression. It is now well-nigh thirty years that we poor devils are blamed for not reading Russian and for apparently not being able to express ourselves in our mother-tongue. The fact is that we would be pleased to read in Russian but it seems our literature goes back no further than Lomonosov and is still extremely limited. It does, of course, present us with several first-class poets, but one cannot expect that all readers should have an exclusive liking for verse. In prose we only have Karamzin's 'History'; the first two or three novels appeared two or three years ago; whereas in France, England and Germany, books follow one another continually, each one more marvellous than the last. We do not even see translations; and if we do, whatever you say I still prefer the originals. Our reviews are interesting for our men of letters. We are compelled to imbibe all our news and ideas from foreign books; so that we begin to think in a foreign language (at least all those who think and follow the progress of human thought do so). Our most eminent men of letters have confessed as much to me.

³ See letter to Vyazemsky, no. 107.

⁴ Ippolit Fedorovich Bogdanovich (1743-1803) is best remembered for his poem *Dushenka* (1783), based on the story of Cupid and Psyche. He broke with classical canons of taste and the inflated style of formal odes and, influenced by La Fontaine, wrote in a lighter, more frivolous vein.

45. Foreword to the first chapter of *Evgeny Onegin*[1]

This is the beginning of a long poem which will, probably, never see completion.

Several cantos or chapters of *Evgeny Onegin* are already completed. Having been written under the influence of favourable circumstances, they bear that imprint of gaiety which marked the first efforts of the author of *Ruslan and Lyudmila*.

The first chapter forms a whole, complete in itself. It contains a description of the social life of a young man in St Petersburg at the end of 1819[2] and is reminiscent of *Beppo* – a humorous work by the sombre Byron.

Far-sighted critics will of course note the insufficiencies of the plan. Everyone is free to judge of the plan of a whole novel on reading its first chapter. They will also start to condemn the anti-poetic character of the hero, reminiscent of *The Prisoner of the Caucasus*,[3] as well as certain stanzas written in the wearisome manner of contemporary elegies, 'in which all is drowned in melancholy'.[4] But may we draw the attention of readers to qualities rarely to be found among satirists:[5] the absence of an offensive character and the maintenance of strict decorum in the humorous description of manners.[6]

[1] Published as a foreword to the first edition of the first chapter of *Evgeny Onegin*, 1825. It was excluded by Pushkin from the 1833 edition of the complete poem.

[2] See page 102.

[3] See pages 25 and 50-1.

[4] Pushkin is here quoting from Küchelbecker's article 'Of the trend of our poetry', published in *Mnemozina*, pt. II (1824).

[5] Pushkin later denied a satiric intention in *Evgeny Onegin*, see no 92.

[6] In the draft, Pushkin went on at this point:

> Juvenal, Petronius, Voltaire and Byron frequently failed to maintain a proper respect for readers and for the fair sex. It is said that our ladies are beginning to read in Russian. We boldly offer them this work, where they will find, under a veneer of satiric humour, observations which are at once just and diverting.

LETTERS

46. To A. A. Bestuzhev   *12 January 1824*
                                                              Odessa

Of course I am angry with you and am ready, by your leave, to scold you all night. You published the very verses which I especially asked you not to publish; you have no idea how annoyed I am.[1] You write that without the three last lines the elegy would be meaningless. Much it matters! . . . I have long given up being angry over misprints, but in the past I have occasionally chattered to excess in verse, and it makes me sad to see that I am treated as though I were dead, with no regard paid either to my wishes or to my poor property. One might expect it of Voeykov,[2] but et tu autem, Brute!

. . . This is the last time that I shall tell you of my complaints and requests, and I embrace you sans rancune and with gratitude for everything else – both prose and verse. You remain the same: i.e. charming, vital, intelligent. Baratynsky is a delight and a marvel; 'The Admission' is perfection itself. I will never publish my elegies in his wake, even if the compositor were to swear on the Gospels to deal more mercifully with me.[3] Ryleev's *Voynarovsky*[4] is incomparably better than all his *Dumy*, his style has matured and is becoming a truly narrative one, which is something we still almost completely lack. Delvig is a splendid fellow.[5] I will write to him. . . . Farewell, my dear *Walter*![6]

[1] The last three lines of the short poem 'Redeyet oblakov . . .' published in *Polyarnaya Zvezda* for 1824 referred to one of the Raevsky daughters. Pushkin omitted these lines when he published this poem in his collection in 1826.

[2] Alexander Fedorovich Voeykov (1778-1839) was a writer and translator who edited several of the literary reviews of the period, including at one time the *Syn Otechestva*. His views on literature were conservative, in line with those of Bulgarin and Grech.

[3] Baratynsky's poem was included in this same issue of *Polyarnaya Zvezda*. In spite of what he said about his attitude to misprints, Pushkin could not resist a side-thrust at the compositors for leaving several mistakes in his poems.

[4] *Voynarovsky* (1825), of which two extracts were included in *Polyarnaya Zvezda*, was a verse tale in the Byronic vein.

[5] Five of Delvig's poems were included in *Polyarnaya Zvezda*.

[6] Pushkin nicknamed Bestuzhev 'Walter' because he thought his tale 'The Castle of Neuhausen' was written in the style of Walter Scott.

47. To F. V. Bulgarin[1]   *1 February 1824*
                                                               Odessa

I am sincerely grateful for the 1st No. of the *Severny Arkhiv*, which I received and for which I believe I am indebted to the respected publisher himself. It is with the same feelings that I have seen your indulgent review of my Tatar poem.[2] You belong to that small group of men of letters whose praise and blame can be, and should be, respected. You will very much oblige me if you will publish in your columns the enclosed two pieces. They were published with misprints in the *Polyarnaya Zvezda* and as a result appeared meaningless.[3] In people this wouldn't matter very much, but poems are not people. . . .

[1] Fadey Venediktovich Bulgarin (1789-1859), a Pole, fought first on the Russian and then on the French side in the Napoleonic wars. After the war he settled in St Petersburg and began to publish literary and historical reviews: the *Severny Arkhiv, Literaturnye Listki*, and, in collaboration with Grech, the *Severnaya Pchela*. His reactionary views recommended him to the government and he became a political informer in Benckendorff's service. He was very suspicious of the 'Lycée spirit' with which Pushkin was imbued, but at this stage professed to admire his work.

Only two letters of Pushkin to Bulgarin survive and the tone of this one is very different from the way in which Pushkin usually spoke of Bulgarin, whom he thoroughly despised.

[2] *The Fountain of Bakhchisarai.*

[3] Bulgarin did as Pushkin asked and published two of the same poems as had appeared in the *Polyarnaya Zvezda* in No. 4 of *Literaturnye Listki* – this time, however, three lines of one of the poems were excised.

48. To L. S. Pushkin   *After 12 January/beginning of February 1824 Odessa*

. . . As you know I have twice asked Ivan Ivanovich,[1] through his Ministers, about leave – and twice a most gracious refusal has followed. It remains either to write to him direct – to so-and-so, at the Winter Palace opposite the Fortress of Peter and Paul, or else quietly to pick up a hat and stick and go to take a look at Constantinople. I am getting to the state where I can hardly bear Holy Russia any longer. . . . If I had money . . . but where am I to get it from? As for fame, it is hard to be content with that alone in Russia. Fame in Russia may flatter some V. Kozlov,[2] who is flattered even by Petersburg contacts, while anybody at all decent despises both the one and the other. Mais pourquoi chantais-tu?[3] I reply to Lamartine's question: I sang as a baker bakes, as a tailor sews, as Kozlov writes, as a doctor kills – for money, for money, for money – such I am in my naked cynicism. Pletnev writes to me that *The Fountain of Bakhchisarai* is in everyone's hands. Thank you, my friends, for your gracious concern for my fame!

. . . a poet should not think of his livelihood, but should, like Kornilovich, write in the hope of snatching a smile from the fair sex.[4] My dear,
I am ill with chagrin – whatever I set eyes on is so nasty, so base, so
stupid; will it continue so for long? Talking of nastiness, I read Lobanov's
Phèdre[5] – I wanted to write a criticism of it, not for the sake of Lobanov
but for the sake of Marquis Racine; but my pen fell from my hand.
And this is causing a stir among you, and this is called by your journalists a most excellent translation of the famous tragedy by M. Racine!
. . . And what does Ivan Ivanovich Racine live by if not by his verse,
full of meaning and precision and harmony? The plot and the characterization of *Phèdre* are the height of stupidity and nullity of invention –
his Theseus is but the first of Molière's cuckolds; Hippolyte, le superbe,
le fier Hippolyte – et même un peu farouche, Hippolyte, the stern
Scythian[6] bastard, is no more than a well-brought-up boy, courteous
and respectful –

> D'un mensonge si noir . . . etc.[7]

Read this much praised tirade right through and you will become convinced that Racine had no idea how to create a tragic character. Compare it to the speech of Parisina's young lover in Byron's poem[8] and you
will see the difference in their intellects. And Théramène is an abbé
and a procurer – Vous-même où seriez-vous, etc. . . . [9] that is the nadir
of stupidity. I am making my peace with Ryleev – *Voynarovsky* is full
of life. What of Kukhlya?[10] I will be writing to Delvig; but if I don't
find time to, tell him to take 'Veshchy Oleg'[11] from Turgenev and publish it. Maybe I shall send him some excerpts from *Onegin*; it is my best
work. Do not believe N. Raevsky who rails at it. He expected romanticism from me and found satire and cynicism and failed to get the feel
of much of it.[12]

[1] Tsar Alexander I.

[2] Vasily Ivanovich Kozlov (1792-1825), a minor writer with social ambitions. He contributed to the literary reviews.

[3] Pushkin is quoting from Lamartine's poem 'Le poète mourant', verse 17:

> 'Mais pourquoi chantais-tu?' – Demande à Philomèle
> Pourquoi, durant les nuits, sa douce voix se mêle
> Aux doux bruits des ruisseaux sous l'ombrage roulant:
> Je chantais, mes amis, comme l'homme respire,
> Comme l'oiseau gémit, comme le vent soupire,
> Comme l'eau murmure en coulant.

Pushkin's matter-of-fact, ironic reply stands in sharp contrast to Lamartine's romantic affirmation. Pushkin always insisted that there should be

nothing against writers living by their pens, but at the time many still regarded literary work as a pastime, in Derzhavin's words 'a glass of sweet lemonade on a summer's day'.

4 Alexander Osipovich Kornilovich (1795-1834) was a member of the Southern secret society and was sentenced to hard labour for his part in the Decembrist revolution. He had published a historical article in the *Polyarnaya Zvezda* for 1824 dedicated to a Baroness A. E. A., in which he said that the smile of her approval would give him fresh strength and would encourage him to renew his labours.

5 M. E. Lobanov's translation of *Phèdre* was produced on 9 November 1823.

6 Pushkin is here using 'Scythian' in the wider sense of 'barbaric'.

7 Hippolyte's speech to Thésée in Act IV, scene ii.

8 Hugo's speech in stanza xiii of *Parisina*. A prose translation of *Parisina* by Bestuzhev was published in St Petersburg in 1821.

9 *Phèdre*, Act I, scene i.

10 Pushkin's usual nickname for Küchelbecker.

11 Pushkin's ballad about Oleg and his steed was written in 1822 and published by Delvig in his almanac, *Severnye Tsvety* for 1825.

12 Pushkin later played down the satiric element in *Evgeny Onegin*, a legacy from his enthusiasm for *Don Juan*. The originality of *Evgeny Onegin* nonplussed several of Pushkin's contemporaries. They were not prepared for its realistic picture of 'ordinary' Russian life; Bestuzhev, for example, found it lacking in social purpose.

49. To A. A. Bestuzhev   *8 February 1824*
Odessa

. . . I am pleased that my *Fountain* splashes. I am not to blame for the structural deficiency. I religiously transposed the young woman's tale into verse,

> Aux douces lois des vers je pliai les accents
> De sa bouche aimable et naïve.[1]

Besides I wrote it solely for my own pleasure and am publishing it because I need the money.

My third and most important point has the epigraph *without ceremony*: you demand half a score of poems of me, as if I had hundreds of them. I'll scarcely be able to muster five, and even then, don't forget my relationship with the censorship. I won't take money from you for nothing; and besides I promised Küchelbecker, who probably needs my poems more than you do.[2] Don't even think of my poem;[3] if it ever is published it will probably be neither in Moscow nor Petersburg.

84

¹ These lines are taken from André Chénier's Eighth Ode, 'La jeune captive'.
² Küchelbecker had asked Pushkin to contribute something to the almanac *Mnemozina*, which he and Odoevsky brought out in 1824. Only one of Pushkin's poems, 'The Demon', was subsequently published in it.
³ *Evgeny Onegin*. In the draft copy of this letter this sentence reads: Don't even think of my poem – it is written in stanzas which are almost freer than those of *Don Juan*, if it is ever published, etc.

50. To Prince P. A. Vyazemsky

8 March 1824
Odessa

. . . I shall pay my old debts and settle down to my new poem.¹ Since I am not of the company of our eighteenth-century writers, I write for myself and publish for money and certainly not for the smile of the fair sex.

. . . I am waiting impatiently for my *Fountain*, that is for your Foreword. I recently read your earlier remarks on Bulgarin, the best of your polemical articles.² I haven't yet seen the Life of Dmitriev.³ But my dear, it is shameful of you to belittle our Krylov. Your opinion should stand as a law for our literature, and yet on account of an unpardonable prejudice you judge contrary to your conscience and patronize the devil knows whom. And what is Dmitriev? All his fables put together are not worth one good fable by Krylov, all his satires one of your epistles, and all the rest of his work Zhukovsky's first poem. You once called him 'Le poète de notre civilisation'. If that is so, what a fine civilization ours is.

¹ Probably *Evgeny Onegin*.
² Bulgarin's article appeared in the *Severny Arkhiv* for 1823, Vyazemsky's reply in *Novosti Literatury*, No. 19 (1823). Vyazemsky argued that the poor state of Russian literature was due to the conditions under which authors had to work – the censorship, etc. And that to say that nobody wrote because there were no readers was like saying that a dumb man did not speak because there was no one to listen – if the tongue were loosened the audience would appear.
³ Vyazemsky's account of Dmitriev's life and work was included in the 1823 edition of Dmitriev's poems. In this article Vyazemsky wrote that Krylov, though he obviously had great talent, had found the ground largely prepared for him by Dmitriev. Vyazemsky must have felt that he was going against the current in his assessment of Krylov and Dmitriev as poets, for almost on the very day Pushkin was writing this letter he was writing, somewhat defensively, to Bestuzhev asserting that he both esteemed and loved Krylov but on aesthetic grounds placed Dmitriev above him.

Pushkin's negative judgement on Dmitriev was probably sharpened by Vyazemsky's diminution of Krylov's achievement and by the fact that Dmitriev had been very cool about *Ruslan and Lyudmila.*

51. To L. S. Pushkin   *1 April 1824*
                                                                Odessa

This is what Vyazemsky writes to me: 'I read in the *Blagonamerenny* that your *Fountain* was read to some learned society prior to publication.[1] What sort of impression does this produce? And there are a thousand manuscript copies of it going round Petersburg. Who will now buy it? My conscience is clear, etc.'

So is mine. But people will say to me: why should you care? You got your 3,000 roubles, as far as you are concerned the whole thing can run to seed. But all the same it is a pity that the booksellers, who acted in a European manner for the first time, should come to grief and sustain a loss – and also in future I won't be able to sell my work at a profit. For all this I am obliged to the friends *of my Fame* – the devil take 'em and it. Here am I trying to avoid dying of starvation, and all they do is shout *'Fame!'* As you see, my dear, I am annoyed at the lot of you. I only ask one thing of you: write and tell me how my *Fountain* sells – or else I'll join the Count Khvostovs[2] and will buy up half the edition myself. What are the journalists doing to me! Bulgarin is worse than Voeykov.[3] How can one publish private letters? Who knows what may pass through my mind as I write to a friend? But they are prepared to publish simply everything – it's sheer piracy. It's decided – I'm dropping all correspondence. I don't want to have anything to do with them. As far as they are concerned they can abuse or praise me with equal stupidity – it's all one to me, I don't hold them worth a farthing. And as for the public, I esteem them on a par with the booksellers – let them buy and lie as much as they like. . . . Neither you nor Father has written a word to me in answer to my elegiac fragments – nor do you send money; but you undermine the sale of my books. A fine state of affairs!

[1] *The Fountain of Bakhchisarai* was read at a meeting of the St Petersburg Independent Society of Lovers of Literature on 7 February 1824; an excerpt from it had already been read to the same society by Ryleev on 1 November 1823.

[2] Count Dmitri Ivanovich Khvostov (1757-1835), a minor poet who was the constant butt of the members of Arzamas. He used to buy up his own works

and generously send them to his friends and to libraries, for nobody else would buy them.

[3] Voeykov was notorious for his practice of publishing works without the author's permission. Bulgarin had published an extract from a letter of Pushkin's to Bestuzhev (dated 8 February 1824) in his *Literaturnye Listki* (1824).

52. To Prince P. A. Vyazemsky   *Beginning of April 1824*
                                           Odessa

I arrived from Kishinev less than an hour ago and found letters, parcels, and *Bakhchisarai*. I don't know how to thank you: the Conversation[1] is delightful, both in ideas and in the brilliant way they are expressed. The judgements are incontrovertible. Your style has progressed splendidly. I have also recently read the life of Dmitriev; all your comments in it are excellent. But this article is a tour de force et affaire de parti. Reading your critical works and letters I also began to have ideas, and think that one of these days I shall write something about our meagre literature, on the influence of Lomonosov, Karamzin, Dmitriev and Zhukovsky.[2] Maybe I'll even publish; then du choc des opinions jaillira de l'argent. Do you know, your Conversation is written for Europe rather than for Russia. You are right as regards Romantic poetry, but have we any of the old . . . classical kind that you attack? That remains an open question. I tell you once again, by the Holy Gospels and the Body and Blood of Christ, that Dmitriev, in spite of all his long-established influence, does not and should not carry more weight than Kheraskov or Uncle Vasily Lvovich. Does he alone represent our classical literature? . . . And in what respect is he a classic? Where are his tragedies, his didactic or epic poems?[3] Is he a classic in his epistles to Severina, or in his epigrams translated from Guichard?[4] . . . Where then are the enemies of Romantic poetry? Where are the pillars of classicism? We'll talk of all this at leisure.

Now let's talk of business, i.e. of money. Slenin offers to pay me what I want for *Onegin*. Russia is indeed part of Europe – and I was thinking this was a mistake on the part of geographers. The matter rests with the censorship, and I'm not joking for this concerns my future and my independence – which I simply must have. . . .

[1] For *The Fountain of Bakhchisarai* Vyazemsky wrote 'Instead of an Introduction: A Conversation between the Publisher and a Classicist from the Viborg side or from Vasilievsky Island', see no. 43.

[2] Compare no. 44.

[3] The accepted *œuvres* of a classic poet.

[4] Jean-François Guichard (1731-1811), French poet and playwright.

53. To V. K. Küchelbecker (?)[1]   *April/first half of May (?) 1824*
                                                         Odessa

Reading Shakespeare[2] and the Bible,[3] though the Holy Ghost sometimes appeals to me, I prefer Goethe[4] and Shakespeare. You ask what
I am doing: I am writing colourful stanzas of a romantic poem[5] – and
am taking lessons in pure Atheism. There is an Englishman here,[6] a
deaf Philosopher, the only intelligent Atheist I have met. He has
covered about 1,000 pages to prove qu'il ne peut exister d'être intelligent Créateur et régulateur, destroying in passing the feeble proofs for
the immortality of the soul. This system, though not as comforting as
is usually thought, is unfortunately the most likely to be true.

[1] Only a fragment of this letter survives and it isn't certain to whom it was
addressed – Küchelbecker and Vyazemsky being the most likely recipients.
It was intercepted and read by the police and served as one of the main
reasons for Pushkin's being expelled from the Civil Service and transferred
from Odessa to his parents' country estate at Mikhailovskoe. He wrote to
Zhukovsky on 29 November 1824: 'I have been exiled on account of a line
in a stupid letter', see pages 35-6. At about this time Vyazemsky wrote to
Pushkin, asking him to keep a good check on his tongue and pen and not
to jeopardize his future.

[2] Pushkin probably read Shakespeare in French. He had the following
editions in his library: *Œuvres complètes de Shakespeare*, translated from the
English by Le Tourneur (Paris, 1821), and *Dramatic Works*, printed from the
text of S. Johnson, George Steevens and Isaac Reed (Leipzig, 1824).

[3] Pushkin possessed French editions of the Bible.

[4] Pushkin had begun to read Goethe earlier than Shakespeare and had used
an epigraph from *Faust* for *The Prisoner of the Caucasus*. When working on
Boris Godunov he read Goethe's Shakespearean play, *Götz von Berlichingen*.

[5] *Evgeny Onegin*, or *The Gipsies*.

[6] Dr William Hutchinson, the personal physician to the Vorontsovs. A few
years later he was ordained into the Church of England.

54. Second draft of letter to A. I. Kaznacheev[1]   *22 May 1824*
                                                                         Odessa

. . . Any complaints on my part would be out of place. I blocked my
own path and chose to aim at something different. For God's sake do

not think that I looked on the writing of poetry with the childish conceit of a rhymester, or as on the relaxation of a man of sensibility: it is simply my craft, a branch of honest trade affording me a livelihood and domestic independence.[2] I do not think that Count Vorontsov will wish to deprive me of one or the other.

I will be told that receiving 700 roubles I have to serve. You know that it is possible to carry on a book trade only in Moscow or Petersburg, for they are the only places where there are journalists, censors and booksellers. I daily have to refuse the most profitable offers simply because I find myself 2,000 versts from the capitals. The government wishes in some measure to compensate me for my losses and I regard the 700 roubles I receive not as a civil servant's salary but as an allowance to an exiled bondman. I am ready to give them up if I cannot be the master of my own time and occupation.

. . . Conscious of my complete unsuitability, I have already disclaimed all the benefits of service and all hope of further success in it.

. . . One more thing: you are perhaps unaware that I suffer from aneurysm.[3] For the last eight years I have been walking round with a mortal complaint. I can send you a certificate from any doctor of your choice. Is it truly impossible for me to be left in peace for the remainder of my life, which I am sure will be short?

---

[1] Alexander Ivanovich Kaznacheev (1788-1881), head of Count Vorontsov's chancellery. He was an exceptionally kind and courteous man and Pushkin used him as an intermediary in his difficult negotiations with Vorontsov. Kaznacheev had tried to prevent Pushkin being sent locust-hunting, see page 33.

[2] Cf. page 69. In another draft of this letter, Pushkin wrote: 'J'ai déjà vaincu ma répugnance d'écrire et de vendre mes vers pour vivre – le plus grand pas est fait. Si je n'écris encore que sous l'influence capricieuse de l'inspiration, les vers une fois écrits je ne les regarde plus que comme une marchandise à tant la pièce.'

[3] Pushkin tried several times to ask for leave to travel on medical grounds, but the furthest he was eventually allowed to go from Mikhailovskoe to cure his (real or assumed) aneurysm was to consult a doctor in Pskov.

55. To Prince P. A. Vyazemsky   *7 June 1824*
                                                          Odessa

. . . What you say about a review has long been brewing in my head.[1] The fact is that it is no good expecting anything of Vorontsov. He is cool about anything which doesn't concern himself; and Maecenases are out of fashion. None of us will want to have *the magnanimous patronage* of an enlightened peer; that went out with Lomonosov. Our literature today is, and must be, honourably independent. We must get together on our own and set to work. But alas! we are all such idlers – the material is there, the materialists are there, but où est le cul de plomb qui poussera ça? . . . One more misfortune: you are a Sectaire, whereas for this one would need a great deal, a very great deal, of tolerance. I would agree to see Dmitriev listed in our bunch, but will you allow me my Katenin?[2] I will repudiate Vasily Lvovich;[3] will you repudiate Voeykov? Yet another misfortune: we are all cursed and scattered over the face of the earth – communication between us is difficult, there is no unanimity; while every minute a golden *opportune* remark slips through our fingers. Our first task must be to take in hand all the reviews and make them *respected*. Nothing would be easier if we were together and could publish on the morrow what we had decided at supper the day before; as it is we have to communicate from Moscow to Odessa a comment on some foolishness on the part of Bulgarin, send it to Birukov in Petersburg, and print it two months later in the *revue des bévues*.[4] No, my dear Asmodaeus, let's postpone this. . . .

I shall give your wife the first canto of *Onegin* to give to you. Maybe with the change at the Ministry it will get published.[5]

[1] From 1819, Pushkin had discussed with his friends – especially Vyazemsky – the desirability of publishing a periodical review. His hopes were not realized till 1836, when he began to publish *Sovremennik* – a year before he died. On 30 April 1820, Vyazemsky had written to Pushkin: 'While we have no review with moral and political aims, we cannot write cheerfully. We are all pouring water from one empty vessel into another and play with words as with spillikins.'

[2] See no. 6, note 1. Pushkin did not realize at this time how negatively Katenin had reacted to *The Fountain of Bakhchisarai* and to Vyazemsky's introduction to it.

[3] Pushkin's uncle.

[4] In January 1823, Pushkin had suggested to his brother that they should publish a collection of literary bloomers called *Revue des bévues*.

[5] A new Minister of Education and consequently head of the censorship, Admiral A. S. Shishkov, had been appointed. Pushkin was optimistic about the change, in spite of Shishkov's previous clashes with the members of Arzamas as President of the Russian Academy and the Discussion Society of Lovers of the Russian Word.

56. To L. S. Pushkin   *13 June 1824*
Odessa

. . . With a change at the Ministry,[1] I am expecting a change of censorship. But it is a pity . . . la coupe était pleine. Birukov and Krasovsky were unbearably stupid, self-willed and repressive. This couldn't have lasted long. . . . Joking apart, I am expecting it to benefit literature in general and am sending him a kiss, not like a Judas of the Arzamas but like the Thief-Romantic.[2] I shall try to shoulder my way through the gates of the censorship with the first chapter or canto of *Onegin*. Perhaps we shall creep through. You ask for details of *Onegin* – what a bore, my dear. Some other time. At the moment I am not writing anything; I have other things to worry about. Unpleasantness of all kinds; everything is dull and dusty. Princess Vera Vyazemsky[3] has arrived here, she is a kindly dame, but I would have been more pleased had it been her husband. I have received the Zhukovsky.[4] He was a pleasant person. God rest his soul!

[1] See no. 55, note 5.
[2] Pushkin is adapting a sentence from the Orthodox prayer of Confession before Communion, 'for I will not tell the secret to thy enemies nor give thee a kiss like Judas, but like the thief I will acknowledge thee'.
[3] During her stay in Odessa, which lasted over two months, Princess Vyazemsky continually wrote to her husband of Pushkin, being always very concerned for his welfare. He made her a confidante in his troubles and their friendship lasted till his death.
[4] The 1824 edition of Zhukovsky's poems. Pushkin refers to him as if he were dead because Zhukovsky had written very little in the last few years.

57. To Prince P. A. Vyazemsky   *24/25 June 1824*
Odessa

. . . I see by your letters to Princess Vera that you feel Küchelbeckery and depressed; you are sad about Byron[1] and I am so glad of his death, as a lofty subject for poetry. Byron's genius grew pale with advancing years. In his tragedies, not excluding *Cain*, he is no longer that flaming demon who created the Giaour and Childe Harold. The first two cantos of *Don Juan* are superior to the rest. His poetry was perceptibly changing. Everything about him was back to front: there was nothing gradual about his development, he suddenly ripened and matured – sang and fell silent, and he never recaptured his early notes. We no longer heard Byron after the fourth canto of *Childe Harold*; some other poet was writing, with great human talent. Your idea of honouring his death with a fifth canto on his Hero is splendid, but it is beyond my powers.[2] I am sick of Greece. One can discuss the fate of the Greeks as one can that of my brother Negroes,[3] and one can wish them both liberation from intolerable slavery; but that all the enlightened peoples of Europe should rave about Greece is unforgivably childish. The Jesuits stuffed us with Themistocles and Pericles and we fancied that the filthy race of brigands and shopkeepers are their lawful descendants, and the heirs of their reputation in the schools.[4] You will say that I have changed my views. You should come to us to Odessa and should take a look at the compatriots of Miltiades, then you would agree with me – and look at what Byron himself wrote a few years ago in his notes to *Childe Harold*, where he refers to the opinion of Fauvel,[5] who was, I seem to remember, the French consul in Smyrna. However, I promise you some verses on the death of His Excellency.[6]

[1] Byron died on 19 April 1824; see pages 34-5 for the reactions to his death throughout Europe.

[2] In his letters to his wife at this time, Vyazemsky several times expressed the hope that Pushkin would write something on Byron's death.

[3] Pushkin liked to slip in unexpected references to his Ethiopian blood.

[4] It is interesting to compare Pushkin's outburst to the words of a guard on a Greek train, to whom Patrick Leigh Fermor talked in Greece in the early 1960s:

> And those old Greeks, our celebrated ancestors, are a nuisance and I'll tell you why. They haunt us. We can never be as great as they were, nobody can. They make us feel guilty. We can't do anything, people think, because of a few old books and temples and lumps of marble. And clever foreigners who know all about the ancients come here expecting to be surrounded by Apollos and gentlemen in helmets and laurel leaves, and what do they see? Me: a small dark fat man with a moustache and eyes like boot buttons! . . . What's Hecuba to him or he to Hecuba? (*Roumeli*, pp. 62-3.)

[5] Pushkin, in referring to Byron's citation of Fauvel's unfavourable view of the Greeks, failed to mention that Byron did not agree with Fauvel's attitude. Byron wrote:

> M. Fauvel, the French Consul, who has passed thirty years principally at Athens, and to whose talents as an artist, and manners as a gentleman, none who have known him can refuse their testimony, has frequently declared in my hearing, that the Greeks do not deserve to be emancipated; reasoning on the grounds of their 'national and individual depravity!' while he forgot that such depravity is to be attributed to causes which can only be removed by the measure he reprobates.

M. Roque, a French merchant of respectability long settled in Athens, asserted with the most amusing gravity, 'Sir, they are the same *canaille* that existed *in the days of Themistocles*!' an alarming remark to the 'Laudatur temporis acti'. The ancients banished Themistocles; the moderns cheat Monsieur Roque; thus great men have ever been treated! . . . but if I may say this without offence, it seems to me rather hard to declare so positively and pertinaciously, as almost everybody has declared, that the Greeks because they are very bad, will never be better.

And much more in the same vein. (Notes to *Childe Harold's Pilgrimage*, Canto II.)

6 Pushkin mourned Byron's death in verses x-xiii of his elegy 'To the Sea' – 'the earth had emptied'. See page 36.

58. To A. A. Bestuzhev

29 June 1824
Odessa

. . . Judge for yourself: I happened once to be madly in love. In such a case I usually write elegies as another may wet his bed; but is it a friendly gesture to hang out my wet sheets in public? God forgive you but you disgraced me by publishing the last three lines of my 'Elegy' in the current number of the *Polyarnaya Zvezda*.[1] The devil possessed me to write a few sentimental lines apropos *The Fountain of Bakhchisarai* and to mention in them my elegiac beauty. Imagine my dismay when I saw them in print:[2] the review might fall into her hands. What might she think, seeing with what readiness I talk about her *with one of my Petersburg friends*? How is she to know that I did not mention her by name, that the letter was unsealed and published by Bulgarin, that the damned 'Elegy' was sent to you by the devil knows whom, and that no one is to blame? I must admit that I value a single opinion of this woman more than those of all the reviews in the world and of all our readers combined. My head has begun to spin . . . I am sad, my dear, that you don't write anything. Who then is going to write? M. Dmitriev and A. Pisarev?[3] They are fine ones! Had the late Byron joined issue with the semi-defunct Goethe, Europe would not have lifted a finger to work them up against each other, either in order to provoke them or to throw cold water over their heads. The age of polemic is over.[4] Who can be interested in Dmitriev's opinion of Vyazemsky's opinion or in Pisarev's opinion of himself? I had to join in,[5] as I was called as a witness by M. Dmitriev. But I won't any more. My *Onegin* grows. But who the devil will print it? I thought your censorship had grown wiser under Shishkov, but I see that under the old man all is as it was.[6]

[1] See no. 46 and note 1.
[2] See no. 51 and note 3.
[3] M. A. Dmitriev, the nephew of the writer I. I. Dmitriev, a minor poet and critic, who at this time was a defender of the classical school of literature. A. I. Pisarev was a satirist whose views on literature coincided with those of M. Dmitriev; together they launched an attack on Vyazemsky's introduction to *The Fountain of Bakhchisarai*. Later M. Dmitriev grew to admire Pushkin's poetry.
[4] Cf. no. 6 and note 2.
[5] See no. 43.
[6] See no. 55 and note 5. On 14 July Pushkin wrote to A. I. Turgenev, 'I don't know whether they will admit this poor Onegin into the heavenly kingdom of print'.

59. Draft letter to V. L. Davydov[1] (?)   *Between June 1823 and July 1824*
Kishinev/Odessa

I hear with surprise that you consider me to be opposed to the liberation of Greece and a champion of Turkish slavery.[2] It seems my words were strangely reported to you. But whatever you may have been told, you should not have believed that I could ever feel unsympathetic to the noble efforts of a renascent people. . . .[3]

[1] Vasily Lvovich Davydov (1792-1855), a Decembrist. He had served in the 1812 war and had retired from the army with the rank of Colonel. He had then become a founder member of the Southern secret society. He did not take part in the actual rising in December 1825, but for his conspiratorial activities was sentenced to hard labour for life, later commuted to twenty years. He was a friend of Pushkin's.
[2] Judging by no. 57 it is not surprising that this idea should have got around.
[3] In another draft of the same letter Pushkin wrote: 'Je ne suis ni un barbare ni un apôtre de l'Alcoran, la cause de la Grèce m'intéresse vivement, c'est pour cela même que je m'indigne en voyant ces misérables revêtus du ministère sacré de défenseurs de la liberté.'

60. Draft letter to Prince P. A. Vyazemsky   *5 July 1824*
Odessa

As historians the French are not a whit inferior to the English. If there is any virtue in precedence, then remember that Voltaire was the first to break new ground – and to carry the torch of Philosophy into the dark archives of History. Robertson said that had Voltaire taken the trouble to indicate the sources for his assertions he, Robertson, would never have written his History.[1]

Lémontey is a genius of the nineteenth century. Read his Survey of the reign of Louis XIV[2] and you will place him above Hume and Robertson. Rabaut de Saint-Étienne[3] is rubbish.

The Romantic age has not yet dawned for France. Delavigne flounders in Aristotle's age-old nets[4] – he is a pupil of the playwright Voltaire rather than of nature.

Tous les recueils de poésies nouvelles dites Romantiques sont la honte de la littérature française.

Lamartine is good in 'Napoleon', in 'The Dying Poet',[5] and in general good in having achieved some kind of new harmony.

Nobody loves the delightful André Chénier more than I, but he is a classic par excellence – he exudes the spirit of ancient Greek poetry.[6] Mark my word: the first genius in the fatherland of Racine and Boileau will be carried away by such desperate liberty, will become such a literary Carbonari, that your Germans . . . But at present there is less poetry in France than here.

---

[1] In his Preface to the *History of the Reign of Charles V*, the Scottish historian William Robertson wrote:

> I have carefully pointed out the sources from which I have derived information, and have cited the writers on whose authority I rely with minute exactness, which might appear to border upon ostentation, if it were possible to be vain of having read books, many of which nothing but the duty of examining with accuracy whatever I laid before the public would have induced me to open.

Pushkin possessed a copy of this history translated into French by J. B. A. Suard, published in Paris in 1817. The introduction to this work, called by Robertson 'a view of the progress of society in Europe, from the subversion of the Roman Empire, to the beginning of the sixteenth century', might well have been influenced by Voltaire's 'Essai sur les Mœurs et l'Esprit des Nations et sur les Principaux Faits de l'Histoire, depuis Charlemagne jusqu'à Louis XIII' (this was the opinion of John Morley in his life of Voltaire published in 1872). Robertson does not, however, mention Voltaire by name and the source of the remark quoted by Pushkin remains untraced.

[2] Pierre-Édouard Lémontey, *Essai sur l'établissement monarchique de Louis XIV* (1818).

95

[3] Jean-Paul Rabaut de Saint-Étienne, revolutionary and historian.

[4] The Rules based on Aristotle's *Poetics*.

[5] 'Napoléon' and 'Le poète mourant' were two of the *Nouvelles Méditations poétiques* (1824).

[6] See draft of no. 38 and note 3.

Section III

'SHAKESPEARIAN STRIDES' IN MIKHAILOVSKOE

WHEN Pushkin arrived at his parents' home at Mikhailovskoe in August he found the whole family there. Unaware of the circumstances of his return, they gave him a warm welcome; but his father's warmth soon evaporated when he heard that Pushkin was in disgrace and under police supervision. In fact he quickly offered to report to the authorities on his son's movements and Pushkin found himself virtually under house arrest.

Mikhailovskoe was not a grand country house. It was a one-storey wooden building, sparsely furnished and inadequately heated. Pushkin's parents were extremely bad at managing their affairs and the whole estate had been allowed to run down. Life was therefore neither calm nor comfortable and the strain on family relationships proved such that on 19 November Pushkin's parents packed and left for St Petersburg taking his brother and sister with them. Pushkin remained alone with his old nurse.

During these few months of family strain, Pushkin – still convinced that he had been punished 'for a line in a stupid letter' – had been writing round desperately in an attempt to find some loophole of escape. His friends were afraid that he would protest too much and make matters worse for himself, and Zhukovsky sent him an impassioned appeal to behave sensibly and save himself for his high destiny as a poet:

To everything that has happened to you, and to all that you have brought on yourself, I have only one answer: POETRY. You have not got talent; you have genius. You are rich, you have an inalienable means to transcend undeserved misfortune and to make good that which you have deserved; you above anybody can and must have moral dignity. You were born to be a great poet; be worthy of it. In this phrase lies your entire ethic, your entire happiness, your entire reward. The circumstances of life, both happy and unhappy, are its shell. You will say that I am preaching to a drowning man from the calm of the shore. No! I am standing on a deserted shore and I see an athlete struggling in the waves and I know he will not drown if he uses all his strength and I am only showing him the better shore that he will reach if he himself wishes it. Swim athlete! (November, 1824.)

And more in the same vein.

Zhukovsky's warm solicitude and genuine concern proved helpful, and after his parents' departure Pushkin calmed down and settled to a routine of country life. He describes it in several letters. He would read and write in bed, rise late, go riding – often composing poetry as he rode, but not always managing to get it written down – play billiards against himself and, most important, spend hours talking to his nurse (see Section I, pages 5-6). Pushkin read everything that he wrote aloud to his nurse – she was his tame audience of one – and he gleaned from her much that was invaluable to him in writing about the Russian countryside and the Russian past: proverbs, legends, customs and superstitions, all of which helped to bind his work firmly to his native soil. In these winter evenings there were nurtured not only Pushkin's magical poems based on Russian folklore, but the whole rich vocabulary of his writing, both in prose and verse, in which the Russian language grew to its maturity. As John Bayley has written, 'the goose, the sled, and the snow-storm were named for a Russian child by Pushkin' (*Tolstoy and the Novel*); one corner-stone of Pushkin's own Russian education was Arina Rodionovna.

These country days were later transmuted by Pushkin into the fourth chapter of *Evgeny Onegin* in which he describes Onegin's experience of rural solitude. The dummy billiards, the rides, the household accounts, the time spent reading, the time spent sitting with wine at hand in the hope that a friend would call – all are included.

Pushkin became a familiar figure in the neighbourhood, noted for his eccentric clothes. He used to walk around visiting country fairs and markets in red shirt, baggy trousers and straw hat, and carrying a heavy walking-stick. Or he would drop in on his neighbours, the Osipovs, at Trigorskoe; always a welcome guest. The Osipovs were a large clan of young people, presided over by Mama, Praskovya Alexandrovna, and they provided Pushkin with plenty of light relief and family junketings and, during the stay of a cousin, Anna Petrovna Kern, with a brief but passionate period of enchantment.

Pushkin had just completed *The Gipsies*, begun in the south, and one evening he read it out at the Osipovs to a rapt audience. Anna Kern was particularly responsive and the flame which sprung up between her and Pushkin inspired one of his best known lyrics – 'I remember a miraculous moment'. But the fire did not last and Anna went home reconciled to her elderly, uninspiring husband.

The Osipovs provided entertainment, but for more serious matters Pushkin had to rely on letters. These are punctuated with requests for various supplies, both mental and physical: Scott's novels and Limburg cheese, Fouché's memoirs and pickles, the works of Schiller and a cork-screw. One of the recurring themes in the letters was Pushkin's growing conviction of the need for a periodical like the *Edinburgh Review*, in which he and his friends could publish their work and express their views on literature and contemporary events. J. L. Talmon has commented on the Romantics' deep conviction in the power of the printed word (*Romanticism and Revolt*) and Pushkin was no exception. Many years were to pass before his hopes would be realized.

11 January 1825 was a red-letter day for Pushkin. His old Lycée friend, Ivan Pushchin, braved official displeasure and spent a day with him in Mikhailovskoe. Many years later, when in exile himself for his part in the Decembrist rising, Pushchin described this day in vivid detail in his notes on Pushkin (*Zapiski o Pushkine*). He had arrived in deep snow.

I look round: I see Pushkin in the porch, barefoot, with only a night-shirt on, with his arms raised. I need not say what I felt at that moment. Jumping out of the sledge I grab hold of him and drag him into the room. It is bitterly cold outside, but in such moments a man does not catch cold. We look at one another, we kiss, we remain silent. He forgot that he should put something on, I did not think of my fur coat and hat covered in frost. It was about eight in the morning. I don't know what went on. The old woman who had run up found us in each other's arms in the same condition as we were as we came into the house: one – almost naked, the other – covered in snow. Finally the tears broke (even now, after thirty-five years, tears make it difficult to write in glasses), we came to our senses.

Pushchin noticed Pushkin's poorly furnished, untidy bedroom, strewn with sheets of discarded paper and the ends of quill pens, and remembered that in school he had also written with stubs of pens which it was hard to hold in one's fingers. He noticed that the house was cold.

Over coffee and pipes, Pushkin told him that he had been despatched from Odessa because Vorontsov was jealous of him and because of his epigrams and religious views. Pushchin had brought a manuscript copy of Griboedov's *Woe from Wit* and Pushkin began to read it aloud with expressive gusto, but he was interrupted by the arrival of a monk from a local monastery 'to check' on his visitor. Pushkin immediately grasped a volume of Saints' lives and poured out tea and rum for the monk, who accepted the refreshment readily. When the 'investigator' left, Pushkin continued his reading from *Woe from Wit* and also dictated to Pushchin the opening stanzas of *The Gipsies* for publication in *Polyarnaya Zvezda*.

In the course of the day they cracked several bottles of champagne, toasting the Lycée and their absent friends. At three in the morning the bells of the waiting sledge were heard in the yard and they had to part. They clinked glasses with the premonition that they were seeing each other for the last time, though they made plans to meet in Moscow. As Pushchin ran out to his sledge, Pushkin was standing in the porch holding up a candle and, as the horses leapt forward up the hill, Pushchin heard him call 'Goodbye my friend!'

A year passed and Pushchin was exiled to Siberia. On his arrival in prison a short poem in an unknown script was handed to him by a friend. It was by Pushkin, written on 13 December 1826. In it he recalled Pushchin's visit to Mikhailovskoe and wished he could now be of the same comfort to him. Pushchin wrote that his gratitude to Pushkin overflowed at that moment and he wished he could embrace him, as they had embraced in the snow-filled porch.

On 29 December 1824 the censorship passed the first chapter of *Evgeny Onegin* for publication. It came out in February 1825, prefaced by a conversation in verse between a bookseller and the poet. In this imaginary dialogue Pushkin distinguished between three driving forces behind the writing of poetry: inspiration, the love of fame or of women, the need for money. The tone both of it and of much of the description of Evgeny's upbringing and daily routine as a St Petersburg dandy at the end of 1819 was delicately frivolous and, though Pushkin denied a close connection and any satiric intent, it showed obvious kinship to that of Byron's *Don Juan*. Pushkin was now writing the later chapters and as the poem grew it changed in character, gaining in breadth of application and depth of feeling like a river, widening and deepening as it flows towards the sea.

The reception the first chapter of *Evgeny Onegin* met with from some of Pushkin's friends was disappointing. Both Bestuzhev and Ryleev found it too light-hearted and lacking in social importance. They were committed men preparing for revolution. To them the pen was a weapon for the political education of their generation and they felt that little was achieved by describing Evgeny at his dressing-table. Ryleev urged Pushkin to resist Byron's influence. Pushkin had himself learned his lesson as far as Byron was concerned; this was no longer a problem. Letters went to and fro between him and his friends on the proper subject for poetry. Bowles and Byron were called as witnesses (see no. 92). But Pushkin never drew demarcation lines between poetic and prosaic subjects; his strength lay in the absolute clarity with which he rendered the smallest detail of the daily scene. He resembles Chaucer and Shakespeare in this: his cocks, frost-bitten fingers, and pots and pans are real.

In spite of his friends' objections *Evgeny Onegin* sold very well and as it grew the chapters were awaited with increasing eagerness. It soon became clear that it would find an echo in countless hearts and be of the greatest significance to Russian writers. The Russian reading public grew with *Evgeny Onegin* and when it was completed the whole territory of the nineteenth-century Russian novel lay open to its masters. The closeness of observation, the truthfulness to life as it is lived and felt, the clarity and economy of its form, set a standard; and subsequently every great Russian writer has acknowledged the essential lessons which were to be learnt from Pushkin, and from no work more than from *Evgeny Onegin*.

On 10 August 1825, Pushkin had completed the sixth chapter. The young poet Lensky had been killed by Onegin in a duel, hauntingly prophetic of Pushkin's own death. In the closing stanzas of this chapter Pushkin bade farewell to his youth and mentioned in passing that prose was beginning to occupy his mind in place of poetry. This was one of several straws in the wind which indicated the direction in which Pushkin's work was moving.

He now made a rigorous overhaul of his shorter poems and prepared a new collection, giving his brother and his friend, Pletnev, precise and vivid instructions as to how it was to be printed (see no. 91). It proved fortunate for Pushkin that the task of preparing his manuscripts for publication now passed from his brother to Pletnev, to whose capable and devoted care he was in future to entrust the publication of all his work.

This collection appeared in January 1826. It contained one of Pushkin's most famous lyrics, 'The Prophet', an adaptation of lines from the prophecies of Isaiah. Solemn and sonorous, it sounded like a testimony of dedication to his calling:

> With fainting soul athirst for Grace,
> I wandered in a desert place,
> And at the crossing of the ways
> I saw a sixfold seraph blaze;
> He touched mine eyes with fingers light
> As sleep that cometh in the night:
> And like a frightened eagle's eyes,
> They opened wide with prophecies . . .

(trans. Maurice Baring)

At the same time Pushkin was beginning to collect material on the rebellion of Emelyan Pugachev in the reign of Catherine the Great which, together with his intensive reading of Scott, was eventually to lead him to try his own hand at a historical novel and, following that, at the writing of straight history. But Pushkin's prose period was still some way ahead and it was historical drama that was to dominate his creative energy during these two years at Mikhailovskoe. In *The Gipsies* Pushkin had introduced short dramatic scenes into his poem so as to highlight the significant moments of the action. He was now ready to take Shakespearian strides. In a letter written between 20 and 24 April 1825, Pushkin mentioned for the first time that he was writing blank verse pentameters. He had begun *Boris Godunov*.

The study of Shakespeare had for some time been absorbing Pushkin. Unfortunately his English was inadequate (he complained of this to Vyazemsky in November 1825) and he had to resort to Letourneur's French translation. At the same time he read A. W. Schlegel's lectures on dramatic art and literature, which were in the vanguard of Shakespeare's conquest of the stages of Europe. Pushkin had long ago rejected the principles of neo-classic tragedy and had been anxious to break the hold of the French on the Russian theatre; but he also saw clearly the limitations of Byron's romantic tragedies. He wrote to Nikolai Raevsky (see page 155):

> . . . je n'ai pas lu Calderón ni Vega mais quel homme que ce Schakespeare! je n'en reviens pas. Comme Byron le tragique est mesquin devant lui!

Byron had only created one character – his own, handing out the different traits of that character to his *dramatis personae*, giving to one his

104

pride, to another his hatred, to a third his melancholy. In this way from one powerful and energetic personality he had created several insignificant ones. Pushkin ended this letter 'Je sens que mon âme s'est tout-à-fait développée, je puis créer.'

For the subject of his first tragedy Pushkin chose well. In Boris Godunov he found a historical character who combined Macbeth's visionary guilt and despair with Richard III's cunning and Henry IV's shrewdness. Boris ascended the throne over the body of a murdered child, the Tsarevich Dimitri killed in Uglich. That poison in his soul brings him to his downfall. His secret fears spring up to meet him, incarnated in a pretender claiming to be Dimitri, and Boris cannot summon the energy and courage needed to meet the challenge. His soliloquy 'I have attained the highest power' is that of a man on a razor's edge. Power has brought little satisfaction. He finds himself held responsible for every national misfortune, named the murderer of every dying man and is unable to combat with his accusers. Preyed upon by hallucinations, he seeks the advice of magicians and astrologers. He does not however, like Macbeth, advance on the path of guilt until hardened by blood: on the contrary, Pushkin shows him weakened and despairing, supporting with difficulty the burden of kingship. This was an aspect of kingship that Shakespeare often stressed – the human frailty beneath the robes of state, the consciousness of responsibility, the ever-present fear of treachery. Like Shakespeare's arch-hypocrite Richard III, Boris had, at his election to the throne, feigned a desire to retreat from the world and from absolute rule; but with heartfelt conviction he now exclaims, 'How heavy art thou, crown of Monomakh!' This speech awakens a sympathy for Boris similar to that we feel at the soaring flights of Macbeth's terrified imagination. And this sympathy is increased by the fact that Boris is opposed not, like Macbeth, by the rightful heir to the throne but by an upstart monk led by dreams along the cruel road of usurpation.

Shakespearian echoes abound in Pushkin's handling of Boris's character. Towards the end of the play, when he stands in fear of losing the throne, Boris allows a blessed simpleton to speak to him as none of his entourage would dare; it is the Fool speaking to Lear. When, on his death-bed, Boris bequeaths the throne to his son, he gives him advice very similar to that of Henry IV to Prince Hal, the advice of a usurper to an heir who succeeds in his own right.

Apart from the character of Boris there were other aspects of the play which lent themselves admirably to Shakespearian treatment. For example, Pushkin was very concerned with the problem of dynastic succession – it was as relevant to his contemporaries as to Shakespeare's. At the very time he was writing Nicholas I succeeded to the throne of his brother, Alexander I, only after suppressing the Decembrist rising. The historical period Pushkin chose for his tragedy also resembled that of Shakespeare's history plays. Boris's accession to the throne was the prelude to a series of usurpations known as the 'Time of Troubles' which bridged the gap between the dynasties of Ryurik and Romanov, and which could be closely paralleled to the dynastic struggles of the Houses of York and Lancaster.

In writing of these public events Pushkin also made full dramatic use of the part played by the crowd in the internecine struggles of its rulers. The crowd symbolizes the shifting foundation on which autocracy rests: at times eagerly swayed from anger to pity, as is the Roman mob in *Julius Caesar*; or silent and obstinate as in *Richard III*; ignorant as in *Coriolanus*; or humorous, as its representatives in *Henry IV* or *Henry V*. In its first draft the play ended with the crowd, typically compliant, cheering the usurper, 'Long Live Tsar Dimitri!' When the play was submitted to the censorship (see page 182) the censor crossed this stage direction through and substituted 'The people are silent'. It was a lucky chance. Pushkin accepted the ending and it became famous. It seemed to stand as an ominous portent of the fate which awaited the Pretender, a fate similar to that which had struck down the house of Godunov. A silent condemnation.

In style and structure, too, *Boris Godunov* owes much to Shakespeare. In it Pushkin made full use of all the flexibility and freedom from neo-classical restrictions which Shakespearian drama affords. His comic scenes do not form a sub-plot but are directly connected with the main action of the tragedy, serving to throw it into sharper relief. In the best of these scenes – at the frontier tavern – Pushkin managed to catch the spirit of Shakespeare's humour and to adapt it to a Russian setting with complete success. He followed Shakespeare's practice too in other ways: in intermingling blank verse and prose, with prose used chiefly in the comic scenes and blank verse in the tragic; in the long period of time which the play covers; and in the constant changes of scene from court to monastery, from patriarch's palace to frontier tavern, and from public square to private garden, with corresponding transitions of mood from calmness and serenity to storm and anguish.

On 7 November 1825 Pushkin completed *Boris Godunov*. He wrote to Vyazemsky:

> My tragedy is finished; I read it aloud to myself and clapped my hands and shouted, 'What a Pushkin, what a son of a bitch!'

It always remained his favourite work and he was very apprehensive about putting it before a public which he feared would fail to understand it. In one of the many draft prefaces he wrote for it, he explained why he had set such store by the reception his tragedy would meet:

> I sincerely confess that I would be distressed by the ill success of my tragedy, as I am firmly convinced that the popular rules of Shakespearian drama are better suited to our stage than the courtly habits of the tragedies of Racine and that any unsuccessful experiment can slow down the reformation of our stage. (See page 248.)

While he was confined to the country there was no chance of arranging for his play to be produced; besides, political events were about to cast a dark shadow over Pushkin and his friends and all literary plans would have to be put aside, some temporarily, some for ever.

Twelve days after Pushkin was shouting for joy on completing a masterpiece, Alexander I died at Taganrog. The succession was uncertain as Alexander had no sons and the next in succession, his brother Constantine, had a few years earlier renounced his rights in favour of his younger brother, Nicholas. However at this moment both brothers were prepared to swear allegiance to each other and both were unpopular, though Nicholas was the more feared, as he had the reputation of being a martinet. Both the Southern and Northern secret societies, which had long been laying revolutionary plans, saw their chance in the interregnum, although immediately there were arguments as to the form their show of strength should take.

Finally 14 December 1825 was fixed as the day for the ceremony of the oath of allegiance to be sworn to Nicholas by the Senate and the Synod – and on that day the Decembrists decided to act, to bring out the regiments they had in their command on to Senate Square in St Petersburg and tell them to shout for Constantine and a Constitution, a simple slogan with which to launch a rebellion.

Much idealism, much youthful ardour were consumed on that December day, but it ended in fiasco and tragedy. Many of the finest young nobles and intellectuals of the time broke their lives on that day, seemingly to no purpose, for it hardened the grip of the reactionary elements and proved a prelude to a harsh reign. Five of the leaders – Ryleev, Pestel, Kakhovsky, Bestuzhev-Ryumin and Muraviev-Apostol were subsequently hanged. One hundred and twenty conspirators, which included some of Pushkin's closest friends – Pushchin, Küchelbecker, Bestuzhev – were exiled to hard labour, many for life. A potentially brilliant group of young men was thrown apart with harsh finality. Even those like Pushkin, who were not immediately involved, never recovered their youthful optimism. The 19 October Lycée reunions of foundation pupils became occasions for remembering the absent and the dead. And yet this sacrifice had enormous significance and Ryleev was right when he wrote:

I foresee that there will be no success, but an upheaval is necessary, for it will awaken Russia, and we with our failure will teach others.

The events of 14 December threw Pushkin into a fervour of anxiety, both for his friends and for himself. Manuscript copies of his poems were found among the papers of almost all the leading conspirators, and they quoted them as having inspired their revolutionary ardour. He was their laureate, their 'poet of freedom'. An official was at once despatched to check on Pushkin's activities in the district of Pskov, but nothing could be laid to his charge. Once again Zhukovsky was writing, urging Pushkin to wait patiently for quieter times:

You were born to be a great poet and could be the glory and treasure of Russia . . . I love both you and your Muse and wish that Russia should love you both. I will end as I began: do not ask for permission to come to Petersburg. The time for it is not ripe. Write *Godunov* and other such works: they will open the door to freedom.

(12 April 1826)

In May 1826 Pushkin lost an old friend and protector: Karamzin died. He had been one of Pushkin's mentors from early youth and even though there was much they did not agree on – which led to temporary estrangement – Pushkin always regarded him with loving respect. While he was writing *Boris Godunov*, he had been especially impressed by the magisterial authority of Karamzin's History and had closely followed his reading of the course of events. It now grieved him to read the inadequate tributes being published on the occasion of his master's death (see page 176).

At last, on 3 September 1826, Pushkin was granted permission to proceed to Moscow and was given orders to present himself directly on arrival at the staff headquarters of His Imperial Majesty. He could 'travel in his own equipage, at freedom, not in the position of a prisoner, and under the escort of a courier only'. It only remained to prepare for the journey. Pushkin packed his manuscripts and his pistols, tried to console his weeping nurse, and left Mikhailovskoe.

On 8 September Pushkin met the Emperor Nicholas I at the Moscow Kremlin. A burdensome privilege was about to descend on his shoulders for Nicholas had decided that from now on he, personally, would act as Pushkin's censor. This meant that in future Pushkin would have to seek the Imperial *imprimatur* for every word he wrote.

1824

———◆•◆◆•◆———

DRAFT NOTE

61. Imaginary conversation with Alexander I

If I were the Tsar I would summon Alexander Pushkin and say to him: 'Alexander Sergeyevich, you write excellent poetry.' Alexander Pushkin would bow to me with a touch of embarrassed modesty, and I would continue:

'I read your ode 'Freedom'.[1] It is written in a somewhat rambling style and is not thought out deeply enough, but there are three stanzas here which are very good. Although you have behaved irresponsibly, you nevertheless have not tried to blacken me in the people's eyes by the spreading of a foolish slander.[2] You may hold superficial opinions, but I can see that you have respected the truth and the personal honour even of the Tsar.'

'Oh, your Majesty, why recall that infantile ode? You would do better at least to read the third and sixth cantos of *Ruslan and Lyudmila*, if not the whole poem, or the first part of *The Prisoner of the Caucasus*, or *The Fountain of Bakhchisarai. Onegin* is in the press, may I have the honour of sending two copies to your Majesty's library to Ivan Andreyevich Krylov,[3] and if your Majesty will find time . . .'

'I do not repudiate my bad poems, placing reliance on my reputation, but as regards my good ones, I must admit that I have not the strength to repudiate them. An unforgiveable weakness.'

'But are you not also an atheist? That will never do.'

'Your Majesty, how can one judge a man by a letter written to a friend?[4] Can one give a schoolboy's jest the weight of a crime, and judge two empty phrases as one would a public sermon? I always did and do still consider you to be the best of the present rulers of Europe (however, we have yet to see what will come of Charles X[5]), but your last act[6] towards me – I make bold to call on your own feelings in the matter – contradicts your principles and your enlightened cast of thought.'

'Admit that you always placed your hopes on my magnanimity.'

'That would be no affront to your Majesty, but you see that I would have been mistaken in my reckoning. . . .'

But here Pushkin would have flared up and would have blurted out a whole lot of unnecessary remarks, and I would have grown angry and would have banished him to Siberia, where he would have written a poem called *Yermak* or *Kochum*[7] in various rhyming measures.

December 1824

[1] Pushkin wrote this ode in 1817. He did not expect to publish it but it was circulated in manuscript in hundreds of copies; and when it reached the notice of the government it proved a major cause for his exile to the south of Russia (see page 11). A. I. Turgenev wrote of it to Vyazemsky in 1819 but said he was afraid to send him a copy as 'Les murs peuvent avoir des yeux et même des oreilles'.

[2] The rumour that Alexander I was involved in the murder of his father, Paul I, which Pushkin describes in the closing stanzas of the ode. The manuscript copy of this section of the Imaginary Conversation is very confused. The reading given here is that of the 1949 Academy edition, which also cites the alternative reading in which the Emperor accuses Pushkin of slander: 'I noticed that you tried to blacken me in the eyes of the people by spreading a foolish slander. I see that you are capable of holding superficial opinions, and that you held truth and even the personal honour of the Tsar in small regard.'

[3] At that time librarian at the Imperial Public Library.

[4] See pages 35-6. This letter speeded his despatch from Odessa to Mikhailovskoe.

[5] He had succeeded to the French throne on 16 September 1824.

[6] Pushkin's exile to Mikhailovskoe.

[7] Yermak Timofeyevich was the sixteenth-century conqueror of Siberia and Kochum a Siberian Khan. In the event of being sent to Siberia Pushkin envisaged himself settling to poems on 'local' subjects, as he had done when exiled to the south of Russia.

LETTERS

62. To Prince P. A. Vyazemsky   *8 or 10 October 1824*
                                                    Mikhailovskoe

I won't tell you anything about my life here. It's dull, that's all. . . . Talking of verse, today I finished the poem, *The Gipsies*. I don't know what to say of it. At the moment I am sick of it.[1] . . . I am sending you a short intercession for the repose of the soul of God's servant Byron – I almost decided on a whole requiem, but it's dull writing for oneself.[2] . . . Send me some poems, I am dying of boredom.

[1] It was characteristic of Pushkin to feel negative about a piece of work he had just completed. His elation on the completion of *Boris Godunov* was unusual, see no. 116.

[2] He is referring to the verses on Byron contained in his poem 'To the Sea'; to the chagrin of the Vyazemskys he balked at writing a full-scale elegy. He seems to imply here that it would not be passed by the censorship anyway.

63. Draft of letter to P. A. Pletnev *End of October 1824*
Mikhailovskoe

... I am confidently and happily relying on you concerning my *Onegin*![1] Summon my Areopagus: you, Zhukovsky, Gnedich and Delvig – I wait on your judgement and will humbly accept your verdict.

I am sorry that Baratynsky is not among you: they say he is writing.[2]

[1] Pushkin had entrusted Pletnev with the publication of the first chapter of *Evgeny Onegin*.

[2] Pushkin's high opinion of Baratynsky is clear from all he wrote about him. Baratynsky was at this time writing his narrative poem *Eda*, published in 1826.

64. Draft of letter to Princess V. F. Vyazemsky *End of October 1824*
Mikhailovskoe

... A l'égard de mes voisins je n'ai eu que la peine de les rebuter d'abord; ils ne m'excèdent pas – je jouis parmi eux de la réputation d'*Onéguine*[1] – et voilà, je suis prophète en mon pays. Soit. Pour toute ressource je vois souvent une bonne vieille voisine[2] – j'écoute ses conversations patriarcales. Ses filles assez mauvaises sous tous les rapports me jouent du Rossini que j'ai fait venir. Je suis dans la meilleure position possible pour achever mon roman poétique, mais l'ennui est une froide Muse – et mon poème n'avance guère – voilà pourtant une strophe que je vous dois – montrez-la au *Prince Pierre*.[3] Dites-lui de ne pas juger du tout par cet échantillon. ...

[1] In *Evgeny Onegin*, Chapter II, stanza 5, written while he was in Odessa, Pushkin describes how Onegin frightens off his country neighbours:

> Our neighbour is a boor, and crazy;
> Freemason, too! red wine, we think,
> In glasses, is his only drink ...
> (trans. Oliver Elton)

[2] Praskovya A. Osipov, see page 100.

[3] Prince Vyazemsky.

65. To L. S. Pushkin *1-10 November 1824*
Trigorskoe

. . . Is Petersburg astir? How was your arrival and how is *Onegin*?[1]

NB send me (1) Œuvres de Lebrun,[2] odes, élégies, etc. – you will find them at St Florent[3] (2) Sulphur matches (3) Cards, i.e. playing cards . . . (3) [*sic*] The Life of Emelka Pugachev[4] (4) Muraviev's Journey in the Tauris[5] (5) Mustard and cheese; but that you can bring yourself. How are our literary nabobs and how are the scoundrels?

I am toiling for the greater glory of the Koran[6] and have written a few other things – which I am too lazy to send.

[1] Chapter I of *Evgeny Onegin* had been submitted to the censorship.
[2] P. D. E. Lebrun (1729-1807), French lyric poet sometimes referred to as Lebrun-Pindare, known for his epigrams.
[3] Bookseller in St Petersburg.
[4] *Lozhny* [*The False*] *Peter III* (Moscow, 1809). Two copies remained in Pushkin's library. Pushkin later made an extensive study of Pugachev, both for his novel, *The Captain's Daughter*, and for his history of the Pugachev rebellion.
[5] See no. 38
[6] Pushkin's lyrics, dedicated to Praskovya A. Osipov, called 'Imitations of the Koran'.

66. To L. S. Pushkin *1-10 November 1824*
Mikhailovskoe

. . . here is a little picture for *Onegin*[1] – find a skilled and speedy artist.

If you have a different picture let the *positioning* of everything be exactly the same. The same scene, do you understand? That I must have, without fail.

And send me some galoshes. . . .

[1] Pushkin annotated his sketch (see plate 20) as follows: the left-hand figure (clearly representing himself, seen from the back) had to be 'handsome'; the right-hand figure (representing Evgeny) had to be '*leaning on the granite*'; 'a boat' and 'the fortress of Peter-and-Paul' had to appear in the background. An illustration based on this sketch was first published in 1829, not in the first edition of chapter I of *Evgeny Onegin*.

67. To L. S. Pushkin *First half of November 1824*
Mikhailovskoe

. . . Will you send me the German review of the *Prisoner of the Caucasus*[1] (ask Grech for it) and some books, for God's sake some books. . . . What of *Onegin*? . . . Poetry, poetry, poetry! Conversations de Byron![2] Walter Scott![3] That is food for the soul. Do you know how I spend my time? Before dinner I write my Memoirs;[4] I dine late; after dinner I go riding; in the evening I listen to fairy tales[5] – and in this way compensate for the shortcomings of my cursed education. How delightful these tales are! Each one is like a poem! Oh, my God, I nearly forgot! Here is a job for you: find a historical, matter-of-fact account of Stenka Razin, the only poetic figure in Russian history.[6]

Goodbye, my dear. How is Baratynsky's Finnish girl?[7] I am waiting.

[1] Carl Friedrich von der Borg, *Poetische Erzeugnisse der Russen* (Riga and Dorpat, 1823).

[2] Thomas Medwin, *Les Conversations de Lord Byron* (Paris, 1824), in Pushkin's library.

[3] Pushkin read Scott's novels extensively (see pages 198-202). His mounting interest in them was in line with his current preoccupation with history, which had been stimulated by his work on *Boris Godunov*.

[4] Pushkin destroyed these personal papers after the suppression of the Decembrist rising.

[5] These evening sessions with his nurse, Arina Rodionovna, bore golden fruit.

[6] A Cossack who led an uprising in the seventeenth century. He is the subject of one of the most popular Russian folk-songs of the Volga region.

[7] The heroine of Baratynsky's poem *Eda* was a Finnish girl.

68. To L. S. Pushkin   *20-24 November 1824*
                                            Mikhailovskoe

. . . Are you having a flood?[1] The very thing for cursed Petersburg! Voilà une belle occasion à vos dames de faire bidet. I am sorry for Delvig's *Tsvety*.[2] Will this hold him up for a long time in Petersburg sludge? How about the cellars? I must admit that my heart aches on their account too. Will a Noah not be found among you to plant a vineyard? . . . Publish, publish *Onegin* with the Conversation.[3] . . . Send me a Bible, a Bible! And it must without fail be in French.[4] My way of life doesn't change; I don't write any poetry, but carry on with my Memoirs and am reading *Clarissa*.[5] What an unbearably boring fool she is! . . . Will *Onegin* have the little illustration?

[1] This catastrophe, which took place in St Petersburg on 7 November, later formed the subject of Pushkin's masterpiece *The Bronze Horseman*.

[2] The publication of Delvig's Almanac, *Severnye Tsvety* for 1825, was held up by the flood.

[3] The first chapter of *Evgeny Onegin*, published in 1825, had a short foreword (see no. 45) and a verse preface 'Conversation between a bookseller and the poet'.

[4] A French edition of the Bible is listed in Pushkin's library.

[5] In his library Pushkin had Richardson's *Pamela, Clarissa Harlowe* and *Sir Charles Grandison* in the three-volume London edition of 1824 (vols. 6-8 of Ballantyne's Novelists' Library). See also his comment on *Clarissa* in *Journey from Moscow to Petersburg* (pages 344-5).

69. To V. A. Zhukovsky[1]   *29 November 1824*
                                                Mikhailovskoe

. . . I was exiled for a line in a stupid letter.[2] . . . I received an excruciatingly funny letter yesterday from Vyazemsky. How has he managed to remain gay in Russia?

You will see the Karamzins – I love both you and them passionately.

[1] On 31 October Pushkin had written a desperate letter to Zhukovsky describing his violent quarrels with his father and begging for his help (see pages 99-100). Zhukovsky wrote a soothing and encouraging letter back on 12 November, to which this letter is a reply.

[2] See no. 53.

70. To Prince P. A. Vyazemsky   *29 November 1824*
                                                Mikhailovskoe

. . . I am amazed at how you got hold of Tania's letter.[1] NB Explain this to me. In answer to your criticism: to be 'unsociable' is not the same as to be a 'misanthrope', i.e. one who hates people, but means to be someone who steers clear of people. Onegin is not sociable with his country neighbours; Tania thinks the reason for this is that 'in the depths of the country everything bores him', and that only the scintillating can hold any attraction for him. . . . What's more, if her meaning is not quite clear it makes the letter all the more truthful; it is a letter written by a woman, what is more she is seventeen, what is more she is in love! My dear, what about your prose about Byron? I can hardly wait.[2]

[1] Vyazemsky had written to Pushkin (6 November 1824) that Tania's letter – *Evgeny Onegin*, III, xxxi – was a delight and a masterpiece but that he found a contradiction in the fact that she says to Onegin that he has the

reputation of being unsociable and at the same time that he is bored in the depths of the country without scintillating neighbours.

² This was never written.

71. To L. S. and O. S. Pushkin

4 December 1824
Mikhailovskoe

. . . Mikhail brought everything safely but no Bible. The Bible for a Christian is what its history is for a nation. The Introduction to Karamzin's History used to begin with this sentence (in reverse).¹ He changed it in my presence. . . . I can't get this flood out of my mind, it is by no means as diverting as appeared at first sight. If you feel like helping some victim, do so out of *Onegin* money. But please do so without any fuss, either spoken or in print.². . . Send me Baratynsky's *Eda*. What a Finn he is! But if she is more charming than my Circassian girl,³ I shall hang myself by the two pine trees and will never speak to him again.

¹ The opening words of Karamzin's *History of the Russian State* are: 'History is in a certain sense the holy book of nations.'
² Lists of donations were being published in the *Russky Invalid*.
³ Heroine of *The Prisoner of the Caucasus*.

72. To A. G. Rodzyanko¹

8 December 1824
Mikhailovskoe

. . . Let us talk about poetry i.e. yours. How goes your romantic poem *Chupka*?² You villain! Don't interfere with my trade – write satires, on me if you like, but don't upset my romantic stall. By the way, Baratynsky has written a poem (don't be angry – about a Finnish girl) and they say this Finnish girl is a perfect dear. And I have written one about *a Gipsy*. What about that! So serve us up your *Chupka* quickly – What a Parnassus! What heroines! Oh what an honest company! I can imagine how Apollo, looking at them, would cry out: 'Why are you bringing me the wrong girl?' Whom do you want then, accursed Phoebus? A Greek? An Italian? In what way are the Finnish girl or the Gipsy worse?

¹ Arkady Gavrilovich Rodzyanko (1793-1846). He served in the Guards and met Pushkin at meetings of the Green Lamp. Pushkin later visited him at his estate near Poltava, where he lived in retirement.

² Rodzyanko replied on 10 May 1825 that his poem, *Chupka*, had expired unfinished, never getting beyond the fragments he had read out to Pushkin.

73. Draft letter to D. M. Schwartz¹   *About 9 December 1824*
                                                       Mikhailovskoe

. . . I have now been four months in the depths of the country – it is dull, but what can one do about it; there is neither sea nor the blue southern sky, nor the Italian opera. But to make up for it there are neither locusts nor milords Vorontsov either. My isolation is complete – idleness triumphs. I have few neighbours in the vicinity, I am acquainted with only one family, and even them I see rather seldom² – I spend all day on horseback – in the evening I listen to my nurse's fairy tales, she is the prototype for Tatiana's nurse; you saw her once, I think. She is my only friend – and it's only when I'm with her that I'm not bored. . . .

¹ Dimitri Maximovich Schwartz (1797-1839), a friend of Pushkin's in Odessa.
² At this point in the draft Pushkin included the phrase 'an absolute Onegin', which he then crossed out. He was clearly in two minds about identifying himself with his hero.

74. To L. S. Pushkin   *About 20 December 1824*
                                                       Mikhailovskoe

. . . I sent you a letter with Rokotov¹ – get hold of it without fail. In it, in my youthful foolishness, I sent you a Yuletide ditty.² That feather-brained youth R. might scatter it – and it won't be a bit funny if I get jailed pour des chansons. For Christ's sake, I beg you to drag *Onegin* out of the censorship as quickly as possible³ . . . I need money. Don't haggle too long over verses – cut, tear, or chop up all 54 stanzas but get some money, for God's sake get some money! . . .

Send me some notepaper and plain paper, and if you send wine send cheese with it, and (speaking like Delille⁴) don't forget the twisted steel which pierces the tarred head of the bottle, i.e. the corkscrew.

¹ Ivan Matveyevich Rokotov, a neighbour of Pushkin's.
² 'Noël', a short poem with political overtones. It hasn't survived.
³ The first chapter of *Evgeny Onegin* was passed by the censorship on 29 December 1824.

[4] Jacques Delille (1738-1813), French abbé and poet, translated Virgil and Milton, given to periphrasis.

75. To Baron A. A. Delvig[1]
December 1824
Mikhailovskoe

. . . I was ill when I arrived in Bakhchisarai. I had heard before of the strange monument erected by the enamoured Khan. K . . .[2] described it to me poetically, calling it la fontaine des larmes. On entering the palace I saw the ruined fountain, with water dripping from a rusty iron pipe. I walked round the palace feeling very annoyed on seeing the neglect into which it had fallen and the semi-European alterations made in some of the rooms. N. N.[3] practically forced me to go with him up the ancient stairway to the ruins of the harem and to the Khan's graveyard . . . I was plagued by fever.

As regards the memorial of the Khan's mistress of which Muraviev-Apostol speaks, I forgot about it when I wrote my poem, or I would certainly have made use of it.

[1] This letter was first published in *Severnye Tsvety* for 1826 and reprinted in the third edition of *The Fountain of Bakhchisarai* (1830). It is not included in the Academy edition of Pushkin's correspondence.
[2] One of the Raevsky daughters disguised for the purposes of mystification.
[3] General Raevsky.

1825

ARTICLES

76. Of Madame de Staël and Mr A. Mukhanov[1]

Of all the works of Mme de Staël, her book *Dix Années d'exil*[2] deserved the particular attention of the Russian public. The quick and penetrating observation, comments striking in their novelty and truth, the writer's pen moved by gratitude and goodwill – all do credit to the mind and sensibility of an exceptional woman. The following has been written of her:

> One can clearly see, reading her book *Dix Années d'exil* that, touched by the kind welcome of the Russian boyars, she did not write of everything that met her gaze (i.e. in speaking of Petersburg society prior to 1812). I dare not on that score rebuke the eloquent and gracious foreigner, who was the first to give the Russian people their due, they who are the perennial objects of the ignorant slander of foreign writers.

It is in that very forbearance which the author of the above lines finds impossible to censure that the chief delight lies of that part of the book devoted to the description of our country. Mme de Staël left Russia as she would a holy sanctuary,[3] a family, into which she had been welcomed with trust and cordiality. Fulfilling the debt of a noble heart, she speaks of us with respect and discretion, praises us with warmth of spirit, reproves us with tact, and *does not wash our dirty linen in public*. Let us, in our turn, thank our celebrated guest; let us honour the fine memory she has left us, as she honoured our hospitality. . . .

From Russia Mme de Staël travelled to Sweden through the dismal wastes of Finland. In the autumn of her days, separated from everything she held dear, kept in exile for seven years by the active despotism of Napoleon, playing an anguished part in the political situation of Europe, she obviously could not at that time (the autumn of 1812) preserve that transparency of spirit which is necessary for a full appreciation of the beauties of nature. It is not surprising, then, that the blackened cliffs, the impenetrable forests and the lakes filled her with depression.

Her incomplete notes end with a sombre description of Finland. . . .
Mr A. M. (in *Syn Otechestva*, No. 10), *skimming once again through the pages of Mme de Staël's book, stumbled* on the above-mentioned passage and translated it in rather ponderous prose, adding to it the following *Comment on Mme de Staël's reveries*:

Leaving aside the disclosure of a feather-brained levity, a lack of observation and a complete ignorance of the locality, which cannot fail to astound readers *familiar with the works of the author of 'De l'Allemagne'*, I for my part was astonished by the story itself, in all respects similar to the vulgar verbiage of those *finicky Frenchies who, a little while ago, arriving in Russia with a meagre supply of information and great expectations, were so joyfully welcomed by our generous and at times misplacedly good-natured countrymen (our contemporaries in all but their ways of thinking)*.

What language and what a *tone!* What have two pages of Observations to do with *Delphine, Corinne, Considérations sur les principaux événements de la Révolution française, etc.* And what is there in common between *finicky* (?) *Frenchies* and Necker's daughter, exiled by Napoleon and protected by the magnanimity of the Russian Emperor?

'Those who have read the works of Mme de Staël' continues Mr A. M. 'in which she often throws her weight about, etc. . . . will no doubt find it strange that the limitless forests, etc., made no other impression on the author of *Corinne*, than that of deadly monotony!' After that Mr A. M. sets himself up as an example. 'No!' he says, 'I can never forget the turmoil of my soul, expanding to absorb such powerful impressions. I shall always remember the mornings, etc.' There follows a description of the northern scene in language utterly different from that of Mme de Staël.

He then advises the late authoress *to ask her coachmen, through the services of some interpreter, of the real reason for the fires*, etc.

The witticism on the proximity of wolves and bears to the University of Åbo did not amuse Mr A. M. – but Mr A. M. grows flippant himself. He says:

Would you have thought that the 400 students studying there are in training to become hunters? In which case she might as well have called this Academy a dog-kennel. Surely Mme de Staël could find herself some other methods of searching out the reasons holding up the spread of enlightenment than, dressed up as Diana, forcing the reader to trot with her through the forests of Finland over freshly fallen snow after bears and wolves. And anyway why look for them in their lairs? Finally, from the fear overcoming *our timid lady's spirit*, etc.

Of this *lady* one should speak in language both polite and cultured. Napoleon paid this *lady* the compliment of exile, monarchs that of trust, Europe that of her esteem, and Mr A. M. that of a puny article in a review, which is at the same time not particularly witty and most indecent.

'If you wish to be esteemed you must know how to esteem others.'[4]

Old Arzamasian

9 June 1825

[1] Published in *Moskovsky Telegraph*, Pt. 3, No. 12 (1825), in answer to Mukhanov's article in the *Syn Otechestva*. Mukhanov, who was adjutant to the Governor-General of Finland, had signed his article by initials only so that Pushkin did not know the identity of the author. Mukhanov had been hurt by Mme de Staël's comments on Finland.

[2] *Dix Années d'exil* was published posthumously in 1818. It was banned in Russia, but Pushkin had a copy in his library and referred to it several times in his works.

[3] Mme de Staël was in Russia for eight weeks in 1812, in exile from Napoleonic France. She left for Finland on the day after the Battle of Borodino.

[4] A line adapted from one of Vyazemsky's poems.

77. Of M. Lémontey's introduction to the translation of I. A. Krylov's fables[1]

Count Orlov's venture[2] pleased the lovers of our literature, although they knew that a method of translation at once so brilliant and so inadequate[3] would to some extent spoil the fables of our inimitable poet. Many awaited M. Lémontey's introduction with great impatience; and it is in fact a very remarkable one, if not completely satisfying. Generally speaking, where the author was forced to write from hearsay his judgements may at times seem mistaken; while by contrast his own guesses and conclusions are surprisingly just. It is a pity that this famous writer barely touched on some subjects on which his opinions would have been so intriguing. One reads his article (that is in translation, published in *Syn Otechestva*; we have not had the opportunity of seeing the French original) with involuntary disappointment, as one sometimes hears the conversation of a very intelligent man who, being constrained by some proprieties, leaves too much unspoken and too often remains silent.

Having thrown a rapid glance over our literary history, the author says a few words on our language, recognizes it to be primitive, has no doubts that it is capable of being perfected, and, quoting the assurances of Russians, presumes it to be rich, mellifluous, and fertile in shades of meaning.

It would not be difficult to substantiate these opinions. As a literary instrument Slavonic is unquestionably superior to all other European languages:[4] its fate has been exceptionally fortunate. In the eleventh century the lexicon of classical Greek, a veritable treasure-house of harmony, was laid open to it. Greek endowed it with its carefully thought-out laws of syntax, its splendid nuances, its majestic flow of speech, in brief – adopted it, freeing it in this way from time's slow, perfecting processes. Sonorous and expressive of itself, it inherited at that time flexibility and correctness. Colloquial speech had of necessity to draw apart from the language of literature; but with time they flowed together again, *and that is the element that we have inherited for the expression of our thoughts.*

M. Lémontey is mistaken in thinking that Tatar rule left the Russian language rusty. A foreign tongue is spread not by fire and the sword but by its own richness and superiority. What new concepts calling for new words could a nomadic tribe of barbarians, having neither literature, trade, nor legislation, have brought us? Their advance left no trace on the language of the cultured Chinese, and our ancestors groaning under the Tatar yoke for two centuries prayed to the Russian God in their own language, cursed their stern overlords, and passed their plaints on from mouth to mouth. We have ourselves seen an example of a similar situation in contemporary Greece. What effect has the preservation of its language on a subjugated nation? The investigation of that question would lead us too far afield. Be that as it may, barely fifty Tatar words were incorporated into the Russian language. The Lithuanian wars likewise had no effect on our language's fate; it remained our unhappy land's one inviolable possession.

In the reign of Peter I it began to be noticeably mutilated by the unavoidable introduction of Dutch, German and French words. This fashion also had its influence on writers at that time patronized by Emperors and Princes; but fortunately there appeared Lomonosov.[5]

M. Lémontey at one point speaks of Lomonosov's all-embracing genius, but his view of the great Peter's illustrious fellow worker is taken from the wrong angle.

Combining exceptional will-power with exceptional powers of understanding, Lomonosov embraced all branches of knowledge. The thirst for knowledge predominated among the many passions that charged his spirit. Historian, rhetorician, mechanic, chemist, mineralogist, artist and poet, he experienced and penetrated all things. He is the first to investigate closely our country's history and to establish the rules of its official language, he draws up laws and *exempla* of classical eloquence, together with the unfortunate Rikhman he foresees Franklin's discoveries,[6] sets up a factory, constructs the machines himself, graces art with works in mosaic, and finally reveals to us the true sources of our poetic language.

At times, in the case of a few born poets, poetry is the single passion which embraces and engulfs all the attention, all the efforts, and all the impressions of their lives; but when we begin to study Lomonosov's life we shall find that the factual sciences were always his main and favourite pursuit, while on the other hand the writing of poetry, though at times a recreation, was for him more often a dutiful exercise. In our first lyric poet we looked in vain for flaming fits of passion and imagination. His diction even, figurative and picturesque, owes its chief merit to its deep grounding in written Slavonic, and to its happy mingling of it with the vernacular. That is why his versions of the psalms and other close renderings of the exalted poetry of the Scriptures are his best works. (It is interesting to see with what sting Tredyakovsky[7] mocks at Lomonosov's Old Slavonic expressions, how pompously he advises him to adopt the grace and sparkle of the speech of good society! But it is surprising that Sumarokov[8] in one line of verse defined with great accuracy Lomonosov's true achievement as a poet: 'He is our country's Malherbe and to Pindar can be likened.' Enfin Malherbe vint, et le premier en France, etc.[9]) They will remain eternal memorials of Russian literature; we will for a long time to come have to learn our poetic language from them; but it is strange to complain that society does not read Lomonosov, and to expect that a man who died seventy years ago should continue to this day to be the public's favourite. As if the great Lomonosov's fame stands in need of the trivial honours bestowed on a fashionable writer.

Having mentioned the singular use of French in the educated circles of our society, M. Lémontey both wittily and fairly remarks that it was on account of this that the Russian language preserved its rare freshness, simplicity and, so to speak, spontaneity of expression. I do not wish to justify our indifference to the success of our country's literature, but there is no doubt that though our writers may forfeit much enjoyment on account of this indifference, it is at least to the advantage of both our language and literature. Who deflected French poetry from its classical models? Who powdered and rouged Racine's Melpomène and even the aged Corneille's stern muse? The courtiers of Louis XIV. What laid the cold veneer of politeness and wit on all the writers of the eighteenth century? The society of Mesdames du Deffand, Boufflers, d'Épinay, women who were both charming and cultured. But Milton and Dante did not write for the *favouring smile of the fair sex*.

A stern and just sentence on the French language does honour to the author's impartiality. True enlightenment is unprejudiced. Citing the fate of this prosaic language as an example, M. Lémontey maintains that our language must also expect to enter *the comity of Europe* through its prose-writers rather than through its poets. The Russian translator took offence at this; but if the original reads 'civilisation Européenne'[10] then the author is largely right.

Let us assume that Russian poetry has already reached a highly civilized level: the enlightenment of the age demands food for thought, thinking minds can no longer be satisfied with the play of harmony and imagination. But learning, politics and philosophy have as yet not found expression in Russian; we have no metaphysical vocabulary. Our prose is as yet so little formed that even in simple correspondence we are forced to *create* forms of speech for the expression of the most ordinary concepts, so that in our indolence we more readily express ourselves in a foreign language, whose syntactical forms have long been formulated and are widely known.

M. Lémontey, going into several details concerning our Krylov's life and habits, said that he does not speak any foreign language and understands only French. That is *not true*! The translator sharply objects in his note. Actually Krylov knows the principal European languages, and over and above that, like Alfieri, learnt classical Greek at the age of fifty. In other countries such a characteristic trait of a famous man would have been blazoned in all the reviews, but we in the biographies of our famous writers content ourselves with stating the year of their birth and the details of their government service and then complain of foreigners' complete lack of knowledge of all that concerns us.

In conclusion I will say that we must thank Count Orlov for choosing a truly national poet for the role of introducing Europe to the literature of the north. Naturally no Frenchman will dare to place anyone above La Fontaine, but we, I think, may be allowed to prefer Krylov. Both of them will always remain their countrymen's favourites. Someone has justly remarked that simplicity (naïveté, bonhomie) is the innate virtue of the French people; in contrast, the distinctive traits of our temperament are a certain gay craftiness, a spirit of mockery, and a vivid way of expressing ourselves. La Fontaine and Krylov are representatives of the spirits of the two nations.

N. K.[11]

12 August 1825

PS I considered it superfluous to mention certain obvious mistakes, pardonable in a foreigner, for instance the association of Krylov with Karamzin (an association for which there is no foundation), the idea that our language is unsuitable for metrical versification, etc.

[1] Published in *Moskovsky Telegraph*, Pt. V, No. 17 (1825). Lémontey's introduction to a French edition of Krylov's fables was published in Paris in 1825 and was reprinted in Russian in the *Syn Otechestva*, Nos. 13 and 14 (1825). Pushkin thought highly of Lémontey's *Essai sur l'établissement monarchique de Louis XIV, etc.* (Paris, 1818) (see his letter to Vyazemsky, 5 July 1824).

[2] Count G. V. Orlov was responsible for the publication in Paris of this collection of French and Italian translations of Krylov's fables.

[3] The translations were versifications of literal renderings from the Russian.

[4] Lomonosov said of Russian that it possessed the vivacity of French, the strength of German, the softness of Italian, the richness and concision of Greek and Latin (quoted by Maurice Baring in *The Oxford Book of Russian Verse*).

[5] See pages 345-9.

[6] Academician Georg-Wilhelm Rikhman was killed by lightning when conducting electrical experiments with Lomonosov in St Petersburg in 1753. Benjamin Franklin's observations concerning the electrical nature of lightning were made public in the 1753 issue of *Poor Richard's Almanack*.

[7] Vasily Kyrilovich Tredyakovsky (1703-69), poet and philologist, altered the direction of Russian prosody by breaking free from the use of strict syllabic scansion, to which Russian with its irregular accentuation was ill adapted. He corresponded with Lomonosov on prosody.

[8] Alexander Petrovich Sumarokov (1718-77) was a poet and playwright of the neo-classical school and helped to establish several literary genres, both dramatic and poetic, in Russia. His views on poetic diction had considerable influence.

[9] Sumarokov's line is from his 'Epistle on Prosody'; Boileau's from *L'Art poétique*.

[10] The phrase Lémontey used is 'sociabilité européenne'.

[11] Pushkin used some consonants from his surname for his signature for this article.

DRAFT NOTES

78. From draft criticism of A. A. Bestuzhev's article 'A survey of Russian literature in 1824 and the beginning of 1825'[1]

... We have criticism? Where is it to be found? Where are our Addisons, La Harpes, Schlegels, Sismondi? What have we critically analysed? Whose literary opinions have been accepted by the whole nation? Whose criticism can we cite, on whose authority lean?

But Mr Bestuzhev himself says further on, 'we see plenty of critics, anticritics and critics of critics, but few efficient critics.'

[1] Published in *Polyarnaya Zvezda* for 1825. Bestuzhev claimed that Russia had criticism but no literature.
  See also Pushkin's letter to Bestuzhev, no. 102.

79. Draft on Classical and Romantic poetry.

Our critics have not yet decided on a clear definition of the difference between the classical and Romantic kinds (in literature).[1] We have French journalists to thank for our confused understanding of this subject, for they tended to assign to Romanticism everything which seemed to them marked with the stamp of visionary idealism and Germanic ideology, or which was based on popular superstitions and legends, which is a most inaccurate definition. A poem can display all these qualities and at the same time belong to the classical kind. If instead of the *form* of a poem we are going to take as a basis only the *spirit* in which it was written then we will never disentangle ourselves from definitions. A hymn by J. B. Rousseau differs in spirit, of course, from an ode by Pindar, Juvenal's satire from that of Horace, *Ierusalemma Liberata* from the *Aeneid* – but yet they all belong to the classical kind. To this kind belong all those poems whose *forms* were known to the Greeks and Romans, or of which they have left us models, consequently herein are included: epics, didactic poems, tragedies, comedies, odes, satires, epistles, *heroides*, eclogues, elegies, epigrams and fables.

What forms of poetry then are to be assigned to the Romantic school? All those which were not known to the Ancients, and those whose earlier forms have suffered change or been replaced by others.

I do not hold it necessary to speak of the poetry of the Greeks and Romans: every educated European should have a sufficient understanding of the immortal works of the majestic ancients. Let us glance at the lineage and gradual development of the poetry of contemporary nations.

The Western Empire declined rapidly, dragging down with it learning, literature and art. Finally it fell; the lamp of learning went out, ignorance darkened bloodstained Europe. Latin barely survived; in the dust of monastic libraries the monks scraped the poems of Lucretius and Virgil off the parchments and wrote their chronicles and legends in their place.[2]

Poetry awoke under the midday sky of France – rhymes echoed in the romance language; this new ornament of verse, of such little importance at first sight, had a powerful influence on the literatures of young nations. The ear was pleased by the double repetition of sounds – a mastered difficulty always gives us pleasure – it is natural to the human mind to love measure and co-ordination. The troubadours played with rhyme, devising for it all sorts of metrical variations. They thought up the most complicated forms: there appeared the virelay, the ballade, the rondeau, the sonnet, etc.

This led necessarily to a straining in expression, a form of preciosity quite unknown to the ancients; petty wit replaced feeling, which cannot find expression in triolets. We find miserable traces of this in the greatest geniuses of our own time.

But the mind cannot remain satisfied with the toys of harmony alone, the imagination demands pictures and tales. The troubadours turned to new sources of inspiration, they sang of love and war, they revived popular legends – the lay, the novel and the fabliau were born.

A dim conception of classical tragedy combined with church festivals occasioned the composition of mystery plays (mystères). They are nearly all written to one model and follow one pattern, but unfortunately there was no Aristotle at that time to fix immutable laws for the dramatic form which mystery plays should take.

Two circumstances had a decisive influence on the spirit of European poetry: the advance of the Moors and the Crusades.

The Moors endowed it with raptures and the softnesses of love, with an appetite for the marvellous and with the gorgeous eloquence of the East; the knights transmitted their piety and simplicity, their concept of heroism and the free morals of the camps of Godfrey and Richard.[3]

Such was the humble beginning of Romantic poetry. If it had got no further than these experiments the stern verdicts of French critics would have been justified; but its shoots blossomed quickly and richly, and soon it appears as a rival to the ancient Muse.

Italy appropriated to herself the epic; semi-African Spain took possession of tragedy and the novel; England in the face of such names as Dante, Ariosto and Calderón proudly put forward those of Spenser, Milton and Shakespeare; in Germany (strangely enough) a new form of satire rose to distinction, caustic, jocular, of which *Reineke Fuchs* remains as an example.

At that time in France poetry was still in a state of infancy: the foremost poet of the time of François I rima les triolets, fit fleurir la ballade.[4]

The scales were already heavily tipped in prose's favour: Montaigne and Rabelais were the contemporaries of Marot.

In Italy and Spain popular poetry was in existence before the appearance of its masters. They followed a trodden road: there were poems written before Ariosto's *Orlando*, tragedies before those of de Vega and Calderón.

In France the Age of Enlightenment caught poetry in its infancy, lacking a sense of direction, lacking force. Educated men in the age of Louis XIV rightly despised its insignificance and reverted to ancient models. Boileau published his Koran – and French literature bowed to his will.

This neo-classical poetry, which was born in the lobby and never got beyond the drawing-room, could not shed some of its innate habits, and we see in it all the affectation of Romanticism, tricked out in strict classical forms.

PS One should not consider however that in France there remained no examples of pure romantic poetry. The tales of La Fontaine and Voltaire, and the latter's *La Pucelle*, bear its mark. I am not going to speak of their countless imitators (whose works are for the most part mediocre; it is easier to surpass one's masters in the neglect of all decencies than in poetic quality).

[1] See letters to Vyazemsky, no. 104, and to Bestuzhev, no. 118.
[2] A characteristically eighteenth-century view of the Middle Ages.
[3] During the Crusades.
[4] Boileau *L'Art poétique*:

> Marot bien-tost après fit fleurir les Ballades,
> Tourna des Triolets, rima des Mascarades . . .

80. Fragment of note on 'Demon'[1]

I think that the critic is mistaken. Many are of the same opinion, others have even pointed out the person whom Pushkin was supposedly wanting to depict in his strange poem. It seems they are mistaken. At any rate I see the 'Demon' as having a different and more moral aim.

At the best time of one's life the heart, as yet unchilled by experience, is responsive to beauty. It is credulous and tender. Gradually the endless contradictions of existence breed doubts, a painful but not a protracted condition. It passes, having destroyed for ever the hopes and the finest poetic preconceptions of the soul. No wonder that that great man Goethe calls the eternal enemy of mankind *the spirit of negation*.[2] And did not Pushkin wish to embody in his demon this spirit of *denial or doubt* and in this pleasant picture sketched its distinctive features and its unhappy influence on the morals of our age?

[1] Unfinished draft of note written because of widespread rumours that in this poem, written in 1823, he had described Alexander Raevsky. Pushkin wanted to avoid autobiographical identification but he protested too much. His relationship with Raevsky, which became particularly strained when they were rivals for the love of Countess Vorontsov, may also be at the root of his poem 'Kovarnost' written on 18 October 1824.

[2] In *Faust*, scene 3, Mephistopheles describes himself as the spirit who eternally denies.

81. Draft note to elegy 'André Chénier'[1]

André Chénier was thirty-one years old when he died, a victim of the French revolution. For a long time his fame was confined to a few words said of him by Chateaubriand, to two or three fragments, and to a general regret at the loss of all else. His works were at last found, and appeared in 1819. One cannot help feeling sad.

[1] Pushkin wrote his elegy on André Chénier in 1825 (see his letters to Vyazemsky, no. 107). Several stanzas of the elegy were banned by the censorship and were subsequently circulated in manuscript under the title 'On 14 December'. Pushkin denied giving them this title but it none the less caused him much trouble, see pages 184-5.

André Chénier only published two poems in his lifetime, which attracted no attention. He was guillotined on 27 July 1794. In 1802 Chateaubriand launched his poetic fame in *Le Génie du christianisme* in which he quoted a few lines of his poetry and spoke of his rare talent for writing eclogues and idylls which were worthy of Theocritus. It was here also that Chateaubriand told the story of Chénier's last words on the scaffold which Pushkin refers to in no. 117. Pushkin had a copy of the first edition of the complete works of Chénier (Paris, 1819) in his library.

82. Draft note on tragedy[1]

Of all forms of composition the ones most lacking in verisimilitude (invraisemblables) are the dramatic, and of dramatic works, the tragic, as the spectator must forget, for the most part, the time, the place and the language; must accept, by an effort of the imagination, poetry and ideas expressed in an accepted idiom. French writers felt this and drew up their arbitrary rules – of action, place, time. Since the holding of the audience's attention is the first concern of dramatic art, unity of action must be adhered to. But those of place and time are too arbitrary – what inconveniences arise from circumscribing the place of action. Conspiracies, declarations of love, councils of state, festivities – all take place in one room! Excessive speed and concentration of action, confidants . . . *a parte* are as unreasonable. . . . And it all does not matter. Is it not simpler to follow the Romantic school, which is marked by the absence of all Rules but not by the absence of art?

Interest is All.

The mixing of the comic and tragic kinds, tension, the occasionally necessary refinement of popular turns of phrase.

[1] Draft note written at the time when Pushkin was working on *Boris Godunov*, see his draft prefaces, no. 174, and Notes on popular drama (1830), no. 179.

LETTERS

83. To K. F. Ryleev   *25 January 1825*
                                          Mikhailovskoe

. . . Pushchin will bring you an excerpt from my *Gipsies*.[1] I hope you will like it. I am waiting impatiently for the *Polyarnaya Zvezda*. And do you know why? Because of *Voynarovsky*.[2] Our literature stood in need of this poem. Bestuzhev writes a lot to me about *Onegin*[3] – tell him he is wrong: does he really mean to banish everything light and gay from the province of poetry? What will become of satires and comedies? One would consequently have to tear up *Orlando Furioso* and *Hudibras*, and *Pucelle*, and *Ver-Vert*, and *Reineke Fuchs*, and the best part of *Dushenka*,[4] and La Fontaine's tales, and Krylov's fables, etc. etc. etc. etc. That's a bit severe. Descriptions of society life also come within the province of poetry. But enough of *Onegin*.

I agree with Bestuzhev's opinion of Pletnev's critical article[5] – but do not fully subscribe to the severe sentence passed on Zhukovsky.[6] Why should we bite the breast that suckled us simply because we have cut our teeth? Say what you will, Zhukovsky has had a decisive influence on the spirit of our literature; and, besides, his style in translating will always remain a model. Oh this republic of letters! For what does it slay, for what crown?

[1] See page 34.

[2] Ryleev's *Voynarovsky* was published in Moscow in 1825, a romantic narrative poem on Mazeppa's rebellion against Peter the Great, referring obliquely throughout to current politics (in the dedication Ryleev declared 'I am a citizen, not a poet'). It was influenced both in style and content by Pushkin's *Prisoner of the Caucasus*.

[3] This letter does not survive but see no. 92 for Pushkin's disputes with both Bestuzhev and Ryleev over the first chapter of *Evgeny Onegin*.

[4] *Orlando Furioso* by Ariosto; *Hudibras* by Samuel Butler; *La Pucelle d'Orléans* by Voltaire (an old favourite of Pushkin's); *Ver-Vert, Histoire d'un perroquet de Nevers*, a tale of an indiscreet nunnery parrot by J. B. L. Gresset; *Reineke Fuchs* translated from a medieval tale by Goethe; *Dushenka* by I. F. Bogdanovich.

[5] Pletnev had published an article on Russian poets in the *Severnye Tsvety* for 1825. See Pushkin's comment in the next letter to Vyazemsky.

[6] See also letter to Vyazemsky 25 May 1825. Vyazemsky was pleased by Pushkin's warm words on Zhukovsky.

84. To Prince P. A. Vyazemsky

25 January 1825
Mikhailovskoe

. . . Rousseau's obscene epigrams are a hundred times better than his odes and hymns.[1] . . . I am expecting my brother and Delvig in a day or two, for the moment I am absolutely alone; . . . I lounge about in the ingle-nook and listen to old fairy tales and songs. Poetry doesn't come. I think I told you that my poem *The Gipsies* is not at all good: don't you believe it – I lied – you will be very pleased with it. *Onegin* is in the press; my brother and Pletnev are seeing to the edition; I didn't expect it to squeeze through the censorship – all honour to Shishkov.[2] . . . What do you think of Pletnev's article? What a jumble! You sleep, Brutus! Tell me which of you it was in Moscow that so hotly took up arms for the Germans against Bestuzhev (whom I haven't read).[3]

[1] Jean-Baptiste Rousseau (1671-1741), French poet and satirist.
[2] The Minister of Education, in charge of the censorship.

[3] Bestuzhev had written critically of German poets in reviewing Sir John Bowring's *Specimens of the Russian Poets* (1821-3) in *Literaturnye Listki* (1824).

85. To Prince P. A. Vyazemsky   *28 January 1825*
                                                              Trigorskoe

... I have read Chatsky[1] – there is much that is clever and amusing in the verse, but the comedy as a whole lacks a plan and a central idea, nor is there any truth in it. Chatsky is not a bit intelligent – but Griboedov is, very intelligent.

[1] See following letter, no. 86.

86. To A. A. Bestuzhev   *End of January 1825*
                                                       Mikhailovskoe

Ryleev will bring you my *Gipsies*.[1] Tell my brother off for not keeping his promise – I didn't want this poem known in advance;[2] now there is nothing I can do about it – I am forced to publish it before it is dismembered completely.

I have heard Chatsky read aloud, but only once, and not with the attention it deserves.[3] This is what I had time to notice in passing.

A dramatist must be judged by his own rules. Therefore I do not censure either the plan, or the mainspring of the plot, or the proprieties, of Griboedov's comedy. He aimed at character-drawing, and at presenting a sharp picture of manners. Seen in this light Famusov and Skalozub are magnificent. Sophia is not sketched in clearly: on the one hand she seems a tart, on the other a Moscow Miss. Molchalin is not sufficiently vile; shouldn't he have been made a coward as well? It's an old trick, but a cowardly civilian in high society, juxtaposed to Chatsky and Skalozub, could be very amusing. Les propos de bal, the gossip, Repetilov's account of the club, Zagoretsky, regarded as a thorough knave by everybody and yet received everywhere – are all strokes of true comic genius. The question arises: in the comedy *Woe from Wit*, who is the intelligent character? The answer is: Griboedov. And do you know what Chatsky is? An impassioned, noble young man and a good sort, who has spent some time in the company of a very intelligent man (that is, of Griboedov) and has imbibed his ideas, his witticisms, and his satiric quips. All he says is very intelligent. But to whom does he say it all? To Famusov? To Skalozub? To Muscovite

132

Grandmamas at a ball? To Molchalin? That is unforgivable. The first mark of an intelligent man is that he knows at a glance whom he is dealing with, and does not cast pearls before Repetilov and his like. By the way, what is Repetilov? He combines in himself two, three, or ten characters. Why make him beastly? It suffices that he is so feather-brained and so ingenuously stupid; it would be enough for him constantly to acknowledge his own stupidity rather than, as he does, his knaveries. Such meekness is quite new to the stage, but who among us has not been embarrassed on hearing similar penitents? Among the masterful features of this delightful comedy, Chatsky's incredulity concerning Sophia's love for Molchalin is charming! And how natural! That is what the whole comedy should have turned on, but it seems Griboedov did not wish it so – that is up to him. I say nothing of his verses: half of them should become proverbs.[4]

Show this to Griboedov – I may be mistaken about something. As I listened to his comedy I did not criticize. I revelled in it. These comments came to me later, when I was no longer able to check up on them. At any rate I am speaking frankly, without circumlocution, as to a true master.

It seems you don't like 'Oleg';[5] that's a mistake on your part. The aged Prince's comradeship with his steed and his solicitude for its fate are signs of a touching simplicity of spirit, and in the very simplicity of the incident there lies a great deal of poetry. . . .

I did not get the number of Bulgarin's *Literaturnye Listki* with your review of Bowring.[6] Order it to be sent.

[1] See page 34.
[2] Bestuzhev had heard Pushkin's brother reciting *The Gipsies* and had written about it in his survey of Russian literature published in *Polyarnaya Zvezda* for 1825.
[3] He and Pushchin had read Griboedov's *Woe from Wit* – of which the hero is Chatsky – aloud together on 11 January, see page 102.
[4] More than a score of them have.
[5] Pushkin's heroic ballad, 'The Lay of Oleg the Seer', in which Prince Oleg is fatally bitten by a snake which had lurked in the skull of his dead charger.
[6] See no. 84 and note 3.

87. To L. S. Pushkin   *End of January/first half of February 1825*
                              Mikhailovskoe

. . . I am waiting for the stir over *Onegin*; in the meantime I am rather bored. You don't send me *Conversations de Byron*[1] – oh well, all right; but, my dear, if it is at all possible, beg, borrow or steal Fouché's Memoirs,[2] and send them to me here. I would give the whole of Shakespeare for them; you cannot imagine what a man Fouché is! In my opinion he is more fascinating than Byron. These memoirs should prove to be a hundred times more instructive, more intriguing, more vivid than those of Napoleon,[3] i.e. from a political point of view, because I don't understand a damned thing about war. Napoleon grew stupid on his rock (God forgive me!). In the first place he lies like a child (i.e. obviously); (2) he judges people not like a Napoleon, but like a Parisian pamphleteer, some Pradt[4] or Guizot.[5] Somehow I have a very, very shrewd suspicion that Bertrand[6] and Montholon[7] were bribed! Especially as it is precisely the most important information that is missing. Have you read Napoleon's memoirs? If not, read them: apart from everything else they read like a splendid novel, mais tout ce qui est politique n'est fait que pour la canaille.

Enough nonsense, now let's talk of serious matters . . . I have no new poetry – I am writing my memoirs, but even much-despised prose bores me.

. . . Advise Ryleev, in his new poem,[8] to include our grandfather in Peter I's suite. His Negro mug will have a curious effect on the whole picture of the battle of Poltava.[9]

[1] See no. 67.

[2] Joseph Fouché, Duc d'Otrante (1759-1820), French Minister of Police. He advised Napoleon to abdicate after Waterloo and then himself assumed the leadership of the provisional government. He was exiled from France in 1816. His *Mémoires*, published in Paris by A. de Beauchamp in 1824, were declared to be faked.

[3] *Mémoires pour servir à l'histoire de France sous Napoléon*, 'écrits à Sainte-Hélène par les généraux, qui ont partagé sa captivité, et publiés sur les manuscrits entièrement corrigés de la main de Napoléon' (Paris, 1823-5). The generals were Comte Charles Tristan de Montholon and Baron Gaspard Gourgaud.

[4] Dominique de Pradt (1759-1837), French Bishop and diplomat, chaplain to Napoleon.

[5] François Guizot (1787-1874), French historian and statesman.

[6] Comte Henri Bertrand (1773-1844), French general who accompanied Napoleon to Elba and St Helena.

[7] See note 3 above.

[8] *Voynarovsky*, see no. 83 above. Ryleev did not mention Pushkin's ancestor, Hannibal.

[9] Pushkin did not bring Hannibal into his own poem on Poltava, but he did make him the subject of his first short story – *The Arap of Peter the Great*, which he wrote in 1827. The tone of Pushkin's comment makes it

clear that he enjoyed causing a *frisson* by the mention of his Ethiopian ancestor – the exoticism appealed. See Section I, pages 3-4.

88. To Prince P. A. Vyazemsky   *19 February 1825*
                                                     Mikhailovskoe

... *Onegin* is printed; I think he has already made his début in the world.
. . . I get all the other reviews – and more than ever feel the need of something in the nature of the *Edinburgh Review*.[1] Christ! I'm sick of literature – my guts ache for some of your prose. How's the edition of Fonvizin?[2]

[1] This was a recurring theme in Pushkin's letters for years. He did not achieve his wish until 1836 (the last year of his life) when he was given permission to publish the *Sovremennik*.
[2] Vyazemsky's biography of the eighteenth-century Russian dramatist Fonvizin was begun in 1819 but not published till 1848.

89. To N. I. Gnedich   *23 February 1825*
                                            Mikhailovskoe

I think Onegin has you to thank for the patronage of Shishkov and for his happy release from Birukov. I see that your friendship towards me has not changed and that comforts me.

My present circumstances do not allow me even to hope for letters from you; but I am waiting for your poems, either in print or in manuscript. The Greek songs are delightful, and a tour de force.[1] The witty introduction calls for discussion. There is an obvious similarity between the lyric poets of the two nations – but why should this be so? . . . My brother has told me that you will soon finish your Homer.[2] That will be the first classical, European achievement in our fatherland (the devil take this fatherland). But what will you undertake, when you have had a rest from the *Iliad*, in the full flowering of your genius, which has grown to maturity in the Temple of Homer, as Achilles' did in the Centaur's cave. I expect an epic poem of you. You once wrote to me that 'Svyatoslav's shade is wandering over the world unsung'. What of Vladimir? Of Mstislav? Of Donskoy and Yermak? Of Pozharsky?[3] The history of a people belongs to the poet.

With your ship laden with treasure from Greece entering the harbour where a crowd awaits it, I am ashamed to write to you of my pedlar's stall No. 1 – I have begun a lot and finished nothing. I sit by the sea and wait for a change in the weather.[4] I am not writing anything and read little, because you publish little.

23 February, the anniversary of Alexander Ypsilanti's proclamation of the Greek Rising.

[1] Gnedich's translation of twelve modern Greek folk-songs was published in 1825. In the introduction Gnedich compared Greek and Russian folk-songs, finding much in common between them.
[2] Gnedich had been working on a translation of the *Iliad*.
[3] Svyatoslav, Vladimir, Mstislav, Dimitri Donskoy, Yermak Timofeevich and Dimitri Pozharsky were all heroes of Russian history between the tenth and the seventeenth centuries. Such subjects were very popular at the time with poets like Ryleev and Bestuzhev, who saw in them opportunities for political comment – Gnedich was not of their number.
[4] Pushkin is here referring to the political climate. A change was not forthcoming.

90. To L. S. Pushkin
14 March 1825
Trigorskoe

. . . My dear, send me some mustard, some rum, some pickles – and the following books: *Conversations de Byron, Mémoires de Fouché, Talia, Starina*,[1] and Sismondi (littérature),[2] and Schlegel (dramaturgie),[3] if they have them at St Florent.[4] I should also like to have the new Collected Edition of Russian Verse[5] but 75 roubles is a lot, I wouldn't give that much for all Russia. Anyway have a look at it.

Kachenovsky has rebelled against me.[6] Write and tell me whether the tone of his criticism is seemly – if not, I shall send an epigram.

There is heresy amongst you. It is said that verse is not the most important part of poetry.[7] What then is the most important? Prose? One must wipe this out from the start with fire and the sword.

[1] *Talia* and *Starina* were literary almanacs.
[2] J. C. L. Simonde de Sismondi (1773-1842), Swiss historian and economist. Pushkin wanted his *De la littérature du Midi de l'Europe* (1813).
[3] A. W. von Schlegel's lectures on Dramatic Art and Literature, *Über dramatische Kunst und Literatur* (Heidelberg, 1809-11).
[4] St Petersburg bookseller.
[5] An anthology of new Russian poems published in two parts in 1824-26 by A. F. Voeykov.
[6] Kachenovsky had published an article (not by himself) in the *Vestnik Evropy* in which it was implied that Pushkin was a negative force in literature; it also pronounced that Onegin's bad upbringing was unrepresentative

and therefore not of national significance. Pushkin was never slow to riposte with an epigram.

[7] In the arguments conducted in the columns of the *Moskovsky Telegraph* and other periodicals in 1824-5, the view had been expressed by several Romantic critics, including Küchelbecker, that the essence of poetry did not lie in its form (versification) but in the inspiration – the afflatus – behind it. Pushkin, who retained a classicist's respect and concern for form, was scornful of this extreme Romantic view.

91. To L. S. Pushkin and P. A. Pletnev   *15 March 1825*
                                                 Mikhailovskoe

Brother Lev and Brother Pletnev!

The day before yesterday I received my manuscript. Today I am sending all my poems, both new and old. I have hurriedly rinsed through my dirty linen and tacked up some new things but hope that, with your help, Madam Public will not slap my face as though I were an obscene washerwoman.

May I ask you to correct all spelling and punctuation mistakes, slips of the pen, and any expressions that don't make sense – I haven't an eye for these things. As regards the order of the pieces, use your own judgements. Only don't imitate the edition of Batyushkov[1] – exclude, blot with vigour. I give you my permission, I even ask you to do so. But for this job take Zhukovsky as an assistant, *pace* Bulgarin, and also Gnedich,[2] *pace* Griboedov. Either have no epigraph, or one from A. Chénier.[3] A vignette wouldn't be a bad thing; in fact, one could have one; in fact, there must be one; in fact, for Christ's sake, let there be one, namely: Psyche, grown pensive over a flower.[4] . . . But then these are but externals. . . .

What am I to tell you as to the editing? Print each piece on a separate page, correctly, cleanly, like the last edition of Zhukovsky;[5] and, please, with no ⌒⌒⌒ or — * — or ─────. All that fussiness is ugly and reminds one of Asia. The titles in large print – and à la ligne. But print every piece separately, even if it only consists of four lines (should it consist of two lines, then one can have another à la ligne).

Sixty pieces! Will that be enough for one volume? Should I perhaps send you 'Tsar Nikita and his forty daughters'[6] to fill it out?

Brother Lev! Do not annoy the journalists! It's bad policy!

Brother Pletnev! Do not write *kind* reviews! Bare your teeth and beware of being oversweet.[7]

Forgive me, children! I'm drunk.

[1] The edition of Batyushkov's verse and prose published in two parts in 1817.
[2] Neither Zhukovsky nor Gnedich in fact played any part in preparing this edition of Pushkin's poems for the press.
[3] Pletnev chose a line from Propertius for an epigraph: 'Aetas prima canat veneres, extrema tumultus' (*Elegies* II, 10, 7). The collection consisted of 100 poems, of which forty-seven were published for the first time. It came out in December.
[4] No vignette was used.
[5] The 1824 edition of Zhukovsky's poems.
[6] A joke poem, written in 1822; not passed by the censorship.
[7] A reflection on Pletnev's kindness. He was incapable of following Pushkin's advice.

92. To A. A. Bestuzhev
24 March 1825
Mikhailovskoe

. . . I am not writing to Ryleev. I am going to wait for *Voynarovsky*. Tell him that he is right as regards Byron's opinion. I wanted to speak against my conscience but it didn't work. Both Bowles and Byron have talked rubbish in their controversy; I have a reasonable refutation to make to them. Would you like me to send it to you? It's dull to copy it out.[1] Why do you think that I flatter Ryleev? I spoke out loud and clear concerning my opinion of his *Dumy* and of his poems. I know full well that as regards poetic language I am his teacher[2] – but he treads his own road. He is a poet at heart. I am seriously afraid of him, and much regret not having shot him when I had the chance – but then, who the devil could have known? I am waiting impatiently for *Voynarovsky* and will send him all my comments. For Christ's sake! He must write – and more and more!

Your letter shows great intelligence, and yet you are not right. You still regard *Onegin* from the wrong angle,[3] for after all it is my best work. You compare the first chapter with *Don Juan*. Nobody esteems *D.J.* more than I do (the first five cantos, I haven't read the rest), but it has nothing in common with *Onegin*. You speak of the Englishman Byron's satire and compare it to mine, and demand of mine the same qualities! No, my dear, you ask too much. Where is my *satire*? There isn't a trace of it in *Evgeny Onegin*. I would have burst my banks if I had embarked on satire. The very word *satirical* should not have appeared in the preface. Wait for the other cantos. . . . Oh! If only I could lure you to Mikhailovskoe . . . you would see that if one must compare *Onegin* to *D.J.*, one should do so only in one respect: in trying to decide which

138

is the more charming and lovely (gracieuse), Tatiana or Julia.[4] The first canto is simply a quick introduction and I am pleased with it (which is a thing that very rarely happens to me).[5] With this I close our polemic ... I am waiting for your tales. Start writing a novel. What is holding you back? Just think: you will be the first among us in all senses of the word. And Europe too will recognize your worth – first, on account of your real talent; and secondly, because of the novelty of your subjects, the local colour, etc. .... Think of it at leisure, my friend ... but then you are set on being a Captain in the cavalry!

[1] Bestuzhev and Ryleev had both reacted unfavourably to the first chapter of *Evgeny Onegin*. Bestuzhev wrote to Pushkin on 9 March, complaining that it was no more than a picture of a commonplace St Petersburg dandy. Pushkin had etched in his picture of society with charm, but he had not penetrated beneath its surface. He compared him unfavourably to Byron, whose sketches of St Petersburg in *Don Juan*, though not drawn from life, were deepened by philosophical observations and sharpened by satire. What Pushkin was doing was not enough; he was wasting his time carving apple-pips when he should be aspiring to be a Praxiteles – a strange echo of Dr Johnson's comment to Hannah More, talking of Milton's sonnets: 'Milton, Madam, was a genius that could cut a Colossus from a rock; but could not carve heads upon cherry-stones.' Bestuzhev ended his letter in a general burst of enthusiasm for English literature: 'il n'y a point de salut hors la littérature Anglaise.'

Ryleev wrote more briefly but quite as decidedly: he was prepared to argue till doomsday that the first chapter of *Evgeny* was inferior to *The Fountain of Bakhchisaray* and *The Prisoner of the Caucasus*. He disagreed with Byron's opinion (quoted by Pushkin in a letter that does not survive) that a poet who describes a game of cards is superior to one who describes trees. Each poet has his own gift, his own Muse.

The argument on the first chapter of *Evgeny Onegin* was thus linked to the celebrated dispute between Byron and Bowles, who had squared up across the card-table at which Belinda had lost her cherished lock. Bowles declared – in his observations on Pope's poetic character, written in 1806, and reiterated in *Invariable Principles of Poetry* (1819) – that

All images drawn from what is BEAUTIFUL and SUBLIME in the works of NATURE, are MORE beautiful and sublime than images drawn from Art, and are therefore more poetical. In like manner those PASSIONS of the HUMAN HEART which belong to nature in general, are *per se*, more adapted to the HIGHER SPECIES of poetry than those which are derived from *incidental* and *transient manners*.

Byron parried: 'To the question "whether the description of a game of cards be as potential, supposing the execution of the artists equal, as a description of a walk in the forest?" it may be answered, that the *materials* are certainly not equal; but that "the *artist*", who has rendered the "game of cards poetical", is by *far the greater* of the two.' (Letter of 1821.) Byron went on to say, however – which Ryleev had not taken into account – that 'all this "ordering" of poets is purely arbitrary on the part of Mr Bowles. There may or may not be, in fact, different "orders" of poetry, but the poet is always ranked according to his execution, and not according to his branch of the art.'

Byron greatly admired Pope and was annoyed at Bowles's diminution of his talent ('those miserable mountebanks of the day, the poets, disgrace themselves and deny God, in running down Pope, the most *faultless* of poets.' Byron to Murray, 4 November 1820).

[2] In his letter to Pushkin of 10 March, Ryleev had written that Pushkin flattered him: 'you will always remain my master as far as the language of poetry is concerned.'

[3] See pages 102-3.

[4] Heroine of *Don Juan*, Canto I.

[5] This was true, judging from his letters; his delight with *Boris Godunov* was exceptional (see no. 116).

93. To L. S. Pushkin   *27 March 1825*
                                                         Mikhailovskoe

. . . Did you receive my Poems? This is what the foreword[1] should consist of: (1) Many of these poems are rubbish and do not deserve the attention of the Russian public, but as they have been printed by God knows whom, and the devil knows under what titles, with the compositor's corrections and the publisher's mistakes – here they are and gobble them up, although they are muck . . . putting it mildly. (2) We (that is the publishers) have had to throw out many items from the complete collection, which might have been considered too obscure, having been written in circumstances little known or of little interest to our highly esteemed (Russian) public; or which might have proved diverting to only a few individuals; or which were too immature, seeing that Mr Pushkin saw fit to publish his little rhymes in 1814 (i.e. when he was fourteen); or – as you please. (3) Please let there not be the slightest praise of me. It lacks propriety and I had forgotten to mention it to Vyazemsky in connection with *The Fountain of Bakhchisarai.*[2] (4) Everything must be expressed Romantically, without any buffoonery. In fact the very opposite of the latter. In all this I rely on Pletnev . . . send me a copy of this foreword to Mikhailovskoe, for safety's sake, and I shall send you my comments.

[1] The 1825 edition of Pushkin's poems had only a short prefatory note put in by the publishers.

[2] Vyazemsky had written very warmly when introducing *The Fountain of Bakhchisarai*.

94. To Prince P. A. Vyazemsky   *End of March/beginning of April 1825*
                                       Mikhailovskoe

. . . My brother will send you my verses, I am copying out *Onegin* for you – hoping it will help you smile.[1] For the first time a reader's smile me sourit (forgive this flat joke: it runs in the blood! . . .). And besides you must be grateful to me – never in my life have I copied anything out for anyone, not even for Princess Golitsin[2] – from which it follows that I am in love with you. . . .

Are you still interested in Russian literature? . . . My poems have been sent to St P. to Birukov. They are nearly all known already; but they needed to be brought together. Of all those which had to be consigned to oblivion, I most regret my epigrams – about fifty of them, and all original – but, unfortunately, I can say like Chamfort:[3] Tous ceux contre lesquels j'en ai fait sont encore en vie, and – enough – I don't want to quarrel with the living.

I deleted those verses from the 'Epistle to Chaadaev' which you didn't like – only for your sake, out of respect for you, and not lest they upset other stomachs.[4]

Give my regards to Davydov,[5] who has forgotten me. My sister Olga is in love with him, and rightly so. Apropos – or not: talking to her of *The Fountain of Bakhchisarai*, he criticized Zarema's eyes. I would agree with him if it wasn't the East we were discussing. I modelled myself on the Eastern style of speech as far as that is possible for us rational, cold Europeans. Talking of that – do you know why I don't like Moore?[6] Because he is excessively Eastern. He imitates in a childish, ugly fashion the childishness and ugliness of Sadi, Hafiz and Mahomet. A European, even when in raptures over Oriental splendour, should retain the taste and eye of a European – that is why Byron is so delightful in *The Giaour*, *The Bride of Abydos*, etc.

[1] Vyazemsky's son, Nikolai, had died in January, aged seven. Shortly after that Vyazemsky himself had been dangerously ill.
[2] Princess Eudoxia Ivanovna Golitsin, whom Pushkin very much admired.
[3] Sébastien Chamfort (1741-94), French writer and wit. Pushkin had the *Œuvres complètes de Chamfort, de l'Académie Française*, 3 vols. (Paris, 1812), in his library.
[4] Pushkin deleted the uncomplimentary reference to 'the American' Tolstoy, who was a friend of Vyazemsky (see pages 56-7).

⁵ Denis Vasilievich Davydov (1784-1839), the celebrated partisan leader of the Napoleonic war; poet and writer.
⁶ See nos. 18 and 117.

95. To Prince P. A. Vyazemsky   *7 April 1825*
                                                    Mikhailovskoe

Today is the anniversary of Byron's death – last night I ordered a Mass to be sung today for the repose of his soul. My priest was surprised at my piety and gave me a piece of sacramental bread for the repose of the servant of God, the Boyar George. I am sending it to you.

I am copying out *Onegin*. He also will get to you without delay.¹ . . . I suffer from spleen and haven't a single thought in my head.

¹ Pushkin was copying out the second chapter of *Evgeny Onegin* for Vyazemsky in order to cheer him up in his convalescence.

96. To L. S. Pushkin   *7 April 1825*
                                            Trigorskoe

. . . I ordered a Mass for the repose of Byron's soul (today is the anniversary of his death). A. N.¹ did too and intercessions were offered in both churches, at Trigorskoe and Voronich. It reminds one a little of la Messe de Frédéric II pour le repos de l'âme de M-r de Voltaire.² I am sending Vyazemsky the sacramental bread given me by Father Shkod,³ for the poet's repose.

¹ Anna Nikolaevna Vulf, one of the Osipov relations at Trigorskoe.
² Pushkin was not insensible of the irony of the situation in both cases – pious gestures from unexpected quarters.
³ The nickname of Pushkin's parish priest, Illarion Raevsky.

97. To L. S. Pushkin   *22 and 23 April 1825*
                                            Mikhailovskoe

Fouché,¹ Œuvres dram. de Schiller,² Schlegel,³ *Don Juan* (canto 6 and following),⁴ the new Wal. Scott,⁵ all the issues of *Sibirsky Vestnik*⁶ – and all this through St Florent and not through Slenin. Wine, wine, rum (12 bottles), mustard, Fleur d'oranger, a suitcase. Limburg cheese. (A book on riding – I want to break in stallions, in free imitation of Alfieri and Byron.)

How pleased I was by the Baron's[7] arrival. He is very charming. All our young ladies fell in love with him – and he remains as indifferent as a block of wood, likes lying on the bed, marvelling at the Chigirinsk Starosta.[8] He asks to be remembered to you, kisses you a hundred times, and wishes you a thousand good things (for example, oysters).

[1] See no. 87.
[2] *Œuvres dramatiques*, traduites par M. de Barante (1821). It did not remain in Pushkin's library.
[3] A. W. Schlegel, *Vorlesungen über dramatische Kunst und Literatur* (1809), translated into French, *Cours de littérature dramatique*, 3 tomes (Paris, 1814), in Pushkin's library.
[4] *Don Juan*, Cantos VI-VIII.
[5] Probably the French translation of *Peveril of the Peak*, *Peveril du Pic* (Paris, 1824), in Pushkin's library.
[6] Review published by G. I. Spassky, which in 1825 was renamed the *Aziatsky Vestnik*.
[7] Delvig. He spent a few days with Pushkin.
[8] Part of a long, unfinished poem by Ryleev, published in *Polyarnaya Zvezda* for 1825.

98. To Prince P. A. Vyazemsky

Around 20 April 1825
Mikhailovskoe

... By the way, why didn't you want to reply to Delvig's letters?[1] He is a man worthy of respect from every point of view and cannot be compared to our Petersburgian literary scoundrels. Please, for my sake, support his *Tsvety*[2] for next year. We will all do our best for them.

[1] This was a misunderstanding; Vyazemsky had no intention of hurting Delvig.
[2] *Severnye Tsvety*, the literary almanac edited by Delvig.

99. To V. A. Zhukovsky

20-24 April 1825
Mikhailovskoe

To answer your question, man to man:[1] I have been going round with my aneurysm for ten years and with God's help can carry on for about another three. Therefore the matter is not urgent, but I feel stifled in Mikhailovskoe. If the Tsar would let me go abroad[2] even before I am cured that would be a blessing for which I should be eternally grateful to him and to my friends. Vyazemsky writes to me that my friends have lost faith in my relations with the powers that be: they need not have

done so. I promised N. M.[3] not to write anything against the government for two years – and I have kept my word. 'The Dagger' was not
written against the government, and although the style of the verses is
not of the purest, their intention is innocent.[4] Now I am sick of it all,
and if I am left in peace I shall probably think only of blank verse
pentameters.[5] Boldly relying on your judgement, I am sending you a
draft letter to the Most White;[6] I do not think there is anything
shameful either in my action itself, or in its expression. I write in
French because it is the language of business transactions and it comes
easier to my pen. However, Thy Will be done; if you think it inappropriate
it can be translated, and my brother will copy it out and sign it for me.

These are all trifles. I have said nothing to you about your poems. . . .
Do you know what will happen? After your death they will print everything with mistakes and with the addition of poems by Küchelbecker.
It's appalling to contemplate. Delvig will tell you of my literary activities – I am sorry that you are not here to advise me, or simply, not
here – your presence is an inspiration. For God's sake finish 'Vodolaz'.[7]
You ask what is the aim of *The Gipsies*.[8] There now! The aim of poetry
is – poetry, as Delvig says (if he didn't crib it from someone else).
Though Ryleev's *Dumy* are aimed in the right direction, they constantly
miss their mark.

[1] Zhukovsky had asked Pushkin to answer his questions on his aneurysm
in an adult, and not in a frivolous and incoherent, fashion (Zhukovsky to
Pushkin, 15-20 April 1825, St Petersburg).
[2] Pushkin was not allowed to go abroad to seek a cure for his aneurysm,
but was directed to get medical advice at the neighbouring town of Pskov.
So much for an attempt to slip away.
[3] Karamzin.
[4] See pages 26-7.
[5] Pushkin was writing *Boris Godunov*.
[6] Blank verse is called 'white verse' in Russian; the Most White is Tsar
Alexander I.
[7] A translation of Schiller's 'Der Taucher' (1797), completed in 1831.
Zhukovsky later called it 'The Goblet'.
[8] Zhukovsky had said in his letter that he knew nothing more perfect than
The Gipsies as far as style was concerned, but wanted to know 'its aim'.

100. To L. S. Pushkin   *First half of May 1825*
                                                            Mikhailovskoe

. . . I was inexpressibly touched by the blind poet's[1] signature. His tale
is delightful – whether he is angry with me or not, I shall still say that

'I wished to pardon, pardon could not' is worthy of Byron. The apparition and the end are magnificent. The epistle is perhaps even better than the poem – at least the terrible part in which the poet describes how he grew blind will remain for all time an example of the poetry of agony. I would like to reply to him in verse; if I have time I'll include my answer with this letter.

. . . What do you think of my comments on *Voynarovsky*?[2] I hope you won't think that I'm criticizing it, for I must admit that I like it very much. I'm even annoyed at not having it by me.

If you can, send me the latest work by Genlis[3] – and *Childe Harold* by Lamartine[4] (what rubbish that must be); and, in general, something new. . . .

I have at last managed to decipher Zhukovsky's letter. How devilishly delightful his heavenly spirit is! He is a saint, even though he was born a Romantic and not a Greek, and a man – and what a man!

. . . The idea of publishing 'Napoleon' is rich, but the censorship . . . the best stanzas will go under.[5]

[1] Ivan Ivanovich Kozlov (1799-1840); a poet and translator. He lost his sight in 1821. He was devoted to both Pushkin and Byron and wrote several poems under Byron's influence; he also translated *The Bride of Abydos*. Pushkin reciprocated Kozlov's feelings for him and always wrote of him warmly. He is here commenting on Kozlov's Byronic tale, *The Monk*, published in 1824. An epistle, 'To my friend V. A. Zhukovsky', was published with the poem, in which Kozlov described his gradual loss of sight.
[2] By Ryleev. Pushkin had sent his copy on to Ryleev with his comments.
[3] Stéphanie, Comtesse de Genlis (1746-1830) published her Memoirs in 1825.
[4] Lamartine's *Le Dernier Chant du Pèlerinage d'Harold*, written as a fifth Canto for Byron's poem, published 1825.
[5] The censorship excluded stanzas 4-6 and 8 from Pushkin's ode 'Napoleon'.

101. To K. F. Ryleev   *Second half of May 1825*
                                            Mikhailovskoe

I think you will already have received my comments on *Voynarovsky*.[1] I will add one thing: the absence of comment on my part is to be taken as praise, exclamation marks as signs of excellence, etc.[2] Assuming that when you wrote well you did so consciously, I did not think it necessary to point it out to you.

What am I to say to you of your *Dumy*? There are vivid lines to be found in all of them; the closing stanzas of 'Peter in Ostrogozhsk' are remarkably original. But, on the whole, they are all weak in inventiveness and structure. In their composition, they all follow one pattern – loci topici:³ the description of the setting, the Hero's speech, and the moral. There is nothing that is national, nothing Russian, in any of them except the proper names (that is excluding 'Ivan Susanin', the first Duma, which made me begin to suspect that you had real talent). You were wrong in 'Oleg' not to correct *the Russian crest*. St George's ancient crest could not have appeared on the shield of the pagan Oleg; our most recent one, the double-headed Eagle, is the Byzantine crest and was adopted by us during Ivan III's reign, not before. The chronicler⁴ simply says: 'He also hung his shield on the gates as a sign of victory'.

. . . You are bored in Petersburg and I am bored in the country. Boredom is inherent to a rational being. What can one do about it? Farewell Poet – when shall we meet?

¹ See no. 100 above.
² Pushkin is here referring to his marginalia in his copy of *Voynarovsky*, which he had sent on to Ryleev.
³ Set pattern or rule.
⁴ The Primary Chronicle for the year 907 A.D.

102. To A. A. Bestuzhev   *End of May/beginning of June 1825*
                                                Mikhailovskoe

Replying to the first paragraph of your Survey.¹ In Rome the age of *genius* was preceded by an age of mediocrity² – it is wrong to deprive men like Virgil, Horace, Tibullus, Ovid and Lucretius of the title of genius, even though they all, with the exception of the last two, walked the highway of imitation (my mistake – Horace was not an imitator). We know of no Greek criticism. In Italy, Dante and Petrarch preceded Tasso and Ariosto, who in their turn were followed by Alfieri and Foscolo. In England, Milton and Shakespeare wrote before Addison and Pope, after whom came Southey, Walter Scott, Moore and Byron; from all this it is difficult to deduce any conclusion or any rule. What you say can fully be applied only to French literature.

We have literary criticism but no literature. Where did you get that idea? On the contrary, it is criticism that we lack. That accounts for the reputation of Lomonosov (I respect him as a great man but, naturally, not as a great poet. He understood the true source of the Russian

language and its beauty; that is his main contribution) and Kheraskov
. . . Derzhavin's idol[3] – ¼ gold, ¾ lead – has not yet been valued. His
'Ode to Felitsa' is on a par with 'Velmozha' ['The Ruler'] and the ode
'God' with the ode 'On the death of Prince Meshchersky'. The ode
'To Zubov' has only been discovered recently. Knyazhnin peacefully
enjoys his fame, Bogdanovich is numbered among great poets, and so
is Dmitriev. We do not have a single commentary, a single book of
criticism. We have no assessment of Krylov – Krylov, who is as far
above La Fontaine as Derzhavin is above J. B. Rousseau.[4] What then
do you mean by criticism? . . . No, we should turn your sentence round
and say: we have some sort of literature but no criticism. What is more,
you agree with me a little further on. (The only nation where criticism
preceded literature was Germany.)

Why have we no Geniuses and few men of talent? First, we have Derzhavin
and Krylov – secondly, where does one find many men of talent?

We get no encouragement – Thank God! Don't we? Derzhavin and
Dmitriev were made Ministers[5] as a mark of *encouragement*. The Age of
Catherine is the Age of Encouragement, which does not make it inferior to any other. Karamzin, I think, is encouraged; Zhukovsky cannot complain, no more can Krylov. Gnedich pushes ahead with his
heroic task in the quiet of his study; let us see when his Homer will
appear.[6] I see only myself and Baratynsky in the ranks of the un-
encouraged – and I don't say 'Thank God!'

Encouragement can give wings only to unexceptional talents. Leaving aside
the Augustan age, the marks of princely patronage can be seen in the
poems of Tasso and Ariosto. Shakespeare wrote his best comedies to
Elizabeth's *order*. Molière was Louis's valet; the immortal *Tartuffe*, the
fruit of the most strenuous effort of comic genius, owes its existence
to the monarch's intervention. Voltaire wrote his *best* poem under
Frederick's patronage.[7] . . . Derzhavin enjoyed the patronage of three
Tsars. You expressed yourself badly. This is what I think you meant
to say:

We can be rightly proud that though our literature yields to others
in profusion of talent, it differs from them in that it does not bear the
stamp of servile self-abasement. Our men of talent are noble, and independent. Flattery's voice fell silent with Derzhavin – and how did he
flatter? . . . Go through our reviews, and all current literature. . . . Of
our poetry one can say what Mirabeau said of Sieyès:[8] Son silence est
une calamité publique. We surprise foreigners – they give us our due,
not understanding how this state has come about. The reason is plain.

Our writers are drawn from the highest class of society. Aristocratic pride merges with the author's self-esteem. We do not wish to be patronized by our equals. And that is what that scoundrel Vorontsov fails to understand. He imagines that a Russian poet will appear in his lobby bearing a Dedication or an Ode, whereas he comes demanding respect as a nobleman with a six-hundred-year-old name – it's the devil of a difference.[9]

All you say of our upbringing, of foreign and internecine (splendid!) imitators is excellent, firmly stated and sincere in its eloquence. By and large, you seem to be bubbling over with ideas. You do not say all that you think of *Onegin*; I think I know why, and am grateful – but why not reveal your opinion clearly.[10] We shall never have any literary criticism while we continue to be guided by our personal relationships; and you are worthy of creating it.

Your 'Tourney'[11] is reminiscent of those of W. Scott. Drop those Germans and turn your attention to us Orthodox. You have written enough *fast-moving* tales with Romantic leaps in the action, which are all very well for Byronic poems. A novel demands *chat*; everything must be expressed. . . .

Ryleev is bound to show you my comments on his *Voynarovsky*; and you send me your objections. In the meantime, I embrace you with all my soul.

One final word: in 1822 you were able to complain of the fog enveloping our literature;[12] yet this year you didn't even say thank you to old Shishkov.[13] Whom are we to thank for livening us up, if not him?

[1] Pushkin is commenting on Bestuzhev's article 'A survey of Russian literature in 1824 and at the beginning of 1825', published in *Polyarnaya Zvezda* for 1825. Pushkin's quotations from Bestuzhev are not all cited accurately.

[2] Bestuzhev said that all national literatures had developed according to certain natural laws and that in every case they began with an age of geniuses called forth by the scope before them – the urge to fill a vacuum.

[3] See page 464 for Pushkin's description of his first meeting with Derzhavin. Throughout this letter his attitude to Derzhavin wavers: genius or idol, three parts lead to one part gold. In speaking of Derzhavin's idol, Pushkin is referring to Derzhavin's poem of that name – 'Moy Istukan'. He considered that 'The Waterfall' was Derzhavin's best poem. See letter to Delvig, no. 103 and page 170.

[4] Jean-Baptiste Rousseau (1671-1741), minor French poet.

[5] Derzhavin was Minister of Justice from 1802 to 1803 and Dmitriev from 1810 to 1814.

[6] Karamzin received an annual pension of 2,000 roubles, Zhukovsky of

4,000 roubles, Krylov, from 1812, of 1,500 roubles – later increased. On 11 March 1825, Gnedich received a pension of 3,000 roubles to enable him to complete his translation of the *Iliad*. He had reached the last book.

[7] Pushkin is probably thinking of *La Pucelle d'Orléans* – an old favourite of his – which Voltaire revised in Berlin in 1750-3.

[8] Honoré, Comte de Mirabeau; E. J. Sieyès, known as Abbé Sieyès.

[9] Pushkin is still bristling against Vorontsov, see pages 32-3.

[10] See pages 102-3 and no. 92.

[11] Bestuzhev's short story 'The Tourney at Revel' was published in *Polyarnaya Zvezda* for 1825. It was clearly influenced by Scott.

[12] In his article 'A glance at old and new literature in Russia', published in *Polyarnaya Zvezda* for 1823.

[13] A. S. Shishkov, the newly appointed Minister of Education and consequently in charge of the censorship. It was he who handled *Onegin*; but Pushkin's hopes of a new spirit prevailing in that institution under his aegis were not realized.

103. To Baron A. A. Delvig[1]　　　　　　　　*1-8 June 1825*
　　　　　　　　　　　　　　　　　　　　　　Mikhailovskoe

. . . After you left I re-read all Derzhavin and here is my final verdict. That old eccentric was illiterate in Russian and knew nothing of the spirit of the Russian language (that is why he is inferior to Lomonosov). He had no idea of style or harmony, or even of the laws of versification. That is why he must infuriate any discriminating ear. He not only cannot sustain an Ode, he cannot even sustain a stanza (you yourself know the exceptions). What then is there in him? Ideas, descriptions, and truly poetic impulses. Reading him, one seems to be reading a bad, free translation of some wonderful original. I swear his Genius thought in Tatar[2] – and he could not spare the time to learn Russian usage. Eventually, when he comes to be translated, Derzhavin will astonish Europe and we, out of national pride, will not let on all we know about him (let alone about his Ministry).[3] One should keep about eight of his odes and a few odd fragments, and burn the rest of his work. His genius can be compared to that of Suvorov[4] – it's a pity that our poet so often crowed like a cock. Enough of Derzhavin. What is Zhukovsky doing? Let me know his opinion of the second chapter of *Onegin*,[5] and of what I have at present on my embroidery frame.[6] What operation has Krylov had? God give him many happy years! His 'Miller' is good, as is 'Demyan and Foka'.[7] . . . Have you seen N. M.?[8] How is his History progressing? At what point will he end? At the election of the Romanovs? The ungrateful ones! Six

Pushkins signed the Electoral Charter! And two more had to put their marks, not being able to write![9] And I, their literate descendant, what am I? Where am I? . . .

[1] In this letter Pushkin writes at greater length – and more impatiently – of Derzhavin's poetry.
[2] Derzhavin's paternal ancestor was a Tatar.
[3] Derzhavin was Minister of Justice from 1802 to 1803, see no. 102 and note 5 above.
[4] The point of contact between Derzhavin and Field-Marshal Suvorov remains unexplained.
[5] The second chapter of *Onegin* was not yet published. Delvig had brought a copy to St Petersburg.
[6] *Boris Godunov.* A curious image – Pushkin and embroidery don't match up.
[7] Krylov's fable 'The Miller' was published in *Polyarnaya Zvezda* for 1825; 'Demyan's Fish-soup (Ukha)' – a very well-known fable – was written in 1813. A new edition of Krylov's fables was published in 1825 by Slenin.
[8] Karamzin. He was working on the twelfth, and final, volume of his History, which was supposed to conclude with the election of the first Romanov to the throne (1613). He died while writing the fifth chapter. The eleventh volume, which Pushkin used so extensively for *Boris Godunov*, was published in 1824.
[9] In fact seven Pushkins signed or put their mark to the Electoral Charter. Pushkin often referred with family pride to this fact but was vague about the number involved.

104. To Prince P. A. Vyazemsky   *25 May/mid-June 1825*
                                                       Mikhailovskoe

You ask me whether I am pleased with what you said of me in the *Telegraph*.[1] What a question. European articles so rarely appear in our reviews! And your pen is guided both by taste and by the partiality of friendship. But you are too kind to me in connection with Zhukovsky. My work is not just the successor of his; I am truly his pupil, and succeed only in so far as I do not venture out on his road but wander along a byway. No one has ever had or ever will have a style to equal his in power and variety. He has remarkable strength in combating difficulties.[2]

Translating has spoilt him, has made him lazy; he does not want to create for himself – but like Voss he has a genius for translating.[3] Also, it is ludicrous to speak of him as having faded while his style is still maturing. That which has been will be again and I still look for the Resurrection of the dead.

I have read what you wrote on *The Monk*;[4] you fulfilled your heart-felt duty. This poem is, of course, full of feeling and is *more intelligent* than *Voynarovsky*; but Ryleev's style has more panache or sweep. He has an executioner in it with rolled-up sleeves for whom I would give much.[5] On the other hand, his *Dumy* are rubbish and the title comes from the German *dumm*, and not from the Polish,[6] as it seemed at first glance. . . . Your calembours are very charming – the girls here find them very entertaining, but I am still waiting for what you will write on Byron. Thank you for Casimir.[7] (How would one write a calembour on him? Think that one out.) I believe you like Casimir, and I don't. Of course he's a poet, but still he's no Voltaire or Goethe . . . it's a far cry from a snipe to an eagle! The first genius *there* will be a Romantic and will turn French heads in God knows what direction. Incidentally, I have noticed that everybody here (even you) has the most hazy notion of what Romanticism is.[8] We'll have to talk about it at leisure, but not now; I am desperately tired. I have written to everyone – even Bulgarin.

You offer to act as a pander between me and Polevoy.[9] The fact is that I shall be glad to help him, but will probably fail to carry out a single condition – therefore I don't want his money. But you keep an eye on him – for God's sake! There are occasions when he talks non-sense too. For instance, 'Don Quixote eradicated knight-errantry from Europe'!!! 'Except for Dante there has been no Romanticism in Italy.'[10] Yet it was precisely in Italy that it arose. What then is Ariosto? And his predecessors, from *Buovo d'Antona*[11] to *Orlando Innamorato*? How can one write so wildly! As for you, don't disdain to write snippets for the reviews: Napoleon busied himself with them and was the best journalist in Paris (as, I seem to remember, Fouché remarked).

[1] Vyazemsky had published an article on Zhukovsky and Pushkin in the *Moskovsky Telegraph*, No. 4 (1825), in which he praised Pushkin for the latter's championship of Zhukovsky, saying it did him credit both as a writer and as a man. Vyazemsky also wrote that though Pushkin in no way resembled Zhukovsky, he was none the less his heir – his work was the result of Zhukovsky's.

[2] Pushkin is here quoting Vyazemsky.

[3] Johann Heinrich Voss (1751-1826), German poet and translator, chiefly of the classic poets.

[4] By Kozlov. Vyazemsky wrote on it in *Moskovsky Telegraph*, No. 8 (1825).

[5] In the annotated copy of *Voynarovsky* that Pushkin had sent Ryleev, by the line on the executioner he had written, 'Sell me this line'. Ryleev had, in his turn, been inspired by Byron's description in *Parisina*.

⁶ In fact Ryleev took the word from the Ukrainian, meaning a lyrical narrative poem.

⁷ Casimir Delavigne.

⁸ Pushkin felt that the terms 'Romanticism' and 'classicism' had not been sufficiently clearly defined in Russia. He himself made several attempts but never came to a satisfactory conclusion. His own work cut across these categories.

⁹ Vyazemsky wanted Pushkin to contribute to the *Moskovsky Telegraph*, which Polevoy was editing.

¹⁰ Pushkin is criticizing views expressed by Polevoy in his article 'On the *Polyarnaya Zvezda* for 1825' published in *Moskovsky Telegraph*, No. 8 (1825), and supplement No. 5.

¹¹ Medieval Italian version of *Bevis of Hampton*. There was also an early Russian version of this widespread tale – *Bova Korolevich*.

105. Draft letter to K. F. Ryleev   *Second half of June/August 1825*
                                                   Mikhailovskoe

I am vexed that Ryleev doesn't understand me – what is the matter? That literature is not encouraged among us and that we should thank God for it?¹ Why speak about it? Pour réveiller le chat qui dort? It's unnecessary. We have the indifference of the government and the oppression of the censorship to thank for the present spirit in our literature. What more do you want? Glance in the reviews for the last six years and see how many times I am mentioned, how many times I have been praised both deservedly and not – and of our friend² there is not a murmur, as if he didn't exist. Why is that? Surely not from some journalist's pride or radicalism; no – everyone knows that even if he were to boot-lick nobody would thank him for it or give him 5 roubles, so it's best to remain a gentleman gratis. You are angry with me for boasting of my six-hundred-year-old nobility (NB my nobility is older).³ Don't you see that the spirit of our literature depends to a certain extent on the social position of the writers. We cannot lay our compositions at the feet of our noble lords, because we hold ourselves equal to them by birth. Hence the pride, etc. One shouldn't judge Russian writers by the same criteria as foreign ones. There they write for money, and here (except for me) they write from vanity. There they earn their living by writing poetry and here Count Khvostov ruined himself by doing so.⁴ There if you have nothing to eat, you write a book; here if you have nothing to eat, you enter government service and don't write. My dear, you are a poet, and I am a poet, but I judge more prosaically and apparently prove to be right. Goodbye, my dear, what are you writing?

[1] See no. 102 above. In the first half of June, Ryleev had written to Pushkin concerning his comments on Bestuzhev's article, saying that he disagreed with him on several points: 'Your main mistake was to equate approval with patronage.' Ryleev believed that every writer, even a genius, requires approval, whereas patronage might even produce a negative reaction.

> The spirit grows weak in courts and genius withers; the task of good government lies in not inhibiting genius; let him freely produce whatever inspires him. Then there is no need for pensions, or honours, or Court Chamberlain's keys; then he will not be penniless and consequently hungry, then he will be provided for.

Ryleev numbered Pushkin among the geniuses.

[2] Alexander I.

[3] Ryleev was amused at the aristocratic attitude that Pushkin had adopted, and saw in this pride in his lineage an imitation of Byron.

[4] Count D. I. Khvostov used to publish his works at his own expense and then buy up remainder copies to send to his friends.

106. To Prince P. A. Vyazemsky   *Beginning of July 1825*
                                              Mikhailovskoe

I think you must have already received my reply to the *Telegraph*'s offer.[1] If he needs my poems, send any you come across (except *Onegin*); but if he wants my name as an associate, I will not agree out of honourable pride, i.e. ambition. The *Telegraph* fellow is decent and honest but proves a fibber and an ignoramus, and fibbing and ignorance in a review reflects on its publishers; and I am not prepared to take my share. In spite of the change in the Ministry and the improvement in the censorship,[2] I still cannot answer for Krasovsky and his fraternity;[3] perhaps I could undertake to supply the review with a number of items, and then, if God and Birukov so will it, it will be the review that will be the loser. I was always inclined to play the aristocrat, but since the Pushkins have begun to die out[4] I have become even more stiff-necked. I deal in my poems en gros, but am locking up my pedlar's stall No. 1. Besides, between us, my brother Lev is on my hands, what Father gives him does not run to girls and champagne; so let the *Telegraph* deal with him and God grant them both an increased turnover, with my blessing. . . .

. . . It is cold and muddy here, and I await the decision concerning my fate.

¹ N. A. Polevoy had asked Pushkin to collaborate in the publication of the *Moskovsky Telegraph*. Pushkin's article on Mme de Staël (see no. 76) was published in this review shortly afterwards.

² See no. 102 and note.

³ The censors. Pushkin's hopes were centred on Birukov, as Krasovsky was very reactionary.

⁴ Several of his relations had recently died.

107. To Prince P. A. Vyazemsky   *13 July 1825*
                                                            Mikhailovskoe

. . . and how is your Byron . . . getting on (Toi dont le monde encore ignore le vrai nom!)?¹ I have just read your comments on Denis's comments on Napoleon's comments² – marvellously good! Your lively and original style is here even more lively and more original. You did well to stand up openly for gallicisms. A day must come when someone will say out loud that Russian metaphysical language is still in a primitive state. God grant that one day it will develop on similar lines to French (the clear, precise language of prose – that is, the language of ideas). I have about three stanzas on the subject in *Onegin*.³ Following your article is one of mine on Mme de Staël.⁴ But don't spread that abroad. . . . In the meantime, my dear, I have undertaken a literary task which will make you want to embrace me: a Romantic Tragedy! Mind you keep it quiet: very few people know about it. Have you read my poem, 'A. Chénier in Prison'?⁵ Judge of it as a Jesuit – according to its intentions. . . .

¹ Vyazemsky was planning an article on Byron but was distracted from his task by a seaside holiday. Pushkin is quoting from Lamartine's 'L'Homme', an epistle to Byron (1819):

> Toi dont le monde encore ignore le vrai nom,
> Esprit mystérieux, mortel, ange ou démon.

² Vyazemsky had published a short article in *Moskovsky Telegraph*, No. 12 (1825), on the partisan hero Denis Davydov, who had protested at the disparaging attitude adopted by Napoleon in his memoirs towards the contribution of the Russian partisans in the 1812 war. In it Vyazemsky praised Davydov's style of writing, and defended his use of occasional gallicisms.

³ *Evgeny Onegin*, III, 26-9.

⁴ See no. 76.

⁵ Published in the 1826 edition of Pushkin's poems simply as 'André Chénier', the section 'Hymn to Freedom' having been deleted by the censorship.

1 Pushkin at the Lycée,
aged 12–14. Print by
E. Heitman (1822). Used as
frontispiece to the first edition
of *The Prisoner of the Caucasus*.

2 A. I. Turgenev. Pencil drawing by
B. F. Sokolov (1816).

3 L. S. Pushkin, the poet's brother.
Pencil drawing by A. O. Orlovsky.

4 The Lycée at Tsarskoe Selo.

5 Pushkin reciting his verses at an examination at the Lycée on 8 January 1815 in the presence of Derzhavin. Oil painting by I. E. Repin (1911).

108. Draft letter to N. N. Raevsky[1]
Second half of July
(after 19 July) 1825
Mikhailovskoe

. . . Voilà ce qui me regarde: Mes amis se sont donnés beaucoup de mouvement pour obtenir une permission d'aller me faire traiter, ma mère a écrit à Sa Majesté et là-dessus on m'a accordé la permission d'aller à Pskof et d'y demeurer même, mais je n'en ferai rien; je n'y ferai qu'une course de quelques jours. En attendant je suis très isolé: la seule voisine que j'allais voir est partie pour Riga et je n'ai à la lettre d'autre compagnie que ma vieille bonne et ma tragédie; celle-ci avance et j'en suis content. En l'écrivant j'ai réfléchi sur la tragédie en général. C'est peut-être le genre le plus méconnu. [1] Les classiques et les romantiques ont tous basé leurs lois sur la *vraisemblance*, et c'est justement elle qu'exclut la nature du drame. Sans parler déjà de temps, etc., quel diable de vraisemblance y a-t-il dans une salle coupée en deux moitiés dont l'une est occupée par deux mille personnes, qui sont censées n'être pas vues par ceux qui sont sur les planches. (2) *La langue.* Par exemple le Philoctète de La Harpe dit en bon français après avoir entendu une tirade de Pyrrhus: Hélas! j'entends les doux sons de la langue Grecque, etc.[2] Voyez les anciens: leurs masques tragiques, leur double personnage – tout cela n'est-il pas une invraisemblance conventionnelle? (3) Le temps, le lieu, etc. etc. Les vrais génies de la tragédie ne se sont jamais souciés de la vraisemblance. Voyez comme Corneille a bravement mené le Cid. Ha, vous voulez la règle des 24 heures? Soit, et là-dessus il vous entasse des événements pour 4 mois. Rien de plus inutile à mon avis, que les petits changements de règles reçues: Alfieri[3] est profondément frappé du ridicule de *l'a-parte*, il le supprime et là-dessus allonge le monologue et pense avoir fait faire une révolution dans le système de la tragédie; quelle puérilité!

La vraisemblance des situations et la vérité du dialogue – voilà la véritable règle de la tragédie. (Je n'ai pas lu Calderón ni Vega) mais quel homme que ce Schakespeare! je n'en reviens pas. Comme Byron le tragique est mesquin devant lui! Ce Byron qui n'a jamais conçu qu'un seul caractère (les femmes n'ont pas de caractère, elles ont des passions dans leur jeunesse; et voilà pourquoi il est si facile de les peindre), ce Byron donc a partagé entre ses personnages tel et tel trait de son caractère; son orgueil à l'un, sa haine à l'autre, sa mélancolie au troisième, etc., et c'est ainsi que d'un caractère plein, sombre et

155

énergique il a fait plusieurs caractères insignifiants – ce n'est pas là de la tragédie.[4]

On a encore une manie: quand on a conçu un caractère, tout ce qu'on lui fait dire, même les choses les plus étrangères, en porte essentiellement l'empreinte (comme les pédants et les marins des vieux romans de Fielding).[5] Un conspirateur dit: *Donnez-moi à boire* en conspirateur – ce n'est que ridicule. Voyez le Haineux de Byron (*ha pagato*[6]), cette monotonie, cette affectation de laconisme, de rage continuelle, est-ce la nature? De là cette gêne et cette timidité du dialogue. Voyez Schakespeare. Lisez Schakespeare, il ne craint jamais de compromettre son personnage, il le fait parler avec tout l'abandon de la vie, car il est sûr en temps et lieu de lui faire trouver le langage de son caractère.

Vous me demanderez: votre tragédie est-elle une tragédie de caractère ou de coutume? J'ai choisi le genre le plus aisé, mais j'ai tâché de les unir tous deux. J'écris et je pense. La plupart des scènes me demandent de l'inspiration, j'attends ou je passe par-dessus – cette manière de travailler m'est tout-à-fait nouvelle. Je sens que mon âme s'est tout-à-fait développée, je puis créer.

[1] Pushkin was replying to a letter from Raevsky, written 10 May 1825, in which he had said:

> Merci pour votre plan de tragédie. Que pourrais-je vous en dire? Ce n'est pas les conceptions brillantes qui vous manquent; mais la patience dans l'exécution. Il vous sera donc donné d'ouvrir encore la carrière d'un théâtre national. Quant à la patience, j'aurais voulu vous voir consulter les sources où Karamzine a puisé au lieu de vous en tenir à son seul récit. N'oubliez pas que Schiller fit un cours d'astrologie avant d'écrire son *Wallenstein*. Je vous avoue ne pas trop comprendre pourquoi vous voulez n'employer que les vers blancs dans votre tragédie. . . . Que votre tragédie soit bonne ou mauvaise j'y prévois d'avance d'importants résultats pour notre littérature; vous donnerez de la vie à notre héxamètre qui jusqu'à présent est si lourd, si inanimé; vous prêterez au dialogue un mouvement qui le fera ressembler à une conversation et non pas à des phrases de vocabulaire comme jusqu'à présent; vous achèverez de populariser chez nous, ce langage simple et naturel que notre public est encore à ne pas comprendre, malgré les beaux modèles des Tsigany [*The Gipsies*] et des Razboyniky [*The Robber Brothers*]. Vous achèverez de faire descendre la poésie de ses échasses.

[2] The hero of the neo-classical tragedy, *Philoctète* (1781), by J. F. de La Harpe.

[3] Vittorio Alfieri (1749-1803) retained a strictly classical form for his tragedies.

[4] For further comments on Byron as a dramatist see nos. 139 and 142.

[5] Fielding's pedants seem to have got entangled here with Smollett's sailors. Pushkin possessed the works of both authors in his library.

[6] Pushkin is referring to Giacopo Loredano in *The Brothers Foscari* (1821). Upon the death of the older Foscari, Loredano says, 'he has paid me . . . nature's debt and *mine*'. These are the closing words of the play.

109. To Prince P. A. Vyazemsky   *10 August 1825*
                                                      Mikhailovskoe

. . . How's your Byron going?[1] Send it to me before you publish it, and aren't there any poems by the late poet Vyazemsky, even if only epigrams? . . . I am sorry that Küchelbecker has been discouraged from writing in the reviews,[2] he is a sensible man when he holds a pen in his hand – even if slightly touched. . . . When shall we embark on a review! I long to.[3] . . .

[1] See no. 107 and note 1. Pushkin often urged Vyazemsky to write more.
[2] Küchelbecker was finding it difficult to find work.
[3] A constant refrain in Pushkin's letters.

110. To Prince P. A. Vyazemsky   *14-15 August 1825*
                                                      Mikhailovskoe

My dear, poetry is your native language,[1] one can hear that by your pronunciation, but who is to blame that you speak it as rarely as ladies in 1807 spoke Slavonic.[2] . . . Your letters are much more important for my peace of mind than an operation would be for my aneurysm. They liven me up like an intelligent conversation, like Rossini's music, like the sexy flirtation of an Italian girl. . . .

[1] In Vyazemsky's letter of 4 August, he had said that he had completely lost the habit of writing poetry and wrote it as a foreign language – one could guess his ideas and feelings but none of the enchantment of eloquence would be transmitted.
[2] After the treaty of Tilsit (1807) between Napoleon and Alexander I, the Russians became temporarily very Francophile and it was fashionable to speak French or at least pepper one's speech with gallicisms.

III. To V. A. Zhukovsky   *17 August 1825*
                                               Mikhailovskoe

. . . My tragedy is growing and I hope to finish it by the winter, consequently my reading consists solely of Karamzin and the chronicles.
What a marvel these last two volumes of Karamzin are![1] What vigour!
C'est palpitant comme la gazette d'hier, as I wrote to Raevsky. One
request, my dear: could you send me either the life of *Iron Cap* or of
some other *holy simpleton*.[2] I searched in vain for the Blessed Vasily[3] in
Chety Meney[4] – and I badly need it.

[1] Volumes X and XI of Karamzin's History.
[2] Pushkin needed some documentation on a holy simpleton of the time of
   Boris Godunov. Inspired by St Paul's words 'We are fools for Christ's sake'
   (1 Cor. 4: 10), such men wandered through the countryside living on
   alms, and their predictions were held to be God-inspired. They were fear-
   less of authority and allowed themselves complete freedom in speaking
   home-truths to the powerful. Iron Cap – or Big Cap – was one such.
   He died in 1589, nine years before Boris Godunov became Tsar, but he
   had met Boris. Pushkin, inspired perhaps by the outspoken comments
   of the Fool in *King Lear*, used him in his play to proclaim Boris's guilt
   publicly.
       Vyazemsky had written to Pushkin on 6 September:
       'Karamzin is very pleased with your notes on tragedy. . . . He says that in
       drawing the character of Boris you must bear in mind a wild contradiction
       between piety and criminal passions. Godunov continually re-read the
       Bible for self-identification. This contradiction is dramatic.'
   It is the same clash of conscience and criminal violence that makes the
   character of Macbeth so interesting. This 'dramatic contradiction', as Karamzin called it, gave point to the confrontation of Boris and the simpleton.
[3] Another simpleton of the sixteenth century, who had several encounters
   with Ivan the Terrible.
[4] The *Menologion* compiled by Makary, Metropolitan of Moscow (1482-1563).

II2. To P. A. Katenin   *First half of September*
                                             (not later than the 14th) 1825
                                             Mikhailovskoe

. . . Heu fugant, Posthume, Posthume, labuntur anni,[1] but what is
worse is that both passions and imagination fly away with them. Take
my advice, my dear, closet yourself up, and settle down to writing a
Romantic tragedy in eighteen acts (like the tragedies of Sophia

Alexeevna).[2] You will cause a revolution in our literature, and nobody is more worthy of the task than you. . . .

What do you think of the first act of *Venceslas*?[3] I think it is wonderfully good – I admit I haven't read old Rotrou, I don't know any Spanish,[4] but I am enchanted by Zhandr. Is the tragedy completed?

What shall I tell you of myself, of my pursuits? I have given up poetry for the time being and am writing my mémoires, that is I am copying out in fair hand a dull, rambling, rough notebook. I have four cantos of *Onegin* ready, and a whole lot more bits and pieces, but I cannot attend to them at present. I am pleased the first canto is to your liking – I like it myself; though actually I am fairly indifferent to all my poems, as I am to my former misdemeanours with K.,[5] with the theatrical Major,[6] etc. I won't do it again! Addio, Poeta, a rivederla, ma quando?

[1] Pushkin misquotes Horace's line,

> Eheu fugaces, Postume, Postume,
> labuntur anni . . . (*Odes*, II, xiv).

[2] Peter the Great's sister – an amateur of court theatricals, both acting and writing plays herself.

[3] *Venceslas* (1647) by Jean de Rotrou (1609-50). Rotrou was patronized by Richelieu and praised by Voltaire, who called him 'le véritable fondateur du théâtre français'. It was translated into Russian blank verse by A. A. Zhandr.

[4] Pushkin may here be referring to Rotrou's source for the plot of *Venceslas*, from the work of the seventeenth-century Spanish playwright Francisco de Rojas Zorrilla.

[5] Probably P. P. Kaverin, an officer and friend of Pushkin in his early St Petersburg days; a member of the Green Lamp society.

[6] Major Denisovich, with whom Pushkin had had a quarrel in the theatre in St Petersburg which had almost ended in a duel.

113. To Prince P. A. Vyazemsky[1]   *13 and 15 September 1825*
     Mikhailovskoe

Eat it yourself! Have you noticed that all our critical polemics in the reviews are based on *Eat it yourself*?[2] Bulgarin says to Fedorov: You are lying. Fedorov says to Bulgarin: You are lying yourself. Pinsky says to Polevoy: *You are an ignoramus.* Polevoy retorts: *You are an ignoramus yourself.* One shouts: You are cribbing! The other: You are cribbing yourself! And they are all right. And so, my dear, eat it yourself; you yourself are looking for midday at two in the afternoon. . . .

I am heartily grateful to Karamzin for arranging to send me *Iron Cap*;[4] and in exchange I will send him by post my motley cap, which I am tired of wearing. In fact, wouldn't it be a good idea if I were to become a Holy Simpleton; it might make me more blessed! I finished the second part of my tragedy today – I think there will be four in all. My Marina is a pleasant wench. . . . Thank you for sending Karamzin's comment on Boris's character. It came in very useful. I had been looking at Boris from a political point of view and failed to notice the poetic side of his character;[5] I shall settle him down to the Gospels, shall make him read the story of Herod[6] and such like. You want to know the *plan*? Take the end of the tenth and the whole of the eleventh volume[7] and there you have it. . . .

I am sorry that Mukhanov (if it is Raevsky's adjutant) wrote about Mme de Staël;[8] he is a friend of mine and I wouldn't have brought him into it, but he is to blame. Mme de Staël is ours – she must not be touched. But actually I have spared him. . . .

[1] This is an answer to Vyazemsky's letter of 25 August/6 September, in which he 'boxed Pushkin's ears' for his constant complaints and for his refusal to go to Pskov to have treatment for aneurysm. Vyazemsky considered that even in prison it was better to have two rooms than one and that if Pushkin got bored with Pskov he could always return to Mikhailovskoe. Pushkin, obviously having hoped to use the excuse of aneurysm in order to get permission to travel for treatment abroad, was piqued at the failure of his scheme and refused to take advantage of the offer to go to Pskov. Like Zhukovsky, Vyazemsky tried hard to cool Pushkin down and urged him – for once – to swim with the current.

[2] So much criticism of criticism was being published at this time that Polevoy complained in his 'Survey of Russian literature in 1824', published in the February issue of the *Moskovsky Telegraph*, that at least a third of the letterpress of Russian literary periodicals was taken up by this kind of wrangling – criticisms and anti-criticisms bouncing to and fro like rubber balls. B. M. Fedorov was a journalist; M. M. Karniolin-Pinsky, a teacher.

[3] A literal translation of the French proverb 'Chercher midi à quatorze heures' which Vyazemsky had quoted in writing to Pushkin, to act out of season.

[4] and [5] See no. 111 and note 2, above.

[6] Appropriate to a king who had gained his throne by causing the murder of the infant heir.

[7] Of Karamzin's History.

[8] The article which had appeared in *Syn Otechestva*, No. 10 (1825), on Mme de Staël, which Pushkin objected to, was by A. A. Mukhanov, not by Pushkin's friend P. A. Mukhanov. See no. 76 for Pushkin's sharp riposte.

114. To Prince P. A. Vyazemsky   *Second half of September*
(not later than the 24th) 1825
Mikhailovskoe

Having nothing to do, I read him [Gorchakov[1]] a few scenes of my comedy.[2] Ask him not to talk about them, or everybody will start discussing it; and I shall grow sick of it as I did of my *Gipsies*, which I could not finish for this very reason. . . .

[1] Prince Alexander Mikhailovich Gorchakov (1798-1883) was at the Tsarskoe Selo Lycée at the same time as Pushkin. He was staying in the vicinity of Mikhailovskoe on leave from London, where he was First Secretary at the Russian Embassy, and Pushkin rode over to see him and read him a few scenes from *Boris Godunov*, not with particular success as Gorchakov found some of his expressions (e.g. 'spittle') coarse. Pushkin wrote of him among other Lycée friends in '19 October 1825', but after that never mentioned him again – the meeting, which had started with an embrace, had proved depressing.
[2] Pushkin used this term in an archaic sense for his play, and even included it on the title-page of the version he submitted to the Tsar. This led to the wording of the Tsar's, or his official's, notoriously insensitive comment (see pages 181-2) and Pushkin removed it from the published text.

115. To V. A. Zhukovsky   *6 October 1825*
Trigorskoe

. . . Let us sit on the sea-shore and wait for a change in the weather.[1] I shall not die; that is impossible. God would not want *Godunov* to perish with me. Give me a time limit, I will eagerly accept your prophecy; let my tragedy redeem me[2] . . . but has our insensitive age any time for tragedies? At any rate, leave me some hope.

[1] Pushkin's usual euphemism for political change.
[2] Zhukovsky had written to Pushkin (mid-September 1825) in support of Vyazemsky's pleas, urging him to seek medical advice in Pskov. Once his health was restored he could settle to *Godunov* with renewed spirit, and the fame this work would bring him would serve to overcome his circumstances. 'You do not understand yourself; you are rebelling as a child against misfortune, which is nothing but the fruit of your own childishness. . . . Stop acting as an epigram; be a poem.'

116. To Prince P. A. Vyazemsky   *About 7 November 1825*
Mikhailovskoe

. . . I congratulate you, my dear fellow, on the appearance of a Romantic tragedy, in which the chief character is Boris Godunov! My tragedy is finished; I read it aloud to myself and clapped my hands and shouted, 'What a Pushkin, what a son of a bitch!' My Holy Fool is a comic fellow; Marina . . . is a Pole, and is very beautiful. . . . The others are all very charming too, except Captain Margeret, who is continually swearing – he won't be passed by the censorship. Zhukovsky says that the Tsar will pardon me on account of my tragedy – I doubt it, my dear. Although it is written in a good spirit, I just could not hide all my ears under the Fool's Cap, they stick out!

117. To Prince P. A. Vyazemsky   *Second half of November 1825*
                                          Mikhailovskoe

I am tired of writing letters to you, because I cannot drop in on you casually in carpet-slippers and shirt-sleeves. . . . You show intelligence, whatever one talks about; and compared to you I am the fool of fools. Let us agree that you will write to me without waiting for replies. Is it your article on Byron's Abbey?[1] What a marvel *Don Juan* is! I only know the first five cantos; but having read the first two, I immediately said to Raevsky[2] that it is Byron's chef-d'œuvre, and was delighted when I later saw that W. Scott was of my opinion.[3] I need a knowledge of English – it is one of the disadvantages of my exile that I have no opportunity of learning while the time is ripe.[4] Curse my persecutors! And I, like A. Chénier, can tap my own forehead and say: Il y avait quelque chose là.[5] . . . Forgive this poetic bragging and prosaic spleen. I cannot contain myself, I am so angry: I haven't had a good sleep or . . .

Why do you regret the loss of Byron's notebooks? The devil take 'em. Thank God they are lost! He confessed, unconsciously, in his poems, carried away by poetic rapture. In the cold blood of prose he would have lied and dissembled, now trying to shine with sincerity, now flinging mud at his enemies. They would have unmasked him as they unmasked Rousseau[6] – and then malice and slander would triumph again. Leave curiosity to the crowd and take your stand with Genius. Moore's action is better than his *Lalla Rookh*[7] (as far as poetry is concerned). We know Byron well enough. We have seen him throned in glory; seen him in the sufferings of his great spirit; seen him on his catafalque at the heart of resurgent Greece. Fancy wanting to see him on his chamber-pot. The crowd eagerly laps up confessions, memoirs, etc., for in its baseness it delights in the degradation of the great, in the weaknesses of the powerful. It is overjoyed at the disclosure of any nastiness. *He is as petty as we are, he is as vile as we are.* You lie, scoundrels: he may be petty and vile, but not in the way you are – in a different way! It is both tempting and pleasant to write one's Mémoires.[8] There is nobody one loves as much, or knows as well, as oneself. It is an inexhaustible subject. But it presents difficulties. It is possible not to lie; but to be sincere is a physical impossibility. The pen will sometimes stop, as a runner draws up at an abyss, before something an outsider would read with indifference. It is not difficult to defy ('braver') the judgement of men; it is impossible to defy the judgement of one's own conscience.

[1] A note – signed V. – on Newstead Abbey had appeared in the *Moskovsky Telegraph*, Pt. V, No. 20 (1825), in which the author expressed regret at the 'forced and criminal suppression' of Byron's memoirs and letters edited by R. C. Dallas and of the notebooks destroyed by Thomas Moore. Pushkin attributed this note to Vyazemsky. Dallas's edition of Byron's private correspondence had been stopped by a court injunction on 7 July 1824, but Galignani had already acquired the rights and the volume was published, both in English and French editions, in Paris in 1825. Pushkin had a copy of the French edition in his library.

[2] Pushkin had first experienced the impact of Byron when staying with the Raevskys (see pages 23-5).

[3] Scott, in his tribute to Byron's memory published in *The Pamphleteer* (1824), vol. xxiv, and reprinted in the Galignani edition mentioned in note 1 above, wrote:

> As various in composition as Shakespeare himself (this will be admitted by all who are acquainted with his *Don Juan*), he has embraced every type of human life and sounded every string on the divine harp, from its slightest to its most powerful and heart-astounding tones. There is scarce a passion or a situation which has escaped his pen. . . . Neither *Childe Harold* nor any of the most beautiful of Byron's earlier tales contains more exquisite morsels of poetry than are to be found scattered through the Cantos of *Don Juan*, amidst verses which the author appears to have thrown off with an effort as spontaneous as that of a tree resigning its leaves to the wind.

[4] Pushkin had been made particularly aware of his lack of English while working on *Boris Godunov*, because of its dependence on Shakespeare.

[5] André Chénier was reputed to have said of himself, when on the scaffold, 'Pourtant, il y avait quelque chose là.'

[6] *The Confessions* of Jean-Jacques Rousseau (1782).

[7] On Byron's death, Thomas Moore – in the presence of six witnesses – destroyed the memoirs which Byron had entrusted to him. Memoirs apart, Pushkin had a very low opinion of *Lalla Rookh* (see no. 18).

[8] Pushkin was to burn his own 'Memoirs' on the suppression of the Decembrist rising.

118. To A. A. Bestuzhev   *30 November 1825*
                                                        Mikhailovskoe

I was very pleased to get your letter; I was beginning to think I had made you sulk; and I am also pleased to hear of your studies. In our day the study of modern languages should replace that of Latin and Greek – such is the spirit of the age and its demands. You – yes, and I think Vyazemsky – are the only men of letters among us to be learning, all the others are unlearning. A pity! The high example set by Karamzin should have brought them to reason. You are going to Moscow. While there, have a talk with Vyazemsky about a review; he himself feels the crying need for one – and it would be a splendid thing to do. You scold me for not publishing.[1] I'm sick of print – of misprints, criticism, vindications, etc. . . . but actually my poems will appear shortly. And I'm sick of them: Ruslan is a milksop; the Prisoner is a greenhorn, and before the real poetry of the Caucasian scene my poem[2] is like Golikov's prose.[3] . . . This is important: I have written a tragedy and am very pleased with it, but am very afraid of sending it out into the world – our timid palate will not accept true Romanticism. By Romanticism we understand Lamartine. Read what I may of Romanticism, I still cannot get to the right thing; even Küchelbecker is wrong.[4] What are his *Spirits*?[5] I haven't read them yet. I am waiting for your new tale, but you should embark on a whole novel – and write it unconstrainedly as if you were speaking or writing a letter, or your style will keep on relapsing into Kotzebueism.[6] My regards to our planner Ryleev, as the late Platov[7] used to say, but I honestly prefer poetry without a plan to a plan without poetry. My friends, here's to your health and inspiration.

[1] Pletnev was urging Pushkin to publish a new edition of his longer poems as a companion volume to the collection of short poems, at that time in the press. He did not do this till 1835.

[2] *The Prisoner of the Caucasus.*

[3] I. I. Golikov, best known for *The Acts of Peter the Great*, in twelve volumes. His style was heavy and ornate.

[4] See Notes on Küchelbecker's articles published in *Mnemozina* (no. 123). In his articles Küchelbecker looked for national individuality in Romantic poetry and criticized his Russian contemporaries for being too imitative, Zhukovsky of Schiller (and of other German Romantic writers) and

Pushkin of Byron. Küchelbecker found both Schiller and Byron excessively subjective and repetitive; on his Parnassus Shakespeare stood supreme, the universal genius embracing the whole of life, spanning heaven and hell, 'immeasurably profound and infinitely various, at once powerful and tender, strong and sensuous, terrifying and enchanting' (*Mnemozina*, III).

Pushkin followed Küchelbecker in rejecting the influence of Byron for that of Shakespeare; but Küchelbecker's view of the poet as a being above human kind, a demi-god in moments of inspiration, was too rarefied for him. And Pushkin could not have agreed with the view that 'the more poetry transcends daily affairs and rises above the base language of the crowd, who know nothing of inspiration, the more splendid it is' (*Mnemozina*, II). Pushkin was a realist and he enriched his language by drawing as widely as possible on that of ordinary men.

5 *Shakespeare's Spirits*, a dramatic joke in two acts (1825), inspired by Shakespeare's fairy characters – Oberon, Puck, Ariel, etc.
6 A by-word for the sentimental and the prolific.
7 Count M. I. Platov, a Hetman of the Don Cossacks and a hero of the Napoleonic war.

119. To P. A. Katenin   4 December 1825
                                        Mikhailovskoe

Your letter pleased me for many reasons: (1) that it was written from Petersburg,[1] (2) that *Andromache* is at last to be produced,[2] (3) that you are planning to publish your poems,[3] (4) (and this should have come first) that you love me as of old. Maybe the present change will bring me closer to my friends. As a loyal subject I must of course grieve at the death of the Tsar; but as a poet I am pleased at the accession of Constantine I.[4] There is much Romanticism about him: his stormy youth, his campaign with Suvorov, his enmity towards the German Barclay, are all reminiscent of Henry V.[5] What is more he is intelligent, and after all it is better to deal with intelligent people; in short, I hope for great benefits from him. How good it would be if this winter I could be both a spectator and a participant in your triumph! I say a participant because I could not feel detached about your success; but will they remember me? God knows. I feel truly ashamed that you have been told so much about my *Gipsies*. It does for the public but I would like to introduce you to something worthier of your attention. I am tired of *Onegin*[6] and he is dormant; but actually I have not dropped him. . . . Think of me at the first night of *Andromache*.

[1] Katenin had been exiled from St Petersburg in 1822 and was allowed to return in 1825.

[2] *Andromache* was in fact not performed till 3 February 1827 and was then published in the same year.

[3] These were not published till 1832.

[4] Pushkin was unaware of the events at that time taking place in St Petersburg, see pages 107-8.

[5] Pushkin's views on current events were at this time coloured by his intensive reading of Shakespeare's history plays, he saw parallels everywhere. See letter to Delvig, no. 126.

[6] He was at work on Chapter IV, which he had begun at the end of October 1824 and wrote intermittently, not completing it till 6 January 1826. In the meantime he wrote *Boris Godunov*, *Count Nulin*, etc. Chapter IV was published with Chapter V in January 1828.

120. To V. K. Küchelbecker[1]   *1-6 December 1825*
                                                    Mikhailovskoe

Before thanking you I want to scold you. When I received your comedy I hoped also to find a letter – I shook and shook and waited to see whether at least a quarter of a sheet would fall out; in vain – nothing did, and in an angry spirit I read *The Spirits*,[2] first to myself and then aloud. Do you want my criticism? No, you don't, do you? All the same I shall criticize. You admit that the character of the poet is not plausible – the admission is praiseworthy, but you should have justified and excused this implausibility in the comedy itself and not in the foreword. . . . Caliban, on the other hand, is delightful. I cannot understand why you should want to parody Zhukovsky. Tsertelev[3] might be forgiven, but not you. You will say that the laugh is on the parodist and not on his subject. My dear, remember that even if you write for us, you publish for the mob; it takes things literally. It sees your disrespect towards Zhukovsky and is delighted. . . . I would say that the versification is careless and at times unnatural, and the expressions are not always good Russian. . . . I forgive all this for the sake of Caliban who is marvellously good. You see, my dear, I am as frank as ever with you; and I am sure you will not be angry with me on account of it.

[1] This letter never reached Küchelbecker; the events of 14 December intervened.

[2] *Shakespeare's Spirits.*

[3] Prince N. A. Tsertelev, a minor critic.

121. To P. A. Pletnev[1]   *4-6 December 1825*
Mikhailovskoe

. . . For God's sake don't let them ask the Tsar to allow me to live in Opochka or Riga; what the devil's the good of them? *He must be asked for permission for me to go either to the capitals*[2] *or abroad.* It is on your account, friends, that I should like to come to the capital – I would like to brag with you again before I die; but of course it would be more sensible to go overseas. What is there for me to do in Russia? . . . Get me sent for, my fine fellows, otherwise somebody else will have to read you my tragedy. Incidentally, Borka[3] also has a Holy Fool in his novel. And he is very Byronic – talking about himself! But you will see that my Fool is much nicer than Borka's . . . Küchelbecker's *Spirits* is trash; there are very few good lines and no imagination. The only decent thing is the foreword. Don't tell him this – he will be upset.[4]

[1] This letter was written immediately on getting news of the death of Alexander I, only a few days before the Decembrist rising, see pages 107-8.
[2] St Petersburg and Moscow.
[3] Boris Mikhailovich Fedorov, a minor writer, in whose novel *Prince Kurbsky* the first chapter is about an encounter between Kurbsky and a Holy Fool, who prophesies to him.
[4] See no. 120 above. Pushkin had found something to praise in his anxiety not to hurt Küchelbecker.

1826

DRAFT NOTES

122. Draft on the national spirit in literature

It has for some time been customary among us to speak of a national spirit, to demand a national spirit, to complain of the absence of a national spirit in works of literature; but no one has thought of defining what he understands by the words 'national spirit'.

One of our critics,[1] I think, considers that a national spirit consists in choosing subjects from our country's history; others[2] see the national spirit in the vocabulary [which the authors use], i.e. are pleased that writing in Russian they make use of Russian expressions.

But can one deny a strong national spirit to Shakespeare's *Othello, Hamlet, Measure for Measure*, etc.; Vega and Calderón are constantly shifting their action to all corners of the world and take the plots of their tragedies from Italian novelle and French lays. Ariosto sings the praises of Charlemagne, of French knights, and of a Chinese princess. Racine based his tragedies on ancient history.

Can one deny that all these writers have a strong national quality? On the other hand, as Vyazemsky rightly remarked,[3] 'what national spirit is there in a Russiad and a Petriad except for the proper names?' What national spirit is there in Xenia,[4] who in the middle of Dimitri's encampment discusses parental authority with a confidante, in iambic pentameters?

National spirit in a writer is a quality which can only be fully appreciated by his fellow countrymen – for others it either does not exist or might even seem to be a fault. A learned German waxes indignant at the courtesy of Racine's heroes;[5] a Frenchman laughs at seeing Calderón's Coriolanus challenging his enemy to a duel.[6] All these, however, bear the stamp of a national spirit.

Its climate, its form of government, its faith, give to each nation distinguishing features which are more or less reflected in poetry's mirror. There is a cast of mind and quality of feeling, there are a multitude of customs and traditional beliefs and habits, which belong exclusively to a single nation.[7]

168

1 Bulgarin in *Russkaya Talia* (1825) rhapsodized on the many subjects Russian history had to offer to the poet and dramatist.

2 Pushkin had in mind Bestuzhev's article in *Polyarnaya Zvezda* (1824) (see no. 44) and Küchelbecker's in *Mnemozina* (1824) (see no. 123).

3 In Vyazemsky's introduction to the first edition of *The Fountain of Bakhchisarai* (1824).

4 In Ozerov's *Dimitri Donskoy* (1807). Vyazemsky in writing of Ozerov in 1817 had said that after the events of 1812 *Dimitri Donskoy*, in which many of those events were prefigured, would, more than ever, be seen to be a national tragedy.

5 A. W. von Schlegel in *Über dramatische Kunst und Literatur*. Pushkin had a French edition published in Paris (1814) in his library.

6 Sismondi's comment in *De la littérature du Midi de l'Europe* on Calderón's *La gran Comedia de las Armas de la Hermosura*. (The third, 1829, edition remained in Pushkin's library, but he had asked his brother for a copy in 1825.)

7 Pushkin returned to these questions when he wrote his *Little Tragedies* in 1830. See also his note on *Romeo and Juliet*, no. 159.

123. Notes on Küchelbecker's articles published in *Mnemozina*

The article on 'The trend of our poetry'[1] and the 'Conversation with Mr Bulgarin',[2] published in *Mnemozina*, have served as a basis to all that has been said against Romantic literature in the last two years.

These articles are written by a learned and intelligent man. Be it right or wrong, he always gives the reasons for his point of view and evidence to substantiate his judgements, which is rather rare in our literature.

Nobody has ventured to contradict him, either because everyone agrees with him, or because nobody feels he can contend with an athlete who is, apparently, both strong and experienced.

Nevertheless many of his judgements are mistaken in every respect. He divides Russian poetry into the lyric and the epic kinds. In the first category he includes the works of all our ancient poets, in the second Zhukovsky and his school.

Now let us suppose that this division is a fair one and then let us see by what criteria the critic judges the degree of merit pertaining to these two kinds.

'Strength, freedom, inspiration – are the three essentials of any poetry.' We are citing this opinion because it coincides absolutely with our own.

What constitutes *strength* in poetry? Is it strength in invention, in the disposition of the plan, in the style?

Freedom? In style, in plan – but what freedom is there in Lomonosov's style and what plan does a solemn ode require?

Inspiration? That is the disposition of the soul to the most lively reception of impressions and consequently to the quick grasp of concepts, thus facilitating their explanation.

Inspiration is as needed in poetry as in geometry.[3] The critic confuses inspiration with ecstasy.

No, definitely not:[4] *ecstasy* excludes *calm*, which is an absolute condition for *beauty*. Ecstasy does not require any intellectual power capable of relating the parts to the whole. Ecstasy is fleeting, inconstant, and consequently incapable of creating anything which is truly great and perfect (without which there can be no lyric poetry). Homer is immeasurably greater than Pindar, the ode, not to mention the elegy, stands on the lowest rungs of poetry[5] – but, tragedy, comedy, satire, all demand more imaginative creation (fantaisie) – a genius's knowledge of nature.

But there is no *plan* in an ode and there cannot be one; the plan of *L'Inferno* alone is the fruit of great genius. What plan is there in Pindar's Olympian odes? What plan in the 'Waterfall', Derzhavin's best work?

The ode excludes steady application, without which there can be nothing truly great.

Ecstasy is a heightened state of the imagination alone. One can have inspiration without ecstasy, but ecstasy cannot exist without inspiration.

---

[1] 'Of the trend of our poetry, especially lyric poetry, in the last decade', *Mnemozina*, Pt. II (June 1824).

[2] 'Conversation with Bulgarin', *Mnemozina*, Pt. III (October 1824).

[3] Pushkin is adapting d'Alembert's words 'L'imagination dans un Géomètre qui crée, n'agit pas moins que dans un Poète, qui invente'. (*Esprit, maximes et principes* (Geneva, 1789); in Pushkin's library.)

[4] In his article 'Conversation with Bulgarin' Küchelbecker wrote of Horace 'He was practically never a truly ecstatic poet. And what would you call a versifier who is a stranger to true inspiration?'

[5] In both articles Küchelbecker defends the ode as an elevated lyrical mode as opposed to the elegy, which predominated in Russian lyric poetry in the 1820s. See *Evgeny Onegin*, IV, verses xxxii-xxxiii, and Pushkin's foreword to the first chapter of *Evgeny Onegin*, no. 45.

124. From Preface to Onegin's Journey, intended as a penultimate chapter to *Evgeny Onegin*

The omitted stanzas invariably aroused disapprobation and banter (which, incidentally, was both justified and witty). The author frankly admits that he omitted a whole chapter from his novel, in which Onegin's journey through Russia was described. It rested with him whether this omission should be indicated by dots or by the numbering; but in order to avoid temptation he decided it was better to change the numbering of the last chapter of *Evgeny Onegin* from nine to eight, and to sacrifice one of the concluding stanzas. . . .

P. A. Katenin (whose splendid poetic talent does not prevent him from being at the same time an astute critic) noted that this omission, even though it may be to the reader's advantage, is none the less harmful to the plan of the work as a whole, as because of it the transition from Tatiana, a provincial girl, to Tatiana, a distinguished lady, becomes too sudden and unexplained: a comment which proves him an experienced artist. The author himself felt the justice of this comment but resolved to omit the chapter for reasons important to himself and not to the public. A few fragments were published.[1]

[1] In these discarded stanzas Pushkin described life in Odessa, the fair in Nizhni-Novgorod, the Arakcheev military settlements, etc. When he wrote them in Mikhailovskoe he intended them for Chapter VII and some were published as such in the *Moskovsky Vestnik* in March 1827. The stanzas describing the Crimea were published in the *Literaturnaya Gazeta* (1 January 1830). They were all then further revised in Boldino in 1830 and some stanzas were worked into Chapter VIII; but the stanzas on the Arakcheev settlements, which were notorious for their repressive discipline, were prudently dropped.

LETTERS

125. To V. A. Zhukovsky   *Second half of January 1826*
                                      Mikhailovskoe

. . . They say you wrote some verses on the death of Alexander[1] – a rich subject! But during ten years of his reign your lyre remained silent. That is the clearest reproach to him. Nobody had more right than you to say that the lyre's voice is the voice of the people. Therefore I wasn't entirely to blame for irritating him to his very grave.

[1] Zhukovsky only mentions Alexander I in his poem 'Choir of the girls of Catherine's Institute' (1826).

126. To Baron A. A. Delvig   *Beginning of February 1826*
Mikhailovskoe

. . . Of course I am not implicated in anything, and if the government
has time to think about me it will easily be convinced on that score.
But I somehow feel ashamed to petition, particularly at the present
moment; my cast of mind is known. Having been persecuted for the
last six years, disgraced by dismissal from the service, exiled into the
depths of the country for two lines in an intercepted letter, I certainly
couldn't feel kindly disposed to the late Tsar, though I fully acknowledged his true merits. But I never preached either rebellion or revolution – on the contrary. Writers as a class, as Alfieri remarked,[1] are more
inclined to speculation than to action, and if 14 December proved it
to be otherwise here, there is a special reason for that. Be that as it
may, I would like to be *fully* and *sincerely* reconciled with the government and of course that depends on it alone. In this wish, as far as I
am concerned, there is more prudence than pride. I await with impatience the decision concerning the fate of the hapless [conspirators[2]]
and the public disclosure of their plot. I have firm faith in the magnanimity of our young Tsar. Let us not be superstitious and one-sided,
as are the French tragedians, but let us rather regard this tragedy as
Shakespeare would have done. . . .

[1] In Vittorio Alfieri, *Del Principe e delle lettere* (1795), which Pushkin had in
a French translation of 1818 in his library.
[2] Pushkin had many close friends among them.

127. To P. A. Katenin   *First half of February 1826*
Mikhailovskoe

. . . The coming Almanac[1] delights me beyond words if it will have the
effect of rousing you to poetry. My soul pines for your verses. But do
you know what: instead of an almanac, wouldn't it be better if we
started a periodical like the *Edinburgh Review*? It is absolutely essential
for us to hear the voice of true criticism; besides, who better than you
could take general opinion in hand and give our literature a new and
true direction? At present, apart from you we have no critics. Many
(including myself) owe a great deal to you; you cured me of one-sided
literary opinions, and one-sidedness is the ruin of thought. If you
would agree to set down your conversations on paper you would bring

great benefit to Russian letters: what do you think of the idea? What of *Andromache* and your collected poems?

¹ The almanac planned by Katenin's friend, N. I. Bakhtin, did not materialize.

128. To P. A. Pletnev¹   *3 March 1826*
                                                        Mikhailovskoe

Karamzin is ill! My dear, that is one of the worst things that could happen; for God's sake reassure me or I'll be twice as afraid when unsealing the papers. Gnedich won't die before finishing the *Iliad*² – or I'll say in my heart there is no Phoebus. You know that I am a prophet. You won't get *Boris* till you get me to Petersburg. Dash it all, it's scandalous – a Sle-Pushkin³ is given a gown and a watch, and a sort of medal; as for the complete Pushkin, he gets a fig. So be it: I will renounce the evening dress and the trousers and even the Academic quarter-rouble⁴ (which is my due) – let them at least allow me to leave this damned Mikhailovskoe. . . . And you are a fine one! You write to me: copy out and hire the Opochka scriveners and publish *Onegin*. I have other things than *Onegin* on my mind. The devil take *Onegin*! I want to publish myself and launch myself into the world. God help me!

¹ This letter is a reply to Pletnev's letter of 6 February 1826, in which he wrote of Karamzin's illness and of his fears that Gnedich would die before he had completed his translation of the *Iliad*.
  Pletnev, who always had Pushkin's interests much at heart, was desperate at Pushkin's refusal to send him either *Godunov* or the rest of *Onegin* for publication, giving as his excuse that he could not settle to copying out his manuscripts; and he urged him to hire a scrivener from the neighbouring village. Pushkin's manuscripts were so difficult to read that Pletnev felt there would be fewer mistakes in the published texts of his works if he hired a professional to do this job.
² Gnedich's translation of the *Iliad* came out in 1829; he had been working on it for nearly thirty years.
³ F. N. Slepushkin (1783-1848), a peasant poet, whose work Pushkin thought showed genuine and original talent. He was awarded various prizes by the Emperor and the Russian Academy. Pushkin is punning on his surname.
⁴ Members of the Academy were given tallies after every session which they attended, which they could afterwards redeem for cash.

129. To P. A. Pletnev   *7(?) March 1826*
                                            Mikhailovskoe

. . . You know, if we are going to publish anything, let's embark on the
Gipsies.[1] I hope that my brother will at least copy it out – then you send
the manuscript to me and I will supply an introduction and maybe
notes – and then away with it. For otherwise every time I think of
them or read of them in a review my blood boils.[2] For a novelty let's
include in the collection of my poems the other tale which is like *Beppo*,
which I have in hand.[3]. . . What lectures do you want *Boris* for?[4] In
my *Boris* they swear obscenely in all languages. It's not a tragedy suitable for the fair sex. . . .

[1] In his letter of 27 February 1826, Pletnev told Pushkin that the edition
of his poems had sold out and that the booksellers were clamouring for
more. He asked Pushkin whether he wanted to publish another edition of
his poems (with additions, as some of those in the original edition would
now be excluded by the censorship), *Boris*, *Onegin*, or *The Gipsies*. 'But I
beg you, do not delay.' *The Gipsies* was published in the spring of 1827.

[2] Pushkin's brother had learnt *The Gipsies* by heart and had then written
out a text from memory which he had given to the bookseller, Slenin, for
publication. Pushkin was annoyed as he had entrusted all matters concerning the publication of his work to Pletnev.

[3] *Count Nulin*, which he had written in two mornings – 12 and 13 December
1825. It was published at the end of 1827. See page 255 and no. 182.

[4] Pletnev was asking for *Boris Godunov* on behalf of Zhukovsky, who wanted
to read it himself and to use it in lessons in Russian literature that he was
giving to the Grand-Duchess Elena Pavlovna.

130. To Prince P. A. Vyazemsky   *27 May 1826*
                                                      Pskov

. . . It's time we despatched Bulgarin, and the *Blagonamerenny*, and our
friend Polevoy.[1] At present I have other things to think about, yet by
God, sometime I'll start on a review. I am sorry that you don't get on
with Katenin, for he's a find for a review.[2] I read in the papers that
Ancelot[3] is in Petersburg. Who the devil is he? I also read that thirty
men of letters gave him a dinner. Who are these immortals? I have
been counting up on my fingers and cannot get to thirty. When you
get to Petersburg, get a grip on this Ancelot (I cannot remember a
single line of his) and don't let him loose among the pot-houses of our
native literature. In our dealings with foreigners we have neither pride
nor shame – in front of Englishmen we make a fool of Vasily Lvovich;[4]

in front of Mme de Staël we force Miloradovich to excel in the mazurka.[5]
. . . Of course I despise my native land from head to foot – but I am
annoyed if foreigners share my views. How can you, being untethered,
stay in Russia? If the Tsar grants me *freedom* I won't stay a month.
We live in a miserable age, but when I think of London, of railways,
steam ships, English reviews or Parisian theatres and brothels, then
my remote Mikhailovskoe fills me with melancholy and fury. In the
fourth canto of *Onegin*[6] I have described my life; sometime you will
read it, and will ask with a charming smile: 'And where is my poet?
He has marked talent.' And, my dear, will hear in reply: 'He has fled
to Paris and will never return to accursed Russia – oh the clever lad!'

[1] Pushkin was not satisfied with the opportunity offered by Polevoy of collaborating in the *Moskovsky Telegraph* for he did not feel in tune with him.
He wanted, with the help of Vyazemsky, to found another review, which
would act as a counterbalance to the literary standpoint of *Severnaya Pchela*
published by Bulgarin, the *Blagonamerenny* published by Izmailov (which
in fact stopped publication in 1826), and the *Moskovsky Telegraph*, published
by Polevoy.

[2] See Pushkin's letter to Katenin, no. 127, on the same matter.

[3] Jacques Arsène François Polycarpe Ancelot (1794-1854), French poet and
dramatist, had come to Russia in the official French party to the coronation
of Nicholas I. See pages 26-7 for his account of Pushkin and of Pushkin's
revolutionary poem 'The Dagger'. What he wrote may have proved very
embarrassing to Pushkin at this time. In general, his account of Russia
was a superficial one and was not well received. Pushkin had a copy in
his library.

[4] Pushkin's uncle.

[5] Mme de Staël made no mention of this episode in her book *Dix Mois d'exil*
(1821). Count Miloradovich was Governor of St Petersburg (1819-25) and
was killed while attempting to put down the Decembrist rising. See also
Pushkin on Mme de Staël, no. 76.

[6] *Evgeny Onegin*, IV, xxxvii-xxxix and xliii-li.

131. To Prince P. A. Vyazemsky   *10 July 1826*
                                              Mikhailovskoe

Your short letter upset me for many reasons. First, what do you call
my epigrams aimed at Karamzin? That there should be one suffices,[1]
written at a time when Karamzin had turned his back on me and had
deeply hurt both my self-esteem and my sincere feelings for him. To
this day I cannot think of this calmly. My epigram is sharp, but in
no way offensive; the others, as far as I know, are both stupid and rabid

in feeling: is it possible that you ascribe them to me? Secondly, whom do you call rascals and scoundrels? Oh, my dear . . . you hear the accusations and come to your decision not having heard the defence: that is an unfair trial. If Vyazemsky thinks that, then what will the others think? It's sad, brother, so sad that I could go and hang myself.

When I read in the reviews the articles on Karamzin's death,[2] I feel enraged: how cold and stupid and base they are. Can it be that not a single Russian soul will pay a worthy tribute to his memory? The fatherland has the right to demand it of you. Write his life, that will be a thirteenth volume for his history of Russia; Karamzin belongs to history. But say *everything*, and for that you will sometimes need to use the eloquence which is defined by Galiani in his letter on the censorship.[3] . . .

[1] Several epigrams on Karamzin were attributed to Pushkin and it is not known which one he here acknowledges as his. When out of sorts Pushkin was in the habit of venting his spleen in epigrams, aimed at times at people he both loved and esteemed. It was a safety-valve he took no pains to control.

[2] Karamzin had died on 22 May 1826. Vyazemsky wrote of it in a letter to Pushkin (12 June/second half of June 1826), saying that in spite of what Pushkin had written in epigrams about Karamzin he was certain that he would be grieving in heart and mind. In the same letter he advised Pushkin to have another attempt at writing to the Emperor for permission to seek a cure in St Petersburg, Moscow, or abroad, giving an assurance that in future he would control both his tongue and his pen.

Vyazemsky replied to Pushkin's suggestion that he should write something on Karamzin on 31 July from Revel, saying that it was too early to write anything more major than an obituary and too late to write an obituary. He suggested that Pushkin, who had often said that he wanted to write prose, would find in Karamzin an excellent subject.

[3] Abbé Ferdinand Galiani, *Correspondance inédite* (Paris, 1818), Vol. II, pp. 131-2, letter to Madame d'Épinay: 'Savez-vous ma définition *du sublime oratoire*? C'est l'art de tout dire, sans être mis à la Bastille, dans un pays où il est défendu de rien dire.'

Section IV

'THE NEW PUSHKIN'

'GENTLEMEN, here is the new Pushkin. Let us forget the old.'
With these words Nicholas I is said to have presented Pushkin
to his courtiers as he ushered him out of his study, having just announced
to him that in future he would personally act as his censor. On arriving
in Moscow Pushkin had been driven under escort straight to the
Chudov monastery where the Tsar was in temporary residence, not
even being allowed to tidy himself up after his journey. The Tsar had
been quick in coming to the point and the conversation proceeded
along these lines:

'You were a friend of quite a number of those men that I sent to
Siberia.'
'Yes, Your Majesty, I have held a number of them in the greatest
friendship and esteem, and my feelings have not changed.'

'What are you writing at present?'
'Almost nothing, Sire. The censorship is too severe.'
'Why do you write things that the censor cannot pass?'
'The censors ban even the most innocent works. They condemn
indiscriminately.'

The Tsar then pressed his main question home:

'Would you have been apprehended in the rising of 14 December if
you had been in Petersburg?'
'Without the slightest doubt, Your Majesty. All my friends were in
the plot. It would not have been possible for me to desert them.
Only my absence saved me, and thank God it did.'

The Tsar appeared to be satisfied. He had clearly decided on a magnanimous gesture to please public opinion. His brother, Alexander I,
had exiled Pushkin; he would bring him back. He underlined this fact.
He gave Pushkin permission to travel freely in Russia, except to St
Petersburg for which he would still require a special permit.

Pushkin withdrew, a free man in shackles. There is an apocryphal story that he had in his pocket a draft of his poem 'The Prophet' concluding with four challenging lines, later deleted, which he planned to hand defiantly to the Tsar in the event of further restrictions being imposed upon him. However, in view of the truce concluded, he thought better of it, only to find to his dismay that the incriminating draft was missing. A moment's panic, the draft found lying on the stairs he had just come down, retrieved and destroyed. An improbable story, but it makes a good epilogue to an interview so dramatically stage-managed.

Pushkin spent that evening with Vyazemsky, finding him deeply depressed by the fate of the Decembrists and anxious to leave Russia. The Tsar spent it at a ball given by the French Ambassador, and was heard to remark, 'I have had a long talk today with the most intelligent man in Russia: Pushkin.' Within two days Pushkin had already walked out of step. He had brought to Moscow his new work which excited him more than any other – *Boris Godunov* – and at once arranged to read it to groups of his friends, but in his zest he omitted to obtain the Tsar's permission to do so. On 10 September he read it at Sobolevsky's and on 12 October at Venevitinov's. These readings produced immediate repercussions (see no. 133).

Mikhail Pogodin has left a vivid account of the reading at Venevitinov's.

It is impossible to convey the effect which this reading produced on all of us. To this day, almost forty years having passed, my blood courses faster at the memory of it. . . . We had been expecting to see a majestic high priest of Art and here was a man of medium height, one might almost say a little man, with long hair curling at the ends, lacking any kind of pretension, with lively, darting eyes and a quiet, pleasant voice. He wore a black frock-coat, a dark-coloured waistcoat, buttoned up to the neck, and a carelessly knotted cravat. Instead of the high-flown language of the gods we heard language that was simple, lucid and everyday, and at the same time poetically enchanting!

We heard the first scenes through quietly and calmly, or rather, in a certain perplexity. But the further he read the stronger the sensations became. The scene between the chronicler and Grigory staggered everybody. It seemed to me that my well-beloved Nestor had risen from the grave and was speaking through Pimen's lips, I heard the living voice of the ancient Russian chronicler. . . . Some of us felt flushed; others shivered. One's hair stood on end. It was impossible to contain oneself. One man would suddenly jump up from his chair, another would cry out. One minute silence, then an outburst of exclamations. . . .

The reading came to an end. We looked at one another for a long moment, then we rushed towards Pushkin. Embraces, noise, laughter, flowing tears, congratulations. *Eheu, eheu*, fill up the goblets!

Champagne was brought, and Pushkin grew animated, seeing the effect he had produced on this select company of young people. Our excitement pleased him. With mounting passion he began to read us songs about Stenka Razin. . . .

Oh what a fantastic morning that was, leaving its imprint on the whole of one's life. I cannot remember how we parted or how we finished the day, or how we went to bed. For there could not have been many of us who slept that night, so shaken were we to the core of our being.

(Russky Arkhiv, 1865)

Unfortunately this was one of the few occasions in Pushkin's lifetime that *Boris Godunov* met with joyous acclaim, that his friends echoed his own glad cry on completing it: 'What a Pushkin!' There followed a long series of obstacles: theatrical presentation was not allowed, publication was delayed, when it finally appeared both critics and public were cool. It did not prove a catalyst to dramatic activity on Shakespearian lines. It had to wait for Mussorgsky to make an opera of it before it conquered Russian hearts.

In the meantime there was trouble with the Tsar. Benckendorff wrote to enquire why Pushkin had given public readings before submitting the play to the Tsar for censorship. Rapped on the knuckles, Pushkin submitted his manuscript. On the whole the Tsar was pleased with it but he would have preferred it to have been written in another genre. In Benckendorff's covering letter to the returned manuscript (14 December 1826) he wrote:

His Majesty has deigned to read your work with great pleasure and on the report which I had submitted on the matter he added the following words in his own hand: 'I consider that Mr Pushkin's aim would have been achieved if he had, with the *necessary expurgations*, changed his Comedy [Pushkin's own heading for it, later altered] into a historical narrative or novel in the manner of Walter Scott.'

So much for the tragedy that was intended to revolutionize the Russian stage.

The sting of the Tsar's insensitive comment was sharpened by the fact that for Pushkin it was precisely in its form that the central importance of *Boris Godunov* lay. In the draft prefaces he wrote for it when he was preparing it for publication a few years later (see nos. 150 and 174) he stressed that he hoped it would serve to introduce a Shakespearian type of drama to the Russian stage, far too long dominated by French-inspired models. To achieve this the play had to be produced, even if it was technically unwieldy because of the multiplicity of short scenes. It had to be seen and heard, experienced in the theatre, for its tragic grandeur to be fully appreciated. But if the censor had been hesitant about publication, he had no doubts about production. 'It is obvious', he wrote, 'that it is both impossible and undesirable to stage it, for we do not allow the Patriarch and monks to be represented on the stage.' The final irony lay in the fact that it was probably Bulgarin, Pushkin's bitterest enemy, who was behind this prohibition, for the Tsar had asked him to vet the play and Pushkin later spotted suspicious plagiarisms in Bulgarin's novel *The False Dimitri*, published in 1831.

There were, however, compensations at this time for Pushkin in renewed contacts with fellow writers. There was much talk of his participating in the new review – *Moskovsky Vestnik* – edited by Pogodin. This was to be launched by a group of Moscow writers, united by a twin devotion to Goethe and Schelling. This association was not to be a long-lived one, for Pushkin was out of his native element in discussions on German metaphysics, but it gave him a temporary platform and he busied himself in writing round to friends for contributions.

Russian literary journalism was about to take on a new pattern. Setting aside Bulgarin and Grech as beyond the pale, the critics who had previously been ranged in the rival camps of Classic and Romantic were now becoming polarized into two new categories: what one might call 'gentlemen and players'. Pushkin and his friends, so recently in the vanguard of the young and rebellious, were now the literary establishment, showing a tendency to deprecate the upstarts whom they did not altogether trust, like Pogodin and Polevoy. The greatest challenge to Pushkin and to his friends such as Vyazemsky, Baratynsky and Pletnev was yet to come in the emergence of Vissarion Belinsky and his school of social realists, for then the traditional cultural criteria of European literature would be replaced by those demanded by Russian social conditions and literature would of necessity, as the only platform available, become 'committed', a sounding board for ideas on social and political reform.

In these early Moscow days Pushkin was very moved to meet the leading Polish poet Adam Mickiewicz, whom the Emperor forced to live outside Poland. They were of an age and had much in common and took to each other with warm spontaneity on both sides. In an unfinished poem, 'He lived among us', which he wrote several years later, Pushkin recorded the pleasures of this brief association, the seminal quality of their conversations on life and literature, and also the pain of what followed.

Cut off from Poland, Mickiewicz grew restless in Russia and applied for permission to go abroad. Pushkin appealed on his behalf to the authorities and helped to achieve for him what was denied to himself – an exit permit. Mickiewicz, having wandered through various European countries, finally settled in Italy. Exile and the sense of hopelessness produced by the suppression of the Polish rising in 1830 proved very embittering and Russophobia began to dominate Mickiewicz's work. This change from the youthful optimism in the ultimate brotherhood of nations, which had so encouraged Pushkin and his circle, created a sombre impression on them, which was confirmed by Herzen's account of his meeting with Mickiewicz in Rome (see page 305). However, when Pushkin died the old generous note was heard in the tribute Mickiewicz published anonymously in *Le Globe* (Paris, 25 May 1837), signed 'un ami de Pouchkine':

> La balle qui frappa Pouchkine porte un coup terrible à la Russie intellectuelle . . . personne ne remplacera Pouchkine. Il n'est pas donné à un pays de produire plus d'une fois un homme qui réunit à si haut degré les qualités les plus diverses et qui semblent s'exclure mutuellement. Pouchkine, dont les lecteurs admiraient le talent poétique, étonnait l'auditoire par la vivacité, la finesse et la lucidité de son esprit. Il était doué d'une mémoire prodigieuse, d'un goût délicat et exquis. . . . J'ai connu le poète russe d'assez près, et pendant un assez long temps. Je lui trouvais un caractère trop impressionnable, et parfois léger, mais toujours franc, noble et capable d'épanchement. Ses défauts paraissaient tenir aux circonstances au milieu desquelles il se trouvait, ce qui était bon en lui, venait du fond de son cœur.

As a mark of personal involvement in the tragedy, Mickiewicz challenged Georges d'Anthès, the man who had shot Pushkin, to a duel.

In spite of the stimulus of these friendships, both old and new, the fizz at being at the centre of things again soon subsided and Pushkin found himself longing to get back to Mikhailovskoe from which, only a few months ago, he had sped with such relief. But when he got back there he could not settle to work, and was soon off again to Moscow and then, by special permit, to St Petersburg. This restlessness of spirit seemed to spring from his need to settle down in a fundamental respect: in short, to marry. He began to draw up a short list.

Soon after his interview with the Tsar, Pushkin had been commissioned to write a report on state education. His previous experience in official report writing had been unhappy (see page 33). This time he wrote in a more sober mood and, while the seventh chapter of *Evgeny Onegin* awaited completion, struggled on with his assignment. The Tsar's comment on the completed document was that Pushkin had laid too much stress on genius and knowledge and not enough on discipline and morality. There was something of the flavour of his own school report in this summary (see pages 6-7); it was clear that once again the Tsar and Pushkin did not see eye to eye on priorities. Pushkin commented to his friend Alexey Vulf, 'It would have been easy for me to write what they wished, but one ought not to miss such an opportunity to do some good.'

The fate of the Decembrists still cast long shadows. On 26 December 1826 at Princess Zinaida Volkonsky's Pushkin met her sister-in-law, Princess Maria Volkonsky, the Maria Raevsky with whom he had first read Byron in the Crimea. She was on her way to join her husband in exile in Siberia, a journey later immortalized by Nekrasov in his poem 'Russian Women'. Nekrasov described this sad crossing of the ways at which so many buried memories were touched on and quickened, when Pushkin and Maria Volkonsky walked up and down the room searching for comforting words to say to each other; and told how Pushkin promised that when he had completed his planned researches on Pugachev in the Urals, he would drive on and drop in on the Volkonskys in Siberia. He did not manage to fulfil this promise and they never met again.

Pushkin himself had some trouble to smooth out over some verses of his poem 'André Chénier', which had been circulated in manuscript under the title of 'On 14 December'. Pushkin was summoned to the Tsar and, while acknowledging the lines as his, denied that he had given them that title. The investigations dragged on; the men on whom the verses were found were severely punished; Pushkin remained under surveillance, his morale at a low ebb.

He applied again for permission to go to St Petersburg and it was granted. Pushkin's parents, now proud of his fame, wanted him to stay with them but he refused, in spite of his mother enticing him with the promise of his favourite dish of baked potatoes!

In St Petersburg Pushkin was back with his past and although he was surrounded by friends all concerned for his welfare – Delvig, Vyazemsky, Zhukovsky, Yakovlev, Illichevsky, Krylov – he could not find the still point at which he could rest and write. To his friends' distress he reverted to the dissolute habits of his early twenties, gambling away money he could not afford. On 16 July 1827, he wrote a short lyric 'Arion' in which he pictured himself as a shipwrecked mariner, a sole survivor sitting in the sun drying out his clothes and singing songs as of old. But in fact he was not singing enough in St Petersburg and so he set off for Mikhailovskoe once more, with debts on his mind.

This was to be his first summer largely devoted to prose. On 31 July he began to write his first short novel – *The Arap of Peter the Great*. He had long intended to set his ancestor's 'negro mug' into some imaginative frame. His choice of a prose tale as a medium was the result of several converging factors: the poetic springs were temporarily dry; the preoccupation with minutiae closely observed and recorded, so noticeable in *Evgeny Onegin*, called for the wider elbow-room of prose; the influence of Scott was beginning to exercise its gravitational pull. Pushkin worked on the tale during the summer of 1827 but left it unfinished, and once again set off for St Petersburg.

It was on this journey that he had the deeply affecting chance encounter with his old Lycée friend, Küchelbecker, which he described so poignantly in his diary (see page 216). Like the brief moments together with Maria Volkonsky, this fleeting embrace with his friend as he was driven away into imprisonment and exile emphasized and made tangible the break with the past which Pushkin was experiencing and brought with it poetic drought and spiritual malaise.

A terse lyric, 'Anchar' ('The Upas Tree'), which Pushkin wrote a year later, gave expression to the iron in his soul at this time. It describes a tyrant who despatches a slave to fetch poison for his arrows; the slave brings it and dies; the tyrant dips his arrows into the poison and prepares to attack his neighbours. The poem is short but it is heavy with the hopelessness of man's self-perpetuating destructive impulses. In the original draft the tyrant was referred to as Tsar, but

185

Benckendorff saw to it that this was emended to the more generalized 'Prince' – the original cut too near the bone.

There was, however, some improvement in Pushkin's position. The Tsar's relations with Pushkin were temporarily less strained. He turned a blind eye to Pushkin's authorship of the blasphemous *Gavriiliada* (see page 32), a manuscript copy of which had been seized by the police, and hushed up the case once he had extracted from Pushkin a written confession of his authorship (for Pushkin had at first been inclined to repudiate his youthful *jeu d'esprit*). He even defended Pushkin against one of Bulgarin's routine attacks and ordered Benckendorff to discipline his assistant.

As the autumn of 1828 approached the poetic sap at last came flooding back. Within a month Pushkin had completed *Poltava* on which he had been working in a desultory way since spring. He was at it day and night: on 3 October he rounded off Canto I, on 9 October, Canto II, on 16 October, Canto III, on 27 October, the dedication, addressed it is thought to Maria Volkonsky, in which he said that her parting words to him were sacred to his soul.

Pushkin's method of composition when in flow has been vividly set down by M. V. Yuzefovich in his reminiscences. Pushkin had described to him how he had written *Poltava* in the autumn of 1828.

> The lines would come to him even when he was asleep and he would jump out of bed in the middle of the night to write them down in the dark. When gripped by hunger he would hasten to the nearest inn, but his poems would pursue him and he would hurriedly eat the first thing that came to hand and rush back home to put down the thoughts that had occurred to him while out dining.

He wrote hundreds of lines a day, and if poetry would not come he drafted the work in prose, crossing and recrossing out the lines till no white gaps were left on the paper. Prince Mirsky has remarked (*Pushkin*, 1926) that 'poets, unlike fruit, ripen from soft to hard'. This kind of ripening can be observed in *Poltava*.

The character of Peter the Great dominated Pushkin's imagination for years and each time he wrote of him he illuminated different facets of this massive personality. In *Poltava* he exalted the hero; in *The Bronze Horseman* he would decry the tyrant. *Poltava* is a heroic poem, full of energy, and there are few more stirring descriptions in the literature of warfare than that of Peter coming out of his tent, surrounded by his chosen lieutenants, 'the fledgelings of his nest', and galloping on his

6   V. A. Zhukovsky, inscribed to Pushkin on the completion of *Ruslan and Lyudmila*, 26 March 1820. Lithograph by Esterreich (1820).

7   N. A. Karamzin. Oil painting by A. D. Venetsianov (1828).

8 Prince P. A. Vyazemsky.
Pencil drawing by
O. A. Kiprensky (1835).

9 Baron A. A.
Delvig. Pencil
drawing attributed to
V. P. Langer.

charger along the drawn-up ranks of his army 'as powerful and joyous as battle itself'. He almost attains apotheosis.

Contrasting with Peter, Pushkin describes Charles XII of Sweden, being carried in a litter – pale, motionless, wounded, plunged deep in thought. Then with a weak motion of his hand Charles moves his regiments against the Russians. It is a supremely dramatic moment. The whole passage must have been in Tolstoy's mind when he wrote his classic description of Napoleon coming out on to the battlefield surrounded by his marshals and giving the order to start the battle of Austerlitz with a wave of his shapely white hand:

> Before dawn he had slept for a few hours, and refreshed, vigorous, and in good spirits, he mounted his horse and rode out into the field in that happy mood in which everything seems possible and everything succeeds. He sat motionless, looking at the heights visible above the mist, and his cold face wore that special look of confident, self-complacent happiness that one sees on the face of a boy happily in love. The marshals stood behind him not venturing to distract his attention. He looked now at the Pratzen heights, now at the sun floating out of the mist.
>
> When the sun had entirely emerged from the fog, and fields and mist were aglow with dazzling light – as if he had only awaited this to begin the action – he drew the glove from his shapely white hand, made a sign with it to the marshals, and ordered the action to begin.
>
> (*War and Peace*, Bk. III, ch. xiv. Trans. L. and A. Maude)

Though the plot of *Poltava* is not centred on Peter the Great but on Mazeppa, Byron's Romantic hero who betrayed Peter, this part of the poem is far less memorable than the heroic part. It is written in a minor key, in a style similar to that of Pushkin's southern tales with, as in *The Gipsies*, short scenes in dialogue introduced into the narrative which add to its compactness and concentration. In the third Canto its muted cadences are scattered by the drum-rolls and trumpet fanfares of the battle. The verse suddenly becomes sharp, clear, challenging: Beethoven could have done it justice.

In December 1828, Pushkin was in Moscow on a brief visit and at a ball first saw his future wife: Natalia Nikolaevna Goncharov, who was at that time only sixteen but already remarkably beautiful. Just over a year later, in April 1829, he proposed to her and irreversibly allied himself to trouble.

To achieve the Goncharovs' consent to his marriage involved difficult and prolonged negotiations. They had three daughters and were not particularly well off and they were determined to achieve the best possible terms. Pushkin's finances were always uncertain and were constantly being undermined by his taste for gambling. Even if he was Russia's leading poet, in the Goncharovs' eyes he was not nearly as eligible as he might be: of noble stock but untitled and with unusual Ethiopian connections; financially definitely unsound; of unprepossessing appearance. They bargained hard.

In the middle of the negotiations, with Mme Goncharov taking the line that Natalia was too young for marriage, Pushkin went off to the Caucasus to see some action in the Russo-Turkish war. His movements were immediately followed by the secret police, but he was given permission to join the army. He made contact with his brother who had been serving at the front for some time under the command of Pushkin's old friend Nikolai Raevsky. On the day after his arrival at the camp, he saw some action: the Kurds attacked the Cossack lines, Pushkin still in civilian clothes, with top hat on his head, sprang on to a horse and charged off waving a sabre. He was taken for a Lutheran minister, and survived! (He drew a quick ink sketch of himself in action in his account of his journey to Erzerum.)

Erzerum fell to the Russians on 27 June and Pushkin spent a short time there with the Russian army, but this was not solving his personal problems with the Goncharovs nor was it being creatively fruitful and he soon headed for home. In 1836 he published a few impressions of this foray of which the most memorable paragraph is that in which he describes how, on his way south, near the Armenian border, he met a wagon trundling the other way: it contained the body of Griboedov, murdered on a diplomatic mission in Teheran (see pages 383-4). He ended 1829 on a gloomy note. On 26 December he wrote a short lyric full of the foreboding of death, which filled his mind whether he was strolling along the busy streets or entering a crowded church.

> Ring out the old, ring in the new,
> Ring happy bells, across the snow:
> The year is going, let him go . . .   (Tennyson)

It was 1830. This was to be Pushkin's 'Annus Mirabilis', the year in which he was to write more masterpieces than in any other. It started with the appearance of a new outlet for his opinions, the publication on 5 January of the first number of *Literaturnaya Gazeta*. Pushkin's closest friend Delvig had, after a long struggle, obtained permission to publish it, provided it was kept strictly non-political. Zhukovsky, Vyazemsky, Baratynsky, all contributed. And, of course, Pushkin was at the centre of activities, writing many of the critical comments but publishing them anonymously so as to avoid the censorship. He and Delvig saw the *Literaturnaya Gazeta* as a platform for attacks both against their old enemies, Bulgarin and Grech, entrenched in the *Severnaya Pchela,* and also against the new men who were ever more vociferously expressing resentment at the aristocratic detachment of Pushkin's circle. Pushkin and his friends would prove they had fight in them and before long, on 6 April, Pushkin fired an extra large cannon-ball in the form of a detailed pen-portrait of Bulgarin, disguised as Vidocq, the notorious French police spy. The name was to stick to Bulgarin like a burr (see no. 171).

On 6 May Pushkin's proposal of marriage was at last accepted. His father invited Vyazemsky to toast the event in champagne and agreed to hand over to Pushkin 200 serfs from the Boldino estate. Pushkin had become a man of property. Simultaneously, as a sign of his Imperial pleasure at the match, the Tsar agreed to the publication of *Boris Godunov* 'on Pushkin's own responsibility'.

Standing on the brink of matrimony Pushkin experienced cold feet and wrote (pretending that he was translating the passage from the French):

> I am to be married, i.e. I sacrifice my independence, my carefree, capricious independence, my luxurious habits, my aimless wanderings, my solitude, my inconstancy. . . . I never bothered about happiness, I could manage without. Now I need it for two, and where am I to find it?

He then sketched in his bachelor existence, still bearing a close resemblance to the way he had described Evgeny Onegin's method of passing the time, with one difference, his literary enthusiasm was now centred on two new authors: Scott and Fenimore Cooper, an important pointer to his growing preoccupation with prose.

> I come home – I sort my books and papers, tidy my dressing table, dress casually if going out to friends, or with extreme care if dining in a restaurant, where I will read a new novel or the reviews. If, on the other hand, Walter Scott and Cooper have written nothing, and there is no criminal case reported in the papers, I will order a

bottle of champagne on ice, and will observe how the wine-glass frosts over, drinking slowly, taking pleasure in the fact that the dinner costs me 17 roubles and that I can afford to indulge myself in this frivolity. I go on to the theatre . . . [and so on]

In the summer fate played a curious trick on Pushkin and laid down the conditions for his most intensively creative autumnal equinox. He usually went to the country in the summer, to Mikhailovskoe; but his nurse had died and the house stood empty, and so he went instead to his new estate at Boldino. And there he was caught by an outbreak of cholera which raged all round and isolated him in forced seclusion for three months' quarantine. He fretted but he wrote 'as I have not written for a long time' (see letter to Pletnev, no. 204).

On 7 July he had written a poetic testimony as an answer to the growing volume of angry criticism he was leaving behind:

Poet! Do not value the public's love. The momentary din of rapturous plaudits will pass, you will hear the judgement of the fool and the laughter of an indifferent crowd, but you must remain firm, calm and stern. You are a tsar: live alone. Walk a free road wherever a free mind leads you, cultivate the fruits of your favourite ideas, do not expect your honourable endeavours to be rewarded. The rewards lie within yourself. You yourself are your own highest tribunal, you can judge your own work more severely than anyone else. Are you, an exacting artist, pleased with it yourself? You are? Then let the crowd berate it and spit on the altar where your flame burns and with childish high spirits shake your tripod.

Now in Boldino he completed *Evgeny Onegin*.

It had taken Pushkin seven years, four months and seventeen days to write *Evgeny Onegin*, as he calculated on 25 September 1830. There is no poem which in its multifarious refraction of Russian life has embedded itself as deeply in the national consciousness. It belongs both in whole and in part to every Russian and everyone can quote from it, either a few lines or by the ream, now as much as in Pushkin's lifetime. It mirrors the intimate details of everyday existence, it touches the deepest chords of feeling, it is both profoundly sad and lightly frivolous. It is jam-making and unrequited love; snowfall and wasteful death. It is Pushkin's own salad days, and the hours spent at his nurse's fireside, and – most tragically – it is his death, foreseen with chilling accuracy in the death of Lensky.

Pasternak has described the extraordinary way in which Pushkin seemed to encompass Russian life in his verse:

> We go on endlessly re-reading *Eugene Onegin* and the poems. . . . It's as if the air, the light, the noise of life, of real substantial things burst into his poetry from the street as through an open window. Concrete things – things in the outside world, things in current use, names of things, common nouns – burst in and take possession of his verse, driving out the vaguer parts of speech. Things and more things, lined up in rhymed columns on the page.
>
> As if these tetrameters, which later became so famous, were units on a yardstick used to measure Russia's life, as if he took the measure of the whole of her existence, as you draw the outline of a foot or give the size of a hand to make sure that the glove or the shoe will fit.
>
> (*Dr Zhivago*, Ch. IX, trans. by Max Hayward and Manya Harari)

Reality had invaded *Evgeny Onegin*; at times the characters seemed even to have acquired a life of their own outside Pushkin's control. 'Tatiana has gone and got married, I cannot think why', he wrote.

His interest in characterization in depth and his desire to convey the texture of daily life, the flavour of a historical moment, led Pushkin to attempt two new media and in the same autumn he wrote the *Tales of Belkin* and completed the *Little Tragedies*, the former between 9 September and 20 October and the latter between 23 October and 6 November.

Pushkin was a master at attempting a new form and at the same time writing with the aplomb of an old hand. There had been little prose fiction of any quality written in Russian before the *Tales of Belkin* – Karamzin's sentimental tale of *Poor Liza* was an exception – but there was a large reading public for prose and all the major European novelists were read, often in French translations. The picaresque novel, the sentimental novel – Tatiana's mother, a typical example of slightly old-fashioned provincial gentry, was 'mad on Richardson', the Gothic novel – the contemplative heroine of *Dubrovsky* was 'steeped in Ann Radcliffe's mysterious horrors' – and most recently the historical novel, all had their eager public. Sir Walter Scott, who had set aside narrative poetry once he had embarked on the Waverley novels, was at the time the leader in the field.

Prose presented Pushkin with fresh challenges and he was drawn to it by its precision, its down-to-earth realism. He spoke of it as 'humble prose', and his prose style always remained extremely economical, even austere, pared down to the bone. The chief significance of Pushkin's prose to later Russian writers, to the masters who took the novel and the short story to the heights of achievement, lay in his choice of subject-matter and in the simplicity of his language. He shone a sharp clear light on isolated moments in the vast expanse of Russian life and showed them to be important in human terms, using for this the language of daily life, without – as Tolstoy was to remark – using a single superfluous word. The *Tales of Belkin* were written with complete lack of pretentiousness, and Pushkin himself remained withdrawn in them. The stories are all told to a fictitious author, Ivan Petrovich Belkin, by different narrators, who are all neutral observers, each with a keen eye for significant detail.

When they first appeared the *Tales of Belkin* were not a success. But before long an abundant harvest was to spring from Pushkin's short stories. Lermontov, Turgenev, Goncharov and Tolstoy were to find inspiration in his feel for the inner life and daily experience of officers and gentlemen, of peasant girls and of refined and sensitive young women, for the life lived in country houses and in barracks; Gogol, Dostoevsky and Chekhov, on the other hand, were to find it in his compassionate studies of 'little men': the minor official, the posting inn-keeper, the undertaker, whether in the back streets of St Petersburg or in remote provincial towns – Dostoevsky's 'humiliated and oppressed'.

The *Tales of Belkin* are miniatures, as are the *Little Tragedies*. In *Boris Godunov* Pushkin was concerned with power-politics, with the effect on a nation's destiny of the clash of rival ambitions; in the *Little Tragedies* he is concerned only with isolated moments of private human experience. Whereas in *Boris Godunov* he had dealt largely with unique historical figures, he now focused on universal types, consumed by a single, overriding passion. He had first conceived of the subjects in 1826, immediately after completing *Boris Godunov*, and they were included in a list he drew up around 1827 of subjects for future plays: 'The Miser; Romulus and Remus; Mozart and Salieri; Don Juan; Jesus; Berald of Savoy; Paul I; The Demon Lover [a subject which eventually fell to Lermontov to handle]; Dimitri and Marina; Kurbsky.'

The Covetous Knight, the first of these plays, deals with men's passion for wealth. Pushkin ascribed to it a fictitious source which long mystified its critics, describing it as a translation of a tragi-comedy by Shenstone. To understand his intention in this play one should read it in the light of his criticism of *The Merchant of Venice* in which he contrasts the dramatic methods of Shakespeare and Molière (see pages 464-5). Pushkin's covetous knight has two complementary loves: gold and power, the one dependent on the other. He desires not so much the tangible products of wealth as the knowledge that the power to obtain such possessions lies in his cellars. He worships gold because it raises him above his fellow men and allows him to contemplate the vast estates and palaces that could be his. For the same reason Shylock seeks wealth because it is the one thing that gives him self-confidence in the face of the hate and disdain of the Venetians. Furthermore in *The Covetous Knight* the type of miserly Jew is separated from the character of the avaricious knight, and the cringing shiftiness of the one is opposed to the cruel yet magnificent vision of the other. In its short span the play rises to great intensity of feeling.

The same can be said of *Mozart and Salieri* in which again Pushkin deals with the effect on man of one consuming passion, in this case envy. Salieri, the hardworking and talented composer, is counterpoised to the playful genius, Mozart. Salieri, overcome by the glory of Mozart's music, poisons him because he feels he is called by destiny to save musicians who have to work for that inspiration which comes to Mozart without effort. It is the study of the conflict between envy and admiration, of the impact of natural genius on trained mastery.

The Stone Guest is concerned with Don Juan's tireless quest for love, his controlling passion. Here, using such hybrid sources as Molière's *Le Festin de pierre*, Da Ponte's libretto for Mozart's *Don Giovanni*, and Shakespeare's scene of Richard of Gloucester's wooing of Lady Anne, Pushkin produced a concentrated drama of characteristic originality and managed to cast over it a strongly evocative Spanish atmosphere, of tersely expressed explosive passions and of balmy nights scented with lemon and laurel in which these passions flourish. This imaginative power of conjuring up settings which he had never seen was one of the qualities which so impressed Dostoevsky about Pushkin's art, as he stressed in his speech commemorating him. Pushkin was indeed Keats's 'chameleon poet'.

In form the *Little Tragedies* were modelled on the *Dramatic Scenes* of Barry Cornwall, which Pushkin admired (see page 483), and in kind they resemble the closet drama of many Romantic poets, for Pushkin's hopes of reforming the Russian theatre were frostbitten by his frustrations over *Boris Godunov*. Apart from the haunting *Rusalka*, which he started at this time and left unfinished in 1832, he wrote no further plays. The Russian theatre was in fact a great disappointment to him: there was no vitality, no creation, no criticism. Pushkin was never to know that creative reciprocity of actor, dramatist and audience as had existed in the Elizabethan theatre. He was never to see the knowledge of dramatic method he had acquired from books put to use on the stage. The uphill struggle against tradition and prejudice proved too daunting, the odds were too heavily weighted against him. Ironically *The Covetous Knight* was due to be staged in St Petersburg on 1 February 1837, but in view of Pushkin's death the production was cancelled 'as a precaution against any political demonstrations on the public's part'.

The amazing fecundity of the autumn of 1830 was inexhaustible. In September Pushkin had written the first of his verse fairy tales – 'The Tale of the Priest and his servant, Balda'; in October he wrote a light-hearted tale in the style of *Beppo* – *The Little House in Kolomna* – and sketched out and began a satiric novel of rural life – *The History of the Village of Gorukhino*; on 6 November he completed a free translation of John Wilson's [Christopher North's] *The City of the Plague*. With cholera raging all round, the subject was a topical one and Pushkin's involvement gave Wilson's work a new dimension. Pushkin wrote as one keenly aware of 'Time's winged chariot hurrying near'. In an autobiographical fragment, 'Cholera', he wrote laconically, describing how he passed his time: 'I busy myself with my affairs, re-read Coleridge, make up stories, avoid visiting neighbours.' One could hardly guess from those few words what creative energy was being expended.

Finally, on 5 December, the quarantine was lifted and Pushkin went back to St Petersburg to suffer within a month the bitterest blow of his life.

Baron Delvig had run into serious difficulties with the censorship over the publication in his review, the *Literaturnaya Gazeta*, of four lines of verse by Casimir Delavigne on the victims of the 1830 revolution in France. He was interrogated several times by Benckendorff who, in an outburst of rage, threatened to have him, Pushkin and Vyazemsky sent to Siberia. The review was proscribed. Delvig did not have Pushkin's stamina in the face of such pressure; his gentle kindliness, his self-effacing humility, were quite unfitted to battling with authority and he suffered a nervous collapse. Within a month he was dead. Pushkin was shattered by this loss: they had loved each other from their schooldays and Delvig could understand the range and scope of Pushkin's writing better than anyone else. 'Nobody in the world was closer to me than Delvig', he wrote to Pletnev (see page 304).

In the meantime *Boris Godunov* had at last been published and had met with a hostile reception in the press. In happier days the failure of his favourite work to kindle the public's imagination would have disappointed Pushkin bitterly; now he was mentally prepared for the fact that the excited plaudits of the friends who had heard *Boris Godunov* in 1826 would not be echoed, and he had drawn the sting by repeatedly saying so in the preface he drafted for it. Benckendorff, on the other hand, informed him that the Tsar had read the play with great satisfaction – maybe indeed for the first time. It was cold comfort.

On 18 February 1831 Pushkin married Natalia Goncharov, with Vyazemsky as his best man, and embarked on a new life of 'responsibility'. The Tsar, who approved of the match, encouraged him by installing him to a nominal post at the Ministry of Foreign Affairs with a salary of 5,000 roubles a year, and by allowing him access to the state archives to collect material for a history of Peter the Great, which Pushkin wanted to write. Proteus-like, Pushkin was now emerging as a serious historian and he visualized himself keeping regular hours researching in the library.

In this same year Pushkin formed a new friendship which would prove very fruitful for Russian literature. Gogol came to call on the newly married Pushkins at Tsarskoe Selo. He brought with him his collection of short stories of Ukrainian life, *Evenings on a Farm near Dikanka*. Pushkin was impressed by them and encouraged Gogol to get them published and was then delighted to hear that the compositors had split their sides laughing as they set up the type (see nos. 208 and 294).

Gogol's attitude to Pushkin had varying facets: as a writer he reigned supreme, as a man he was sometimes disturbing, over-worldly, dancing his life away at balls. However, both Gogol's masterpieces, *The Government Inspector* and *Dead Souls*, owe the central point on which they turn to Pushkin. It was Pushkin who was to suggest to Gogol the splendid scheme of accumulating a nominal property by buying up the rights to dead serfs at bargain prices; and it was Pushkin who told him of an impostor who posed as a government inspector and fleeced all the officials of a provincial town as well as causing domestic upheaval in the Mayor's family. A manuscript note of 1832 remains in Pushkin's handwriting, in which he outlines the story of Crispin, a quick-witted Figaro of a man, who arrives at X-town for the fair and is taken for a superior personage. The Governor of the town (he dropped to Mayor in Gogol's comedy) is an honest fool; the Governor's wife flirts with Crispin and he becomes betrothed to their daughter. Pushkin had also heard of another story of an incident in a town in the district of Novgorod, which involved an impostor posing as a civil servant and fleecing the inhabitants. Lastly, Pushkin himself, when in the district of Orenburg collecting material on Pugachev, was reported as being in fact bent on a secret inspection of the local officials. Out of these three situations *The Government Inspector* was born.

Pushkin and Gogol met creatively in a shared sense of humour; in many other ways as writers they were strikingly different. Gogol's genius was closer to that of Dickens, he tended towards the fantastic and the grotesque, he was a master of comic caricature and of the use of symbolism to point his moral. His style was decorative, with an affinity to the imaginative world of Hieronymus Bosch, all very different from Pushkin's economy. But for Gogol his meeting with Pushkin was the happiest of chances and he never forgot Pushkin's encouragement when he was at the brink of his career as a writer. When Pushkin lay dead a few years later, he wrote:

> Every month, every week, brings in a new loss; but there could have been no worse news from Russia. The whole delight of my life, all my chiefest joy, vanished with him. I undertook nothing without his advice. I did not write one line without imagining him in front of me. What would he say, what would he notice, what would make him laugh, on what would he bestow his final and permanent approval – that alone is what occupied and animated my powers. A secret, trembling pleasure, such as cannot be experienced on earth, enfolded my soul . . . God! My present work [*Dead Souls*], suggested by him, is his creation. . . . I have not the strength to continue. I have tried to take up the pen several times, and the pen has fallen from my hand. Indescribable anguish!
>
> (To P. A. Pletnev, 16 March 1837, Rome)

On 27 October 1833 Pushkin completed *Angelo*, his reworking of Shakespeare's *Measure for Measure*. Pushkin transposed Shakespeare's play into a long narrative poem interspersed with a few dramatic scenes. He concentrated on the central theme of the play – the confrontation of Angelo and Isabella and the tragic dilemma to which their meeting gives rise. Contrasting Shakespeare's and Molière's dramatic methods (see pages 464-5) Pushkin had set Angelo up as an example in juxtaposition to Tartuffe. The former was a man of conflicting impulses divided within himself, seen in the round, whom an unexpected temptation exposes as a hypocrite; the latter, the personification of hypocrisy, whose every action bears that one hallmark. Now in dealing with Angelo himself, Pushkin extracted the kernel of the play and discarded its shell, but in so doing he sacrificed its life.

Shakespeare's comedy is untidy and cynical, it has a maddening plot depending on a pantomime of false monastic habits and substituted heads; but the fecund life of the Viennese stews – the pimps, the prostitutes, the potboys – provides an animated background against which the figures of Angelo and Isabella face each other in a passionate struggle of carnal lust against determined chastity. Pushkin's economy did not serve him well here; he had come much nearer Shakespeare when creating in his spirit than when attempting to translate him, however freely.

When *Angelo* was published it justifiably disappointed Belinsky, who saw in it the falling-off of Pushkin's poetic powers. In fact, however, at the very same time he was completing *Angelo* Pushkin was writing what was perhaps his *chef-d'œuvre*: *The Bronze Horseman*. It was begun on 6 October and completed on the 31st.

The Bronze Horseman combines the eloquent majesty of *Poltava* and the compassion and tenderness of *Evgeny Onegin*. It is both a great State poem and an indictment of the despotic power of that State. It celebrates with splendid sonority a great achievement – the creation of St Petersburg, a noble and beautiful city – and at the same time mourns the victims of that creation.

The equestrian statue of Peter the Great by Falconet which Catherine the Great had raised to his memory, inscribing on it the words 'Petro Primo Catherina Secunda', rears up on its granite rock by the Neva with imperious bravado. The Emperor rides the crest of the wave, trampling a serpent underfoot, his arm taking in, in a sweeping gesture, the site he had chosen for *his* city. But St Petersburg was built on marshy foundations, hundreds died of fever while it was being constructed, and its location made it subject to floods, some very serious.

In Pushkin's poem the hero, Evgeny – a very different figure from Onegin – is a minor clerk whose fiancée, Parasha, lives in a cottage in the low-lying suburbs on the banks of the Neva. On the day the Neva bursts its banks she is drowned and Evgeny, gradually becoming obsessed by the dominant figure of the Bronze Horseman, goes mad and flees as behind him he hears the heavy galloping tread of the statue pursuing him relentlessly through the city streets. Nothing that Pushkin wrote before or since is as resonant as this poem – it rings true as a bell throughout. Classicism and Romanticism had come together in perfect fusion and an image was created that in its pity and terror has haunted generations of Russian artists.

In *The Bronze Horseman* Pushkin held a mirror up to despots and Nicholas I flinched at the reflection. He refused to let it be published unless some alterations were made, while Pushkin, in his turn, refused to make any changes. As a result it was not published till after Pushkin's death and then only in a version toned down by Zhukovsky.

In 1834 Pushkin again wrote a masterpiece set in St Petersburg, *The Queen of Spades*, the best of his short stories. This brief exemplum is as sparklingly frosty as a winter night in St Petersburg. It tells, with characteristic economy, the tale of an obsessed gambler, Hermann. The scene is set in a few sentences: 'There was a card party in the rooms of Narumov, an officer of the Horse Guards. The long winter night had passed unnoticed and it was after four in the morning when the company sat down to supper. Those who had won ate with hearty appetites; the others sat absent-mindedly in front of empty plates.'

Soon the secret held by Countess X – the winning sequence of three cards – is tossed into the conversation. Hermann, relentlessly determined to learn this secret, breaks into the Countess's bedroom as she sits wigless, exposed in her moribund senility, ready for bed; the Countess dies of shock. Hermann edges his way into her crowded funeral service; the Countess winks at him from her coffin. Hermann dreams three, seven, ace, and gambles; he wins heavily on three and seven but when he thinks he is playing an ace, he turns up the Queen of Spades and the card winks at him. Hermann goes mad. The story has tremendous impact. And it haunts.

Dostoevsky was one of the first critics to mark out *The Queen of Spades* as a masterpiece, and something of the pale intensity of Hermann, the outsider determined to prove himself, found its way into Raskolnikov. Tolstoy also rated it at the highest value and maybe when at the end of *War and Peace* he was taking leave of Natasha, now plump and matronly surrounded by children for whom 'the first ball' lay ahead, he remembered Pushkin's image of time passing and of its little ironies, how Pushkin had parted with Lizaveta Ivanovna, the Countess's sad, repressed companion, with the words: 'Lizaveta Ivanovna in her turn is bringing up a poor relative.'

Pushkin's last few years were orientated to history and prose and in this orientation Scott's novels played an important role. Scott's reputation enjoyed a European heyday in the twenties and early thirties. In many respects the far-flung interest in antiquarian detail to be found in the Waverley novels was an extension of that fascination with 'local colour' which formed so integral a part of the Byronic movement. The exoticism of the Mediterranean was now replaced by that of Midlothian.

Scott loved the living past. He searched for relics of bygone days remaining in the nooks and crannies of the present. When he stood on some spot made famous by historical fact or legend, he crowded it in his mind's eye with the people who by their actions had drawn it into history. He accumulated detailed information on the armour, clothing, architecture and customs of the past and whenever possible he searched out eye-witnesses of the events he was describing in order to give his tales an authentic flavour. Scott's best novels are those in which he deals with events which took place in Scotland about fifty years before the time of writing. They have a vitality lacking in his incursions into the Middle Ages and into the sixteenth century. Scott also made it a rule to use historical events and personalities only in the background or in secondary roles; the chief characters were to be fictitious, so that the movement of his novel would not be controlled by the established data of history. It was the spirit of the past he tried to recapture, not its factual framework.

Throughout Europe Scott's novels were translated, adapted, imitated, dramatized, turned into opéra bouffe: 'Salut Ivanhoé! débris de la croisade! Honneur à toi! Salut épopée! Iliade!' When Scott visited Paris in 1826 a covey of Russian princesses danced in tartan in his honour (Scott's *Journal*, 6 November 1826). Byron carried his shelf of the Waverley novels with him in all his perambulations for they brought Auld Lang Syne into his head, 'with Scotch plaids, Scotch snoods, the blue hills and clear streams' (*Don Juan*, Canto X, xviii). Victor Hugo, Merimée, Dumas, Alfred de Vigny, all turned to historical documents for subject-matter; Goethe was in the vanguard of Scott's admirers in Germany.

The swirl of tartanry was intoxicating but Scott's influence went deeper than this and had a serious and lasting effect on historical studies, focusing attention on the picturesque detail of given moments of history, the local circumstances surrounding particular events.

It was this serious side of Scott's influence which played an important part in Pushkin's career. Pushkin had been insisting for a long time that more attention should be paid to Scott. From 1826 to 1833 Scott's name frequently reappeared in his letters and in his requests for new books to be sent to him. At the same time Pushkin's own involvement with history was growing. Since 1831 he had been the official historiographer of Peter the Great and also engaged in the collection of materials on the Pugachev rebellion in the reign of Catherine II; he now, almost inevitably, conceived the idea of a historical novel ('à la Walter Scott', as the Tsar had once recommended) in which Pugachev would play an important but not the central role. He followed Scott's example and chose a subject sufficiently far removed in time for an objective view to be possible and sufficiently close for there to be some living witnesses, even if they proved to be old crones. He asked for permission to go to the Urals and to the provinces of Orenburg and Kazan to collect local material and verbatim reports.

On 18 August 1833 Pushkin left St Petersburg and by 1 October he was back in Boldino and writing fast. In the course of his travels in Pugachev country he had met a very old woman who had once slept with Pugachev and remembered him well. Pushkin gave her a gold rouble for her story. The rumour had been put about in the town in which she lived that Pushkin was either a foreign nobleman trying to stir up a fresh rebellion by distributing gold or the Devil himself. 'It must be the Antichrist,' they said, noticing his swarthy complexion, and 'he has claws instead of finger-nails' (wearing his nails long was always one of Pushkin's foibles). The old woman needed a lot of reassurance once these rumours got about.

On 20 November 1833 Pushkin had returned to St Petersburg to a new humiliation. The Tsar, anxious to ensure the presence of the beautiful Mme Pushkin at court functions, appointed Pushkin as Kammerjunker, a court position usually reserved for eighteen-year-old aristocratic boys, not for major poets (see no. 269). Pushkin was caught in a tightening knot of difficulties. His relations with the Tsar deteriorated; he lost his right to use the state archives, which put an end to his historical studies; he was, as usual, beset with financial troubles. In the last of his fairy tales, The Golden Cockerel, which he completed on 20 September 1834, Pushkin allegorized the tyranny of Tsars. His fairy tales had been an escape to bygone days of cakes and ale, when men were heroes, and golden cocks and fish were in control of events. The golden cock flew off his perch and killed the cruel Tsar Dadon; but sadly Pushkin was waking to find that fairy tales were dreams.

Pushkin worked on his historical novel, The Captain's Daughter, returning once again to Boldino to write. In it the massive proportions of a

Waverley novel are reduced to a slim volume, a clipped, almost hurried narrative. As in Scott's novels a fictitious family takes the centre of the stage, and important historical personages are glimpsed in the wings. The antiquarian flavour has gone but there are vivid details of local colour, realistically drawn from life. The chapters are all equipped with epigraphs from old folk-songs, plays and proverbs, which set the mood and crystallize the point of what follows. The story is told in the first person by the hero, Grinev, with the author hiding behind a curtain of mystification, pretending he had heard the tale from one of Grinev's descendants – the tradition of Jedediah Cleishbotham is carried on.

One episode in *The Captain's Daughter* is taken directly from *The Heart of Midlothian*, when the heroine, Maria, sets off alone on a long journey to St Petersburg to intercede with Catherine II for the life of the hero. She encounters the Empress 'incognito', a sympathetic, homely lady in the palace park, and wins her favour. The lady's identity is revealed as Maria is ushered into the imperial presence and the benevolent monarch hands out a reprieve. It is Jeanie Deans and Queen Caroline all over again.

But the salt of the novel does not lie in either the hero or the heroine: he is too noble in sentiment, honest in manner, self-consciously tender-hearted, and at the same time totally lacking in distinction; she is too 'good' and too prone to swooning. Pushkin's heart lay elsewhere, with the rebel, Pugachev, and with the serf, Savelich.

From his first appearance in the novel ('I could make out nothing save the dense swirl of the blizzard. . . . Suddenly I caught sight of something black . . . it seems to be moving. It must be a wolf or a man'), when he guides the hero to shelter, to his last wink from the scaffold a second before losing his head, the black-bearded, glowing-eyed Pretender, Pugachev, dominates the novel. He is a powerful character, sympathetically conceived. The Russian poet Marina Tsvetaeva maintained that the special relationship which existed between Grinev and Pugachev from the moment that Grinev gave him his hare-skin coat expressed Pushkin's own feelings for Pugachev, into whose rebellion he had researched in such detail, and she has vividly described the devastating effect which Pugachev's image has on that of Catherine II:

Against the flaming backcloth of Pugachev – of fires, robberies, blizzards, sledges, feasts – this woman, in her mob-cap and comforter, sitting on a bench among sundry little bridges and leaves, seemed to me like some enormous white fish. And not even a salted one at that.

('Pushkin and Pugachev', 1937)

As he parts from Pugachev Grinev himself finds it difficult to define his feelings: 'I cannot describe what I felt at parting company with this terrible man, this monster of evil to all but me. Why not confess the truth? At that moment a strong instinctive liking drew me to him.'

The other outstanding character is the old servant Savelich, untiring in his protection of Grinev. At the height of the rebellion, when Pugachev has barely finished meting out punishment to his victims, and their bodies are still swinging on the gallows, he rushes forward and demands satisfaction for the fur-coat Pugachev had wheedled out of his master. Belinsky compared him to Caleb, the extraordinary servant of the Master of Ravenswood, and they certainly have their reckless devotion to their masters in common, but Savelich's real importance (and this Belinsky would have appreciated) was that he was the first serf to be brought into the foreground of a Russian novel and treated with sympathy and humour. Many others followed him.

Gogol's comment on *The Captain's Daughter*, which Pushkin completed on 19 October 1836, was:

> Compared to *The Captain's Daughter* all our novels and short stories seem like sickly-sweet pulp. Purity and artlessness attain such heights in it that reality itself seems artificial and caricatured. For the first time characters that are truly Russian have come into being: the simple commander of the fortress, his wife, the young lieutenant, the fortress itself with its single cannon, the confusion of the period, and the unassuming greatness of ordinary people. It is not only truth itself but something even better.

But the general public received the novel with reserve, for Pushkin had outgrown them.

On 7 September 1835 Pushkin visited Mikhailovskoe for the first time after a very long absence, but with Arina Rodionovna's room standing empty he felt melancholy and wrote nothing except the enigmatic fragment 'Egyptian Nights', in which with wry humour he sketched in the character of a poet, Charsky (The Enchanter), in which some of his own feelings at the pretences which society was forcing him into can be glimpsed.

He wrote of the serious disadvantages and troubles which being a poet brought with it:

The public regards a poet as its private property; it holds the opinion that he is born for its profit and pleasure. Should he return from the country, the first person he meets asks him whether he has brought the public some little novelty. Should he be plunged in thought concerning his disordered affairs or the illness of someone dear to him, he is immediately met with a banal smile and the exclamation: 'he must be writing something!'

As a result Charsky did everything he could to avoid appearing to be a poet:

In his study which was furnished like a lady's bedroom, there was nothing to remind one of a writer: there were no books strewn on or under the tables; the sofa was not bespattered with ink; there was none of that disorder which bespeaks the presence of the Muse and the absence of a broom and brush. . . . He affected to be either a passionate horse-lover or a desperate gambler, or a most refined gastronome, although he could not distinguish between horses of mountain or Arab breed, never remembered which suit was trumps, and in secret preferred baked potatoes to any concoctions of a French cuisine. He led the most dissipated form of life, hanging around at all the balls. . . . And yet he was a poet and his passion was unfathomable. When inspiration (which he would dismiss as 'trash') possessed him, he locked himself in his study and wrote from morning till late at night. He confessed to his genuine friends that only then did he know real happiness. . . . The world and the opinions of the world and his own whims ceased to exist for him – he wrote poetry.

And then *at last*, the Tsar gave Pushkin permission to publish a literary review, provided it completely eschewed politics. A new era of activity seemed to lie ahead.

1826

LETTERS

132. To Prince P. A. Vyazemsky

9 November 1826
Mikhailovskoe

. . . The country somehow suits my mood. There is a kind of poetic delight in coming back freely to an abandoned prison. You know that I do not affect sentimentality but the welcome of my domestics – the boors – and my nurse honestly warms the cockles of my heart more than fame, the pleasures of self-esteem, distractions, etc. . . . Moscow left an unpleasant impression on me, but still it's better to see you than to correspond with you. What is more, there is the review[1] . . . I didn't say anything to you concerning your firm intention of joining up with Polevoy, but by God it's sad. And so the decent writers among us will never produce anything together! Always alone. Polevoy, Pogodin, Sushkov,[2] Zavalevsky,[3] whoever edits the review, it's all one. The fact is that we must take possession of one review and rule autocratically, in sole sway. We are too lazy about translating, reprinting and advertising, etc., etc. That's the drudgery of a review, that's the reason for having an editor; but he must (1) know Russian grammar, (2) write sense, i.e. make his adjectives agree with his nouns and combine them with verbs. And that's exactly what Polevoy can't do. For Christ's sake read the first paragraph of his obituaries of Rumyantsov and Rostopchin[4] and agree with me that he can't possibly be entrusted with the editing of a review which is graced with our names. But then all is not lost. Maybe I and not Pogodin will be the master of the new review. Then willy-nilly you will send Polevoy to . . .

PS I have just re-read my pages on Karamzin – there is nothing I can publish.[5] Gather up your spirits and write . . . I found Yazykov's verses[6] here. You will be astonished how he has developed. And what will become of him? If we are to envy anyone, he's the one we should envy. Verily, verily I say unto you, he'll button up all of us old folk.

---

[1] A group of writers in Moscow, headed by Pogodin, all admirers of the German philosopher Schelling, had received permission on 6 November 1826 to publish a new review – the *Moskovsky Vestnik*. The first number appeared on 1 January 1827, and contained a scene from *Boris Godunov* (in

Pimen's cell). Several of Pushkin's friends, including Delvig, Kozlov and Yazykov, contributed to the *Moskovsky Vestnik* but Vyazemsky remained loyal to Polevoy's *Moskovsky Telegraph*. However, Pushkin still hankered for a chance to edit a review himself though he realized it would involve him in routine jobs which did not appeal.

2 N. V. Sushkov, a minor writer, a friend of Griboedov.

3 N. S. Zavalevsky was a friend of Pushkin's in the south of Russia.

4 Count N. P. Rumyantsov and Count F. V. Rostopchin had both died in 1826 and Polevoy had written a joint obituary in *Moskovsky Telegraph*.

5 A few pages of personal reminiscences concerning Karamzin had remained of the memoirs Pushkin had begun to write in Mikhailovskoe but which he had largely destroyed after December 1825.

6 'Trigorskoe'. On Yazykov see no. 133 and notes.

133. To N. M. Yazykov[1]   *9 November 1826*
                                               Mikhailovskoe

I have just come from Moscow and have just seen *your* 'Trigorskoe'. I am hastening to embrace and congratulate you. You have not written anything better but you will – much better. May God grant you health, caution, and a prosperous and peaceful life! The Tsar has freed me from the censorship. He himself is my censor. An enormous advantage, of course.[2] Because of this we will print *Godunov*. Of the censorship regulations[3] we will speak anon. Write to me. . . .

1 This is the first surviving letter from Pushkin to Yazykov. They had met in the summer when Yazykov, on vacation from the University of Derpt (Estonia), had come to stay with Praskovya Osipov at Trigorskoe. They spent an idyllic month of country delights in each other's company, during which much poetry was read and more inspired, including this long poem 'Trigorskoe' which Yazykov dedicated to Praskovya Osipov. Both poets looked back to these summer days, sweet with the aroma of home-made jam, as to a particularly happy interlude. Pushkin was very impressed by the love of life and the energy which pulsed through Yazykov's poetry at this time. It was doomed to be short lived. In 1837 Yazykov fell incurably ill and in 1846 he died, an embittered man of reactionary opinions, sunk in melancholy.

2 The full implications of the Tsar's decision to act as his censor had not yet dawned on Pushkin. He found that he had to recall everything that he had sent to the censorship by the usual channels. Nothing could bypass the scrutiny of the Tsar, which meant in practice that of his chief of secret police, Count Benckendorff. See no. 246.

3 The Tsar had endorsed the new censorship regulations on 10 June. There was a general tightening-up. Yazykov complained that it was difficult to get books on history and political science in the St Petersburg University

library; Katenin wrote of the ban placed on books on philosophy and logic. This period of extreme repression lasted for two years.

134. To Count A. C. Benckendorff   *29 November 1826*
Pskov

. . . as I have in fact read my tragedy to several people in Moscow[1] (not out of disobedience, of course, but only because I had not clearly understood the Emperor's exalted wishes), I consider it my duty to forward it to Your Excellency, in the exact form in which it was read by me, so that you yourself can see the spirit in which it was written; I had not dared before to submit it to the Emperor, intending first to rid it of some improprieties of expression.[2] As I have no other copy, may I make so bold as to ask Your Excellency to return it to me. . . .

[1] Benckendorff wrote to Pushkin on 22 November 1826, rebuking him for giving public readings of *Boris Godunov* before it had been seen by the Emperor, see pages 180-1.
[2] The Emperor was charmed by Pushkin's reply and asked to see the play. See page 181 for his subsequent comment on it.

135. To Prince P. A. Vyazemsky   *1 December 1826*
Pskov

. . . I am being driven![1]. . . I will explain later. In the country I wrote in prose,[2] which is despised, and inspiration does not come. . . .

[1] Pushkin was in trouble, see letter to Benckendorff, no. 134.
[2] Pushkin had been asked by the Tsar to write a paper on state education – a task outside his usual province.

136. To N. M. Yazykov   *21 December 1826*
Moscow

I received your letter in Pskov and wanted to answer you from Novgorod – you, the worthy poet of them both.[1] However, I am writing from Moscow, where I brought your 'Trigorskoe' yesterday. You will know from the papers that I am taking part in the *Moskovsky Vestnik*, therefore you will be doing so too. . . . You must be with us.[2] . . .

Are you pleased about the review? It's time to strangle the almanacs.

Delvig is with us. Only Vyazemsky has remained firm and faithful to the *Telegraph* – it's a pity, but what can one do?[3]

[1] In his early poetry Yazykov often wrote of Russia's heroic past implying, as Ryleev did, that the present was less heroic. He was particularly interested in the history of the ancient cities of Novgorod and Pskov.

[2] Pushkin threw himself into helping to prepare the new review for the press, reading proofs and writing round for contributions. Yazykov was not as enthusiastic, as he did not consider a journalist's trade fitting to a poet.

[3] Vyazemsky enjoyed working for the *Moskovsky Telegraph* and filled issues with his contributions. He said both Pushkin and Mickiewicz assured him that he was a born pamphleteer.

1827

DRAFT ARTICLES

137. On the almanac *Severnaya Lira*[1]

Almanacs have become the representatives of our literature. In time people will turn to them to judge of its movements and successes. A few pleasant poems, some curious prose translations from eastern languages, the names of Baratynsky and Vyazemsky, all guarantee the success of the *Severnaya Lira*, the pioneer of the Moscow almanacs. . . .

The prosy article on Petrarch and Lomonosov[2] could have been interesting and witty. Indeed these two great men had much in common. They both were the founders of their country's literature, they both thought of grounding their fame on works of great moment, but contrary to their own desires are better known as national poets. Separated from one another by time, by the circumstances of their lives, by the political condition of their countries, they resemble one another in their firmness and indefatigibility of spirit, in their quest for education, and, finally, in the respect which they could command in the eyes of their fellow countrymen. . . .

[1] The *Severnaya Lira* was published in January 1827. This article was intended for the *Moskovsky Vestnik*. Pushkin made no mention of the contributions by F. Tyutchev, which were published in this almanac.
[2] By S. E. Raich, one of the editors of the almanac. The founder of the Friends of Wisdom Society.

For Pushkin on Lomonosov see pages 345-9.

138. On Baratynsky

The collected edition of Baratynsky's poems, which has been so long and so impatiently awaited, has at last appeared. We hasten to take this opportunity of expressing our opinion of one of our first-class poets and one who is (possibly) still underrated by his fellow countrymen.[1]

Baratynsky's first works brought him to people's notice. Connoisseurs were astonished to see maturity and harmony in his first attempts.

This premature development of all his poetic talents was perhaps

dependent on circumstances but it already foretold that which the poet
has now fulfilled for us in so brilliant a manner.

Baratynsky's first poems were elegies and he reigns supreme in this
form. It has recently become fashionable to disparage elegies,[2] as in the
past there has been an attempt to scoff at odes; but even if flaccid
imitators of Lomonosov and Baratynsky are equally unbearable, it does
not necessarily follow that the lyric and elegiac kinds must be excluded
from the ranks of the poetic oligarchy.

But, what is more, we have hardly any pure elegies. Among the
ancients the elegy used to have a distinguishing metre, but sometimes
approached the idyll, sometimes merged into tragedy, and sometimes
took on a lyric movement (of which at the present time we find examples
in Goethe).

[1] An edition of Baratynsky's poems came out in Moscow in November 1827;
Baratynsky had been planning it since 1824. Pushkin probably intended
to publish this article in the *Moskovsky Vestnik*.
[2] Pushkin is referring to Küchelbecker's article in *Mnemozina* on the trend
of Russian poetry, which he criticized, see no. 123.

139. On Byron's plays

English critics disputed Byron's dramatic talent; I think they were
right. Byron, so original in *Childe Harold*, in *The Giaour* and in *Don Juan*,
becomes an imitator as soon as he embarks on drama – in *Manfred* he
imitated *Faust*,[1] replacing the crowd scenes and the [witches'] sabbath
with others which he considered more elevated; but *Faust* is among the
greatest creations of the poetic spirit, being a representative example
of contemporary poetry, in the way that the *Iliad* is a monument of
classical antiquity.

It seems that in his other tragedies Alfieri was Byron's model – *Cain*
only has the form of drama, but on account of the inconsequence of its
scenes and its abstract dialectic in fact belongs, like *Childe Harold*, to
the poetry of scepticism. Byron threw a one-sided glance at the world
and at human nature, then turned away from them and became absorbed in himself. In *Cain* he conceived, created and described one sole
character (his own in fact), and related everything else to this gloomy
and powerful figure, one that is so strangely fascinating. However,
when he began to create his tragedy, he handed out to each of the
dramatis personae one of the component parts of this complex and

strong personality – and in this way broke up his majestic creation into several small and insignificant figures.

Byron was conscious of his mistake and at a later date took up *Faust* again, imitating it in his *Deformed Transformed* (thinking in this way to improve on *le chef-d'œuvre*).

[1] Pushkin wrote of this again in his article on Katenin (1833), see no. 256. Byron himself acknowledged his debt to *Faust*.

NOTES

140. Excerpts from letters, thoughts and comments[1]

True taste consists not in the instinctive rejection of this or that word or turn of phrase, but in a sense of proportion and decorum.

A learned man without talent is like the poor mullah, who cut up and ate the Koran, hoping to be filled with the spirit of Mahomet.

Monotony in a writer proves him to have a one-track mind, even though it might run deep.

People complain of the indifference of Russian women to our poetry, seeing as a reason for that their lack of knowledge of their native language; but what lady could fail to understand the poetry of Zhukovsky, Vyazemsky or Baratynsky? The fact is that women are the same the world over. Nature having endowed them with acute minds and with a most highly charged sensibility, well nigh denied them a sense of style. Poetry slides over them without touching their souls; they are insensitive to its harmony. Notice how they sing modern romances, how they mangle the most natural verses, upset the metre, destroy the rhyme. Listen to their literary judgements and you will be surprised by the distortion and even the crudeness of their understanding. . . . Exceptions are rare.

Nobody has more sensibility in his thoughts and more taste in his feelings than Baratynsky.

. . . Tredyakovsky came to be beaten several times. In Volynsky's papers it says that he demanded an ode on the occasion of some holiday from the court poet, Vasily Tredyakovsky, but the ode was not ready [in time] and the fiery Secretary of State punished the negligent poet with the rod.

One of our poets used to say proudly, 'Though some of my verses may be obscure they are never prosaic'. Byron could not explain some of his lines. There are two kinds of obscurity; one arises from a lack of feelings and thoughts, which have been replaced by words; the other from an abundance of feelings and thoughts, and the inadequacy of words to express them.

Un sonnet sans défaut vaut seul un long poème.[2] A good epigram is better than a bad tragedy. . . . What does this prove? Can one say that a good lunch is better than bad weather?

The traveller Ancelot[3] speaks of a grammar, establishing the rules of our language – which has not yet been published; of some Russian novel which has brought fame to its author – still in manuscript; and of a comedy, the best in the whole Russian repertory – as yet neither performed nor published. What an entertaining literature!

Inspiration is the inclination of the spirit to the most lively reception of impressions and to the grasping and exposition of ideas. Inspiration is as necessary to geometry as to poetry.

Byron said that he would never undertake to describe a country that he had not seen with his own eyes. None the less in *Don Juan* he describes Russia, and consequently some errors in local colour are found. For example, he speaks of the dirt in the streets of Ismail.[4] Don Juan sets off for Petersburg 'in a *kibitka* (a cursèd sort of carriage without springs, which on rough roads leaves scarcely a whole bone)' and mentions ruts and flints.[5] Ismail was taken in winter, in severe frost. On the streets the bodies of the enemy were covered over by snow, and the conqueror rode over them, marvelling at the tidiness of the town: 'God be praised, how clean!' A winter *kibitka* does not jolt and a road in winter is not flinty. There are other mistakes which are more important. Byron both read and enquired a lot about Russia. I believe he loved her and knew her recent history well. In his poems he often speaks of Russia, of our customs. The dream of *Sardanapalus* reminds one of a famous political cartoon published in Warsaw at the time of the 17..

war.[6] He portrayed Peter the Great in the person of Nimrod.[7] In 1813 Byron intended to come to the Caucasus by way of Persia.

Subtlety is not a proof of wisdom. Fools and even madmen are at times extraordinarily subtle. One can add that subtlety rarely combines with genius, which is usually ingenuous, or with greatness of character, which is always frank. . . .

The publication of *The History of the Russian State* (as was right and proper) created a great stir and made a profound impression. 3,000 copies were sold in one month, a thing which Karamzin himself did not expect. Society rushed to read the history of the fatherland. It was a revelation. Ancient Russia seemed to have been discovered by Karamzin as America had been by Columbus. For a time nothing else was spoken about anywhere. I must admit that it is impossible to imagine anything more stupid than some of the opinions of society it was my lot to hear; they were well designed to cure anyone of a desire for fame. . . . He was not reviewed in the journals: we have no one capable of studying and appraising Karamzin's enormous work. Kachenovsky fastened himself on the Introduction. Nikita Muraviev, a clever young hot-head, analysed the Introduction (the Introduction!). Mikhail Orlov in a letter to Vyazemsky criticized Karamzin for not including at the beginning of his work some brilliant hypothesis on the origin of the Slavs; that is, he demanded of a historian something other than history. Some wits at supper translated the first chapters of Livy in the style of Karamzin. At the same time nobody thanked the man who had shut himself up in his study at a time of most flattering successes, and devoted twelve whole years of his life to silent and tireless labours. The notes to the *History of Russia* bear witness to the breadth of Karamzin's learning, acquired by him in those years when, for ordinary men, the limits of education and knowledge have long been fixed, and jockeying for position takes the place of attempts at self-education. Many forgot that Karamzin published his History in Russia, an autocracy, and that the Tsar in freeing him from the censorship was, by this mark of trust, placing on Karamzin the obligation of extreme delicacy and restraint. I repeat that *The History of the Russian State* is not only the work of a great writer but is also an act of heroism by an honest man.[8]

Delvig's idylls seem to me remarkable. What a powerful imagination one must have in order to transport oneself so completely from the nineteenth century into the Golden Age, and what an extraordinary feeling for the graceful, so to fathom Greek poetry through Latin imitations or German translations: that luxuriance, that voluptuousness, that negative, rather than positive, charm that allows for nothing strained in feeling, nothing subtle or confused in thought, nothing superfluous or unnatural in description![9]

French literature was born in the entrance hall and never got further than the drawing room.

[1] Published in the Almanac *Severnye Tsvety* for 1828, which came out on 22 December 1827.
[2] Boileau, *L'Art poétique*, II.
[3] J. A. P. F. Ancelot, *Six Mois en Russie* (1827). The books in question are a grammar by N. Grech, a novel by Bulgarin, *Ivan Vyzhigin*, and Griboedov's *Woe from Wit*. This last proved worth waiting for.
[4] *Don Juan*, Canto VIII, lxxiii.
[5] *Don Juan*, Canto IX, xxx-xxxi.
[6] *Sardanapalus*, Act IV, scene i. The cartoon Pushkin refers to was published in London, not in Warsaw, in 1795, showing Suvorov handing Catherine the Great the heads of women and children after the taking of Warsaw.
[7] Byron's only mention of Nimrod is in *Don Juan*, Canto V, lx, in which he refers to him as the founder of Babylon. Peter is not mentioned.
[8] This paragraph formed part of Pushkin's autobiographical notes which he largely burnt after the Decembrist rising.
[9] Delvig modestly did not include this paragraph in the printed text of these notes.

141. Draft foreword to 'Excerpts from letters, thoughts and comments'[1]

One day my uncle fell ill. A friend visited him. 'I'm bored,' said my uncle, 'I would like to write but do not know what to write about.' 'Write whatever comes into your head,' answered his friend, 'thoughts, literary and political comments, satirical portraits, etc. That is very easy. That is how Seneca and Montaigne wrote.' The friend left and my uncle followed his advice. In the morning his coffee was badly made and that annoyed him; then he philosophically reflected that he had been upset by a mere trifle and he wrote, 'Sometimes we are upset by mere trifles.' At that moment he was handed a review, he glanced through and saw an article on dramatic art, written by a defender of Romanticism. My uncle being a classicist to the marrow thought and wrote, 'I prefer Racine and Molière to Shakespeare and Calderón, despite the cries of the latest critics.' My uncle wrote down a further dozen or so thoughts on similar lines and went to bed. On the following day he sent them to a journalist, who thanked him politely and my uncle then had the pleasure of re-reading his thoughts in print.[2]

One of the reasons why we avidly lap up the memoirs of the great is our own self-love, we are pleased if we resemble a remarkable man in any way: in opinions, in feelings, in habits, even in weaknesses and vices; probably, if they had left us their confessions, we would find more resemblances between our opinions, habits and weaknesses, and those of quite insignificant people.

Prince Vyazemsky's prose is extremely vivid. He possesses the rare talent of expressing his thoughts in an original way – and fortunately he does think, which is fairly uncommon among us.

There is a different kind of boldness. . . .
Calderón calls lightning flashes fiery tongues of heaven, speaking to the earth. Milton says that the flame of hell only served to make visible the eternal darkness of the pit.
We think such expressions have boldness because they convey to us, in a forceful and unusual way, clear ideas and poetic images.
The French to this day marvel at Racine's boldness in using the word 'pavé', dais:

Baiser avec respect le pavé de tes temples.[3]

And Delisle boasts that he used the word 'vache'.[4] Despicable literature, that panders to such petty and arbitrary criticism! One pities the fate of poets (of whatever merit) if they are obliged to win fame by such victories over the prejudices of taste!
There is a higher form of boldness. The boldness of invention, of creation, in which a vast plan is encompassed by creative thought – such is the boldness of Shakespeare, Dante, Milton, Goethe in *Faust*, Molière in *Tartuffe*.

When repeated a bon mot appears foolish. How can one translate epigrams? Not, that is, those of the Anthology, in which poetic beauty is unfolded, not one by Marot in which a lively tale is condensed, but such as Boileau describes: Un bon mot de deux rimes orné.[5]

214

¹ These notes were extras to no. 140, present in the draft but not included in the printed version.
² Pushkin's uncle, V. L. Pushkin, had published a set of aphorisms in *Literaturny Muzey* for 1827 (March 1827) which he called 'Comments on people and society'.
³ Prologue to *Esther*.
⁴ 'La Vache gonfle en paix sa mamelle pendante,' in 'L'Homme des champs'.
⁵ *L'Art poétique*, II.

142. Of Byron and his imitators[1]

No work of Lord Byron created such a stir in England as *The Corsair*, in spite of the fact that it yields to many others in merit: to *The Giaour* in the flaming portrayal of passion, to *The Siege of Corinth* and *The Prisoner of Chillon* in the touching unfolding of the heart, to *Parisina* in tragic power, and finally to the third and fourth cantos of *Childe Harold* both in depth of thought and in loftiness of truly lyrical flight, and to the amazing Shakespearian variety of *Don Juan*. *The Corsair* was indebted for its incredible success to the character of the hero, hauntingly reminiscent of the man whose fatal will at that time ruled over one half of Europe and threatened the other.

At any rate the English critics assumed Byron to have had this intention, but it is more likely that the poet here too presented the character who appeared in all his works, and one which he finally assumed himself in the person of Childe Harold. Be that as it may, the poet never clarified his intention, the comparison with Napoleon being pleasing to his self-esteem.

Byron took little trouble over the plans of his works, at times giving them no thought at all: a few scenes, loosely connected, sufficed him for that infinitude of thoughts, feelings and images.

The critics questioned his dramatic power, and Byron was always disappointed by this. The fact is that he fully comprehended and loved only one character.

That is why, despite great poetic beauties, his tragedies are in general of lower quality than his genius, and the dramatic parts of his poems (except possibly in *Parisina*) have no merit.

What, then, are we to think of a writer, who takes only the plot of *The Corsair*, which is worthy of nothing but an absurd and banal tale, and on this childish framework writes a dramatic trilogy, replacing Byron's enchanting and profound poetry by inflated ugly prose, worthy

of our miserable imitators of the late Kotzebue? For that is what Mr
Olin has done in writing his Romantic tragedy *The Corsair* – an imitation of Byron. One asks: what struck him in Byron's poem – can it be
that it was the plot?[2] O miratores[3] . . .

[1] Comment written on V. N. Olin's Romantic tragedy *Corsair*, (1827),
inspired by Byron's poem. Pushkin intended to publish this review in the
Moskovsky Vestnik. Compare his letter to Raevsky, 1825, no. 108.
[2] Olin, for his part, had written critically of *The Fountain of Bakhchisarai*,
noting particularly the lack of plot.
[3] 'O imitatores', Horace, 19th Epistle of Bk. I.

DIARY

143.

15 October 1827. . . . At the next halt[1] I picked up Schiller's *Der Geister-
seher*, but had hardly had time to read the opening pages when suddenly
four troikas with a courier drew up. 'I expect they are Poles,'[2] I said
to the inn-keeper. 'Yes,' she replied, 'they are being taken back.' I went
out to have a look at them.

One of the men under arrest was leaning up against a column. He
was approached by a tall, pale, thin, young man with a black beard,
in a frieze overcoat, who looked a real Jew-boy – and I took him for
a Jew and the close association of Jews and spies produced in me the
usual reaction: I turned my back on him, thinking he had been summoned to Petersburg for information or explanations. Seeing me, he
gave me a quick lively glance. Involuntarily I turned towards him.
We look at each other intently – and I recognize Küchelbecker.[3] We
flung into each other's arms. The guards pulled us apart. The courier
caught me by the arm, threatening and cursing – I didn't hear him.
Küchelbecker felt faint. The guards gave him some water, put him in
the cart and galloped away. I went on my way. At the next halt I
heard that they were being taken from Schlüsselburg – but where?

[1] Pushkin was on his way from Mikhailovskoe to St Petersburg.
[2] Some members of a Polish nationalist society had been involved in the
Decembrist rising.
[3] Küchelbecker was being moved from Schlüsselburg fortress to the Dina-
burg fortress. He was kept in prison till 1835 and then sent to a penal settle-
ment in Siberia, where he died in 1846. This was his last meeting with
Pushkin but they remained in correspondence and Pushkin used to send
him books.

LETTERS

144. To Count A. C. Benckendorff   *3 January 1827*
                                                         Moscow

It was with feelings of profound gratitude that I received Your
Excellency's letter, informing me of the Gracious mention of His Majesty
concerning my dramatic poem.[1] I agree, as the Emperor thought fit
to remark, that it resembles a historical novel rather than a tragedy.
I regret that it is beyond my powers to change that which I have
written. . . .

[1] Benckendorff wrote to Pushkin on 14 December 1826, informing him that
the Tsar had read *Boris Godunov* with great pleasure, see pages 181-2 and no.
191, though certain passages the Tsar wished altered or expurgated were
marked in the manuscript. Benckendorff went on to say that the play was
certainly not fit for the stage but could be published if a few alterations
were carried out.

145. To Baron A. A. Delvig   *2 March 1827*
                                                         Moscow

. . . You reproach me concerning the *Moskovsky Vestnik* and German
metaphysics. God knows how much I hate and despise it, but what is
one to do? A group of hot-headed, stubborn youngsters have come
together: to the parish priest his own, to the devil his own. 'Gentlemen,'
I say, 'fancy wanting to pour out of one empty vessel into another –
all that is well enough for the Germans, surfeited as they are with
positive knowledge, but for us . . .' . . . And time is a commodity that
I will not waste on any *Vestnik*.[1] So much the worse for them if they
do not listen to me.

[1] Pushkin's association with the Schlegel-enthusiasts of the *Moskovsky Vestnik*
was short-lived.

146. To Baron A. A. Delvig   *31 July 1827*
                                                         Mikhailovskoe

. . . Here is the promised elegy, my dear. Now you have an excerpt
from *Onegin*, an excerpt from *Boris*, and this piece. I will try to send
something else. Remember that I have the *Moskovsky Vestnik* on my
hands and I can't leave it in the hands of fate and Pogodin. If I finish

the epistle addressed to you on your grandfather's skull we'll publish that as well.[1] I am in the country and hope to write a lot, at the end of the autumn[2] I shall be with you; as yet I lack inspiration, in the meantime I have started on prose.[3] Write and tell me what you are doing. How are your prose and your poetry? Has chivalric Reval awakened your drowsy Muse?[4] Is Bulgarin with you? Incidentally, Somov tells me of his 'Evening with Karamzin'. Don't print it in your *Tsvety*. Honestly, it's indecent. Of course a dog is free to bark at a bishop, but let it bark in the yard and not in your room. Our silence on Karamzin is shameful enough as it is,[5] without Bulgarin being the one to break it. That would be even more shameful. . . .

[1] On 17 October 1827 – Delvig's name-day – Pushkin came to see Delvig in St Petersburg and brought him as a present a skull of one of his ancestors, which Yazykov had acquired in Riga, and with it a marvellous poem 'The Skull', which he dedicated to him. At dinner toasts were drunk to Delvig out of this skull. In all respects a Byronic gesture. In order to get his poem through the censorship quickly Pushkin signed his poem 'I', saying that nobody would guess that ' "I" was I', and it was published in the *Severnye Tsvety* for 1828 with this signature.
[2] Pushkin always wrote best in the autumn.
[3] His short story about his ancestor – *The Arap of Peter the Great*.
[4] Delvig was very prone to indolence, see no. 273.
[5] See no. 131. Delvig did not print Bulgarin's article in his almanac.

147. To M. P. Pogodin   *Second half of August 1827*
                                             Mikhailovskoe

. . . I have run away to the country, sensing the imminence of rhyme. . . .

148. To M. P. Pogodin[1]   *31 August 1827*
                                             Mikhailovskoe

Victory, victory! The Tsar has passed *Faust*[2] except for two lines. . . . Now let's turn to another subject. You want to edit *Uraniya*!!! et tu, Brute!! . . . Think what that will look like. You, the editor of a European review in Asiatic Moscow, you, an honest man of letters among the stall-keepers of literature, you! . . . No, you will not want to soil your hands in almanac mud.[3] *You have accumulated many articles which do not fit into a review:* but what sort? Quod licet *Uraniae*, licet even more the *Moskovsky Vestnik*; not only *licet*, but *decet. And there are other reasons.*

Which? Money? There will, there will be money. For God's sake don't abandon the *Vestnik*. I promise you *unreservedly* that I will take an active part in its publication next year; and for that reason am definitely severing all my ties with the almanac men of both capitals. Our chief mistake has been that we wanted to be too serious; our poetry section is renowned; the prose could be even better but the trouble is there is too little light matter in it. You must surely have a tale for *Uraniya*. Give it to the *Vestnik*. Talking of tales: they must, without fail, form a substantial part of the review, just as fashions do in the *Telegraph*.[4] Tales are a rarity here, which isn't the case in Europe. They constituted Karamzin's initial glory; and these are still being discussed among us.

Your Indian tale, 'The Crossing',[5] will attract general attention in a European review as a curious example of erudition; but here, among us, they see it only as a tale and pompously think it stupid. Do you sense the difference? The *Moskovsky Vestnik* is, in my unbiased opinion, the best of the Russian reviews. The only thing that is praiseworthy in the *Telegraph* is its zealous industry – and the only good things are Vyazemsky's articles – as far as that is concerned, I would give three serious articles from the *Moskovsky Vestnik* for one of Vyazemsky's articles in the *Telegraph*. His criticism is either superficial or unfair, but the trend of his incidental ideas and their expression are strikingly original; he thinks, angers one, and makes one think and laugh: important qualities, especially for a journalist! . . .

[1] Mikhail Petrovich Pogodin (1800-1875), a Slavophile historian, writer and journalist. He was the Editor of the *Moskovksy Vestnik* (1827-30). He had admired Pushkin's work from the start. They first met at Venevitinov's on 11 September 1826 (see pp. 180-1) and began to collaborate on the *Moskovksy Vestnik*. Their mutual interest in history drew them together and they met frequently 1826-31, but their literary and political views gradually diverged and the friendship cooled. Nonetheless Pushkin invited Pogodin to contribute to the *Sovremennik*. Pogodin was shattered by Pushkin's death and wrote: 'This is an irreplaceable loss for our literature. He is our first national poet.' (21 February 1837)

[2] 'Scene from Faust', published 1828.

[3] Pushkin clearly felt that they should concentrate all their resources on making the *Moskovsky Vestnik* a success rather than spreading themselves in too many almanacs. He did, however, contribute regularly to Delvig's *Severnye Tsvety* and, reluctantly, to *Uraniya* for 1826. Pogodin did not publish *Uraniya* for 1828.

[4] Pictures of foreign fashions in clothes, furniture, carriages, etc., were included as a supplement with each number of the *Moskovsky Telegraph*.

[5] Published in *Moskovsky Vestnik* (1827), trans. from German by V. P. Titov.

1828

NOTE

149. From a Preface to *Ruslan and Lyudmila* printed in the second edition
(1828) and excluded from the 1835 edition

The author was twenty years old when he finished *Ruslan and Lyudmila.*
He began his poem while still a pupil at the Tsarskoe Selo Lycée and
completed it while leading a most dissipated life, which to a certain
extent serves as an excuse for its shortcomings. . . .

. . . you know that we received from our ancestors a small and poor
literary legacy, of *folk-tales* and *songs*. What can one say of them? If
we treasure even the most ugly old coins, should we not also carefully
preserve the literary remains of our ancestors? Without doubt. We like
to recollect everything which belongs to our infancy and to that happy
period of our childhood when some song or story gave us innocent
delight and contained within itself a wealth of experience. You can
see for yourselves that I have nothing against the collecting and seeking
out of Russian tales and songs; but when I discovered that our men of
letters took a very different view of them, loudly proclaiming the greatness, mellifluousness, power, beauty and wealth of our ancient songs,
that they had begun to translate them into German, and, finally, had
grown so enamoured of *tales* and *songs* that new-fangled Yeruslans and
Bovas began to gleam through nineteenth-century poetry, well then –
I wish you good-day, gentlemen. . . .

DRAFT ARTICLES

150. On *Boris Godunov*[1]

Thank you for the interest you have taken in the fate of *Godunov*;[2] your
impatience to see it is very flattering to my self-esteem; but now that,
through a combination of favourable circumstances, the opportunity
of publishing it has presented itself, I foresee new difficulties, which I
had previously not suspected.

Having been expelled from Moscow and Petersburg society since 1820, I could only observe the direction our literature was taking by reading the reviews. Following the heated arguments about Romanticism, I imagined that we had indeed tired of the decorum and perfection of classical antiquity and of the pale, monotonous copies of its imitators, that our jaded taste demanded other, stronger sensations and was seeking them in the turbid but boiling sources of a new, native poetry. It seemed to me, however, rather strange that our infant literature, not presenting any models in any form, should already by its few attempts have had time to blunt the taste of the reading public; but I thought that French literature, known to us all so intimately from childhood, was probably responsible for this phenomenon. I frankly admit that I have been brought up to fear the respected public and see nothing shameful in pleasing it and in following the spirit of the age. This first admission leads me to a second, more important one: so be it, I confess that in literature I am a sceptic (to say no worse) and that to me all its sects are equal, each exhibiting both good and bad sides. Should the literary conscience be superstitiously subject to conventions and forms? Why should the writer not comply with the accepted literary customs of his people, just as he complies with the laws of his language? He must be in command of his subject in spite of the difficulties presented by rules, as he is compelled to master his language, in spite of the shackles of grammar.

Firmly believing that the obsolete forms of our theatre demand reform, I ordered my Tragedy according to the system of our Father Shakespeare; and having sacrificed two of the classical unities on his altar,[3] have barely kept to the third.[4] Apart from this notorious trio, there is a unity not mentioned by French critics (who probably do not suspect that one can question the absolute necessity for it), that of style – the fourth absolute condition of French tragedy – of which the theatres of Spain, England and Germany are free. You realize that I too have followed such a tempting example.

What more is there to say? I have replaced the respected Alexandrine by the blank pentameter – in some scenes I have even descended to despised prose. I have not divided my tragedy into acts – and was already thinking that the public will say 'thank you very much'.

Voluntarily disclaiming the benefits offered by a form of art justified by experience and confirmed by habit, I tried to compensate for their lack, of which I was sensible, by the true representation of the people of the period and of the development of historical characters and events, in short, I wrote a truly Romantic tragedy.

At the same time, studying more carefully the critical articles appearing in the reviews, I began to suspect that I was cruelly mistaken in thinking that an urge for Romantic reform had appeared in our literature. I saw that people take the general term 'Romanticism' to imply works bearing the stamp of melancholy and reverie and that, following this arbitrary definition, one of the most original writers of our time,[5] who is not always right but who is always to be excused by the pleasure he gives his enchanted readers, did not hesitate to include Ozerov in the company of Romantic poets; that, finally, the Aristarchuses of our reviews unceremoniously set on one plane Dante and Lamartine, and autocratically divide European literature into classical and Romantic,[6] conceding to the first the languages of the Latin south and attributing to the second the Germanic tribes of the north, so that Dante (il gran padre Alighieri), Ariosto, Lope de Vega, Calderón and Cervantes, find themselves in the classical phalanx, to whom, thanks to this unexpected reinforcement bestowed by the editor of the *Moskovsky Telegraph*, the victory will undoubtedly belong.

All this has gravely shaken my self-assurance as an author. I began to suspect that my tragedy was an anachronism.

At the same time reading the trivial poems extolled as being Romantic, I did not see in them the slightest trace of the sincere and free-flowing current of Romantic poetry, but only the preciosity of neo-classical France. This impression was soon confirmed.

You read in the first book of the *Moskovsky Vestnik* an extract from *Boris Godunov*, the scene of the chronicler – the character of Pimen is not my invention. In him I drew together those characteristics in our ancient chronicles which captivated me: the innocence of soul, the disarming humility, the almost child-like quality which is at the same time combined with wisdom, the pious devotion to the Divine Right of the Tsar, the complete absence of self-regard and partiality, which breathe in these precious memorials of bygone days, among which the embittered chronicle of Prince Kurbsky differs from the others as the stormy life of this exile from Ivan[7] differed from the humble lives of tranquil monks.

It seemed to me that this character would be at the same time new and familiar to the Russian heart; that the touching kindness of the ancient chroniclers, so vividly apprehended by Karamzin and reflected in his immortal work, would grace the simplicity of my verses and would earn the indulgent smile of readers – but what happened? Attention was drawn to Pimen's political opinions and they were found out of date; some doubted whether blank verse could be called poetry. Mr Z. suggested exchanging the scene from *Boris Godunov* for pictures from the *Damsky Zhurnal*. And that was the sum of the respected public's stern judgement.

What follows from this? That Mr Z. and the public are right and that the gentlemen of the press are to blame for the incorrect information which led me into temptation. Brought up under the influence of French literature the Russians have grown used to rules, sanctioned by its criticism, and look unwillingly at everything which does not comply with these laws. Innovations are dangerous and, it seems, unnecessary.

Do you want to know what else holds me back from publishing my tragedy? Those parts of it that might give rise to hints, *allusions*. Thanks to the French we cannot understand that a dramatist can fully renounce his own line of thought in order to transfer completely into the period he is describing. The Frenchman writes his tragedy with the *Constitutionnel* or the *Quotidienne*[8] in front of his eyes, in order to force Sylla, Tibère, Léonidas,[9] to express in hexameters his own opinions on Villèle[10] or Canning. By means of this intricate method, on the French stage today one hears many eloquent journalistic forays but true tragedy does not exist. Note that in Corneille you do not find allusions, nor are there any in Racine apart from those found in *Esther* and *Bérénice*. The chronicler of the French theatre saw in *Britannicus* a bold hint at the diversions of the court of Louis XIV: 'Il ne dit, il ne fait que ce qu'on lui prescrit,' etc.;[11] but is it likely that a refined courtier like Racine would dare to draw such an opprobrious parallel as between Louis and Nero? Being a true poet, Racine, in writing these splendid lines, was steeped in Tacitus and in the spirit of Rome; he portrayed ancient Rome and the tyrant's court, not having in mind the ballets at Versailles. As was said of Shakespeare in a similar case by either Hume or Walpole[12] (I don't remember which), the very audacity of such an allusion serves as proof that it did not enter Racine's head.

---

[1] Pushkin cast his preface to *Boris Godunov* in the form of a letter, similar to the one he had drafted to Raevsky in 1825 (see no. 108). He intended to send it to the Editor of the *Moskovsky Vestnik*. It was not published.

[2] The thanks expressed here are addressed to S. P. Shevyrev who had written so enthusiastically about the one scene of *Boris Godunov* which had

already appeared in print in his 'Survey of Russian literature in 1827' in the *Moskovsky Vestnik* (1828), No. 1. Shevyrev had emphasized the impatience with which the publication of the whole play was awaited.

3 Of time and place.

4 Of action.

5 Vyazemsky in his introduction to Ozerov's works. In a postscript to this written fifty years later (1876), Vyazemsky wrote that Pushkin did not like Ozerov and that they frequently had heated arguments about this. 'Above all Pushkin would not forgive me for saying that Ozerov was to some extent a Romantic dramatist.' Pushkin would not accept him as a Romantic, 'but then', adds Vyazemsky, 'at that time the meaning of *Romanticism* was not fully or firmly defined. Nor is it to this day.'

6 Pushkin is referring to Polevoy's article published in *Polyarnaya Zvezda* for 1825, in which he drew a demarcation line between the classical south and the Romantic north. See also his letter to Vyazemsky, no. 104, and his draft article on classical and Romantic poetry, no. 79.

7 Prince Kurbsky fled from the court of Ivan the Terrible and then conducted a famous correspondence with him.

8 *Le Constitutionnel*, a French newspaper of liberal tendencies; *La Quotidienne*, a French monarchist newspaper.

9 All characters in French plays of the 1820s.

10 French royalist Prime Minister, 1822-8.

11 *Britannicus*, Act IV, scene iv.

Boileau wrote to Monsieur De Losme de Montchenay in September 1707:

> la Tragédie et la Comédie . . . ont quelquefois rectifié l'homme plus que les meilleures Prédications. Et pour vous en donner un exemple admirable je vous dirai qu'un très grand Prince qui avoit dansé à plusieurs Ballets, ayant vu jouer le Britannicus de Mr Racine où la fureur de Néron à monter sur le théâtre est si bien attaquée, il ne dansa plus à aucun Ballet, non pas mesme au temps du Carnaval.

12 In his 'Notes on several characters of Shakespeare' (1786) Horace Walpole wrote:

> Racine had been taught by Corneille to avoid all the faults of their predecessors, and was taught by his own judgment and by that of his friend Boileau, to avoid the faults of Corneille. The latter was inspired with majesty by Roman authors and Roman spirit; Racine with delicacy by the polished court of Louis XIV. Shakespeare had no tutors but nature and genius.

> In his Preface to the second edition of the *Castle of Otranto*, which is included in the 1823 edition in Ballantyne's Novelists' Library which Pushkin possessed, Walpole defends Shakespeare against Voltaire's strictures for the mixing of tragic and comic kinds and says that he was not constricted as Voltaire was by the tastes of the Parisian 'parterre'.

151. A reply to an article in the *Ateney*[1]

In the fourth number of the *Ateney* there appears an analysis of the fourth and fifth chapters of *Onegin*.

The author sees in Romanticism an excuse providing an escape route for the poet.[2]

Analysing the novel's characters, he finds them to be generally immoral. He blames Onegin for behaving in an open and correct manner towards Tatiana, who is in love with him, and for squeezing Olga's hand with the evil intention of teasing his friend.

He considers it odd that the quiet (?), *dreamy* (?) (it would be fairer to say – passionate, enamoured) Lensky wants to challenge Onegin to a duel for what amounts to a trifle and that he calls his phlegmatic fiancée a coquette and a flighty child (on the grounds that young men usually shoot each other for serious matters and lovers are never roused to jealousy by trifles).

He is indignant with Tatiana for falling madly in love with Onegin at first sight and for writing a love letter to him, which is, of course, a very indecent thing to do.

Finally, he finds that these two chapters are quite worthless, about which I won't argue with him. . . .[3]

[1] The article in the *Ateney*, No. 4 (1828), was signed V. and was by M. A. Dmitriev. Pushkin did not publish his reply but later incorporated some of the points in his notes to *Evgeny Onegin*. N. A. Polevoy in his Memoirs recalls how, in St Petersburg in 1828, Pushkin read him these remarks of his off scraps of blue paper. Polevoy tried to persuade him to publish them but Pushkin firmly declared: 'I have never published a single reply to any criticisms of my works; but I do not refrain from writing them for my own satisfaction.'

[2] Dmitriev wrote: 'The appellation "Romantic" excuses a poem from all claims to sense and from the legitimate demands of taste.'

[3] Pushkin then goes on to discuss individual points of style and grammar criticized by Dmitriev.

152. Of poetic diction

There comes a time in a mature literature when minds grown tired of monotonous works of art and of a conventional and refined vocabulary address themselves to fresh popular fantasies and to unfamiliar vernacular expressions, which were previously despised. Just as at one time in France blasé men of fashion were enraptured by Vadé's[1] muse, so today Wordsworth and Coleridge have a large following. But Vadé had neither imagination nor poetic sensibility and his entirely light-hearted, witty works are expressed in the language of fishwives and market-porters. The works of the English poets, on the other hand, are full of deep feeling and poetic ideas, expressed in the language of honest, ordinary men.[2] Thank God, that time has not yet dawned for us, for the so-called language of the gods is still so fresh in our ears that we call anyone a poet who can write a dozen rhymed iambic lines. Not only have we not yet considered making poetic diction approximate more closely to noble simplicity, but we even try to inflate the style of our prose. Nor can we yet understand poetry freed from all conventional poetic adornments. The efforts of Zhukovsky and Katenin were unsuccessful not in themselves but in the effect which they produced. There were few, very few, people who appreciated the merit of the translations from Hebel[3] and even fewer, the power and originality of 'The Murderer',[4] a ballad which can stand comparison with the best works of Buerger and Southey.[5] The murderer's invocation to the moon, the sole witness of his crime, 'Stare down, bald-head', a verse filled with truly tragic power, appeared ludicrous to superficial people who did not realize that sometimes horror is increased when it is expressed through laughter. The ghost scene in *Hamlet* is all written in jocular and even vulgar language, but one's hair stands on end at Hamlet's jokes.

[1] J. J. Vadé (1720-57), French writer credited with introducing the manners and language of the market-place into literature.
[2] Pushkin's knowledge of English had improved sufficiently for him to widen his range of reading in English poetry; he no longer relied on French translations. There are several indications at this period that he was reading Wordsworth and Coleridge. He would have every sympathy with their aim of bringing 'language really used by men' into poetry.
[3] Zhukovsky translated the following poems by J. P. Hebel: 'Das Habermuss', 'Der Karfunkel', 'Der Wächter in der Mitternacht', 'Die Vergänglichkeit', 'Der Morgenstern', 'Der Sommerabend', 'Sonntagsfrühe'.
[4] By Katenin (1815). See Pushkin's article on Katenin (1833), no. 256.
[5] Pushkin himself tried his hand at translating Southey: lines 1-25 of 'Madoc' and lines 1-32 of 'Hymn to the Penates'.

153. On *The Ball* by Baratynsky

Our poets cannot complain of unnecessary severity on the part of the critics or the public – on the contrary. Hardly has a bent for versifying and a knowledge of the language and its uses been noticed in a young writer, than we hurry to welcome him with the title of Genius for his smooth rhymes, we cordially thank him in the name of humanity[1] in the reviews, we unhesitatingly compare a faulty translation or a pale imitation to the immortal works of Goethe and Byron (in this way we have collected several of our own Pindars, Ariostos and Byrons, and thirty odd other writers *bestowing honour on our age*). Amusing but harmless benevolence: a true talent will trust its own judgement, based on a love of art, more than the ill-considered verdict of scribbling Aristarchuses. Why deprive golden mediocrity of the harmless pleasures of journalistic triumph?

Baratynsky enjoys this customary indulgence of our reviews less than any other of our poets. Is this because truthfulness of mind and feelings, accuracy of expression, taste, clarity and harmony affect the crowd less than the 'exagération' of modern poetry or because our poet by some of his epigrams aroused the indignation of a brotherhood not given to meekness? Be that as it may, the critics displayed in their attitude towards him unscrupulous indifference and even hostility. Not mentioning the famous quips of the late *Blagonamerenny*, a well-known joker, let us note that the appearance of *Eda*, a work remarkable for its novel simplicity, for the charm of its plot, for the vivid quality of its descriptive colour, and for the light but masterly sketching-in of characters, only provoked an indecent little article in the *Severnaya Pchela*[2] and a feeble protest, I believe, in the *Moskovsky Telegraph*.[3] How did the *Moskovsky Vestnik* react to the collected works of our leading elegiac poet?[4] Meanwhile Baratynsky has quietly been perfecting his style – his most recent works are the fruits of a mature talent. It is time for Baratynsky to take up the place which has long been his on the Russian Parnassus.

His most recent poem, *The Ball*, printed in the *Severnye Tsvety*,[5] confirms our opinion. This brilliant work is suffused with original colour and is of extraordinary charm. In this quick-moving tale, the poet has combined humour and passion, metaphysics and poetry, with astonishing artistry. . . .[6]

---

[1] Pushkin was laughing at one of Polevoy's reviews in the *Moskovsky Telegraph*, No. 21 (1827). He suggested to Shevyrev that the next round should be thanks in the name of the universe.

[2] In the *Severnaya Pchela*, No. 20 (1826), by Bulgarin.

[3] In *Moskovsky Telegraph*, Pt. VIII (1826), by Polevoy.

[4] Shevyrev wrote critically of Baratynsky in *Moskovsky Vestnik*, No. 1 (1828). This annoyed Pushkin.

⁵ Only a section of Baratynsky's poem was published in the *Severnye Tsvety* for 1828. The complete poem came out with Pushkin's *Count Nulin* as a separate volume, *Two Verse Tales*, in December 1828.
⁶ Pushkin goes on to analyse Baratynsky's poem in more detail.

LETTERS

154. To M. P. Pogodin   *19 February 1828*
                                                            St Petersburg

. . . In a few days I will send you some prose – but for Christ's sake don't offend my little orphan verses by misprints, etc.

I am writing to Shevyrev¹ separately. It's a sin on his part that he doesn't respond to Baratynsky, but let God be his judge.

¹ Stepan Petrovich Shevyrev (1806-64), poet, critic and translator, was co-editor with Pogodin of the *Moskovsky Vestnik* and from 1834 Professor of Russian literature at Moscow University. In the first issue of the *Moskovsky Vestnik* for 1828 he wrote a critical 'Survey of Russian literature for 1827' in which he fiercely attacked Bulgarin and spoke with rapture of Pushkin's work, particularly of the scene from *Boris Godunov* which had already been published.
   Shevyrev recalled that in Pushkin's presence no one would dare to say anything critical of Baratynsky's poetry. At this time Pushkin was very preoccupied with Baratynsky's work.

155. To N. M. Yazykov¹   *14 June 1828*
                                                            St Petersburg

Send me some poetry, for God's sake, some poetry! My soul craves for it. . . .

¹ With this letter Pushkin sent Yazykov a short poem, saying how he longed to join him in Derpt, but that financial worries shackled him to St Petersburg.

156. To M. P. Pogodin   *1 July 1828*
                                                            St Petersburg

. . . I haven't sent you anything for the *Moskovsky Vestnik*. It's true there was nothing to send; but give me time – autumn is at the gates. I will bury myself in the country and will send you my quit-rent in full.¹ Our review, too, must be published next year. Between you and me, it is of course the leading, the only review in Holy Russia. We must with patience, conscientiousness, nobility of spirit, and especially with pertinacity, justify the expectations of the true friends of literature and the approval of the great Goethe. All praise and honour to our dear Shevyrev. You did well to publish the letter of our German Patriarch.[2] It will, I hope, give Shevyrev more weight in public opinion, which is exactly what we need. It is time for intelligence and knowledge to oust Bulgarin and Fedorov.[3] Here, at my leisure, I tease them about the disparity between their views and Goethe's. . . .

[1] Compare No. 146 and note 2. Pushkin was to express the way in which autumn moved him to composition most memorably in his poem 'Autumn' a fragment, 1833, which ends:

> Thoughts flock to me in droves; they dance about and caper;
> Swift rhymes to meet them rush; my fingers restive grow,
> They boldly seek a pen; the pen, a sheet of paper . . .
> A moment, and the verse will smoothly, freely flow.

Pushkin then compares the sudden frenzy of activity to that on a Tall ship about to put out to sea:

> 'Tis done. The sails fill out. Upon her travels leaving,
> The ship begins to move, the swelling waters cleaving . . .
>   (Translated by Irina Zheleznova)

One is reminded of what John Aubrey wrote of Milton: 'All the time of writing his *Paradise Lost*, his veine began at the Autumnall Aequinoctiall, and ceased at the Vernall.'

[2] Shevyrev had published an article on Goethe's *Faust* in the *Moskovsky Vestnik*, No. 21 (1827). This article was sent to Goethe and he replied in a letter to N. I. Borchard (Weimar, 1 May 1826) which was published both in German and Russian in the *Moskovsky Vestnik*, No. 9 (1828). In his letter Goethe had some complimentary things to say of Russian literature and its publication created quite a stir.

[3] B. M. Fedorov, a minor writer, who was critical of Pushkin's lack of moral tone and carped at *Evgeny Onegin*.

1829

———◆◆◆◆◆———

NOTES

157. From the Introduction to the first edition of *Poltava*[1]

... Mazeppa is one of the most remarkable personalities of that epoch. Some writers[2] wanted to make of him a heroic fighter for liberty, a new Bogdan Khmelnitsky.[3] History shows him to have been ambitious, rooted in cunning and crime, the slanderer of his benefactor, Samoilovich, the butcher of his unhappy mistress's father, a traitor to Peter before his victory, a betrayer of Charles after his defeat; his memory, subject to the Church's anathema, cannot escape the curse of mankind.

Someone[4] in a Romantic tale portrayed Mazeppa as an old coward, blenching before an armed woman, inventing refined tortures suited to French melodrama, etc. It would be better to expound and explain the real character of the rebel Hetman, without arbitrarily distorting a historical figure.

1 January 1829

[1] Pushkin began writing *Poltava* on 5 April 1828. He completed it on 27 October, see page 186.
[2] Ryleev, for example, in *Voynarovsky*.
[3] A Cossack Hetman (1593-1657), for a time a semi-independent prince of the Ukraine.
[4] E. Aladin in *Kochubey* (1828).

158. Note

We have a literature but as yet no criticism. Our journalists abuse each other with the name *Romantic* as old women berate rakes as freemasons or Voltairians – having no notion either of Voltaire or of freemasonry.

1830

NOTES

159. Note on Shakespeare's *Romeo and Juliet*[1]

Many of the tragedies attributed to Shakespeare are not his, but were only touched up by him. The tragedy *Romeo and Juliet*, although differing absolutely from his usual method, so obviously belongs to his dramatic canon and bears so many marks of his free and sweeping brush-strokes, that it must be recognized as Shakespeare's work. The Italy contemporary to the poet is reflected in it, its climate, passions, festivals, voluptuousness, sonnets, its magnificent language full of scintillating concetti. That is what Shakespeare understood by dramatic local colour. After Juliet and Romeo, those two delightful creations that grace Shakespeare's art, Mercutio, the model young gentleman of the time, polished, affectionate, noble Mercutio, is the most wonderful character in the whole tragedy. The poet chose him to represent the Italian people, who were the people most in fashion in Europe, the French of the sixteenth century.

[1] Published in *Severnye Tsvety* for 1830 with the heading 'taken from Pushkin's manuscript', but judging from the manuscript this seems to be a completed note rather than an extract. It was printed with the translation of Act III, scene i, of *Romeo and Juliet*, possibly by Pletnev, who had already published a translation of a part of the play in *Severnye Tsvety* for 1829.

160. Of the translation of *Adolphe*, the novel by B. Constant[1]

Prince Vyazemsky has translated and will soon publish a delightful novel by Benjamin Constant. *Adolphe* belongs to the category *of two or three novels*

> In which the age its face might see,
> And our contemporaries be,
> With some fair share of truth, depicted:
> The soul without morality,
> The temper egoistic, dry,
> And in excess to dreams addicted;

The bitter, angry cast of thought,
A-boil with deeds – that came to naught.
(*Evgeny Onegin*, VII, xxii,
translated by Oliver Elton)

Benjamin Constant was the first to present that character which was to be made universally popular by Lord Byron's genius.[2] We are impatiently awaiting the appearance of this book. It will be interesting to see how Prince Vyazemsky's experienced and lively pen mastered the difficulties of its metaphysical language, always harmonious and urbane and often inspired. In this respect the translation will be a truly creative work and an important event in our literary history.

[1] Published unsigned in the 'Miscellany' section of the *Literaturnaya Gazeta*, No. 1 (1830).

The censor had objected as he thought that *Adolphe* was on the list of proscribed foreign books and he had refused to pass this note. Delvig wrote to Odoevsky, who reassured the censor, and Vyazemsky's translation dedicated to Pushkin came out in 1831. In his dedication Vyazemsky wrote: 'Accept my translation of our favourite novel. . . . We so often spoke together of this splendid work that settling down to translate it at my leisure in the country I mentally put myself under your direction.'

At the same time the novel was also translated by Polevoy and was published in the first issues for 1831 of the *Moskovsky Telegraph*.

[2] In *Childe Harold*.

161. On Homer's *Iliad*[1]

The translation of the *Iliad*, so long and so impatiently awaited, has at last appeared! When writers spoilt by fleeting success have for the most part concentrated on brilliant trifles, when talent shuns work and fashion sets at naught the lofty models of the ancient world, when poetry is no longer a form of dedicated service but only a frivolous pastime, we regard with feelings of the deepest respect and gratitude a poet who proudly gave the best years of his life to something which claimed his entire attention, to disinterested inspiration, to the completion of a single, sublime task. The Russian *Iliad* is before us. We turn to studying it so that in time we can give an account to our readers of the book which is bound to exercise such an important influence on our native literature.[2]

[1] Published in the *Literaturnaya Gazeta*, No. 2 (1830). Gnedich's translation had come out at the end of December 1829; it was his life-work. On the

same day as Pushkin published this note, Gnedich wrote to thank him for it: 'I am unlikely ever again in my life to read anything about my work expressed in so generous a spirit and which would be so comforting and sweet to my ears.'

2 When the *Iliad* translation was published, Pushkin immediately drafted a letter to Gnedich, which he then largely incorporated in this note. The draft ended with an image he had used in an earlier letter to Gnedich, no. 89, 23 February 1825: 'All right-thinking people sensed the importance of this translation and awaited it with impatience. You ask for my works. At the time when your sailing ship, laden with the riches of Homer, is entering harbour to the thunder of our welcome, there is no need to speak of my trifles on the death of Napoleon I.'

162. On literary criticism[1]

In one of our reviews[2] they think fit to say that we cannot have a *Literaturnaya Gazeta* for the simple reason *that we have no literature.* If that were true we should not stand in need of criticism. However, our literary productions, few though they be, do appear, live and die, lacking the appreciation they deserve. Criticism in our reviews either restricts itself to dry bibliographical facts, satirical observations, witty or otherwise, and general friendly commendations; or it simply becomes a domestic correspondence between the publisher and his contributors, the proof-reader, etc. 'Clear a space for my new article,' writes a contributor. 'With pleasure,' answers the publisher. And all that is printed.[3]

People will say that criticism should concern itself solely with works having obvious merit; I do not think so. Some works are nothing on their own account, but are made remarkable by their success or influence; and in this respect moral observations are more important than literary ones. Last year several books were published (*Ivan Vyzhigin*[4] among others) of which many instructive and interesting things could have been said by way of criticism. But where were they analysed and elucidated? Living authors apart, Lomonosov, Derzhavin and Fonvizin still await posthumous evaluation. Grandiloquent epithets, unqualified praise, banal exclamations, can no longer satisfy judicious people. Besides the *Literaturnaya Gazeta* was essential not so much for the public as for some of our authors unable, for a variety of reasons, to publish under their own names in any Petersburg or Moscow review.[5]

[1] Published unsigned in Miscellany, *Literaturnaya Gazeta*, No. 3 (1830).

[2] In *Severnaya Pchela*, No. 3 (1830).

[3] Examples taken from *Vestnik Evropy*, No. 24 (1828), and No. 23 (1829), from exchanges between N. Nadezhdin and the Editor, M. Kachenovsky.

[4] By F. Bulgarin.

[5] This remark provoked several attacks in the *Severnaya Pchela*, etc., including parodies by Polevoy, on the exclusiveness of the aristocratic group of writers such as Vyazemsky, Baratynsky and Delvig (see pages 182-3).

163. Draft, provoked by articles appearing in *Galatea*, published by S. Raich[1]

A. Have you read the review by N. N. in the last number of the *Galatea*?

B. No, I don't read Russian criticism.

A. That is mistaken of you. There is nothing that can give you a better insight into the state of our literature.

B. What! Do you really think that the reviews in periodicals 'are the final Court of Appeal for our works of literature?

A. Not at all! But it gives one some idea of the relations of the various writers one to another, of their greater or lesser fame, and, finally, of the opinions prevailing among the public.

B. I do not need to read the *Telegraph* in order to know that Pushkin's poems are in fashion – and that no one among us understands Romantic poetry. . . .

A. . . . If all writers whom the public esteems would undertake the task of guiding public opinion, criticism would soon be a very different thing from what it is now. Wouldn't it be interesting to read, for example, Gnedich's opinion on Romanticism or Krylov's on modern elegiac poetry? Wouldn't it be pleasant to find Pushkin analysing Khomiakov's tragedy?[2] These gentlemen are in close touch and probably hand on to one another their comments on new works. Why not make us participators in their critical discussions?

B. The public is rather indifferent to literary success and finds little of interest in true criticism. It will occasionally watch a fight between two journalists or hear in passing an infuriated author's monologue – and will shrug its shoulders.

A. Have it your own way, but I always stop, watch, and hear it out to the end and applaud the man who has knocked out his opponent.

If I was an author myself, I would consider it faint-hearted to fail to reply to attacks, whatever their nature. What aristocratic pride to allow every street urchin to fling mud at one! Take an English lord: he is ready to meet the polite challenge of a gentleman and fight with Kuchenreuter pistols or to strip off his frock-coat and box with a coachman. That is true courage. But we are too refined and too ladylike both in our literary dealings and in our social behaviour.

B. Criticism is not publicized among us. The writers of the highest circles probably do not read Russian reviews and do not know whether they are being praised or blamed.

A. Pardon me, Pushkin reads all the numbers of the *Vestnik Evropy* in which he is abused, which, to use his own vigorous expression, is like *overhearing through a door what is being said of him in the entrance-hall.*

B. I say, how fascinating!

A. A form of curiosity which is, at any rate, quite understandable! Pushkin even replies to his critics in epigrams. What more can you ask?

B. But satire is not criticism – an epigram is not a refutation.[3] I am working on behalf of literature, not simply for my personal satisfaction.

[1] Polevoy also replied to Raich in the *Moskovsky Telegraph*.
[2] *Yermak.*
[3] Pushkin is laughing at his own tendency to resort to epigrams in preference to critical polemics with men whom he generally considered to be second-rate. He often drafted replies to criticism for his own satisfaction, but did not publish them.

164. *Yury Miloslavsky*, or the Russians in 1612, by M. N. Zagoskin[1]

Today by a *novel* we understand a fictitious narrative describing a historical epoch. Walter Scott gave the lead to a whole host of imitators. But how far removed are they all from the Scottish wizard![2] Like Agrippa's pupil,[3] having summoned up the demon of the past they could not control him and became the victims of their own audacity. Weighed down by a heavy burden of local customs and superstitions and mundane impressions, they stagger into the age into which they wish to transport the reader. Under the plumed *beret* you recognize a head dressed by your own barber; through a ruff à la Henri IV peeps the starched cravat of today's dandy. Gothic heroines are educated under Madame Campan,[4] and the public men of the six-teenth century read *The Times* and *Le Journal des débats.* How many absurdities, unnecessary details, important omissions; how much refine-ment! And, above all, how little life![5] And yet these pallid productions are read in Europe. Is it because, as Madame de Staël declared,[6] people know only the history of their own time and, consequently, are not in a position to notice the absurdity of the anachronisms found in novels? Is it because the representation of the past, even if it is weak and inaccurate, holds indefinable charm for the imagination, dulled by the monotonous motley of the actual, the everyday?

We hasten to notice that these reproaches do not apply to *Yury Miloslavsky.* Mr Zagoskin accurately transplants us into the year 1612. Our good common people, the boyars, the cossacks, the monks, the unruly informers and vagabonds – all are comprehended, they all act and feel as people must have acted and felt in the troubled days of Minin and Avraam Palitsin.[7] How vivid and enthralling the scenes of life in Old Russia are! How much truth and good-natured fun there is in the delineation of the characters. . . . The plot of the novel effortlessly fills the widest possible framework of historical events. The author does not hurry with his story, he lingers over details and digresses without ever wearying the attention of the reader. The dialogue (lively and dramatic wherever written in the vernacular) proves the author a master of his craft. But Mr Zagoskin's indisputable talent noticeably betrays him when he touches on historical characters. Minin's speech in the square in Nizhni Novgorod is weak; it lacks the passion of popular oratory. The boyars' duma is portrayed coldly. One can also note two or three slight anachronisms and a few errors in language and dress. . . . But these few errors and others, mentioned in the first number of this year's *Moskovsky Vestnik,*[8] cannot harm the brilliant, fully deserved success of *Yury Miloslavsky.*

[1] Zagoskin's novel came out in 1829 and was very well received. See Push-kin's letter to him of 11 January 1830 (no. 189), and also his letter to Vyazemsky (no. 190). This article was published in *Literaturnaya Gazeta,* No. 5 (1830).

[2] In the draft version of this article Pushkin at this point named two excep-tions: Fenimore Cooper and Manzoni, having in mind the former's *The Spy* (1821) and the latter's *I Promessi Sposi* (1825-6).

[3] Heinrich Cornelius Agrippa von Nettesheim (1486-1535), an alchemist, subject of a ballad by Goethe, 'Der Zauberlehrling', and one by Southey, 'Cornelius Agrippa; a ballad of a young man that would read unlawful books, and how he was punished. Very pithy and profitable.'

⁴ Madame Campan was First Lady of the Bedchamber to Marie Antoinette. In 1794 she opened a girls' boarding school at St Germain, and in 1807 Napoleon appointed her head of a school for the daughters, sisters and nieces of the officers of the Légion d'Honneur. Pushkin had her *Mémoires sur la vie privée de Marie Antoinette* (1822) in his library.

⁵ In the draft Pushkin mentioned Alfred de Vigny's *Cinq-Mars* (1826) as one such pale imitation of Scott, see page 453.

⁶ Mme de Staël in *Considérations sur les principaux événements de la Révolution Française* (London, 1818), Pt. I, ch. 2: 'Les hommes ne savent guère que l'histoire de leur temps . . .'

⁷ Kuzma Minin and Avraam Palitsin were Russian leaders in the wars against the Poles and Swedes in the early seventeenth century known as the Time of Troubles, which preceded the establishment of the Romanov Dynasty. Zagoskin's novel is about this period.

⁸ Review by the novelist S. T. Aksakov.

165. Of Sanson's Memoirs[1]

The French reviews announce the pending appearance of *The Memoirs of Sanson, the Paris Executioner*.[2] One might have expected that. That is where our thirst for novelty and sensationalism has led us.

After the enticing *Confessions*[3] of eighteenth-century philosophy appeared the no less enticing political revelations. We were not satisfied with seeing famous people in nightcap and dressing-gown; we wanted to follow them into their bedrooms and further. When this also bored us there appeared a crowd of shady characters with their scandalous tales. But we did not stop at the shameless memoirs of Harriette Wilson,[4] Casanova,[5] and 'La Contemporaine'.[6] We seized on the fake admissions of a police spy[7] and on their elucidation by a branded convict. The journals are full of extracts from Vidocq. The poet Hugo was not ashamed to seek in him inspiration for a novel,[8] filled with fire and filth. Only an executioner was missing in the ranks of contemporary men of letters. Finally he also turned up, and to our shame let it be said that the success of his memoirs appears beyond dispute.

We do not envy people who, basing their calculations on our immoral curiosity, dedicated their pens to the repetition of stories by the (probably) illiterate Sanson. But let us confess, living as we do in an age of confessions, that we are awaiting the Memoirs of the Paris Executioner with impatience, even if with disgust. Let us see what there is in common between him and ordinary folk. With the cry of what animal will he express his thoughts? What will this work tell us of that which permeated Count Maistre's[9] poetic and fearsome pages? What will this man have to say to us who was present for forty years of his bloodstained life at the last shudders of so many victims, the famous and the obscure, the saintly and the odious? All – all of them, his momentary acquaintances, will pass in order before us to the guillotine, where he, the savage mountebank, plays his unchanging role. Martyrs, criminals, heroes – the royal martyr and his murderer, and Charlotte Corday, and the charmer Du Barry, and the mad Louvel, and the rebel Berton, and the doctor Castaing, who poisoned his intimates, and Papavoine, who murdered children – we will see them again in the last terrible moment. One after another heads will roll before us, all of them pronouncing their last words. . . . And having satiated our savage curiosity, the executioner's book will take its place in libraries, waiting for the learned annotation of a future historian.

[1] Published unsigned in Miscellany, *Literaturnaya Gazeta*, No. 5 (1830).
[2] *Mémoires pour servir à l'histoire de la Révolution Française par Sanson* (1830). These were not in fact written by Sanson or by his father Charles-Henri Sanson (both executioners) but by Louis-François L'Héritier, to whom Henri Sanson had given the family papers and whom he had authorized to write under his name.
[3] By Jean-Jacques Rousseau (1781 and 1788).
[4] *The interesting memoirs and amorous adventures of H. W.* [Harriette Wilson], *one of the most celebrated women of the day* (1825). In the course of the one year at least 35 editions had appeared. Even Gladstone found time to read it.
[5] Published in 1826.
[6] The pseudonym of the French adventuress Elzélina Van-Aylde Jonghe, calling herself Ida Saint-Elme. *Mémoires d'une contemporaine* (Brussels, 1827).
[7] Of François Vidocq (1828), see no. 171. These were also written up by L'Héritier.
[8] *Le Dernier Jour d'un condamné* (1829) mentions two of Sanson's victims: De Castaing and Papavoine.
[9] Joseph de Maistre, *Les Soirées de Saint-Pétersbourg* (1821), which included a descriptive sketch of an executioner.

166. Of Prince Vyazemsky's critical articles[1]

Some periodicals which have been accused of conducting indecent polemics have named Prince Vyazemsky as the instigator of the abuse now reigning in our literature. A false pointer. The critical articles of Prince Vyazemsky are stamped with his subtle, observant and original intelligence. One often does not agree with his ideas, but they force one to think. Even when his opinion is clearly contradictory to our accepted

notions he irresistibly fascinates us by the extraordinary power of his
argument and by the skill of the sophistry itself. . . .

¹ Published unsigned in Miscellany, *Literaturnaya Gazeta*, No. 10 (1830).
There had been attacks on Vyazemsky in the *Moskovsky Telegraph*, No. 1,
and in *Severnaya Pchela*, No. 12. The accusation levelled against Vyazemsky
'the literary aristocrat' and his 'famous friends' stemmed from the same
source as those already directed at Pushkin: Bulgarin and Polevoy.

167. Draft on the latest guardians of morality

But isn't it ludicrous that they should consider what is and what is
not customary in Society, what our 'parquet ladies' can or cannot read,
what expression belongs to the drawing-room (or the boudoir, as these
gentlemen call it)? Isn't it diverting to see them acting as chaperones
for high social circles, among whom they probably have neither the
time nor the need to put in an appearance? Isn't it strange to meet in
learned publications pompous discussions on the disgusting immorality of
certain expressions with reference to 'parquet ladies'? Isn't it shameful to
observe respected professors blushing at worldly jokes? How are they to
know that in the best circles affectation and pomposity are more intolerable and more indicative of petit-bourgeois values than is 'vulgarité', and
it is exactly that which betrays their ignorance of society? How are they to
know that the outspoken and original expressions of the crowd are repeated in the highest circles without offence, while the affected circumlo-
cutions of provincial politesse would simply cause general and instinctive
amusement? Good society can exist outside the highest circles, everywhere,
in fact, where honest, intelligent and educated people are to be found.

    This zest to show themselves to be members of high society has some-
times led our journalists into amusing blunders. One thought that it
was impossible to speak of fleas in the presence of ladies. And whom
did he choose to rebuke strongly on that account? A young and brilliant
courtier. In one review they vigorously attacked the impropriety of a
poem in which it says that a young man dared by night to enter the
room of a sleeping beauty;¹ and while the bashful reviewer was dis-
secting it as if it were the most immodest tale by Boccaccio or La
Fontaine, all the ladies of Petersburg had read it and knew whole
sections of it by heart. Recently a historical novel² commanded general
attention and for a few days drew our ladies away from 'fashionable
tales'³ and historical memoirs. What happened? The review pointed
out to the author that in his crowd scenes were found the dread words:

son of a bitch. Is it possible? What will the ladies say if their eyes chance to fall on this unheard-of expression? What would they have said to Fonvizin who read his *Adolescent* to the Empress Catherine, in which the rude Prostakova calls Yeremeyevna *a daughter of a bitch* on every page? What would today's guardians of morality say of the reading of *Dushenka*[4] and of the success of this delightful work? What do they think of the humorous odes of Derzhavin, of the charming tales of Dmitriev? Isn't *The Modern Wife*[5] as immoral as *Count Nulin*?

[1] Pushkin is replying to Nadezhdin's criticism of *Count Nulin* in the *Vestnik Evropy*, No. 3 (1829).

[2] *Yury Miloslavsky* by Zagoskin, reviewed by Bulgarin in *Severnaya Pchela*, No. 9 (1830).

[3] The fashionable tales of the Marquis of Normanby, for example *Clorinda*, *Matilda* or *Granby*, all written in the 1820s.

[4] By I. Bogdanovich (1783), an adaptation of La Fontaine's *Les Amours de Psiché et de Cupidon*. Very popular light verse.

[5] By I. I. Dmitriev (1791), a satirical play.

168. On Yazykov[1]

. . . The poetry section is graced by Yazykov.[2]

From the moment he first appeared this poet has astonished us by the fire and force of his language. No one masters cadence and phrasing with more authority. There seems to be no subject which he could not grasp and express poetically with characteristic vividness. It is regrettable that so far he has barely stepped out from the confines of one over-narrow kind; and it is surprising that the publisher of the review, who is renowned for a style faulty to the point of absurdity,[3] should think that he could in some form of parody imitate Yazykov, whose style is firm, precise and expressive.

[1] From a review of *The Nevsky Almanakh for 1830*, published unsigned in *Literaturnaya Gazeta*, No. 12 (1830).

[2] See page 205.

[3] Nikolai Polevoy, who published some parodies of Yazykov in the *Moskovsky Telegraph* in 1829.

169. *The History of the Russian People* by Nikolai Polevoy, Vol. I (Moscow, 1829)[1]

I

. . . Karamzin is our first historian and our last chronicler. His critical judgements put him in the rank of historians, his artlessness and apophthegms in that of the chroniclers. His criticism consists in the learned collation of legends, in the penetrating search for truth, in the clear and true portrayal of events. There is not one epoch, or one important occurrence, that is not satisfactorily traced by Karamzin. Where his story is not satisfactory is where he lacked source material: he did not replace it by arbitrary guesswork. His moral speculations in their ingenuous simplicity give his whole narrative the inexpressible charm of an old chronicle. He used them as tropes but did not endow them with any great significance. 'Let us note that for judicious minds these apophthegms are either half-truths or commonplaces, which have little value in a historical work, where we look for action and character,' he says in his Preface, which has been so much criticized and as yet so little understood. One should not see in such chance reflections the forcing of the narrative towards some preconceived end. . . .

II

The influence of W. Scott is felt in all branches of contemporary letters. The new school of French historians was formed under the influence of the Scottish novelist. He pointed out to them completely new sources, previously unsuspected in spite of the existence of historical drama, founded by Shakespeare and Goethe. Mr Polevoy was forcibly struck by the merits of Barante and Thierry[2] and followed their line of thought with the boundless enthusiasm of a young neophyte. Captivated by the fact that truth brought before us in the artless simplicity of a chronicle had the vivid quality of fiction, he fanatically denied the existence of any other kind of history. We judge not by Mr Polevoy's own words, as one cannot from them come to any positive conclusion, but by the spirit in which the *History of the Russian People* is, in the main, written, by Mr Polevoy's efforts to preserve the rich colours of the past, and by his frequent borrowing from the chronicles. . . .

[1] Nikolai Alekseevich Polevoy (1796-1846) writer, journalist, critic. Editor of the *Moskovsky Telegraph* (1825-34). Pushkin took an interest in the *Moskovsky Telegraph* in 1826 (see p. 153) and contributed to it, but his relations with Polevoy subsequently cooled. Polevoy took up a 'bourgeois' position against what he called the literary aristocracy of Pushkin's circle and linked up with Bulgarin. See pages 260-1 for one of Pushkin's replies to criticism levelled against him by Polevoy's camp. However, Polevoy wrote to Pushkin on 1 January 1831, that he was Russia's 'one and only' poet. They did not meet after 1834 but Polevoy grieved bitterly at Pushkin's death.

These two articles on Polevoy's *History* were published in *Literaturnaya Gazeta* (1830), Nos. 4 and 12. Polevoy's *History* was directed against Karamzin's, which Pushkin very much admired; this caused Pushkin to rally to Karamzin's defence.

[2] French nineteenth-century historians.

170. Note in *Literaturnaya Gazeta*[1]

England is the motherland of caricature and parody. Every remarkable event provides occasion for a satirical drawing; every work which meets with success is subjected to parody. The art of imitating the style of famous writers has in England been brought to perfection. Walter Scott was once shown verses, supposedly written by him. 'I think these are my verses,' he said laughing, 'I have been writing so many for so long that I daren't disclaim even this nonsense!' I do not think that any of our famous writers could mistake a parody, such as were printed recently in one of the Moscow reviews,[2] for his own work. This type of jest demands rare flexibility of style; a good parodist has every style at his command, and ours has barely one. But actually we have one very successful example: Mr Polevoy very amusingly parodied Guizot and Thierry.[3]

[1] Published unsigned in Miscellany, *Literaturnaya Gazeta*, No. 12 (1830).
[2] Polevoy had published verse parodies of Pushkin and his circle in the *Moskovsky Telegraph*.
[3] In his *History of the Russian People*, see no. 169 above.

171. Of Vidocq's Memoirs[1]

In one of the issues of the *Literaturnaya Gazeta* there was mention of the *Memoirs of a Paris Executioner*;[2] the moral tracts of Vidocq, a police detective, are phenomena no less repulsive and no less intriguing.

Imagine a man without name or moorings, living day by day as an informer, married to one of those unfortunate people whom, because of his calling, he is obliged to have under surveillance; a thorough rogue, as shameless as he is vile; and then imagine, if you can, what sort of moral tracts a man like that can write.

In his memoirs Vidocq calls himself a patriot, un bon Français, as if Vidocq could ever have a fatherland! He insists that he did his military service[3] and that he not only has the permission, but in fact has been ordered to wear a variety of uniforms, and therefore struts about with the insignia of the Légion d'Honneur, arousing the indignation of such honest paupers as half-pay officers sitting out in cafés. He insolently boasts of his friendship with the illustrious dead who were in contact with him[4] (Who has not been young? And Vidocq is an obliging and practical man), he talks with extraordinary pomposity of good society, as if he could have an entrée to it, and passes stern strictures on famous writers, partly in the hope of earning their scorn, partly by design. Vidocq's judgements on Casimir Delavigne and on B. Constant will be intriguing by the very fact of their incongruity.

Who could have believed it? Vidocq is ambitious! He gets enraged reading the unfavourable comments of journalists on his style (the style of M. Vidocq!). He takes the opportunity of denouncing his *enemies*, accusing them of amoral behaviour and free-thinking, and argues (not in jest) of noble feelings and independent opinions: an irritability, ludicrous in any other scribbler, but comforting in Vidocq, as we see by it that human nature, in its vilest degradation, still retains reverence for concepts sacred to human kind.

An important question presents itself.

The works of Vidocq, the spy, of Sanson, the executioner, etc., do not shame either established religion, or the government, or even what is generally understood by morality; but at the same time one cannot but consider them an insult to public decency. Should not civic authority give serious attention to this new kind of temptation, which has slid by completely unnoticed by legislators?

---

¹ Published unsigned in Miscellany, *Literaturnaya Gazeta*, No. 20 (1830). Pushkin first offered the article to Pogodin for publication in the *Moskovsky Vestnik* but Pogodin was reluctant to publish it. Pushkin took the opportunity of writing on this book – written not by Vidocq himself but, like the *Memoirs of Sanson*, largely by L'Héritier – in order to represent Bulgarin in the role of Vidocq. The likeness was so accurately drawn that nobody could have any doubt as to whom Pushkin had in mind. Bulgarin had published a personal attack on Pushkin, thinly disguised as a French writer, in *Severnaya Pchela*, 11 March 1830, and in reply to this article of Pushkin's he launched out again, this time commenting on his Negro ancestry.

² See no. 165.

³ Bulgarin had served in the French army in 1812.

⁴ Pushkin had Griboedov in mind.

172. Draft letter to the Editor of the *Literaturnaya Gazeta*¹

Though giving full credit to your newspaper's good intentions and impartiality, I must admit that I could not agree with the opinions that it proclaims concerning criticism and polemics.

First, what do all these endless discussions on *politeness* mean? If the critics in our reviews offended only by being rude, there would not be much harm in that.

It has become usual among our writers, who have won the public's trust and respect, not to reply to criticism. It is rare for any of them to give voice, and if one does it will not be on his own account. This is a custom which is harmful to literature. Such 'anti-criticisms' would be doubly useful: in the correcting of faulty judgements and in the spreading of sound opinions concerning art. You will say that the larger part of literary criticism in periodicals consists of personalities and abuse, that the public is fairly indifferent to literary successes.

There will be those who will object that the attacker is sometimes so despicable that an honest man can on no account come into any contact with him without defiling himself. In that case explain yourself, apologize to the public. You have been subjected to abuse by Vidocq. Explain why you are not prepared to reply to him. . . .

[1] Pushkin is replying to Vyazemsky's article published in *Literaturnaya Gazeta*, No. 18 (1830), in which Vyazemsky expressed the view that it was not fitting for gentleman-writers to engage in disputes with ill-bred opponents. Pushkin did not agree with Vyazemsky – except in so far as it applied to publishing replies to criticism of his own works – and on several occasions returned to the discussion of the value of polemics in literary reviews.

173. Draft notes on criticism in general

Criticism is a science.

Criticism is the science of discovering the beauties and defects in works of art and literature. It is based (1) on an absolute knowledge of the rules by which the artist or the writer has been guided in his work, (2) on a study in depth of examples, and on the alert observation of contemporary phenomena.

I do not speak of disinterestedness – but anyone who is guided in his criticism by anything other than a pure love of art debases himself to the level of the mob, which is slavishly controlled by the lowest mercenary considerations.[1]

Where there is no love of art, there is no criticism. 'If you wish to become a connoisseur in the arts,' says Winckelmann, 'try to love the artist and seek for beauties in his works.'

Among us criticism is largely in the hands of journalists, i.e. entrepreneurs, people who know their own job but are not *critics* or even men of letters.

In other countries authors write either for the crowd or for a minority. [Footnote: who lovingly study the new work and pronounce a judgement on it, and in this way, without being subject to the public's verdict, the work acquires its due value and place in general estimation.] Here the latter is impossible, so one has to write for oneself.

[1] Pushkin felt strongly about a poet's need for absolute independence and personal integrity.

174. Draft prefaces to *Boris Godunov*[1]

I

Voici ma tragédie puisque vous la voulez absolument, mais avant que de la lire j'exige que vous parcouriez le dernier tome de Karamzine.[2] Elle est remplie de bonnes plaisainteries et d'allusions fines à l'histoire de ce temps-là, comme nos sous-œuvres de Kiov et de Kamenka.[3] Il faut les comprendre *sine qua non*.

A l'exemple de Shekspeare je me suis borné à développer une époque et des personnages historiques sans rechercher les effets théâtraux, le pathétique romanesque, etc. . . . le style en est mélangé. Il est trivial et bas là où j'ai été obligé de faire intervenir des personnages vulgaires et grossiers – quant aux grosses indécences, n'y faites pas attention: cela a été écrit au courant de la plume, et disparaîtra à la première copie. Une tragédie sans amour souriait à mon imagination. Mais outre que l'amour entrait beaucoup dans le caractère romanesque et passionné de mon aventurier, j'ai rendu Dmitri amoureux de Marina pour mieux faire ressortir l'étrange caractère de cette dernière. Il n'est encore qu'esquissé dans Karamzine. Mais certes c'était une drôle de jolie femme. Elle n'a eu qu'une passion et ce fut l'ambition, mais à un degré d'énergie, de rage qu'on a peine à se figurer. Après avoir goûté de la royauté, voyez-la, ivre d'une chimère, se prostituer d'aventuriers en aventuriers – partager tantôt le lit dégoûtant d'un juif, tantôt la tente d'un cosaque, toujours prête à se livrer à quiconque peut lui présenter la faible espérance d'un trône qui n'existait plus. Voyez-la braver la guerre, la misère, la honte, en même temps traiter avec le roi de Pologne de couronne à couronne et finir misérablement l'existence la plus orageuse et la plus extraordinaire. Je n'ai qu'une scène pour elle, mais j'y reviendrai, si Dieu me prête vie. Elle me trouble comme une passion. Elle est horriblement polonaise, comme le disait la cousine de Mme Lubomirska.

Gavrila Pushkin[4] est un de mes ancêtres, je l'ai peint tel que je l'ai trouvé dans l'histoire et dans les papiers de ma famille. Il a eu de grands talents, homme de guerre, homme de cour, homme de conspiration surtout. C'est lui et Pleshcheev qui ont assuré le succès du Samozvanets [the Pretender] par une audace inouïe. Après je l'ai retrouvé a Moscou, l'un des 7 chefs qui la défendaient en 1612, puis en 1616 dans la Duma siégeant à côté de Kozma Minine, puis *voevode* à Nizhni, puis parmi les députés qui couronnèrent Romanof, puis ambassadeur. Il a été tout, même incendiaire, comme le prouve une Gramota [Charter] que j'ai trouvée à Pogoreloye Gorodishche[5] – ville qu'il fit brûler (pour la punir de je ne sais quoi) à la mode des proconsuls de la Convention Nationale.

Je compte revenir aussi sur Shuisky.[6] Il montre dans l'histoire un singulier mélange d'audace, de souplesse et de force de caractère. Valet de Godounof, il est un des premiers Boyards à passer du côté de Dmitri. Il est le premier qui conspire et c'est lui-même, notez cela, qui se charge de retirer les marrons du feu, c'est lui-même qui vocifère, qui accuse, qui de chef devient enfant perdu. Il est prêt à perdre la tête, Dmitri lui fait grâce déjà sur l'échafaud, il l'exile, et avec cette générosité étourdie qui caractérisait cet aimable aventurier il le rappelle à sa cour, il le comble de biens et d'honneurs. Que fait Shuisky qui avait frisé de si près la hache et le billot? Il n'a rien de plus pressé que de conspirer de nouveau, de réussir, de se faire élire Tsar, de tomber et de garder dans sa chûte plus de dignité et de force d'âme qu'il n'en eut pendant toute sa vie.

Il y a beaucoup du Henri IV[7] dans Dmitri. Il est comme lui brave, généreux et gascon, comme lui indifférent à la religion – tous deux abjurant leur foi pour cause politique, tous deux aimant les plaisirs et la guerre, tous deux donnant dans des projets chimériques – tous deux en butte aux conspirations. . . . Mais Henri IV n'a pas à se reprocher Xenia – il est vrai que cette horrible accusation n'est pas prouvée et quant à moi je me fais une religion de ne pas y croire.

Griboyedov a critiqué le personnage de Job; le patriarche, il est vrai, était un homme de beaucoup d'esprit, j'en ai fait un sot par distraction.

En écrivant ma Godunov j'ai réfléchi sur la tragédie, et si je me mêlais de faire une préface, je ferais du scandale – c'est peut-être le genre le plus méconnu. On a tâché d'en baser les lois sur la vraisemblance, et c'est justement elle qu'exclut la nature du drame; sans parler déjà du temps, des lieux, etc., quel diable de vraisemblance y a-t-il dans une salle coupée en deux dont l'une est occupée par 2,000 personnes, censées n'être pas vues par celles qui sont sur les planches?

La langue. Par exemple le Philoctète de La Harpe dit en bon français après avoir entendu une tirade de Pyrrhus: 'Hélas, j'entends les doux sons de la langue grecque.'[8] Tout cela n'est-il pas d'une invraisemblance de convention? Les vrais génies de la tragédie ne se sont jamais souciés d'une autre vraisemblance que celle des caractères et des situations. Voyez comme Corneille a bravement mené le Cid: ha, vous voulez la règle des 24 heures? Soit. Et là-dessus il vous entasse des événements pour 4 mois. Rien de plus ridicule que les petits changements de règles reçues. Alfieri est profondément frappé du ridicule de l'*a parte*, il le supprime et là-dessus allonge le monologue. Quelle puérilité!

Ma lettre est bien plus longue que je ne l'avais voulu faire. Gardez-la, je vous prie, car j'en aurai besoin si le diable me tente de faire une préface.

II

My decision to place my work before the public is taken with aversion.

Although I was generally fairly indifferent to the success or failure of my work, yet I must confess that the failure of *Boris Godunov* would affect me, and that it will fail I am almost certain. As Montaigne, I can say of my work: c'est une œuvre de bonne foi.[9]

This tragedy which I wrote in strict isolation, removed from the chilling presence of society, the fruit of constant labour and of con-scientious study, has afforded me all the pleasure that an author is allowed: an occupation quickened by inspiration, an inner conviction that I was straining every nerve, and finally the approval of a [chosen] few.

My tragedy is already known to almost all those whose opinion I value. Among my audience only one was absent,[10] him to whom I owe the germ of my tragedy, whose genius animated and upheld me, whose encouragement seemed to me the sweetest of rewards and was my only solace in my solitary hours.

III

The study of Shakespeare, Karamzin, and our ancient chroniclers gave me the idea of presenting in dramatic form one of the most dramatic epochs of modern history. Untouched by any other influence I imitated Shakespeare's free and broad portrayal of characters, and his casual and simple delineation of types. I followed Karamzin's lucid unfolding of events and tried to glean from the chronicles both the mental outlook and language of those days. These are rich sources! I do not know whether I proved capable of using them. At least my labours were both zealous and conscientious.

For a long time I could not make up my mind to publish my play. Up till now my self-esteem was little disturbed by the good or ill success of my poems, or by the favourable or stern judgement of the journals concerning some verse-tale. It was not blinded by over-flattering reviews, and reading the most offensive criticism I tried to fathom the critic's point of view, to comprehend with the utmost sang-froid of what in fact he was accusing me. And if I never replied to any such, this arose not from disdain but solely from a conviction that il est indifférent for our literature whether a certain chapter of *Onegin* is better or worse than another. But I sincerely confess that I would be distressed by the ill success of my tragedy, as I am firmly convinced that the popular rules of Shakespearian drama are better suited to our stage than the courtly habits of the tragedies of Racine and that any unsuccessful experiment can slow down the reformation of our stage. (A. S. Khomiakov's *Ermak*[11] is a lyrical rather than a dramatic work. It owes its success to its splendid verse-style.)

Now to embark on a few personal explanations. The verse form I have used (iambic pentameter) has been generally accepted by the English and the Germans. I believe with us it was first used in *The Argonauts*;[12] A. Zhandr uses it extensively in the fragment of a splendid tragedy in free verse.[13] I have retained the caesura in the second foot as in the French pentameter and, I think, was mistaken in doing so, having thus voluntarily deprived my verse of its distinctive variety. There are some coarse jokes and scenes of low life. It's as well if a poet can avoid them – a poet should not voluntarily assume the mores of the market-place – but if he cannot, there is no need for him to try to replace them with something else.

Having discovered in the history of the period one of my ancestors playing an important part in this unhappy epoch, I brought him on to the stage con amore, having no thoughts for the finer points of decorum. Of all the things in which I imitated Byron, aristocratic pride was the most ludicrous. Our aristocracy consists of a newly created nobility; the old nobility has declined, its rights are brought down to the level of those of other ranks, the great estates have long since been broken up, destroyed. In the eyes of the sensible crowd there are no advantages attached to belonging to the old aristocracy, and a privately held respect for the glory of one's ancestors can only serve to draw on one accusations of eccentricity or of the pointless imitation of foreign ideas.

IV

My decision to place *Boris Godunov* before the public is taken with the greatest aversion. The success or failure of my tragedy will influence the reformation of our dramatic art. I am anxious that its own short-comings should not be ascribed to Romanticism in general and that it should not in this way slow down progress.

However, I am encouraged by the success of *Poltava*. . . .

V

Je me présente ayant renoncé ma manière première – n'ayant plus à allaiter un nom inconnu et une première jeunesse, je n'ose plus compter sur l'indulgence avec laquelle j'avais été accueilli. Ce n'est plus le sourire de la mode que je brigue. Je me retire volontairement du rang de ses favoris, en faisant mes humbles remerciements de la faveur avec laquelle elle avait accueilli mes faibles essais pendant dix ans de ma vie.

VI

Lorsque j'écrivais cette tragédie, j'étais seul à la campagne, ne voyant personne, ne lisant que les journaux, etc. – d'autant plus volontiers que j'ai toujours cru que le romantisme convenait seul à notre scène; je vois que j'étais dans l'erreur. J'éprouvais une grande répugnance à livrer au public ma tragédie, je voulais au moins la faire précéder d'une préface et la faire accompagner de notes. Mais je trouve tout cela fort inutile.

VII

Pour une préface.[14] Le public et la critique ayant accueilli avec une *indulgence passionnée* mes premiers essais et dans un temps où la sévérité et la malveillance m'eussent probablement dégoûté de la carrière que j'allais embrasser, je leur dois reconnaissance entière, et je les tiens quittes envers moi – leur rigueur et leur indifférence ayant maintenant peu d'influence sur mes travaux.

¹ The first draft preface to *Boris Godunov*, written in the form of a letter to N. N. Raevsky, is a revision of Pushkin's letter to Raevsky, no. 108, of July 1825, and is dated 30 January 1829. The other drafts were also written in the years 1829-30, when the decision to publish *Boris Godunov* was taken. Pushkin himself set off for Erzerum and left Pletnev and Zhukovsky in charge of all the necessary negotiations.

² Volume IX of Karamzin's History, the source of *Boris Godunov*.

³ The discussions among the southern Decembrists which Pushkin had heard while in exile.

⁴ He died in 1638.

⁵ In the province of Tver.

⁶ Pushkin planned to write a further play on Dmitri and Marina and also one on Prince Shuisky.

⁷ Henry of Navarre, the subject of Voltaire's *La Henriade* (1723).

⁸ In La Harpe's *Philoctète* (1783), Philoctète on meeting Pyrrhus says,

> Répondez, que je puisse entendre votre voix,
> Reconnoître des Grecs l'accent et le langage.

and Pyrrhus replies,

> Soyez donc satisfait: nous sommes Grecs.

To which Philoctète,

> Ô ciel!
> Après un si long tems d'un exil si cruel,
> Ô que cette parole à mon oreille est chère!

⁹ The opening words of the note to reader in Montaigne's *Essais* are: 'C'est ici un livre de bonne foi, lecteur.' See also Pushkin's letter to Benckendorff, no. 191.

¹⁰ Karamzin.

¹¹ First published in *Moskovsky Vestnik* in 1828, first separate edition in 1832.

¹² By Küchelbecker.

¹³ Only the first act of his tragedy *Wenceslas* was published in the almanac *Talia* in 1825. It was a transposition of a French play by Jean de Rotrou, *Venceslas* (1648). Pushkin omits to mention the earlier example of Russian blank verse, Zhukovsky's translation of Schiller's *Die Jungfrau von Orleans* (1821).

¹⁴ This last draft belongs to the second edition of *Boris Godunov*, which Pushkin planned to bring out in 1831.

175. Refutations to criticism

Being a Russian writer, I always considered it my duty to keep up my reading of current literature and always read with particular care all the criticism which my works had provoked. I honestly admit that praise affected me as a clear and, probably, sincere sign of goodwill and friendliness. I make bold to say that when reading the most hostile critiques I always tried to see my critic's point of view and to follow his arguments, without disputing them with an impatience born of self-love but rather wishing to agree with him in a complete self-abnegation of authorship. Unfortunately I noticed that more often than not we failed to understand each other. As regards the critical articles written with the sole aim of insulting me at whatever cost, I will only say that they made me very angry, at any rate while I read them, and that therefore their authors can rest satisfied having ascertained that their labours were not in vain. If in the course of sixteen years of authorship I never replied to a single review (not to mention abuse), the reason for that certainly did not lie in contempt.

The condition of criticism is itself indicative of the general level of literary culture. The analyses of the *Vestnik Evropy* and the judgements of the *Severnaya Pchela* satisfy us. We have no need as yet of Schlegels or even of La Harpes. To scorn criticism only because it is still in its infancy is to scorn a young literature because it has not yet matured. This would be unjust. But just as our literature can proudly place before Europe Karamzin's History, a few odes by Derzhavin, a few fables by Krylov, a paean on the year 1812,[1] a few flowers of northern elegiac poetry, so our criticism can show a few random articles, filled with lucid thought, profound opinions and significant wit. But they are isolated instances, appearing at intervals, and have not yet acquired either weight or permanent influence. Their time is not yet ripe.

Nor did I fail to answer my critics because I lacked the desire to do so, buoyancy or the spirit of pedantry; nor because I considered that these critics did not have any influence on the reading public. But I must admit I was ashamed to repeat elementary or commonplace truths in order to refute the critics, to discourse on grammar, rhetoric and the ABC, and – what is more difficult – to clear myself where there was no accusation, and to say proudly: 'Et moi, je vous soutiens que mes vers sont très bons';[2] or, through having nothing better to do, to stand trial before the public and attempt to amuse it (for which I haven't the slightest inclination). For example, one of my critics, who is by the way a kind and well-intentioned man, discussing, I think, *Poltava*, quoted some passages and instead of putting forward any criticisms affirmed that such verses were *poor recommendation*.[3] What could I reply to that?! And that's how most of the comrades behaved. Our critics usually say: this is good because it is excellent, and this is ugly because it is bad. And one can never lure them out of this position.

The final, and main, reason is laziness. I was never able to get sufficiently roused by obtuseness or dishonesty to take up my pen and embark on objections. Now, in the unbearable hours of incarceration in quarantine,[4] having with me neither books nor a friend, I thought to pass the time by writing replies to all the criticisms that I could remember, and my own observations on my works. I make bold to assure the reader (if God sends me one) that never in my life could I have thought of a more stupid occupation than this.

Ruslan and Lyudmila was on the whole favourably received. Apart from one article in the *Vestnik Evropy*,[5] in which it was very superficially criticized, and apart from some most pertinent *questions*[6] exposing the poem's structural weakness, I believe there was not a bad word said about it. Nobody even noticed that it is a frigid work. It was accused of being immoral because of a few voluptuous descriptions, some lines which I excluded from the second edition:

> O terrible sight! The feeble wizard
> Fondles with wrinkled hand . . .

the introduction to one of the cantos, I don't remember which:

> In vain you hid in the shadow, etc.

and the parody of the *Twelve Sleeping Beauties*. I deserved to be soundly rebuked for the last of these, for showing a lack of aesthetic sensibility. It was unforgivable (particularly at my age) for the pleasure of the mob to parody an example of primitive poetry. There were other rather shallow criticisms. Is there a single place in *Ruslan* which could be compared in the licence of its humour to the pranks of, for example, Ariosto, of whom I was constantly being reminded? Even the part I omitted was a very toned-down imitation of Ariosto (*Orlando*, Canto V, st. viii).

The Prisoner of the Caucasus – the first unsuccessful attempt at characterization, with which I coped with difficulty. It was received better than anything else I had written, thanks to certain elegiac and descriptive verses. But on the other hand Nikolai and Alexander Raevsky and I had a good laugh at it.

The Fountain of Bakhchisarai is weaker than *The Prisoner* and, like it, reflects the reading of Byron, on whom I was mad at the time. The

scene between Zarema and Maria has dramatic quality. I believe it
wasn't criticized. A. Raevsky roared with laughter at the following
lines:

> He often raises his sabre
> To fatal carnage – and having swung it up
> Remains suddenly motionless
> Gazes round wildly
> Grows pale . . .

Young writers in general are unable to describe the physical stress of
passion. Their heroes always shudder, laugh wildly, gnash their teeth,
etc. All of which is ludicrous, like a melodrama.

I can't remember who drew my attention to the fact that it is unlikely that the robbers could have swum across a river, being shackled
together. This entire incident is true and took place in 1820, while I
was in Ekaterinoslav.

For a long time our critics left me in peace. This does them credit:
my circumstances were far from favourable. Through habit they still
considered me to be a very young man. The first unfavourable articles,
I remember, began to appear on the publication of the fourth and
fifth chapters of *Evgeny Onegin*. The analysis of these chapters, published
in the *Ateney*, surprised me by their good tone, good style, and by
the curiously carping objections. The most rhetorical tropes and figures
arrested the critic's attention. . . .
The study of ancient songs, stories, etc., is essential for a thorough
knowledge of the distinctive qualities of the Russian language. Our
critics err in despising them. . . .

The daily speech of the common people (not reading foreign books
and, thank God, not expressing their ideas in French as we do) is also
worthy of the deepest research. Alfieri studied Italian in the markets
of Florence: it would be no bad thing if we occasionally listened to
the Muscovite women who bake sacramental bread. Their speech is
extraordinarily pure and correct.

The absence of certain stanzas has repeatedly provoked criticism.
There is nothing surprising in the fact that there are stanzas in *Evgeny
Onegin* which I either could not or would not print. But being omitted

they break the continuity of the story and so the places where they should have been found are indicated. It would have been better to have replaced these stanzas with others or to have spliced those that I have retained. But I confess that I am too lazy for that. I also humbly confess that there are two stanzas omitted in *Don Juan*.[7]

The sixth canto [of *Evgeny Onegin*] was not subjected to analysis, they even did not note the Latin misprint in the *Vestnik Evropy*. Incidentally, I have not opened a Latin book since I left the Lycée and I have completely forgotten my Latin. Life is short, there is no time to re-read books. Marvellous books come crowding in one after another, but nobody nowadays writes in Latin. On the other hand, for fourteen centuries the Latin language was essential and was rightly judged the first requisite of an educated man.

One lady remarked to me of *The Gipsies* that in the whole poem there is only one honest man, and that is the bear. The late Ryleev was disturbed by the fact that Aleko led the bear about and even passed round a hat for money from the gaping crowd. Vyazemsky echoed this criticism. (Ryleev asked me to make at least a smith of Aleko, as being more fitting.[8]) The best thing would have been to have made him an official of the eighth grade or a landowner, instead of making him a gipsy. In that case, it is true, the whole poem would not have existed: *ma tanto meglio.*

My tragedy will probably have no success.[9] The reviews are angry with me. I lack the chief attractions as far as the public is concerned, that of being young and a literary novelty. Furthermore, the main scenes have already been published or mangled in *imitations*.[10] Opening at random a historical novel by Bulgarin, I found that he makes Prince V. Shuisky announce the appearance of the Pretender to the Tsar. In my play, Boris Godunov speaks privately to Basmanov about the abolition of the order of precedence in rank, likewise in Mr Bulgarin's book. All these are dramatic fictions and not traditions handed down by history.

The spirit of the age calls for important changes in the theatre. Perhaps they will cheat the hopes of the reformers. The poet, *inhabiting the peaks of creativity*, perhaps sees more clearly both the shortcomings of legitimate demands and that which is hidden from the eyes of the restless mob, but it would be vain for him to take up the struggle. In this way Lope de Vega, Shakespeare and Racine surrendered themselves to the current, but a genius, whatever path he chooses to follow, remains a genius – the judgement of posterity will sift his gold from dross.

Count Nulin has caused me a lot of trouble.[11] It was found to be obscene, if you'll excuse the term: that is in the reviews, of course, not one of the journalists was ready to defend it; in society it was favourably received. A young man has the temerity to enter a young lady's bedroom at night and gets slapped in the face. What horror! How can one dare to write such disgusting filth? The author asks what the ladies of Petersburg would have done in Natalia Pavlovna's shoes? What insolence! Speaking of my poor tale (written, let it be said in passing, in an absolutely sober and seemly manner) all classical antiquity and all European literature was brought to bear against me! I can well believe in the prudery of my critics; I can well believe that *Count Nulin* strikes them as reprehensible. But how can one cite the Ancients when speaking of decency? And can it be that the authors of humorous tales – Ariosto, Boccaccio, La Fontaine, Casti, Spenser, Chaucer, Wieland, Byron – are known to them only by hearsay. Have they not at least read Bogdanovich and Dmitriev? What miserable pedant will dare to censure *Dushenka* for immorality and indecency? What grim fool will start pompously condemning *The Modern Wife*, that delightful example of a light and facetious tale? And Derzhavin's erotic poems – innocent, great Derzhavin? Setting aside inequality in poetic merit, *Count Nulin* must yield to them in the freedom and vivacity of the jokes.

These critics have found a curious method of assessing the level of morality in a given poem. One of them has a fifteen-year-old niece, another a fifteen-year-old friend, and whatever according to the judgement of the parents is not yet suitable for them to read is pronounced indecent, immoral, obscene, etc.! As if literature exists solely for sixteen-year-old girls! A sensible tutor will probably not hand either them or even their brothers the complete works of any classic poet, especially from among the ancients. That is what anthologies, selected passages, etc., are for. But the public is not a fifteen-year-old girl nor a thirteen-year-old boy. It can, thank God, read without any misgivings both tales by the worthy La Fontaine and an eclogue by the worthy Virgil, and all that the critics read themselves – if our critics read anything except the proofs of their reviews.

All these gentlemen, so sensitive on matters of decorum, remind one of Tartuffe, bashfully throwing a kerchief over Dorine's bared bosom, and deserve the servant-girl's amusing retort:

> Vous êtes donc bien tendre à la tentation,
> Et la chair sur vos sens fait grande impression?
> Certes, je ne sais pas quelle chaleur vous monte:
> Mais à convoiter, moi, je ne suis pas si prompte,
> Et je vous verrais nu du haut jusques en bas,
> Que toute votre peau ne me tenterait pas.
>
> (*Tartuffe*, Act III, sc. ii)

An immoral work is one of which the aim or the effect is the subversion of rules which form the basis of social well-being or the dignity of man. Poems whose aim is to heat the imagination by libidinous descriptions degrade poetry, transforming its divine nectar into an inflammatory potion and the Muse into a loathsome Canidia. But a jest, inspired by warm-hearted high spirits and a passing whim of the imagination, can seem immoral only to those who have a childish and blurred conception of morality, confusing it with moralizing and seeing literature solely as a pedagogic exercise.

Incidentally, I began writing at thirteen and publishing almost at the same time. There is much I would like to destroy as unworthy even of my ability, whatever that might be. Other things weigh on my conscience like a rebuke. At any rate I should not be responsible for the reprinting of the sins of my youth, and more especially for the follies of others. . . .

---

[1] Zhukovsky's 'Minstrel in the Russian camp'.
[2] 'Et moi, je vous soutiens que mes vers sont fort bons', Molière, *Le Misanthrope*, Act I, scene ii.
[3] This was said by S. Raich, writing on *Evgeny Onegin*, ch. VII in *Galatea*, No. 14 (1830).
[4] In the beginning of October 1830 Boldino was surrounded by outbreaks of cholera and Pushkin could not leave the village, see pages 190 ff.
[5] *Vestnik Evropy*, No. 11 (1820).
[6] Article in *Syn Otechestva*, No. 38 (1820), which consisted of a series of questions drawing attention to the poem's shortcomings.
[7] In certain sections of *Evgeny Onegin* censorship cuts have played havoc with the text. For example, in Canto I stanzas ix, xiii, xiv, and xxxix-xli are omitted, Canto IV starts with stanza vii, and so on. Pushkin's suggestion that perhaps he was secretly imitating Byron is characteristic of his self-

depreciatory humour. His alternative explanation that he was too lazy to rewrite or replace anything is in line with his dislike of copying out his poems for his friends: he clearly disliked going back over his traces.

8 Ryleev wrote this in a letter to Pushkin in April 1825; Vyazemsky in a review of *The Gipsies* in *Moskovsky Telegraph*, No. 10 (1827).

9 This and the following comment are, in the 1936 Academia edition of Pushkin's works, included with the draft prefaces to *Boris Godunov*. They were both first published in *Russkaya Starina*, No. 12 (1884).

10 Pushkin noticed plagiarisms in Bulgarin's *Dimitri Samozvanets* (1830). It is thought that it was Bulgarin who wrote the censorship report on *Boris Godunov* for the Tsar in 1826.

11 Written in answer to Nadezhdin's review in *Vestnik Evropy*, No. 3 (1829). (On *Count Nulin* see also no. 182.)

176. Notes on *Poltava*[1]

Habent sua fata libelli. *Poltava* had no success. Probably it did not deserve any, but I had been spoilt by the reception which my previous, far weaker works had met with. Furthermore it is a completely original work, which is what we are struggling for.

Our critics took it upon themselves to explain to me the reasons for my lack of success – and this is how they did it.[2]

They first informed me that it had never been heard of that a woman should fall in love with an old man, and that therefore Maria could not have loved the aged Hetman (NB although this is historically proved).

'Well come now, come now, Cheston; though I know, I don't believe.'[3] I could not be satisfied with this explanation: love is the most wilful of passions, not to mention the ugliness and folly which is daily preferred to youth, brains and beauty. Think of the legends of mythology, Ovid's metamorphoses, Leda, Philyra, Pasiphae, Pygmalion, and admit that all these stories are not foreign to poetry. And Othello, an old Negro, captivating Desdemona with tales of his wanderings and battles? And Mirra, inspiring the Italian poet to write one of the best of his tragedies?[4]

People have said to me that Maria . . . was led on by vanity and not by love: what an honour for the daughter of a Judge to be a Hetman's mistress! Furthermore people have said that my Mazeppa is *a cruel and stupid gaffer*. I confess that I showed Mazeppa to be cruel; I don't find him kind, especially at the moment when he busies himself over the execution of the father of the young girl he has seduced. On the other hand, a man's stupidity makes itself felt either in his actions or in his words: in my poem Mazeppa acts exactly as he did in history, and his speeches explain his historical character. People have pointed out that my Mazeppa is too rancorous, that a Ukrainian Hetman is not a student and would not wish to revenge himself for a slap in the face or for the tweaking of his moustache. Again historical fact is denied by literary criticism – again 'though I know, I don't believe'! Mazeppa, brought up in a Europe in which ideas on the honour of a gentleman were at their height, could long have remembered the slight he had received at the hands of the Tsar of Moscow and have repaid him when the occasion arose. His whole character is contained in this trait: secretive, harsh, unswerving. To tweak the moustache of a Pole or a Cossack was like pulling a Russian's beard. I recollect that Khmelnitsky for all the slights he had received at the hands of Chaplinsky was granted, by a judgement of the Cossack administration, his enemy's cut-off moustache by way of retribution (see Konissky's Chronicle).[5]

In my poem the old Hetman, foreseeing disaster, when alone with his confidant, blames the young Charles and calls him, I seem to remember, a naughty lad and a madcap: the critics pompously rebuked *me* for a superficial evaluation of the King of Sweden. I say somewhere that Mazeppa was attached to no one: the critics referred to the Hetman's *own words*, assuring Maria that he loves her *more than fame and more than power*. How can one answer such criticisms?

The words *moustache, to squeal, get up, Mazeppa, oh ho, it's time*, struck the critics as *low* expressions appropriate to boatmen. What can one do!

In the *Vestnik Evropy* they noted that the title of the poem is a mistaken one, and that I probably did not call it 'Mazeppa' so as not to remind people of Byron. A fair comment, but there was also another reason: an epigraph. Similarily *The Fountain of Bakhchisarai* was, in manuscript, called 'The Harem', but the melancholy epigraph (which of course is better than the whole poem) tempted me.

Incidentally, talking of *Poltava*, the critics also mentioned Byron's *Mazeppa*; but what did they make of it! Byron knew Mazeppa only from Voltaire's *History of Charles XII*. He was struck only by the picture of a man tied to a wild horse galloping across the steppes. It is, of course, a poetic conception, and besides see what he has made of it. But do not look here either for Mazeppa, or for Charles, or for that sombre, hateful, tormenting character who appears in almost all Byron's works, but who (unhappily for one of my critics) is absent precisely in *Mazeppa*.

Byron did not even think of him: he presented a series of pictures, each more striking than the last – that is all. But what a burning creation! What a wide-sweeping and rapid brush! Had the story of the seduced daughter and the executed father fallen to his pen then, probably, no one after him would have dared to touch this terrible subject.

Having read the following lines in *Voynarovsky*[6] for the first time:

> The wife of the martyr Kochubey
> And their seduced daughter

I was amazed how a poet could pass by such a fearful event. It is neither clever nor magnanimous to burden historical characters with fictitious horrors. Slanders, even in poems, have always struck me as unpraiseworthy. But in the description of Mazeppa it was unforgivable to omit such a striking historical trait. Nevertheless, what a hideous subject! Not one redeeming feature! Enticement, enmity, treachery, cunning, cowardice, violence . . . Delvig was amazed that I could embark on such a subject. Strong characters and a deep tragic shadow cast over all these horrors, that is what captivated me. I wrote *Poltava* in a few days,[7] I could not have worked on it longer and would have dropped it all.[8]

[1] The first, and longer, of these notes was published in *Dennitsa* (1831). In manuscript this note began with the words: 'The most mature of all my poetic tales is that in which almost everything is original . . . *Poltava*, which Zhukovsky, Gnedich, Delvig, and Vyazemsky preferred to all the others previously written by me. And *Poltava* was not a success.'

[1] Bulgarin in *Syn Otechestva*, Nos. 15 and 16 (1829); Nadezhdin in *Vestnik Evropy*.

[3] From Ya. Knyazhnin's comedy *The Boaster* (1786).

[4] Alfieri, *Mirra* (1791).

[5] Khmelnitsky, a Ukrainian Hetman of the seventeenth century. Chaplinsky was a Pole who slighted Khmelnitsky and as a result had one of his moustaches cut off. G. Konissky (1717-95), Archibishop of Mohilev and Belorussia.

[6] By Ryleev.

[7] See page 186.

[8] In the ninth issue of the *Sovremennik* (1838), Pletnev published a translation of Byron's *Mazeppa* together with a letter he had had from Pushkin in October 1829, which is very close indeed to the text of these two notes, for which it might have served as a draft.

177. An attempt to reply to some non-literary accusations[1]

Averse from controversy as I am, both by principle and inclination, I make no profession of non-resistance.

(Southey)[2]

One of our leading writers was asked why he never replied to criticism. He replied: the critics never understand me, nor do I understand them. If we are going to be judged in front of the public it will probably not understand us either. This reminds one of an old epigram:

> Un sourd fit un sourd ajourner,
> Devant un sourd en un village,
> Et puis s'en vint haut étonner
> Qu'il avoit volé son fromage;
> L'Autre répond du labourage.
> Le Juge étant sur ce suspens,
> Déclara bon le mariage,
> Et les renvoya sans dépens.[3]

One can *fail to answer one's critics* (as the Editor of the *History of the Russian People* pronounces in a lordly fashion)[4] when the attacks are of a purely literary nature and serve only to harm the sales of the criticized book. But out of self-respect one should not, on account of laziness or good-nature, allow personal insults or slanders – unfortunately too common of late – to pass unnoticed. The public does not merit such want of respect.

If in the course of sixteen years of authorship I never replied to a single review (not to mention abuse), the reason for that certainly did not lie in contempt.

The condition of criticism is itself indicative of the general level of literary culture. If the judgements of our reviews satisfy us, it proves that we have no need as yet of Schlegels or even of La Harpes. To scorn the critics is to scorn the public (which God forbid). Just as our literature can proudly place before Europe Karamzin's History, a few odes, a few fables, a paean on the year 1812,[5] a translation of the *Iliad*,[6] a few flowers of elegiac poetry; so our criticism can show a few random articles, filled with lucid thought and arrogant wit. But they are isolated instances, appearing at intervals, and have not yet acquired either weight or permanent influence. Their time is not yet ripe.

Nor did I fail to answer my critics on account of any lack on my part either of buoyant spirits or of pedantry; nor because I considered that these critics did not have any influence on the reading public. I noticed that the most groundless judgement, the most stupid abuse, gains weight from the magic influence of print. We still *cling to the sanctity of the printed word.*[7] We still think: how can this be stupid or unfair, after all it has been published! But I must admit I was ashamed to stand trial before the public and to try to laugh it to scorn (for which I have not the least inclination). I was ashamed to repeat elementary or commonplace truths in order to refute the critics, to discourse on the ABC and on rhetoric, to clear myself where there was no accusation, and – what is most difficult – to say proudly: 'Et moi, je vous soutiens que mes vers sont très bons.'[8]

As it is usual for our critics to say: this is good because it is excellent, and this is ugly because it is bad. And one can never lure them out of this position.

The final, and main, reason is laziness. I was never able to get sufficiently roused by obtuseness or dishonesty to take up my pen and embark on objections and proofs. Now, in the unbearable hours of incarceration in quarantine, having with me neither books nor a friend, I thought to pass the time by writing replies not to reviews (that I simply can't make up my mind to do) but to accusations of a non-literary character, which are at present much in fashion. I can assure the reader (if God sends me one) that never in my life could I have thought of a more stupid occupation than this.

[1] In this article Pushkin rewrote his previous 'Refutations to criticism' (no. 175). He originally intended also to include his comments on *Count Nulin* (see page 255) and on Vidocq (see no. 171). He began to write it on 2 October 1830. See also his letters to Delvig (no. 201) and to Vyazemsky (no. 202).

[2] R. Southey to the Editor of the *Courier*, Keswick, 5 January 1822.

[3] Pushkin freely translates this epigram by Pelisson from *Bibliothèque poëtique ou Nouveaux Choix des plus belles pièces de vers*, vol. II (Paris, 1745).

[4] N. Polevoy in *Moskovsky Telegraph*, No. 9 (1830).

[5] Zhukovsky's 'Minstrel in the camp of Russian warriors'.

[6] By Gnedich.

[7] From I. Dmitriev's satire *A Stranger's Talk* (1794).

[8] From *Le Misanthrope*, Act I, scene ii, by Molière, spoken by Oronte: 'Et moi je vous soutiens, que mes vers sont fort bons'.

178. Of Alfred de Musset

While the harmonious but monotonous Lamartine was preparing some new pious *Méditations* under the well-deserved title of *Harmonies* [*poétiques et*] *religieuses,* while the haughty Victor Hugo was publishing his brilliant but pretentious *Les Orientales,* while the poor sceptic Delorme was resurrecting himself in the form of a regenerate neophyte,[1] and a strict morality and decorum was proclaimed by edict throughout the whole of French literature, there suddenly appeared a young poet with a small volume of tales and songs,[2] who created a great sensation. It seems Musset committed himself to singing only of mortal sins, murder and adultery. The voluptuous images which fill his poems perhaps surpass in their vivid quality the most revealing descriptions by the late Parny. He hasn't a thought for morality, mocks at moralizing, and, unfortunately, most charmingly shows the least possible respect for the haughty alexandrine, breaking it up and turning it topsy-turvy in a manner both pitiful and terrible to behold. He sings of the moon in verses[3] such as only a poet of the blessed sixteenth century would have dared to write, before the existence of Boileau and La Harpe, Hoffman and Colnet.[4] How then was the young rogue received? One trembles for him. One can in one's mind's eye see the indignation of the reviews and all the ferules raised against him. Nothing of the sort. The candid prank of the charming rascal was so astonishing and so pleasing that the critics not only did not abuse him but even took it upon themselves to excuse him, announcing that the *Spanish Tales* prove nothing, that it is possible to describe brigands and murderers, even without aiming to explain how unpraiseworthy these professions are – and to remain at the same time a good and honest man; that vivid images of carnal pleasure are pardonable in a twenty-year-old poet; that, probably, his family reading his poems will not come to share the press's horror or see him as a monster; that, in short, poetry is a fiction and has nothing in common with the prose of real life. Thank God! It's high time. Would it not be odd in the nineteenth century to resurrect the formality, starchiness and hypocrisy ridiculed in his day by Molière, and to treat the public in the way grown-ups treat children, not allowing them to read books which they enjoy themselves, and tacking on moral precepts to any trifle, in and out of season. The public finds this laughable and will surely not say thank you to her guardians.

As we have already said, the Italian and Spanish tales are outstanding on account of their extraordinary vivacity. Of them 'Porcia', I believe, has the most merit: the scene of the nocturnal assignation; the picture of the jealous man, whose hair turns grey in an instant; the two lovers' conversation at sea – all that is delightful. The dramatic sketch 'Les marrons du feu' holds out the promise of a Romantic dramatist for

France. And in the tale 'Mardoche', Musset is the first French poet to catch the tone of Byron's frivolous works, which is no laughing matter in itself. If we interpret Horace's words as the English poet understood them, we will agree with his opinion: it is difficult to describe ordinary subjects well.

NB in the epigraph to *Don Juan* –

Difficile est proprie communia dicere[5] – 'Communia' does not mean ordinary objects, but those *common to all*. (He is speaking of the subjects of tragedy known to all, common property, as opposed to invented subjects. See *ad Pisones* (*Ars Poetica*).) The subject of *Don Juan* belongs exclusively to Byron.

[1] In 1829 Sainte-Beuve brought out the work of a supposedly dead poet, Joseph Delorme, the *Vie, poésies et pensées de Joseph Delorme* and in 1830 he published, again anonymously, another collection of poems *Les Consolations*. See no. 205.

[2] Alfred de Musset's first collection of poems and dramatic scenes *Contes d'Espagne et d'Italie* (1830).

[3] In 'Ballade à la Lune'.

[4] François-Benoît Hoffman and C. J. M. de Colnet du Ravel, French critics.

[5] Byron's epigraph to *Don Juan* taken from Horace's *Ars Poetica*, line 128. Byron also wrote of this line in *Hints from Horace*, lines 183-90.

179. Notes on popular drama and on M. P. Pogodin's *Martha, the Governor's Wife*[1]

Dramatic art was born in the public square – for the entertainment of the people. What do people like, what astonishes them? What language do they understand?

From the public squares and fairs (the freedom of the Mysteries) Racine transports it to the courtyard. How did it make its first appearance?

(Corneille, a Spanish poet.[2])

Sumarokov, Ozerov – (Katenin).

Shakespeare, Goethe – his influence on the contemporary French stage, on us.

The blessed ignorance of the critics, derided by Vyazemsky; they gave verbal assent and recognition to Romanticism, but in fact not only do not keep to it, but even attack it in a childish fashion.

What is worked out in a tragedy? What is its aim? Man and the people. The fate of Man, the fate of the people. That is why Racine is great, despite the confined form of his tragedy. That is why Shakespeare is great, despite his unevenness, his carelessness, and ugliness of finish.

What is necessary to a dramatist? A philosophy, impartiality, the political acumen of an historian, insight, a lively imagination. No prejudices or preconceived ideas. *Freedom.*

A faulty notion of poetry in general and of dramatic poetry in particular. What is the aim of drama? What is drama? How did it develop?

Though there has been so much clarification and widening of scope in the field of aesthetics since the days of Kant and Lessing, we still hold to the notions of the ponderous pedant Gottsched;[3] we still repeat that the *beautiful* consists in the imitation of the beauties of nature and that the chief merit of art lies in its *usefulness.* Why then do we like painted statuary less than those in plain marble and bronze? Why does a poet prefer to express his ideas in verse? And wherein lies the usefulness of Titian's Venus or the Apollo Belvedere?

Verisimilitude is still considered to be the principal condition of dramatic art and to form its basis. What if it were proved to us that it is precisely verisimilitude which is excluded by the very essence of dramatic art? Reading a poem or a novel, we can often lose ourselves in the thought that the events described are fact and not fiction. Reading an ode or an elegy, we can think that the poet portrayed his real feelings in actual circumstances. But wherein lies the verisimilitude in a building, divided into two parts, of which one is filled with spectators? . . .

If we will understand verisimilitude as something strictly observed in the costumes, and in period and local colour, we shall see here as well that the greatest dramatists did not submit to this rule. Shakespeare's Roman lictors retain the customs of London Aldermen. Calderón's brave Coriolano challenges the consul to a duel and throws down his gage. In Racine, the semi-Scythian Hippolyte speaks the language of a young, well-brought-up Marquis. Corneille's Romans are either Spanish knights or Gascon barons. And Corneille's Clytemnaestra[4] is escorted by a Swiss Guard. And in spite of all this, Calderón, Shakespeare and Racine stand on unattainable heights, and their works form the constant object of our study and admiration.

What kind of verisimilitude then are we to demand of a dramatist?

264

In order to answer this question let us first see what drama is and what is its aim.

Drama was born in the square and was a form of popular entertainment. The people, just as children do, demand diversion and action. The play appears to them as an extraordinary and strange adventure. The people demand strong sensations, for them even executions are spectacles. Laughter, pity and fear are the three chords of our imagination shaken by the magic of drama. But laughter soon grows weak, and it is impossible to base a complete dramatic action on this alone. The ancient dramatists paid little regard to this mainspring.

Popular satire monopolized it completely and it acquired dramatic form as something more closely connected to parody. In this way comedy was born, which in time became perfected. Let us note that high comedy is not based solely on laughter, but on the development of character, and that it frequently approaches tragedy.

Tragedy usually presented grievous crimes, superhuman suffering, even physical suffering (for example, Philoctetes, Oedipus, Lear). But habit blunts the senses – the imagination grows accustomed to murders and executions, and comes to look on them with indifference, whereas the presentation of passions and of the outpourings of the human spirit are always new, always intriguing, lofty and instructive. Drama began to rule over the passions and the soul of man.

The truth concerning the passions, a verisimilitude in the feelings experienced in given situations – that is what our intelligence demands of a dramatist.

Drama left the square and at the demand of a cultivated and select society transferred to the palace. The poets moved to the court. But in fact drama remains true to its original purpose – that of working on the crowd and satisfying its curiosity. What can attract the attention of an educated and enlightened spectator more than a representation of the great events of state. That is why history is brought into the theatre and kings and their peoples are brought before us by the dramatic poet.

In the palace drama changed; its voice was lowered. It no longer stood in need of screams. Having shed the mask of exaggeration which, imperative to a public square, is superfluous in a room, it became simpler, more natural. More refined feelings no longer demanded powerful shocks. It ceased to represent revolting sufferings, it grew unused to horrors, and gradually grew decorous and grand.

Therein lies the important difference between Shakespearian popular

265

tragedy and court drama of Racine. The author of popular drama was more educated than his audience; he knew that, and presented them with his freely conceived works in the assurance of his own superiority, which the public acknowledged. It was an unspoken understanding.

At court, on the contrary, the poet felt himself to be inferior to his public. His audience was more educated than he, at least both he and they thought so. He did not give free and bold play to his imagination. He tried to guess the demands of the refined taste of people who belonged to a class to which he was a stranger. He feared to humiliate some high official, or insult some of the haughty members of his audience – from which sprung timid primness, ludicrous pomposity – finding expression in the proverb (un héros, un roi de comédie), and the habit of regarding the members of the highest class with a kind of fawning servility and of attributing to them a curious, inhuman manner of expressing themselves. Racine's Nero (for example) will not simply say, 'je serai caché dans ce cabinet' – but 'Caché près de ces lieux je vous verrai, Madame.'[5] Agamemnon, waking his confidant, says to him: 'Oui, c'est Agamemnon . . .'[6]

We have got used to this, and it seems to us that's how things should be. But one must confess that in Shakespeare's tragedies if the heroes speak like stable-boys it does not strike us as strange,[7] as we feel that even the illustrious must speak of simple things as simple men.

[Not in 1949 Academy edition:
Drama abandoned common speech and adopted a select and refined dialect.]

I neither intend nor dare to define the advantages and the disadvantages of one or other kind of tragedy – to dwell on the fundamental differences between the systems of Racine and Shakespeare, Calderón and Goethe. But rather hasten to survey the history of dramatic art in Russia.

Among us drama was never a popular need. Dimitri of Rostov's Mystery plays and the tragedies of Tsarina Sophia Alexeyevna were performed at court and in the halls of the chief boyars and were occasional feasts rather than regular entertainments. The first companies to appear in Russia did not attract the crowd, which neither understood dramatic art nor was used to its conventions. Sumarokov appeared, the most unfortunate of imitators. His tragedies, crammed with nonsense, written in a barbarously debased form of speech, were liked by

Elizabeth's court, as imitations of Parisian entertainments. These limp, frigid works could have no influence whatsoever on popular taste. [Not in 1949 Academy edition: The theatre remained a field foreign to our way of life.] Ozerov felt this. He tried to give us a national tragedy – and imagined that for this it would suffice to choose a subject from national history,[8] forgetting that France's poet[9] took all his subjects from Roman, Greek and Hebrew history, and that Shakespeare's most popular tragedies are derived from Italian novelle.

Even after *Dmitri Donskoy*,[10] and after *Pozharsky*,[11] the work of an immature talent, we still had no tragedy. Katenin's *Andromache* (perhaps our Melpomene's best work on account of the force of genuine feeling in it and its truly tragic spirit) did not, however, rouse the stage, which had remained empty since Semenova's death, from its slumbers.

Yermak,[12] an idealized and lyrical product of an ardent, youthful imagination, is not a dramatic work. Everything about it is foreign to our customs and our spirit, everything, even the very enchantment and beauty of the poetry.

Comedy was more fortunate. We have two dramatic satires.[13]

Why then have we no popular tragedy? It would do no harm to decide whether one could exist. We saw that popular tragedy was born in the market-place, took shape, and only then was summoned into aristocratic society. With us the process would have been reversed. We would have wanted Sumarokov's courtly tragedy to descend to the public square – but over what obstacles! Could our tragedy, modelled on Racine's tragedies, shed its aristocratic habits? How could it pass from its measured, haughty and decorous dialogue to the rude frankness of popular passion, to the free judgements of the market-place? How could it suddenly shed its servile tone; how could it manage without the rules to which it is accustomed, that forced adaptation of everything Russian to everything European? Where would it learn the dialect which is understood by the people? What are the passions of this people, of what nature are the sinews of its heart? Where will it find an echo? In short, where are the spectators, where is the public?

Instead of the public it will meet the same small, confined circle – and will offend its supercilious habits (dédaigneux) and it will meet with petty and captious criticism, instead of understanding, response and applause. Insurmountable obstacles will rise up in its path – and

267

in order to set up its stage it will have to change and overthrow the customs, manners and ideas of centuries. . . .

However, there is before us an attempt at writing popular tragedy.

Before we start to assess *Martha, the Governor's Wife* let us thank the anonymous author[14] for the conscientiousness with which he has done his work, a guarantee of real talent. He wrote his tragedy moved not by considerations of self-love, eager for pursuing success, nor in order to please the general public, who are not only unprepared for Romantic tragedy but are positively hostile to it (not to mention the reviews, whose pronouncements have a decisive influence not only on the public but even on writers, who though they may make light of them none the less fear to be mocked and abused in print). He wrote his tragedy as a result of a deep inner conviction, having given himself over completely to independent inspiration, isolating himself in his work. In the present state of our literature nothing which is truly worthy of attention can be created without such self-denial.

The author of *Martha, the Governor's Wife* aimed at unfolding an important historical event: the fall of Novgorod, which decided the unification of Russia under single rule. History presented him with two great figures: the first Ivan, already delineated by Karamzin in all his terrible and icy grandeur, the second Novgorod, whose features had to be guessed at.

The dramatic poet – impartial as Fate – had to depict, as sincerely and profoundly as a thorough investigation of the truth combined with the liveliness of a youthful, fiery imagination would allow, the suppression of dwindling freedom as a carefully planned blow, which established Russia on its broad foundation. He had to avoid dodging the issue and, in leaning to one side, sacrificing the other. Neither he himself, nor his political opinions, nor his secret or open prejudices, were to find expression in his tragedy – but only the people of the past, their minds, their prejudices. It is not his business to excuse, condemn, or prompt. It is his business to resurrect a past age in all its truth. Did the author of *Martha, the Governor's Wife* fulfil these primary and essential conditions?

We reply: he did – and if not fully, then he was betrayed not by his desires, nor by his convictions, nor by his conscience, but by human nature itself, which is always imperfect.

268

[There follows a close analysis of Pogodin's characterization of Ivan the Terrible.]

1 An incomplete article, written in the autumn of 1830. Not published in Pushkin's lifetime. It reflects Pushkin's reading of Guizot's life of Shakespeare, which formed the introduction to the French translation of Shakespeare's works by Letourneur (Paris, 1821) that Pushkin used while working on *Boris Godunov*, and of A. W. Schlegel's *Über dramatische Kunst und Literatur* (1809-11).

2 Pushkin is alluding to Corneille's predilection for the Spanish dramatists and to his use of themes taken from Spanish plays.

3 Johann Christoph Gottsched (1700-66) introduced the neo-classicism of Boileau into German literature in his *Versuch einer critischen Dichtkunst für die Deutschen* (1730).

4 Clytemnaestra does not appear in any play by Corneille. Pushkin must have had Racine's *Iphigénie* in mind, in which in Act V Clytemnaestra enters under guard. The reference to 'Swiss Guards' probably refers to the Renaissance costume in which the play was produced.

5 *Britannicus*, Act II, scene iii.

6 Opening words of *Iphigénie*.

7 See also 'Of Walter Scott's novels', no. 184.

8 Pushkin had a low opinion of both Sumarokov and Ozerov.

9 Racine.

10 By Ozerov.

11 *Pozharsky, or the Liberation of Moscow*, by M. Kryukovsky (1807).

12 By A. S. Khomiakov. Single scenes were published between 1828 and 1830, the whole play in 1832.

13 *The Adolescent* by Fonvizin and *Woe from Wit* by Griboedov.

14 It was intended that this play, written according to the dramatic principles recommended by Pushkin – in blank iambic pentameters, untrammelled by the Unities, attempting to capture the language of the common people, and with the crowd playing a central role, should be published anonymously. It did not in fact appear till 1832. In May 1830 Pogodin read the first act aloud to Pushkin and he gave him the manuscript of the rest, which Pushkin read in the autumn in Boldino. In writing these notes on it Pushkin returned to the ideas on drama which had preoccupied him when drafting his prefaces to *Boris Godunov* (see no. 174). Pushkin continued to show an interest in the play and spoke on its behalf to Benckendorff.

180. Baratynsky[1]

Baratynsky is one of our outstanding poets. He is unique in that he thinks. He would stand out as being original everywhere as he reasons along his own lines, justly and independently, and at the same time has strong and deep feelings. The harmony of his verses, the freshness of his style, the liveliness and accuracy of his locutions, must astonish anyone having the least measure of taste and sensibility. Apart from charming elegies and minor poems, which everyone knows by heart and which are so continually and unsuccessfully imitated, Baratynsky has written two tales[2] which would have won him fame in Europe but which here were noticed only by experts. The verses Baratynsky wrote in his early youth were at one time received with rapture. The recent, more mature pieces, which approach nearer to perfection, had less success with the public. Let us try to explain the reasons. The first cause must lie in the very perfection and maturity of his work. The understanding and feelings of the eighteen-year-old poet are still closely akin to those of any man, and young readers understand him and, with delight, recognize in his works their own feelings and thoughts expressed in a clear, vivid and harmonious manner. . . . But years go by – the young poet matures, his talent grows, his understanding grows deeper, his feelings alter. His songs are no longer the same, but the readers remain the same, except that their hearts may have grown colder and less responsive to the poetry of life. The poet grows apart from them and gradually isolates himself completely. He creates for himself and if he occasionally publishes his work he meets with coolness and with neglect and finds an echo to his words only in the hearts of a few poetry lovers, who are astray in the world and, like him, live in isolation.[3] The second reason lies in the absence of criticism and of a standard of taste. There is no popular demand for literature among us. Writers acquire fame through extraneous circumstances – the public is little concerned with them – the body of readers is limited – and it is ruled by the reviews which judge of literature as of political economy and of political economy as of music, that is by hit-and-miss methods, by hear-say, following no fundamental principles or knowledge, and mostly according to personal consideration. Being the object of their disfavour, Baratynsky never defended himself, did not reply to a single article in the reviews. It is true that it is rather difficult to defend oneself where there has been no direct accusation, and on the other hand it is rather easy to despise childish malice and vulgar mockery – but none the less their judgements have a decisive influence.

The third reason – Baratynsky's epigrams. These masterly, model epigrams did not spare the rulers of the Russian Parnassus. Our poet not only failed to descend to polemics in the journals and did not once combat with our Aristarchuses, in spite of the unusual force of his power of dialectic, but he could not resist occasionally expressing his opinion in these little satires which are so amusing and scathing. We dare not rebuke him on their account. It would be too sad if they did not exist. [Pushkin's footnote: An epigram, defined by the legislators of French poetics as 'un bon mot de deux rimes orné',[4] is effective at the first minute, as any pointed remark, but dates quickly and loses all its force through repetition. The opposite is true of Baratynsky's epigrams. The satirical idea takes on either a fanciful or a dramatic form and develops more freely and more forcefully. Having smiled at it as a witticism, we then re-read it with pleasure as a work of art.]

This unconcern as to the fate of his works, this unchanging indifference to success and praise, not only as far as journalists were concerned but also in the public's attitude, are very remarkable. He never tried to pander cravenly to the prevailing taste of the time and to the demands of passing fashion, he never resorted to charlatanism, 'exagération', for creating a striking effect, he never neglected to make those thankless efforts which are rarely remarked on, efforts concerned with finish and precision, he never trailed in the steps of the Spirit of the Age, gleaning his scattered ears of wheat: he went his own way, independent and alone. It is time for him to take his rightful place and stand next to Zhukovsky and above the singer of the Penates and the Tauride.[5]

Re-read his *Eda* (which our critics found to be *worthless*[6] because, like children, they demand that a poem should have incident), re-read this simple, entrancing tale, and you will see with what depth of feeling the development of a woman's love is traced in it. . . .

---

[1] Not published in Pushkin's lifetime. Written in Boldino in October/November of 1830 and probably intended for the *Literaturnaya Gazeta*.

[2] *Eda, a Finnish tale* (1826) and *The Ball, a tale in verse* (1828).

[3] Baratynsky, writing to Pushkin (end of February/beginning of March 1828) on the criticism being levelled against *Evgeny Onegin*, Chapters IV and V, said that the public could not appreciate the splendid poetic simplicity of his design, which seemed to them to indicate paucity of invention, and that they failed to notice that in the poem 'old and new Russia, life in all its changes, passes before their eyes'. He then went on:

> I think that among us in Russia a poet can only hope for a major success with his first immature efforts. All young people support him, finding in him almost their own feelings, their own thoughts, clothed in brilliant colours. The poet matures, writes with deep thought, with great profundity: he becomes boring to the officers, and the Brigadiers don't make their peace with him because poetry is, after all, not prose.

Now, in writing of Baratynsky, Pushkin made these ideas his starting point.

4 *L'Art poétique*, II.
5 K. N. Batyushkov.
6 Bulgarin in *Severnaya Pchela*, No. 20 (1826).

181. Draft for an article on Russian literature[1]

Respect for the past – that is a trait which distinguishes a cultured from a primitive man; nomadic tribes have neither a history nor a noble class.

Embarking on a study of our literature we would like to look back and glance with curiosity and veneration at its ancient monuments, comparing them with that infinity of poems, romances, both heroic and amatory, both naïve and satiric, with which medieval European literature is flooded.

It would be pleasant to observe the history of our people through these primary intellectual and creative pastimes and to compare the influences of the Scandinavian invasions with those of the Moors. We would see the difference between the naïve satire of the French trouveurs and the subtle mockery of the strolling players, between the market-place jokes of a semi-religious Mystery and the pranks of our ancient comedies.

But unfortunately we have no ancient literature. Behind us lies a dark steppe and on it rises a single monument: *The Lay of Igor's Campaign*.

Our literature appeared suddenly in the eighteenth century, like the Russian nobility without ancestors or a pedigree.

1 Pushkin returned to these ideas later, in writing on the insignificance of Russian literature, see no. 272.

182. Note on *Count Nulin*[1]

At the end of 1825 I was living in the country. Re-reading *Lucrece*, a rather weak poem of Shakespeare's, I thought: what if it had occurred to Lucrece to slap Tarquin's face? Maybe it would have cooled his boldness and he would have been obliged to withdraw, covered in confusion. Lucrece would not have stabbed herself, Publicola would not have been enraged, Brutus would not have driven out the kings, and the world and its history would have been different.[2]

And so we owe the republic, the consuls, the dictators, the Catos, the Caesars, to a seduction similar to one which took place recently in our neighbourhood, in the Novorzhev district.[3]

I was struck by the idea of parodying both history and Shakespeare; I could not resist the double temptation and in two mornings had written this tale. I am accustomed to date my papers – *Count Nulin* was written on 13 and 14 December.

History does repeat itself strangely.

[1] Not published in Pushkin's lifetime.

[2] Pushkin is here referring to the Argument with which Shakespeare prefaces his poem, in which he sums up the events which followed the rape and mentions Publius Valerius, known as Publicola, who does not figure in the poem itself.

[3] Pushkin's friend, Alexey Vulf, was said to have seduced the daughter of a local parish priest.

183. Projected preface to the last chapters of *Evgeny Onegin*[1]

It is rather difficult here for an author to find out for himself the impression his work has made on the public. From the reviews he can only glean the opinions of publishers, which are unreliable for a variety of reasons. The opinions of friends are, naturally, biased and strangers will obviously not start criticizing his work to his face, even if it deserves no better.

At the appearance of the seventh chapter of *Onegin* the reviews were, on the whole, very unfavourable. I would have been quite ready to accept their verdict if it had not been so completely contrary to what they had said of the previous chapters of my novel. After the excessive and undeserved praise which was showered on six parts of the same work, it was strange for me to read, for example, the following comment:[2]

. . . Can one expect to hold the public's attention with such works as, for instance, the VIIth chapter of *Evgeny Onegin*? At first we thought it was a form of mystification, simply a joke or a parody, and were not satisfied that this VIIth chapter was the work of the author of *Ruslan and Lyudmila*, until we were assured of the same by the booksellers. . . . There is not a single idea, a single expression of feeling, a single description worthy of attention in this wishy-washy chapter VII! It is a complete débâcle, a chute complète. . . .

Our readers will ask what are the 57 small pages of chapter VII about. [Pushkin's footnote: . . . These are very good verses but they contain a superficial point of criticism. A poet can write of the most trivial object: there is no need for the critic to analyse what the poet describes but how he describes it.] The point is, dear reader, that all that this chapter is about is the fact that Tania is taken to Moscow from the country! etc.

In one of our journals it was said that chapter VII could not meet with any success as our age and Russia were on the march forward and the poet had remained marking time. An unfair judgement (that is, in the conclusion it reaches). The century can go forward in the sciences and in philosophy, and the civil administration can be improved and change – but poetry remains the same. It has one sole aim, and its means do not alter. And whereas the conceptions, the writings and the discoveries of the great masters of ancient astronomy, physics, medicine and philosophy have dated and are daily being replaced by others, the works of true poets remain fresh and eternally green.

A poetic work may be weak, unsuccessful, mistaken – but it is the poet's talent that is to blame and not the fact that the march of time has left him behind.

Probably the critic wanted to say that Evgeny Onegin and all his kind are no longer novel, and that the public, as well as the journalists, has grown tired of him.

Be that as it may, I make bold to test its patience once again. Here are another two chapters of *Evgeny Onegin* – the last at any rate that I shall print. . . . Let me assure those who would seek enthralling events in them that there is even less action than in all the previous chapters. I wanted to do away with the eighth chapter entirely and put in its place a solitary roman numeral, but I was afraid of the critics. Furthermore, many excerpts from it have already been published. The thought that a playful parody might be taken as a sign of disrespect to a great and sacred memory also held me back. But Childe Harold stands in such high esteem that in whatever tone one speaks of him the idea that one could possibly be insulting him would never have occurred to me.

28 November 1830
Boldino

---

[1] Pushkin wrote this introduction for an intended edition of the original chapter VIII of *Evgeny Onegin* – which he subsequently omitted and referred

to as 'Onegin's Journey' – and chapter IX, which he then renumbered chapter VIII (the final chapter).

Pushkin had started work on chapter IX on 24 December 1829, and completed it on 25 September 1830 in Boldino. It was published in January 1832 as 'the last chapter of *Evgeny Onegin*' with an epigraph from Byron: 'Fare thee well, and if for ever/Still for ever fare thee well' and with the following foreword:

> Omitted stanzas invariably aroused disapprobation and banter (which, incidentally, was both justified and witty). The author frankly admits that he omitted a whole chapter from his novel, in which Onegin's journey through Russia was described. It rested with him whether this omission should be indicated by dots or by the numbering; but in order to avoid ambiguity he changed the numbering of chapter nine to eight....
>
> P. A. Katenin (whose splendid poetic talent does not prevent him from being at the same time an astute critic) noted that this omission, even though it may be to the readers' advantage, is none the less harmful to the plan of the work as a whole, as because of it the transition from Tatiana, a provincial girl, to Tatiana, a distinguished lady, is too sudden and unexplained. This is a comment which proves him an experienced writer. The author himself felt the justice of this comment but resolved to omit the chapter for reasons important to himself and not to the public.

Only a few stanzas of 'Onegin's Journey' were published.
² By Bulgarin, *Severnaya Pchela*, Nos. 35 and 39 (1830).

184. Of Walter Scott's novels¹

The chief fascination of Walter Scott's novels lies in the fact that we grow acquainted with the past, not encumbered with the *enflure* of French tragedies, or with the prudery of the novels of sentiment, or with the dignité of history, but in a contemporary, homely manner. Ce qui me dégoûte c'est ce que – here on the contrary it's ce qui nous charme dans le roman historique, c'est que ce qui est historique est absolument ce que nous voyons. Shakespeare, Goethe, Walter Scott, have no slavish passion for kings and heroes. They don't (as French heroes do) resemble menials mimicking *la dignité et la noblesse*. Ils sont familiers dans les circonstances ordinaires de la vie, leur parole n'a rien d'affecté, de théâtral même dans les circonstances solennelles – car les grandes circonstances leur sont familières.

On voit que Walter Scott est de la petite société de rois d'Angleterre.

¹ Not published in Pushkin's lifetime. Pushkin's first published comment on Walter Scott appeared in his second article on Polevoy's *History of the*

Russian People (see page 241). In 1835, when he re-read Scott in Mik-hailovskoe, he found that his high opinion of him remained unaltered, see his letter to his wife, no. 290, and both his imaginative and his historical prose owed a great deal to Scott's influence (see pages 198-202).

See also Pushkin's article on Chateaubriand's translation of Milton's *Paradise Lost* (no. 307).

185. Notes in the *Liternaturnaya Gazeta* (1830)[1]

When Macpherson published *The Poems of Ossian* (whether a transla-tion, an imitation, or his own composition is a question which I believe has not yet been settled) everybody read and re-read them with delight. 'Nobody was as yet *depressed* by the thought (says Villemain[2]) that mar-velling at these poetic cantos, they were marvelling at [the work of] a contemporary. All experienced *flawless pleasure*, that is they read the splendid poems and were under no obligation to thank *any living man* for them.' Then they began to guess, to investigate, and came to the conclusion (whether correct or not) that the poems of Ossian were forgeries, quite new works; in short, that they had been written by Macpherson himself.

The famous critic Dr Johnson, an exceedingly rude man, fiercely attacked Macpherson and called him a cheat and a malicious forger. A heated literary war boiled up. Here is an example of the polemics of the day: Dr Johnson's answer to Macpherson's letter, in which he had proudly said how grieved he was by the English critic's hurtful disbelief in him:

Mr James Macpherson,

I received your foolish and impudent letter. Any violence offered me I shall do my best to repel; and what I cannot do for myself, the law shall do for me. I hope I shall never be deterred from detect-ing what I think a cheat, by the menaces of a ruffian.

What would you have me retract? I thought your book an im-posture; I think it an imposture still. For this opinion I have given my reasons to the publick, which I here dare you to refute. Your rage I defy. Your abilities, since your Homer, are not so formidable; and what I hear of your morals inclines me to pay regard not to what you shall say, but to what you shall prove. You may print this if you will.

20 January 1775

In explanation of certain words in this letter it must be said that Macpherson, beguiled by the success of *Ossian,* had made an extremely unsuccessful translation of Homer's *Iliad* in Ossianic diction.

We publish this letter to serve as an example to our critics. And why cannot we have our own *Addisons* and our own *Johnsons*?

[1] Published anonymously in *Literaturnaya Gazeta,* No. 5 (1830), ascribed to Pushkin.

[2] A. F. Villemain, *Cours de littérature française* . . . Tableau du dix-huitième siècle, Part II (Paris, 1828), lecture VI: 'Jusque-là, Messieurs, tout allait bien, on n'avait pas le chagrin, en admirant des chants poétiques, d'admirer un contemporain. (*On rit*) Il y avait une satisfaction sans mélange à lire de belles choses, et à n'être pas obligé d'en savoir gré à quelqu'un qui fût là présent.' (One is given the audience reaction for good measure.)
Villemain then quotes Dr Johnson's letter (in French) and continues: 'Pour l'intelligence de quelques mots de cette lettre, je ne dois pas oublier, Messieurs, de vous dire que Macpherson, enchanté et enrichi par le succès de son *Ossian,* avait essayé de traduire Homère.'

186. Miscellaneous Notes

French critics have their own conception of Romanticism. They class as Romantic all those works which bear the mark of melancholy or reverie. Some even term neologism and errors of grammar Romanticism. In this way André Chénier, a poet steeped in antiquity, whose very defects stem from his desire to impose Greek verse forms on the French language, has been classed by them as a Romantic poet.[1]

At the moment at which love vanishes, the heart still fondly treasures its memory. In the same way Byron's gladiator agrees to die, but his imagination is ranging along the shores of his native Danube.[2]

Milton once said, 'I am satisfied with a few readers if they are worthy of understanding me.' This proud assertion on the poet's part is sometimes heard in our own times only with a slight alteration. Some of our contemporaries explicitly or by hints make it clear that they are 'satisfied with a few readers, provided there are a lot of purchasers'.[3]

Translators – the post-horses of enlightenment.

[1] Not published in Pushkin's lifetime.
[2] *Childe Harold,* IV, cxi.
[3] Published unsigned in *Literaturnaya Gazeta,* No. 16 (1830).

LETTERS

187. To N. I Gnedich   *6 January 1830*
                                                                 St Petersburg

I am pleased, I am delighted that the few lines I timidly threw together
for the Gazette could touch you so much.[1] The fact that I do not know
Greek prevents me from undertaking a full-scale analysis of your *Iliad*.
Your reputation does not require it, but it would be a good thing for
Russia. . . .

[1] On reading these words, Gnedich wrote to Pushkin (6 January 1830) : 'an
entire panegyric, the length of that of Pliny to Trajan, could not have
moved me as much as these *few lines*! I am unlikely ever again in my life
to read anything about my work, which will be expressed with such
generosity and which will be so comforting and sound so sweet to me!'

188. To Count A. C. Benckendorff   *7 January 1830*
                                                                 St Petersburg

. . . Tandis que je ne suis encore ni marié, ni attaché au service, j'aurais
désiré faire un voyage soit en France, soit en Italie. Cependant s'il ne
me l'était pas accordé, je demanderais la grâce de visiter la Chine avec
la mission qui va s'y rendre.[1]

Oserais-je vous importuner encore? Pendant mon absence, M-r
Joukovsky avait voulu imprimer ma tragédie,[2] mais il n'en a pas reçu
d'autorisation formelle. Il me serait gênant, vu mon manque de fortune,
de me priver d'une quinzaine de milles roubles que peut me rapporter
ma tragédie, et il me serait triste de renoncer à la publication d'un
ouvrage que j'ai longtemps médité et dont je suis le plus content.[3]

[1] Permission was not granted to either request. Pushkin was told that the
composition of the mission to China had already been arranged and that
no changes could be made without the approval of the court at Peking.
As regards the journey to Europe, Benckendorff wrote: 'Sa Majesté
l'Empereur n'a pas daigné acquiescer à Votre demande d'aller visiter les
pays étrangers, croyant que cela dérangerait trop Votres affaires pécuniaires
et Vous détournerait en même temps de Vos occupations.' So much for
that. The only time Pushkin had been allowed to leave Russian territory
was when he went a little way into Turkey with the Russian army in the
summer of 1829.

A. O. Smirnov recalled that Pushkin told her that his interest in China
had been aroused by reading Voltaire's play *L'Orpheline de la Chine*, which
had nothing Chinese about it, and that he wanted to go there so as to

write his own Chinese tragedy and vex Voltaire's ghost. Naturally, as far as Pushkin was concerned, it was second best to travelling in Western Europe.

2 *Boris Godunov* was published in December 1830.

3 In the draft of this letter the sentence read: 'Il me serait pénible de renoncer à la publication d'un ouvrage que j'ai le plus médité et du seul dont je suis content . . . et quant aux idées politiques, elles sont parfaitement monarchiques.'

189. To M. N. Zagoskin[1]   *11 January 1830*
                                                              St Petersburg

I am interrupting my absorbed reading of your novel in order to thank you most sincerely for having sent me *Yury Miloslavsky*, a flattering token of your goodwill towards me. I congratulate you on your complete and deserved success, and the public on one of the best novels of the present epoch. Everybody is reading it. Zhukovsky spent a whole night over it. The ladies are delighted with it. There will be an article on it by Pogorelsky in the *Literaturnaya Gazeta*.[2] If all is not said in it, I shall try to add the rest. Farewell. May God grant you many years – i.e. may God grant us many novels.

1 Mikhail Nikolaevich Zagoskin (1789-1852), novelist and dramatist, best known for *Yury Miloslavsky, or the Russians in 1612*. It was one of the first historical novels to be written in Russia, a genre in which Pushkin was particularly interested at this time, and was an immediate success.

2 In thanking Pushkin most warmly for this letter (20/25 January 1830), Zagoskin wrote that though he was pleased that Pogorelsky (pseud. of A. A. Perovsky) planned an article he would be even more pleased if Pushkin were to decide to add his own comments. Pogorelsky's article did not materialize and Pushkin wrote one instead, see no. 164.

190. To Prince P. A. Vyazemsky   *End of January/*
                                               beginning of February 1830
                                               St Petersburg

. . . Thank you very much for your prose – serve up more of it.[1] You criticize *Miloslavsky*[2] and I praised it. Every cloud has a silver lining. Of course there is much that it lacks, but it has a lot too: vitality and gaiety such as Bulgarin could never dream of. . . .[3]

1 Vyazemsky had sent Pushkin some contributions, both prose and verse, for *Literaturnaya Gazeta*. He was critical of the quality of the review and

suggested that Pushkin should reprint a foreign review of some outstanding book (letter of 15/25 January 1830).

[2] Vyazemsky did not himself criticize *Yury Miloslavsky* but in one of his articles quoted at considerable length some critical remarks on it from the *Ateney*.

[3] Pushkin was thinking of Bulgarin's historical novels, *Ivan Vyzhigin* (1829) and *Dimitri Samozvanets* (1830).

191. To Count A. C. Benckendorff   *16 April 1830*
Moscow

. . . Encore une grâce: En 1826 j'apportai à Moscou ma tragédie de Godunov écrite pendant mon exil. Elle ne vous fut envoyée, telle que vous l'avez vue, que pour me disculper. L'Empereur ayant daigné la lire m'a fait quelques critiques sur des passages trop libres et, je dois l'avouer, Sa Majesté n'avait que trop raison. Deux ou trois passages ont aussi attiré son attention, parce qu'ils semblaient présenter des allusions aux circonstances alors récentes,[1] en les relisant actuellement je doute qu'on puisse leur trouver ce sens-là. Tous les troubles se ressemblent. L'auteur dramatique ne peut répondre des paroles qu'il met dans la bouche des personnages historiques. Il doit les faire parler selon leur caractère connu. Il ne faut donc faire attention qu'à *l'esprit dans lequel est conçu l'ouvrage entier*, à l'impression qu'il doit produire. Ma tragédie est une œuvre de bonne foi et je ne puis en conscience supprimer ce qui me paraît essentiel. Je supplie Sa Majesté de me pardonner la liberté que je prends de la contredire; je sais bien que cette opposition de poète peut prêter à rire, mais jusqu'à present j'ai toujours constamment refusé toutes les propositions des libraires; j'étais heureux de pouvoir faire en silence ce sacrifice à la volonté de Sa Majesté. Les circonstances actuelles me pressent, et je viens supplier Sa Majesté de me délier les mains et de me permettre d'imprimer ma tragédie comme je l'entends. . . .[2]

[1] The Decembrist rising.

[2] In Benckendorff's reply (28 April 1830) he wrote:

. . . Sa Majesté l'Empereur, par une sollicitude toute paternelle pour Vous, Monsieur, a daigné charger moi le général Benckendorff, non le chef de la gendarmerie, mais l'homme dans lequel il se plaît à mettre sa confiance, de vous observer et de vous guider par ses conseils; jamais aucune police n'a eu ordre de vous surveiller. Les avis que je Vous ai donné de temps en temps, comme ami, n'ont pu que Vous être utiles, et j'espère que Vous Vous en convaincrez toujours davantage. Quel est

donc l'ombrage qu'on peut trouver dans votre position sous ce rapport?
Je Vous autorise, Monsieur, de faire voir cette lettre à tous ceux à qui
Vous croirez devoir la montrer.

Pour ce qui regarde Votre tragédie de Godounoff, Sa Majesté
l'Empereur Vous permet de la faire imprimer sous Votre propre
responsabilité.

192. To Princess V. F. Vyazemsky *Before 28 April 1830*
Moscow

Vous avez raison de trouver l'*Âne*[1] délicieux. C'est un des ouvrages les
plus marquants du moment. On l'attribue à V. Hugo – j'y vois plus de
talent que dans le *Dernier Jour*[2] où il y en a beaucoup.... Mon mariage
avec Natalie (qui par parenthèse est mon cent-treizième amour) est
décidé. Mon père me donne 200 paysans que j'engage au lombard....

[1] *L'Âne mort et la femme guillotinée* by Jules-Gabriel Janin (1829). Pushkin
had a copy in his library.
[2] *Le Dernier Jour d'un condamné* by Victor Hugo (1829).

193. To Prince P. A. Vyazemsky *2 May 1830*
Moscow

... Come here, my dear fellow, and fall in love with my wife, and we
will talk about a newspaper or an almanac. Delvig is certainly lazy,
but none the less his *Gazeta*[1] is good; you have livened it up considerably.
Support it while we have no other. It would be shameful to surrender
the field to Bulgarin.[2] The fact is that a purely literary paper cannot
exist among us, it must enter into an alliance either with Fashion or
with Politics. It goes against one's conscience somehow to compete with
Raich[3] or Shalikov.[4] Has Bulgarin really been granted a monopoly of
political news? Is it true that among us no review apart from the
Severnaya Pchela dare announce the fact that there was an earthquake
in Mexico and that the Chamber of Deputies is in recess till September?
Is it really not possible to obtain permission for this? Ask some junior
ministers, or Benckendorff. This is not a question of political opinions
but of the dry setting-down of events. ...

[1] *Literaturnaya Gazeta.* Both Pushkin and Vyazemsky tried to help Delvig as
much as possible in the publication of his review.
[2] Pushkin had just published his review of Vidocq's memoirs (*Literaturnaya*

Gazeta, No. 20), in which though he wrote of Vidocq his sights were firmly and unmistakably set on Bulgarin.

³ S. E. Raich was the editor of *Galatea*.

⁴ Prince P. I. Shalikov, a sentimental minor poet, editor of *Damsky Journal*.

194. To P. A. Pletnev   *Around 5 May 1830*
                                                         Moscow

My dear fellow! Victory! The Tsar has given me permission to print *Godunov* in all its pristine beauty. This is what Benckendorff writes to me: 'Pour ce qui regarde votre tragédie de Godounoff, Sa Majesté vous permet de la faire imprimer sous votre propre responsabilité.'¹ . . . I am thinking of writing a preface.² My hands itch to crush Bulgarin. But is it becoming for me, Alexander Pushkin, appearing before Russia with *Boris Godunov*, to start talking about Fadey Bulgarin?³ I think it is unbecoming. What do you think? Decide. Tell me: has the *Severnaya Pchela's* review influenced the sales of *Onegin*?⁴ I am curious to know. . . . What effect, in general and in particular, did the article on Vidocq have? Please write and tell me. Oh, my dear fellow, what a little wife I have acquired! . . . The Tsar is very charming to me.⁵

¹ See pages 280-1.

² See no. 174 for the many versions of this draft preface. Pushkin's anxiety that *Boris Godunov* should be a success, and his eagerness to win acceptance for his ideas on drama, caused him to attempt over and over again to write a preface, using as a basis ideas expressed several years earlier when he was embarking on his play in a letter to N. N. Raevsky, see no. 108. In fact the play was published without a preface.

³ Pletnev replied on 21 May advising Pushkin not to cumber his introduction to *Boris Godunov* with references to Bulgarin. His introduction should be in harmony with his work and this could only be achieved by a clear and true statement on dramatic poetry in general. There were two 'Shakespearian' points that he would particularly like to see emphasized. First, the author's right to make his characters say what it would be natural for them to say in life, regardless of the sensibilities of the audience. Secondly, the author's right to combine prose, blank verse, and rhymed verse in one piece, thus allowing every character to speak appropriately.

⁴ Bulgarin wrote a slashing review of *Evgeny Onegin* Chapter VII in *Severnaya Pchela*, Nos. 35 and 39.

⁵ Pushkin's friend, Elizaveta Khitrovo (see page 283), confirmed this impression in a letter written in mid-May: 'Je suys sûre, d'après ce que je sais des idées de l'Empereur sur vous que si vous désiriez une place de quelque manière auprès de lui on vous la donnerait . . . L'Empereur est si bien disposé que vous n'avez besoin de personne.' It was a short honeymoon.

10 I. I. Pushchin visiting Pushkin at Mikhailovskoe, 11 January 1825.
Oil painting by N. N. Gé.

11 Presumed to be I. I. Pushchin.
Pastel drawing by Vernet (1817).

12 P. A. Pletnev. Water-colour,
artist unknown.

13 A. S. Pushkin. Oil
painting by V. A. Tropinin
(1827).

14 Self-portrait in pencil
(1827).

195. To Count A. C. Benckendorff   7 *May 1830*
                                                    Moscow
Mon Général,
   C'est à la sollicitude de Votre Excellence que je dois la grâce nouvelle[1]
dont l'Empereur vient de me combler: veuillez recevoir l'expression de
ma profonde reconnaissance. Jamais dans mon cœur je n'ai méconnu
la bienveillance, j'ose le dire, toute paternelle que me portait Sa
Majesté, jamais je n'ai mal interprété l'intérêt que toujours vous avez
bien voulu me témoigner. . . .

[1] Permission to publish *Boris Godunov*.

196. To E. M. Khitrovo[1]   *Between 19 and 24 May 1830*
                                         Moscow

D'abord permettez-moi, Madame, de vous remercier pour *Hernani*.
C'est un des ouvrages du temps que j'ai lu avec le plus de plaisir. Hugo
et Sainte-Beuve sont sans contredit les seuls poètes français de l'époque,
surtout Sainte-Beuve – et à ce propos, s'il est possible d'avoir à Pétersbourg les *Consolations*[2] de ce dernier, faites une œuvre de charité, au
nom du ciel envoyez-les moi. . . . Être gentilhomme de la Chambre
n'est plus de mon âge, et puis que ferai-je à la cour? Ni ma fortune ni
mes occupations ne me le permettent.[3] . . .

[1] Elizaveta Mikhailovna Khitrovo (1783-1839) was the favourite daughter
of Field-Marshal Prince Kutuzov. Her first husband, Count Tiesenhausen,
was mortally wounded at Austerlitz and she then married General Nikolai
Khitrovo, at the time Russian Ambassador to Florence. He died in 1819.
She returned to Russia in 1823 ready to marry again – there was something of the Wife of Bath in her character (her *décolletage*, which displayed
her splendid shoulders, was much remarked on). She and her daughter,
Countess Ficquelmont, both established salons in St Petersburg, the mother
receiving in the morning and the daughter in the evening. These salons
became the social centres of Russian literary and political life. Elizaveta
Khitrovo often received in her bedroom and the writers who visited her
almost daily each had a favourite perch: Pushkin's armchair, Zhukovsky's
divan, Gogol's chair, etc.
   Among Elizaveta Khitrovo's qualities were immense kindness and the
staunchest loyalty to her friends; she always campaigned for them passionately with no thought for any personal difficulties that might result. Her
feelings for Pushkin were most tender: she worshipped and cherished him.
Their correspondence began in March 1830. She wrote to him: 'Comme
j'aime qu'on vous aime!' (18-21 May 1830); and though this devotion
sometimes became overpowering, Pushkin did not wish to hurt her and

continued to visit her regularly. When he referred to her in his letters he often sounded a humorous note.

[2] See Pushkin's article on *Les Consolations*, no. 205.

[3] The final word in this matter was not to be Pushkin's. He was appointed as Kammerjunker on 1 January 1834, an insulting post for a man of his age and position.

197. To P. A. Pletnev   *31 August 1830*
                                            Moscow

. . . Autumn is approaching. It is my favourite season – my health usually improves – the time for my literary labours sets in – and now I must fuss round about a dowry and about the wedding, which God alone knows when we will celebrate. All this isn't very comforting. I am going to the country.[1] God knows whether I'll have time to work there, and will have the peace of mind without which one can't create anything but epigrams on Kachenovsky.[2]

[1] Pushkin always wrote best in the autumn. See his letter to Pletnev no. 204.

[2] The editor of the *Vestnik Evropy*, a literary critic of the neo-classical school and hostile to the Romantic writers. In 1837 he became Rector of Moscow University.

198. To P. A. Pletnev   *9 September 1830*
                                            Boldino

. . . Around me there is cholera morbus. And do you know what sort of a wild beast that is? Before one can say 'knife' it may come and call on Boldino and bite us all – and hey presto! I'll set off to join Uncle Vasily, and you to write my biography. Poor Uncle Vasily![1] Do you know what his last words were? I came to him, found him unconscious, he came to, recognized me, wept a little, then was silent: '*How dull Katenin's articles are!*'[2] and not another word. What do you think of that? That's what it means to die like a trooper on one's shield, le cri de guerre à la bouche! You cannot imagine what fun it is to run away from a fiancée and settle down to write poetry. A wife is not the same as a fiancée. Nothing like! A wife's like a brother. One can write as much as one likes in her presence. But a fiancée ties up one's tongue and arms more effectively than the censor Shcheglov[3] . . .

Oh my dear fellow, how delightful the country here is! Just imagine:

steppe upon steppe; not one neighbour; one can ride to one's heart's content, write at home as much as one wants, nobody will interfere. I'll cook up all sorts of things for you, both in prose and verse. . . .[4]

PS. What about my tragedy? I have written a little elegiac preface. Shall I send it to you? But remember that you have promised to write one for me: a sensible, long one.[5] And how much will the tragedy cost? 10 or 12?[6]

[1] Pushkin's uncle, Vasily Lvovich Pushkin, died on 20 August.
[2] Katenin's articles on literature were being published in the *Literaturnaya Gazeta*.
[3] N. P. Shcheglov was a Professor of Physics at St Petersburg University and so was ill suited to act as censor for works of literature. He died of cholera in 1831.
[4] See note 1 to no. 197. This is a very different tune from the one Pushkin used to sing in Mikhailovskoe, when he was forced to live in the country.
[5] *Boris Godunov* was published without a preface.
[6] Roubles.

199. To N. N. Goncharov[1]   *11 October 1830*
                                                  Boldino

. . . Boldino a l'air d'une île entourée de rochers. Point de voisins, point de livres.[2] Un temps affreux. Je passe mon temps à griffoner et à enrager. Je ne sais ce que fait le pauvre monde, et comment va mon ami Polignac.[3] Ecrivez-moi de ses nouvelles, car ici je ne lis point de journaux. Je deviens si imbécile que c'est une bénédiction.

[1] Pushkin's fiancée, Natalia.
[2] In a note he wrote on the epidemic, Pushkin said that he kept away from neighbours and spent his time writing stories and re-reading Coleridge.
[3] Prince de Polignac (1780-1847), Minister of Foreign Affairs under Charles X of France, who had just been deposed. Pushkin thought he would be executed.

200. To P. A. Pletnev   *End of October, but not later than the 29th, 1830*
                             Boldino

. . . And even poems don't germinate, although it's a lovely autumn, both rain and snow and mud to the knees. . . . I don't read your reviews. Who is being knocked by whom? Tell Delvig that he should stand firm; and that I shall definitely come to his aid in the winter, that is if I don't peg out here. Meanwhile he can already order a vignette, a woodcut depicting me naked, as Atlas, holding up the *Literaturnaya Gazeta* on my shoulders. How's my tragedy? Stand up for it, brave friends! Don't let those hounds of reviewers tear it apart. I wanted to dedicate it to Zhukovsky with the following words: I had wanted to dedicate my tragedy to Karamzin, but as he is no longer among us, I am dedicating it to Zhukovsky. Karamzin's daughters said I should dedicate my favourite work to the memory of their father. And so, if it is still possible, print on the title-page:

> To the Memory precious to Russians
> Of Nikolai Mikhailovich
> Karamzin
> This work, inspired by his genius,
> Is dedicated with veneration and gratitude.
> > A. Pushkin

201. To Baron A. A. Delvig   *4 November 1830*
Boldino

. . . I have, my dear fellow, written heaps of polemic articles,[1] but not receiving the reviews I am out of touch with the age and do not know what is going on – and which one should strangle, Polevoy or Bulgarin.

[1] Pushkin did not know when writing this letter that the publication of the *Literaturnaya Gazeta* had been stopped and Delvig had been dismissed as editor. See note 7 to letter to Pletnev (no. 204) below.

202. To Prince P. A. Vyazemsky   *5 November 1830*
Boldino

. . . I have written a few things here.[1] But it is a pity that I have not been getting the reviews. I was in the vein for abuse and would have dealt with them in their own manner. You and I will say of these polemics: 'there's a drop of our honey in here too.'[2] I am glad that you have embarked on Fonvizin.[3] Whatever you say of him, or concerning him, will be good, simply for being said. . . .

[1] See letter to Pletnev, no. 204.
[2] Quotation from Krylov's fable, 'The Eagle and the Bee'.
[3] Vyazemsky had long been planning a biography of Fonvizin; it was finally passed by the censorship in 1835 but was not published till 1848.

203. To M. P. Pogodin   *End of November 1830*
                                    Boldino

... As consolation I found your letters and *Martha*. And read it through twice straight off. Hurrah! I must confess I was afraid that the first impression would be weakened later; but no – I am still of the same opinion: *Martha* has quality of a high European order. I shall analyse it as fully as possible.[1] I will find doing that both instructive and pleasurable. There is one fault: the style and the language. You make endless mistakes.[2] And you treat the language as Ivan treated Novgorod.[3] There are scores of grammatical mistakes – truncations and abbreviations – which are alien to the spirit of the language. But you know, in fact, there is little harm in that. Our language needs to be given more freedom (of course in keeping with its spirit) and your freedom is more to my liking than our prim correctness. Will your *Martha* be published soon? I am not sending you any comments (concerning details) as you will not have time to change what needs changing. Leave that to the next edition. Meanwhile I will say that only one place struck me as undramatic: Boretsky's conversation with Ivan. Ivan does not retain his majesty (not in the way he speaks but in his attitude to the traitor). Boretsky (although he comes from Novgorod) is too familiar in his behaviour; he might have bargained like that with one of Ivan's boyars, but not with Ivan himself. You have no sympathy for Ivan. Having traced his policy dramatically (that is, intelligently, vividly, profoundly), you could not imbue it with the pulling power of your emotion. You were even forced to make him express himself in rather pompous language. That is my chief criticism. As for the rest – the rest one will have to praise to the peal of Ivan the Great,[4] which your humble sexton will carry out with all zeal.

How delightful the scene with the ambassadors is! How well you have understood Russian diplomacy! And the popular assembly? And the Governor? And Prince Shuisky? And the feudal princes? I assure you that these are all of *Shakespearian* quality!

I shall say only a few words about the style, leaving it to the reviews who will probably raise a row royal (and deservedly so); and see that you follow their advice. I shall, however, send you, for yourself, a detailed criticism, taking it line by line. Forgive more and goodbye. Greetings to Yazykov.[5]

---

[1] See no. 179 for Pushkin's extensive comments on Pogodin's tragedy *Martha, the Governor's Wife.*

² As soon as Pushkin managed to be cleared of the cholera quarantine he returned to Moscow and Pogodin immediately came to see him. He noted in his diary (11 December) that Pushkin again praised *Martha* warmly but that he was surprised by Pushkin's strictures on his language.
³ Ivan III conquered the city of Novgorod, which was a republic, and annexed it to the Tsardom of Moscow.
⁴ The belfry in the Moscow Kremlin.
⁵ The poet, N. M. Yazykov.

204. To P. A. Pletnev   *9 December 1830*
                                                               Moscow

. . . What news of *Godunov*?¹ I'll tell you (as a secret) that I wrote in Boldino as I haven't written for a long time.² This is what I've brought here: the two *final* chapters of Onegin, the eighth and the ninth,³ absolutely ready for publication. A tale⁴ written in ottava rima (400 lines) which we'll publish Anonyme. Several dramatic scenes, or little tragedies, namely: *The Covetous Knight, Mozart and Salieri, A Feast in the time of the Plague,* and *Don Juan.*⁵ Besides that I have written about thirty short poems. Good? That is still not all (this is an absolute secret): I wrote five tales in prose⁶ which make Baratynsky whinny and buck – which we'll also publish Anonyme.⁷ It will be impossible to do so under my name for Bulgarin will damn them. And so Russian literature is handed over body and soul to Bulgarin and Grech! A pity – but what was Delvig thinking of? Fancy his wanting to print the sugary trifle by that unbearable Delavigne.⁸ But all the same, Delvig will have to clear himself before His Majesty. He can prove that there has never been even a shadow of ill-will, let alone of rebelliousness, towards the Government in his *Gazeta*. Talk this over with him. Or else the scribbler-spies will rend him to death.⁹

¹ *Boris Godunov* was in the press.
² The autumn spent in quarantine in Boldino had yielded an exceptional harvest. Apart from all the items listed above, Pushkin had begun *The History of the Village of Gorukhino* (left unfinished) and had written many draft articles and notes on literary topics.
³ Renumbered Chapters VII and VIII when 'Onegin's Journey' was dropped.
⁴ *The Little House in Kolomna.*
⁵ *The Stone Guest.*
⁶ *The Tales of Belkin.*
⁷ Pogodin wrote to Shevyrev at this time that Pushkin had secretly read

him many new works which he wanted to publish anonymously (presumably to avoid sending them to the Tsar for censorship).

[8] The publication in Delvig's *Literaturnaya Gazeta*, No. 61 (28 October 1830), of four lines of verse on the French Revolution of 1830 by Casimir Delavigne had led to the temporary proscription of this review. Delvig had once before been summoned to Benckendorff, rebuked for his attacks on Bulgarin and told that a strict watch would be kept on the *Literaturnaya Gazeta*. Benckendorff admitted to Delvig that he was once again acting on representations made by Bulgarin. Delvig was desperate and wrote to Pushkin (about 17 November):

> As soon as you receive this letter, my most dear friend, sit down and copy out all the items you have prepared for the *Severnye Tsvety*. They will help me now more than ever before. The *Literaturnaya Gazeta* brought no profit and besides is proscribed because some new lines of Delavigne were published in it. People who are genuinely devoted to their Tsar and have a clear conscience, seek nothing and bow to no man, thinking that their loyalty and their conscience will protect them in all eventualities. This is not so . . . I am looked upon as a Carbonari, I am a Russian, brought up by the Tsar, the father of a family and relying on the Tsar for help for my mother, brothers and sisters –
>
> I embrace you and expect consolation from you, not in the form of expressions of sympathy – I know that you love me – but poems, poems, poems! I need them! Do you hear, you Boldino landowner!

The offending four lines of poetry were:

> France, dis-moi leurs noms! Je n'en vois point paraître
> Sur ce funèbre monument:
> Ils ont vaincu si promptement
> Que tu fus libre avant de les connaître.

[9] Pushkin did not realize how near the mark he had struck. Though the *Literaturnaya Gazeta* resumed publication within the month it was with a new editor, O. M. Somov. Delvig was devastated, his health rapidly deteriorated, and he died in the following month, see nos. 215 and 216.

1831

ARTICLES AND NOTES

205. *Vie, poésies et pensées de Joseph Delorme* (Paris, 1829) and *Les Consolations*, poésies par Sainte-Beuve (Paris, 1830)[1]

About two years ago a book appeared in Paris entitled *Vie, poésies et pensées de J. Delorme*, which caught the attention of the critics and the public. In place of a foreword it had an account, which read like a novel, of the life of a poor young poet who had died, it was maintained, in poverty and obscurity. The friends of the deceased put before the public poems and reflections, which had been found among his papers, excusing both their shortcomings and the errors of judgement of their author, Delorme, on account of his youth, his diseased state of mind, and his physical suffering. An extraordinary talent was revealed in the poems, vividly reflected in the strange choice of themes. Never, in any language, had naked spleen been exposed with such dry precision; never had the errors of pitiful youth, left at the mercy of the passions, been voiced with such disillusionment. Gazing at a stream shaded by the dark branches of trees, Delorme contemplates suicide in these words:

> Pour qui veut se noyer la place est bien choisie.
> On n'aurait qu'à venir, un jour de fantaisie,
> A cacher ses habits au pied de ce bouleau,
> Et, comme pour un bain, à descendre dans l'eau:
> Non pas en furieux, la tête la première;
> Mais s'asseoir, regarder; d'un rayon de lumière
> Dans le feuillage et l'eau suivre le long reflet;
> Puis, quand on sentirait ses esprits au complet,
> Qu'on aurait froid, alors, sans plus traîner la fête,
> Pour ne plus la lever, plonger avant la tête.
> C'est là mon plus doux vœu, quand je pense à mourir.
> J'ai toujours été seul à pleurer, à souffrir;
> Sans un cœur près du mien j'ai passé sur la terre;
> Ainsi que j'ai vécu, mourons avec mystère,
> Sans fracas, sans clameurs, sans voisins assemblés.

L'alouette, en mourant, se cache dans les blés;
Le rossignol, qui sent défaillir son ramage,
Et la bise arriver, et tomber son plumage,
Passe invisible à tous comme un écho du bois:
Ainsi je veux passer. Seulement, un . . . deux mois,
Peut-être un an après, un jour . . . une soirée,
Quelque pâtre inquiet d'une chèvre égarée,
Un chasseur descendu vers la source, et voyant
Son chien qui s'y lançait sortir en aboyant,
Regardera: la lune avec lui qui regarde
Éclairera ce corps d'une lueur blafarde;
Et soudain il fuira jusqu'au hameau, tout droit.
De grand matin venus, quelques gens de l'endroit,
Tirant par les cheveux ce corps méconnaissable,
Cette chair en lambeaux, ces os chargés de sable,
Mêlant des quolibets à quelques sots récits,
Deviseront longtemps sur mes restes noircis,
Et les brouetteront enfin au cimetière;
Vite on clouera le tout dans quelque vieille bière,
Qu'un prêtre aspergera d'eau bénite trois fois;
Et je serai laissé sans nom, sans croix de bois!

A son is born to his friend Victor Hugo; Delorme greets him:

Mon ami, vous voilà père d'un nouveau-né;
C'est un garçon encor: le Ciel vous l'a donné
Beau, frais, souriant d'aise à cette vie amère;
A peine il a coûté quelque plainte à sa mère.
Il est nuit; je vous vois: . . . à doux bruit, le sommeil
Sur un sein blanc qui dort a pris l'enfant vermeil,
Et vous, père, veillant contre la cheminée,
Recueilli dans vous-même, et la tête inclinée,
Vous vous tournez souvent pour revoir, ô douceur!
Le nouveau-né, la mère, et le frère et la sœur,
Comme un pasteur joyeux de ses toisons nouvelles,
Ou comme un maître, au soir, qui compte ses javelles.
A cette heure si grave, en ce calme profond,
Qui sait, hors vous, l'abîme où votre cœur se fond,
Ami? qui sait vos pleurs, vos muettes caresses;
Les trésors du génie épanchés en tendresses;

L'aigle plus gémissant que la colombe au nid;
Les torrents ruisselants du rocher de granit,
Et, comme sous les feux d'un été de Norwège,
Au penchant des glaciers mille fontes de neige?
Vivez, soyez heureux, et chantez-nous un jour
Ces secrets plus qu'humains d'un ineffable amour!

– Moi, pendant ce temps-là, je veille aussi, je veille,
Non près des rideaux bleus de l'enfance vermeille,
Près du lit nuptial arrosé de parfum,
Mais près d'un froid grabat, sur le corps d'un défunt.
C'est un voisin, vieillard goutteux, mort de la pierre;
Ses nièces m'ont requis, je veille à leur prière.
Seul, je m'y suis assis dès neuf heures du soir.
A la tête du lit une croix en bois noir,
Avec un Christ en os, pose entre deux chandelles
Sur une chaise; auprès, le buis cher aux fidèles
Trempe dans une assiette, et je vois sous les draps
Le mort en long, pieds joints, et croisant les deux bras.
Oh! si, du moins, ce mort m'avait durant sa vie
Été longtemps connu! s'il me prenait envie
De baiser ce front jaune une dernière fois!
En regardant toujours ces plis raides et droits,
Si je voyais enfin remuer quelque chose,
Bouger comme le pied d'un vivant qui repose,
Et la flamme bleuir! si j'entendais crier
Le bois de lit!... ou bien si je pouvais prier!
Mais rien: nul effroi saint, pas de souvenir tendre;
Je regarde sans voir, j'écoute sans entendre;
Chaque heure sonne lente, et lorsque, par trop las
De ce calme abattant et de ces rêves plats,
Pour respirer un peu je vais à la fenêtre
(Car au ciel de minuit le croissant vient de naître),
Voilà, soudain, qu'au toit lointain d'une maison,
Non pas vers l'orient, s'embrase l'horizon,
Et j'entends résonner, pour toute mélodie,
Des aboiements de chiens hurlant dans l'incendie.

Among these diseased confessions, these desires born of lamentable weaknesses, and these tasteless imitations of the venerable Ronsard, long since subject to ridicule, we are astonished to find poems brimming with freshness and purity. With what melancholy charm, for instance, he describes his muse!

Non, ma Muse n'est pas l'odalisque brillante
Qui danse les seins nus, à la voix sémillante,
Aux noirs cheveux luisants, aux longs yeux de houri;
Elle n'est ni la jeune et vermeille Péri,
Dont l'aile radieuse éclipserait la queue
D'un beau paon, ni la fée à l'aile blanche et bleue,
Ces deux rivales sœurs, qui, dès qu'il a dit *oui*,
Ouvrent mondes et cieux à l'enfant ébloui.
Elle n'est pas non plus, ô ma Muse adorée!
Elle n'est pas la vierge ou la veuve éplorée,
Qui d'un cloître désert, d'une tour sans vassaux,
Solitaire habitante, erre sous les arceaux,
Disant un nom; descend aux tombes féodales;
A genoux, de velours inonde au loin les dalles,
Et, le front sur un marbre, épanche avec des pleurs
L'hymne mélodieux de ses nobles malheurs.

Non; – mais, quand seule au bois votre douleur chemine,
Avez-vous vu là-bas, dans un fond, la chaumine
Sous l'arbre mort? auprès, un ravin est creusé;
Une fille en tout temps y lave un linge usé.
Peut-être à votre vue elle a baissé la tête;
Car, bien pauvre qu'elle est, sa naissance est honnête.
Elle eut pu, comme une autre, en de plus heureux jours
S'épanouir au monde et fleurir aux amours;
Voler en char, passer aux bals, aux promenades;
Respirer au balcon parfums et sérénades;
Ou, de sa harpe d'or éveillant cent rivaux,
Ne voir rien qu'un sourire entre tant de bravos.
Mais le ciel dès l'abord s'est obscurci sur elle,
Et l'arbuste en naissant fut atteint de la grêle.
Elle file, elle coud, et garde à la maison
Un père vieux, aveugle et privé de raison.

It is true that he concludes the whole delightful picture with a medical description of consumption; his muse coughs up blood,

une toux déchirante
La prend dans sa chanson, pousse en sifflant un cri,
Et lance les graviers de son poumon meurtri.

In our opinion the following elegy can stand as the most consummate
poem in the whole collection, worthy of being placed next to the best
productions of André Chénier:

Toujours je la connus pensive et sérieuse;
Enfant, dans les ébats de l'enfance joueuse
Elle se mêlait peu, parlait déjà raison;
Et, quand ses jeunes sœurs couraient sur le gazon,
Elle était la première à leur rappeler l'heure,
A dire qu'il fallait regagner la demeure;
Qu'elle avait de la cloche entendu le signal;
Qu'il était défendu d'approcher du canal,
De troubler dans le bois la biche familière,
De passer en jouant trop près de la volière:
Et ses sœurs l'écoutaient. Bientôt elle eut quinze ans,
Et sa raison brilla d'attraits plus séduisants:
Sein voilé, front serein où le calme repose,
Sous de beaux cheveux bruns une figure rose,
Une bouche discrète au sourire prudent,
Un parler sobre et froid, et qui plaît cependant;
Une voix douce et ferme, et qui jamais ne tremble,
Et deux longs sourcils noirs qui se fondent ensemble.
Le devoir l'animait d'une grave ferveur;
Elle avait l'air posé, réfléchi, non rêveur:
Elle ne rêvait pas comme la jeune fille,
Qui de ses doigts distraits laisse tomber l'aiguille,
Et du bal de la veille au bal du lendemain
Pense au bel inconnu qui lui pressa la main.
Le coude à la fenêtre, oubliant son ouvrage,
Jamais on ne la vit suivre à travers l'ombrage
Le vol interrompu des nuages du soir,
Puis cacher tout d'un coup son front dans son mouchoir.
Mais elle se disait qu'un avenir prospère
Avait changé soudain par la mort de son père;
Qu'elle était fille aînée, et que c'était raison
De prendre part active aux soins de la maison.
Ce cœur jeune et sévère ignorait la puissance

Des ennuis dont soupire et s'émeut l'innocence.
Il réprima toujours les attendrissements
Qui naissent sans savoir, et les troubles charmants,
Et les désirs obscurs, et ces vagues délices
De l'amour dans les cœurs naturelles complices.
Maîtresse d'elle-même aux instants les plus doux,
En embrassant sa mère, elle lui disait *vous*.
Les galantes fadeurs, les propos pleins de zèle
Des jeunes gens oisifs étaient perdus chez elle;
Mais qu'un cœur éprouvé lui contât un chagrin,
A l'instant se voilait son visage serein:
Elle savait parler de maux, de vie amère,
Et donnait des conseils comme une jeune mère.
Aujourd'hui la voilà mère, épouse, à son tour;
Mais c'est chez elle encor raison plutôt qu'amour.
Son paisible bonheur de respect se tempère;
Son époux déjà mûr serait pour elle un père;
Elle n'a pas connu l'oubli du premier mois,
Et la lune de miel qui ne luit qu'une fois,
Et son front et ses yeux ont gardé le mystère
De ces chastes secrets qu'une femme doit taire.
Heureuse comme avant, à son nouveau devoir
Elle a réglé sa vie. . . . Il est beau de la voir,
Libre de son ménage, un soir de la semaine,
Sans toilette, en été, qui sort et se promène
Et s'asseoit à l'abri du soleil étouffant,
Vers six heures, sur l'herbe, avec sa belle enfant.
Ainsi passent ses jours depuis le premier âge,
Comme des flots sans nom sous un ciel sans orage,
D'un cours lent, uniforme, et pourtant solennel;
Car ils savent qu'ils vont au rivage éternel.

Et moi qui vois couler cette humble destinée
Au penchant du devoir doucement entraînée,
Ces jours purs, transparents, calmes, silencieux,
Qui consolent du bruit et reposent les yeux,
Sans le vouloir, hélas! je retombe en tristesse;
Je songe à mes longs jours passés avec vitesse,
Turbulents, sans bonheur, perdus pour le devoir,
Et je pense, ô mon Dieu! qu'il sera bientôt soir!

The public and the critics were grieving at the untimely end of a talent promising so much, when they suddenly discovered that the deceased was alive and, thank God, in good health. Sainte-Beuve, already well known for his *History of French Literature in the Sixteenth Century* and his learned edition of Ronsard, had conceived the idea of publishing his first poetical efforts under the assumed name of J. Delorme, fearing probably the strictures and severity of the censorship on moral grounds. Mystification of such a sad character, because of its gay dénouement, should have harmed the success of his poems; however, the new school recognized and adopted this new comrade-in-arms with delight.

J. Delorme's views on French versification are expounded in his *Reflections*. The critics praised the truth, erudition and novelty of these comments. It seems to us that Delorme places too much importance on the innovations of the so-called *Romantic* school of French writers, who themselves place too much importance on poetic form, on the caesura, on rhyme, on the use of certain archaic words and idiomatic expressions, etc. All that is very well, but it is too reminiscent of the nappies and rattles of babyhood. There is no doubt that French versification is most arbitrary and, I make bold to say, most unsoundly based. How, for instance, will you justify the exclusion of the hiatus, which is so unbearable to French ears, in the running on of two words (as: été où aller), which they themselves seek in proper names for the sake of harmony: Zaïre, Aglaë, Eléonore. Let us note in passing that the French derive their rules on the hiatus from elision in Latin. According to the custom of Latin versification a word ending in a vowel loses it before another vowel. Boileau replaced this rule by one on the hiatus:

> Gardez qu'une voyelle à courir trop hâtée,
> Ne soit en son chemin pas une autre heurtée.[2]

Secondly, how can one always rhyme by sight and not by sound? Why should rhymes always agree in number (singular or plural) when their pronunciation is the same in both cases? However, the reformers have not touched on all this yet, though their attempts to do so have hardly been fortunate.

Last year Saint-Beuve published another volume of poems entitled *Les Consolations*. In them Delorme appears to have reformed on the advice of his friends, staid and moral people. Already he only quietly doubts, rather than desperately denies, the consolations of religion;

already he does not visit Rose, but admits to having, at times, depraved desires. As far as his diction goes, he has sown his wild oats. In short, both taste and morality should be pleased with him. One can even hope that in his third volume Delorme will appear as pious as Lamartine, and as a person of complete respectability.

Unfortunately we have to admit that in rejoicing at the changed man we mourn the poet. Poor Delorme was endowed with a virtue of great importance, denied to almost all French poets of the present generation, i.e. *sincerity of inspiration*. Now the French poets have systematically said to themselves: soyons religieux, soyons politiques – and some even say, soyons extravagants – and the chill of design, strain and constraint is felt in every one of their works, in which we see the movement of fleeting, unfettered impulse; in short, there is no true inspiration. God forbid that we should become the advocates of immorality in poetry (we do not use the word with the childish connotation with which it is used by some journalists among us)! Poetry by its nature, when at its highest and most free, should have no aim except itself, and should not, moreover, debase itself through the power of the word to the undermining of eternal truths on which man's happiness and greatness depend or to the transformation of its divine nectar into a lascivious, inflammatory potion. But the description of human weaknesses, errors and passions is not immoral, just as anatomy is not murder; and we do not see anything immoral in the elegies of the unhappy Delorme, in his confessions, which lacerated the heart, in his inhibited descriptions of his passions and lack of faith, in his complaints against fate, against himself. . . .

---

[1] First published in *Literaturnaya Gazeta*, No. 32 (1831), signed 'P'. Pushkin mentioned this article in a letter to Pletnev (no. 221) and planned to include it in a collection of his articles.

[2] *L'Art poétique*, I. The second line should read: 'Ne soit d'une voyelle en son chemin heurtée.'

206. Note

Our so-called 'aristocratic' writers have instituted a fashion which is very harmful to literature, of not replying to criticism. It is rare for any one of them to give voice, and even then it will not be on his own account. What sort of behaviour is that? Do they really scorn their brother writers; or do they really imagine themselves to be aristocrats?

They are very much mistaken: the reviews labelled them as such by way of a joke, ironically (see *Severnaya Pchela, Severny Merkuri*, etc.), and even if they do belong to good society, being well brought up and decent people, that is another matter and has nothing to do with literature.

One aristocrat[1] (still using the word ironically) excused himself by saying that it was unfitting for a man, who had any self-respect or cared for public opinion, to involve himself with certain people; that it constituted the same difference as existed between a duel and a fight; that, finally, no one had the right to insist that a man should speak to someone whom he did not wish to address. All this is no excuse. If you have gone into a public house then do not get annoyed if the talk there matches the company: if a rascal flings mud at you in the street it is ludicrous to challenge him to a duel instead of simply giving him a thrashing. And in refusing to speak to a man who has addressed you, you are being insulting and proud, which is unworthy of a good Christian.

[1] Vyazemsky, in an article in *Literaturnaya Gazeta*, No. 18 (1830).

207. A review of reviews[1]

Some of our writers see Russian reviews as the mouthpieces of popular enlightenment, as guides to public opinion, etc., and consequently insist that they should be accorded the same respect as is enjoyed by *Le Journal des débats* and *The Edinburgh Review*.

'Define the meanings of words,' Descartes used to say. A review in the sense in which it is understood in Europe is the voice of an entire party, a pamphlet appearing periodically, published by men of recognized knowledge and talent, having their own political leanings and their own influence on the course of events. The body of journalists is a seed-bed for public servants – they are conscious of this and, hoping to capture public opinion, they are afraid of lowering themselves in the public eye by dishonesty, vacillation, cupidity, or insolence. Because of the extent of the competition, ignorance and mediocrity cannot gain a monopoly among reviews, and a man lacking real talent cannot sustain 'l'épreuve' of print. Look at who publishes these warring reviews in France and England. In the former, Chateaubriand, Martignac, Peronet; in the latter, Gifford, Jeffrey, Pitt. I appeal to the conscience of our men of letters: what is there in common between these men and our reviews and journalists? By what right, may I ask, can the *Severnaya Pchela* direct Russian public opinion; or what sort of a voice can the *Severny Merkuri*[2] have?

[1] Not published in Pushkin's lifetime.
[2] The *Severny Merkuri* was published between 1830 and 1832 by M. A. Bestuzhev-Ryumin; it was little better than Bulgarin's *Severnaya Pchela*. Pushkin and Bestuzhev-Ryumin were at daggers drawn, the latter having on many occasions launched attacks on Pushkin's work, particularly on *Evgeny Onegin*.

208. A letter to the editor of the Literary Supplement to the *Russky Invalid*[1]

I have just read *Evenings by the Dikanka*. It astonished me. Here is real gaiety, which is sincere, unforced, without affectation, without pomposity. And in places what poetry! What sensibility! All that is so unusual for our contemporary literature that I have not yet come to my senses. I have been told that when the publisher[2] came into the printing works where the *Evenings* were in the press, the compositors began to suppress their giggles and snorts, covering their mouths with their hands. The foreman explained their hilarity, confessing that the compositors were dying of laughter in setting up his book. Molière and Fielding would doubtless have been glad to have amused their compositors. I congratulate the public on a truly gay book, and sincerely wish the Author success in the future. For God's sake take his side if the reviewers, in their customary manner, attack the *indecency* of his expressions, the *mauvais ton*, etc. It is high time that we laughed les précieuses ridicules of our literature to scorn, those people who are for ever talking of their 'fair readers', which they have never had, of the highest social circles, to which they are not invited. . . .

[1] Published in *Russky Invalid*, No. 79 (1831), as an addition to a review of Gogol's *Evenings on a Farm near Dikanka*, Book I, by L. Yakubovich.
[2] Gogol himself. He wrote to Pushkin (21 August 1831) that, when he visited the printers where his book was being set up, all the compositors had begun to giggle and splutter and the foreman explained that they had found his book most amusing, from which Gogol concluded that he was a writer 'absolutely to the mob's taste'. See Pushkin's reply to Gogol (25 August 1831), no. 234, and his comment in *Sovremennik* on the second edition of *Evenings on a Farm near Dikanka*, no. 294.

LETTERS

209. To P. Y. Chaadaev

Voici, mon ami, celui de mes ouvrages que j'aime le mieux.[1] Vous le lirez, puisqu'il est de moi – et vous m'en direz votre avis. En attendant, je vous embrasse et vous souhaite une bonne année.

[1] This letter was sent with a copy of *Boris Godunov*, which had been published the day before.

210. To Prince P. A. Vyazemsky

Your poems[1] are delightful – I don't feel like giving them to an almanac,[2] better let's send them to Delvig.[3] The waggon trains, the piglets and the brigadier are extraordinarily amusing. Yakovlev[4] is publishing an almanac for Shrove week called *The Pancake*. It will be a pity if his first pancake will prove a lump.[5] . . . In the *Pchela*[6] they offer me peace terms, reproaching us (you and me) with unyielding hostility and of perpetually courting Nemesis. All this is splendid; one thing I am sorry about – in my *Boris* they have cut out the crowd scenes[7] and French and native obscenities; incidentally, it's odd reading a lot of what is printed. The *Severnye Tsvety* are somewhat pale. What a joker Delvig is: he hasn't written anything himself for a whole year and publishes his almanac in the sweat of our brows.[8] I will be with you in a few days and will bring some champagne with pleasure – I am glad that the bottle's on me.[9] I have made peace with Polignac. His second term of imprisonment in Vincennes, the meridian drawn along the floor of his cell,[10] his reading of Walter Scott,[11] all that is romantically touching – but all the same the Chamber[12] is right. I am displeased with the advocates'[13] speeches – they are all timid. Only Lamennais[14] could aborder bravement la question. . . .

[1] 'Winter caricatures'.
[2] *Dennitsa* for 1831, edited by M. A. Maximovich. However Pushkin did forward the poems to Maximovich as Vyazemsky had asked.
[3] For *Severnye Tsvety*.
[4] P. L. Yakovlev. The almanac did not appear.
[5] The traditional fate of the first pancake in a frying. A Russian proverb.
[6] Bulgarin's *Severnaya Pchela*, the publication always most hostile to Pushkin.

Pushkin is referring to an article on Russian journalism in issue No. 155 (1830).

7 They were shortened, not cut out.

8 The almanac for 1831 was published on 24 December 1830. Delvig had not contributed anything to this issue; and Pushkin had not yet grasped the gravity of his friend's condition.

9 Pushkin had wagered Vyazemsky a bottle of champagne that Polignac would be executed; he lost his bet. Polignac was first imprisoned and then exiled.

10 Polignac was moved by the fact that he was confined in the same cell at Vincennes as he had occupied in 1804 and found on the floor the meridian line which he himself had drawn (*Le Temps*, 30 August 1830).

11 Mentioned in *Le Corsaire*, 30 August 1830.

12 The Chamber of Peers who tried Polignac for treason.

13 At the trial of Charles X's ministers.

14 Félicité-Robert de Lamennais, philosopher and theologian. He was a passionate publicist all his life, forcibly expressing his increasingly liberal views on both Church and State.

211. To M. P. Pogodin   *3 January 1831*
                                             Moscow

. . . They write to me from Petersburg that Godunov has met with success. That's another marvel. Bring out *Martha*. . . .

212. To P. A. Pletnev   *7 January 1831*
                                             Moscow

. . . Now let's talk of business. My dear fellow, I have seen *Tsvety*: a strange thing, an incomprehensible thing! Delvig hasn't included a single line of his own in them.¹ He has treated us like a landowner treats his peasants. We slave away – and he sits on the lavatory pan and criticizes us. This is neither good nor prudent. He opens our eyes to the fact that we have been made fools of. . . . They write to me that my *Boris* is a great success: a strange thing, and an incomprehensible thing! At any rate I certainly never expected it. What is the reason for it? The reading of Walter Scott?² The voice of the connoisseurs, of the chosen few? The clamour of my friends?³ The opinion of the court? Be it as it may, I cannot understand the success of my tragedy among you. Can the same be said of Moscow? Here they bemoan my utter, utter decline; that my tragedy is an imitation of Victor Hugo's *Cromwell*,⁴ that unrhymed poetry is not poetry, that the Pretender

301

should not have revealed his secret to Marina so carelessly, that it was a very irresponsible and impudent action on his part – and similar profound critical comments. I am waiting for the translations of it[5] and the judgement of the Germans, but am not bothered about the French. They will look for political allusions to the Warsaw rebellion in *Boris*, and will say to me as our own folk do: 'Spare us, Sir.' It will be interesting to see the response of our Schlegels, of whom only Katenin knows his business.[6] . . . By the way: Baratynsky's poem[7] is a marvel. Addio.

[1] See letter to Vyazemsky, no. 210 and note 8, above.
[2] On the widespread interest in Scott see pages 198-9.
[3] See pages 180-1 for account of the rapturous acclaim given to *Boris Godunov* by Pushkin's friends when he first read his play to them.
[4] See Pushkin's article on Chateaubriand's translation of *Paradise Lost*, no. 307.
[5] A German translation of *Boris Godunov* by Carl von Knorring was published in the second issue of *Russische Bibliothek für Deutsche* (Reval, 1831).
[6] The reception of *Boris Godunov* by Russian critics was not an enthusiastic one. In this work, which meant so much to him, Pushkin was definitely ahead of his time. The play puzzled rather than pleased and Pushkin was criticized for leaning too heavily on Karamzin's History. The famous actor, V. A. Karatygin, referred to it as a gallimaufry à la Shakespeare. Katenin, in spite of Pushkin's trust in his judgement, was as puzzled by the play's form as the rest; it seemed to him like chopped-up history rather than a play: 'It is unsuited to the stage, it cannot be called a poem or a novel or a dramatized history; there is nothing it can be called.' (Letter of 1 February 1831.) And he had many other objections. There was no help to be gained from that quarter.
[7] 'The Concubine' (1831).

213. To P. A. Pletnev   *13 January 1831*
                                                                 Moscow

. . . What about our *Gazeta*?[1] We must give it some thought. It had grown very dull; it could not very well be otherwise for it reflects Russian literature. Recently the talk in it was only of Bulgarin; that's just as it should be: in Russia only Bulgarin writes. Here is a text for a glorious philippic. If I was not lazy, and not engaged,[2] and not extremely kind, and could read and write, I would write a literary survey every week. But I don't have the patience, the malice, the time, or the *inclination*. However, we shall see.

Money, money: that's the most important thing. Send me some

money. And I'll say thank you. But why don't you write to me, you shameless man?

¹ *Literaturnaya Gazeta.* There was a general loss of heart in the *Gazeta* after the removal of Delvig from the editorship; but it had been a useful plat-form for Pushkin and he was anxious to keep at least this review going as a mouthpiece for his ideas on literature and for his campaigns against Bulgarin, Grech, etc.
² Pushkin got married on 18 February.

214. To Count A. C. Benckendorff   *18 January 1831*
                                                          Moscow

I was honoured to receive, with a feeling of deepest gratitude, the favourable comment of the Sovereign Emperor on my historical play.¹ Written during the last reign, *Boris Godunov* owes its appearance not only to the personal patronage which the Tsar conferred on me, but also to the freedom boldly given by the monarch to Russian writers at a time and in circumstances in which any other government would have tried to restrict and fetter the publication of books.²

Allow me also heartily to thank your Excellency, as the voice of the Supreme will and as a person who has always taken such indulgent interest in me.³

¹ Benckendorff had written to Pushkin on 9 January 1831, that the Tsar had read *Boris Godunov* with particular pleasure.
² Pushkin was probably referring to the July Ordinances restricting the freedom of the press for which Polignac was responsible and which had precipitated the French Revolution of 1830.
³ Pushkin could hardly have been more studiously polite and deferential.

215. To Prince P. A. Vyazemsky   *19 January 1831*
                                                        Moscow

Yesterday we received the sad news from Petersburg – Delvig has died of fever.¹ Today I am going to Saltykov,² he probably knows every-thing already. Leave *Adolphe*³ with me – I'll send you the necessary comments in a day or two.

¹ Delvig was Pushkin's closest friend and his death, probably of typhus, was a shattering blow. On 14 January Pletnev wrote to Pushkin a full account of the rapid course of Delvig's illness – it had lasted eight days. It was thought that he was too mentally run down to put up a fight for life.

Delvig had left unfinished when he died a review of *Boris Godunov* for the *Literaturnaya Gazeta*, his last piece of writing.

[2] M. A. Saltykov, Delvig's father-in-law.

[3] Vyazemsky's translation of Benjamin Constant's *Adolphe* was published in 1831.

216. To P. A. Pletnev *21 January 1831*
Moscow

What can I say to you, my dear! I received the terrible news on Sunday. On the next day it was confirmed. Yesterday I went to Saltykov to tell him everything – and hadn't the courage. In the evening I got your letter. I feel sad and desolate. This is the first death that I have mourned over. Towards the end of his life Karamzin and I were estranged, I grieved deeply for him as a Russian, but nobody in the world was closer to me than Delvig. Of all the ties of my childhood he alone remained – and our poor little circle gathered round him. We are orphaned without him. Count on your fingers how many there are of us. You and I, Baratynsky, that is all.

Yesterday I spent the day with Nashchokin[1] who is deeply shaken by his death – we spoke of him, referring to him as the late Delvig and this epithet was both strange and fearful. There's nothing one can do about it! We must accept. The late Delvig. So be it.

Baratynsky[2] is ill with grief. It isn't so easy to lay me out. Keep well and let's try to stay alive.

[1] Pavel Voinovich Nashchokin (1800-54), a man of exceptional kindness and good humour, was a school-friend of Pushkin's brother and became a very close friend of Pushkin's from the time he came to Moscow from Mikhailovskoe. Many years later Nashchokin recalled Pushkin's words to him on this occasion: 'Well, Voinich, hold on – they are beginning to fire into our ranks!' (Letter to N. M. Konshin, 1844.)

[2] Baratynsky was also a very close friend of Delvig's.

217. To E. M. Khitrovo *21 January 1831*
Moscow

. . . De tous les polonais il n'y a que Mickévicz[1] qui m'intéresse. Il était à Rome au commencement de la révolte,[2] je crains qu'il ne soit venu à Varsovie, assister aux dernières crises de sa patrie. . . .

Les Français ont presque fini de m'intéresser. La révolution devrait être finie et chaque jour on en jette de nouvelles semences. Leur roi,[3] avec son parapluie sous le bras, est par trop bourgeois. Ils veulent la république et ils l'auront – mais que dira l'Europe et où trouveront-ils Napoléon?

La mort de Delvig me donne le spleen. Indépendamment de son beau talent c'était une tête fortement organisée et une âme de la trempe non commune. C'etait le meilleur d'entre nous. Nos rangs commencent à s'éclaircir.

Je vous salue bien tristement, Madame.

[1] Adam Mickiewicz (1798-1855), Polish Romantic poet. See page 183 for Pushkin's friendship with Mickiewicz. When Mickiewicz left Russia for good he finally settled in Rome – he was not allowed to live in Poland. Alexander Herzen met him in Rome in 1848 and left this moving account in *My Past and Thoughts*, Part V, ch. 36:

> . . . I was really interested in one person only – Adam Mickiewicz; I had never seen him before. He was standing by the fireplace with his elbow on the marble mantelpiece. . . . Many thoughts and sufferings had passed over his face, which was rather Lithuanian than Polish. The whole impression made by his figure, by his head, his luxuriant grey hair and weary eyes, was suggestive of unhappiness endured, of acquaintance with spiritual pain, and of the exaltation of sorrow – he was the moulded likeness of the fate of Poland. . . . It seemed as though Mickiewicz was held back, preoccupied, distracted by something: that 'something' was the strange mysticism into which he retreated further and further. . . . He knew little of the literary movement (in Russia) after Pushkin, having stopped short at the time that he left Russia. (Translated by Constance Garnett, revised by H. Higgens, 1968.)

[2] The Polish rising, which lasted from January to September 1831, was followed by a period of intensified repression.
[3] Louis-Philippe.

218. To E. M. Khitrovo   *About, and not later than, 9 February 1831*
                              Moscow

. . . Qu'il me tarde de m'y retrouver [à Pétersbourg] et que je suis soûl de Moscou et de sa nullité tartare![1] Vous me parlez du succès de *Boris Godunov*: en vérité je ne puis y croire. Le succès n'entrait en rien dans mes calculs – lorsque je l'écrivis. C'était en 1825 – et il a fallu la mort d'Alexandre, la faveur inespérée de l'Empereur actuel, sa générosité et sa manière de voir si large et si libérale – pour que ma tragédie pût être publiée. D'ailleurs ce qu'il y a de bon est si peu fait pour frapper le respectable public (c'est-à-dire, la canaille qui nous juge) et il est si facile de me critiquer raisonnablement, que je croyais ne faire plaisir qu'aux sots, qui auraient eu de l'esprit à mes dépens. Mais il n'y a qu'heur et malheur dans ce bas monde et *delenda est Varsovia*.

[1] Pushkin often complained that he found Moscow stifling but he had to stay there to settle his wedding plans.

219. To N. I. Krivtsov[1]

10 February 1831
Moscow

My dear friend, I am sending you my favourite work.[2] You have in the past been indulgent over my early efforts – look on my more mature works favourably too. . . .

[1] See letter to N. I. Krivtsov, no. 3.
[2] *Boris Godunov.*

220. To P. A. Pletnev

26 March 1831
Moscow

. . . I received the books from Bellizard's[1] and am grateful. Could you ask him to send me the following as well: Crabbe, Wordsworth, Southey and Shakespeare,[2] to Khitrova's house on the Arbat. . . . Tell Somov to send me, if he can, last year's *Literaturnaya Gazeta* (I don't need this year's; I shall come for it myself) and *Severnye Tsvety*, our Delvig's last memorial.[3] We will discuss the almanac. I wouldn't mind editing the last *Severnye Tsvety* with you. But I am embarking on something else as well, which we will also discuss.[4] I was told that Zhukovsky is very pleased with *Martha, the Governor's Wife*; if that is so, let him use his influence with Benckendorff or with whomever else he wishes, to get permission to publish the whole play, a very remarkable work, despite the unevenness in the quality of the whole and the weaknesses in versification.[5] Pogodin is a very, very business-like and honest young man, a real German in his pure love of learning, his industry and his moderation. He should be supported and so should Shevyrev,[6] whom it would be no bad thing to seat on Merzlyakov's vacated chair, a kindly soak but a shocking ignoramus.

[1] A bookseller on the Nevsky Prospect in St Petersburg.
[2] The following editions of these authors remained in Pushkin's library, see

Appendix: *The Poetical Works of George Crabbe*, complete in one volume (Paris, 1829); *The Poetical Works of Robert Southey*, complete in one volume (Paris, 1829); *The Dramatic Works of Shakespeare*, printed from the text of Samuel Johnson, George Steevens and Isaac Reed, complete in one volume (Leipzig, 1824). No volume of Wordsworth survived, but Pushkin referred to his work several times and had clearly read some. In 1830 he wrote a sonnet inspired by Wordsworth's 'Scorn not the sonnet, critic', using Wordsworth's line as an epigraph. Pushkin's English had improved and he no longer had to rely on French translations. His interest in English poetry consequently widened.

³ Pushkin and Pletnev planned to publish *Severnye Tsvety* for 1832 to raise money for Delvig's two young brothers.

⁴ Pushkin was again laying plans for a literary review. At this time he was thinking of calling it 'Dnevnik' (The Diary).

⁵ See no. 179.

⁶ Stepan Petrovich Shevyrev (1806-64), whom Pushkin met when he came to Moscow in 1826, was at this time living in Italy. He had been present at Pushkin's reading of *Boris Godunov* and Pushkin had read him some other of his works. They discussed literary matters together. Shevyrev did not get the university chair that Pushkin thought he deserved.

221. To P. A. Pletnev   *11 April 1831*
                                             Moscow

. . . I think that if we all form a group, literature cannot fail to get warmed up and something must happen: an almanac, a review and newspapers! Vyazemsky is bringing you *The Life of Fonvizin*, well-nigh the most remarkable book to be written since we began writing books here (excluding Karamzin, however).

222. To P. A. Pletnev   *About 14 April 1831*
                                             Moscow

. . . I won't say anything to you of Gogol¹ because up till now I haven't had time to read him. . . . Embrace Zhukovsky for his sympathetic interest which I never doubted. I haven't written to him because we are not in the habit of corresponding.² I am waiting impatiently for his new ballads.³ And so 'his past is coming into its own again'.⁴ Thank God! But you don't mention whether his ballads are translations or original compositions. Dmitriev, thinking of criticizing him, gave Zhukovsky most salutary advice. Zhukovsky, he said, makes the old women in his village massage his legs and tell him stories, then he puts them into verse. In the poetry of the fantastic, Russian legends yield nothing to those of Ireland and Germany. If he is still inspired advise him to read the *Menologion*,[5] particularly the legends of the Kievan miracle-workers, which are gems of simplicity and invention!

[1] On 22 February 1831, Pletnev wrote to Pushkin:

> You must be introduced to a young writer who promises to be very good. Maybe you noticed in the *Severnye Tsvety* an extract from a historical novel signed OOOO and in *Literaturnaya Gazeta* an article – 'Thoughts on teaching geography', a story – 'The Woman', and a chapter from a Malorussian tale ('The Fearsome Boar') – 'The Schoolmaster'. They were written by Gogol – Yanovsky. He was educated in the Nezhinsky Lycée Bezborodko. At first he took a post in the civil service but a passion for teaching brought him under my banner: he also became a schoolmaster. Zhukovsky is enraptured by him. I cannot wait to bring him to you for your blessing. He has a disinterested love of learning and, as an artist, is ready to make any sacrifice for its sake. This touches and delights me.

[2] Pushkin and Zhukovsky usually corresponded only when Pushkin was in trouble and Zhukovsky, fearing for his safety, urged tact and patience.
[3] Translations from Southey and Schiller and other German poets – Hebel, Bürger, Uhland. Zhukovsky wrote nothing of his own at this time.
[4] Pushkin is quoting from one of Zhukovsky's own poems, written in 1823.
[5] Pushkin had been reading it while working on *Boris Godunov*.

223. To E. M. Khitrovo   *8 May 1831*
                                              Moscow

Le roman de Zagoskine[1] n'a pas encore paru. Il a été obligé d'en refondre quelques chapitres où il était question des Polonais de 1812. Les Polonais de 1831 sont bien plus embarrassants, et leur roman n'est pas à sa fin.

[1] *Roslavlev*, which came out in June. The action of the novel was set at the time of the Napoleonic wars.

224. To E. M. Khitrovo   *18-25 May 1831*
                                              St Petersburg

Voici vos livres, Madame, je vous supplie de m'envoyer le second volume de *Rouge et noir*.[1] J'en suis enchanté. *Plock et Plick*[2] est misérable.

C'est un tas de contresens, d'absurdités qui n'ont pas même le mérite de l'originalité. *Notre-Dame*[3] est-elle déjà lisible? Au revoir, Madame.

[1] Stendhal's *Le Rouge et le noir*, Chronique de 1830, was published in 1830. A copy of the 1831 edition remained in Pushkin's library. Contemporary readers judged this novel as a political and social tract.

[2] Eugène Sue's *Plick et Plock*, Scènes maritimes, published in 1831. This was the work of a subsequently prolific writer.

[3] Victor Hugo's *Notre-Dame de Paris*, published in 1831. The first volume of the 1832 Brussells edition remained in Pushkin's library. It was received with passionate enthusiasm when it appeared in St Petersburg, copies were snapped up and everybody spoke about it.

225. To E. M. Khitrovo   *9(?) June 1831*
                                             St Petersburg

. . . Voici, Madame, les livres que vous avez eu la bonté de me prêter. On conçoit fort bien votre admiration pour la *Notre-Dame*. Il y a bien de la grâce dans toute cette imagination. Mais, mais – – je n'ose dire tout ce que j'en pense. En tout cas la chute du prêtre[1] est belle de tout point, c'est à en donner des vertiges. *Rouge et noir* est un bon roman, malgré quelques fausses déclamations et quelques observations de mauvais goût.

[1] Book XI, ch. 2, the fall of Claude Frollo from the top of Notre-Dame.

226. To Prince P. A. Vyazemsky   *11 June 1831*
                                             Tsarskoe Selo

. . . Zhukovsky is still writing. He has translated several ballads by Southey,[1] Schiller[2] and Uhland,[3] including 'The Diver', 'The Glove', 'Polycrates' ring', etc. He has also translated Walter Scott's unfinished ballad[4] 'The Pilgrim', and has added his own ending – it is charming. He is now writing a tale in hexameters,[5] like his 'Red Carbuncle',[6] with the same characters: Grandpa, Louisa, the pipe, etc. All these will appear in the new edition of his collected ballads, which are being published by Smirdin in two little volumes. That is all we have to comfort ourselves with in the present bitter circumstances. . . .

[1] 'God's Judgement on a wicked Bishop', 'Donica', and 'Queen Orraca and the Five Martyrs of Morocco'.

[2] 'Der Taucher', 'Der Handschuh', 'Der Ring des Polykrates' and 'Klage der Ceres'.

³ 'Lob des Frühlings' and 'Das Schloss am Meere'.
⁴ Scott's 'The Gray Brother. A fragment'. Zhukovsky called his translation of it 'The Confession' and added a few verses of his own.
⁵ 'There were two and one more'.
⁶ 'Der Karfunkel' by Hebel, translated by Zhukovsky in 1816.

227. To M. P. Pogodin   *27-30 June 1831*
Tsarskoe Selo

Write 'Peter';¹ do not be afraid of his cudgel. In his day you would have been one of his *assistants*; in our own day at least be his portrait-painter.

¹ Pogodin wrote his tragedy *Peter* between January and July 1831 under Pushkin's guidance and spurred on by Pushkin's enthusiasm for *Martha*. It was not immediately passed by the censorship and was not published till 1873 – two years before Pogodin's death.

228. To P. A. Pletnev   *3 July 1831*
Tsarskoe Selo

. . . I have copied out my five tales and the introduction,¹ i.e. the works of the late Belkin, the dear man. What should I do with them? . . .

¹ Passed by the censor on 1 September and published at the end of October.

229. To Prince P. A. Vyazemsky   *3 July 1831*
Tsarskoe Selo

. . . I have seen in the papers that Turgenev has set out for Moscow to see you; can't you come back here with him? That would be delightful. We would start up something in the Almanac line and would draw on Turgenev a little.¹ I have no news of your *Adolphe*.² . . . Do not ask about literature: I don't get a single review except the *St Petersburgskiye Vedomosty*, and don't read that. I have read *Roslavlev*³ and very much want to know why on earth you criticize it. I haven't heard or seen the conversations about Boris;⁴ I don't listen in to other people's conversations. I am not writing anything at the moment, I am waiting for autumn to come. . . .

¹ A. I. Turgenev, see page 15. Turgenev had just come back to St Petersburg

from abroad. He had an encyclopedic knowledge of European literature.
2 Vyazemsky's translation of *Adolphe* by Benjamin Constant was in the press
at the time.
3 Novel by Zagoskin.
4 An anonymous pamphlet, 'Of *Boris Godunov* . . . a conversation', published
in Moscow in 1831. See letter to Nashchokin (no. 232) below. Belinsky
reviewed it in one of his early critical articles.

230. To P. Y Chaadaev[1]   *6 July 1831*
                                                Tsarskoe Selo

Mon ami, je vous parlerai la langue de l'Europe, elle m'est plus
familière que la nôtre et nous continuerons nos conversations com-
mencées jadis à Sarsko-Selo[2] et si souvent interrompues.

. . . Votre manuscrit[3] est toujours chez moi; voulez-vous que je vous
le renvoye? Mais qu'en ferez-vous à Nécropolis?[4] Laissez-le-moi encore
quelque temps. Je viens de le relire. Il me semble que le commencement
est trop lié à des conversations antécédentes, à des idées antérieurement
développées, bien claires et bien positives pour vous, mais dont le
lecteur n'est pas au fait. Les premières pages sont donc obscures et je
crois que vous feriez bien d'y substituer une simple note ou bien d'en
faire un extrait.[5] J'étais prêt à vous faire remarquer aussi le manque
d'ordre et de méthode de tout le morceau, mais j'ai fait réflexion que
c'est une lettre, et que le genre excuse et autorise cette négligence et
ce laisser-aller. Tout ce que vous dites de Moïse,[6] de Rome,[7] d'Aristote,[8]
de l'idée du vrai Dieu, de l'Art antique,[9] du protestantisme[10] est
admirable de force, de vérité ou d'éloquence. Tout ce qui est portrait
et tableau est large, éclatant, grandiose. Votre manière de concevoir
l'histoire m'étant tout à fait nouvelle, je ne puis toujours être de votre
avis; par exemple je ne conçois pas votre aversion pour Marc-Aurèle,
ni votre prédilection pour David (dont j'admire les psaumes, si toute-
fois ils sont de lui).[11] Je ne vois pas pourquoi la peinture forte et naïve
du polythéisme vous indignerait dans Homère.[12] Outre son mérite
poétique, c'est encore, d'après votre propre aveu, un grand monument
historique. Ce que l'Iliade offre de sanguinaire, ne se retrouve-t-il pas
dans la Bible? Vous voyez l'unité Chrétienne dans le catholicisme,
c'est-à-dire dans le pape. N'est-elle pas dans l'idée du Christ, qui se
retrouve aussi dans le protestantisme? L'idée première fut monarchique;
elle devint républicaine. Je m'exprime mal, mais vous me comprendrez.
Écrivez-moi, mon ami, dussiez-vous me gronder. Il vaut mieux, dit

l'Ecclésiaste, entendre la correction de l'homme sage que les chansons de l'insensé.[13]

[1] This is the only surviving letter from Pushkin to Chaadaev (see page 10) though he had written many. It was taken out of Chaadaev's possession when his papers were seized and examined, but to his delight was returned to him shortly before Pushkin's death. Pushkin was replying to a letter of Chaadaev's of 7 July, in which Chaadaev expressed anxiety concerning Pushkin's health and safety in view of the cholera epidemic raging round St Petersburg. (See also Pushkin's comment, written in the form of a letter, on Chaadaev's First Philosophical Letter published in the *Teleskop* (October 1836), which remained in Zhukovsky's keeping and which Chaadaev never saw, no. 321.)

[2] Pushkin is thinking of their early days together at Tsarskoe Selo.

[3] Pushkin wanted to help Chaadaev publish these two letters in a separate edition and had brought the manuscript from Moscow to St Petersburg, but they were not passed by the censor and did not appear till 1862. They were later published as Letters 2 and 3 in *Œuvres choisies de Pierre Tchadaïeff*, 'publiés pour la première fois par le P. Gagarin de la compagnie de Jésus' (Paris/Leipzig, 1862). More letters later came to light among Chaadaev's papers and these were seen to be Letters 6 and 7 in a series which comprised eight.

[4] Chaadaev writing in Moscow signed his letters as coming from Necropolis.

[5] The second letter opens with a reference to ideas raised in his first letter (not published till 1836) and in others which were lost.

[6] Moses stood high in Chaadaev's Pantheon, as having shown mankind the true God:

> la plus gigantesque et la plus imposante de toutes les figures historiques. . . . L'influence que ce grand homme a exercée sur le genre humain est bien loin d'être comprise et appréciée comme elle devrait l'être. Sa physionomie est restée trop voilée dans le jour mystérieux qui la couvre. . . . Il se peut aussi qu'il ait trouvé chez sa nation ou chez d'autres peuples l'idée d'un Dieu national, et qu'il ait fait usage de cette donnée, comme de tant d'autres qu'il aura trouvées dans ses antécédents naturels, pour introduire dans la pensée humaine son sublime monothéisme . . . de conserver pour le monde entier, pour toutes les générations à venir, la notion du Dieu unique... que les temps et les générations ne pouvaient avoir pour lui aucune sorte de valeur; que sa mission n'avait pas été d'offrir un modèle de justice et de perfection morale, mais de placer dans l'esprit humain une immense idée que l'esprit humain n'avait pu produire de lui-même.

[7] Chaadaev wrote of Rome:

> . . . ce n'est point Rome qui a péri, c'est la civilisation tout entière. L'Égypte des Pharaons, la Grèce de Périclès, la seconde Égypte des Lagides, et toute la Grèce d'Alexandre, qui s'étendait par delà l'Indus, enfin le judaïsme lui-même, depuis qu'il s'était hellénisé, tout cela

s'était fondu dans la masse romaine et ne faisait plus qu'une seule société, qui représentait toutes les générations antérieures depuis l'origine des choses, qui contenait tout ce qu'il y a eu de forces morales et intellectuelles développées jusque-là dans la nature humaine. Ce n'est donc point un empire, c'est la société humaine qui a été anéantie et qui a recommencé de ce jour. . . .

[8] Curiously Chaadaev, whose outlook on religion and philosophy was strongly biased in favour of Roman Catholicism, had developed an antipathy to Aristotle. He referred to him as 'ce mécanicien de l'intelligence'.

[9] Chaadaev wrote of ancient art:

Vous savez que ce sont les Grecs qui ont fait de l'art une vaste idée de l'esprit humain. Or, en quoi consiste cette magnifique création de leur génie? Ce qu'il y a de matériel dans l'homme a été idéalisé, agrandi, divinisé; l'ordre naturel et *légitime a été interverti*; ce qui devait se trouver originairement à la région inférieure du monde intellectuel a été mis au niveau des plus hautes pensées de l'homme, l'action des sens sur l'esprit a été augmentée à l'infini, la grande *ligne* de démarcation qui sépare le divin de l'humain dans la raison a été rompue . . . à la place de la primitive poésie de la raison et de la vérité, une poésie des sens et du mensonge s'est introduite dans l'imagination, et cette faculté puissante, faite pour nous figurer l'infigurable et nous faire voir l'invisible, ne s'est plus employée dès lors qu'à rendre le palpable plus palpable encore, le terrestre plus terrestre encore. . . . Voilà donc ce qu'a fait l'art des Grecs. C'est l'apothéose de la matière, on ne peut le nier.

[10] Chaadaev regarded Protestantism as a disruptive rather than as a reforming or purifying force:

Elle a replacé le monde dans la *désunité* du paganisme; elle a de nouveau rétabli les grandes individualités morales, l'isolement des âmes et des esprits que le Sauveur était venu détruire. . . . Le fait propre de tout schisme dans le monde chrétien est de rompre cette mystérieuse *unité*, dans laquelle est comprise toute la divine pensée du christianisme et toute sa puissance. C'est pour cela que l'Église catholique jamais ne transigera avec les communions séparées. Malheur à elle et malheur au christianisme, si le fait de la division est jamais reconnu par l'autorité légitime! Tout ne serait bientôt derechef que chaos des idées humaines, mensonge, ruine et poussière.

[11] Chaadaev wrote: 'On saura une fois pour toutes que Moïse a donné le Dieu véritable aux hommes, tandis que Socrate ne leur a légué que le doute pusillanime; que David est le modèle parfait du plus saint héroïsme, tandis que Marc-Aurèle n'est au fond qu'un exemplaire curieux d'une grandeur artificielle et d'une vertu d'apparat.'

[12] Writing of Homer Chaadaev says: 'C'est qu'en effet il y a une séduction étonnante dans cette poésie toute terrestre, toute matérielle, prodigieusement douce au vice de notre nature, qui relâche la fibre de la raison, qui

la tient stupidement enchaînée à ses fantômes et à ses prestiges, et la
berce et l'endort de ses illusions puissantes.'
[13] Ecclesiastes, VII, 5.

231. To P. A. Pletnev
Before 11 July 1831
Tsarskoe Selo

... A few days ago I sent you by Gesling the tales of my friend, the late
Belkin.[1] Did you get them? I shall send the preface later. ... What of
your plan for the *Severnye Tsvety*[2] in aid of Delvig's brothers? I am con-
tributing *Mozart*[3] and a few oddments; Zhukovsky, his tale in hexameters.[4] Write to Baratynsky;[5] he will send us some treasures. He is
at his country place. One can't hope for poems from you, but if only
you pulled yourself together and wrote something about Delvig it
would be splendid![6] In any case we need prose; if you don't contribute
anything it will run aground. There is no need for a survey of literature.
What the devil is there in our literature? One will have to scold
Polevoy and Bulgarin. ...

[1] They were published anonymously to avoid Pushkin's special censorship
arrangement with the Tsar.
[2] *Severnye Tsvety* for 1832, published in December 1831.
[3] *Mozart and Salieri*, see page 193 and no. 241.
[4] 'A Battle with a Serpent (a tale written in imitation of Schiller).'
[5] Only one of his poems was published in this almanac, 'My Elysium'.
Baratynsky was hardly writing any poetry at this time.
[6] Pletnev did not contribute to this almanac.

232. To P. V. Nashchokin
21 July 1831
Tsarskoe Selo

... You write to me of some critique in the form of a conversation,[1]
which I have not yet read. If you read our reviews you would see that
everything that passes for criticism among us is equally stupid and
laughable. For my part I have retreated. It is impossible to reply
seriously; and I am not prepared to play the fool before the public.
What is more, neither the critics nor the public deserve serious replies.
Now that autumn's here I shall settle down to my literary work, and
in the winter will bury myself in the archives to which the Tsar has
given me access.[2] The Tsar treats me very graciously and courteously ...

[1] See no. 229 and note 4.

15 Pushkin's sketch for an illustration for *Evgeny Onegin*, from a letter to his brother, 1–10 November 1824.

16 Self-portrait in manuscript of Chapter 1 of *Evgeny Onegin*, Odessa, June 1823.

17 Portrait of Pushkin in the last year of his life, by A. Linev.

18 Pushkin's study in the flat in which he died, 12 Moyka, St Petersburg (now a Pushkin Museum), photographed in 1967.

² Pushkin had approached the Tsar orally on this matter and was given access to the state archives in order to write a history of Peter the Great and his successors (up to Peter III). He received a civil servant's salary of 5,000 roubles a year for this work. The news of his novel role as 'historiographer royal' spread quickly among his friends, Chaadaev being one of the first to wish him God-speed in his task. From now to the end of his life he spent most of his time collecting material from various archives. He had settled in St Petersburg and rarely travelled anywhere, except for regular visits to Boldino or Mikhailovskoe in the autumn. Every morning he set off to the archive department, taking exercise by walking there and back to a late luncheon.

Pushkin had conceived the idea of this work as early as 1827 but before he finally settled to it he also wrote a history of the Pugachev rebellion in the reign of Catherine the Great. He was determined not to hurry, to immerse himself completely in the period, and only when he had done this to write something which would combine facts with literary excellence. Death caught up with him when he had scarcely begun writing. The Tsar then offered the post to Vyazemsky but he refused it.

233. To Prince P. A. Vyazemsky   *14 August 1831*
                                                    Tsarskoe Selo

... We are waiting for you. We really should start a review, but what kind? A quarterly. We'll issue a book, no – a tome, once in three months ...

234. To N. V. Gogol   *25 August 1831*
                                                    Tsarskoe Selo

... Congratulations on your first triumph, with the snorts of the compositors and the explanations of the foreman.¹ I am impatiently awaiting something else: the comments of the journalists and the verdict of the sharp-witted watchman.² All is well here: no riots, floods, or cholera. Zhukovsky is writing furiously. I feel autumn in the air, and am getting ready to settle down to work.

¹ See no. 208 on the reactions of the compositors to *Evenings on a Farm near Dikanka*.
² N. A. Polevoy.

235. To Prince P. A. Vyazemsky   *3 September 1831*
                                                    Tsarskoe Selo

... You write of the review: but who the devil will allow us to publish one? Von Fock has died, in a trice N. I. Grech will have taken his place.¹

A fine look-out for us! There's no point in even thinking of a political newspaper, and if we were to try a monthly or a quarterly, or one appearing three times a year, there would be nothing but trouble. *Without fashions* it won't sell, and *with fashions* we'll be lined up with Shalikov, Polevoy, etc., which would be shaming. What do you think? *With* or *without*?[2] . . . Zhukovsky is still writing; he has acquired six notebooks and has started six poems at one go; such is the force of his flux. Hardly a day passes without his reading me something new; this year he must have written a whole volume. That would be good for the review. I have started the same thing . . . yesterday I defecated a fairy tale a thousand lines long;[3] and another is rumbling in my guts. And the cholera continues. . . . What you say of *Roslavlev* is absolutely true;[4] it amuses me to read the reviews in our papers: one starts with Homer, another with Moses, and another with Walter Scott. They write volumes[5] on a novel which you assessed completely in three lines, to which, however, one could add another three: *that the situations, although forced, are intriguing and the conversations though fictitious are lively, and that the whole can be read with pleasure.* . . .

[1] Maxim Yakovlevich von Fock was Benckendorff's right-hand man at the Secret Police and had Pushkin under surveillance. Nikolai Ivanovich Grech was not in Benckendorff's service but, together with Bulgarin, made himself useful to him.
[2] In his reply (11 September 1831) Vyazemsky was scornful of the idea of attempting to deal with fashions in a quarterly review; by the time the issue came out the fashions would only be fit for Outer Siberia.
[3] 'The Tale of Tsar Saltan' was published in 1832.
[4] By Zagoskin. In his letter to Pushkin of 24 August, Vyazemsky wrote that he had sweated his way through Zagoskin's novel and so felt free to criticize it. He summed it up by saying that there was not one thought, or one feeling, or one situation in it which bore the stamp of truth.
[5] In *Moskovsky Telegraph* and *Teleskop*.

236. To Prince P. A. Vyazemsky   *Middle of October (about the 15th) 1831 Tsarskoe Selo*

. . . Busy yourself over the *Severnye Tsvety*,[1] send us your poems and prose. And hasn't Yazykov got something? I hear that he and Kireevsky are embarking on a review.[2] God speed! But will they have fashions?[3] This is an important point. At any rate there will be somewhere for us to appear in print – and Kosichkin is glad of it.[4] Zhukovsky has written heaps of good things, and is still at it. He is translating one canto of 'Marmion'; splendid.[5] What do you think of Gogol? My *Tales*[6] are being published. The *Severnye Tsvety* will be interesting. . . .

[1] For 1832.
[2] *Evropeets*, edited by Ivan Vasilyevich Kireevsky, Yazykov and Baratynsky. Two issues of it appeared in 1832 and then it was suppressed, see no. 243.
[3] Pushkin was still concerned as to whether one should have fashion-plates in a literary review, to help on sales. They figured in the *Moskovsky Telegraph*, the *Damsky Zhurnal*, and the Literary Supplement of the *Russky Invalid*.
[4] Pushkin's own pseudonym for an article aimed at Bulgarin, published in the *Teleskop* (1831), pt. iv.
[5] Zhukovsky translated Canto II of 'Marmion' and called it 'The Underground Trial'.
[6] *The Tales of Belkin.*

237. To P. V. Nashchokin   *22 October 1831*
                                                                                    St Petersburg

. . . I am waiting for Vyazemsky;[1] I am not sure that I won't start up something literary, a review, an almanac, or something of the sort. I feel lazy. Incidentally, I am editing the *Severnye Tsvety* in aid of our late Delvig's brothers; make sure it is bought up. It will be a good deed on our part. My *Tales* have been published.[2] You will get them in a day or two. . . .

[1] He was in Moscow.
[2] On 24 October 1831.

238. To Baron E. F. Rozen[1]   *October/mid-November 1831*
                                                                                    Tsarskoe Selo, or
                                                                                    St Petersburg

Here, dear Baron, is the *Feast in the time of the Plague* from Wilson's tragedy[2] à effet. Having embarked on publishing a third volume of my shorter poems I am not sending you some of them, as they will probably appear before your *Alcyone*.[3] I am burning with impatience to read your preface to *Boris*;[4] I think, for the second edition,[5] I shall write you a letter, that is if you will permit me to do so, and will expound in it the ideas and rules by which I was guided when writing my tragedy.

317

[1] Baron Egor Fedorovich Rozen (1800-60), literary journalist, minor poet, dramatist and librettist (he wrote the libretto for Glinka's opera *Life of the Tsar*). He thought of himself as a specialist on theatrical matters.

[2] Based on *The City of the Plague* by John Wilson (pseud. of Christopher North), 1816. It was written in Boldino, see page 194.

[3] An almanac for 1832, published by Rozen.

[4] Rozen was planning a German translation of *Boris Godunov*, but it was not published. His preface for it was published separately, in German in 1833 and in Russian in 1834.

[5] *Boris Godunov* did not go into a second edition in Pushkin's lifetime. Pushkin several times embarked on this form of introduction to *Boris Godunov*, see no. 174.

239. To N. M. Yazykov   *18 November 1831*
St Petersburg

. . . I congratulate the whole brotherhood on the birth of *Evropeets*.[1] I am ready, for my part, to serve you in whatever way I can, either with prose or verse. . . . Hurry Vyazemsky up, let him send me his prose and verse; shame on him and on Baratynsky. We are arranging a memorial to Delvig.[2] And that is how he is remembered by his own friends! It really is shameful. . . .

[1] See letter to Vyazemsky of middle of October above. Kireevsky wrote of his plans to Shevyrev in Rome (26 October). He wanted to include in his almanac the best of the European literary reviews, so as to draw Russian literature closer to that of other European countries. There were to be no fashions (!) and it would not be blotted by the name of Bulgarin. He mentioned that Pushkin had also once planned to start a review and, if he were to do so, the *Evropeets* would become redundant. The review was suppressed before Pushkin had had time to contribute to it, see page 194.

[2] *Severnye Tsvety* for 1832.

240. To F. N. Glinka[1]   *21 November 1831*
St Petersburg

We have embarked on the publication of the last *Severnye Tsvety* in memory of our Delvig. Of all his friends only you and Baratynsky are not numbered in the poetic requiem; the very two poets with whom, apart from his Lycée friends, he was most closely associated. I am told that you are angry with me;[2] that is no excuse: anger is one thing and friendship another. Those who are causing bad blood between us by God knows what gossip are a fine lot. On my part I have an entirely clear conscience in my sincere and deep respect for you and for your splendid talent. I still rely on your goodwill and your verses. Maybe I shall see you soon; at any rate it is pleasant for me to end my letter with this hope.

1 Fedor Nikolaevich Glinka (1786-1880). Pushkin had met him shortly after leaving the Lycée and Glinka had formed a high opinion of Pushkin's early poetry. Exiled for complicity in the Decembrist rising, he retained a reputation for idealism and exceptional kindness and goodwill.
2 Pushkin had written an epigram, 'A meeting of insects', in which Glinka figured as a ladybird – an allusion to his piety for in Russian a ladybird is called 'God's little cow'. Glinka replied with a warm, friendly letter (28 November), expressing his devotion to Pushkin and enclosing some contributions for the almanac.

1832

NOTES

241. Note for *Mozart and Salieri*[1]

At the first performance of *Don Giovanni*,[2] while the whole theatre, packed with astonished connoisseurs, was silently drinking in Mozart's harmony, somebody whistled—everyone turned round indignantly to see the famous Salieri walk out of the hall, maddened by all-consuming envy.

Salieri died eight years ago.[3] Some German reviews said that on his death-bed he confessed to the terrible crime of having poisoned Mozart. A man who could, through envy, hiss at *Don Giovanni* was capable of poisoning its creator.

[1] This note was not published in Pushkin's lifetime. It was intended for his Little Tragedy *Mozart and Salieri*, which he first planned in 1826 and wrote in 1830, see page 193.

[2] In Prague on 29 October 1787. The first performance in Vienna, at which Salieri could have been present, was on 7 May 1788.

[3] Antonio Salieri died in 1825. The rumour that he was responsible for Mozart's death was scotched, but it was true that he disliked Mozart and was not sorry when he died.

242. Note[1]

Everyone knows that the French are the most anti-poetical of people. Their best writers, the most famous representatives of this witty and rational nation, Montaigne, Voltaire, Montesquieu, La Harpe and Rousseau himself, proved how alien and incomprehensible they found a feeling for beauty.

If we look at the critical judgements current among the people and accepted by them as literary axioms, we will be astonished at how insignificant and unjust they are. They hold Corneille and Voltaire, as dramatists, to be the equals of Racine; J. B. Rousseau still retains the title 'great'. The unbearable Béranger, a versifier of stilted and mannered ditties lacking both passion and inspiration, which in gaiety and wit lag far behind Collé's[2] delightful trifles, is now considered their leading lyric poet. I don't know whether they have at last admitted to the jejune and faded uniformity of Lamartine,[3] but ten years have not passed from the time when they unabashedly placed him on a level with Byron and Shakespeare. *Cinq Mars*, a mediocre novel by the Comte de Vigny, is classed with the great works of Walter Scott.[4]

Naturally their blame is as ill judged as their praise. Sainte-Beuve is the least known of all the young talents of our age, and yet he is perhaps the most remarkable. His poems are certainly very original and, what is more important, are shot through with real inspiration. They were favourably mentioned in the *Literaturnaya Gazeta*,[5] receiving praise which seemed exaggerated. Now Victor Hugo, a poet and man of real gifts,[6] has taken upon himself to justify the opinion of the Petersburg review by publishing a book of poems entitled *Les Feuilles d'automne*, apparently written in imitation of Sainte-Beuve's *Les Consolations*.

[1] Note not published in Pushkin's lifetime.
[2] Charles Collé (1709-83), dramatist and song-writer.
[3] Pushkin had hardened in his views on Lamartine since his comment on French poetry written in 1824, see no. 60. See also his note on Alfred de Musset (1830) page 261.
[4] See Pushkin's article on Chateaubriand's translation of *Paradise Lost*, no. 307.
[5] Pushkin's own article, see no. 205.
[6] For Pushkin's comments on Victor Hugo see his letter to E. M. Khitrovo (no. 196) and his article on Chateaubriand's translation of *Paradise Lost*, mentioned in note 4 above.

LETTERS

243. To I. V. Kireevsky[1]   *4 February 1832*
                                                 St Petersburg

Please be generous enough to forgive me for not having thanked you till now for the *Evropeets* and for not having sent you my humble tribute-money. The blame for this lies in the cursed dissipation of Petersburg life[2] and on the almanacs, which drained my treasury, so that I didn't have even a couplet put by for a rainy day, except for a tale which I saved, an excerpt from which I am sending for your review.[3] God grant long life to your review! Judging by the first two issues the *Evropeets* should live for many years. Up to now our reviews have been arid and trivial or intelligent but dry; it seems that the

Evropeets[4] will be the first to combine good sense with attractive qualities. Now a few words on magazine economy: in the first two issues you published two major pieces by Zhukovsky, and a heap of poems by Yazykov – that is misplaced profligacy. There should have been at least three issues between the Sleeping Princess and Stepanida the Mouse.[5] Two pieces by Yazykov would have been sufficient. Save him for a rainy day. Otherwise you will squander all you have and will be forced to live on Raich[6] and Pavlov.[7] Your article[8] on *Godunov* and 'The Concubine'[9] cheered all hearts; at long last we have lived to see some true criticism. NB avoid learned terms; try to translate them, that is, paraphrase them. That will be both pleasant for the unlearned and useful for our language, which is still in its infancy. Baratynsky's article is good[10] but too subtle and long drawn out (I am speaking of his answer to criticism). Your comparison of Baratynsky and Mieris[11] is amazingly vivid and accurate. His elegies and poems are like a series of charming miniatures; but can this charm of finish, precision of detail, delicacy and truth in nuances, guarantee his future success in comedy, which demands, just as stage décor does, a bold and sweeping brush? I hope the *Evropeets* will wake him from his inactivity. . . . My cordial greetings to you and Yazykov.

[1] Ivan Vasilyevich Kireevsky (1806-56), a literary journalist who was much harassed by the government in his publishing efforts. This eventually drove him to despair. Herzen wrote of him in *My Past and Thoughts*:

> The prematurely aged face of Ivan Kireevsky bore deeply bitten traces of the suffering and conflict which had been followed by the mournful calm of the sea-swell above a foundered ship. His life was a failure. He threw himself with ardour – in 1833, if I remember rightly – into a monthly review, *The European*. The two numbers that appeared were excellent, but on the publication of the second *The European* was prohibited. He inserted an article upon Novikov in the *Dennitsa*: the *Dennitsa* was seized and the censor, Glinka, was put under arrest . . . he could not stand it, and went away to the country, burying in his heart profound distress and yearning for activity. This man too, firm and true as steel, was consumed by the rust of that terrible time. Ten years later he went back to Moscow from his hermit's life, a mystic and an Orthodox believer.

(Part IV, chapter 30; translated by Constance Garnett, revised by H. Higgens, 1968.)

Kireevsky much admired Pushkin and said of him that he had met with no other Russian skull that contained so much brain-matter. He was one of the few people to greet *Poltava* enthusiastically.

2 Marriage was beginning to present its problems.

3 *The Little House in Kolomna.*

4 There were not to be any more.

5 Extract from the unfinished 'War of the Mice and the Frogs'. This and 'The Sleeping Princess' were both by Zhukovsky.

6 S. E. Raich, editor of *Galatea*, a third-rate poet.

7 N. F. Pavlov, translator and minor poet, an inveterate gambler. Pavlov addressed a poem 'To N. N.', *Teleskop*, No. VI (1831), with the following epigraph from Balzac: 'La vanité a un souffle qui dessèche tout'. The poem started and ended with the words: 'You did not understand the poet and cannot understand him'. It seems to have been aimed directly at Pushkin's wife.

8 'Survey of Russian literature for 1831', *Evropeets*, nos. 1 and 2.

9 Poem by Baratynsky, later called 'The Gipsy'.

10 In the second number of the *Evropeets*, headed 'Anti-criticism'.

11 Franz von Mieris the elder (1635-81), a Dutch painter of domestic scenes and portraits. He specialized in small canvases and was renowned for the brilliance of his detail, particularly in the painting of costumes. One of his famous pictures – The Oyster Meal (1659) – hangs in the Hermitage Museum in Leningrad.

244. To Count A. C. Benckendorff   *7 February 1832*
                                                                St Petersburg

Your Excellency has demanded an explanation of me[1] as to how it was that my poem 'Anchar' came to be published in an almanac without having previously been scrutinized by His Imperial Majesty: I hasten to answer Your Excellency's inquiry.

I was always firmly convinced that the highest *favour*[2] that was un-expectedly bestowed on me did not at the same time deprive me *of the right*, granted by the Tsar to all his subjects, to publish that which has been approved by the censorship. During the last six years, both with and without my knowledge, my poems have been published in all the reviews and almanacs without any obstacles, and no comment on this score was ever made either to me or to the censorship. Feeling guilty at constantly troubling His Majesty I even asked for your good word on one or two occasions, when the censorship was hesitating, and was fortunate in finding you more indulgent than it. . . .

1 On 7 February Benckendorff had sent Pushkin an official inquiry, asking why there had appeared, in the almanac *Severnye Tsvety* for 1832, several poems of his, including the 'Anchar' (The Upas Tree), without their previously having been sent for clearance to the Emperor. None of the

poems published (including the Little Tragedy, *Mozart and Salieri*) had caught the attention of the secret police except for 'Anchar'. In the original version of the poem the Tyrant, who poisons his neighbours and destroys his slaves, was referred to as 'the Tsar' – later altered to 'the Prince'. This potentially offensive allusion had caught Benckendorff's wary eye and was the cause of the trouble.

[2] Of acting as Pushkin's personal censor.

245. To I. I. Dmitriev   *14 February 1832*
                                              St Petersburg

... I am glad that I succeeded in pleasing you with my verses, despite their being blank.[1] You must love rhyme as a faithful servant who has never quarrelled with you and has always submitted to your slightest whim. The liveliness of your activity and interest must be consoling to every Russian; and, to judge by physiological signs, this is a pledge of longevity and health. Long life to you, dear Sir! Outlive our generation as your powerful and harmonious verses will outlive the puny productions of today.

You probably already know that the review, The *Evropeets* has been banned as a result of a denunciation.[2] Kireevsky, kind and modest Kireevsky, has been represented to the government as a madcap and a Jacobin! Everybody here hopes that he will clear himself and that his slanderers – or at any rate the slander – will be put to shame and exposed.

[1] Dmitriev had written to Pushkin (1 February): 'Your *Godunov* and *Mozart and Salieri* prove to us that you are not only a Protean Poet, but a diviner of hearts and a painter and musician. So far, after Karamzin (in his minor verse), only Pushkin can make me read *blank* verse and forget about rhyme.'

Mozart and Salieri was staged twice in the St Petersburg Bolshoy theatre (27 January and 1 February 1832) but it did not meet with success and was not produced again in Pushkin's lifetime.

[2] The *Evropeets* was banned on account of two articles by Kireevsky himself: one on nineteenth-century literature and one on Griboedov's *Woe from Wit*. The Tsar was personally responsible for the decision. He informed Benckendorff that under cover of writing on nineteenth-century literature Kireevsky was writing on politics, which had been specifically forbidden. The article should never have been passed by the censor. In writing of *Woe from Wit*, Kireevsky showed too much love of things foreign as opposed to things Russian.

246. Draft letter to Count A. C. Benckendorff   *18-24 February 1832*
St Petersburg

At your Excellency's command I am forwarding to you a poem[1] which has been accepted by an almanac and has already been passed by the censorship. I have delayed its publication pending your permission.

May I make so bold as to take this opportunity of asking your Excellency permission to explain my position frankly. In 1827[2] it pleased His Majesty the Sovereign Emperor to announce to me that *I should have no censor but His Majesty*. This unheard-of favour imposed on me the obligation of submitting for His Majesty's examination those works which were worthy of his attention if not by their quality then at least by their aim and contents. I have always felt pained and guilty at troubling the Tsar with trifling poems important only to me, as they brought me an income of 20,000, and this necessity alone forced me to make use of the right granted me by the Sovereign.

Now your Excellency . . . has ordered me to submit to your Excellency those of my poems which either I or the papers might wish to publish. Allow me to state to your Excellency how this request brings with it various inconveniences.

(1) Your Excellency is not always in residence in Petersburg, whereas the book *trade*, like every other trade, has its *deadlines*, its market-days; with the result that because a book is published in March and not in January the author may stand to lose several thousand roubles, and the publisher of a review, several hundred subscribers.

(2) Being alone subject to a censorship which depends solely on you – I, contrary to the right given me by the Sovereign, will be subject to a more repressive censorship than any other writer, as – quite simply – this censorship will regard me with prejudice and will everywhere find hidden meanings, allusions and difficulties – and accusations concerning allusions and hidden meanings have no bounds and no justifications, if the word *free* is understood as meaning constitution, and the word *arrow*, autocracy.

I make bold to ask one favour: that in future I should have the right to refer my shorter poems to the ordinary censorship.

---

[1] 'Anchar'.
[2] Actually it was in September 1826, see page 179.

247. To Count A. C. Benckendorff   *24 February 1832*
St Petersburg

. . . May I take the liberty of troubling your Excellency again with a most humble request for permission to examine in the Hermitage the library of Voltaire,[1] who used various rare books and manuscripts, sent to him by Shuvalov,[2] for the compilation of his *History of the Russian Empire under Peter the Great.*

At your Excellency's command I am forwarding to you one poem,[3] which I have given to an almanac and which has already been passed by the censorship. I have delayed its printing pending your Excellency's permission.

[1] Catherine the Great acquired Voltaire's library in 1779 and kept it in the Hermitage; it is now in the Leningrad State Public Library.

[2] Prince Ivan Ivanovich Shuvalov sent Voltaire many documents, engravings, medals, etc., when he was writing his *History of Russia at the time of Peter the Great.* This work was included in the collection of Voltaire's work which Pushkin had in his library (Geneva 1759-63).

[3] 'Anchar'.

248. To Count A. C. Benckendorff   *27 May 1832*
St Petersburg

Général,

Mademoiselle Küchelbecker m'a fait demander si je ne prendrais pas sur moi d'être l'éditeur de quelques poèmes manuscrits que son frère lui a laissés. J'ai cru qu'il fallait pour cela l'autorisation de Votre Excellence et que celle de la censure ne suffisait pas. J'ose espérer que cette permission que je sollicite ne pourra me nuire : ayant été camarade de collège de G. Küchelbecker, il est naturel que sa sœur, en cette occasion, se soit adressée à moi plutôt qu'à tout autre.[1]

Maintenant permettez-moi de vous importuner pour quelque chose qui m'est personnel. Jusqu'à présent j'ai beaucoup négligé mes moyens de fortune. Actuellement que je ne puis être insouciant sans manquer à mes devoirs, il faut que je songe à m'enrichir et j'en demande la permission à Sa Majesté. Mon service auquel Elle a daigné m'attacher, mes occupations littéraires m'obligent à demeurer à Pétersbourg, et je n'ai de revenu que ce que me procure mon travail. L'entreprise littéraire dont je sollicite l'autorisation et qui assurerait mon sort, serait d'être à la tête du journal dont M-r Joukovsky m'a dit vous avoir parlé.[2]

Je suis avec respect, Général,
de Votre Excellence
le très humble et très obéissant serviteur
Alexandre Pouchkine

[1] Permission was not granted.
[2] For many years Pushkin had corresponded with Vyazemsky on the crying
need for a new literary and political review. Now, as it appears from the
diary of N. A. Mukhanov, he felt that Vyazemsky was no longer the right
man to work with: he had become too embittered ('aigri'), and despised
Russian reviews. S. S. Uvarov, who was in on the discussions, felt Pushkin
was temperamentally unsuited to edit a good review as he lacked the
necessary determination and diligence.

As a result of this letter Pushkin received provisional permission to publish
a periodical called *Dnevnik* (Diary), in which he could include news of
political events. A. I. Turgenev, who was in Paris at the time, immediately
sent Journalist-Pushkin an 'Album littéraire. Choix d'articles extraits des
meilleurs Écrits périodiques publiés en France, sur la Littérature, les Arts
et les Sciences.' Delighted notices of the coming publication began to
appear but though Pushkin approached Kireevsky, Yazykov, and others,
asking them to collaborate with him, he was worried by the restrictions
he would have to observe in handling material of a political nature. The
Dnevnik did not see the light of day.

[At about the same time as the above letter Pushkin sent the following, using
a draft he had written in July/August 1830. Those lines of the draft that he
now omitted are printed in square brackets.]

To Count A. C. Benckendorff   *About 27 May 1832*
                                      St Petersburg

Ten years ago only a very few amateurs among us concerned themselves
with literature. They saw in it a pleasant and honourable exercise but not,
as yet, a branch of industry; there were as yet very few readers; the book
trade was confined to some translated novels and the reprinting of books
interpreting dreams and song-books.

[Karamzin, a person who had an important influence on Russian enlightenment and who had devoted his life solely to learning, was the first to have
experience of the business side of literature. In this, as in everything else,
he was the exception to all we were used to see here.

During the reign of the late Emperor, writers were left at the mercy of
an arbitrary and oppressive censorship – only rarely did a work get into
print. All the writers (an important class in our society for at least it consists
of literate people) joined the ranks of the disaffected. The government did
not wish to notice this, partly out of magnanimity (unfortunately people
either did not understand this or did not wish to do so) and partly out of
unforgivable negligence. I could claim that during the last five years of

327

the late Tsar's reign I had much more influence on the whole body of writers than had the Ministry, in spite of the immeasurable disparity in our resources.]

The unfortunate circumstances which accompanied the accession to the throne of the present Emperor drew his Majesty's attention to the estate of writers. He found this class to be utterly at the mercy of fate and oppressed by an ignorant and arbitrary censorship. There was not even a law of copyright. [Last year, having failed to find justice, I lost 3,000 roubles through the reprinting of one of my works[1] (this being only the first example).]

The protection of copyright and the establishment of Censorship Rules are among the most important benefactions of the present reign.

Literature took on a new lease of life and entered on its normal path, i.e. the commercial. Now it forms a branch of industry, under legal protection.

Of all forms of literature, periodical publications bring in the most profit and the more varied their contents, the wider their circulation.

Political news, being of general interest, draws the majority of readers.

[The newspapers of Petersburg, Moscow, Odessa and Tiflis, and the *Severnaya Pchela*, are so far the only publications in which political news is published.]

The *Severnaya Pchela*, published by two well-known men of letters,[2] having about 3,000 subscribers [bringing in to its publishers 80,000 roubles each, whereas a purely literary review can barely cover publication costs] must naturally exercise a strong influence on the reading public and consequently on the book trade.

Every journalist has the right to voice his own opinion on a newly published book in as strong terms as he wishes. The *Severnaya Pchela* avails itself of this right and does well to do so; it would be both impossible and unjust to force a journalist by law to be either indulgent or unprejudiced. It remains for the author of a slated book to wait for the judgement of the reading public or to seek for justice and defence in another paper.

But *purely literary* reviews have instead of 3,000 subscribers barely 300 and consequently their voice has little effect.

In this way the literary trade finds itself in the hands of the publishers of the *Severnaya Pchela* and criticism as well as politics has become their monopoly.

[1] *The Prisoner of the Caucasus.*
[2] Bulgarin and Grech.

249. To I. V. Kireevsky   *11 July 1832*
                                                               St Petersburg

I stopped corresponding with you, fearing to bring down on you extra displeasure or unnecessary suspicion, in spite of my conviction that coal cannot be blackened by soot.[1] Today I have the chance to send you a letter by hand[2] and I am going to speak frankly to you. The suppression of your review created a strong impression here; everybody was on your side, that is, on the side of complete innocence; the denunciation, as far as I could discover, struck not from Bulgarin's dunghill but like a bolt from the blue.[3] Zhukovsky, with his passionate integrity, came out on your side; Vyazemsky wrote a bold, intelligent and convincing letter to Benckendorff.[4] You alone did not act, and in this case you are absolutely wrong. As a citizen you have been deprived by the government of one of the rights of all its subjects; you should have cleared yourself out of self-respect and, I make bold to say, out of respect for the Sovereign; since an attack by him is not the same as one by Polevoy or Nadezhdin, I don't know if it's too late but in your place I should even now not hold back from clearing myself; start your letter by saying that 'having long waited for an inquiry from the government you remained silent up till now, but, etc.' I swear this wouldn't be out of order.

Meanwhile I would like to ask you and your brother[5] and Yazykov for a great favour. I was the other day given permission to publish a political and literary newspaper.[6] Don't desert me, brothers! If you undertake the task of jotting down a few words about any book you happen to have read for my begging bowl, God will not desert you. Nikolai Mikhailovich[7] is lazy, but as I am having as little poetry as possible, my request won't cause even him any trouble. Write me a few words (do not be afraid of harming thereby my political reputation) about the proposed newspaper. I seek your advice and help.

PS. Joking apart: you are wrong in thinking that you can harm anybody by your letters. I would be as pleased to correspond with you as I am flattered by your friendship. I await your reply impatiently – maybe I'll be in Moscow in a day or two.

[1] Pushkin had not written to Kireevsky since 4 January. Now he himself was in trouble again, see his letter to Benckendorff, no. 246.

[2] Those who were aware that their letters were watched took advantage of opportunities to send them 'by hand'. This letter had been delivered in this way.

[3] A hint that the Tsar himself – Jove, the Thunderer – and not Bulgarin was responsible for the ban. Pushkin is adapting a proverb. The Emperor was very displeased at two of Kireevsky's articles published in the *Evropeets*: one on the nineteenth century and one on the Moscow production of Griboedov's *Woe from Wit*. He suspected that in the article on the nineteenth century Kireevsky, while pretending that he was writing only of literature, was in fact covertly writing of politics: 'the word *enlightenment* stands for *freedom, mental activity* stands for *revolution*, and *a skilfully discovered*

centre for nothing other than *a constitution*.' The Emperor clearly felt he had cracked a code. In view of this he considered that the article had no business to appear in a literary magazine in which the publication of anything of a political nature was strictly forbidden and the censorship should never have passed it. The trouble with the review of *Woe from Wit* was that in it Kireevsky showed enthusiasm for foreign ideas.

4 There was widespread indignation at the ban on the *Evropeets*. A. V. Nikitenko heard of it at an evening gathering at Pletnev's (Pushkin was also present) and wrote in his diary: 'What will there be left for us to do in Russia? Nothing but drinking and rioting. It's depressing and shameful and sad!' Baratynsky was devastated. He wrote to Kireevsky (14 March 1832): 'Like you, I have lost all incentive to undertake any literary work. The proscribing of your review has made me splenetic and judging by your letter it has plunged you into melancholy.'

All representations were in vain. It was not what was written that was considered dangerous but what could be read between the lines. Here revolution was writ plain.

As a result of Zhukovsky's intervention Kireevsky was given the chance to offer explanations of his views. He declared that he wanted to establish links with European thinkers and politicians and did not conceal that he considered the emancipation of the serfs as an essential condition of Russia's moral development. This finally sealed his reputation as a dangerous man and he was placed under police surveillance.

5 P. V. Kireevsky, collector of Russian folk-songs.

6 This permission was cancelled before the publication had time to be launched.

7 Yazykov.

250. To M. P. Pogodin   *11 July 1832*
                                                       St Petersburg

. . . I am infuriated by the barbarism of our literary trade. Smirdin has tied himself up in various obligations,[1] has bought up novels, and such like, and won't discuss any terms. Tragedies don't sell these days, says he in his technical jargon. Let's sit it out. I am told that you were criticized somewhere for *The Governor's Wife*: I hope that this will have no influence on your work. Remember that for ten consecutive years I was praised for God knows what, and then was decried for *Godunov* and *Poltava*. Our criticism is, of course, of an even lower order than our literary public, let alone our literature. One can fume at it but on no account trust it – that is an unpardonable weakness. Your *Martha* and your *Peter* are filled with true dramatic power, and if they ever get passed by the theatrical censorship[2] I foresee for you such popular success as we, cold northern spectators of vaudevilles by Scribe[3] and ballets by Didelot,[4] cannot even imagine.

Do you know that the Tsar has given me permission to edit a political paper? An important matter, for the monopoly of Grech and Bulgarin has fallen. You understand that you won't be spared from this affair. But as the review is a commercial venture I daren't start doing anything either as regards offers or contracts until I have sorted things out systematically. I don't want to sell you the skin off a live bear, or to collect subscriptions for a history of the Russian people which exists only in my stupid head. . . .[5]

[1] Smirdin had just opened a new bookshop on the Nevsky Prospect which impressed Vyazemsky by its comfort – all mahogany and bronze, gleam and comfort. It became a centre for writers and journalists to gather for readings and for publishers to meet their authors. Pushkin was a frequent visitor.
[2] *Martha, the Governor's Wife* was not passed for public performance as the Emperor would not allow Russian Tsars to be presented on the stage.
[3] Augustin Eugène Scribe (1791-1861), a prolific French dramatist specializing in light comedy.
[4] Charles Louis Didelot, the famous ballet-master (see *Evgeny Onegin*, I, xviii).
[5] Polevoy had collected subscriptions for his history of the Russian people before writing it.

251. To M. P. Pogodin   *First half of September 1832*
                                             St Petersburg

What sort of manifesto[1] would you like to see? The political part is officially insignificant; the literary section is insignificant in content: news of the rate of exchange, of arrivals and departures – there you have the whole plan. I wanted to break the monopoly,[2] and have succeeded. The rest interests me little.[3] My paper will be a little worse than the *Severnaya Pchela*. I have no intention of pleasing the public; to quarrel with the reviews is all right once in five years, and even then it is better for Kosichkin[4] and not me to do it. I have no intention of including poetry, as even Christ forbade men to cast pearls before the public: that is what the chaff of prose is for. One thing spurs me on: I want to destroy, to show up the entire disgusting banality of contemporary French literature. For once to say aloud that Lamartine is duller than Young,[5] and has not got his depth, that Béranger is not a poet, that V. Hugo has no life in him, i.e. no truth, that the novels of A. Vigny are worse than the novels of Zagoskin, that their reviews are uninformed, that their critics are little better than ours in the *Teleskop* and *Telegraph*. I am deeply convinced that in comparison to the eighteenth century the nineteenth century is sunk in mire (I mean, of course, in France). The prose barely redeems the muck they call poetry.

We will speak anon of your client Godunov.[6] I am coming to Moscow in a few days to see you.

[1] In connection with Pushkin's projected review *Dnevnik*. At one stage Pushkin had wanted Pogodin to work with him but now he was intent on cooling off the widespread interest that had been aroused in the venture.

[2] Particularly of Bulgarin and his *Severnaya Pchela*.

[3] The difficulties which surrounded the obtaining of permission to publish a review had sapped Pushkin's spirit. His tone throughout this letter is flat and hopeless, bitter with irony. It was clear that only those things which interested him least would be passed for publication – the rates of exchange and social comings and goings.

[4] His own pseudonym.

[5] This is Pushkin's only mention of Young. He had the French 1818 edition of *Night Thoughts* in his library. It was as popular in Russia as elsewhere.

For Pushkin's changing views on Lamartine see no. 242. Lamartine for his part was interested in Pushkin's poetry and in 1836 asked Vyazemsky to send him some to read.

[6] Pogodin was also writing a play on Boris Godunov. He completed it in 1833 but it was not published till 1868.

252. To N. N. Pushkin   *Around, and not later than,*
                                         30 September 1832
                                         Moscow

. . . I have thought of an idea for a novel,[1] and I shall probably get busy on it; but at the moment my head is spinning with thoughts of the paper.[2] . . .

[1] *Dubrovsky*. See notes to the following letter to P. V. Nashchokin.

[2] The *Dnevnik*.

253. To P. V. Nashchokin   *2 December 1832*
                                            St Petersburg

. . . I have the honour to announce to you that the first volume of *Ostrovsky*[1] is ready and will be sent to Moscow in a few days for your perusal and for Korotky's criticism.[2] I wrote that in two weeks but was then stopped by fiendish rheumatism from which I suffered for the next fortnight, so that I could not lift my pen or put two ideas together in my head. . . . My review has been brought to a halt because the permit took so long in coming. It will not be published this year. Actually I'm glad. I'll be able to look around and get ready for next year and in the meanwhile I will practise small economies. . . . Tell Baratynsky that Smirdin is in Moscow and that I talked to him of the publication of the *Complete Poetical Works of E. Baratynsky*.[3] I spoke of 8 or 10 thousand, but Smirdin was afraid that Baratynsky would not agree, so Baratynsky can come to terms with him. Let him try. . . .

[1] Renamed *Dubrovsky*. The novel remained unfinished. The first chapter is dated 21 October 1832; chapter XIX, the last Pushkin wrote, was completed 22 January 1833. Pushkin had got his subject – a legal action between a poor nobleman, Ostrovsky, and his neighbour – from Nashchokin. He received the transcript of the case from Nashchokin's friend, D. V. Korotky. *Dubrovsky* was first published in 1841.

[2] This concerned the handling of court procedure in which Korotky was well versed.

[3] Not published till 1835.

254. To E. M. Khitrovo   *August/first half of September or*
                                          end of October/December 1832
                                          St Petersburg

. . . Comment n'avez-vous pas honte d'avoir parlé si légèrement de *Karr*.[1] Son roman a du génie et vaut bien le marivaudage de votre Balzac.[2] . . .

[1] Jean Alphonse Karr (1808-90), French novelist. His first novel was *Sous les tilleuls*, published in 1832. Pushkin had several novels by Karr in his library.

[2] Balzac had embarked on *La Comédie humaine* in 1829. His novels were becoming very popular with the Russian public.

1833

DIARY

255.

29 November. Yesterday they staged *Les Enfants d'Édouard*[1] here with great success – they say the tragedy will be banned. Heeckeren[2] is surprised at the boldness of the allusions. . . . Bligh[3] did not notice them. I think Bligh is right.

3 December. Yesterday Gogol read me a story, 'How Ivan Ivanovich quarrelled with Ivan Timofeyevich',[4] which is both original and very funny.

14 December. The Bronze Horseman has been returned to me with the Emperor's comments. The word 'idol' has not been passed by the supreme censor; the lines 'And before the younger capital ancient Moscow has paled, like a purple-clad dowager before a new empress' have been crossed through. Many places are marked with a query. All of which makes a big difference to me.

[1] By Casimir Delavigne, concerning the murder of the Prinçes in the Tower. It was first performed by a French company in St Petersburg on 8 November 1833. The audience saw links with the murder of Paul I, but the play was not proscribed and was later staged in Russian.

[2] Baron von Heeckeren, the Dutch Ambassador and guardian of Georges D'Anthès.

[3] English Chargé d'affaires.

[4] Published in 1834. Pushkin made a slip in the title of the story, which is 'How Ivan Ivanovich quarrelled with Ivan Nikiforovich'.

ARTICLE

256. On the works of P. A. Katenin[1]

The works and verse translations of Pavel Katenin were published the other day.

The publisher (Mr Bakhtin) at the beginning of his most remarkable preface mentions that P. A. Katenin, almost from the very beginning of his literary career, was met with the most unfair and the most intemperate criticism.

It seems to us that Mr Katenin (like all our writers in fact) has more cause to complain of the silence of the critics than of their severity, or prejudiced captiousness. We have as yet no criticism in the true sense of the word; it would be unfair of us to expect it. We have, in fact, hardly any literature; and there can be no judgement on nothing, in the words of an irrefutable proverb. If the public can be satisfied with what passes among us for criticism, that only proves that we are not in need of Schlegels or even of La Harpes.[2]

As regards the unfair coolness of the public for Katenin's works, that is, in all respects, to his credit: it proves firstly the aversion of the poet for the petty ways of winning acclaim, and secondly his independence. He never tried to pander to the ruling taste of the public, on the contrary he always went his own way, creating for himself whatever he pleased in whichever form it suited him. He even took this proud independence to such lengths as to abandon a branch of poetry as soon as it became fashionable and to withdraw where he would not be affected either by the prejudices of the crowd or by sampling the works of some writer, who had others in his wake. In this way, having been one of the first apostles of Romanticism and the first to introduce popular language and subjects into the pale of elevated poetry, he was the first to repudiate Romanticism and to turn to classic idols, just when the novelty of the literary reformation had begun to please the reading public.

Mr Katenin's first remarkable piece of work was his translation of Bürger's delightful *Lenore*. It was already well known among us through Zhukovsky's inaccurate but charming imitation, which changed it in the way that Byron changed *Faust* in *Manfred*, weakening the spirit and form of its original. Katenin felt this and decided to show us 'Lenore' in all the energetic beauty of the original version; he wrote 'Olga'. But the simplicity and even the coarseness of its expression, 'the scoundrel' in place of 'airy chain of shadows', the gibbet in place of rustic scenes bathed in summer moonlight, were all an unpleasant surprise to its unconditioned readers, and Gnedich took it upon himself to express their views in an article, the unfairness of which was exposed by Griboedov.[3] After 'Olga' came 'The Murderer', maybe the best of Katenin's ballads. The impression it made was even worse: the murderer, in a fit of madness, blamed the moon, the witness of his crime, for being *bald!* Readers, brought up on Florian and Parny, burst out laughing and judged the ballad to be unworthy of any criticism.

Such were Katenin's early misfortunes which came to influence his later works as well. He had definite successes in the theatre. His poems appeared from time to time in the reviews and almanacs and these were at last given their due, though even then in a niggardly and unwilling fashion. Among them 'Mstislav Mstislavich', a poem full of fire and movement, and 'The Old True Tale', which is full of artlessness and true poetry, are outstanding.

In the book now published enlightened readers will notice 'An Idyll', in which bucolic nature is caught with such charming truth – not as in Gesner,[4] where it is prudish and mannered, but ancient, simple, spacious and free; a melancholy 'Elegy'; a masterful translation of three cantos from the *Inferno*; and a collection of songs on *El Cid*, that intriguing, poetical, popular chronicle. Specialists give due praise to Katenin's learned handling of the hexameter and its resulting sonorousness, and to the general mechanics of his verse, matters too often neglected by our best poets.

[1] Published in the Literary Supplement to the *Russky Invalid*, No. 26 (1 April 1833). Signed, and dated 14 March 1833.

Katenin's works were published in two volumes in 1832 and Pushkin had been very active collecting subscriptions. He had a high opinion of Katenin as a critic, see his letter to him, no. 127. See also 'Of poetic diction', no. 152.

[2] Pushkin had written this in 1830.

[3] 'Of the free translation of Bürger's ballad "Lenore" ' in *Syn Otechestva*, No. 27 (1816). Gnedich wrote that Katenin's version was an offence to the ear, to good taste, and to reason. Katenin was defended by Griboedov in *Syn Otechestva*, No. 30 (1816).

[4] Salomon Gesner (1730-88), Swiss poet, notably of idyllic verse.

MISCELLANEOUS NOTES

257. On *The Bronze Horseman*[1]

Mickiewicz described the day which preceded the floods in Petersburg in some splendid lines in one of his best poems, 'Oleczkiewicz'. It is a pity, however, that his description is not an accurate one. There was no snow, the Neva was not covered with ice. Our description is the more correct, although it lacks the Polish poet's vivid colours.

* * *

Grammar does not dictate rules to the language, but clarifies and confirms its usages.

[1] *The Bronze Horseman* was written at Boldino between 6 and 31 October 1833. It was not published in Pushkin's lifetime as the Tsar disapproved of it, except for the lines on St Petersburg which were published in *Biblioteka dlya Chteniya*, I (1834). The whole poem was printed in the first issue of the *Sovremennik* in 1837, which was dedicated to Pushkin's memory, with alterations which had been called for by the censorship supplied by Zhukovsky.

LETTERS

258. To P. S. Sankovsky[1]   *3 January 1833*
                                                             St Petersburg

. . . M-r Kasassi[2] m'avait apporté une bien aimable lettre de votre part; vous m'y demandiez des vers pour un almanach que vous aviez l'intention de faire paraître pour cette année-ci. J'ai tardé à vous répondre pour une bonne raison: je n'avais rien à vous envoyer et j'attendais toujours un moment d'inspiration comme on dit, c'est-à-dire, un moment de griffomanie. Et bien, l'inspiration n'est pas venue, je n'ai pas écrit un vers depuis deux ans[3] – et voilà comment la bonne intention que j'avais de vous faire hommage de mes pauvres rimes est allée paver l'enfer. Pour Dieu, ne m'en voulez pas, et plaignez-moi de ne jamais faire ce que j'aurais dû ou voulu. . . .

[1] Pavel Stepanovich Sankovsky (1798-1832) was a great admirer of Pushkin. They had met in 1829 when Pushkin had travelled to Persia (he is mentioned in the *Journey to Arzrum*). Sankovsky spoke fluent French and Italian and had been the editor of the *Tifliskiye Vedomosti*, the first official Russian newspaper in the Caucasus. Pushkin was unaware that Sankovsky had died the previous October.
[2] Ivan Antonovich Kasassi had served as Major in the Dragoons till 1830 and then in the military police in Tiflis, in which capacity he was in charge of some political prisoners, including A. A. Bestuzhev.
[3] Pushkin is exaggerating but, in comparison to 1830, 1831 and 1832 were indeed lean years.

259. To P. V. Nashchokin   *About, and not later than, 25 February 1833*
St Petersburg

. . . My life in Petersburg is neither fish, flesh, nor good red herring. Life's concerns prevent me from getting bored, but I lack leisure, the freedom of a bachelor existence, which is essential for a writer. I am caught up in the social whirl,[1] my wife is in great vogue – all this demands money, money comes to me through work, and work requires solitude. This is how I plan my future. In the summer, after my wife's lying-in, I will send her to her sisters in the country in Kaluga,[2] while I go to Nizhny[3] and maybe to Astrakhan. We'll meet in the course of the journey and will talk our fill. I need this trip both morally and physically.

[1] Gogol wrote to A. S. Danilevsky on 8 February, 'One only sees Pushkin at balls. He'll fritter his whole life away like this if some event, or rather necessity, will not drag him off to the country.' Pletnev was also very upset by this and complained bitterly to Zhukovsky on 17 February that Pushkin was being lazy, doing nothing but reading over his letters and going to balls.

[2] Pushkin's wife did not go to Kaluga.

[3] In connection with his work on the Pugachev rebellion. Pushkin went to Nizhny-Novgorod and other towns on the Volga, but he did not get as far as Astrakhan.

260. Second draft to A. N. Mordvinov[1]   *30 July 1833*
St Petersburg

. . . During the last two years I have been engaged solely on historical research and have not written a single line of pure literature.[2] It is essential for me to spend about two months in complete solitude in order to have a rest from these important studies and to finish a book,[3] which I began long ago and which will bring me in some money, of which I am in need. I am myself ashamed at spending time on trivial pursuits, but what am I to do? They alone afford me independence and the means of living with my family in Petersburg, where my work, thanks to the Sovereign, bears a more important and useful character.[4]

Apart from my salary, appointed me by His Majesty's generosity, I have no regular income; whereas the cost of living in the capital is high and, with the increase of my family, expenses mount too.

Perhaps the Tsar wishes to know precisely which book it is that I want to finish writing in the country: it is a novel, the greater part

of the action of which takes place in Orenburg and Kazan, and that
is why I would like to visit both these districts.[5]

[1] Alexander Nikolaevich Mordvinov was standing in for Count Benckendorff
and was handling Pushkin's request for permission to travel to the Urals
in search of material on the Pugachev rebellion for his novel *The Captain's
Daughter*. Pushkin was given leave to travel for four months.
[2] See note 3 to letter to Sankovsky, no. 258 above.
[3] *The Captain's Daughter*, published in 1836 in the fourth issue of *Sovremennik*.
Before completing his novel Pushkin wrote a straight history of the Pugachev rebellion.
[4] A reference to his work on Peter the Great for which he had the Tsar's
permission.
[5] See pages 198-202 for the influence Scott had on Pushkin's method of
collecting material for a novel.

261. To N. N. Pushkin   *8 September 1833*
                                                       Kazan

... I have been busy here with old men, contemporaries of my hero.[1] I
rode round the outskirts of the town, went over the fields of battle,
asked questions, took notes, and am very pleased that I did not visit
these parts in vain. ...

[1] Pugachev. Pushkin was following the method which proved so successful
with Scott, searching out eye-witness accounts of the events he wanted to
describe.

262. To N. N. Pushkin   *2 October 1833*
                                                       Boldino

... In the village of Berda where Pugachev quartered for six months,
I had une bonne fortune – I found a seventy-five-year-old Cossack
woman[1] who remembers those days as you and I remember 1830. I
fastened upon her. ...

[1] When she was fourteen or fifteen Pugachev had made her his mistress.
She did not remember much about Pugachev, but recounted all she did
remember with gusto and sang some songs about him. She later told a lady
visitor, E. Z. Voronin, who called two months later, that all the village
women were afraid of the man who had come to ask her all those questions
and, noticing his long finger-nails (!), had taken him for Antichrist. Pushkin
found this material remarkably fresh and vivid and used it both for his
novel and for his History.

263. To N. N. Pushkin   *8 October 1833*
                                                          Boldino

... I have already been in Boldino a whole week. I am sorting out my
notes on Pugachev but poetry is still dormant. ...

264. To N. N. Pushkin   *11 October 1833*
                                                         Boldino

... Do you know what they say of me in the neighbouring districts? This
is how they describe my method of work: when Pushkin writes poetry,
in front of him stands a quart of the *best* liqueur – he knocks back one
glass, a second, a third – and then he's off! That's fame for you. ...[1]

[1] During this stay in Boldino Pushkin was writing *The History of the Pugachev
Rebellion*, *The Bronze Horseman*, 'The Tale of the Fisherman and the Little
Golden Fish', 'The Tale of the Dead Tsarevna and the Seven Heroes',
'Angelo' (an adaptation of part of *Measure for Measure*), *The Queen of Spades*,
and some shorter pieces.

265. To N. N. Pushkin   *21 October 1833*
                                                        Boldino

... I am working in a lazy, slipshod fashion. All these days I have had
a headache and I was consumed by the spleen. Now I feel better. I
have embarked on a lot, but have no enthusiasm for anything; God
knows what's the matter with me. I am growing old and weak witted....

266. To N. N. Pushkin   *30 October 1833*
                                                        Boldino

... I wake up at seven, have coffee, and stay in bed till three. Lately
I began to write and have already written heaps. At three I go riding,
at five I have a bath, and then dine on potatoes and buckwheat
porridge. I read till nine. There you have my day and they all follow
the same pattern.

267. To Prince V. F. Odoevsky[1]   *30 October 1833*
                                                        Boldino

It is my fault, Your Excellency! It is entirely my fault. Having arrived
in the country I thought I would settle to writing. But nothing of the

kind. Headaches, domestic troubles, indolence – the indolence of a gentleman and a landowner – overcame me to such a degree that heaven preserve me from the like again. Do not expect Belkin. Joking apart, he really appears to be dead; he will not be present at the house-warming, either in Gomozeyka's drawing-room or in Panka's attic.[2] It seems he is not worthy of being in their company. . . .

. . . My regards to Gogol. How goes his comedy?[3] It's got something.

[1] Prince Vladimir Fedorovich Odoevsky (1803-69) was a man of many parts: a writer, philosopher and musical critic. He was closely associated with Pushkin as a literary journalist. In 1833 he kept open house every Saturday after the theatre – guests were not expected to arrive before 11 p.m. The company forgathered in two small rooms and then proceeded to the library, where Princess Odoevsky presided over an enormous silver samovar. Pushkin, Vyazemsky and Zhukovsky were frequent callers. The guests formed a cross-section of St Petersburg society: diplomats, actors, writers, travellers, etc.

[2] Pushkin was replying to a suggestion made by Prince Odoevsky (in a letter of 28 September) that Pushkin (under his pseudonym Belkin) should collaborate with him (writing under the name Gomozeyka) and Gogol (whom he referred to as Panka) and publish a three-storeyed almanac: 'Belkin' would take the cellar, 'Gomozeyka' the drawing-room floor, and 'Panka' the attic. Pushkin declined, saying that 'Belkin' had died.

[3] *The Vladimir Third Class.*

268. To Count A. C. Benckendorff[1]   *6 December 1833*
St Petersburg

. . . Although I have tried to avail myself as rarely as possible of the treasured permission I have been granted to call on the Sovereign Emperor's attention, I now make bold to ask for his supreme assent. I once thought of writing a historical novel pertaining to the times of Pugachev, but having found a great deal of material I put aside the idea and in the meantime wrote a history of the Pugachev rebellion.[2] I make bold to ask through your Excellency for permission to submit it for the Sovereign's examination. I do not know whether it will be possible for me to publish it, but I dare to hope that this historical fragment will prove of interest to His Majesty, particularly respecting the military events of that time, of which up to now little has been known.[3]

[1] Pushkin was invited to call on Benckendorff on 11 December. At this meeting, the manuscript of *The Bronze Horseman* was returned to him with

excisions and queries marked, the poem as it stood not having been passed for publication.

2 Pushkin had intended to call his work *The History of Pugachev*. The Tsar, however, wished it to be called *The History of the Pugachev Rebellion*. Pushkin complied and it was published at the Tsar's expense, which was fortunate in view of Pushkin's pressing financial difficulties.

3 In the draft of this letter Pushkin had added the following sentence which he now discarded: 'At any rate I have, according to my conscience, carried out the duty of a historian: have searched diligently for the truth and have presented it in all sincerity, without attempting to flatter either the sovereign power or the prevailing current of opinion.'

1834

━━━━━◆◆◆◆◆━━━━━

DIARY

269.

1 January. The day before yesterday I was made a Kammerjunker (which is somewhat indecent at my age), but the court wishes that Natalia Nikolaievna should dance at the Anichkov palace. So I will become a Russian Dangeau.[1]

7 January. . . . The Emperor said to Princess Vyazemsky: 'J'espère que Pouchkine a pris en bonne part sa nomination. Jusqu'à présent il m'a tenu parole, et j'ai été content de lui, etc.' The other day the Grand Duke[2] congratulated me at the theatre: 'Thank you very much, Your Highness. Up till now everyone has laughed at me, you are the first to congratulate me.'

7 April. . . . My *Queen of Spades*[3] is in great vogue. Gamblers punt on a three, a seven and an ace. . . . Gogol on my advice has begun a history of Russian criticism.[4]

18 December. The day before yesterday I went at last to the Anichkov palace. I shall describe everything in detail for the sake of a future Walter Scott. . . . On the whole I enjoyed the ball. The Tsar was very natural and homely in his bearing. The young sons of Canning and Wellington were also there. . . .

[1] Philippe de Courcillon, Marquis de Dangeau (1638-1720), wrote his Memoirs – *Journal de la cour de Louis XIV* – covering the years 1684-1720, which were entirely concerned with court matters and the trivia of court etiquette.
[2] Grand-Duke Mikhail Pavlovich.
[3] Published in the March issue of *Biblioteka dlya Chteniya*.
[4] Nothing remains of this work.

ARTICLES

270. The beginning of an autobiography[1]

I have several times embarked on making daily entries into a diary and have always given up through laziness. In 1821 I began to write my autobiography[2] and worked at it in the course of several years. At the end of 1825, at the disclosure of the ill-fated conspiracy, I was forced to burn these notes. They might have involved many people and, perhaps, increased the number of victims. I cannot but regret their loss; I spoke in them of people who afterwards became figures of historical importance with the candour of intimacy or of short acquaintance. Now they are surrounded by a certain theatrical pomp, which will probably affect both my style and the way I think.

On the other hand I will be more cautious in my testimony and if in future my diary will as a result be less lively, it will at the same time be more accurate.

[1] Probably written in Boldino in the autumn of 1834. Published posthumously.

[2] Largely written in 1824-5 in Mikhailovskoe and destroyed after the Decembrist rising, see his letters to L. S. Pushkin (no. 67) in November 1824, and to Katenin (no. 112) in September 1825.

271. A Journey from Moscow to Petersburg[1]

Having found out that the new Moscow road was now completed I got the idea of going to Petersburg where I had not been for more than fifteen years. I booked at the express coach office (the coaches seeming to me to be much steadier than the previous type of postchaise) and on 15 October at ten o'clock in the morning I drove out of the Tver gate.

. . . Having decided to go on a journey and placing a rather rash reliance on inns, I wanted to arm myself with a book rather than with pies and cold veal, as I feared the conversation of my fellow passengers in the coach. In prison or on a journey any book is like a gift from God, and one which you could not bring yourself to open on returning from the English club or when dressing for a ball will seem as enchanting as an Arabian tale, if it falls into your hands in prison or in an express coach. I will go further: in such cases the more boring the book the better. You will gulp an interesting book down too quickly, and it will cut too deeply into your memory and imagination; it will be impossible to re-read it. On the other hand when you read a dull book you pause and rest – it gives you the opportunity of nodding and daydreaming; recollecting yourself you take it up again, re-read passages which you missed through inattention, etc. A dull book is more diverting.

One's conception of dullness is very relative. A dull book can be a very good one; I am not speaking of learned works for this also applies to books written solely with a literary purpose. Many readers will agree with me that *Clarissa*[2] is very tiring and dull, but in spite of this Richardson's novel is of exceptional merit.

That is what journeys are good for.

And so, having decided on the journey, I went in to my old friend . ., whose library I have grown accustomed to use. I asked him for a dull book which would, none the less, be of some interest. My friend wanted to give me a satiric novel with a moral,[3] affirming that nothing could be duller, and that the book was very interesting in view of its reception by the public; but thanking him I said I knew from experience the unreadable quality of satiric novels with a moral. 'Wait,' he said, 'I have a book for you.' With this he pulled out from under the complete works of Alexander Sumarokov and Mikhail Kheraskov a book which appeared to have been published at the end of the last century. 'Please treasure it,' he said in a mysterious voice. 'I hope that you will fully appreciate and justify my trust.' I opened it and read the title: *A Journey from St Petersburg to Moscow*, St P., 1790, with the epigraph:

A grim monster, savage, gigantic, hundred-mouthed, and bellowing.
Telemakhida, Book XVIII, verse 514.

The book, which had at one time caused a scandal and had drawn down Catherine's wrath on its author – leading to the death penalty and exile to Siberia, is now a bibliographical rarity, having lost its fascination, and is to be found only by chance on the dusty shelves of a bibliophile or in the sack of a bearded hawker.

I thanked . . sincerely and took *A Journey* with me. Its contents are known to everyone. Radishchev wrote several fragments, giving to each the name of one of the stages on the road from Petersburg to Moscow. In them he poured out his thoughts without any plan or order. In Chernaya Gryaz while they were changing horses I started reading the book at the last chapter and in this way made Radishchev travel with me from Moscow to Petersburg.

LOMONOSOV

At the end of his book Radishchev included a passage on Lomonosov. It is written in a pompous and heavy style. Radishchev secretly intended to damage the inviolate fame of Russia's Pindar. It is worth noting that Radishchev carefully concealed his intention under cover of respect and he handled Lomonosov's fame with much more circumspection than he meted out to the sovereign power, which he attacked with such insane audacity. He filled more than thirty pages with banal praise of the poet, rhetorician and grammarian, in order to include at the end of his passage the following seditious lines:

> We wish to show with regard to Russian literature, that he who laid out the road to the temple of glory is the first cause for the attainment of that glory, even if he himself could not enter the temple. Is Bacon of Verulam not worthy to be remembered because he could only show how to advance learning? Are the courageous writers who have risen against oppression and tyranny not worthy of gratitude because they could not themselves free mankind from fetters and captivity? And shall we fail to honour Lomonosov because he did not understand the rules of dramatic poetry and wore himself out in writing epics, because in his poems he was wanting in sentiment, because he was not always penetrating in his judgements, and because even in his odes he sometimes employed more words than ideas?
>
> [trans. L. Wiener.]

Lomonosov was a great man. Between Peter I and Catherine II he stands alone as a pioneer champion of education. He founded our first university. Or rather, he was himself our first university. But in this university the Professor of Poetry and Rhetoric was no more than a meticulous official, not a poet inspired from above, nor an orator with the power to fascinate. The uniform and limited moulds into which he poured his ideas make the movement of his prose tiring and heavy. That semi-Slavonic, semi-Latinate scholastic pomp became well-nigh obligatory; fortunately Karamzin freed the language from its foreign yoke and gave it back freedom, returning it to the living sources of popular speech. In Lomonosov there is neither feeling nor imagination. His odes, modelled on those of German poets of his day who have long since been forgotten even in Germany, are tiring and bombastic. [In draft: His influence was harmful, and still makes itself felt on our lean literature. Preciosity, a grandiose style, an aversion for simplicity and accuracy – these are the marks left by Lomonosov. Have we been writing in a language which is understood by everybody for long? Are we now convinced that Slavonic is not Russian and that we cannot arbitrarily combine them. . . . I know that Lomonosov did not think this and advised the study of Slavonic as an essential condition for a thorough knowledge of the Russian language.] His influence on literature was harmful and it is still felt to this day. An inflated style, preciosity, an aversion for simplicity and accuracy, the absence of any national characteristics and of any originality, these are the marks left by Lomonosov. Lomonosov himself did not value his own poetry and was far more concerned about his chemical experiments than about official odes on the solemn occasions of royal name-days, etc. With what scorn he speaks of Sumarokov, so devoted to his art, *of this man who can think of nothing but his poor rhyming*. . . . But then with what feeling he speaks of science, of education! See his letters to Shuvalov, Vorontsov, etc.

. . . Tredyakovsky was certainly a respectable and honourable man. His philological and grammatical researches are very remarkable. He had a wider understanding of Russian versification than either Lomonosov or Sumarokov. His love of Fénelon's epic does him credit, and his idea of translating it in verse and his choice of the verse form itself prove his extraordinary feeling for elegance. There are many fine lines and happy locutions in the *Telemakhida*. Radishchev wrote a whole article on them (see A. Radishchev's collected works). . . . Altogether it is more profitable to study Tredyakovsky than our other early writers. Sumarokov and Kheraskov do not match up to Tredyakovsky – habent sua fata libelli.

Patronage is still customary in the English literary scene. The worthy Crabbe, who died last year, presented all his splendid poems to his Grace the Duke, etc. In his humble dedications he respectfully mentions the favours and the high patronage which he enjoyed, etc. In Russia you will not meet with anything of the kind. Among us, as Mme de Staël noticed, literature was for the most part the occupation of noblemen (En Russie quelques gentilshommes se sont occupés de littérature).[4] This gave a special character to our literature; our writers cannot seek for favour or patronage from men whom they account their equals, or present their works to a lord or magnate in the hope of getting 500 roubles or a signet-ring studded with precious stones. What follows from this? That the thoughts and sensibilities of present-day writers are more honourable than those of Lomonosov and Kostrov? I beg to question that.

Nowadays a writer, blushing at the very thought of dedicating his book to a man who is two or three grades above him in rank, is not ashamed to shake hands with a journalist who is decried by public opinion[5] but who can still either harm a book's sale or tempt purchasers by a favourable notice. Nowadays the meanest scribbler, capable of committing any act of private meanness, loudly proclaims his independence and writes anonymous lampoons on people, before whom he would cringe in their studies.

Furthermore literature has recently become a lucrative trade and the public is in a position to pay more than his Grace so-and-so or his Excellency thus-and-thus. Be that as it may, I repeat, such outward signs mean nothing; Lomonosov and Crabbe are worthy of all honest men's respect, in spite of their humble dedications and Messrs. .. are none the less to be despised, in spite of the fact that in their books they preach independence and even though they dedicate their works not to a kind and wise lord, but to some rogue and liar, no better than themselves.

[In draft: France's brilliant literature in the reign of Louis XIV was confined to the lobby. . . . Nowadays manners are different in France but the ranks of writers only desist from fawning before the ministers because the public has more money to give them. To make up for it they toady to the reigning fashion! What talent in France today has not been stained with dirt and blood in order to please the mob which demands dirt and blood? Can one compare J. Janin with Crabbe?

Even now we have very few writers who do not belong to the rank of the nobility. Nevertheless they have gained control of all branches of literature existing among us. This is an important symptom and will certainly have important consequences. Writers who are members of the nobility (or those who consider themselves à tort ou à raison to be members of the top layers of society) are gradually beginning to draw away from the others on the grounds of some sort of *lack of respectability*. It is strange that just at the time when in all Europe Gothic prejudice against learning and literature, supposedly incompatible with honour and nobility, has almost entirely disappeared, among us it is only just beginning to appear. Already one of our most prolific writers has announced that he is not prepared to spend any more time on literature, because it is not *work suited to a nobleman*. A pity! Of course the reason for this is partly the unflattering association with certain upstarts, but can the dishonourable behaviour of two or three pensioned-off *scoundrels* be sufficient excuse for all officers to hand over their swords and resign from the honourable calling of warriors!

Radishchev says that in no branch of knowledge did Lomonosov make any new discoveries, and in the same breath compares him to – Lord Bacon! Such were the curious ideas held in the eighteenth century on the greatest thinker of recent times, a man who effected a tremendous revolution in the sciences, putting them on the road which they still follow today.

If Lomonosov can be called the Russian Bacon it can only be on the same level as calling Kheraskov the Russian Homer. What is the point of such a sobriquet? Lomonosov is the Russian Lomonosov – that serves him well enough.]

ON THE CENSORSHIP

Having settled down to dinner at Pozharsky's pleasant inn, I read the section headed Torzhok. It is concerned with the freedom of the press; and it is interesting to read the arguments on this subject of a man who allowed himself this liberty to the full, having printed on his own press a book in which the audacity of his thoughts and expressions exceed all bounds.

[In draft: I feel it my duty to say that I am convinced that it is absolutely necessary for an educated, moral and Christian society, ruled by whatever laws or government, to have a censorship.]

A French journalist wanted to prove the unreasonableness of a censorship by way of a witty sophism.[6] If, he says, the ability to speak was a new invention, then there is no doubt that the government would not delay establishing a censorship on the tongue: they would issue certain rules and two people in order to talk of the weather would have to get preliminary permission to do so.

Obviously, if the *word* was not the common property of all mankind and only of a millionth part of it, governments would have to restrict the rights of the powerful class of speaking people by law. But *literacy* is not a natural gift bestowed by God to all mankind, as is speech or sight. An *illiterate* man is not a monster and does not stand outside the eternal laws of nature. And among the literate not all have the same *opportunity* or the same *ability* to write books or articles. To print a sheet costs about 35 roubles, paper also costs something. Consequently not everyone can afford to print (not to mention having the talent to do so, etc.). The writers of all nations of the world form numerically the smallest section of the population. It is clear that the most powerful, the most dangerous aristocracy is that of men who for whole generations, whole centuries, impose their ideas, their passions, their prejudices on others. What significance has the aristocracy of birth and wealth in comparison with the aristocracy of talented writers? No wealth can outbid the influence of a popularly accepted idea. No power, no government can withstand the destructive force of the ammunition of the printing press. [In draft: Take a look at France today: Louis-Philippe, who was brought to the throne by the grace of a free press, is already compelled to restrict this freedom, in spite of the despairing cries of the opposition.] Respect the writers' class but do not allow it to gain complete control over you.

An idea! What a mighty word! Wherein lies man's greatness if not in ideas? Let thought be as free as man should be, but *within the bounds of law and in the full observance of conditions laid down by society.*

'We do not argue about this', say the opponents of censorship, 'but books like citizens are responsible for themselves. There are laws for both. What need then is there for a preliminary censorship? Let a book go to press and then if it is found to be injurious, you can pursue it, seize it, and kill it, and can send the author or the publisher to prison and impose an agreed fine on them.'

But an idea becomes a citizen, responsible for itself, as soon as it has been born and expressed. Are not *a speech* and *a manuscript* subject to the law? Every government has the right to forbid the propagation by speakers in public squares of whatever comes into their heads, and can put a stop to the distribution of manuscripts, although they are written by hand and have not come off the printing press. The law not only punishes, it also warns. That is in fact its benevolent aspect.

A person's influence is momentary and isolated; the influence of a book is multifold and universal. The laws against the abuse of the press do not attain their end; they do not warn of evil and rarely cauterize it. Censorship alone can fulfil both these functions.

---

[1] In planning this article, which he wrote between December 1833 and April 1834, Pushkin envisaged a running commentary on Radishchev's famous *Journey from St Petersburg to Moscow* (1789) which, by way of being reflections on a journey made by coach with chapters headed with the

names of the stages en route, was in fact a passionate indictment of autocracy and serfdom. Pushkin's traveller journeys in the opposite direction
to Radishchev and comments on his book, working backwards from the
end.

Pushkin was interested in Radishchev all his life and wrote of him many
times. The fourth verse of his celebrated poem 'Exegi monumentum',
written on 21 August 1836, originally read:

> I will be loved for generations
> Because I sang with new rhythms
> And because, following in Radishchev's footsteps,
> I praised freedom and mercy.

The position Pushkin adopts in this article is contrary to Radishchev's
in many particulars and it has been suggested that he did this in order to
ease its passage through the censorship, and thus, by means of quotations,
achieve the dissemination of certain ideas from Radishchev's proscribed
book. However, making every allowance for discretion, it is clear that Pushkin's views in the 1830s were not as radical as Radishchev's in 1789. The
optimism which the first flush of the French Revolution had produced in
Europe, of which Wordsworth's joy was a characteristic example, had been
put under heavy pressure by later events, and Pushkin's political outlook,
always volatile and unpredictable, had been darkened by the general
repression which had followed the failure of the Decembrist rising and
by the personal difficulties of his delicate relationship with the Tsar – his
every move watched, his every word weighed.

In spite of all Pushkin's care and excisions in making his fair copy, this
article was not passed by the censorship and only parts of it were published
posthumously in 1841.

2 See also no. 68.

3 F. Bulgarin's *Ivan Vyzhigin*.

4 In writing of the Russians in *Dix Années d'exil* Mme de Staël noted the
lack of original literature (and what there was being too influenced by
the French) and ascribed this to the absence of a middle class, from which
writers and artists usually spring. She noted with pleasure, however, that
while on her journey from Kiev to Moscow: 'Plusieurs gentilshommes des
environs vinrent à mon auberge me complimenter sur mes écrits, et j'avoue
que je fus flattée de me trouver une réputation littéraire à cette distance de
ma patrie.' (Chapter XII.)
Pushkin's quoted remark is an amalgam of these comments.

5 Pushkin had Bulgarin in mind.

6 The jumping-off point for this comment is Benjamin Constant's proposition in Chapter VIII of *Réflexions sur les constitutions, la distribution des
pouvoirs, et les garanties, dans une monarchie constitutionnelle* (1814): 'Supposons
une société antérieure à l'invention du langage, et suppléant à ce moyen
de communication rapide et facile par des moyens faciles et plus lents. La
découverte du langage aurait produit dans cette société une explosion
subite. . . .' After that Pushkin was on his own.

272. On the insignificance of Russian literature[1]

If Russian literature presents few works worthy of the attention of literary criticism, it must (as any other phenomenon in the history of mankind) attract the attention of conscientious seekers after truth. Russia was for a long time alien to Europe. Having received the light of Christianity from Byzantium, she did not participate either in the political upheavals or in the intellectual development of the Roman Catholic world. The great age of the Renaissance had no influence on her; our ancestors were not inspired by the chaste raptures of chivalry, and the beneficent ferments caused by the Crusades did not find an echo in the rigid lands of the north. . . . A great destiny was prepared for Russia; her measureless plains swallowed up the power of the Mongols and checked their advance on the very brink of Europe; the barbarians did not dare to leave an enslaved Russia in their rear and returned to their Eastern steppes. A growing culture was saved by a lacerated Russia in extremis. . . . [Footnote: And not by Poland, as some European reviews were till quite recently still maintaining; but as regards Russia Europe was always as ignorant as she was ungrateful.]

The clergy, spared by the Tatars' extraordinary percipience, alone – for two dark centuries – kept alight the pale embers of Byzantine culture. In the silence of the monasteries the monks wrote their unbroken chronicles. The priests addressed the princes and boyars in epistles, comforting their hearts in the heavy days of trial and hopelessness. But the inner life of the enslaved people did not develop. The Tatars were not like the Moors. Having conquered Russia they did not bring her as a gift either algebra or Aristotle. The overthrow of their yoke, the quarrels between the royal princes and the local dukes, between the central power and the free cities, between autocracy and the boyars and between the conquerors and the indigenous inhabitants, were not favourable to the free growth of culture. Europe was flooded by an incredible quantity of poems, legends, satires, novels, mystery plays, etc. – but in our ancient archives and libraries there is practically nothing apart from the chronicles to feed the curiosity of researchers. A few tales and songs continually renewed by oral tradition have preserved some semi-obliterated national features, while the *Lay of Igor's Campaign* rises as a solitary monument in the desert of our ancient literature.

But even in the age of storm and crisis the tsars and boyars were united on one question: on the absolute necessity of drawing Russia closer to Europe. From this arose Ivan Vasilyevich's relations with England, Godunov's correspondence with Denmark, the terms offered to the Prince of Poland by the aristocracy of the seventeenth century, Alexey Mikhailovich's embassies. . . . Finally there came Peter.

Russia entered Europe like a ship newly launched – to the sound of hammers and the thunder of guns. But the wars which Peter the Great undertook were beneficent and fruitful. The successful transformation of the whole nation was the result of the battle of Poltava, and European culture weighed anchor on the shores of the conquered Neva.

Peter did not live to bring to a conclusion the things he had started. He died in his prime, in the heyday of his creative work. He had cast a fleeting but penetrating glance at literature. He set up Theophan, encouraged Kopievich, took a dislike to Tatishchev[2] on account of his levity and latitudinarian ideas, and foresaw the *eternal student* in the pale schoolboy Tredyakovsky.[3] A son of a Moldavian Hospodar was brought up on his campaigns;[4] while the son of a fisherman from Kholmogor, who had fled from the shores of the White Sea, was knocking at the gates of the Zaikonospassky school.[5]

The new literature, the fruit of a new kind of society, had soon to be born.

At the beginning of the eighteenth century French literature captured all Europe. It was to have a prolonged and decisive influence on Russia. Before all else it is necessary for us to examine it.

Having looked through a countless number of short poems, ballads, rondeaux, virelays, sonnets and poems, allegorical, satirical and chivalric tales, fairy-stories, fabliaux, mystery plays, etc., with which France was flooded at the beginning of the seventeenth century, one cannot but admit how sterile and insignificant was this seeming plenitude. A difficulty overcome with artistry, a happy use of repetition, a delicate turn of phrase, an artless jest, a candid aphorism, are the short, sharp rewards of the weary seeker.

Romantic poetry was blossoming out richly and majestically in all Europe. Germany had long had its Nibelungen; Italy – its triune poem;[6] Portugal – the *Lusiad*; Spain – Lope de Vega, Calderón and Cervantes; England – Shakespeare, and among the French Villon was singing of taverns and the gallows in bawdy couplets and was held to be the leading national poet! His successor Marot, a contemporary of Ariosto and Cameons,

Rima des triolets, fit fleurir la ballade.[7]

353

Prose already had the ascendancy. The sceptic Montaigne and the cynic Rabelais were contemporaries of Tasso.

Men, endowed with talent, and being amazed at the mediocrity and, it must be said, *vulgarity* of French poetry, took it into their heads that it was the poverty of the language that was to blame, and began to try to reform it on the model of ancient Greek. A new school was formed, whose opinions, aim and efforts remind one of our Old Slavonic school, among whom there also were some men of talent. But the efforts of Ronsard, Jodelle and Du Bellay were in vain. The language refused to follow a road alien to it and continued on its accustomed way.

Finally there came Malherbe, who was assessed with such brilliant accuracy and with such abolute justice by the great critic:

> Enfin Malherbe vint et le premier en France
> Fit sentir dans les vers une juste cadence,
> D'un mot mis à sa place enseigna le pouvoir
> Et réduisit la Muse aux règles du devoir.
> Par ce sage écrivain la langue réparée
> N'offrit plus rien de rude à l'oreille épurée –
> Les stances avec grâce apprirent à tomber
> Et le vers sur le vers n'osa plus enjamber.[8]

But today Malherbe is no more remembered than Ronsard, these two talents who sacrificed all their powers to the perfection of verse forms. Such is the fate awaiting writers who worry more about the technique of language, the external form of a word, than about the thought [it expresses] – in which lies its real life, unaffected by usage!

How amazing was the sudden appearance, among all the general mediocrity of French poetry, the lack of true criticism and the vacillations of opinion, and among the general lowering of taste, of a crowd of truly great writers, throwing such lustre over the end of the seventeenth century. Was it the political generosity of Cardinal Richelieu or the proud patronage of Louis XIV which gave rise to this phenomenon? Or is an epoch accorded to each nation by fate in which a galaxy of men of genius suddenly appears, blazes and vanishes? Be that as it may, after a crowd of mediocre and pathetic poetasters, completely lacking in talent, with whom the age of ancient French poetry closed, there appeared at one and the same time Corneille, Pascal, Bossuet and Fénelon, Boileau, Racine, Molière and La Fontaine. And their

sway over the minds of the entire educated world is far easier to understand than is their sudden appearance.

Among other European peoples poetry existed before the appearance
of the immortal men of genius, who endowed humanity with their
great works. These men of genius followed a trodden road. But the
exalted intellects of seventeenth-century France found their national
poetry still in swaddling bands, and scorning its helplessness turned to
the models of classical antiquity. Boileau, a poet endowed with a
powerful talent and a penetrating intellect, published his code, and
literature bowed to his will. Old Corneille remained the sole repre-
sentative of romantic tragedy, which he had so splendidly brought out
on to the French stage.

Despite its seeming insignificance Richelieu was conscious of the
importance of literature.[9] The great man, who had humiliated French
feudalism, wanted likewise to bind French literature to his will. The
writers (a poor, mocking and insolent company) were summoned to
court and pensions were showered on them as on the courtiers. Louis
XIV followed the cardinal's system. Soon literary activity was centred
round his throne. Every writer was given his appointed task. Corneille
and Racine solaced the king with commissioned tragedies, the historiographer Boileau sang his victories and appointed to his service
writers worthy of his notice, Bossuet and Fléchier preached the word
of God in the royal chapel, at court the valet de chambre Molière
mocked at his fellow courtiers. The Academy laid down as its first rule:
the great king's praise. There were exceptions: the impoverished nobleman La Fontaine (in spite of the prevailing piety) published in Holland
gay tales about nuns, and an eloquent bishop in a book filled with bold
philosophical speculations included a biting satire of [Louis's] celebrated reign.[10] . . . But then La Fontaine died without a pension, and
Fénelon died in his diocese, banished from the court for a mystical
heresy.

From here sprang polite, refined literature, brilliant, aristocratic – a
trifle mannered, but accessible on that account to all the nobility of
Europe, for the highest society, as one of our recent writers has fairly
said, forms a single family in all Europe.

But at the same time the great age passed. Louis XIV died, having
outlived his fame and his contemporaries. New ideas, new trends
found an echo in minds eager for novelty. A spirit of censure began
to manifest itself in France. Minds, setting at nought the flowers of

literature and the noble exercise of the imagination, prepared for the destined role of the eighteenth century.

Nothing could stand in greater contrast to poetry than the philosophy to which the eighteenth century gave its name. It was directed against the reigning religion, the unfailing source of poetry among all peoples, and its favourite weapons were cold and cautious irony and wild and vulgar mockery. Voltaire, the giant of this age, mastered the art of versifying as an important branch of man's mental activity. He wrote an epic with the intention of besmirching catholicism.[11] For sixty years he plied the theatres with tragedies in which, not worrying about the verisimilitude of his characters or the correctness of his means, he forced his dramatis personae in and out of season to express the rules of his philosophy. He flooded Paris with charming trifles in which philosophy spoke in a mocking voice which all could understand, distinguishable from prose only on account of its rhyme and metre. And this frippery appeared as the height of poetry. Finally there came the time when in his old age he became a poet, when all his destructive genius poured with its full force into a cynical poem, in which all the elevated feelings precious to mankind were sacrificed to the demon of laughter and irony, classical Greece was derided, the sanctity of both Testaments was abused. . . .[12]

Voltaire's influence was phenomenal. The traces of le grand siècle (as the French called the age of Louis XIV) are fading. Poetry grown lean is being transformed into the petty baubles of wit. The novel is becoming a dull sermon or a gallery of seductive pictures.

All the great intellects follow in Voltaire's footsteps. The meditative Rousseau declares himself his pupil; the hot-headed Diderot is his most zealous apostle. England welcomes the Encyclopedia in the persons of Hume, Gibbon, and Walpole. Catherine enters into friendly correspondence with him. Frederick first quarrels and then makes it up with him; society is under his sway. Europe journeys to Ferney to do homage. Finally Voltaire dies, joyfully bestowing his blessing on Franklin's grandson and welcoming the New World in words such as have never been heard before. . . .[13]

Voltaire's death does not stay the flood. All that yet remained inviolable is dragged by Beaumarchais on to the stage to be stripped naked and lacerated. Louis XVI's ministers descend into the arena with the writers. The old monarchy roars with laughter and applauds.

Society is mature for wholesale destruction. As yet all is peace, but already in the distance the young Mirabeau's voice is to be heard thundering dully from the depths of the prisons through which he is driven, like the sound of a distant storm. . . .

Europe, deafened and enchanted by the fame of French writers, affords them her flattering attention. German professors from the eminence of their chairs proclaim the rules of French criticism. England is led by France in the field of philosophy, and poetry in the land of Shakespeare and Milton becomes as dry and insignificant as it is in France. Richardson, Fielding and Sterne uphold the honour of the prose novel. Italy repudiates Dante's genius, Metastasio imitates Racine.

Let us turn to Russia.

---

[1] This article, based on his earlier observations on classical and Romantic poetry (1825), see no. 79, was not published in Pushkin's lifetime. It was written at the same time and in the same notebook as 'Journey from Moscow to Petersburg' and consequently sometimes printed as part of it.

It is possible that Pushkin stopped writing on arriving at Russian literature because his article was forestalled in the press by Belinsky's extended survey of Russian literature, headed 'Literary Musings', in *Molva*, Nos. 38-52 – an event of great importance for Russian letters. A new major critic had appeared on the scene, a radical challenge had been thrown down both to the gentlemen critics with whom Pushkin was associated and to those reactionary professionals, Bulgarin and Grech. Russian literary criticism was from this point to be centrally concerned with questions of social and political significance, it would be a committed criticism dedicated to social reform and to realism in writing.

'Literary Musings' was the second appearance of Vissarion Grigorievich Belinsky in print, the first being a short review of *Boris Godunov* published in 1831. Belinsky, born in 1811 in Chembar, Province of Penza, the son of an army doctor, was at the time working as a French translator for Nadezhdin, the publisher of the *Teleskop*. In this series of articles Belinsky passionately proclaimed the paucity of Russian literature and the dependence of what existed on the French. Even Pushkin, he complained, had changed, 'through whose powerful songs had first blown the very air of Russian life, whose playful, varied talent was so cherished and loved by Russia, for whose harmonious sounds she listened with such craving and to which she responded with such love, Pushkin – the author of *Poltava* and *Godunov* and now Pushkin – the author of *Angelo* and of other dead, spiritless tales.'

The plan of Pushkin's article was:

(1) A rapid survey of French literature in the seventeenth century.
(2) The eighteenth century.
(3) The beginnings of Russian literature – Cantemir plans his satires in Paris and translates Horace – He dies aged twenty-eight – Lomonosov, captivated by the harmony of rhyme, writes in his early youth an ode filled with life, etc. – and turns to the sciences, dégoûté by Sumarokov's fame – Sumarokov – In those days

357

Tredyakovsky alone understands his trade – Meanwhile the eighteenth century allait son train. Voltaire.

(4) Catherine, a pupil of the eighteenth century, is the only one to give her age a jolt forward. She humours the philosophers. The Decree. No more than the people will literature agree to follow her lead. Derzhavin, Bogdanovich, Dmitriev, Karamzin, Catherine, Fonvizin and Radishchev.

The age of Alexander – Karamzin retires to write his History. Dmitriev is a minister. All-round mediocrity. At the same time French literature, which has grown very shallow, envahit tout.

Voltaire and the giants have not got a single follower in Russia but the pygmies without any talent, the mushrooms that have grown up round the roots of the oaks – Dorat, Florian, Marmontel, Guichard, Mme de Genlis, hold Russian literature in thrall. Sterne is foreign to all of us except to Karamzin. Parny and the influence of sensual poetry on Batyushkov, Vyazemsky, Davydov, Pushkin and Baratynsky. Zhukovsky and the year 1812, German influence predominates.

The present influence of French criticism and budding literature. Exceptions.

² Vasily Nikitich Tatishchev (1688-1750), a historian and government administrator.
³ Vasily Kyrilovich Tredyakovsky (1703-69), philologist and poet. Tredyakovsky, who had studied at the Sorbonne, was one of the first to replace Old Slavonic by contemporary spoken Russian as a literary language. Working with Lomonosov, he also brought in important changes in Russian poetic metres, urging the replacement of the old syllabic measures by metric patterns based on stress, and was the first to introduce hexameters into Russian in his translation of Fénelon's *Télémaque*.
⁴ Antiokh Dmitrievich Kantemir (1708-44), poet, satirist and diplomat. He was Russian Minister in England 1732-8.
⁵ Mikhail Lomonosov was at a school attached to the Zaikonospassky monastery in Moscow from 1730 to 1735.
⁶ *La Divina Commedia.*
⁷ Boileau's *L'Art poétique.*
⁸ Ibid.
⁹ In the draft copy this sentence was preceded by the following paragraphs:

Someone among us has said that French literature was born in the lobby and never got beyond the drawing room. These words were repeated in the French reviews and were described as a deplorable point of view (opinion déplorable). It is not a point of view but it is quite literally the historical truth. Marot was Francis I's valet de chambre. Molière was Louis XIV's valet de chambre. Boileau, Racine and Voltaire (especially Voltaire) certainly reached the drawing room but they did so none the less by way of the lobby. There is no need to speak of contem-

porary poets. Their place is of course in the market-place, on which fact
we congratulate them.

The influence which French writers exercised on society must be
attributed to their attempt to conform to the reigning taste and views
of the public. It is remarkable that not one of the well-known French
poets came from Paris. Voltaire, exiled from the capital on Louis XV's
secret order, advises writers in a semi-jocular, semi-pompous manner
to remain in Paris if they value the patronage of Apollo and of the god
of taste.

Not one of the French poets dared to take an independent stand, not
one, as Milton had, forswore the plaudits of his contemporaries. Racine
stopped writing when he saw the ill success of *Athalie*. The public (of
whom Chamfort wittily asked: how many fools must one have to form
a public?), the superficial and ignorant public was the writer's one guide
and governess. When the writers ceased to crowd the lobbies of lords
they turned to the crowd in order to get renewed confidence, pandering
to its pet ideas, or else they bluffed independence and eccentricity, with
the sole aim of acquiring money for themselves! They are not, and
never were, inspired by a disinterested love of art or beauty. A despicable
race!

10 Fénelon's *Télémaque* (1699).
11 *La Ligue ou Henri le Grand* (1723), revised as *La Henriade* (1728).
12 *La Pucelle d'Orléans*, always Pushkin's favourite among Voltaire's works.
13 In December 1776 Benjamin Franklin had been sent as one of three com-
missioners to France to ask for Louis XVI's assistance for the Americans
in their struggle for independence. He had with him his grandson, William
Temple Franklin, and in 1778 he took him to see Voltaire, who addressed
him with the words 'God and freedom'.

DRAFT ARTICLE

273. Delvig[1]

Delvig was born in Moscow (6 August 1798). His father, who died a
Major-General in 1828, was married to Miss Rakhmanov.

Delvig received his early education in a private boarding-school; he
entered the Tsarskoe Selo Lycée at the end of 1811. His talents developed
slowly. His memory was weak; his intelligence indolent. When he was
rising fourteen he did not know a single foreign language and showed
no aptitude for any branch of study. The only thing that was noticeable
in him was his lively imagination. He once conceived the idea of telling
some of his friends of the 1807 campaign, pretending to have been an
eye-witness of the events of that time. His account was so vivid and
true to life and affected the imaginations of his young audience to

359

such an extent that for several days a group of eager listeners gathered round him, demanding fresh details about the campaign. A rumour of this reached our principal, A. F. Malinovsky, who wanted to hear from Delvig himself the account of his adventures. Delvig was ashamed to admit to his innocent and inventive fabrication and decided to keep up the pretence, which he did with remarkable success, so that none of us doubted the truth of his tales, till he himself confessed to having made them up. When he was five he thought of describing some miraculous vision and confounded his whole family with his account. A tendency to lie when found in children endowed with a lively fancy does not prevent them from being sincere and frank. Delvig, describing his mysterious visions and the imaginary dangers to which he had apparently been exposed in his father's supply train, never lied to defend himself over some misdemeanour in order to evade a dressing-down or a punishment.

The love of poetry awoke in him early. He knew almost by heart the collection of Russian poems published by Zhukovsky. He did not part with Derzhavin's works. He read Klopstock, Schiller, and Hölty with one of his friends, who was a walking dictionary and a living and breathing critical commentary.[2] He learnt Horace in class, under Professor Koshansky. Delvig never took part in games which required agility and strength; he preferred strolling along the avenues of Tsarskoe Selo and conversation with his friends whose intellectual tastes corresponded to his own. His first attempts at writing verse were imitations of Horace. The odes To Dion, To Lileta, To Dorida, were written in his fifteenth year and were printed in his collected works without any alterations. In them is already noticeable that extraordinary feeling for harmony and that classical elegance to which he was always faithful. . . . Incidentally, nobody at that time paid any attention to the early, unleavened efforts of this splendid talent! Nobody welcomed the inspired youth, while at the same time the mediocre verses of one of his friends,[3] noteworthy only on account of a certain lightness and clarity of decorative detail, were praised and lauded as some sort of miracle. But such is Delvig's fate: he was not appreciated, when he made his first, early appearance in his short-lived career; and he is still not appreciated, even now that he lies at rest in his premature grave.

I was travelling with Vyazemsky from Petersburg to Moscow. Delvig wanted to accompany me as far as Tsarskoe Selo.

We left town on the morning of 10 August 1830. Vyazemsky was to catch us up on the way.

Delvig usually slept very late and it was almost impossible to wake him early. But on this occasion he got up at eight o'clock and as a result he felt dizzy and had a headache. We had to go into a low-ceilinged inn. Delvig had breakfast. We went on and he felt better, his headache went, and he became cheerful and talkative.

The breakfast at the inn reminded him of a story which he planned to write. Delvig took a long time thinking over even the slightest of his works. He liked to develop his poetic ideas in conversation and we knew his splendid works several years before they were written. But when he finally read them, expressed in sonorous hexameters, they seemed new and unexpected.

In this way his 'Russian Idyll', written in the very year of his death, was first told me in the hall of the Lycée after a dull mathematics lesson.

PS. La raison de ce que D. a si peu écrit tient à sa manière de composer.

[1] Draft of an unfinished article on Delvig, first published posthumously. Soon after Delvig's death Pushkin had written to Pletnev that he wanted to collaborate with him and Baratynsky in writing a biography of Delvig, but this plan did not materialize.
[2] V. K. Küchelbecker.
[3] A. D. Illichevsky, a selection of whose poems was published in 1827.

LETTERS

274. To P. V. Nashchokin   *Middle of March 1834*
                                                    St Petersburg

... *The Bronze Horseman* has not been passed, which means financial loss and difficulties! To make up for it *Pugachev*[1] has been passed, and is being published at the Tsar's expense. This has cheered me up completely, especially as, of course, in appointing me to be a Kammerjunker the Tsar was thinking of my rank and not of my age – and surely did not mean to wound me. ....[2]

[1] *The History of the Pugachev Rebellion.*
[2] There was a resilience in Pushkin's nature, even in his darkest days, which

made him rally quickly and optimistically to the slightest sign of kindness and favour.

275. To M. P. Pogodin[1]   *About, but not later than, 7 April 1834*
                                                St Petersburg

I am pleased to have the chance to talk frankly with you. The Society of the Lovers [of Russian Literature] have treated me in a way which makes it impossible for me to have any further dealings with them. They elected me a member together with Bulgarin,[2] at the same time as he was unanimously blackballed at the English club (the Petersburg one) as a spy, turncoat and slanderer; and at the very time when in answer to his abuse I was forced to print my article on Vidocq,[3] for I had to prove to the public, who had every right to wonder at my patience, that I have every right to despise Bulgarin's opinion without demanding satisfaction from a disgraced scoundrel, who prates of honour and morality. And what happens? At the same time I read in Shalikov's paper[4] that *Alexander Sergeyevich and Fadey Venediktovich, these two leading lights of our literature,* have been honoured, etc. etc. Say what you like: it was a slap in the face. . . .

. . . It was my duty immediately to return the certificate I had been sent. I did not do this, because at the time I had other things to think of than certificates – but I do feel quite unable to have any further contact with the Society of Lovers [of Russian Literature].

You ask me of *The Bronze Horseman,* of Pugachev and of Peter.[5] The first will not be published. Pugachev will come out in the autumn. I am embarking on Peter with fear and trembling, as you on your Chair of History.[6] In general, I am writing a lot for myself and publish unwillingly and solely for money: what's the good of appearing before a public which does not understand one, so that for six months afterwards four fools can pour abuse on one, only just short of obscenity, in their reviews. There was a time when literature was an honourable and aristocratic profession. Now it's a lousy market. So be it.

---

[1] Pogodin, the Secretary of the Society of Lovers of Russian Literature, had written to Pushkin (24 March 1834) asking him to send one of his poems to be read to the society prior to publication.

[2] In 1829.

[3] See no. 171.

[4] *Moskovskie Vedomosti,* edited by Prince P. I. Shalikov.

[5] *The History of Peter I.*

[6] Pogodin had been appointed to a Chair of History at Moscow University.

276. To M. L. Yakovlev[1]　　　*About, but not later than, 12 August 1834*
　　　　　　　　　　　　　　　　　St Petersburg

And why?[2] Voltaire was a very respectable man, and his relations with Catherine are a matter of history.

[1] M. L. Yakovlev was the head of the Government printing department which was publishing *The History of the Pugachev Rebellion.*
[2] Pushkin had received a note from Yakovlev saying 'Cannot one do without Voltaire?', concerning a reference to him in Pushkin's history. Pushkin was forced to comply, see next letter.

277. To M. L. Yakovlev　　　　　　*Middle of August 1834*
　　　　　　　　　　　　　　　　　St Petersburg

. . . It will be necessary (you are right, beloved of the Muses!) to throw out Voltaire's name from the introduction, much though I love him.

278. To N. N. Pushkin　　　　　　*20-25 September 1834*
　　　　　　　　　　　　　　　　　Boldino

I will soon have been in the country a fortnight and I have not yet had a letter from you. I'm bored, my angel. Poems don't come, and I am not copying out my novel.[1] I am reading Walter Scott and the Bible, and think of you all, all the time. . . .

[1] *The Captain's Daughter.*

279. To N. M. Yazykov　　　　　　*26 September 1834*
　　　　　　　　　　　　　　　　　Boldino

. . . Talking of this and that, we decided that it would be a very good thing if I were to get going on an almanac, or even better, on a review. I have nothing against it, but for that I must be certain of your co-operation. What think you of it, Sir? You can see for yourself that the hack-writers trample on us. It is time – indeed, indeed it is – to deliver a sharp rebuff. . . .

280. To A. A. Fuchs[1]　　　　　　*19 October 1834*
　　　　　　　　　　　　　　　　　St Petersburg

. . . I hope in a few days to send you my disgustingly awful history of Pugachev. Don't scold me. It seems that poetry has dried up in me. I

am entirely given over to prose: and then what prose! . . . I honestly
feel ashamed, especially in front of you. . . .

[1] Alexandra Andreyevna Fuchs, a poet living in Kazan. She had sent Pushkin
a copy of her poems.

281. To N. V. Gogol   *Second half of October 1834*
                                           St Petersburg

I read it[1] through again with great pleasure; I think it may be passed
in its entirety. It would be a pity to leave out the flogging: I think it's
essential for the full effect of the evening's mazurka. It may go through,
with God's grace.[2] God speed.

[1] Gogol's short story 'The Nevsky Prospect', published in *Arabesques* (1835).
[2] It was cut out by the censorship.

1835

DIARY

282.

February. Since January I have been very busy with Peter . . . the public is very critical of my Pugachev and, what is worse, is not buying it.

LETTERS

283. To I. I. Dmitriev

14 February 1835
St Petersburg

. . . You scoff at our generation and certainly have the full right to do so. I will not start to defend the historians and poets of my time: in the past the former had less charlatanry and were more learned and industrious and the latter had more sincerity and spiritual warmth. As regards financial returns, allow me to point out that Karamzin was the first among us to set an example of a big turnover in the literary trade. . . .

284. To I. I. Dmitriev

26 April 1835
St Petersburg

I want to express my most sincere thanks to your Excellency for your kind word[1] and for your comforting approval of my historical fragment. It is being criticized, and rightly so: I wrote it for myself, not thinking that I would be able to publish it, and was concerned only with the clear exposition of events, in themselves rather confused. Readers love anecdotes, touches of local colour, etc., all of which I have pushed into the notes. As for those thinkers who are indignant because Pugachev appears as Emelka Pugachev and not as Byron's Lara, I willingly refer them to Mr Polevoy, who, probably, for a reasonable sum, will undertake to idealize this character according to the very latest fashion. . . .

[1] Dmitriev had written to Pushkin on 10 April to thank him for his inscribed copy of the *History of the Pugachev Rebellion*, mentioning some of the criticisms he had heard with which he did not agree.

285. Draft letter to Count A. C. Benckendorff *April/May 1835*
St Petersburg

J'ose soumettre à la décision de Votre Excellence.

En 1832 Sa Majesté a daigné m'accorder la permission d'être l'éditeur d'un journal politique et littéraire.[1]

Ce métier n'est pas le mien et me répugne sous bien des rapports, mais les circonstances m'obligent d'avoir recours à un moyen dont jusqu'à présent j'ai cru pouvoir me passer. Je demeure à Pétersbourg où grâce à Sa Majesté je puis me livrer à des occupations plus importantes et plus à mon goût, mais la vie que j'y mène entraîne à des dépenses, et les affaires de famille étant très dérangées, je me vois dans la nécessité soit de quitter des travaux historiques qui me sont devenus chers,[2] soit d'avoir recours aux bontés de l'Empereur auxquelles je n'ai d'autres droits que les bienfaits dont il m'a déjà accablé.

Un journal m'offre le moyen de demeurer à Pétersbourg et de faire face à des engagements sacrés. Je voudrais donc être l'éditeur d'une gazette[3] en tout pareille à la *Severnaya Pchela* et quant aux articles purement littéraires (comme critiques de longue haleine, contes, nouvelles, poèmes, etc.), qui ne peuvent trouver place dans un feuilleton, je voudrais les publier à part (un volume tous les 3 mois dans le genre des Reviews Anglaises).

Second draft to Count A. C. Benckendorff *April/May 1835*
St Petersburg

En demandant la permission d'être l'éditeur d'une gazette littéraire et politique je sentais moi-même tous les inconvénients de cette entreprise. Je m'y voyais forcé par de tristes circonstances. Ni moi, ni ma femme, nous n'avons encore notre fortune; celle de mon père est si dérangée que j'ai été obligé d'en prendre la direction pour assurer un avenir au reste de ma famille. Je ne voulais devenir journaliste que pour ne pas me reprocher d'avoir négligé un moyen qui me donnant 40,000 de revenu me mettait hors d'embarras. Mon projet n'ayant pas eu l'agrément de Sa Majesté, j'avoue que me voilà soulagé d'un grand poids. Mais aussi je me vois obligé d'avoir recours aux bontés de l'empereur qui maintenant est mon seul espoir. Je vous demande la permission, M-r le Comte, de vous exposer ma situation et de remettre ma requête en votre protection. . . .

Pour payer toutes mes dettes et pouvoir vivre, arranger les affaires de ma famille et être enfin libre de me livrer sans tracas à mes travaux historiques et à mes occupations, il me suffit de trouver à faire un emprunt de 100,000. Mais en Russie c'est impossible. . . .

[1] See nos. 248 and 251 for the abortive negotiations for publishing the *Dnevnik*.
[2] His work on Peter the Great.
[3] Permission for publishing the *Sovremennik* was eventually granted, but it was to be a literary and not a political review.

286. To Count A. C. Benckendorff   *1 June 1835*
                                                St Petersburg

. . . Je n'ai pas de fortune; ni moi, ni ma femme n'avons encore la part qui doit nous revenir. Jusqu'à présent je n'ai vécu que des fruits de mon travail. Mon revenu fixe, ce sont les appointements que l'Empereur a daigné m'accorder. Travailler pour vivre n'a pour moi, certes, rien d'humiliant; mais accoutumé à l'indépendance, il m'est tout-à-fait impossible d'écrire pour de l'argent; et l'idée seule suffit pour me réduire à l'inaction. La vie de Pétersbourg est horriblement chère. Jusqu'à présent j'ai envisagé avec assez d'indifférence les dépenses que j'ai été obligé de faire, un journal politique et littéraire, entreprise purement mercantile, me donnant tout de suite les moyens d'avoir 30 à 40,000 de revenu. Cependant cette besogne me répugnait tellement, que je n'ai songé à y avoir recours qu'à la dernière extrémité. . . .

Je me vois dans la nécessité de couper court à des dépenses qui ne m'entraînent qu'à faire des dettes et qui me préparent un avenir d'inquiétude et d'embarras, sinon de misère et de désespoir. Trois ou quatre ans de retraite à la campagne[1] me mettront de nouveau dans la possibilité de venir reprendre à Pétersbourg des occupations que je dois encore aux bontés de Sa Majesté.

[1] Pushkin was not allowed to retire.

287. To V. A. Durov[1]   *16 June 1835*
                                                St Petersburg

I was sincerely pleased to receive your letter which reminded me of our old, pleasant acquaintanceship and I make haste to reply. If the author of the Memoirs[2] will agree to entrust them to me, I will willingly undertake to press for their publication. If he thinks of selling them in manuscript, let him fix the price himself. If the booksellers don't agree to it, I shall probably buy them myself. I think one can guarantee their success. The author's fate is so intriguing, so well known, and so mysterious, that the disclosure of the riddle cannot fail to produce a strong impression on everyone. As far as the style is concerned, the simpler the better. The most important things are truth and sincerity. The subject is so fascinating that it requires no embellishments. They would even prove detrimental. . . .

[1] Pushkin had met Vasily Andreyevich Durov in the Caucasus in 1829.
[2] Vasily Andreyevich had approached Pushkin about his sister's memoirs of the Napoleonic wars in which she had fought in disguise. Nadezhda Andreyevna Durov had fought as a cavalry officer between 1807 and 1814 and had written her memoirs under the pseudonym Alexander Andreyevich Alexandrov. Pushkin always referred to her in the masculine gender.

288. To V. D. Volkhovsky[1]   *22 July 1835*
St Petersburg

. . . I am sending you my latest work, The History of the Pugachev Rebellion. In it I tried to investigate the military operations of that time and concentrated entirely on describing them clearly, which cost me no little effort, as the military leaders acted in a rather confused manner and then wrote their reports in an even more confused way, boasting or defending themselves with equal incoherence. All this had to be collated, checked, etc. I would value your opinion on my book from every point of view.

[1] Vladimir Dimitrievich Volkhovsky (1798-1841) was a friend of Pushkin's at the Lycée. He had then served in the Caucasus and had been a member of the Union of Welfare – one of the political organizations with which many of Pushkin's friends were associated in the 1820s.

289. To N. N. Pushkin   *21 September 1835*
Mikhailovskoe

. . . I borrowed Walter Scott from them[1] and am re-reading him. I am sorry I did not bring an English edition with me.[2] By the way: send me, if you can, the Essays de M. Montaigne – four blue volumes on my long shelves.[3] Find them. Today it's overcast. It's the beginning of autumn. Maybe I'll settle down to work.[4]

[1] The Vrevskys, Pushkin's neighbours.
[2] It is interesting to note that Pushkin now felt fluent enough in English to

read Scott in the original. See Bibliography of Pushkin's library, page 517, for the editions he possessed.

[3] *Essais de Michel de Montaigne*, Nouvelle Édition (Paris, 1828).

[4] Pushkin was always hopeful that inspiration would come in the autumn but this was not to be a propitious year.

290. To N. N. Pushkin   *25 September 1835*
Trigorskoe

... Imagine that up till now I have not written a line;[1] and all because I have no peace of mind. I found everything as of old in Mikhailovskoe except that my nurse is no longer alive and that near the familiar old pine trees a young family of pines has grown in my absence, which makes me sad in the same way as I sometimes feel sad looking at young cavalry officers at balls at which I no longer whirl. There is nothing to be done about it: everything around me tells me that I am growing old. . . .

... I comport myself modestly and decently, I go for walks and rides, read Walter Scott's novels, from which I am in raptures, and sigh for you. . . .

[1] On the following day Pushkin wrote a poem, not published in his lifetime, expressing the emotions he writes of in this letter which had been aroused by the absence of his nurse and the growth of the new trees: 'Again I visited that corner of the earth. . . .'

291. To P. A. Pletnev   *Around, but not later than, 11 October 1835*
Mikhailovskoe

... you have received the 'Journey'[1] from the censorship, but what did the committee decide concerning my most humble request.[2] ... Thanks, enormous thanks to Gogol for his 'Carriage' – the Almanac can travel far in it; but in my opinion 'The Carriage' must not be accepted free; a price must be agreed on; Gogol needs money.[4] You ask for a name for the Almanac: let us call it either Arion or Orion; I like names that don't mean anything, they leave no room for frivolous comment. Likewise make Langer draw a vignette[5] that doesn't mean anything. As long as there are some little flowers, and lyres, and goblets, and some ivy, as in Alexander Ivanovich's flat in Gogol's comedy,[6] it will be very appropriate. I should be pleased to come and see you in November, especially as in all my life I haven't known such a barren autumn. I write carelessly. For inspiration one must have inward peace and I am not at all at peace. You are wrong in becoming indecisive. I always found that everything that you thought worked out well for me. . . . Let us start the Almanac with the Journey, send me the proofs, and I'll send you some poems. Who will be our censor? I am glad that Senkovsky is trafficking under the name of Belkin,[7] but cannot one (quietly, of course, from a corner, say in the *Moskovsky Nablyudatel*) announce that the true Belkin had died and does not accept the sins of his namesake? That really would not be a bad thing.

[1] 'Journey to Arzrum' published in the first issue of *Sovremennik*.
[2] Pushkin had asked for clarification regarding his position in having to face a double censorship – the ordinary one and the extraordinary one of the Tsar.
[3] Published in the first issue of *Sovremennik* instead of in the projected Almanac.
[4] On 7 October Gogol had written to Pushkin:

> . . . I earnestly beg you to send me the copy of my comedy, if you have it with you, which I brought you for your comments. I sit here without money and with absolutely no means of support and I have to give it to the actors for rehearsal. . . . Please be kind and send it quickly and jot down just a few main points off the cuff. I have begun to write *Dead Souls*. The subject will stretch to a fair-sized novel and I think it will be very amusing. But at the moment I have stopped at the third chapter . . . in this novel I would like to show the whole of Russia, at least from one angle.
>
> Do me a kindness and give me a subject for a comedy in five acts and I swear that it will be devilishly funny. For God's sake. I am at starvation point both in mind and body. And send me *The Marriage*. . . .

[5] Valerian Platonovich Langer, a well-known painter.
[6] *The Vladimir, Third Class.*
[7] O. I. Senkovsky had published 'A Tale lost to the World' under the pseudonym of Belkin, which contained some ironic comments on a story by M. P. Pogodin. In the beginning of May Pushkin had drafted a letter to Pogodin in which he wrote: 'I have just received the latest issue of *Biblioteka dlya Chteniya* and found in it some sort of story signed "Belkin" mentioning your name. As I don't intend to read it, I am hastening to tell you that Belkin is not my Belkin and I am not answerable for his nonsense.'

292. Draft letter to Count A. C. Benckendorff   *About, but not before,*
23 October 1835
St Petersburg

I am approaching your Excellency with a complaint and with a most humble request.

I was, owing to the censorship's difficulties in authorizing the publication of one of my poems,[1] compelled to approach the censorship committee in your absence with a request that the misunderstanding which had arisen should be cleared up. But the committee did not deign to reply to my request. I don't know how I could have earned such negligence . . . but not one Russian writer is more restricted than I am. My works, approved by the Sovereign, are suppressed on appearance – they are published with the censor's arbitrary corrections, my complaints receive no attention. I do not dare to publish my works, for I do not dare . . .[2]

[1] *Angelo*. The first version was passed by Nicholas I; the second corrected version was blocked by the censorship. See no. 246 for the trouble Pushkin encountered through having to face a double censorship.
[2] The draft breaks off at this point.

293. To Count A. C. Benckendorff   *31 December 1835*
                                                        St Petersburg

. . . I make bold to trouble your Excellency with a humble request. I should during next year, 1836, like to publish four volumes of articles[1] of a purely literary (stories, poems, etc.), historical and scholarly nature, as well as critical studies of Russian and foreign literature, modelled on the English quarterly reviews. By refusing to take part in any of our reviews I deprived myself of income. The publication of such a review would re-establish my independence and at the same time enable me to continue the researches I have already embarked on. It would serve as a further benefaction on my account on the part of the Sovereign. . . .

[1] The *Sovremennik*. Permission was granted and it began to appear in April 1836.

Section V

THE 'SOVREMENNIK'

On 10 March 1836 Pushkin had submitted the following plan to the censorship committee:

> The review to be called *Sovremennik* will come out once every three months in a single volume. It will contain poetry of all kinds, short stories, articles on manners and morals, etc., criticism (both original and translated) of noteworthy books, both Russian and foreign, and finally articles concerned with the arts and sciences in general. The price will be 25 roubles, 30 roubles including postage.

The plan had been passed. The *Sovremennik* would be strictly literary: the authorities had ruled out politics, Pushkin excluded fashion and social gossip. After years of advocating the need for a Russian *Edinburgh Review* Pushkin sat down in an editorial chair.

Most of the work connected with the publication devolved on Pushkin himself: he wrote round for contributions, edited copy, corrected proofs, supervised sales and wrote reviews, many of which he left unsigned so as to avoid the Tsar's censorship. His friends too rallied round. Prince Odoevsky helped with the editorial work, Zhukovsky, Vyazemsky, Baratynsky and Yazykov sent poetry, Gogol contributed short stories and articles, and A. I. Turgenev wrote a series of letters from Paris. All seemed fruitful and set fair.

Unfortunately, however, this field of activity, which a few years earlier Pushkin had so keenly sought after, had opened up too late for him. The joy had died. The gap left by Delvig remained painfully open, for none of Pushkin's other friends – not even Vyazemsky – had so close a rapport with him on literary matters. He was aware that he no longer spoke for the young. His debts exceeded 100,000 roubles and he was being forced to pawn more and more of his possessions, for his wife had expensive tastes, his children were growing in number, and his father was increasingly dependent on him. His position at court as a middle-aged Kammerjunker was a perpetual humiliation. Pushkin was tired and showed it.

375

The first number of the *Sovremennik* appeared on 11 April 1836, in an issue of 2,400 copies. Included in the contents were the Little Tragedy, *The Covetous Knight*, 'The Journey to Arzrum' (see no. 295), poems by Zhukovsky and Vyazemsky, and Gogol's short story 'The Carriage'. It was met in almost total silence by the critics who saw nothing in it to entertain the public. Bulgarin sarcastically commented that the eagle had deigned to descend from the clouds, the poet had turned journalist. Benckendorff lodged a routine complaint on a minor point. It was all very predictable.

In May, just before his fourth child – Natalia – was born, Pushkin went to Moscow to collect material for the second number of *Sovremennik* and by dint of great effort managed to bring it out in July. But his readers were disappointed for there was nothing of his own in it. The attitude of his immediate circle to Pushkin at this time can be glimpsed in a series of letters (brought to light in 1939) from Karamzin's widow and daughters to his son then living abroad. Mme E. A. Karamzin was a close friend of Pushkin's and they were all very concerned for his family's fortunes. On this occasion Sophia Karamzin, the eldest daughter, reported critically:

> The second number of *Sovremennik* has appeared; they say it is colourless and has nothing in it by Pushkin. . . . There are a few very witty articles by Vyazemsky, including one on *The Government Inspector*; but one has to be as casually carefree and lazy as Pushkin to include scenes from André Mouravieff's *Tiberiada*!
>
> (24 July 1836)

Sophia Karamzin blames Pushkin's carefree laziness for the inadequacies of this number of the *Sovremennik* but laziness was never one of his vices and carefree he certainly was not. There was no doubt that during the summer and autumn of 1836 Pushkin's spirits had sunk to their lowest ebb; his mood in the few poems he wrote was tenebrous and elegiac. A fragmentary plan remains which shows Pushkin's mind travelling back with longing to the days of his youth at the Lycée:

Prologue (the plan of a poem)
I visited your grave – but it is crowded there; les morts m'en distraient – I am now going to call in at Tsarskoe Selo . . . Tsarskoe Selo! (Gray) les jeux du Lycée, nos leçons . . . Delvig and Küchelbecker, la poésie –

Graveyards preoccupied him. On 14 August he wrote a few lines of verse contrasting the crowded confusion of a town cemetery, where the earth seems to be greedily gaping for the dead tomorrow will bring, with the spacious peace and dignity of a country churchyard. In expression these sentiments come very close to Wordsworth's in his essay 'Upon Epitaphs', appended to 'The Excursion' in Galignani's first collected edition of his poetical works (Paris, 1828), which Pushkin might well have had to hand. But for Pushkin these were not random thoughts; about this time he bought himself a grave-plot next to his mother's in the Svyatogorsky monastery near Mikhailovskoe.

Then, suddenly and unexpectedly, on 21 August Pushkin raised his head and asserted his claim on posterity. In resonant verses he declared that he was a great poet whose work would live. As many others had done before him he took his lead from Horace and headed his poem 'Exegi monumentum'. He foresaw that his poetry would penetrate every corner of Russia and would be recited in all the languages contained within its span from the Baltic to Siberia, by Finns, Tungus and Kalmucks alike; and he summed up the reasons why he thought he would be loved: 'Because by means of my lyre I have aroused kind feelings, and, in this harsh age in which we live, praised freedom and called for mercy for the downtrodden.' It was the voice of the youthful Pushkin of 'The Dagger' and the secret societies speaking again, the follower of Byron, the friend of the Decembrists. He seemed to have regained his confidence.

This same buoyancy carried him through the third number of the Sovremennik. It contained some new poems and, more significantly, a large number of articles by Pushkin, for example the one on Voltaire (see no. 302) which was written in a particularly sparkling style. There was also Gogol's brilliant fantasy 'The Nose' and some poems of exceptional quality by a new poet, F. Tyutchev, sent from Germany where he was on a diplomatic posting.

The Karamzins were quick to comment favourably on the improvement – even though they failed to appreciate Gogol's satirical wit:

I will try to send you the third number which has just appeared, which everyone finds to be better than the others and which should serve to restore Pushkin's popularity. I have not got it yet but we have had some splendid things by the editor read to us, and also some delightful pieces by Vyazemsky and Gogol's unspeakable extravaganza 'The Nose'; Sophia is outraged. . . .

(E. A. Karamzin, 20 October 1836)

377

Unfortunately, however, the circulation of *Sovremennik* had dropped sharply, only 1,200 copies (half the original number) were printed, of which 700 were for its regular subscribers.

In the meantime serious fissures were becoming apparent in the surface of Pushkin's family life. In September, Sophia Karamzin was aware of Pushkin's extreme agitation at her name-day party:

> . . . every ingredient for a gay ball was present, judging from all the faces except that of Alexander Pushkin, who remained sad, pensive and care-worn. His melancholy makes me melancholy too. His straying eyes, which were wild and distracted, were fixed with anxious concentration on his wife and d'Anthès alone. D'Anthès continued to play out his old farce, constantly linked up with Ekaterina Goncharov and at the same time casting œillades from a distance at Natalia, with whom he none the less managed to finish up in the mazurka. It was pitiful to see Pushkin standing there facing them, framed in a doorway, silent, pale and menacing.
>
> (19 September 1836)

Georges d'Anthès, a French officer, the adopted son of the Dutch Ambassador, Baron von Heeckeren, was becoming an increasingly bold admirer of Pushkin's wife; Ekaterina Goncharov, Pushkin's unmarried sister-in-law, an increasingly passionate admirer of d'Anthès. The association of d'Anthès and Ekaterina Goncharov was too obviously a screen serving to conceal d'Anthès's relationship with Pushkin's wife.

Pushkin attended the twenty-fifth Lycée reunion on 19 October. He began to read his customary anniversary poem, which incidentally he had not had time to complete, but broke down in tears before he had finished. There was no going back to happier days. There were too many missing faces and his own affairs were tangled and hopeless.

On 4 November several of Pushkin's closest friends, including Zhukovsky, Vyazemsky, Mme Karamzin and Elizaveta Khitrovo, received sealed envelopes addressed to Pushkin containing the following anonymous letter (written in French):

> The Grand-Cross Commanders and Chevaliers of the Most Serene Order of Cuckolds, convened in plenary assembly under the Presidency of the venerable Grand Master of the Order, His Excellency D. L. Naryshkin, have unanimously elected M. Alexander Pushkin coadjutor of the Grand Master of the Order of Cuckolds and historiographer of the Order.
>
> Permanent Secretary: Count I. Borch.

378

Several of the recipients on opening the letters destroyed them but a few were passed on to Pushkin unopened and besides copies had been sent to him direct. The sender – later discovered to have been Prince P. V. Dolgorukov – had made quite sure that Pushkin would receive this communication and that his closest friends would know that he had received it.

Pushkin's reaction was immediate. On 5 November he challenged Georges d'Anthès to a duel. On this occasion friends quickly intervened, Baron von Heeckeren on behalf of d'Anthès and Zhukovsky on behalf of Pushkin. A fortnight's truce was agreed upon. Also involved was Count V. A. Sollogub, who had himself been challenged by Pushkin earlier in the year but had made up the quarrel and had remained a fervent admirer of both Pushkin and his wife. Pushkin now asked him to act as his second.

On 16 November, Sollogub was at a dinner party and found himself sitting next to Pushkin, who suddenly turned to him and said: 'Go to d'Archiac (d'Anthès's second) and make the necessary arrangements for a duel. The bloodier the better. Do not countenance any explanations.' There was a note in Pushkin's voice which made it impossible for Sollogub to argue. He spent a sleepless night. In the words in which he later recounted his emotions on this occasion there is an echo of Lermontov's famous lines on Pushkin's death (see page 482): 'I understood what a responsibility before all Russia lay on me. This was a very different situation from the one in which I had been involved. I had not feared for Pushkin then. Not a single Russian would have lifted his arm against him, but a Frenchman had no cause to feel concern for Russia's glory.' On 17 November, Sollogub called on d'Archiac and found him to be in sympathy with his own feelings: the two seconds now joined the conciliators and, much to everyone's relief, achieved an agreement.

An extraordinary marriage was arranged between Georges d'Anthès and Ekaterina Goncharov, who willingly stepped into the role of decoy, for d'Anthès, undeterred by plans of matrimony, continued to stalk his fiancée's sister. This compromise solution could not last and Pushkin's nerves were stretched almost to breaking point.

At the end of November the fourth number of *Sovremennik* appeared, noteworthy particularly for the publication in it of *The Captain's Daughter*. Sophia Karamzin wrote to her brother of a meeting with Pushkin, who

... broke his grim and embarrassing silence only with a few brief, ironic, abrupt remarks, and from time to time a demonic laugh. ...

To change the subject, the fourth *Sovremennik* has just come out and contains a novel by Pushkin, *The Captain's Daughter*, which they say is delightful.

The success of *The Captain's Daughter* could not sweeten Pushkin's life at this juncture.

D'Anthès married Ekaterina Goncharov as agreed, on 10 January 1837. Pushkin forbade the couple his house and d'Anthès any contact with his wife; but meet they did. A secret rendezvous in a private house was arranged and Pushkin was informed by anonymous letter that it had taken place. On 25 January he wrote a letter to Baron von Heeckeren which made a duel between d'Anthès and himself inevitable. This time Pushkin made sure that no one would have a chance to intervene: two days after his letter had been handed to von Heeckeren, the duel took place.

1836

ARTICLES

294. *Evenings on a Farm near Dikanka*[1]

Our readers will of course remember the impression made on them by the appearance of *Evenings on a Farm*:[2] everyone was delighted by this vivid portrayal of a singing and dancing tribe, by the fresh pictures of the Malorossian scene, by the gaiety which was at once naïve and cunning. How astonished we were to find a Russian book which made us laugh, having not laughed since Fonvizin's time! We were so grateful to the young author that we willingly forgave him the unevenness and incorrectness of his style and the incoherence and improbability of some of the stories, leaving these defects as a perquisite for the critics. The author has justified such indulgence. From that time he has continually developed and improved. He published *Arabesques*,[3] in which is found his 'Nevsky Prospect', his richest work. This was followed by *Mirgorod*,[4] in which everybody greedily lapped up both the 'Old-world Land-owners' – that humorous, touching idyll, which makes one laugh through tears of sorrow and tenderness, and 'Taras Bulba', the opening of which is worthy of Walter Scott. Mr Gogol is still advancing. We desire and hope to have the occasion of speaking of him in our review. [Footnote: In a few days his comedy, *The Government Inspector*,[5] will be presented on our stage.]

[1] Published in the first issue of *Sovremennik*, in the 'New books' section.
[2] *Evenings on a Farm near Dikanka*, published in two parts 1831-2.
[3] Published in two parts in 1835.
[4] Published in two parts in 1835. This was a sequel to *Evenings on a Farm near Dikanka*. Gogol later expanded the first version of 'Taras Bulba' and published it separately in 1842.
[5] 19 April 1836.

295. A Journey to Arzrum [Erzerum] at the time of the 1829 campaign[1]

PREFACE

I recently picked up a book published in Paris last year [1834] called:

381

Voyages en Orient, entrepris par ordre du gouvernement français.[2] The author giving his personal impressions of the 1829 campaign ends his discourse with the following words: Un poète distingué par son imagination a trouvé dans tant de hauts faits dont il a été témoin, non le sujet d'un poème, mais celui d'une satire.

I only knew of two poets who took part in the Turkish campaign: A. S. Khomiakov and A. N. Muraviev. They were both in Count Dibich's army. The former wrote at that time several splendid lyrical poems, the latter meditated on his travels to the Holy Land, which had made such a tremendous impression [on him]. But I have not read any satire on the Erzerum campaign.

I would never have thought that it was me that was in question here had I not in the same book found my name among the generals of the independent Caucasian Corps. 'Parmi les chefs qui la commandaient [l'armée du Prince Paskewitch] on distinguait le Général Mouravieff . . . le Prince Géorgien Tsitsevazé . . . le Prince arménien Beboutoff . . . le Prince Potemkine, le général Raiewsky, et enfin – M. Pouchkine[3] . . . qui avait quitté la capitale pour chanter les exploits de ses compatriotes.'

I must admit that these words of a French traveller were, in spite of the flattering epithets, far more grievous to me than the abuse of Russian reviews.[4] *The seeking of inspiration* always seemed to me a ludicrous and absurd pursuit of the fancy: one can never find inspiration; it must find the poet of its own accord. To arrive at a war prepared to sing its pending glories would make me feel on the one hand very vain, on the other, very unworthy. I do not meddle in military judgements. That is not my business. It may be that the bold march over Sagan-lu, the manœuvre by which Count Paskevich cut off the Seraskier from Osman-Pasha, the rout of two enemy corps in twenty-four hours, the quick march on Erzerum, that all these things crowned with complete success are very deserving of mockery in the eyes of military men (as for example in those of the trade consul Fontanier, the author of the journey to the East); but I would be ashamed to write satires on the celebrated general, who kindly welcomed me to his tent and found time to show me flattering attention among his manifold preoccupations, being someone who does not stand in need of the patronage of the great yet values their friendship and hospitality and asks nothing else of them. An accusation of ingratitude cannot be left undefended, like some worthless criticism or some literary squabble. That is why I have decided to publish this preface and to present my travelling notes as the definitive version of *all* that I wrote of the 1829 campaign.

We stopped for the night in Lars. Here we met a French traveller who scared us about our forthcoming route. He advised us to leave our carriages at Kobi and to proceed on horseback. We drank our first Kakhetine wine with him out of a smelly leather bottle, calling to mind the feasting in the *Iliad*:

And wine from goat skins our delight!

Here I found a soiled copy of the *Prisoner of the Caucasus* and, I must admit, read it through with great pleasure. All that is weak, immature, incomplete, but quite a lot has been understood and well expressed.

Two bullocks were drawing a cart up the steep road. A few Georgians were following the cart. 'Where are you from?' I asked them. 'From Teheran.' 'What are you carting?' 'Griboeda [the mushroom-eater].' It was the body of the murdered Griboedov, which was being brought to Tiflis.[5]

I didn't think that I would ever meet our Griboedov again. I parted with him last year in Petersburg before he left for Persia. He was depressed and had strange premonitions. I was trying to comfort him and he said to me: *Vous ne connaissez pas ces gens-là : vous verrez qu'il faudra jouer des couteaux.* He thought that the death of the Shah and the internal dissension between his seventy sons would be the cause of bloodshed. But the aged Shah is still alive, while Griboedov's prophetic words have come to pass. He perished at the points of Persian daggers, a victim of ignorance and treachery. His mutilated body, which for three days was the plaything of the Teheran mob, was identified only by his hand, which had once been shot through by a pistol bullet.

I had become acquainted with Griboedov in 1817. Everything about him – his melancholy character, his embittered intelligence, his good-nature, his very weaknesses and defects – was extremely attractive. Born with ambition equal to his gifts, he was long caught in the toils of petty needs and of obscurity. The abilities of a public man remained idle; the talent of a poet unrecognized; even his cold and brilliant courage was for a time under suspicion. A few of his friends recognized his worth and would observe the smile of distrust – that inane and unbearable smile – whenever they chanced to speak of him as a man of unusual quality. People only trust Fame and don't understand that there might be amongst them some Napoleon who has not commanded a single company of chasseurs, or another Descartes, who has not written one line for the *Moskovsky Telegraph*. But then our regard for Fame perhaps has its roots in our self-love, for after all our voice plays its part in the establishing of Fame.

Griboedov's life was overshadowed by certain clouds: the results of fiery passions and great events. He felt the absolute necessity of breaking once and for all with his youth and of radically altering his way of life. He said goodbye to Petersburg and to idle dissipation, and went to Georgia where he spent eight years in solitary, indefatigable labours. His return to Moscow in 1824 marked the change in his fortunes and the beginning of an unbroken line of successes. His comedy, *Woe from Wit*, circulated in manuscript, produced an indescribable impression and suddenly placed him on a level with our foremost poets. A little while later, a detailed knowledge of a country where war had broken out opened a new field of activity for him: he was appointed ambassador. Having arrived in Georgia he married the woman he loved . . . I know of no more enviable life than that he led for the last years of his stormy life. Death itself, coming on him in the middle of a bold and uneven battle, held no horror and no suffering for Griboedov. It was swift and glorious.

What a pity that Griboedov left no memoir! The writing of his biography would be a task for his friends; but wonderful men vanish from among us leaving no trace. We are lazy and incurious. . . .

FROM CHAPTER V

In Vladikavkaz I found Dorokhov[6] and Pushchin.[7] They were both going to the spa to recuperate from wounds they had received in the present campaign. On Pushchin's table I found the Russian reviews. The first article I opened was a critique of one of my works.[8] Both I and my verses were roundly attacked in it. I began to read it aloud. Pushchin stopped me, saying I should read it with more mimicry. One should know that the criticism was enlivened by the usual tricks of literary criticism among us: it took the form of a conversation between a deacon, a baker of bread for consecration, and a proof-reader, the Mr Wiseman of this little comedy. Pushchin's request amused me so much that the depression brought on by the reading of the article quite vanished, and we all burst out laughing.

That was my first welcome back to my beloved fatherland.

¹ During his foray into the Russo-Turkish war Pushkin intermittently kept a diary. In the spring of 1835 he revised it with a view to possible publication and wrote this preface (dated 3 April 1835). The diary was not published but the preface appeared on its own in the first issue of the *Sovremennik*.

² *Voyages en Orient, entrepris par ordre du gouvernement français, de 1830 à 1833*, by V. Fontanier (Paris, 1834).

³ Pushkin omits Fontanier's qualifying phrase: 'le plus célèbre des poètes russes.' See his comment in the next paragraph.

⁴ Journalists hostile to Pushkin accused him of failing to celebrate Russian exploits in the 1829 campaign.

⁵ Griboedov had been sent to Teheran as Minister-plenipotentiary after the signing of a Russo-Persian treaty in 1828. He was killed in an attack on the Russian embassy on 11 February 1829.

⁶ P. I. Dorokhov. Pushkin wrote an epigram on him in 1829, celebrating his escapades.

⁷ The brother of Pushkin's close friend.

⁸ Nadezhdin's article on *Poltava*, published in the *Vestnik Evropy*, Nos. 8 and 9 (1829).

296. Alexander Radishchev¹

Il ne faut pas qu'un honnête homme mérite d'être pendu.
(Said by Karamzin in 1819.)

At the end of the first decade of the reign of Catherine II a few young men, barely out of their teens, were sent by her command to the University of Leipzig under the supervision of a tutor and accompanied by a father confessor. They did not benefit from their studies. The tutor thought only of his own gain; the father confessor, a good-natured but uneducated monk, exercised no influence either on their minds or their morals. The young men indulged in pranks and nurtured libertarian views. They returned to Russia where government service and family cares took the place of Gellert's² lectures and student pranks. The majority of them vanished from ken, leaving no trace; two became well known: one displaying utter helplessness and a miserable mediocrity in a position of authority,³ the other winning renown in a very different way.

Alexander Radishchev was born about 1750. He received his first schooling in the Corps of Pages, and won the notice of the authorities as a young man of great promise. University life benefited him little. He did not even bother to learn sufficient Latin and German to enable him at least to understand what his professors were saying. A restless curiosity rather than a thirst for knowledge was the distinguishing mark of his mind. He was shy and dreamy. His close ties with the young Ushakov[4] had a decisive and profound influence on his whole life. Ushakov was not much older than Radishchev, but he had the experience of a man of the world. He was already employed as a secretary by the privy-councillor Teplov and a brilliant career was open to his ambitions, when out of love for learning he left his post and with some young students set off for Leipzig. The affinity of their minds and of their studies brought Radishchev into close contact with him. Together they fell on Helvétius. They eagerly studied the foundations of his banal and barren metaphysic. Grimm, the roving agent of French philosophy, found Russian students in Leipzig poring over the book *De l'esprit* and brought Helvétius the news, flattering to his vanity and pleasing to the whole brotherhood. Now it would appear incomprehensible how the frigid and dry Helvétius could have become the favourite of ardent and sensitive young men, if we did not know how tempting, unfortunately, new ideas and principles, repudiated by law and tradition, are to developing minds. We know eighteenth-century French philosophy too well; it has been scrutinized and appraised from all sides. That which at one time passed for the secret teachings of hierophants was afterwards made public and preached in the market-squares and thus lost the charm of mystery and novelty for all time. Other ideas, equally childish, other hopes, equally unattainable, replace the ideas and hopes of the pupils of Diderot and Rousseau, and the irresponsible lover of talk sees in them the purpose of humanity and the answer to the eternal riddle, failing to see that in their turn they too will be replaced by others.

Radishchev wrote *The Life of V. F. Ushakov*. From this fragment one can see that Ushakov was endowed with a native wit and eloquence, and that he had the gift to inspire affection in others. He died in his twenty-first year as a result of a dissolute life, but he had time on his death-bed to teach Radishchev a terrible lesson. Diagnosed as dying by his doctors, he heard his sentence calmly; soon his agonies became unbearable and he asked one of his friends for poison. Radishchev was opposed to this move but from that time on he was always much preoccupied with the question of suicide.

On returning to Petersburg, Radishchev entered the civil service, at the same time not neglecting his literary work. He married. His fortune sufficed him. In society he was honoured as a *writer*. Count Vorontsov bestowed on him his patronage. He was personally known to the Empress and she established him at her personal chancery. In the normal run of events Radishchev should have reached one of the highest positions in government service. But Fate had something else in store for him.

There were at that time in Russia people known as Martinists. A few old men were still alive in our time who belonged to this semi-political, semi-religious society. A strange mixture of mystical piety and philosophic agnosticism, disinterested love of learning and practical philanthropy, clearly distinguished them from the generation to which they belonged. People who profited by spreading insidious scandal tried to present the Martinists as conspirators and attributed to them criminal political views. The Empress having long looked on the efforts of French philosophers as on the exercises of skilled boxers, and having herself encouraged them by her royal applause, now watched their triumph with alarm and turned a suspicious eye on the Russian Martinists, whom she considered to be the propagators of anarchy and the followers of the Encyclopedists. One cannot deny that many of them belonged to the ranks of the disaffected, but their grudge was confined to a grumbling disapproval of the existing order, to harmless hopes for the future, and to double-edged toasts at Masonic suppers.

Radishchev found his way into their society.[5] The mysteriousness of their conversations kindled his imagination. He wrote his *Journey from St Petersburg to Moscow*, a satiric call to indignation, printed it at his private press and calmly put it into circulation.

If we imagine ourselves back in 1791, if we remember the political situation at that time, if we call to mind the power of our government and of our laws, unchanged since the time of Peter I, and their severity, as yet unmellowed by the silver jubilee of Alexander's reign, an autocrat with a respect for humanity,[6] if we think of the stern personalities who still surrounded Catherine's throne, then Radishchev's offence will appear to be the act of a madman. A petty official, a man without any power, without any prop, dares to take arms against the established order, against autocracy, against Catherine! And take note: a conspirator founds his hopes on the combined forces of his friends; a member of a secret society, in case of failure, either prepares to win clemency by resorting to denunciation or, depending on the large number of his accomplices, hopes for impunity. But Radishchev is alone. He has neither friends nor accomplices. In case of failure – and what success can he hope to have? – he alone is answerable for everything, he alone appears as the law's victim. We never considered Radishchev to be a great man. His action always seemed to us criminal and inexcusable, and *The Journey to Moscow* a very mediocre book; but at the same time we cannot fail to recognize in him a criminal of extraordinary spirit; a political fanatic, erring without doubt but acting with amazing self-lessness and displaying an almost chivalric conscientiousness.

But maybe Radishchev himself did not understand the full import of his mad delusions. How else can one explain his rashness and his strange idea of sending his book to all his acquaintances, among whom was Derzhavin whom he thus put in an awkward position? Be that as it may, his book, at first unnoticed, probably because the opening pages are extremely dull and tedious, soon created a commotion. It reached the hands of the Empress. Catherine was very astonished. For several days she read these bitter, shocking satires. 'He is a Martinist,' she said to Khrapovitsky[7] (see his diary), 'but he is worse than Pugachev, he praises Franklin' – a profoundly interesting comment: the monarch, aiming to unite the polyglot parts of her Empire, could not observe with equanimity the secession of a colony from England's sovereignty.

Radishchev was brought to trial. The Senate condemned him to death (see the Complete Collection of Laws). The Empress softened the sentence. The criminal was deprived of his rank and nobility and was sent in chains to Siberia.

In Ilimsk Radishchev devoted himself to peaceful, literary studies. It was there that he wrote the major part of his works, many of them dealing with Siberian statistics, Chinese trade, etc. There is in existence his correspondence with a powerful noble of the time[8] who was perhaps not unacquainted with the publication of the *Journey*. Radishchev was at that time a widower. His sister-in-law went to join him, so as to share the sad isolation of his exile.[9] In one of his poems he mentions this touching gesture.

The Emperor Paul I, on ascending the throne, recalled Radishchev from exile, restored him to his rank and nobility,[10] dealt mercifully with him and made him promise not to write anything contrary to the spirit of the government. Radishchev kept his word. During the whole of the Emperor Paul I's reign he did not write a single line. He lived in Petersburg, withdrawn from affairs and occupied with bringing up his children. Humbled by experience and years, he even changed the trend of the opinions which had marked his stormy and arrogant youth. He bore no malice in his heart for that which had passed, and became reconciled in all sincerity with the glorious memory of the great Empress.

We will not begin to rebuke Radishchev for weakness or inconstancy of character. Time works its changes on man both physically and spiritually. The grown man repudiates with a sigh or a smile the hopes which agitated the youth. Youthful opinions like youthful faces always have something slightly odd or amusing about them. Only the simpleton does not change, as time does not bring him maturity and he knows no such thing as experience. Could the sensitive and fiery Radishchev fail to recoil from what he saw taking place in France at the time of the *Terror*? Could he fail to be strongly repelled when he heard his one-time favourite ideas preached from the guillotine to the base applause of the rabble? Having once been fascinated by the lion's roar of the giant Mirabeau, he did not want to become an admirer of the sentimental tiger Robespierre.

The Emperor Alexander on ascending the throne remembered Radishchev and pardoning him for what could be accounted the ardour of youth and the folly of the age, saw in the author of the *Journey* a repugnance for many malpractices and some well-intentioned opinions. He appointed Radishchev to the commission for the drafting of laws and ordered him to expound his views concerning certain civilian edicts. Poor Radishchev, carried away by his subject touching so closely on his former speculative studies, remembered the past and in the draft, which he submitted to his superiors, indulged in his bygone hopes. Count Zavadovsky[11] was astonished by the old man's youthful spirit and said to him in friendly rebuke, 'Come, Alexander Nikolaievich, fancy wanting to fulminate as of yore! Or have you not had enough of Siberia?' Radishchev felt these words to be ominous. Disappointed and frightened, he returned home, remembered an even earlier past and the student in Leipzig who first gave him the idea of suicide ... and poisoned himself. It was an end he had long foreseen and predicted for himself!

Radishchev's works in verse and prose (except the *Journey*) were published in 1807. His longest work is a philosophical discourse *On Man, of his mortality and immortality*. His reasoning is banal and it is not enlivened by the style in which it is expressed. In Radishchev, although he defends himself against a charge of materialism, one can still discern a pupil of Helvétius. He is more anxious to set forth than to refute the conclusions of pure atheism. Noteworthy among his literary articles are his critical comments on the *Telemakhida*[12] and on Tredya-kovsky whom he liked for the very reason which made him censure Lomonosov:[13] his repugnance for generally accepted opinions. His best work in verse is 'The Eighteenth Century', a lyrical poem, written in classical elegiac measure. . . .

The first canto of 'Bova'[14] also has merit. The character of Bova is described with originality and his conversation with Karga is amusing. It is a pity that neither in 'Bova' nor in 'Alesha Popovich',[15] another of his poems not included for some unknown reason in his collected works, is there a shadow of national spirit so necessary for works of this kind; but Radishchev wanted to imitate Voltaire because he was always imitating someone. Generally speaking he wrote better verse than prose, as in the latter he had no model, while Lomonosov, Kheraskov, Derzhavin and Kostrov had already had time to fashion our poetic language.

The Journey to Moscow, the cause of his adversity and of his fame, is, as we have already said, a very mediocre work even if one overlooks its barbaric style. His complaints on the wretched condition of the people, on the tyranny of the rulers, etc., are exaggerated and common-place; the sudden gusts of mannered and inflated sensibility are at times ludicrous in the extreme. We could substantiate our opinion with many examples. But it suffices for the reader to open the book at random to convince him of the truth of what we have said.

The whole of contemporary French philosophy is reflected in Radish-chev: Voltaire's scepticism, Rousseau's philanthropy, Diderot's and Raynal's political cynicism;[16] but all in an incoherent and twisted manner, as things seen through a distorting mirror. He is a true repre-sentative of the semi-educated. An ignorant contempt for the past; a short-sighted astonishment at his own day and age; a blind passion for novelty; private superficial information adapted at random to suit every circumstance – that is what we find in Radishchev. He seems to be intent on irritating the Sovereign power by his bitter diatribe. Would it not have been better to point out the good which it is capable of achieving? He inveighs against the power of the landowners as being plainly illegal. Would it not have been better to put before the government and wise landowners some methods by which one could achieve the gradual amelioration of the condition of the peasantry? He rails at the censorship. Would it not have been better to discuss the principles by which the legislator should be guided, so that on the one hand the writers' class should not be oppressed and Thought, the sacred gift of God, should not be the slave or victim of a pointless and wilful decree, and on the other, that the writer should not use this sacred weapon for the attainment of a base or criminal end? But all that would simply have been useful and would not have created any stir, nor was it tempting, as the government not only did not neglect or oppress writers but actually demanded their co-operation, called upon them for active service, gave ear to their judgements, followed their advice – in short, felt a need for the co-operation of enlightened intellectuals. It was neither scared by their boldness nor offended by their frankness.

What was Radishchev's aim? What exactly was it he wanted? It is unlikely that he himself could give satisfactory answers to these questions. His influence was minimal. Everybody read and forgot his book in spite of the fact that there are in it a few sensible ideas, a few well-intentioned assumptions, which it was quite unnecessary to dress up in abusive and bombastic phrases and to print illegally on the presses of a secret printing-house, with an admixture of banal and criminal verbiage. They would have done some real good had they been presented with more sincerity and goodwill, since there is no force of conviction in obloquy and no truth where there is no love.

3 April 1836, St P.

---

[1] This article, completed 26 August 1836, was intended for the third issue of the *Sovremennik*, but it was proscribed by order of the Minister of Education, S. S. Uvarov, who wrote: 'the article in itself is not a bad one and could, with a few alterations, be passed. On the other hand, I find it both inconvenient and absolutely unnecessary to revive the memory of a writer and of a book, which have been completely and rightly forgotten.'

Pushkin had anticipated that there would be difficulties with the censorship in publishing anything on Radishchev and had purposely emphasized the points on which he differed in opinion with him. All he wanted to achieve was to break the veto on the mention of Radishchev's name. (See his letter to Bestuzhev no. 34.)

[2] C. F. Gellert, poet and playwright, was Professor of Philosophy at Leipzig.

[3] O. P. Kozodavlev, Minister of the Interior 1810-19.

[4] F. V. Ushakov, materialist philosopher influenced by Helvétius. He died in 1770.

[5] This was the official charge against Radishchev, but the accusation was untrue.

[6] This was Pushkin's usual opinion of Alexander I.

[7] A. V. Khrapovitsky was a senator and Secretary of State and Catherine

II's close adviser on literary matters. In his diaries covering the years 1782-93 he recorded many of her opinions.

[8] Count A. R. Vorontsov (1741-1805). Radishchev had served under him in the Ministry of Commerce.

[9] They later married.

[10] This in fact is not correct. Radishchev was forced to live in the country under police supervision, not in St Petersburg as Pushkin says.

[11] Count P. V. Zavadovsky, the Chairman of the Commission appointed to draft laws and Minister of Education.

[12] *Telemakhida*, see page 347.

[13] Radishchev criticized Lomonosov for bowing down to unworthy idols and for the metrical monotony of his verse.

[14] This poem was one of two works with which Radishchev broke his silence during the reign of Paul I (see Pushkin's remark above).

[15] Not by Radishchev but by his eldest son, Nikolai.

[16] G. T. F. Raynal's *Histoire philosophique et politique des établissements et du commerce des Européens dans les deux Indes* (1770) influenced Radishchev's thinking in the *Journey*.

297. From article on the Russian Academy[1]

... At present the Academy is preparing a third edition of its Dictionary, the circulation of which grows hourly more necessary. Our splendid language, through being used by uneducated and unskilled writers, is going into a rapid decline. Words are being distorted. Grammar falters. Orthography, which is the heraldry of language, is arbitrarily altered by one and all. In our reviews there is even less correct spelling than common sense. ...

[1] Published unsigned in the second issue of the *Sovremennik* (1836).

298. The French Academy[1]

Scribe[2] has joined the Academy. He took the place of Arnault,[3] who died last year.

Arnault wrote several tragedies which were very successful in their day, and are now completely forgotten. That is the fate of poets who write for the public, humouring its opinions, conforming to its taste, rather than writing for themselves, independently following their own inspiration, out of a disinterested love of their art! Two or three fables, either because of their wit or their grace, give the late Arnault more right to the title of poet than do all his dramatic works. Everybody knows his *Feuille*:

> De la tige détacheé,
> Pauvre feuille desséchée.
> Où vas tu ? – Je n'en sais rien, etc.

The fate of this little poem is remarkable. Kosciuszko recited it before his death on the banks of the Lake of Geneva. Alexander Ypsilanti translated it into Greek, among us it was translated by Zhukovsky and Davydov. . . .

Maybe Davydov himself does not know the lines which Arnault wrote for him, when he heard of this translation. The latter included them in the notes to his published works. . . .[4]

[1] Published unsigned in the second issue of the *Sovremennik* (1836).
[2] A. E. Scribe (1791-1861), a prolific dramatist.
[3] Antoine Vincent Arnault (1766-1834), dramatist and poet patronized by Napoleon.
[4] Arnault had written:

> La 'Feuille' a obtenu dans plus d'une langue les honneurs de la traduction. Celle qui en a été faite en russe, par le général Davouidoff, est, dit-on, remarquable par son élégance et sa fidelité. M. Davouidoff est un de ces hommes qui, nés avec le don de la poésie, ne s'y livrent que par caprice et pour se délasser de la guerre et des plaisirs. Instruit de l'honneur qu'il en avait reçu, l'auteur de ces fables lui en adressa un exemplaire avec cet envoi:
>
> > A vous poëte, à vous guerrier,
> > Qui, sablant le champagne au bord de l'Hippocrène,
> > Avez d'une feuille de chêne
> > Fait une feuille de laurier.

299. The Opinions of M. E. Lobanov on the Spirit of Literature, both abroad and at home[1]
(Read by Lobanov on 18 January 1836 in the Imperial Russian Academy.)

Mr Lobanov[2] thought fit to present his views in a casual, non-academic manner; this short article, in the form of notes contributed to a review, appeared in the 'Literary Supplement to the *Russky Invalid*'. It may turn out that what reads well in a review will appear light-weight when spoken in the presence of the entire Academy, and when it is afterwards formally made public. However, Mr Lobanov's opinions deserve, and in fact demand, the most careful analysis.

'The love of reading and a desire for education (so begins Mr Lobanov's article) have greatly increased in our fatherland in the last few years. Printing presses have multiplied; the number of books has grown; reviews have a large circulation; the book trade is spreading.'

Finding the events *gratifying for one who observes progress in our fatherland*, Mr Lobanov pronounces an unexpected accusation. 'Unprejudiced observers,' he says, 'having in their hearts love for everything that tends towards the good of the fatherland, bringing to mind all they have recently read, cannot say without a shudder that there is in our most recent literature a certain echo of the immorality and absurdity bred by foreign writers.'

Mr Lobanov, not venturing an explanation of what he means by the words 'immorality' and 'absurdity', continues:

Nation borrows from nation, and reason dictates that one should borrow that which is useful and imitate that which is graceful. But what is there to borrow now (I am speaking of pure literature) from the latest foreign writers? They often present absurd, odious and monstrous spectacles, spread pernicious and destructive thoughts of which the reader previously had not the slightest knowledge, and which perforce implant in his soul the seeds of immorality and atheism and, in consequence, of future errors and crimes.

Do the lives and bloody deeds of bandits, hangmen, and their like, now flooding literature in tales, novels, in verse and prose, and satisfying curiosity alone, really serve as models for imitation? Do the abominable scenes, inspiring disgust rather than edifying horror and affronting the soul, really serve the good of mankind? Has the unplumbed source of the noble, the edifying, the good, and the elevated really run so dry that men have turned to the absurd, the *abhorrent* (?), the repugnant, and even to the odious?

In confirmation of these accusations Mr Lobanov cites the famous opinion of the Edinburgh reviewers, 'On the present state of French literature'.[3] In this case the proceedings of the Academy rang with the names of Jules Janin, Eugène Sue, and others; these names being furnished with curious epithets. . . . But what if (in the face of all hopes) Mr Lobanov's article will be translated and these gentlemen will see their names printed in the proceedings of the Imperial Russian Academy? Will not all the eloquence of our orator be in vain? Will they not have every right to be proud of this unexpected honour, unheard of in the annals of European academies, where before only the names of those

living men were mentioned who had won eternal fame for themselves
by their talents, deserts and labours? (The Academy remained silent
about the others.) The critical article of the English Aristarchus was
published in a review, where it occupied a decent position and had
its effect. Here it was translated in the *Biblioteka*, and it was a good
thing to do so. But that's where matters should have stopped. There
are heights from which satiric reproaches should not be heard; there
are callings which impose an obligation of restraint and decency, irre-
spective of censorship surveillance, 'sponte sua, sine lege'.

'For France' writes Mr Lobanov,

> for peoples clouded by the latest philosophy, catastrophic for
> humanity, coarsened in the bloody manifestations of the revolution
> and fallen into a slough of spiritual and intellectual corruption, the
> most loathsome spectacles – for instance, the most odious of tragedies,
> the most abominable chaos of detestable shamelessness and incest,
> *Lucrece Borgia*[4] – do not appear as such; the most destructive ideas
> do not seem to them to be infectious – as they have long since grown
> acquainted and, so to speak, become one with the horrors of the
> revolution.

I would ask: can one pronounce such a terrible anathema on a whole
nation? A nation which has produced Fénelon, Racine, Bossuet, Pascal,
and Montesquieu, and which even now boasts of Chateaubriand and
of Ballanche; a nation which acknowledged Lamartine as its leading
poet; which countered Niebuhr and Hallam by Barante, the two
Thierrys and Guizot; a nation which manifests such strong religious
aspirations, which so triumphantly abjures the pathetic, sceptical ratio-
cination of the past century? Has all this nation really to answer for
the works of a few writers, for the most part young men, turning their
talents to evil ends and basing their mercenary calculations on the
curiosity and nervous sensibilities of the readers? For the public's satisfaction, always demanding novelty and powerful sensations, a lot of
writers have turned to the representation of the horrible, paying little
regard to elegance and truth and to their own convictions. But a moral
sense, like talent, is not given to everyone. One cannot expect of all
writers that they should strive towards the one goal. No law can say:
write just on these subjects and not on others. Thoughts, like actions,
fall into the categories of criminal and those for which one is not
answerable. The law does not interfere with the habits of a private
person, does not require reports on his dinner, his walks, etc.; the law

likewise does not interfere with the subjects chosen by the writer, does not demand that he should describe the morals of a Genevan pastor rather than the adventures of a brigand or a hangman, should extol matrimonial bliss rather than laugh at the misfortunes of wedlock. To demand of all literary works either elegance or a moral aim would be the same as to demand of every citizen that he should lead a blameless life and be well educated. The law only clamps down on crimes, leaving failings and venial offences to the individual conscience. Contrary to the opinion of Mr Lobanov, we do not consider that contemporary writers *put up the brigands and hangmen as examples for imitation.* Le Sage in writing *Gil Blas* and *Guzman d'Alfarache* certainly did not intend to give lessons in theft and imposture. Schiller probably did not write *Die Räuber* with the aim of summoning young men from the universities on to the highways. Why then assume criminal intentions in contemporary writers, when their works can so simply be explained as written with the intent of gripping and astonishing the readers' imagination? The adventures of cunning rogues, fearsome tales of bandits, of the dead, etc., have always intrigued the curiosity not only of children but of grown-up infants, and the story-tellers and poets of old took advantage of this bent in our natures.

We do not consider that the *irascible, unconsidered, incoherent, French literature of the present day is the result of political unrest.*[5] French literature had its own revolution which was alien to the political upheaval, which overthrew the ancient monarchy of Louis XIV. At the revolution's most sombre period, literature consisted of cloying, sentimental and moralizing books. Literary monstrosities had already begun to appear in the last years of the timid and pious 'Restauration'. For the cause of this phenomenon we must look in the literature itself. For a long time humbled by arbitrary rules, imposing on it forms that were too restricting, it went to the other extreme and began to consider the neglect of all rules as the law of freedom. The petty and false theory sanctioned by ancient rhetoricians, that *usefulness* is the necessary condition and goal of literature, brought about its own destruction. People began to feel that the aim of art is to present *the ideal*, and not to *moralize*. But French writers only grasped one side of this undeniable truth, and assumed that moral infamy could also be the end of poetry, i.e. an ideal! Former novelists presented human nature masked by affected pomposity; the reward of virtue and the punishment of vice were an absolute condition of their every fiction; those of the present day, on the contrary, like to present vice as triumphant, at all times and places, and see only two chords in men's hearts: egotism and vanity. Such a superficial view of human nature is obviously a mark of pettiness and will soon prove as ludicrous and cloying as the affectation and pomposity of the novels of Arnaud and Mme Cottin. While this view is still fresh, the public, i.e. the majority of readers, from lack of experience, regard contemporary novelists as the most profound connoisseurs of human nature. But already the 'literature of despair' (as Goethe called it), 'Satanic literature' (in Southey's words), galvanic literature, penal literature, the literature of punch, blood and tobacco, etc., having long been condemned by the higher criticism, begins to fall even in the public's favour.

French literature, having had since the time of Kantemir[6] an influence – direct or indirect – on our awakening literature, should have made itself felt in our time as well. But of late its influence has been slight. It was confined only to translations and some imitations, which did not enjoy much success. Our reviews which, as everywhere, rightly or wrongly direct the public taste, generally proved to be the enemies of the new Romantic school. Original novels, which enjoy rather more success among us, belong to the social and historical school. Le Sage and Walter Scott rather than Balzac and Jules Janin served as their models. Poetry has remained untouched by French influence; it grows closer and closer to German poetry[7] and remains proudly independent of public taste and demands.

'Concentrating on the spirit and direction of our literature,' continues Mr Lobanov,

> every enlightened person, every right-thinking Russian, sees in scientific theories confusion, impenetrable murk and a chaos of disconnected ideas; and in literary judgements complete arbitrariness, unscrupulousness, impudence and even turbulence. Decency, respect, sound judgement, are denied, forgotten, destroyed. Romanticism – a word, which – though as yet vague – has magic in it – has become for many a cover for complete arbitrariness and literary extravagance. Criticism, the gentle instructress and dutiful friend of literature, has now turned to street clowning, to literary piracy, to a method of earning one's keep from the pockets of the gulls by impertinent and aggressive forays, frequently even against public men, renowned for their services both to the state and to literature. Nothing is sacred, neither rank, nor intelligence, nor talent, nor age. Lomonosov passes for a pedant. The greatest genius, bequeathing Russia a mighty song

397

to God, a song which has no equal in any other language, might never have existed as far as our literature is concerned: as one lacking talent, he receives no attention. The name of Karamzin, that profound thinker, that conscientious writer, that man of pure heart, is subjected to mockery. . . .

Of course criticism among us is still in a very immature state. It rarely preserves an appropriate dignity and decency. It may be that its judgements are often inspired by calculation rather than by conviction. Lack of respect towards names illuminated by fame – the first sign of ignorance and feeble wit – is, unfortunately, considered among us to be not only permissible but in fact praiseworthy audacity. But here also Mr Lobanov has made unfair comments. Lomonosov's claim to be a poet was disputed (very unconvincingly) but nobody, at any time as far as I can remember, called him a pedant; on the contrary, it has now become customary to extol him as a man of learning and play down the fact that he was a poet. The great Derzhavin's name is always pronounced with sentiments of well-nigh superstitious partiality. Karamzin's clear, splendid fame belongs to Russia; and not one writer of real talent, not one truly learned man, even among those standing in opposition to him, denied him their tribute of deep respect and gratitude.

We do not number ourselves among the servile admirers of our age, but we must admit that learning has made progress. The speculations of the great European thinkers have not been fruitless, even for us. Scientific theory has freed itself from empiricism, has embraced a wider view, has shown a greater striving for synthesis. German philosophy found, particularly in Moscow, many young, ardent, conscientious followers, and though they spoke in a language difficult for the uninitiated to understand, nevertheless their influence was beneficial, and daily becomes more felt.

I will not start to speak *either* of the reigning taste *or* of what is understood and taught concerning beauty. The former will obviously manifest itself everywhere and in everything and is known to one and all; the latter is so incoherent and distorted in the latest ephemeral systems of thought, each succeeding one destroying its predecessor, or so confused in idle philosophizing, that they prove impenetrable to sound judgement. Now they barely acknowledge that the spirit of beauty, with only a few changes in the forms it assumed, was and remains one and the same for all ages and all peoples; that Homer, Dante, Sophocles, Shakespeare, Schiller, Racine, Derzhavin, in spite of their differences in form, birth, faith and customs, all created beauty for all time; that poets, be they Romantics or classicists, must satisfy the minds, imaginations and hearts of educated and enlightened people and not only of the thoughtless crowd which applauds buffoons without discrimination. No, now they preach that man's mind has made great progress, that it can leave aside great writers, both ancient and modern, that it does not require guides and models, that nowadays every writer is an original genius – and under this heretical banner rout the great writers of antiquity by naming heavy and cloying classic writers (who, none the less, enchanted their fellow countrymen for thousands of years, and will always afford a great deal of elevated pleasure to their readers). Under the banner of this false doctrine, the latest writers continually darken the council of inexperienced youth and are leading morality and literature towards absolute collapse.

Leaving this philippic unanswered, I cannot but pause on the conclusion which Mr Lobanov draws from all he has said:

on account of the numbers of immoral books being written at present the censorship is faced with the unavoidable task of penetrating all the artifices of the writers. It is not easy to destroy the vacillations of opinion in literature and to control impertinence in speech if, actuated by malice, it exalts the absurd and even the harmful. Who then must co-operate in this difficult task? Every honest Russian writer, every enlightened family man, and in particular the Academy, founded for this very purpose. Moved by love to Sovereign and fatherland, it has the right, it has the duty, unfailingly to disclose, attack and destroy evil, wherever it may rear its head in the field of literature. The Academy (as it says in the Statutes, ch. III, par. 2, and in the Loyal Address, par. III) is the institution established *for the supervision of morality, purity and clarity of the language, and should consider the survey of books and critical pronouncements as one of its main duties.* And so, dear sirs, every one of my esteemed fellow members should present for scrutiny and publication at the sessions of this Academy, according to its Statute, surveys of published works and judgements on contemporary books and reviews and, in this way acting for the general good, should fulfil the true purpose of this illustriously established institution.

But where are these masses of immoral books? Who are these impertinent, malicious writers, contriving to overthrow the laws on which the welfare of society rests? And can we reproach the censorship with negligence and slackness? We know otherwise. Contrary to Mr Lobanov's opinion, the censorship must not *penetrate all the artifices* of writers. 'The censorship must pay special attention to the spirit of the book under discussion, to the apparent aim and intentions of the author, and *in its judgement always take as a basis the obvious meaning of the words, not allowing itself to interpret them arbitrarily as having evil intentions.*' (Statute on the Censorship, par. 6.)

Such was the sovereign will, granting us the rights of authorship and legalized freedom of thought! If at first glance this basic rule of our censorship may appear to be an exceptional privilege, on looking at it more carefully we shall see that without it there would be no opportunity of publishing a single line, as every word can be interpreted as having evil intention. *The absurd*, if it is simply absurd and contains nothing contrary to Faith, the government, morality, or personal honour, is not subject to suppression by the censorship. Absurdity, like stupidity, lies open to the mockery of society and does not call for legal action. There are many books passed by the censorship which an enlightened father will not place in his children's hands: books are not written for all ages alike. Certain moralists declare that girls of eighteen should not even be allowed to read novels, from which it does not follow that the censorship should prohibit all novels. The censorship is a beneficent and not a repressive institution; it is a sure guard of private and state security, and not an importunate nursemaid, following at the heels of mischievous children.[8]

Let us close with the sincere wish that the Russian Academy, which has brought real benefit to our splendid language and has made so many notable advances, will encourage and enliven our native literature, rewarding deserving writers by its practical patronage, and punishing the undeserving by its sole fitting weapon: neglect.

[1] Published unsigned in the third issue of the *Sovremennik* (1836).
[2] M. E. Lobanov, dramatist, translator of Racine, and biographer of Krylov.
[3] In the issue for July 1833 (*Edinburgh Review*, Vol. 57). A review of the collected works of Jules Janin and of Victor Hugo, both published in Paris in 1832, which turns into a general survey of the state of the modern French novel. Translated into Russian in the *Biblioteka dlya Chteniya*, Vol. 1 (1834).
[4] By Victor Hugo (1833).
[5] Pushkin is here referring to Gogol's article 'On trends in periodical literature', published in the first issue of the *Sovremennik* (1836). Gogol in fact writes of European literature in general, not French literature in particular:

A restless and agitated taste in literature has spread throughout Europe. Unconsidered, incoherent, infantile, and yet often exalted and passionate, works appeared – the products of political unrest in the country in which they were born. This strange literature, turbulent and disorganized as a comet, agitated Europe, quickly spreading to all corners of the reading world.

[6] Antiokh Dmitrievich Kantemir (1708-44), son of the Hospodar of Moldavia, was brought to Russia at the age of three. A poet of the neo-classical school, he wrote satires which were not acceptable for publication in Russia in his lifetime. He was sent as Ambassador first to England (1732-8) and then to France. His satires were published posthumously, in London in a French translation in 1749 and in Russia in 1762. Kantemir's style was not affected by the metrical reforms introduced by Tredyakovsky and Lomonosov.

[7] Pushkin may have in mind the poetry of F. Tyutchev which he was at that time printing in the *Sovremennik* under the heading 'Poems, sent from Germany by F.T.'.

[8] These were not Pushkin's usual sentiments; he was holding out a sop to Cerberus.

300. *Thracian Elegies:* Poems by Victor Teplyakov, 1836[1]

In our day for a young man who is preparing to visit the glorious East, it would be difficult, on boarding ship, not to remember Lord Byron, and with a pang of involuntary identification not to draw a close parallel between his own fate and that of Childe Harold. If, by any chance, the young man also happens to be a poet and wants to express his emotions, how can he avoid imitating him? Can one blame him for it? Our talent is not a free agent and imitation is not a shameful form of stealing – a sign of mental dullness, but a worthy trust in one's own powers, a hope of finding new worlds, following in the steps of genius, or the experiencing, even more lofty in its humility, of a desire to study one's model and thus to give it a second lease of life.

There is no doubt that Childe Harold's fantastic shade accompanied Mr Teplyakov on the ship which brought him to the shores of Thrace. The sounds of the concluding stanzas,

Adieu, adieu, my native land!

are echoed in the very beginning of his song. . . .

Shortly after, the poet sails past the shores made famous by Ovid's exile: they flash past him for a moment along the sea's horizon. . . .

The poet hails Ovid's tomb, which is out of sight, in verses which are marred by carelessness.

. . . it is all inaccurate, false, or simply meaningless.
Gresset, in one of his epistles,[2] writes:

> Je cesse d'estimer Ovide
> Quand il vient sur de faibles tons
> Me chanter, pleureur insipide,
> De longues lamentations.

The *Tristia* did not merit such severe condemnation. In our opinion it is superior to all Ovid's other works (except the *Metamorphoses*). The *Heroides*, the amatory elegies, and the *Ars Amatoria* itself, the supposed cause of his banishment, yield to the Epistles *ex Ponto*. In the latter, there is more true feeling, more simplicity, more individuality, and less icy wit. How brilliant are the descriptions of a foreign clime and of a foreign land! How lively in detail! And what longing for Rome! What touching complaints! We thank Mr Teplyakov for not attempting to shine with spiritual fortitude at the expense of the poor exile, and for coming vigorously to his defence.

The song which the poet puts in the mouth of Naso's ghost would have greater merit if Mr Teplyakov had aligned it more closely to Ovid's character as it is found, so sincerely expressed in his *lament*. He would not then have said, that at the time of the incursions of the Getae and Bessi the poet
Rushed joyfully into the fatal fray.
Ovid good-naturedly admits that from his youth he had no taste for warfare and that it was difficult for him in his old age to don a helmet over his grey hairs, and at the first news of invasion to grasp a sword in his shaking hand (see *Trist*. Lib. IV, El. 1).

. . . the meditations on the ruins of a Venetian castle have the disadvantage of reminding one of several stanzas from the fourth Canto of *Childe Harold*, verses which are too deeply engraved on our imaginations.

---

[1] Published unsigned in the third issue of the *Sovremennik* (1836). This was the second volume of Teplyakov's poems to appear, volume I having come out in 1832. Teplyakov (1804-42) had himself been exiled from St Petersburg to Cherson in the Crimea in 1826 and worked for a time under Count Vorontsov in Odessa. In 1835-6 Teplyakov was again living in St Petersburg.

[2] 'La Chartreuse' by J. B. L. Gresset.

301. V.L.P.'s Journey[1]

. . . All those who love Catullus, Gresset and Voltaire, all those who love poetry, not only in its lyrical flights or in the melancholy inspiration of elegy, not only in the wide sweep of drama and epic, but also in such products of simple humour as playful quips and intellectual diversions, value poetic sincerity. We are pleased to follow a poet through all the changes and conditions to which his lively and creative soul is subject – in sorrow and in joy, in the flights of ecstasy and when his feelings are in repose, both in Juvenalian indignation and in gentle regret at a neighbour's dullness . . . I venerate *Faust*, but I also love epigrams.

I plead guilty: I would give everything which has been written here in imitation of Lord Byron for the following spontaneous and unimpassioned lines in which the poet makes his hero exclaim to his friends,

> Friends! sisters! I'm in Paris!
> I have begun to live as well as breathe! etc.

There are people who do not acknowledge any poetry that is not passionate or exalted; there are people who consider even Horace to be prosaic (is it because he is calm, intelligent, rational?). Let it pass. But it would be a pity if his delightful odes, which our Derzhavin, among others, imitated, did not exist.

[1] I. I. Dmitriev's humorous poem 'V.L.P.'s Journey' was published in Moscow in 1808 in 50 copies. It dealt lightly with the journey Pushkin's uncle, Vasily Pushkin, had undertaken to Paris and London in 1803-4. The frontispiece shows V. L. Pushkin having an elocution lesson from Talma.
   This note was written in 1836, probably intended for the *Sovremennik*, but was not published till 1855.

302. Voltaire[1]
(*Correspondance inédite de Voltaire avec Frédéric II, le Président de Brosses, et autres personnages*, Paris, 1836)

There has lately been published in Paris the correspondence between Voltaire and the President de Brosses. It deals with the purchase of land effected by Voltaire in 1758.

Every line by a great writer becomes precious for posterity. We scan the manuscript with curiosity, be it nothing more than a jotting from an account book or a note to a tailor asking for the deferment of payment. We are involuntarily struck by the fact that the hand which traced these tame figures, these unimportant words, in the same hand-writing and it may be with the same pen, wrote the mighty works which are the object of our study and delight. But, I think, it fell only to Voltaire to form out of the business correspondence concerning the purchase of land a book which makes you laugh on every page, and to endow deals and title-deeds with all the fascination of a witty pamphlet. Fate provided such an amusing purchaser with a seller no less amusing. The President de Brosses was one of the most remarkable writers of the last century. He is renowned for many learned works, but we consider his best work to be the letters he wrote in Italy between 1730 and 1740, and which have recently been republished under the title: *L'Italie il y a cent ans*. In these letters to friends, de Brosses revealed an amazing talent. True learning never burdened with pedantry, depth of thought, playful wit, pictures sketched haphazardly but with vigour and boldness, put his book in a higher category than any other written in the same kind.

Voltaire, exiled from Paris, forced to flee from Berlin, sought refuge on the shores of Lake Geneva. Fame did not save him from worries. His personal freedom was not secure; he quaked for his capital which he had entrusted to various hands. The patronage of a small bourgeois republic did not serve much to encourage him. He wanted, as a precaution, to make peace with his own fatherland and wished (as he wrote himself) to have one foot in a monarchy and the other in a republic – so as to go from one to the other according to circumstances. The hamlet, Tournay, which belonged to the President de Brosses, caught his attention. He knew the president to be an improvident and extravagant man, always in need of money, and he entered into negotiations with him in the following letter:

J'ai lu avec un extrême plaisir ce que vous avez écrit sur les *Terres australes*; mais serait-il permis de vous faire une proposition qui concerne le Continent? Vous n'êtes pas homme à faire valoir votre terre de Tournay. Votre fermier Chouet en est dégoûté et demande à résilier son bail. Voulez-vous me vendre votre terre à vie? Je suis vieux et malade. Je sçais bien que je fais un mauvais marché; mais ce marché vous sera utile et me sera agréable. Voicy quelles seraient les conditions que ma fantaisie, qui m'a toujours conduit, soumet à votre prudence.

Je m'engage à faire bâtir un joli pavillon des matériaux de votre très-vilain châtau, et je compte y mettre vingt-cinq mille livres. Je vous payeray comptant vingt-cinq autres mille livres.

Tous les embélissements que je ferai à la terre, tous les bestiaux et les instruments d'agriculture dont je l'aurai pourvüe, vous apartiendront. Si je meurs avant d'avoir achevé le bâtiment, vous aurez pardevers vous mes vingt-cinq mille livres, et vous achèverez le bâtiment si vous voulez. Mais je tâcherai de ne pas mourir de deux ans, et alors vous serez joliment logé sans qu'il vous en coûte rien.

De plus, je m'engage à ne pas vivre plus de quatre ou cinq ans.

Moyennant ces offres honnêtes, je demande la pleine possession de votre terre, de tous vos droits, meubles, bois, bestiaux, et même du curé, et que vous me garantissiez tout jusqu'à ce que ce curé m'enterre. Si ce plaisant marché vous convient, Monsieur, vous pouvez, d'un mot, le rendre sérieux: la vie est bien courte pour que les affaires soient longues.

J'ajoute encor un petit mot; j'ay embelli mon trou intitulé *les Délices*. J'ay embelli une maison à Lausane. Ces deux effets, grâce à ma façon, valent actuellement le double de ce qu'ils valaient. Il en sera autant de votre terre. Voyez ce que vous en pensez. Vous ne vous en déferez jamais dans l'état où elle est.

Quoy qu'il en soit, je vous demande le secret.

De Brosses did not delay with his reply. His letter, like Voltaire's, is filled with wit and humour:

Si j'avois été dans votre voisinage, Monsieur, lorsque vous fîtes une acquisition si près de la ville, en admirant avec vous le physique des bords de notre lac, j'aurois eu l'honneur de vous dire à l'oreille que le moral du caractère des habitans demandoit que vous vous plaçassiez sur France, par deux raisons capitales: l'une qu'il faut être chez soy, l'autre qu'il ne faut pas être chez les autres. Vous ne sçauriés croire combien cette république me fait aimer les monarchies: j'avois grand besoin d'une raison pareille. Je vous aurois dès-lors volontiers offert mon château, s'il avoit été digne d'être la demeure ordinaire d'un homme si célèbre: mais il n'a pas même l'honneur d'être une antiquité, ce n'est qu'une vieillerie. Il vous vient en fantaisie de le rajeunir comme Memnon. J'aprouve fort ce projet, dont vous ne sçavés peut-être pas que M. d'Argental avoit eu cydevant l'idée pour votre établissement. Entrons en matière.

At this point de Brosses analyses, one after another, all the conditions offered by Voltaire; agrees with some, contradicts others, revealing in

the process a resourcefulness and acuteness which it seems Voltaire did
not expect from the president. That stirred up Voltaire's pride. He
began to be cunning; the correspondence grew livelier. Finally on 15
December the deal was accomplished.

These letters, containing the negotiations of the bargainers, and a
few others, written on the conclusion of the deal, form the best part
of Voltaire's correspondence with de Brosses. Each is flirting with the
other; both constantly leave aside questions of business for the most
unexpected jokes, for the most sincere judgements on men and contemporary events. In these letters Voltaire appears as Voltaire, that is
as the most courteous of companions; de Brosses – as the acute writer,
who described the government and customs, and the artistic and voluptuous life of Italy with such originality.

But soon the agreement between the new master of the land and its
former owner was broken. The war, like so many other wars, was
begun for trivial reasons. Felled trees angered the impatient Voltaire;
he quarrelled with the president, no less irritable than himself. What
Voltaire's wrath meant has to be seen to be believed! He already
regards de Brosses as an enemy, as a Fréron, as a Grand Inquisitor.
He means to ruin him: 'Qu'il tremble!' He exclaims in fury, 'Il ne
s'agit pas de le rendre ridicule: IL S'AGIT DE LE DÉSHONORER!'
He complains, he weeps, he gnashes his teeth . . . all over 200 francs.
De Brosses, for his part, does not want to yield to the irascible philosopher; in answer to his complaints, he writes a haughty letter to the
famous sage, reproaching him for innate impertinence, advising him
to hold back his hand from using his pen in moments of madness, so
as not to blush later on coming to himself, and ends the letter with
Juvenal's wish for

Mens sana in corpore sano.

Outsiders intervene in the neighbours' quarrel. Their mutual friend,
M. de Ruffey, appeals to Voltaire's conscience and writes him a stinging
letter (which was probably dictated by de Brosses himself): 'Vous
craignez d'être dupe', says M. de Ruffey, 'c'est cependent le beau
rôle à jouer. . . . Vous n'avez jamais eu de procès, ils . . . sont ruineux,
même à gagner. . . . Rappelez-vous l'huître de La Fontaine[2] et la scène v
de l'acte II du *Scapin* de Molière. [The scene in which Leander forces
Scapin to confess on his knees to all his own trickery.] Outre les mauvaises
plaisanteries des avocats, vous avez à craindre celles de la canaille
littéraire, qui sera charmée d'avoir prise sur vous. . . .'

Voltaire was the first to tire and to yield. He sulked for a long time
at the obstinate president and was the instrument of de Brosses's not
being elected to the Academy (which meant a great deal at the time).
Over and above that Voltaire had the satisfaction of outliving him:
de Brosses, the younger of the two by fifteen years, died in 1777, a year
before Voltaire.

In spite of the amount of material collected on Voltaire's life (there
is a whole library of it), he is as yet very little known as a man of affairs,
a capitalist, and a property owner. The correspondence now published
reveals a great deal. 'Il faut voir', writes the editor[3] in his introduction,

> à soixante ans l'enfant gâté de l'Europe, le correspondant de Catherine-
> le-Grand et de Frédéric II, soigner avec une préoccupation et une
> insistance croissantes les plus minutieux détails de son importance
> locale. Il faut le voir faire en habit de gala son entrée dans sa comté
> de Tourney, entre ses deux nièces *toutes en diamants*, harangué par
> le curé et salué par les *sujets*, qui empruntent l'artillerie de Genève
> pour fêter sa prise de possession seigneuriale. – Nul esprit plus in-
> génieux à se créer des luttes et des affaires. Tantôt il importune un
> prince du sang pour se faire lieutenant des chasses; tantôt il s'agite
> en tout sens pour le syndicat de la noblesse de Gex. Il est en d'inces-
> santes hostilités avec tous les hommes d'église du canton. La gabelle
> n'a pas d'ennemi plus actif et plus délié. Il veut être le banquier du
> pays de Gex comme Paris de Montmartel est celui de la Cour. Le
> voici qui entre dans des spéculations sur le sel: il a des gentilshommes
> à lui qu'il fait ses ambassadeurs en Suisse pour cet objet. Puis il est
> remué par tout cela. Il prend au sérieux ces petites agitations. Il
> s'en émeut sincèrement avec cette mobilité de passion qui n'est qu'à
> lui. Ce sont tour-à-tour d'habiles argumentations d'avocat, des
> chicanes de procureur, des finesses de marchand, des hyperboles de
> poète, des accents d'une véritable éloquence. Sa lettre au président
> de Brosses pour de Croze contre le curé de Moens rappelle en
> vérité son Mémoire pour les Calas.[4]

In one of these letters we found some hitherto unknown verses by
Voltaire. They bear the light touch of his inimitable talent. They are
written to a neighbour[5] who sent him some roses.

> Vos rosiers sont dans mes jardins
> Et leurs fleurs vont bientôt paraître.
> Doux asile où je suis mon maître!
> Je renonce aux lauriers si vains,

Qu'à Paris j'aimai trop peut-être.
Je me suis trop piqué les mains
Aux épines qu'ils ont fait naître.

We admit to the element of rococo in our old-fashioned taste: we find more style, more life, more thought, in these seven lines than in half a dozen long French poems, written according to the present taste, in which the thought is replaced by distorted expression, Voltaire's lucid language by the inflated language of Ronsard, his liveliness by unbearable monotony, and his wit by vulgar cynicism or drooping melancholia.

In general, Voltaire's correspondence with de Brosses reveals to us the pleasant side of the creator of Mérope and Candide. His pretensions, his weaknesses, his childish irritability – all these do not harm him in our eyes. We readily forgive him and are prepared to follow in the wake of his fiery spirit and restless sensibility. But no such feeling is born from the reading of the letters appended by the editor to the book under discussion. These new letters were found among the papers of M. de la Touche, the former French Ambassador to the court of Frederick II (in 1752).

At that time Voltaire was not on good terms with his former pupil, *The Solomon of the North* [Footnote: that is what Voltaire called Frederick II in his laudatory Epistles]. Maupertuis, the President of the Berlin Academy, quarrelled with Professor Koenig. The King took the side of the president; Voltaire took up arms for the professor. An anonymous work appeared, with the title: *Letter to the Public*. In it Koenig was censured and Voltaire was not left untouched. Voltaire retorted and published his stinging reply in German reviews. After some time the *Letter to the Public* was republished in Berlin with an engraving of the crown, sceptre and Prussian eagle on the title-page. Voltaire only then realized with whom he had had the rashness to contend, and he began to contemplate a tactful withdrawal. He saw in the King's actions a definite cooling-off in his attitude towards him and foresaw disgrace. 'I try not to think it,' he wrote to d'Argental in Paris,[6] 'but I do not want to be like cuckolded husbands, who try to persuade themselves of their wives' fidelity. In their heart of hearts the poor things are aware of their sorrow.' Despite his despondency, he still could not restrain himself from aiming one more shaft at his enemies. He wrote his most biting satire (*La Diatribe du docteur Akakia*) and published it, having wheedled permission to do so by a trick from the King himself.

What followed is well known. The satire, on Frederick's orders, was burned by the executioner. Voltaire left Berlin, was held up in Frankfurt by Prussian guards, was under arrest for several days, and was obliged to hand over the collection of poems by Frederick, which had been published in a limited edition,[7] among which was to be found a satirical poem against Louis XV and his court.

This whole lamentable story bestows little honour on philosophy. Voltaire in the whole course of his long life never could preserve his personal dignity. In his youth his confinement in the Bastille, his exile and persecution, failed to attract to his person the compassion and sympathy which was hardly ever denied to suffering talent. The confidant of kings, the idol of Europe, the foremost writer of his age, the leader of thought and of contemporary opinion, Voltaire, even in his old age, did not command the respect owed to his grey hairs – the laurels which crowned them were bespattered with mud. Slander, which persecutes fame but which is always destroyed in the face of truth, in his case, contrary to its usual practice, did not dissolve, as it always remained plausible. He lacked self-respect and did not look for the respect of others. What drew him to Berlin? Why did he want to exchange his independence for the capricious favours of a King, who was a stranger to him, and who had no right to coerce him? . . .

To Frederick II's credit one should say that the King on his own initiative, in spite of his native bent for mockery, would not have begun to humiliate his old master, would not have clothed the foremost French poet in motley,[8] would not have betrayed him to the world's gibes, if Voltaire had not brought on himself such shabby humiliation.

Up till now it was believed that Voltaire of his own accord, in a fit of high-minded distress, returned the Chamberlain's key and the Prussian order – the symbols of his inconstant favour – to Frederick; but it now appears that the King demanded them back himself. The roles are reversed: Frederick is indignant and threatening, Voltaire weeps and implores. . . .

To what conclusions does all this bring one? That genius is endowed with its weaknesses – this comforts the mediocre but saddens those of noble spirit, reminding them of humanity's imperfections; that the rightful place for an author is his study; and, finally, that in the long run independence and self-respect alone can raise us above the petty concerns of life and the storms of fate.[9]

[1] Published unsigned in the third issue of the *Sovremennik* (1836). Pushkin wrote to Chaadaev that this article was by him.

² La Fontaine's fable 'L'Huître et les Plaideurs'.

³ J. Théophile Foisset.

⁴ Voltaire had taken up the case of Jean Calas, who had been tortured and executed in 1762 on the trumped-up charge of having murdered his son to prevent him becoming a Catholic. He fought the case for three years and finally managed to have Calas posthumously declared innocent.

⁵ Le Président de Ruffey, 3 March 1759.

⁶ The letter Pushkin is quoting was to Marie-Louise Denis, written on 29 October 1751, the manuscript of which is in the Leningrad State Public Library. Voltaire wrote: '. . . je tâche de n'en rien croire, mais j'ai peur d'être comme les cocus, qui s'efforcent à penser que leurs femmes sont très fidèles. Les pauvres gens sentent au fond de leur cœur quelque chose qui les avertit de leur désastre.'

⁷ *Poésies diverses.*

⁸ In the manuscript Pushkin had added at this point: 'would not have so cruelly betrayed him to the mockery of pages', which ties the passage closely to Pushkin's own experience at the hands of Nicholas I, humiliated as he was by his appointment to the office of Kammerjunker. In fact, the situation here described is Pushkin's not Voltaire's.

⁹ In this concluding paragraph the undercurrent of Pushkin's emotions can again be clearly sensed beneath the surface.

303. John Tanner[1]

For some time the States of North America have been attracting the attention of the more thoughtful Europeans. The reason for this does not lie in political events: America is calmly accomplishing her development in stages, being as yet both safe and prosperous, strong in a peace made secure by her geographical position, proud of her institutions. But several men of profound intellect have of late begun to investigate American customs and decrees, and their observations have raised anew questions which were long accounted settled. The respect felt for this new nation and for its code, the fruit of most advanced enlightenment, was very much shaken. People saw with astonishment democracy in all its disgusting cynicism, with all its cruel prejudices, in its unbearable tyranny. Everything noble and disinterested, everything that raises man's spirit, crushed by implacable egoism and the passion for comfort; the majority, an insolently persecuting society; negro slavery in the midst of education and freedom; class persecution among a people who have no nobility; cupidity and envy on the part of the electorate; timidity and flattery on the part of the legislators; talent forced into voluntary ostracism out of regard for equality; the rich man putting on a ragged coat so as not to offend in the street the proud penury he secretly despises: such is the picture of the American States, recently put before us.

The attitude of the States to the Indian tribes, the ancient owners of the land, now colonized by European emigrants, was also subjected to the stern analysis of recent investigators. The obvious injustice, calumny and inhumanity of the American Congress are indignantly condemned; in one way or another, be it by fire or by the sword, through rum or trickery, or by more moral means, the savage must vanish with the approach of civilization. Such is the irrevocable law. The remnants of the ancient inhabitants of America will soon be completely exterminated; and the wide steppes and the immense rivers, in which they used to catch their food with nets and arrows, will become cultivated fields studded with villages and mercantile harbours, where the steam will rise from ships and the American flag will be unfurled.

The manners of North American savages are known to us from the descriptions of famous novelists. But both Chateaubriand and Cooper showed us Indians in their poetic aspect and touched up the truth with the colours of their imaginations.[2] 'Savages as presented in novels', writes Washington Irving, 'resemble real savages as little as idyllic shepherds do real ones.'[3] This was the very thing readers suspected; and mistrust for the words of the enchanting story-tellers lessened the pleasure afforded by their brilliant works.

In New York, there was recently published the 'Narrative of John Tanner', who had spent thirty years in the wilds of North America, among its savage inhabitants. This 'Narrative' is valuable in many respects. It is the fullest and probably the last document concerning the mode of life of a people of which soon no trace will remain. The chronicle of illiterate tribes sheds true light on that which some philosophers call the natural state of man.[4] Finally, as a simple and unimpassioned testimony, it will bear witness before the world of the methods which the American States used in the nineteenth century for spreading both their dominion and Christian civilization. The authenticity of this 'Narrative' is unquestioned. John Tanner is still alive; many (including De Tocqueville, the author of the famous book, *De la démocratie en Amérique*) have met him, and have bought this book from him personally. In their opinion there cannot have been any forgery. But it suffices to read a few pages to be satisfied on that score: the absolute artlessness and humble simplicity of the narrative vouch for its truth.

John Tanner's father, an emigrant from Virginia, was a clergyman. On the death of his wife he settled in a place called Elk Horn, not far from Cincinatti.

Elk Horn was subject to raids by Indians. One night John Tanner's uncle, having made a plan with his neighbours, approached the Indian camp and shot one of them. The others jumped into the river and swam away. . . .

Tanner's father, starting out one morning to go to a distant village, ordered his two daughters to send little John to school. They remembered this only after dinner. But it was raining, and John stayed at home. The father returned in the evening and on finding out that he had not been at school sent him to bring a cane and flogged him severely. From that time the young Tanner found his father's house uncongenial; he often thought and said to himself: 'I wish I could go and live among the Indians.'

I cannot tell how long we remained at Elk Horn; when we moved, we travelled two days with horses and wagons, and came to the Ohio, where my father bought three flat boats; the sides of these boats had bullet holes in them, and there was blood on them, which I understood was that of people who had been killed by the Indians. In one of these boats, we put the horses and cattle, in another, beds, furniture, and other property, and in the third were some negroes. The cattle boat and the family boat were lashed together; the third, with the negroes, followed behind. We descended the Ohio, and in two or three days came to Cincinnati; here the cattle boat sunk in the middle of the river. When my father saw it sinking, he jumped on board, and cut loose all the cattle, and they swam ashore on the Kentucky side, and were saved. The people from Cincinnati came out in boats to assist us, but father told them the cattle were all safe.

In one day we went from Cincinnati to the mouth of the Big Miami, opposite which we were to settle. Here was some cleared land, and one or two log cabins, but they had been deserted on account of the Indians. My father rebuilt the cabins, and enclosed them with a strong picket. It was early in the spring when we arrived at the mouth of the Big Miami, and we were soon engaged in preparing a field to plant corn. I think it was not more than ten days after our arrival, when my father told us in the morning, that from the actions of the horses, he perceived there were Indians lurking about in the woods, and he said to me, 'John, you must not go out of the house today.' After giving strict charge to my step mother to let none of the little children go out, he went to the field, with the negroes, and my elder brother, to drop corn.

Three little children, beside myself, were left in the house with my step mother. To prevent me from going out, my step mother required me to take care of the little child, then not more than a few months old; but as I soon became impatient of confinement, I began to pinch my little brother, to make him cry. My mother perceiving his uneasiness, told me to take him in my arms and walk about the house; I did so, but continued to pinch him. My mother at length took him from me to give him suck. I watched my opportunity, and escaped into the yard; thence through a small door in the large gate of the wall into the open field. There was a walnut tree at some distance from the house, and near the side of the field, where I had been in the habit of finding some of the last year's nuts. To gain this tree without being seen by my father, and those in the field, I had to use some precaution. I remember perfectly well having seen my father, as I skulked towards the tree; he stood in the middle of the field, with his gun in his hand, to watch for Indians, while the others were dropping corn. As I came near the tree, I thought to myself, 'I wish I could see these Indians.' I had partly filled with nuts a straw hat which I wore, when I heard a crackling noise behind me; I looked round, and saw the Indians; almost at the same instant, I was seized by both hands, and dragged off betwixt two. One of them took my straw hat, emptied the nuts on the ground, and put it on my head. The Indians who seized me were an old man and a young one; these were, as I learned subsequently, Manito-o-geezhik, and his son Kish-kau-ko. Since I returned from Red River, I have been at Detroit, while Kish-kau-ko was in prison there; I have also been in Kentucky, and have learned several particulars relative to my capture, which were unknown to me at the time. It appears that the wife of Manito-o-geezhik had recently lost by death her youngest son, that she had complained to her husband, that unless he should bring back her son, she could not live. This was an intimation to bring her a captive whom she might adopt in the place of the son she had lost. Manito-o-geezhik, associating with him his son, and two other men of his band, living at Lake Huron, had proceeded eastward with this sole design. On the upper part of Lake Erie, they had been joined by three other young men, the relations of Manito-o-geezhik, and had proceeded on, now seven in number, to the

413

settlements on the Ohio. They had arrived the night previous to my capture at the mouth of the Big Miami, had crossed the Ohio, and concealed themselves within sight of my father's house. Several times in the course of the morning, old Manito-o-geezhik had been compelled to repress the ardour of his young men, who becoming impatient at seeing no opportunity to steal a boy, were anxious to fire upon the people dropping corn in the field. It must have been about noon when they saw me coming from the house to the walnut tree, which was probably very near the place where one or more of them were concealed.

It was but a few minutes after I left the house, when my father, coming from the field, perceived my absence. My step mother had not yet noticed that I had gone out. My elder brother ran immediately to the walnut tree, which he knew I was fond of visiting, and seeing the nuts which the Indian had emptied out of my hat, he immediately understood that I had been made captive. Search was instantly made for me, but to no purpose. My father's distress, when he found I was indeed taken away by the Indians, was, I am told, very great.

After I saw myself firmly seized by both wrists by the two Indians, I was not conscious of any thing that passed for a considerable time. I must have fainted, as I did not cry out, and I can remember nothing that happened to me, until they threw me over a large log, which must have been at a considerable distance from the house. The old man I did not now see; I was dragged along between Kish-kau-ko and a very short thick man. I had probably made some resistance, or done something to irritate this last, for he took me a little to one side, and drawing his tomahawk, motioned to me to look up. This I plainly understood, from the expression of his face, and his manner, to be a direction for me to look up for the last time, as he was about to kill me. I did as he directed, but Kish-kau-ko caught his hand as the tomahawk was descending and prevented him from burying it in my brains. Loud talking ensued between the two. Kish-kau-ko presently raised a yell; the old man and the four others answered it by a similar yell; and came running up. I have since understood that Kish-kau-ko complained to his father, that the short man had made an attempt to kill his little brother, as he called me. The old chief, after reproving him, took me by one hand, and Kish-kau-ko by the other, and dragged me betwixt them; the man who had threatened to kill me, and who was now an object of terror, being kept at some distance. I could perceive, as I retarded them somewhat in their retreat, that they were apprehensive of being over-taken; some of them were always at some distance from us.

It was about one mile from my father's house to the place where they threw me into a hickory bark canoe, which was concealed under the bushes, on the bank of the river. Into this they all seven jumped, and immediately crossed the Ohio, landing at the mouth of the Big Miami, and on the south side of that river. Here they abandoned their canoe, and stuck their paddles in the ground, so that they could be seen from the river. At a little distance in the woods, they had some blankets and provisions concealed; they offered me some dry venison and bear's grease, but I could not eat. My father's house was plainly to be seen from the place where we stood; they pointed at it, looked at me, and laughed, but I have never known what they said.

After they had eaten a little, they began to ascend the Miami, dragging me along as before. The shoes I had on when at home, they took off, as they seemed to think I could run better without them. Although I perceived I was closely watched, all hope of escape did not immediately forsake me. As they hurried me along, I endeavoured, without their knowledge, to take notice of such objects as would serve as landmarks on my way back. I tried also, where I passed long grass, or soft ground, to leave my tracks. I hoped to be able to escape after they should have fallen asleep at night. When night came, they lay down, placing me between the old man and Kish-kau-ko, so close together, that the same blanket covered all three. I was so fatigued that I fell asleep immediately, and did not wake until sun-rise next morning, when the Indians were up and ready to proceed on their journey. Thus we journeyed for about four days, the Indians hurrying me on, and I continuing to hope that I might escape, but still every night completely overpowered by sleep. As my feet were bare, they were often wounded, and at length much swollen. The old man perceiving my situation, examined my feet one day, and after removing a great many thorns and splinters from them, gave me a pair of moccasins, which afforded me some relief. Most com-monly, I travelled between the old man and Kish-kau-ko, and they often made me run until my strength was quite exhausted. For several days I could eat little or nothing. It was, I think, four days after we left the Ohio, that we came to a considerable river, running as I suppose, into the Miami. This river was wide, and so deep, that I could not wade across it; the old man took me on his shoulders and carried me over; the water was nearly up to his arm pits. As he carried me across, I thought I should never be able to pass this river alone, and gave over all hope of immediate escape. When he put me down on the other side, I immediately ran up the bank, and a short distance into the woods, when a turkey flew up a few steps before me. The nest she had left contained a number of eggs; those I put in the bosom of my shirt, and returned towards the river. When the Indians saw me they laughed, and immediately took the eggs from me, and kindling a fire, put them in a small kettle to boil. I was then very hungry, and as I sat watching the kettle, I saw the old man come running from the direction of the ford where we had crossed; he immediately caught up the kettle, threw the eggs and the water on the fire, at the same time saying something in a hurried and low tone to the young men. I inferred we were pursued, and have since understood that such was the case; it is probable some of my friends were at that time on the opposite side of the river searching for me. The Indians hastily gathered up the eggs and dispersed themselves in the woods, two of them still urging me forward to the utmost of my strength.

It was a day or two after this that we met a party of twenty or thirty Indians, on their way towards the settlements. Old Manito-o-geezhik had much to say to them; subsequently I learned that they were a war party of Shawneese; that they received information from our party, of the whites who were in pursuit of us about the forks of the Miami; that they went in pursuit of them, and that a severe skirmish happened between them, in which numbers were killed on both sides.

Our journey through the woods was tedious and painful: it might have been ten days after we met the war party, when we arrived at the Maumee river. As soon as we came near the river, the Indians were suddenly scattered about the woods examining the trees, yelling and answering each other. They soon selected a hickory tree, which was cut down, and the bark stripped off, to make a canoe. In this canoe we all embarked, and descended till we came to a large Shawnee village, at the mouth of a river which enters the Maumee. As we were landing in this village, great numbers of the Indians came about us, and one young woman came crying directly towards me, and struck me on the head. Some of her friends had been killed by the whites. Many of these Shawneese showed a disposition to kill me, but Kish-kau-ko and the old man interposed, and prevented

416

them. I could perceive that I was often the subject of conversation, but could not as yet understand what was said. Old Manito-o-geezhik could speak a few words of English, which he used occasionally, to direct me to bring water, make a fire, or perform other tasks, which he now began to require of me. We remained two days at the Shawnee village, and then proceeded on our journey in the canoe. It was not very far from the village that we came to a trading house, where were three or four men who could speak English; they talked much with me, and said they wished to have purchased me from the Indians, that I might return to my friends; but as the old man would not consent to part with me, the traders told me I must be content to go with the Indians, and to become the old man's son, in place of one he had lost, promising at the same time that after ten days they would come to the village and release me.

At last the canoe moored at the place where poor John's kidnappers lived. An old woman came out of a log cabin and ran to meet them. The old man said a few words to her; she cried out, hugged and embraced her little prisoner and dragged him to the cabin.

John Tanner's kidnapper was called Manito-o-geezhik. His youngest son had died a short while before the event here described took place. His wife had announced that she would not live if her son was not found. That is, she demanded she should be found a young prisoner whom she could adopt. Old Manito-o-geezhik with his son, Kish-kau-ko, and with two fellow tribesmen, inhabitants of Lake Huron, set out at once in order to satisfy the old woman's wish at all costs. Three young men, the old man's relatives joined them. All seven came to the villages situated on the shores of the Ohio. On the eve of the raid the Indians crossed the river and hid near the Tanners' house. The young men impatiently waited for the child to appear, and were, on several occasions, ready to shoot at the labourers. The old man could barely restrain them.

Having returned home successfully with their prize, old Manito-o-geezhik summoned his friends and relations the very next day, and John Tanner was ceremonially adopted on the little savage's grave itself.

It was spring. The Indians left their settlements and all set out to hunt big game. Having found a convenient place they began to sur-round it with a stockade of green boughs and saplings, from behind which they were to shoot. They set John to breaking off the little dry twigs and to stripping the leaves from the side where the hunters hid. The little prisoner, tired out by the heat and the work, continually hungry and miserable, was idly carrying out his task. Old Manito-o-geezhik, on finding him once asleep, hit the boy on the head with his *tomahawk* and threw him, as good as dead, into the bushes. Returning to the camp, the old man told his wife: 'Old woman, the boy I brought you is good for nothing; I have killed him and you will find him in such a place.' The old woman and her daughter ran and found Tanner still alive and brought him back to consciousness.

The little foster-child's life was of the saddest. He was made to work beyond his strength; and the old man and his sons constantly beat the poor boy. He was given hardly anything to eat; at night he usually slept between the door and the hearth, and anyone coming in or out invariably kicked him. The old man grew to hate him, and treated him with incredible brutality. Tanner could never forget the following incident.

Once Manito-o-geezhik, having gone out of his hut, suddenly returned and, grabbing the boy by the hair, dragged him behind the door and thrust his face *like a cat's* into a heap of excrement. 'Tanner' writes the American editor of his notes, 'has much of the Indian habit of concealing emotion; but when he related the above to me, the glimmering of his eye and a convulsive movement of his upper lip, betrayed sufficiently that he is not without the enduring thirst for revenge which belongs to the people among whom he has spent his life. Though more than thirty years had elapsed, he intended now to have avenged himself for the injury done him when a boy not eleven years of age.'

Preparations for war began in the winter. Manito-o-geezhik, on setting out for the expedition, said to Tanner, 'Now I am going to kill your father and your brother and all your relations. . . .' In a few days he returned, and showed John an old white hat which he at once recognized: it belonged to his brother. The old man assured him that he had kept his word, and that none of his relatives now remained alive.

Time passed, and John Tanner began to grow accustomed to his fate. Although Manito-o-geezhik continued to treat him severely, the old woman loved him and tried to ease his lot. After two years there occurred an important change. The chief of the Ottawwaw tribe, Net-no-kwa, a relative of the old Indian who had captured John Tanner, bought him to replace a son she had lost. John Tanner was bartered for a keg of whisky and a few pounds of tobacco.

Adopted for the second time, Tanner found his new mother to be an
affectionate and kind protectress. He grew very attached to her; he soon
forgot the habits of his early upbringing and became completely Indian
– and now, when fate brought him once more into the society from
which he had been torn in infancy, John Tanner retained the appearance, character and prejudices of the savages who had adopted him.

Tanner's narrative presents a vivid and sad picture. It has a certain
monotony, a certain sleepy incoherence and lack of thought, giving
some idea of the life of American savages. It is a long tale of shot game,
of blizzards, of long hungry marches, of hunters frozen in their tracks,
of bestial orgies, of quarrels, of enmity, of a life both indigent and hard,
of penury unknown to the enlightened races.

American savages are all in fact hunters. European civilization having
forced them out of their native prairies, gave them powder and shot:
that was the measure of its beneficent influence. A skilled shot is held
among them to be a great man. Tanner describes his first attempt in
the field, in which he was afterwards famous,

I had never killed any game, and, indeed, had never in my life discharged a gun. My mother had purchased at Mackinac a keg of
powder, which, as they thought it a little damp, was here spread out
to dry. Taw-ga-we-ninne had a large horseman's pistol; and finding
myself somewhat emboldened by his indulgent manner toward me,
I requested permission to go and try to kill some pigeons with the
pistol. My request was seconded by NET-NO-KWA, who said, 'it
is time for our son to begin to learn to be a hunter.' Accordingly, my
father, as I called Taw-ga-we-ninne, loaded the pistol and gave it
to me, saying, 'Go, my son, and if you kill anything with this, you
shall immediately have a gun, and learn to hunt.' Since I have been
a man, I have been placed in difficult situations; but my anxiety
for success was never greater than in this, my first essay as a hunter.
I had not gone far from the camp, before I met with pigeons, and
some of them alighted in the bushes very near me. I cocked my
pistol, and raised it to my face, bringing the breech almost in contact
with my nose. Having brought the sight to bear upon the pigeon, I
pulled trigger, and was in the next instant sensible of a humming
noise, like that of a stone sent swiftly through the air. I found the
pistol at the distance of some paces behind me, and the pigeon under
the tree on which he had been sitting. My face was much bruised,
and covered with blood. I ran home carrying my pigeon in triumph.

My face was speedily bound up; my pistol exchanged for a fowling-piece; I was accoutred with a powder horn, and furnished with shot, and allowed to go out after birds. One of the young Indians went with me, to observe my manner of shooting. I killed three more pigeons in the course of the afternoon, and did not discharge my gun once without killing. Henceforth I began to be treated with more consideration, and was allowed to hunt often, that I might become expert.

Soon after this the young hunter distinguished himself in a new exploit.

After we had remained about three months in this place, game began to be scarce, and we all suffered from hunger. The chief man of our band was called As-sin-ne-boi-nainse (the Little Assinneboin), and he now proposed to us all to move, as the country where we were was exhausted. The day on which we were to commence our removal was fixed upon, but before it arrived our necessities became extreme. The evening before the day on which we intended to move, my mother talked much of all our misfortunes and losses, as well as of the urgent distress under which we were then labouring. At the usual hour I went to sleep, as did all the younger part of the family; but I was wakened again by the loud praying and singing of the old woman, who continued her devotions through great part of the night. Very early, on the following morning, she called us all to get up, and put on our moccasins, and be ready to move. She then called Wa-me-gon-a-biew to her, and said to him, in rather a low voice, 'My son, last night I sung and prayed to the Great Spirit, and when I slept, there came to me one like a man, and said to me, "Net-no-kwa, to-morrow you shall eat a bear. There is, at a distance from the path you are to travel to-morrow, and in such a direction (which she described to him), a small round meadow, with something like a path leading from it; in that path there is a bear." Now, my son, I wish you to go to that place, without mentioning to any one what I have said, and you will certainly find the bear, as I have described to you.' But the young man, who was not particularly dutiful, or apt to regard what his mother said, going out of the lodge, spoke sneeringly to the other Indians of the dream. 'The old woman', said he, 'tells me we are to eat a bear to-day; but I do not know who is to kill it.' The old woman, hearing him, called him in, and reproved him; but she could not prevail upon him to go to hunt.

The Indians, accordingly, all moved off towards the place where they were to encamp that night. The men went first by themselves, each carrying some article of baggage; and when they arrived where the camp was to be placed, they threw down their loads and went to hunt. Some of the boys, and I among them, who accompanied the men, remained with this baggage, until the women should come up. I had my gun with me, and I continued to think of the conversation I had heard between my mother and Wa-me-gon-a-biew, respecting her dream. At length, I resolved to go in search of the place she had spoken of, and without mentioning to any one my design, I loaded my gun as for a bear, and set off on our back track. I soon met a woman belonging to one of the brothers of Taw-ga-we-ninne, and of course my aunt. This woman had shown little friendship for us, considering us as a burthen upon her husband, who sometimes gave something for our support; she had also often ridiculed me. She asked me immediately what I was doing on the path, and whether I expected to kill Indians, that I came there with my gun. I made her no answer; and thinking I must be not far from the place where my mother had told Wa-me-gon-a-biew to leave the path, I turned off, continuing carefully to regard all the directions she had given. At length, I found what appeared at some former time to have been a pond. It was a small, round, open place in the woods, now grown up with grass and some small bushes. This I thought must be the meadow my mother had spoken of; and examining it around, I came to an open place in the bushes, where, it is probable, a small brook ran from the meadow; but the snow was now so deep that I could see nothing of it. My mother had mentioned, that when she saw the bear in her dream, she had, at the same time, seen a smoke rising from the ground. I was confident this was the place she had indicated, and I watched long, expecting to see the smoke; but wearied at length with waiting, I walked a few paces into the open place, resembling a path, when I unexpectedly fell up to my middle into the snow. I extricated myself without difficulty, and walked on; but remembering that I had heard the Indians speak of killing bears in their holes, it occurred to me that it might be a bear's hole into which I had fallen, and looking down into it, I saw the head of a bear lying close to the bottom of the hole. I placed the muzzle of my gun nearly between his eyes, and discharged it. As soon as the smoke cleared away, I took a piece of a stick and thrust it into the eyes and into the wound in the head of the bear, and being satisfied that he was dead, I endeavoured to lift him out of the hole; but being unable to do this, I returned home, following the track I had made in coming out. As I came near the camp, where the squaws had, by this time, set up the lodges, I met the same woman I had seen in going out, and she immediately began to ridicule me, 'Have you killed a bear, that you came back so soon, and walk so fast?' I thought to myself, 'how does she know that I have killed a bear?' But I passed by her without saying any thing, and went into my mother's lodge. After a few minutes, the old woman said, 'My son, look in that kettle, and you will find a mouthful of beaver meat, which a man gave me since you left us in the morning. You must leave half of it for Wa-me-gon-a-biew, who has not yet returned from hunting, and has eaten nothing to-day.' I accordingly ate the beaver meat, and when I had finished it, observing an opportunity when she stood by herself, I stepped up to her, and whispered in her ear, 'My mother, I have killed a bear.' 'What do you say, my son?' said she. 'I have killed a bear.' 'Are you sure you have killed him?' 'Yes.' 'Is he quite dead?' 'Yes.' She watched my face for a moment, and then caught me in her arms, hugging and kissing me with great earnestness, and for a long time. I then told her what my aunt had said to me, both going and returning, and this being told to her husband when he returned, he not only reproved her for it, but gave her a severe flogging. The bear was sent for, and, as being the first I had killed, was cooked all together, and the hunters of the whole band invited to feast with us, according to the custom of the Indians.

The description of various hunts and adventures met with while tracking game occupy a great part of John Tanner's 'Narrative'. The tale of shot bears alone forms a novel in itself. That which he tells of the moose, the American reindeer (cervus alces) deserves study by naturalists.

There is an opinion prevalent among the Indians, that the moose, among the methods of self-preservation with which he seems better acquainted than almost any other animal, has the power of remaining for a long time under water. Two men of the band of Wa-ge-to-tah-gun, whom I knew perfectly well, and considered very good and credible Indians, after a long day's absence on a hunt, came in, and stated that they had chased a moose into a small pond, that they had seen him go to the middle of it, and disappear; and then choosing positions, from which they could see every part of the circumference of the pond, smoked, and waited until near evening; during all which time, they could see no motion of the water, or other indication of the position of the moose. At length, being discouraged, they had abandoned all hope of taking him, and returned home. Not long afterwards, came a solitary hunter loaded with meat, who related that having followed the track of a moose for some distance, he had traced it to the pond before mentioned; but having also discovered the tracks of two men, made at the same time as those of the moose, he concluded they must have killed it. Nevertheless, approaching cautiously to the margin of the pond, he sat down to rest. Presently he saw the moose rise slowly in the centre of the pond, which was not very deep, and wade towards the shore where he was sitting. When he came sufficiently near, he shot him in the water. The Indians consider the moose shyer and more difficult to take than any other animal. He is more vigilant, and his senses more acute, than those of the buffaloe or caribou. He is fleeter than the elk, and more prudent and crafty than the antelope. In the most violent storm, when the wind, and the thunder, and the falling timber, are making the loudest and most incessant roar, if a man, either with his foot or his hand, breaks the smallest dry limb in the forest, the moose will hear it; and though he does not always run, he ceases eating, and rouses his attention to all sounds. If in the course of an hour, or thereabouts, the man neither moves, nor makes the least noise, the animal may begin to feed again, but does not forget what he has heard, and is for many hours more vigilant than before.

The agility and indefatigability of the Indians tracking game is almost incredible. This is how Tanner describes elk hunting:

Cold weather had scarce commenced, and the snow was no more than a foot deep, when we began to be pinched with hunger. We found a herd of elks, and chasing them one day, overtook and killed four of them. When the Indians hunt elk in this manner, after starting the herd they follow them at such a gait as they think they can keep for many hours. The elks being frightened, outstrip them at first by many miles; but the Indians, following at a steady pace along the path, at length come in sight of them; they then make another effort, and are no more seen for an hour or two; but the intervals at which the Indians have them in sight, grow more and more frequent, and longer and longer, until they cease to lose sight of them at all. The elks are now so much fatigued that they can only move in a slow trot, at last they can but walk, by which time the strength of the Indians is nearly exhausted, but they are commonly able to come up and fire into the rear of the herd; but the discharge of a gun quickens the motions of the elks, and it is a very active and determined man that can in this way come near enough to do execution more than once or twice, unless when the snow is pretty deep. The elk, in running, does not lift his feet well from the ground, so that, in deep snow, he is easily taken. There are among the Indians some, but not many, men who can run down an elk on the smooth prairie, when there is neither snow or ice.

The obstacles and privations endured by the Indians in these pursuits exceed anything that can be imagined. Finding themselves constantly on the move, they do not eat for days on end and are sometimes compelled after such an enforced fast, to content themselves with boiled boot-leather. Falling into crevices, buried in snow, navigating raging rivers in light canoes, they are in constant danger of losing either their lives or the means for their preservation. Having wetted the rotted wood which serves them as tinder, the hunters often freeze to death in the snowbound prairie. Tanner himself on several occasions felt the approach of icy death.

Early one morning, about midwinter, I startled an elk. I pursued until night, and had almost overtaken him; but hope and strength failed me at the same time. What clothing I had on me, notwithstanding the extreme coldness of the weather, was drenched with sweat. It was not long after I turned towards home, that I felt it stiffening about me. My leggins were of cloth, and were torn in pieces in running through the brush. I was conscious I was somewhat frozen, before I arrived at the place where I had left our lodge standing in the morning, and it was now midnight. I knew it had been the old woman's intention to move, and I knew where she would go; but I had not been informed she would go on that day. As I followed on their path, I soon ceased to suffer from cold, and felt that sleepy sensation which I knew preceded the last stage of weakness in such as die of cold. I redoubled my efforts, but with an entire consciousness of the danger of my situation, it was with no small difficulty that I could prevent myself from lying down. At length I lost all consciousness for some time, how long I cannot tell; and awaking as from a dream, I found I had been walking round and round in a small circle, not more than twenty or twenty-five yards over. After the return of my senses, I looked about to try to discover my path, as I had missed it; but while I was looking, I discovered a light, at a distance, by which I directed my course. Once more, before I reached the lodge, I lost my senses; but I did not fall down; if I had, I should never have got up again; but I ran round and round in a circle as before. When I at last came into the lodge, I immediately fell down, but I did not lose myself as before. I can remember seeing the thick and sparkling coat of frost on the inside of the pukkwi lodge, and hearing my mother say that she had kept a large fire in expectation of my arrival; and that she had not thought I should have been so long gone in the morning, but that I should have known long before night of her having moved. It was a month, before I was able to go out again, my face, hands, and legs, having been much frozen.

Subject to such exertions and dangers the Indians have as their aim the stocking up of beaver and buffalo skins, etc., in order to sell and barter them to American traders. But they rarely make any profit in their trading transactions, the merchants usually taking advantage of their simplicity and weakness for strong drink. Having bartered part of their goods for rum and whisky, the poor Indians give the rest for a song; prolonged drunkenness is followed by hunger and poverty, and the poor Indians are then forced to resume their meagre and thankless trade. This is how John Tanner describes one such orgy.

After we had completed our trade, the old woman took ten fine beaver skins, and presented them to the trader. In return for this accustomed present, she was in the habit of receiving every year a chief's dress and ornaments, and a ten gallon keg of spirits; but when the trader sent for her to deliver his present, she was too drunk to stand. In this emergency, it was necessary for me to go and receive the articles. I had been drinking something, and was not entirely sober. I put on the chief's coat and ornaments, and taking the keg on my shoulder, carried it home to our lodge, placed it on one end, and knocked out the head with an axe. 'I am not', said I, 'one of those chiefs who draw liquor out of a small hole in a cask, let all those who are thirsty come and drink'; but I took the precaution to hide away a small keg full, and some in a kettle, probably in all three gallons; the old woman then came in with three kettles, and in about five minutes the keg was emptied. This was the second time that I had joined the Indians in drinking, and now I was guilty

of much greater excess than before. I visited my hidden keg frequently, and remained intoxicated two days. I took what I had in
the kettle, and went into the lodge to drink with Waw-zhe-kwaw-
maish-koon, whom I called my brother, he being the son of Net-no-
kwa's sister. He was not yet drunk; but his wife, whose dress was
profusely ornamented with silver, had been for some time drinking,
and was now lying by the fire in a state of absolute insensibility.
Waw-zhe-kwaw-maish-koon and myself took our little kettle and sat
down to drink, and presently an Ojibbeway, of our acquaintance,
staggered in and fell down by the fire near the woman. It was late
at night, but the noise of drunkenness was heard in every part of
the camp, and I and my companion started out to go and drink
wherever we could find any to give us liquor. As, however, we were
not excessively drunk, we were careful to hide away the kettle which
contained our whisky, in the back part of the lodge, covering it, as
we thought, effectually from the view of any that might come in.
After an excursion of some hours, we returned. The woman was
still lying by the fire, insensible as before, but with her dress stripped
of its profusion of silver ornaments; and when we went for our kettle
of rum, it was not to be found. The Ojibbeway, who had been lying
by the fire, had gone out, and some circumstances induced us to
suspect him of the theft, and I soon understood that he had said I
had given him something to drink. I went next morning to his lodge,
and asked him for my little kettle, which he directed his squaw to
bring to me. Having thus fixed the theft upon him, Waw-zhe-kwaw-
koon went and recovered the ornaments of his wife's dress.

We leave the reader to judge for himself what improvement in the
morals of savages is brought about by contact with civilization!

Irresponsibility, incontinence, cunning and cruelty are the chief
vices of American natives. Murder is not accounted a crime among
them, but the relatives and friends of the victim will often avenge his
death. John Tanner brought on himself the hate of one Indian and
was several times attacked by him.

'If you had been a man, you would have killed me long ago,'
Tanner once said to him [not in B.M. version: 'but you haven't even
a woman's heart, nor the boldness of a dog. I will never forgive you
for raising your knife at me and then not having the spirit to stab.'].
Courage is held among the Indians to be the chief human virtue; the
coward is despised among them in company with the lazy or weak

hunter. Sometimes if a murder is perpetrated in a drunken state or unintentionally the relatives solemnly pardon the murderer. Tanner recounts a curious incident.

After about ten days, a young man, of the Ottawwaws, whom Be-nais-sa had given me to cook for me, and assist about me in my sickness, went across the creek, to a camp of the Po-ta-wa-to-mies, who had recently arrived, and were drinking. At midnight, he was brought into the lodge drunk, and one of the men who came with him, said to me, as he pushed him in, 'take care of your young man, he has been doing mischief.' I immediately called Be-nais-sa to kindle a fire, when we saw, by the light of it, the young man standing with his knife in his hand, and that, together with his arm, and great part of his body, covered with blood. The Indians could not make him lie down, but when I told him to, he obeyed immediately, and I forbade them to make any inquiries about what he had done, or take any notice of his bloody knife. In the morning, having slept soundly, he was perfectly unconscious of all that had passed. He said he believed that he had been very drunk, and as he was now hungry, he must hurry and get ready something to eat. He was astonished and con-founded when I told him he had killed a man. He remembered only, that in his drunkenness, he had began to cry for his father, who had been killed on that spot, several years before, by white men. He expressed much concern, and went immediately to see the man he had stabbed, who was not yet dead. We learned from the Po-ta-wato-mies that he had found the young man sleeping, or lying in a state of insensibility from intoxication, and had stabbed him, without any words having been exchanged, and apparently without knowing who he was. The relations of the wounded man said nothing to him, but the interpreter of Gov. Cass reproved him very sharply.

It was evident to all that the young man he had wounded could not recover; indeed, he was now manifestly near his end. When our companion returned, we had made up a considerable present, one giving a blanket, one a piece of strouding, some one thing, and some another. With these he immediately returned, and placing them on the ground beside the wounded man, he said to the relatives, who were standing about, 'My friends, I have, as you see, killed this, your brother; but I knew not what I did. I had no ill will against him, and when, a few days since, he came to our camp, I was glad to see him. But drunkenness made me a fool, and my life is justly

427

forfeited to you. I am poor, and among strangers; but some of those who came from my country with me, would gladly bring me back to my parents; they have, therefore, sent me with this small present. My life is in your hands, and my present is before you, take which ever you choose, my friends will have no cause to complain.' He then sat down beside the wounded man, and stooping his head, hid his eyes with his hands, and waited for them to strike. But the mother of the man he had wounded, an old woman, came a little forward, and said, 'For myself and my children, I can answer, that we wish not to take your life; but I cannot promise to protect you from the resentment of my husband, who is now absent; nevertheless, I will accept your present, and whatever influence I may have with him, I shall not fail to use it in your behalf. I know that it was not from design, or on account of any previous hatred, that you have done this, and why should your mother be made to cry as well as myself?' She took the presents, and the whole affair being reported to Gov. Cass, he was satisfied with the course that had been taken.

On the following day, the wounded man died, and some of our party assisted the young man who had killed him, in making his grave. When this was completed, the governor gave the dead man a valuable present of blankets, cloth, etc., to be buried with him, according to the Indian custom, and these were brought and heaped up on the brink of the grave. But the old woman, instead of having them buried, proposed to the young men to play for them. As the articles were somewhat numerous, various games were used, as shooting at the mark, leaping, wrestling, etc., but the handsomest piece of cloth was reserved as the prize for the swiftest in the foot race, and was won by the young man himself who had killed the other. The old woman immediately afterwards called him to her, and said, 'Young man, he who was my son, was very dear to me, and I fear I shall cry much and often for him. I would be glad if you would consent to be my son in his stead, to love me and take care of me as he did, only I fear my husband.' The young man, who was grateful to her for the anxiety she showed to save his life, immediately consented to this arrangement, and entered heartily upon it.

But not all quarrels and murders end so peaceably. John Tanner described one quarrel in which the fearsome and the comic are strangely intermingled,

I learned that my brother, as I always called Wa-me-gon-a-biew, had but just arrived, when he happened to go into a lodge, where a young man, a son of Ta-bush-shish, was beating an old woman. Wa-me-gon-a-biew held his arms; but presently old Ta-bush-shish coming in, and in his drunkenness, probably misapprehending the nature of my brother's interference, seized him by the hair, and bit his nose off. At this stage of the affair, Be-gwa-is, an old chief who had always been very friendly to us, came in, and seeing that a scuffle was going on, thought it necessary to join in it. Wa-me-gon-a-biew perceiving the loss of his nose, suddenly raised his hands, though still stooping his head, and seizing by the hair the head that was nearest him, bit the nose off. It happened to be that of our friend Be-gwa-is. After his rage had a little abated, he recognized his friend, and exclaimed, 'wah! my cousin!' Be-gwa-is was a kind and good man, and being perfectly aware of the erroneous impression under which Wa-me-gon-a-biew had acted, never for one moment betrayed any thing like anger or resentment towards the man who had thus been the unwilling cause of his mutilation. 'I am an old man,' said he, 'and it is but a short time that they will laugh at me for the loss of my nose.'

For my own part, I felt much irritated against Ta-bush-shish, inasmuch as I doubted whether he had not taken the present opportunity to wreak an old grudge upon Wa-me-gon-a-biew. I went into my brother's lodge, and sat by him; his face, and all his clothes, were covered with blood. For some time he said nothing; and when he spoke, I found that he was perfectly sober. 'To-morrow', said he, 'I will cry with my children, and the next day I will go and see Ta-bush-shish. We must die together, as I am not willing to live, when I must always expect to be ridiculed.' I told him I would join him in any attempt to kill Ta-bush-shish, and held myself in readiness accordingly. But a little sober reflection, and the day's time he had given himself to cry with his children, diverted Wa-me-gon-a-biew from his bloody intention, and like Be-gwa-is, he resolved to bear his loss as well as he could.

Within a few days after this drunken quarrel, Ta-bush-shish was seized with a violent sickness. He had for many days a burning fever, his flesh wasted, and he was apparently near dying, when he sent to Wa-me-gon-a-biew two kettles, and other presents, of considerable value, with a message, 'My friend, I have made you look ugly, and you have made me sick. I have suffered much, and if I

die now my children must suffer much more. I have sent you this
present, that you may let me live.' Wa-me-gon-a-biew instructed
his messenger to say to Ta-bush-shish, 'I have not made you sick.
I cannot restore you to health, and will not accept your presents.'
He lingered for a month or more in a state of such severe illness,
that his hair all fell from his head. After this, he began to amend,
and when he was nearly well, we all removed to the prairie; but were
scattered about in different directions, and at considerable distances
from each other.

After our spring hunting, we began to think of going against the
Sioux, and an inconsiderable party assembled, among those who
lived immediately about me. Wa-me-gon-a-biew and I accompanied
them, and in four days we arrived at the little village where Ta-bush-
shish then lived. Before our arrival here we had been joined by Wa-
ge-tote, with sixty men. After we had rested and eaten at our encampment near Ta-bush-shish's lodge, and were about to start, we saw
him come out naked, but painted and ornamented as for a war,
and having his arms in his hands. He came stalking up to us with a
very angry face, but none of us fully comprehended his design, until
we saw him go up and present the muzzle of his gun to Wa-me-gon-
a-biew's back. 'My friend,' said he, 'we have lived long enough, and
have given trouble and distress enough to each other. I sent to you
my request that you would be satisfied with the sickness and pain
you had made me suffer, but you refused to listen to me; and the
evils you continue to inflict on me, render my life wearisome; let
us therefore die together.' A son of Wa-ge-tote, and another young
man, seeing the intention of Ta-bush-shish, presented the point of
their spears, one to one of his sides, the other to the other; but he
took no notice of them. Wa-me-gon-a-biew was intimidated, and
dared not raise his head. Ta-bush-shish wished to have fought, and
to have given Wa-me-gon-a-biew an equal chance for his life, but
the latter had not courage enough to accept his offer. Henceforth I
esteemed Wa-me-gon-a-biew less even than I had formerly done. He
had less of bravery and generosity in his disposition than is common
among the Indians.

If the frequent quarrels of the Indians are cruel and bloody, their
wars on the other hand, are not at all destructive and are on the whole
confined to tiring marches. The chiefs have no authority and the savages
know nothing of military service. Tiring of the march, one after another

they leave the troop, and return to their dwellings without having seen the enemy. The chiefs persevere for a time; but, left alone without warriors, follow the general example and the war ends without any consequences.

John Tanner recounts with obvious pleasure one of his warlike exploits, which almost approached theft but which nevertheless proved his enterprise and fearlessness. Some Indians stole his horse. He set out intending either to find or replace it. In one of the Indian settlements he was visiting he found no hospitality. This offended him and, noticing a good horse belonging to the chief, he decided out of revenge to take it for himself.

I had a halter under my blanket, and watching a favourable opportunity, I slipped it on the head of this horse, mounted him, and flew rather than fled. I was excited to this action, principally by a feeling of irritation at the unfriendly conduct of the people of the village, as it had not been my intention to take any horse but the one which belonged to me. When the horse and myself were out of breath, I stopped to look back, and the Assinneboin lodges were scarcely visible, like little specks on the distant prairie. I now reflected that I was doing wrong, to steal away the favourite horse of a man who had never absolutely injured me, though he had refused the customary dues of hospitality towards a stranger. I got down and left the horse, but had scarce done so, when I saw thirty or forty men on horseback, who had before been concealed in a depression of the prairie; they were in pursuit, and very near me. I had scarce time to fly to a thicket of low hazel bushes, when they were upon me. They rode about for some time on horseback searching, and this delay gave me some little time to choose a place of concealment. At length they dismounted, and dispersed themselves in various directions, seeking for me. Some came near me, and then turned off to search in other directions. My position was such that I could watch their motions without the risk of exposing myself. One young man stripped himself as for battle, sung his war song, laid aside his gun, and came with only his war club directly towards the spot where I lay. He was within about twenty steps of me, my gun was cocked and aimed at his heart, when he turned and went back. It is not probable he saw me; but the idea of being watched by an unseen enemy armed with a gun, and whose position he could not hope to ascertain until he was almost over him, probably overcame his resolution. They

431

continued their unavailing search until near night, and then returned, taking the chief's horse to their village.

I travelled towards home, rejoicing in my escape, and without stopping for the night, either on that or the succeeding one, and the third night arrived at the Mouse River trading house. The traders told me I was a fool that I had not brought the chief's horse; they had heard much of his qualities, and would, as they said have paid me a high price for him.

In the Assinneboin village, ten miles from this trading house, I had a friend called Be-na (pheasant), and when I had passed through I requested him, while I should be absent, to endeavour to discover my horse, or at least to ascertain, and be able to tell me, where I could find Ba-gis-kun-nung. When I returned thither, after visiting Mouse River trading house, Be-na took me immediately into a lodge where a couple of old women lived, and looking through the crevices, he pointed out to me the lodge of Ba-gis-kun-nung, and those of his four sons. Their horses were feeding about, and among them we distinguished the fine black one they had brought from the Mandans in place of mine.

Wa-me-gon-a-biew had been to the trading house, but returned thence to the village before I arrived, and was now waiting for me at the lodge of some of the sons of a brother of Taw-ga-we-ninne, who were of course his cousins, and were very friendly to him. He had sent messengers to Ba-kis-kun-nung, offering him a good gun, a chief's coat, and all the property he had about him, for a horse to ride home on. But when I heard this, I reproved him severely, and told him that if Ba-gis-kun-nung had accepted his presents, it would only have occasioned additional trouble to me, as I should have been compelled to take not only a horse, but those presents also.

Soon after my arrival in the village, I went to Ba-gis-kun-nung, and said to him, 'I want a horse.' 'I shall not give you one,' he answered. 'I will take one from you.' 'If you do I will shoot you.' With this I returned to the lodge of Be-na, and made my preparations for starting at an early hour in the morning. Be-na gave me a new buffaloe robe to ride home on, and I got from an old woman, a piece of leather thong for a halter, having left mine on the chief's horse. I did not sleep in Be-na's lodge, but with our cousins, and very early in the morning, as I was ready to start, I went to Be-na's lodge, but he was not awake. I had a very good new blanket, which

I spread over him without making any noise; then, together with Wa-me-gon-a-biew, I started. When we came in sight of the lodge of Ba-gis-kun-nung, we saw the eldest of his sons sitting on the outside, and watching the horses. Wa-me-gon-a-biew endeavoured to dissuade me from the design of attempting to take one, since we could not do it without being seen, and had every reason to believe they were prepared to use violent measures to prevent us from succeeding in the attempt. I told him I would not listen to his advice, but consented to go with him two hundred yards on our road, and lay down our baggage; then we were to return together, and take the horse. When we had proceeded as far as I thought necessary, I laid down my load; but Wa-me-gon-a-biew, seeing me resolute in my determination, began to run. At the same time that he started to run from the village, I ran towards it, and the son of Ba-gis-kun-nung, when he saw me coming, began to call out as loud as he could in his own language. I could only distinguish the words 'Wah-kah-towah,' and 'Shoonk-ton-gah' (Ojibbeway – horse). I suppose he said, 'an Ojibbeway is taking a horse.' I answered, 'Kah-ween-gwautch Ojibbeway' (not altogether an Ojibbeway). The village was instantly in motion. In the faces of most of those who gathered round, I could see no settled determination to act in any way; but there was encouragement in the countenances of my friend Be-na and a number of Crees who were about him. There was manifest hostility only in the Ba-gis-kun-nungs. I was so agitated that I could not feel my feet touch the ground, but I think I was not afraid. When I got my halter on the head of the black horse, I stood for a moment hesitating to get on him; as in the act of doing so, I must for the moment, deprive myself of the power of using my arms, and could not avoid exposing myself to an attack behind. But recollecting that any thing like indecision, would at this time have a most unfavourable effect, I gave a jump to mount the horse, but jumped so much higher and farther than was necessary, that I fell sprawling to the ground on the other side of the horse, my gun in one hand, my bow and arrows in the other. I regained my feet as soon as I could, and looked round to watch the motions of my enemies; but presently an universal shout of laughter, in which all joined but the Ba-gis-kun-nungs, gave me some confidence, and I proceeded more deliberately to mount. I knew if they could have ventured to make any open attack on me, it would have been at the time I was lying on the ground, and not in a situation to make any dangerous resistance. The loud and hearty laughter of the Indians convinced me also, that what I was doing was not generally offensive to them.

John Tanner threw off his pursuers and remained the calm possessor of his heroically captured steed.

He sometimes puts himself out as a man untouched by prejudice, yet he is constantly revealing his Indian, superstitious nature. Tanner believes in dreams and in the prophecies of old women; he always finds they come true. When he is hungry he dreams of fat bears and tasty fish and in a little while he indeed manages to shoot a wild goat or catch a sturgeon. In difficult circumstances he always dreams of some young man, who gives him good advice or encourages him. Tanner poetically describes one vision which he had in the desert and on the shores of the Little Saskawjewun.

There is, on the bank of that river, a place which looks like one the Indians would always choose to encamp at. In a bend of the river is a beautiful landing place, behind it a little plain, a thick wood, and a small hill rising abruptly in the rear. But with that spot is connected a story of fratricide, a crime so uncommon, that the spot where it happened is held in detestation, and regarded with terror. No Indian will land his canoe, much less encamp at 'THE PLACE OF THE TWO DEAD MEN'. They relate, that many years ago, the Indians were encamped here, when a quarrel arose between two brothers, having she-she-gwi for totem. One drew his knife and slew the other; but those of the band who were present, looked upon the crime as so horrid, that without hesitation or delay, they killed the murderer, and buried them together.

As I approached this spot, I thought much of the story of the two brothers, who bore the same totem with myself, and were, as I supposed, related to my Indian mother. I had heard it said, that if any man encamped near their graves, as some had done soon after they were buried, they would be seen to come out of the ground, and either react the quarrel and the murder, or in some other manner so annoy and disturb their visitors, that they could not sleep. Curiosity was in part my motive, and I wished to be able to tell the Indians, that I had not only stopped, but slept quietly at a place which they shunned with so much fear and caution. The sun was going down as I arrived; and I pushed my little canoe in to the shore, kindled a fire, and after eating my supper, lay down and slept. Very soon, I saw the two dead men come and sit down by my fire, opposite me. Their eyes were intently fixed upon me, but they neither smiled, nor said any thing. I got up and sat opposite them by the fire, and in this situation I awoke. The night was dark and gusty, but I saw no men, or heard any other sounds, that that of the wind in the trees. It is likely I fell asleep again, for I soon saw the same two men standing below the bank of the river, their heads just rising to the level of the ground I had made my fire on, and looking at me as before. After a few minutes, they rose one after the other, and sat down opposite me; but now they were laughing, and pushing at me with sticks, and using various methods of annoyance. I endeavoured to speak to them, but my voice failed me; I tried to fly, but my feet refused to do their office. Throughout the whole night I was in a state of agitation and alarm. Among other things which they said to me, one of them told me to look at the top of the little hill which stood near. I did so, and saw a horse fettered, and standing looking at me. 'There, my brother,' said the jobi, 'is a horse which I give you to ride on your journey to-morrow; and as you pass here on your way home, you can call and leave the horse, and spend another night with us.'

At last came the morning, and I was in no small degree pleased to find, that with the darkness of the night these terrifying visions vanished. But my long residence among the Indians, and the frequent instances in which I had known the intimations of dreams verified, occasioned me to think seriously of the horse the jobi had given me. Accordingly I went to the top of the hill, where I discovered tracks and other signs, and following a little distance, found a horse, which I knew belonged to the trader I was going to see. As several miles travel might be saved by crossing from this point on the Little Saskawjewun to the Assinneboin, I left the canoe, and having caught the horse, and put my load upon him, led him towards the trading house, where I arrived next day. In all subsequent journeys through this country, I carefully shunned 'the place of the two dead'; and the account I gave of what I had seen and suffered there, confirmed the superstitious terrors of the Indians.

John Tanner was twice married. The description of his first love has in his narrative a certain wild charm. His beauty had a name filled with poetical significance but one which would hardly fit into elegies: she was called Mis-kwa-bun-o-kwa, which in Indian means the red sky of the morning.

Soon after I returned, I was standing by our lodge one evening, when I saw a good looking young woman walking about and smoking. She noticed me from time to time, and at last came up and asked me to smoke with her. I answered, that I never smoked. 'You do not wish to touch my pipe; for that reason you will not smoke with me.' I took her pipe and smoked a little, though I had not been in the habit of smoking before. She remained some time, and talked with me, and I began to be pleased with her. After this we saw each other often, and I became gradually attached to her.

I mention this because it was to this woman that I was afterwards married, and because the commencement of our acquaintance was not after the usual manner of the Indians. Among them, it most commonly happens, even when a young man marries a woman of his own band, he has previously had no personal acquaintance with her. They have seen each other in the village; he has perhaps looked at her in passing, but it is probable they have never spoken together. The match is agreed on by the old people, and when their intention is made known to the young couple, they commonly find, in themselves, no objection to the arrangement, as they know, should it prove disagreeable mutually, or to either party, it can at any time be broken off.

My conversations with Mis-kwa-bun-o-kwa (the red sky of the morning), for such was the name of the woman who offered me her pipe, was soon noised about the village. Hearing it, and inferring, probably, that like other young men of my age, I was thinking of taking a wife, old O-zhusk-koo-koon came one day to our lodge, leading by the hand another of his numerous grand-daughters. 'This', said he, to Net-no-kwa, 'is the handsomest and the best of all my descendants; I come to offer her to your son.' So saying, he left her in the lodge and went away. This young woman was one Net-no-kwa had always treated with unusual kindness, and she was considered one of the most desirable in the band. The old woman was now somewhat embarrassed; but at length she found an opportunity to say to me, 'My son, this girl which O-shush-koo-koon offers you, is handsome, and she is good; but you must not marry her, for she has that about her which will, in less than a year, bring her to her grave. It is necessary that you should have a woman who is strong and free of any disease. Let us, therefore, make this young woman a handsome present, for she deserves well at our hands, and send her back to her father.' She accordingly gave her goods to a considerable

436

amount, and she went home. Less than a year afterwards, according to the old woman's prediction, she died.

In the mean time, Mis-kwa-bun-o-kwa and myself were becoming more and more intimate. It is probable Net-no-kwa did not disapprove of the course I was now about to take, as, though I said nothing to her on the subject, she could not have been ignorant of what I was doing. That she was not I found, when after spending, for the first time, a considerable part of the night with my mistress, I crept into the lodge at a late hour, and went to sleep. A smart rapping on my naked feet waked me at the first appearance of dawn, on the following morning. 'Up,' said the old woman, who stood by me, with a stick in her hand, 'up, young man, you who are about to take for yourself a wife, up, and start after game. It will raise you more in the estimation of the woman you would marry, to see you bring home a load of meat early in the morning, than to see you dressed ever so gaily, standing about the village after the hunters are all gone out.' I could make her no answer, but, putting on my moccasins, took my gun and went out. Returning before noon, with as heavy a load of fat moose meat as I could carry, I threw it down before Net-no-kwa, and with a harsh tone of voice said to her, 'here, old woman, is what you called for in the morning.' She was much pleased, and commended me for my exertion. I now became satisfied that she was not displeased on account of my affair with Mis-kwa-bun-o-kwa, and it gave me no small pleasure to think that my conduct met her approbation. There are many of the Indians who throw away and neglect their old people; but though Net-no-kwa was now decrepid and infirm, I felt the strongest regard for her, and continued to do so while she lived.

I now redoubled my diligence in hunting, and commonly came home with meat in the early part of the day, at least before night. I then dressed myself as handsomely as I could, and walked about the village, sometimes blowing the Po-bo-gwun, or flute. For some time Mis-kwa-bun-o-kwa pretended she was not willing to marry me, and it was not, perhaps, until she perceived some abatement of ardour on my part, that she laid this affected coyness entirely aside. For my own part, I found that my anxiety to take a wife home to my lodge, was rapidly becoming less and less. I made several efforts to break off the intercourse, and visit her no more; but a lingering inclination was too strong for me. When she perceived my growing indifference, she sometimes reproached me, and sometimes sought to move me by tears and entreaties; but I said nothing to the old woman about bringing her home, and became daily more and more unwilling to acknowledge her publicly as my wife.

About this time, I had occasion to go to the trading-house on Red River, and I started in company with a half breed, belonging to that establishment, who was mounted on a fleet horse. The distance we had to travel has since been called, by the English settlers, seventy miles. We rode and went on foot by turns, and the one who was on foot kept hold of the horse's tail, and ran. We passed over the whole distance in one day. In returning, I was by myself, and without a horse, and I made an effort, intending, if possible, to accomplish the journey in one day; but darkness, and excessive fatigue, compelled me to stop when I was within about ten miles of home.

When I arrived at our lodge, on the following day, I saw Mis-kwa-bun-o-kwa sitting in my place. As I stopped at the door of the lodge, and hesitated to enter, she hung down her head; but Net-no-kwa greeted me in a tone somewhat harsher than was common for her to use to me. 'Will you turn back from the door of the lodge, and put this young woman to shame, who is in all respects better than you are. This affair has been of your seeking, and not of mine or hers. You have followed her about the village heretofore; now you would turn from her, and make her appear like one who has attempted to thrust herself in your way.' I was, in part, conscious of the justness of Net-no-kwa's reproaches, and in part prompted by inclination; I went in and sat down by the side of Mis-kwa-bun-o-kwa, and thus we became man and wife.

John Tanner left his wife and took another by whom he had three children. In spite of the habit of a lifetime and his passionate love of hunting, the life of toil, of dangers and of ecstasies, which can neither be understood nor explained, the American who had grown wild still thought of returning to the bosom of the family from which he had so long ago been rudely torn. At last he decided to fulfil his lifelong intention and set off to the shores of Big Miami, where his former family had lived.

Arriving at one of the settlements there, he met an old Indian and recognized him to be the young savage who had once kidnapped him. They embraced. Tanner heard from him of the death of the old man, whom he had got to know in such fearsome circumstances. The Indian told him of the details of his capture, of which Tanner had only a dim notion. In answer to his question whether it was true that his father and all his family had fallen victims to the Indians as Manito-o-geezhik had once assured his young prisoner, the Indian replied that the old man had lied, and told him the following.

Manito-o-geezhik, the year after I was taken, at the same season of the year, returned to the same field where he had found me; that, as on the preceding year, he had watched my father and his people planting corn, from morning till noon; that then they all went into the house, except my brother, who was then nineteen years of age; he remained ploughing with a span of horses, having the lines about his neck, when the Indians rushed upon him; the horses started to run; my brother was entangled in the lines, and thrown down, when the Indians caught him. The horses they killed with their bows and arrows, and took my brother away into the woods. They crossed the Ohio before night, and had proceeded a good distance in their way up the Miami. At night they left my brother securely bound, as they thought, to a tree. His hands and arms were tied behind him, and there were cords around his breast and neck; but having bitten off some of the cords, he was able to get a pen-knife that was in his pocket, with which he cut himself loose, and immediately ran towards the Ohio, at which he arrived, and which he crossed by swimming, and reached his father's house about sunrise in the morning. The Indians were roused by the noise he made, and pursued him into the woods; but as the night was very dark, they were not able to overtake him. His hat had been left at the camp, and this they brought, to make me believe they had killed him.

Tanner's father had died about ten years previously, leaving his estate to his eldest son and not forgetting in his will him of whose lot he knew nothing.

At last John Tanner again saw his family who all welcomed him with great joy. His brother gleefully embraced him, cut his hair and tried in every possible way to persuade him to stay at home. The shy American who had become a savage, on his part, invited him to come with him to the Lake of the Woods, extolling to him, through an interpreter, the wild life and the freedom of the prairies. His brothers were married; his sister, Lucy, had ten children. Finally his family's pleas had their effect on him; he decided to leave the Indians and, with his children, to settle in the society to which he belonged by right of birth.

But Tanner's adventures did not finish there. Fate decreed new trials

439

for him. Returning to his savage friends and announcing his decision to them, he aroused strong opposition. The Indians did not agree to hand his children over to him. His wife refused to follow him to a life among people who were strange and hateful to her. The American authorities were forced to intervene in John Tanner's family affairs. By threatening and cajoling they managed to persuade the Indians to allow him to go home with all his family. For the last time he set off with his relatives to the Red River to hunt buffalo, parting for ever from the wild life which held so much attraction for him. On returning he began to make preparations for his journey.

The Indians parted with him on friendly terms. His son did not want to go with him and remained a free savage. Tanner set off with his two daughters and their mother, who did not want to part from them. Let us hear how Tanner describes his last journey.

I did not return to the Lake of the Woods by the way of the Be-gwi-o-nus-ko Se-be, but chose another route, in which I had to travel a part of the way by water, a part by land. In ascending the Bad River, there is a short road by what is called Sturgeon River, and a portage to come again into the principal river. Not far from the mouth of Sturgeon River was, at this time, an encampment, or village, of six or seven lodges. A young man belonging to that band, and whose name was Ome-zhuh-gwut-oons, had not long previous to this been whipped by Mr Cote, for some real or alleged misconduct about the trading-house, and feeling dissatisfied, he, when he heard I had passed up Sturgeon River, started after me in his little canoe, and soon overtook me. After he had joined me, he showed, I thought, an unusual disposition to talk to me, and claimed to be, in some manner, related to me. He encamped with us that night, and the next morning we started on together. This day, when we stopped, and were resting on shore, I noticed that he took an opportunity to meet one of my daughters in the bushes; but she returned immediately, somewhat agitated. Her mother, also, was several times, in the course of the day, in close conversation with her; but the young woman continued sad, and was several times crying.

At night, after we stopped to encamp, the young man very soon left us; but as he remained at a little distance, apparently much busied about something, I went and found him with his medicines all opened about him, and he was inserting a thong of deer's sinew, about five inches in length, into a bullet. I said to him, 'My brother,' (for this was the name he had himself given me) 'if you want powder or balls, or flints, I have plenty, and will give you as much as you wish.' He said that he also had plenty, and I left him and returned to camp. It was some time before he came in; when at last he made his appearance, he was dressed and ornamented as a warrior for battle. He continued during the first part of the night, to watch me much too closely, and my suspicions, which had been already excited, were now more and more confirmed. But he continued to be as talkative, and to seem as friendly as ever. He asked me for my knife, as he said, to cut some tobacco, and instead of returning it to me, slipped it into his own bolt; but I thought, perhaps he would return it to me in the morning.

I laid myself down at about the usual time, as I would not appear to suspect his intentions. I had not put up my tent, having only the little shelter afforded by a piece of painted cloth that had been given me at Red River. When I lay down, I chose such a position as would enable me to watch the young man's motions. I could see, as he sat opposite the fire, that his eyes were open and watchful, and that he felt not the least inclination to sleep. When at length a thunder shower commenced, he appeared more anxious and restless than before. When the rain began to fall, I asked him to come and place himself near me, so as to enjoy the benefit of my shelter, and he did so. The shower was very heavy, and entirely extinguished our fire; but soon after it had ceased, the mosquitoes becoming very troublesome, Ome-zhuh-gwut-oons rekindled it, and breaking off a branch of a bush, he sat and drove them away from me. I was conscious that I ought not to sleep; but drowsiness was gaining some hold on me, when another thunder shower, more violent than the first, arose. In the interval of the showers, I lay as one sleeping, but almost without moving or opening my eyes. I watched the motions of the young man; at one time, when an unusually loud clap of thunder alarmed him, he would throw a little tobacco into the fire, as an offering; at another, when he seemed to suppose me asleep, I saw him watching me like a cat about to spring on its prey; but I did not suffer myself to sleep.

He breakfasted with us as usual, then started by himself, before I was quite ready. My daughter, whom he had met in the bushes, was now apparently more alarmed than before, and absolutely refused to enter the canoe; but her mother was very anxious to quiet her agitation, and apparently very desirous to prevent my paying any particular attention to her. At last, she was induced to get into the canoe, and we went on. The young man kept along before us, and at a little distance, until about ten o'clock, when, at turning a point in a difficult and rapid part of the river, and gaining a view of a considerable reach above, I was surprised that I could see neither him nor his canoe. At this place the river is about eighty yards wide, and there is, about ten yards from the point before mentioned, a small island of naked rock. I had taken off my coat, and I was, with great effort, pushing up my canoe against the powerful current, which compelled me to keep very near the shore, when the discharge of a gun at my side arrested my progress. I heard a bullet whistle past my head, and felt my side touched, at the same instant that the paddle fell from my right hand, and the hand itself dropped powerless to my side. The bushes were obscured by the smoke of the gun, but at a second look I saw Ome-zhuh-gwut-oons escaping. At that time the screams of my children drew my attention to the canoe, and I found every part of it was becoming covered with blood. I endeavoured, with my left hand, to push the canoe in shore, that I might pursue after him; but the current being too powerful for me, took my canoe on the other side, and threw it against the small rocky island before mentioned. I now got out, pulled the canoe a little on to the rock, with my left hand, and then made an attempt to load my gun. Before I could finish loading I fainted, and fell on the rock. When I came to myself again, I was alone on the island, and the canoe, with my daughters, was just going out of sight in the river below. Soon after it disappeared, I fainted a second time; but consciousness at length returned.

As I believed that the man who had shot me was still watching from his concealment, I examined my wounds, and finding my situation desperate, my right arm being much shattered, and the ball having entered my body, in the direction to reach my lungs, and not having passed out, I called to him, requesting him to come, and by putting an immediate end to my life, to release me from the protracted suffering I had in prospect. 'You have killed me,' said I; 'but though the hurt you have given me must be mortal, I fear it may be some time before I shall die. Come, therefore, if you are a man, and shoot me again.' Many times I called to him, but he returned me no answer. My body was now almost naked, as I had on, when shot, beside my pantaloons, only a very old and ragged shirt, and much of this had been torn off in the course of the morning.

442

I lay exposed to the sun, and the black and green headed flies, on a naked rock, the greater part of a day in July or August, and saw no prospect before me, but that of a lingering death; but as the sun went down, my hope and strength began to revive, and plunging into the river, I swam across to the other side. When I reached the shore, I could stand on my feet, and I raised the sas-sah-kwi, or war whoop, as a cry of exultation and defiance to my enemy. But the additional loss of blood, occasioned by the exertion in swimming the river, caused me another fainting fit, from which, when I recovered, I concealed myself near the bank, to watch for him. Presently I saw Ome-zhuh-gwut-oons come from his hiding place, put his canoe into the water, embark, and begin to descend the river. He came very near my hiding place, and I felt tempted to make a spring, and endeavour to seize and strangle him in the water; but fearing that my strength might not be sufficient, I let him pass without discovering myself.

I was now tormented with the most excessive thirst, and as the bank was steep and rocky, I could not, with my wounded arm, lie down to drink. I was therefore compelled to go into the water, and let my body down into it, until I brought my mouth to a level with the surface, and thus I was able to drink. By this time, the evening growing somewhat cooler, my strength was, in part, restored; but the blood seemed to flow more freely. I now applied myself to dressing the wound in my arms. I endeavoured, though the flesh was already much swollen, to replace the fragments of the bone; to accomplish which, I tore in strips the remainder of my shirt, and with my teeth and my left hand I contrived to tie these around my arm, at first loosely, but by degrees tighter and tighter, until I thought it had assumed, as nearly as I could give it, the proper form. I then tied on small sticks, which I broke from the branches of trees, to serve as splints, and then suspended my hand in a string, which passed around my neck. After this was completed, I took some of the bark of a choke cherry bush, which I observed there, and chewing it fine applied it to the wounds, hoping thus to check the flowing of the blood. The bushes about me, and for all the distance between me and the river, were covered with blood. As night came on, I chose a place where there was plenty of moss, to lie down on, with the trunk of a fallen tree for my pillow. I was careful to select a place near the river, that I might have a chance of seeing any thing that might pass; also, to be near the water in case my thirst should again become urgent. I knew that one trader's canoe was expected, about this time, to pass this place, on the way towards Red River, and it was this canoe from which I expected relief and assistance. There were no Indians nearer than the village from which Ome-zhuh-gwut-oons had followed me, and he, with my wife and daughters, were the only persons that I had any reason to suppose were within many miles of me.

I laid myself down, and prayed to the Great Spirit, that he would see and pity my condition, and send help to me, now in the time of my distress. As I continued praying, the mosquitoes, which had settled on my naked body in vast numbers, and were, by their stings, adding greatly to the torment I suffered, began to rise, and after hovering at a little distance above and around me, disappeared entirely. I did not attribute this, which was so great a relief, to the immediate interposition of a Superior Power, in answer to my prayer, as the evening was, at that time, becoming something cool, and I knew it was entirely the effect of change of temperature. Nevertheless, I was conscious, as I have ever been in times of distress and of danger, that the Master of my life, though invisible, was yet near, and was looking upon me. I slept easily and quietly, but not without interruption. Every time I awoke, I remembered to have seen, in my dream, a canoe with white men, in the river before me.

It was late in the night, probably after midnight, when I heard female voices which I supposed to be those of my daughters, not more than two hundred yards from me, but partly across the river. I believed that Omo-zhuh-gwut-oons had discovered their hiding place, and was, perhaps, offering them some violence, as the cry was that of distress; but so great was my weakness, that the attempt to afford them any relief seemed wholly beyond my power. I learned afterwards, that my children, as soon as I fainted and fell on the rock, supposing me dead, had been influenced by their mother to turn the canoe down the river, and exert themselves to make their escape. They had not proceeded far, when the woman steered the canoe into a low point of bushes, and threw out my coat, and some other articles. They then ran on a considerable distance, and concealed themselves; but here it occurred to the woman, that she might have done better to have kept the property belonging to me, and accordingly returned to get it. It was when they came to see these things lying on the shore, that the children burst out crying, and it was at this time that I heard them.

444

Before ten o'clock next morning, I heard human voices on the river above me, and from the situation I had chosen, I could see a canoe coming, like that I had seen in my dream, loaded with white men. They landed at a little distance above me, and began to make preparations for breakfast. I knew that this was the canoe belonging to Mr Stewart, of the Hudson's Bay Company, who, together with Mr Grant, was expected about this time; and being conscious that my appearance would make a painful impression upon them, I determined to wait until they had breakfasted, before I showed myself to them. After they had eaten, and put their canoe again in the water, I waded out a little distance into the river, to attract their attention. As soon as they saw me, the Frenchmen ceased paddling, and they all gazed at me, as if in doubt and amazement. As the current of the river was carrying them rapidly past me, and my repeated calls, in the Indian language, seemed to produce no effect, I called Mr Stewart by name, and spoke a few words of English, which I could command, requesting them to come and take me. In a moment their paddles were in the water, and they brought the canoe so near where I stood, that I was able to get into it.

No one in the canoe recognized me, though Mr Stewart and Mr Grant were both well known to me. I had not been able to wash the blood off my body, and it is probable that the suffering I had undergone, had much changed my appearance. They were very eager and rapid in their inquiries, and soon ascertained who I was, and also became acquainted with the principal facts I have related. They made a bed for me in the canoe, and at my urgent request went to search for my children, in the direction where I had heard them crying, and where I told them I feared we should find they had been murdered; but we sought here, and in other places, to no purpose.

Having ascertained who it was that had wounded me, these two traders agreed to take me immediately to the village of Ome-zhuh-gwut-oons, and they were determined, in case of discovering and taking him, to aid me in taking my revenge, by putting him immediately to death. They therefore concealed me in the canoe, and on landing near the lodges, an old man came down to the shore, and asked them, what was the news in the country they came from? 'All is well there,' answered Mr Stewart; 'we have no other news.' 'This is the manner', said the old man, 'in which white people always treat us. I know very well something has happened in the country

445

you have come from, but you will not tell us of it. Ome-zhuh-gwut-oons, one of our young men, has been up the river two or three days, and he tells us that the Long Knife, called Shaw-shaw-wa-ne-ba-se (the falcon), who passed here a few days since, with his wife and children, has murdered them all; but I am fearful that he himself has been doing something wrong, for he is watchful and restless, and has just fled from this place before you arrived.' Mr Stewart and Mr Grant, notwithstanding this representation, sought for him in all the lodges, and when convinced that he had indeed gone, said to the old man, 'It is very true that mischief has been done in the country we come from; but the man whom Ome-zhuh-gwut-oons attempted to kill, is in our canoe with us; we do not yet know whether he will live or die.' They then showed me to the Indians, who had gathered on the shore.

We now took a little time to refresh ourselves, and to examine my wounds. Finding that the ball had entered my body, immediately under the broken part of my arm, and gone forward and lodged against the breast bone, I tried to persuade Mr Grant to cut it out; but neither he nor Mr Stewart being willing to make the attempt, I was compelled to do it myself, as well as I could, with my left hand. A lancet, which Mr Grant lent me, was broken immediately, as was a pen knife, the flesh of that part of the body being very hard and tough. They next brought me a large white handled razor, and with this I succeeded in extracting the ball. It was very much flattened, and the thong of deer's sinew, as well as the medicines, Ome-zhuh-gwut-oons had inserted in it, were left in my body. Notwithstanding this, when I found that it had not passed under my ribs, I began to hope that I should finally recover, though I had reason to suppose, that the wound being poisoned, it would be long in healing.

After this was done, and the wound in my breast taken care of, we went on to Ak-kee-ko-bow-we-tig (the Kettle Falls), to the village of the chief Waw-wish-e-gah-bo, the brother of Ome-zhuh-gwut-oons. Here Mr Stewart used the same precaution of hiding me in the canoe, and then giving tobacco, which he called every man in the village, by name, to receive; but when there appeared no prospect of finding him, they made me again stand up in the canoe, and one of them told the chief that it was his own brother who had attempted to kill me. The chief hung his head, and to their inquiries about Ome-zhuh-gwut-oons he would make no answer. We, however, ascertained from other Indians, that my daughters and their mother had stopped here a moment, in their way towards Rainy Lake.

When we arrived at the North West Company's house, at Rainy Lake, we found that my daughters and their mother had been detained by the traders, on account of suspicions arising from their manifest agitation and terror, and from the knowledge that I had passed up with them but a few days before. Now, when I first came in sight of the fort, the old woman fled to the woods, taking the two girls with her. But the Company's people sent out and brought them in again. Mr Stewart and Mr Grant now left it to me to say what punishment should be inflicted on this woman, who, as we all very well knew, had been guilty of aiding in an attempt to kill me. They said they considered her equally criminal with Ome-zhuh-gwut-oons, and thought her deserving of death, or any other punishment I might wish to see inflicted. But I told them I wished she might be sent immediately, and without any provisions, away from the fort, and never allowed to return to it. As she was the mother of my children, I did not wish to see her hung, or beaten to death by the labourers, as they proposed; but as the sight of her had become hateful to me, I wished she might be removed, and they accordingly dismissed her without any punishment.

Now John Tanner lives among his educated compatriots. He is engaged in a lawsuit with his stepmother about a few Negroes left to him in a legacy. He sold his intriguing Narrative at a great profit; and probably will soon become a member of the *Temperance Society*. In short, there is hope that Tanner will in time become a real Yankee, on which we heartily congratulate him.

[1] Published in the third issue of the *Sovremennik*, signed 'The Reviewer'. Pushkin wrote to Chaadaev that this article was by him.

John Tanner's narrative, as dictated by the author to Edwin James, was first published in New York in 1830. Pushkin had in his library the French edition which came out in Paris in two volumes in 1835. The opening few pages of Pushkin's article were based on De Tocqueville's *De la démocratie en Amérique*, which Pushkin also had in his library (4th edition, Paris 1836).

In the first issue of the *Sovremennik*, A. I. Turgenev mentions in his Paris diary that he spent an evening reading Tocqueville's book on democracy in America and continues:

Talleyrand calls it the wisest and most remarkable book of our time; and he knows America, and is himself an Aristocrat, as is Tocqueville, all of whose connections are with the Faubourg of St Germain. You will agree with the author's conclusion: 'On remarque aujourd'hui moins de différence entre les Européens et leurs descendants du Nouveau-Monde, malgré l'Océan qui les divise, qu'entre certaines villes du treizième siècle qui n'étaient séparées que par une rivière. Si ce mouvement d'assimilation rapproche des peuples étrangers il s'oppose à plus forte raison à ce que les rejetons du même peuple deviennent étrangers les uns aux autres', etc. The author concludes with the drawing together of two contrasted peoples: the Russians and the Anglo-Americans: 'Leur point de départ est différent, leurs voies sont diverses; néanmoins chacun d'eux semble appelé par un dessein secret de la Providence à tenir un jour dans ses mains les destinées de la moitié du monde.'

Pushkin quoted from John Tanner throughout in Russian, but he did not specify which edition he was using. The version used here is taken from a typed copy of the original, see Bibliography page 531.

[2] Chateaubriand's *Atala* (1801) and a large number of novels by Fenimore Cooper, who was called by his contemporaries 'the American Scott'. Pushkin had the French edition of Cooper's works (Paris, 1830-5) in his library.

[3] From Washington Irving's preface to the French edition of John Tanner's narrative.

[4] Jean-Jacques Rousseau and other believers in the 'Noble Savage'. Edwin James, in introducing Tanner's narrative, criticized this school of thought.

304. *On the Duties of Men* by Silvio Pellico[1]

A new translation of the book: *Dei Doveri degli Uomini*, the work of the famous Silvio Pellico, will shortly be published.[2]

There is a book every word of which has been interpreted, explained, preached on, in all the corners of the earth, applied to every possible human situation and world event, from which one cannot repeat a single expression which would not be known by heart by all men, which would not already be a *popular saying*, which contains nothing still unknown to us; but it is called the Gospels – and such is its perennially renewed delight that if we, being satiated by the world or cast down with melancholy, chance to open it, we have no power to combat its sweet fascination and we steep our spirits in its divine eloquence.

And it is not fortuitous that preparing to say a few words on a book by a humble martyr, we dared to mention the Holy Gospels: only a chosen few (even among the early fathers of the church) have approached in their works – in humility of spirit, in sweet eloquence, and in childlike simplicity of heart – the teaching of the Divine master.

Subsequently the unknown author of *The Imitation of Christ*, Fénelon, and Silvio Pellico belong in highest measure to this select company, whom the angel of God greeted with the name of 'Men of goodwill'.

Silvio Pellico spent ten years in various prisons and on regaining his freedom published his notebooks.[3] There was general astonishment: instead of the expected complaints filled with bitterness appeared the most moving meditations, filled with serenity, love and goodwill.

Let us admit our own uneasy malice. Reading these notes in which there does not fall one word of impatience, reproach, or hatred from the unfortunate prisoner's pen, we involuntarily assumed there to be a hidden intention beneath this unruffled benevolence towards everyone and towards all things; this moderation struck us as artificial. And filled with admiration for the author, we reproached the man for insincerity. The book, *Dei Doveri*, put us to shame, and solved for us the secret of a beautiful soul, the secret of a man and a Christian.[4]

Having named the book of which we were reminded by Silvio Pellico's work, we neither can nor should say more in its praise.

In one of our reviews, in an article by a writer of real talent, a critic who has earned the trust of educated readers,[5] we read with astonishment the following lines about Silvio Pellico's book:

'If *The Duties* had not been published in the wake of *My Prisons*, it would have struck us as a platitudinous, dry, arbitrarily dogmatic form of instruction, which we would have heard through without attention.'

Is it possible that Silvio Pellico stands in need of apology? Can it be that his book, permeated as it is with heartfelt warmth, inexpressible beauty, harmonious eloquence, could to anyone at any time seem *dry* and frigidly dogmatic? Can it be that if it had been written in the quiet of a Thebaid or in a philosopher's library, and not in the sad solitude of a prison, it would have been unworthy of the attention of a man possessed of a heart? We cannot believe that that was indeed what the author of *A History of Poetry*[6] meant.

This is not new, this has been said before – that is one of criticism's most usual charges. But everything has already been said, all ideas have been expressed and repeated in the course of centuries: and what follows from this? That the spirit of man will never create anything new? No, let us not malign it; reason is inexhaustible in its *synthesis* of ideas as language is inexhaustible in its *combination* of words. All words are to be found in the dictionary; but books, appearing hourly, are not repetitions of the dictionary. A single thought is never new in itself; but *thoughts* can be infinitely varied.

449

As the best refutation of Shevyrev's opinion, I quote his own words:

Read it [Pellico's book] with the same faith as that in which it was written and you will step out from a dark world of doubts and depression and discord between head and heart into a world of light, of order and agreement. The problems of life and of happiness will seem simple. You will seem to gather yourself together from among the scattered fragments of passions, habits and whims; and you will become aware of two emotions in your soul, which are unfortunately very rare in this age: a sense of contentment and of hope.

[1] First published unsigned in the third issue of the *Sovremennik* (1836) in the 'New books' section.

[2] Pushkin had French translations of Pellico's *Dei Doveri degli Uomini* and *Le Mie Prigioni* in his library.

[3] Silvio Pellico was arrested in 1820 on a charge of carbonarism and sentenced to fifteen years' imprisonment. He was released in 1830 and published *Le Mie Prigioni* in 1832 and *Dei Doveri degli Uomini* in 1834.

[4] Vyazemsky writing many years later of Pushkin's response to Pellico's book commented on his unfailingly warm response to anything that was imbued with beauty and sincerity of spirit, even if it did not coincide with his own way of thinking.

[5] S. P. Shevyrev.

[6] Volume I published in 1835; it remained incomplete.

305. From 'Letter to the Editor', answering an article by Gogol published in the *Sovremennik*, First Issue (1836)[1]

. . . Speaking of the indifference shown by journalists to important literary events you cite the death of Walter Scott. But Walter Scott's death is not a literary event; and of Walter Scott and his novels enough has been written among us, both relevantly and irrelevantly.

You say that of late the public has shown a marked indifference to poetry and a taste for novels, tales, and such like. But is not poetry always the delight of a chosen few, whereas stories and novels are read by all and sundry everywhere? And where have you spotted this indifference? One can sooner reproach our poets for inactivity than the public for a growing coolness. Derzhavin has come out in a third edition; and there is a rumour that a fourth is in preparation. The title-page of Krylov's fables (published last year) is marked 30,000. The new poets, Kukolnik and Benediktov, were welcomed with delight. Koltsov gained the favourable attention of the general public. . . . Wherein lies the public's indifference to poetry?

A.B.

[1] Gogol's unsigned article on trends in periodical literature in 1834-5 aroused opposition and was taken as expressing the views of the editor of the *Sovremennik* and as forming a programme for the review. In order to disengage himself Pushkin published the above letter under the initials A.B., supposedly writing from Tver. He appended a footnote saying how pleased he was to publish A.B.'s letter and stressing that the fact that the article on the trends in periodical literature appeared in his review did not, of course, mean that he agreed with all the views expressed in it nor that it represented the *Sovremennik's* programme.

306. *The Lay of Igor's Campaign*[1]

The Lay of Igor's Campaign was found in the library of Count A. I. Musin-Pushkin[2] and was published in 1800. The manuscript was burnt in 1812. Experts who had seen it said that its script was semi-cursive, of the fifteenth century. Its first editors appended a translation, which was on the whole satisfactory, although several places remained obscure or altogether unintelligible. Many people subsequently tried to elucidate them. But, although in researches of this kind the last become the first (since the mistakes and discoveries of their predecessors clear the way for those that follow after), the first translation, in which very learned men collaborated, still remains the best.[3] Further investigators vied with each other in obscuring the difficult passages with arbitrary corrections and with guesses having no foundation. For the most important explanations we are obliged to Karamzin who, in his history, solved in passing some of the difficult problems.[4]

Some writers expressed doubts as to the genuineness of this ancient monument of our poetry and aroused heated protests.[5] A happy imitation can deceive the ignorant but it cannot escape the scrutiny of a real expert. Walpole was not deceived when Chatterton sent him the poems of the old monk Rowley, Johnson immediately detected Macpherson. But neither Karamzin, nor Yermolaev, nor A. Kh. Vostokov, nor Khodakovsky, ever doubted the genuineness of *The Lay of Igor's Campaign*. The great sceptic Schlözer, before he had seen *The Lay of Igor's Campaign*, doubted its authenticity, but having read it he admitted it to be a genuinely ancient work and did not even consider it necessary to bring forward proofs of this, so obvious did the truth seem to him! There is no other proof except the words of the poet himself. The

451

authenticity of the lay itself is proved by its spirit of antiquity, which cannot be imitated. Which of our eighteenth-century writers had enough talent for that? Karamzin? But Karamzin was not a poet. Derzhavin? But Derzhavin did not know the Russian language, let alone that of *The Lay of Igor's Campaign*. The others all combined had not as much poetry in them as is contained in Yaroslavna's lament, and in the description of the battle and flight. To whom could it have occurred to take as a subject for a poem an obscure expedition by an unknown prince? Who could have obscured with such skill certain places in his poem by using words since discovered in ancient chronicles or traced in other Slavonic dialects, where they yet remain in all the freshness of common usage? That would be to assume a knowledge of *all* Slavonic dialects. Supposing someone were to possess this knowledge, would such a jumble be natural? Homer, if he existed, distorted by rhapsodists.

Lomonosov did not live in the twelfth century. Lomonosov's odes are written in Russian, with an admixture of certain expressions taken from the Bible, which lay at his elbow. But you will not find in Lomonosov either Polish, Serbian, Illyrian, Bulgarian, Bohemian, Moldavian, or any other Slavonic dialects.

[1] This unfinished article was written in 1836 but not published till 1855. Pushkin knew *The Lay* by heart and was planning to publish an annotated edition. He spoke about it a great deal in the last years of his life and he left among his papers two heavily annotated modern Russian versions of the poem – Zhukovsky's and A. F. Weltman's (1833). A. I. Turgenev wrote to his brother (3 December 1836) that Pushkin had read him some of his detailed and witty comments on the poem, all of which were based on his knowledge of Slavonic dialects.

[2] The manuscript had come into Count Musin-Pushkin's hands in a collection he acquired in 1795 and shortly afterwards a copy of it was made for Catherine II. It was first published in 1800.

[3] A. F. Malinovsky and N. N. Bantysh-Kamensky (the 1800 edition).

[4] Karamzin's *History*, Volume III, chapter vii.

[5] I. I. Davydov, O. I. Senkovsky, and M. T. Kachenovsky. On a visit to Moscow University in September 1832 Pushkin met Kachenovsky and hotly disputed with him the question of *The Lay's* authenticity.

307. On Milton and on Chateaubriand's translation of *Paradise Lost*[1]

For a long time the French disregarded their neighbour's literatures. [Being exclusively faithful to the models of the seventeenth century, they did not recognize any foreign writer as being equal to those who had immortalized their shores. The translators who tried to acquaint them with great foreign authors never dared to be faithful to their originals; but carefully transformed them and in their translations tried to make them appear as absolute Frenchmen.[2]] Convinced of their own superiority over all the rest of mankind, they appreciated famous foreign writers in proportion to the extent they deviated from French customs and rules, as established by French critics.

In the translations published during the last century one cannot read a single preface without coming on the inevitable sentence: we thought to please the public and at the same time render a service to our author by excluding from his book the places which might have offended the cultured taste of a French reader. It is odd to think of who was thus excusing himself before whom! That is what comes from an ignorant passion for nationalism! . . . At long last the critics came to their senses. They began to suspect that M. Letourneur might have been mistaken in his judgement of Shakespeare, and was not being entirely reasonable when he trimmed *Hamlet*, *Romeo* and *Lear* to his own pattern. People began to demand a greater degree of accuracy from the translators, and less delicacy and zeal vis-à-vis the public, they began to want to see Dante, Shakespeare and Cervantes in their true likeness, in their own national dress and with their natural defects. Even the view, confirmed by time and generally accepted, that the translator must try to render the spirit and not the letter (of his original) found its opponents and was expertly refuted.

Now (an unheard-of precedent) the leading writer in France translates Milton *word for word* and announces that line-by-line translation would have been the consummation of his art, had he been able to achieve it! Such humility in a French writer, the prime master of his trade, must have greatly astonished the champions of *improved translations* and will probably have an important influence on literature.

Of all great foreign authors Milton was the most unfortunate as far as France was concerned. Leaving aside the pathetic prose translations[3] in which he was innocently slandered or the verse translation by Abbé Delille,[4] which so disastrously improved on his shortcomings and so mercilessly embellished him, how was he himself portrayed in the tragedies and novels of the latest Romantic school? What was done to him by Alfred de Vigny, unceremoniously placed by French critics on a level with W. Scott? How was he presented by Victor Hugo, another favourite of the Parisian public? Maybe readers have forgotten both *Cinq-Mars* and *Cromwell* and are therefore unable to judge of the

453

absurdity of Victor Hugo's pictures. Let us bring both before the judgement of any educated and right-thinking person.

Let us begin with the tragedy – one of the most absurd productions of a man who is in fact endowed with talent. [The play *Cromwell* was the first Romantic experiment on the Parisian stage. Victor Hugo deemed it necessary to destroy all the rules and all the traditions of French drama as were then reigning behind the scenes in the classical theatre, the Unities of Place and Time, the lofty uniformity of diction, the metre of Racine and Boileau – all were thrown over by him. However it is only fair to mention that V. Hugo did not interfere with the Unity of Action; in his tragedy there is no action, and even less of interest.[5]]

We will not try to follow in the halting steps of the dull and monstrous play; we only want to show our readers how it presents Milton, who, still unknown as a poet, is famed throughout Europe as a political writer for his embittered and overbearing eloquence.

Cromwell, in his palace, is talking to Lord Rochester, disguised as a Methodist [*sic*], and four jesters. Milton is also present with a guide (a superfluous character as it was much later that Milton lost his sight). The Protector says to Rochester:

CROMWELL *montrant ses bouffons à lord Rochester.*
Puisque nous voilà seuls, je veux rire un instant.
Docteur, ce sont mes fous, et je vous les présente.
Lord Rochester et les bouffons s'inclinent.
Quand nous sommes en joie, ils sont d'humeur plaisante.
Nous faisons tous des vers, – il n'est pas même ici
Il montre Milton.
Jusqu'à mon vieux Milton qui ne s'en mêle aussi.

MILTON *avec dépit.*
Vieux Milton, dites-vous! Mylord, ne vous déplaise,
J'ai bien neuf ans de moins que vous-même.

CROMWELL.
                                        A votre aise!

MILTON.
Oui. Vous êtes, Mylord, de quatre-vingt-dix-neuf.
Moi, de seize cent huit.

CROMWELL.
                    Le souvenir est neuf!

454

MILTON *avec vivacité.*

Vous pourriez me traiter de façon plus civile!
Je suis fils d'un notaire, alderman de sa ville.

CROMWELL

Là, ne vous fâchez pas. Je sais aussi fort bien
Que vous êtes, Milton, grand théologien,
Et même, mais le ciel compte ce qu'il nous donne,
Bon poëte, – au-dessous de Vithers et de Donne!

MILTON *comme se parlant à lui-même.*

Au-dessous! Que ce mot est dur! – Mais attendons.
On verra si le ciel m'a refusé ses dons!
L'avenir est mon juge. – Il comprendra mon Ève,
Dans la nuit de l'enfer tombant comme un doux rêve,
Adam coupable et bon, et l'Archange indompté,
Fier de régner aussi sur une éternité,
Grand dans son désespoir, profond dans sa démence,
Sortant du lac de feu que bat son aile immense! –
Car un génie ardent travaille dans mon sein.
Je médite en silence un étrange dessein!
J'habite en ma pensée, et Milton s'y console. –
Oui, je veux à mon tour créer par ma parole,
Du Créateur suprême émule audacieux,
Un monde, entre l'enfer, et la terre, et les cieux!

LORD ROCHESTER *à part.*

Que diable dit-il là?

HANNIBAL SESTHEAD *aux bouffons.*

Risible enthousiaste!

CROMWELL.

Il regarde Milton en haussant les épaules.
C'est un fort bon écrit que votre *Iconoclaste.*
Quant à votre grand diable, autre Léviathan, –
Il rit.
Très-mauvais!

MILTON *indigné, entre ses dents.*

C'est Cromwell qui rit de mon Satan!

455

LORD ROCHESTER *s'approchant de Milton.*

Monsieur Milton!

MILTON *sans l'entendre, et tourné vers Cromwell.*

Il parle ainsi par jalousie!

LORD ROCHESTER *à Milton qui l'écoute d'un air distrait.*

Vous ne comprenez pas, d'honneur, la poésie.
Vous avez de l'esprit, il vous manque du goût.
Écoutez: – les Français sont nos maîtres en tout.
Étudiez Racan! Lisez ses *Bergeries.*
Qu'Aminte avec Tircis erre dans vos prairies,
Qu'elle y mène un mouton au bout d'un ruban bleu.
Mais Ève! mais Adam! l'enfer! un lac de feu!
C'est hideux! Satan nud et ses ailes roussies! . . . –
Passe au moins s'il cachait ses formes adoucies
Sous quelque habit galant, et s'il portait encor
Sur une ample perruque un casque à pointes d'or,
Une jaquette aurore, un manteau de Florence,
Ainsi qu'il me souvient, dans l'Opéra de France,
Dont naguère à Paris la cour nous régala,
Avoir vu le soleil, en habit de gala!

MILTON *étonné.*

Qu'est-ce que ce jargon de faconde mondaine
Dans la bouche d'un saint?

LORD ROCHESTER *à part et se mordant les lèvres.*

Encore une fredaine!
Il a mal écouté par bonheur; mais toujours
Au grave Obededom Rochester fait des tours.

haut à Milton.

Monsieur, je plaisantais! . . .

MILTON.

Sotte est la raillerie!

Further Milton affirms that to govern a kingdom is a trifle, whereas to write Latin verses is quite another matter. A little later on Milton throws himself at Cromwell's feet, begging him not to aspire to the throne, to which the Protector replies: Mr Milton, secretary of state, you are a poet, and in a burst of lyrical enthusiasm you forgot who I am, etc.

In a scene having neither historical truth nor dramatic probability, in a meaningless parody of the ceremonial followed at the coronation of the Kings of England, the chief parts are played by Milton and one of the court jesters. Milton advocates a republic, the jester takes up the gage of a royalist knight. . . .

It is as such a pathetic madman and insignificant windbag that Milton is portrayed by a man who probably did not realize himself what he was doing when he insulted that mighty spirit! In the course of the whole tragedy Milton hears nothing except taunts and curses; but it is true that he himself does not once utter a sensible word. He is an old buffoon whom everybody despises and to whom nobody pays the slightest attention.

No, Mr Hugo! That is not what John Milton was like, the friend and champion of Cromwell, the austere fanatic, the stern author of the *Eikonoklastes* and of *Defensio populi*. He who addressed to Cromwell his famous and prophetic sonnet, 'Cromwell, our chief of men', would not have spoken to him in this language. He, who 'though fall'n on evil days . . . and evil tongues', in poverty, persecuted and blind, retained an inflexibility of soul and dictated *Paradise Lost*, could not have been made a laughing-stock by the dissolute Rochester and by the court jesters.

If Mr Hugo, himself being a poet (albeit a second-rate one), understood Milton so badly, anyone can guess what happened to Cromwell under his pen, for whom he had no sympathy whatsoever! But that does not concern us here. Let us pass from the uneven and crude works of Victor Hugo and his ugly tragedies to the prim and mannered Count de Vigny and to his polished novel.

Alfred de Vigny in his novel *Cinq-Mars* also brings Milton before us in the following circumstances.

A circle of courtiers and scholars gather round Cardinal Richelieu's fair mistress, Marion de Lorme. Scudéry explains her allegorical map of love[6] to them. The guests are delighted at the fort of *Beauty* standing on the river *Pride*, and at the village of *Billet-Doux*, the harbour *Indifference*, etc., etc. Everybody except Molière, Corneille and Descartes, who are also present, showers exaggerated praise on Madeleine de Scudéry. Suddenly the hostess introduces a young English traveller by the name of John Milton to the company, and makes him read extracts of *Paradise Lost* to her guests. Right; but how will the French who do not know English understand Milton's lines? It's quite simple: the parts which he is going to read have been translated into French and copied out on to separate pieces of paper and copies are handed round to the guests. Milton will recite, and the guests will follow. But why should he bother if the lines are already translated? Is it that Milton is a great reciter or is the sound of English so extremely interesting? And what business has Count de Vigny to perpetrate all these clumsy absurdities? He needed Milton to read *Paradise Lost* to Parisian society so that French wits (naturally with the exception of Molière, Corneille and Descartes) could laugh at him, failing to understand the great poet's spirit, from which would follow the subsequent effective scene:

So saying, she took them and distributed them among her erudite visitors. The company seated themselves, and were silent. It took some time to persuade the young foreigner to speak or to quit the recess of the window, where he seemed to have come to a very good understanding with Corneille. He at last advanced to an arm chair placed near the table; he seemed of feeble health, and fell into, rather than seated himself in, the chair. He rested his elbow on the table, and with his hand covered his large and beautiful eyes, which were half closed, and reddened with night watches or tears. He repeated his fragments from memory; his doubting auditors looked at him haughtily, or, at least, patronizingly; others carelessly glanced over the translation of his verses.

His voice, at first suppressed, grew clearer by the very flow of his harmonious recital; the breath of poetic inspiration soon elevated him to himself, and his look, raised to heaven, became sublime as that of the young evangelist, conceived by Raffaello, for the light still shone on it. He narrated in his verses the first disobedience of man, and invoked the Holy Spirit who prefers before all other temples a pure and simple heart, who knows all, and who was present at the birth of time.

This opening was received with a profound silence, and a slight murmur arose, after the enunciation of the last idea. He heard not, he saw only through a cloud; he was in the world of his own creation; he continued.

He spoke of the infernal spirit, bound in avenging fire by adamantine chains, lying vanquished nine times the space that measures night and day to mortal men; of the darkness visible of the eternal prisons, and the burning ocean where the fallen angels float. Then, his voice, now powerful, began the address of the fallen angel. 'Art thou', he said, 'he who in the happy realms of light, clothed with transcendent brightness, didst outshine myriads? From what height

458

fallen? What though the field be lost, all is not lost! Unconquerable will and study of revenge, immortal hate and courage never to submit or yield – what is else not to be overcome.'

Here a lacquey, in a loud voice, announced MM. de Montrésor and d'Entraigues. They saluted, exchanged a few words, deranged the chairs, and then settled down. The auditors availed themselves of the interruption, to institute a dozen private conversations; scarcely anything was heard but expressions of censure, and imputations of bad taste. Even some men of merit, dulled by a particular habit of thinking, cried out that they did not understand it; that it was above their comprehension (not thinking how truly they spoke); and from this feigned humility gained themselves a compliment, and for the poet an impertinent remark – a double advantage. Some voices even pronounced the word, profanation.

The poet, interrupted, put his head between his hands, and his elbows on the table, that he might not hear the noise, either of praise or censure. Three men only approached him, an officer, Poquelin, and Corneille; the latter whispered to Milton:

'I would advise you to change the picture; your hearers are not on a level with this.'

[Translation by W. Hazlitt.]

Milton in spite of the fact that the parts appointed for reading have been translated and that he has to read them in order, racks his memory for something which would make a greater impression on his audience, not worrying whether they will understand or not. But by some miracle (unexplained by Mr de Vigny) he is understood by everyone. Desbarreaux finds him cloying; Scudéry – dull and frigid. Marion de Lorme is very touched by the description of Adam in his original state. Molière, Corneille and Descartes shower him with compliments, etc. etc.

Are we much mistaken in thinking that Milton when passing through Paris would not display himself as an itinerant buffoon, and entertain the company in the house of a lewd woman by the reading of poetry written in a language understood by none of those present, posing and showing off, one minute *closing his eyes*, the next *casting them up to the ceiling*? His conversations with De Thou, Corneille and Descartes would not have been banal and mannered verbiage; but he would have played in society a role that became him, that of an honourable and well-brought-up young man.

After the surprising inventions of Victor Hugo and Count de Vigny, would you like to see a picture, lightly sketched in by another painter? Read in *Woodstock* of the meeting of one of the characters with Milton in Cromwell's study.[7] . . .

A French novelist would naturally not have been satisfied with such a slight and natural portrayal. Milton, occupied with affairs of state, would inevitably suddenly have lost himself in poetical reveries and would have scribbled a few lines of *Paradise Lost* on the margins of some report; Cromwell would have noticed this, would have scolded his secretary, called him a rhymester and dissembler, all of which would produce an *effect* such as poor W. Scott never envisaged.

The translation published by Chateaubriand to a certain extent smoothes over some of the sins of the young French writers, who had so innocently yet so cruelly insulted that mighty shade. We have already mentioned that Chateaubriand translated Milton almost word for word, as close a rendering as French syntax allowed: an arduous and thankless task, passed over unnoticed by the majority of readers and one which can be appreciated only by one or two specialists! But is the new translation a success? Chateaubriand found in Nisard an implacable critic.[8] Nisard, in an article filled with pointed wit, vehemently attacked both Chateaubriand's chosen method of translating, and the translation itself. There is no doubt that in attempting to render Milton *word for word* Chateaubriand could not in his version preserve accurately both the meaning and the idiomatic turns of phrase. A literal translation can never be true to its original. Every language has its own locutions, its accepted rhetorical figures, its assimilated expressions which cannot be translated into another language simply by using the corresponding words. Take a basic phrase: Comment vous portez-vous? How do you do? Try and translate these word for word into Russian.

If even the Russian language, which is so flexible and rich in idioms and locutions, so derivative and adaptable in its relations with foreign languages, is not suitable for line-by-line or word-for-word translations, how can French, so cautious in its habits, so jealous of its traditions, so unfriendly even to those languages which belong to the same family, endure such a test? This is especially true in a tussle with Milton's language – a poet at once refined and naïve, sombre, obscure, expressive, independent and audacious to the point of absurdity.

The translation of *Paradise Lost* is a commercial venture. Chateaubriand, a leading contemporary French writer, the teacher of all the writers of the present generation, having been at one time a prime minister, and several times an ambassador, translated Milton in his old age *for a crust of bread*. Whatever the standard of the work thus undertaken, the work itself and its purpose does credit to the famous old man. He who, overcoming a few scruples, could have peacefully benefited from the generosity of the new government, enjoyed power, honours and wealth, preferred an honourable poverty. Resigning from the upper house, where his eloquent voice had long sounded, Chateaubriand comes to a bookseller with a manuscript for sale, but with an incorruptible conscience. What in the face of that can criticism say? Will it confound the honourable labours by the sternness of its judgement, and disparage his wares like some miserly buyer? But Chateaubriand stands in no need of indulgence: he has appended to his translation two volumes as brilliant as all his former works, and critics can be as stern as they like about its shortcomings, its indisputable beauties, the pages worthy of the great writer's best period, will save this book from the neglect of readers, in spite of all its shortcomings.

English critics were stern in their censure of the *Essai sur la littérature anglaise*. They found it to be too superficial, too incomplete; taking the title on trust they expected to find in Chateaubriand both learned criticism and an absolute knowledge of subjects with which they themselves are closely familiar, but that is not at all what one should have looked for in this brilliant survey. In the field of learned criticism Chateaubriand lacks firmness, he is timid and quite unlike his usual self; he speaks of writers he never read; in his judgements he skims over the surface of his subjects, treating of them at second hand, and somehow scrambles through the dull task of the bibliographer; but inspired pages constantly flow from his pen, he is for ever forgetting his critical researches and freely develops his ideas on the great epochs of history, comparing them with those of which he himself was a witness. There is much sincerity, much heartfelt eloquence, much simplicity (at times childish, but always winning) in these fragments, having no connection with the history of English literature, but forming the most valuable part of the *Essai*.[9]

Chateaubriand's book opens with a rapid and wide-ranging survey of the Middle Ages, which serves as an introduction to the *History of English Literature*:

Social order, separated from political order, is composed of religion, intelligence, and material industry. In every nation, even at the

461

moment of the direst catastrophes and of the greatest events, there will always be a priest who prays, a poet who sings, an author who writes, a philosopher who meditates, a painter, a sculptor, an architect, who paints, chisels, builds, and a workman who labours. These men, surrounded by revolutions, seem to lead a life apart: if you look at them only, you see a real, a genuine, an immutable world, the base of the human edifice, but which appears fictitious and foreign to the society of convention, the political society. The priest, indeed, in his hymns, the poet, the philosopher, the artist, in their compositions, the artisan in his work, mark occasionally the time in which they live, and the recoil of the events which wrung from them in more abundance their sweat, their complaints, and the productions of their genius.

The middle ages present a grotesque picture, which seems to be the production of a strong but wild imagination. In antiquity, each nation springs, if we may so express ourselves, from its own stock; a primitive spirit, insinuating itself everywhere and showing its influence in everything, renders manners and institutions homogeneous. The society of the middle ages was composed of the wrecks of a thousand other societies: Roman civilization, nay paganism itself, had left their vestiges in it; from the christian religion it received its faith and its solemnities; the Gothic, Burgundian, Anglo-Saxon, Danish, Norman barbarians retained the customs and character peculiar to their respective races. All kinds of property were intermingled; all kinds of laws were blended, the allodial, the fief, the mortmain, the code, the digest, the salic, the gombrette, the visigoth law, the common law; all the forms of liberty and servitude jostled one another; the monarchial liberty of the king, the aristocratic liberty of the noble, the individual liberty of the priest, the collective liberty of parishes, the privileged liberty of towns, of the magistracy, of the guilds and artizans and traders, the representative liberty of the nation, Roman slavery, barbarous villenage, the servitude of the *aubaine*. Hence those incoherent spectacles, those usages, which appear contradictory to each other, and which are held together solely by the bond of religion. You would almost take them to be different nations, wholly unconnected with one another, but who have merely agreed to live under one common master and around the same altar.

¹ Pushkin wrote this article for the *Sovremennik*. It was unfinished at his death and published posthumously in the sixth issue in 1837, edited by Zhukovsky. See pages xiii and 486 for comment on this article.

Chateaubriand's translation of *Paradise Lost* came out in 1836, Victor Hugo's play *Cromwell* in 1828 and Alfred de Vigny's novel *Cinq-Mars* in 1826.

² The bracketed sentences are crossed through in manuscript.

³ By N. F. Dupré de Saint-Maur, revised by C. J. Chéron de Boismorand (1792).

⁴ Published 1805.

⁵ The bracketed sentences are crossed through in manuscript.

⁶ The map of love (La Carte du Tendre) appears in *Clélie* (1656) by Madeleine de Scudéry, the sister of the dramatist Georges de Scudéry.

⁷ Pushkin left room in his manuscript for a quotation from Scott's *Woodstock*, but no such incident is described. In fact Milton is only mentioned by name in the novel.

⁸ J. M. N. D. Nisard waged a critical war against the French Romantic school.

⁹ After Pushkin's death, Vyazemsky sent Chateaubriand a translation of this article. Chateaubriand in reply wrote that he had read it with lively interest. France, he said, mourned with Russia the death of this illustrious poet, and Pushkin's approval of his work had filled him with pride.

308. Pushkin's footnote to 'The Nose' by Gogol[1]

For a long time N. V. Gogol refused to consent to the publication of this jest; but we found it to be so rich in the unexpected, in fantasy, in gaiety, and in originality, that we persuaded him to allow us to share with the public the pleasure which his manuscript afforded us.

The Editor

[1] Published in the third issue of the *Sovremennik*. Shevyrev had refused to publish Gogol's tale in the *Moskovsky Nablyudatel*.

309. From 'Table-talk'[1]

Man is, by nature, more prone to criticize than to praise (says Machiavelli,[2] that great expert on human nature).

A stupid criticism does not draw as much attention to itself as stupid praise; a fool sees no merit in Shakespeare and this is attributed to his discriminating taste, peculiarity, etc. The same fool is in raptures over a novel by Ducray-Duminil or Polevoy's History and he is despised, although anyone who thinks will see that his foolishness is more clearly manifested in the first instance.

Othello is not jealous by nature – on the contrary, he is trusting. Voltaire understood this and developing [this fact] in his imitation of Shakespeare gave Orosmane the following line:

Je ne suis point jaloux . . . si je l'étois jamais . . .³

I only saw Derzhavin once in my life but I will never forget the occasion.⁴ It was in 1815 at the public examination at the Lycée. When we heard that Derzhavin would be there we were all very excited. Delvig went out on the stairs to wait for him, in order to kiss his hand – the hand which had written 'The Waterfall'. Derzhavin arrived. He came into the porch and Delvig heard him ask the porter, 'Where's the convenience, m'boy?' Delvig, very disappointed by this prosaic question, gave up his intention and returned to the hall. Delvig told me this story with extraordinary candour and gaiety.

Derzhavin was very old. He was in full-dress uniform and wore velveteen boots. Our examination exhausted him. He sat propping his head up on his hand. His face was expressionless; his eyes dim; his lip drooping – the portrait in which he is shown in a night-cap and dressing-gown is a very good likeness. He dozed till the examination in Russian literature began. At this point he revived, his eyes began to sparkle; he was completely transformed. Naturally, his poems were read, his poems discussed, his poems repeatedly praised. He listened with extraordinary animation. Finally I was called. I read my 'Recollections in Tsarskoe Selo', standing two paces away from Derzhavin. I am powerless to describe my emotions when I came to the verse in which I mention Derzhavin's name, my youthful voice rang out and my heart beat in an ecstasy of delight . . . I do not remember how I finished my reading, I do not remember where I ran off to. Derzhavin was in raptures; he called for me, wishing to embrace me. . . . They looked for me but I was not to be found. . . .

Characters created by Shakespeare are not, as Molière's, types exemplifying some passion or some vice, but living beings, compacted of many passions and many vices; and circumstances unfold to the spectators their varied, many-sided personalities. Molière's Miser is miserly – and that is all; Shakespeare's Shylock is miserly, resourceful, vindictive, a fond father, witty. Molière's Hypocrite trails after his patron's wife – hypocritically; takes on the care of an estate – hypo-

critically; asks for a glass of water – hypocritically. Shakespeare's hypocrite pronounces judgement with proud severity but with equity; he
justifies his cruelty with the thoughtful arguments of a statesman; he
seduces innocence with irresistibly beguiling sophisms, and not by
some ludicrous combination of piety and flirtation. Angelo is a hypocrite – because his public actions contradict his secret passions! And
what depth there is in this character!

But probably Shakespeare's many-sided genius did not express itself
anywhere with such variety as in Falstaff, whose vices strung together
form a diverting and grotesque chain, reminiscent of some ancient
Bacchanalia. Analysing Falstaff's character we see that its predominant
trait is sensuality; probably from his youth, coarse and cheap flirtation
had been his chief preoccupation; but now he is in his fifties, he has
grown fat and senile, gluttony and wine have noticeably stolen a march
on Venus. Secondly he is a coward but, spending days in the company
of young rakes and being constantly subject to their jibes and pranks,
he hides his cowardice under a cover of evasive and mocking bravado.
He is boastful both by habit and by design.

Falstaff is not at all stupid; on the contrary. He also has some of the
habits of a man who has once seen good society. He observes no rules.
He is as weak as an old woman. He needs strong Spanish wine (sack),
a fat dinner, and money for his mistresses; and to get these he is ready
to do anything, provided there is not obvious danger involved.

In my youth chance brought me into close contact with a man in
whom, it seemed, nature wishing to imitate Shakespeare, repeated his
magnificent creation. X[5] was a second Falstaff: sensual, cowardly,
boastful, clever, amusing, immoral, tearful, and fat. One circumstance
gave him an individual charm. He was married. Shakespeare had no
time to marry off his bachelor. Falstaff died among his mistresses, not
having had time to be either a cuckolded husband or the father of a
family; how many scenes lost to Shakespeare's brush!

Here is a glimpse of the home life of my esteemed friend. Once in his
father's absence, his four-year-old son, the image of his father, a little
Falstaff III, was repeating under his breath, 'How bwave daddy is!
How the Empewor loves daddy!' The boy was overheard and asked,
'Who told you this, Volodia?' 'Daddy,' replied Volodia.

Goethe had a great influence on Byron. Faust troubled Childe
Harold's imagination. Byron tried twice[6] to combat with the Giant of
Romantic poetry – and was lamed, like Jacob.

Many wax indignant at the low tone of the literary criticism found in the reviews, at its neglect of the decencies, and so on: their displeasure is unjust. A learned man, who is busy with his own work and is immersed in his thoughts, has not the time to appear in society in order to acquire its superficial culture, in the manner of worldly idlers. We must be indulgent towards his unsophisticated bluntness, which is his bond for conscientiousness and love of truth. Pedantry has its good points. It is only ludicrous and disgusting when pettiness and ignorance speak in its language.

[1] Published after Pushkin's death in the eighth issue of the *Sovremennik* (1837), with some censorship cuts.
[2] In *Discorsi sopra la prima Deca di Tito Livio*.
[3] *La Zayre*, Act I, scene v.
[4] See page 9, plate 2 and *Evgeny Onegin*, VIII, i-ii.
[5] A. L. Davydov, see page 26.
[6] In *Manfred* and in *The Deformed Transformed*.

LETTERS

310. To P. V. Nashchokin   *10-19 January 1836*
                                                 St Petersburg

... My financial affairs are bad – I have been forced to embark on a review. I don't yet know how it will go. Smirdin is already offering me 15,000 to drop my venture and collaborate with him again on his *Biblioteka* [*dlya Chteniya*]. But although that would be profitable, I cannot agree to it. Senkovsky is such a rogue, and Smirdin such a fool, that it's impossible to get involved with them. ...

311. To George Borrow[1]   *End of October 1835/March 1836*
                                                 St Petersburg

Alexander Pushkin received Mr Borrow's book[2] with most profound gratitude and he heartily regrets that he did not have the honour of making his acquaintance.

[1] George Borrow in the course of his travels through Europe acted as an agent for the British and Foreign Bible Society.
[2] *Targum*. Or, Metrical Translations from thirty languages and dialects (St Petersburg, 1835). This included translations of two poems by Pushkin: 'The Black Shawl' (1820) and 'Song' from *The Gipsies*.

312. To N. M. Yazykov   *14 April 1836*
                                              Golubovo

. . . You will receive my *Sovremennik*;[1] I hope that it will earn your approval. One of the critical articles is mine: on Konissky.[2] You must collaborate with me. Your poetry is living water; ours is stagnant. We have poured ours over the *Sovremennik*; sprinkle it with your sparkling drops. Your 'Epistle to Davydov' is charming! . . .

[1] The first issue.
[2] An unsigned article on the collected works of G. Konissky, Belorussian Archbishop.

313. To N. N. Pushkin   *6 May 1836*
                                              Moscow

. . . Send for Gogol and read him the following: I saw the actor Shchepkin,[1] who begs him for Christ's sake to come to Moscow to read aloud *The Government Inspector*. The actors cannot agree without him. He says the comedy will be caricatured and made filthy (for which Moscow always showed an inclination). I would give him the same advice. *The Government Inspector* must not flop in Moscow where they like Gogol better than in Petersburg.[2]

. . . Cleaning up Russian literature means cleaning out privies and depending on the police. Before you know where you are. . . . The devil take them! My blood is turning to bile. . . .

[1] M. S. Shchepkin later became famous in the role of Mayor in Gogol's *The Government Inspector*.
[2] First performed in St Petersburg on 19 April 1836 in the Alexandrinsky theatre in the presence of the Emperor. First performed in Moscow on 25 May 1836 in the Maly theatre.

314. To N. N. Pushkin   *14 and 16 May 1836*
                                              Moscow

. . . When I listen to the conversation of the men of letters here I am astonished how they can be so decent in print and so stupid in conversation. Confess: does that apply to me? I am honestly afraid that it does. Baratynsky, however, is very charming, but there is some sort of coldness between us. . . .

315. To N. N. Pushkin   *18 May 1836*
Moscow

. . . Bryullov[1] has just left me. He goes to Petersburg gritting his teeth;
he is afraid of the climate and of the lack of freedom. I try to comfort
and encourage him; but at the same time my own heart sinks to my
boots when I remember that I am a journalist. Being still a man of
honour, I have already been reprimanded by the police and have been
told *vous avez trompé* and such like. What will happen to me now?
Mordvinov[2] will look on me as on Faddey Bulgarin and Nikolai
Polevoy – as a spy. What devil prompted me to be born in Russia
having a soul and talent! Very amusing, I must say!

[1] K. P. Bryullov, a painter.
[2] A. N. Mordvinov, head of the Secret Police (the Third Department).

316. To P. V. Nashchokin   *27 May 1836*
St Petersburg

. . . The second number of the *Sovremennik* is very good, and you will
thank me for it. I am beginning to love it myself and will probably
apply myself to it energetically. . . .

317. To N. A. Durov[1]   *Around 10 June 1836*
St Petersburg

Here is the opening part of your Memoirs.[2] All the copies are already
printed and are now being bound. I don't know whether it will be
possible to stop the publication. My sincere and unbiased opinion is
that you should leave it as it is. The 'Memoirs of an Amazon' is too
far-fetched and mannered; it reminds one of German novels. 'The
Memoirs of N. A. Durov' is simple, sincere and dignified. Be bold –
step on to the field of literature as courageously as you did on the field
which brought you fame. Half-measures are useless.

[1] Nadezhda Andreyevna Durov had fought in the Napoleonic wars disguised as a cavalry officer. Pushkin published extracts from her memoirs
in the second issue of the *Sovremennik*.
Pushkin had written to Nadezhda Durov's brother on 17-27 March: 'I
have just read the Memoirs as copied out: delightful! Lively, original, and
a splendid style. A certain success.'

468

318. To I. I. Dmitriev   *14 June 1836*
St Petersburg

. . . Your indulgent comment on the *Sovremennik* encourages me in a field which is new to me. I will try in the future to justify your good opinion. . . . May God grant you health and long life! Outlive our young men of letters, as your verses will outlive our young literature. . . .

319. Draft letter to D. V. Davydov   *August 1836*
St Petersburg

You thought that your article on partisan warfare[1] would pass through the censorship whole and unscathed. You were wrong: it didn't escape the red ink. It honestly seems as if the military censors blot out in order to prove that they read.

It's hard, I must say. There's trouble enough with one censor; imagine what it's like depending on four.[2] I don't know wherein lies the offence of Russian writers, who are not only docile but are even themselves in agreement with the spirit of the government. But I do know that they have never been so restricted as now, not even in the last five years of the late Emperor's rule when the whole of literature remained in manuscript thanks to Krasovsky and Birukov. . . .

[1] Published in the third issue of the *Sovremennik*.
[2] Over and above the normal censorship (and, as far as Pushkin's own work was concerned, the Emperor's private check), the *Sovremennik* had to be passed by the ecclesiastical authorities, the Ministry of Foreign Affairs, and – in this case – the military censorship.

320. To N. I. Grech   *13 October 1836*
St Petersburg

I am sincerely grateful for your kind word about my 'Commander-in-Chief'.[1] Barclay's stoical figure is one of the most remarkable in our history. I don't know whether he can be fully justified as far as his military strategy is concerned, but his character will always remain worthy of admiration and respect.

[1] Pushkin's poem on Barclay de Tolly, published in the third issue of the *Sovremennik*.

321. To P. Y. Chaadaev¹   *19 October 1836*
                                           St Petersburg

Je vous remercie de la brochure² que vous m'avez envoyée. J'ai été
charmé de la relire, quoique très étonné de la voir traduite et imprimée.
Je suis content de la traduction: elle a conservé de l'énergie et du
laisser-aller de l'original. Quant aux idées, vous savez que je suis loin
d'être tout-à-fait de votre avis. Il n'y a pas de doute que le Schisme
nous a séparés du reste de l'Europe et que nous n'avons pas participé à
aucun des grands événements qui l'ont remuée: mais nous avons eu
notre mission à nous. C'est la Russie, c'est son immense étendue qui
a absorbé la conquête Mongole. Les tartares n'ont pas osé franchir
nos frontières occidentales, et nous laisser à dos, ils se sont retirés vers
leurs déserts, et la civilisation chrétienne à été sauvée.³ Pour cette fin,
nous avons dû avoir une existence tout-à-fait à part, qui en nous
laissant chrétiens, nous laissait cependant tout-à-fait étrangers au
monde chrétien, en sorte que notre martyre ne donnait aucune distraction à l'énergique développement de l'Europe catholique. Vous
dites que la source où nous sommes allés puiser le christianisme était
impure, que Byzance était méprisable et méprisée, etc. – hé, mon ami!
Jésus-Christ lui-même n'était-il pas né juif et Jérusalem n'était-elle pas
la fable des nations? L'évangile en est-il moins admirable? Nous avons
pris des grecs l'évangile et les traditions, et non l'esprit de puérilité et
de controverse. Les mœurs de Byzance n'ont jamais été celles de Kiov.
Le clergé Russe, jusqu'à Théophane,⁴ a été respectable, il ne s'est
jamais souillé des infamies du papisme et certes n'aurait jamais provoqué
la réformation au moment où l'humanité avait le plus besoin d'unité.⁵
Je conviens que notre clergé actuel est en retard. En voulez-vous savoir
la raison? C'est qu'il est barbu; voilà tout. Il n'est pas de bonne com-
pagnie.⁶ Quant à notre nullité historique, décidément je ne puis être
de votre avis. Les guerres d'Oleg et de Sviatoslav, et même les guerres
d'apanage, n'est-ce pas cette vie d'effervescence aventureuse et d'acti-
vité âpre et sans but qui caractérise la jeunesse de tous les peuples?
L'invasion des tartares est un triste et grand tableau. Le réveil de la
Russie, le développement de sa puissance, sa marche vers l'unité (unité
Russe bien entendu) les deux Ivan,⁷ le drame sublime commencé à
Ouglitch⁸ et terminé au monastère d'Ipatief⁹ – quoi? tout cela ne
serait pas de l'histoire, mais un rêve pâle et à demi oublié? Et Pierre
le Grand qui à lui seul est une histoire universelle! Et Catherine II
qui a placé la Russie sur le seuil de l'Europe? et Alexandre qui vous

a mené à Paris? et (la main sur le cœur) ne trouvez-vous pas quelque chose d'imposant dans la situation actuelle de la Russie, quelque chose qui frappera le futur historien? Croyez-vous qu'il nous mettra hors l'Europe? Quoique personellement attaché de cœur à l'empereur, je suis loin d'admirer tout ce que je vois autour de moi; comme homme de lettres, je suis aigri; comme homme à préjugés,[10] je suis froissé, mais je vous jure sur mon honneur, que pour rien au monde je n'aurais voulu changer de patrie, ni avoir d'autre histoire que celle de nos ancêtres, telle que Dieu nous l'a donnée.

Voici une bien longue lettre. Après vous avoir contredit il faut bien que je vous dise que beaucoup de choses dans votre épître sont profondément vraies. Il faut bien avouer que notre existence sociale est une triste chose. Que cette absence d'opinion publique, cette indifférence pour tout ce qui est devoir, justice et vérité, ce mépris cynique pour la pensée et la dignité de l'homme sont une chose vraiment désolante. Vous avez bien fait de le dire tout haut. Mais je crains que vos opinions historiques ne vous fassent du tort. . . . Enfin je suis fâché de ne pas m'être trouvé près de vous lorsque vous avez livré votre manuscrit aux journalistes. Je ne vais nulle part et ne puis vous dire si l'article fait effet. J'espère qu'on ne le fera pas mousser. Avez-vous lu le 3me No. du *Sovremennik*? L'article Voltaire[11] et John Tanner[12] sont de moi. Kozlovsky[13] serait ma providence s'il voulait une bonne fois devenir homme de lettres. Adieu, mon ami. Si vous voyez Orlof et Rayewsky dites-leur bien des choses. Que disent-ils de votre lettre, eux qui sont si médiocrement chrétiens?

[1] See page 10.
[2] Chaadaev's First Philosophical Letter, published in the *Teleskop*, Vol. XXXV, No. 15 (1836). The Letter was originally written in French but was published in Russian. In this Letter Chaadaev ascribed the manifold ills of Russian society to the fact that Russia had been cut off from the civilizing influence of the Roman Catholic Church, having espoused the Eastern branch of Christianity.
    As a result of the publication of this Letter, which predictably caused an uproar, the Editor of the *Teleskop*, N. I. Nadezhdin, was exiled to Siberia, the *Teleskop* itself was proscribed, the censor who had passed the issue for publication, A. V. Boldyrev, was sacked and discharged from his post at Moscow University. Chaadaev was declared insane and put under daily medical surveillance, the Emperor, on being shown the Letter by Benckendorff, having pronounced it the work of a madman. In 1837 Chaadaev published (in French) his 'Apology of a Madman' with an epigraph from Coleridge: 'O my brethren! I have told most bitter truth but without bitterness.'

This Letter proved to be the opening salvo in the Westerner/Slavophil controversy which divided Russian intellectual opinion for the rest of the century. The Slavophils rejected Chaadaev's thesis completely, but even the leading Westerners, like Herzen, although agreeing with it in part did not share Chaadaev's views on religion.

Herzen wrote of it in *My Past and Thoughts*:

That *Letter* was in a sense the last word, the limit. It was a shot that rang out in the dark night . . . one had to wake up.

What, one may wonder, is the significance of two or three pages published in a monthly review? And yet such is the might of speech, such is the power of the spoken word in a land of silence, unaccustomed to free speech, that Chaadaev's *Letter* shook all thinking Russia. And well it might. There had not been one literary work since *Woe from Wit* which made so powerful an impression. Between that play and the *Letter* there had been ten years of silence, the Fourteenth of December, the gallows, penal servitude, Nicholas . . . suddenly a mournful figure quietly rose and asked for a hearing in order calmly to utter his *lasciate ogni speranza*.

. . . The letter grew and developed, it turned into a dark denunciation of Russia, the protest of one who, in return for all he has endured, longs to utter some part of what is accumulated in his heart.

Chaadaev's melancholy and peculiar figure stood out sharply like a mournful reproach against the faded and dreary background of Moscow 'high life'. . . . However dense the crowd, the eye found him at once. The years did not mar his graceful figure; he was very scrupulous in his dress, his pale, delicate face was completely motionless when he was silent, as though made of wax or of marble – 'a forehead like a bare skull' – his grey-blue eyes were melancholy and at the same time there was something kindly in them though his thin lips smiled ironically. For ten years he stood with folded arms, by a column, by a tree on the boulevard, in drawing-rooms and theatres, at the club and, an embodied veto, a living protest, gazed at the vortex of faces senselessly whirling round him.

Chaadaev and the Slavophils alike stood facing the unsolved Sphinx of Russian life, the Sphinx sleeping under the overcoat of the soldier and the watchful eye of the Tsar; they alike were asking: 'What will come of this? To live like this is impossible: the oppressiveness and absurdity of the present situation is obvious and unendurable – where is the way out?'

(Part IV, chapter 30. Translated by Constance Garnett, revised by Humphrey Higgens.)

This Letter was dated 1 December 1829, and Pushkin had probably read it then (see his letter to Chaadaev, no. 230, about the Second and

Third Philosophical Letters. Before he had sent this letter Pushkin heard from K. O. Rosset of what had happened to Nadezhdin, Boldyrev and Chaadaev. Rosset advised Pushkin not to send his own letter, especially by post. Pushkin held it back, writing on it a saying from Scott's Preface to *Woodstock*: 'Hawks . . . ought not to pick out hawks' eyes.'

[3] See Pushkin's article on the insignificance of Russian literature, no. 272. In the twentieth century the poet Alexander Blok was to make a similar point in his poem 'The Scythians' (1918).

[4] Theophan Prokopovich (1681-1736) who drew up the 'Spiritual Regulations' (1721) which replaced the Patriarchate of Moscow by the Holy Synod, placing the Russian Orthodox Church under the supervision of the State.

[5] At the time of the Turkish invasions of Europe in the sixteenth and seventeenth centuries.

[6] Peter the Great had forced the nobles, but not the clergy, to shave.

[7] Ivan III (ruled 1462-1505), who married Sophia Paleologue, the niece of the last Byzantine Emperor. He threw off the Tatar yoke. And Ivan IV ('the Terrible'), who ruled from 1533 to 1584.

[8] The murder of the Tsarevich Dimitri – the son of Ivan the Terrible – at Uglich in 1591 and the election after the death of Tsar Fedor of Boris Godunov, Ivan's son-in-law, to the throne. The subject of Pushkin's play.

[9] After the Time of Troubles which followed the death of Boris Godunov, Mihkail Romanov was elected to the throne of Russia in 1613. He received the news at the Ipatiev monastery.

[10] In favour of the old aristocracy, tracing its descent back to the Ryurik dynasty, as opposed to the new aristocracy of service. (In the draft of this letter Pushkin had written: 'Voilà déjà 140 ans que la Table of Ranks balaye la noblesse; et c'est l'empereur actuel, qui le premier a posé une digue (bien faible encore) contre le débordement d'une démocratie, pire que celle de l'Amérique (avez-vous lu Tocqueville? je suis encore tout chaud et tout effrayé de son livre).')

[11] See no. 302.

[12] See no. 303.

[13] Prince P. B. Kozlovsky's article 'On hope' was published in the third issue of the *Sovremennik* (1836).

322. To S. L. Pushkin   *20 October 1836*
                                             St Petersburg

. . . je suis moi-même très dérangé, chargé d'une nombreuse famille, la faisant vivre à force de travail et n'osant envisager l'avenir. . . . J'avais compté aller à Mikhailovskoe; je n'ai pas pu. Ça va encore me déranger pour un an, au moins. A la campagne j'aurais beaucoup travaillé; ici je ne fais rien, que de la bile. . . .

323. To P. A. Korsakov[1]   *25 October 1836*
St Petersburg

I hasten to answer your questions. The name of Mironov's daughter is fictitious. My novel is founded on a tradition, which I once heard, that one of the officers, who betrayed his trust and went over to Pugachev's band, was pardoned by the Empress at the request of his old father who had thrown himself at her feet. The novel, as you see, has moved a long way from the facts. I would ask you not to mention the author's real name,[2] but to announce that the manuscript reached you through P. A. Pletnev, whom I have already warned. . . .

[1] P. A. Korsakov was going to act as censor for Pushkin's novel *The Captain's Daughter*, published in the fourth issue of the *Sovremennik*. He had asked whether the heroine was a historical character and whether she had in fact visited Catherine the Great (see pages 201-2).
[2] Pushkin wanted to publish the novel anonymously.

324. To Prince N. B. Golitsin[1]   *10 November 1836*
St Petersburg

Merci mille fois, cher Prince, pour votre incomparable traduction de ma pièce de vers, lancée contre les ennemis de notre pays.[2] J'en avais déjà vu trois, dont une d'un puissant personnage *de mes amis*, et aucune ne vaut la vôtre. Que ne traduisîtes-vous pas cette pièce en temps opportun, je l'aurais[3] fait passer en France pour donner sur le nez à tous ces vociférateurs de la Chambre des Députés.

Que je vous envie votre beau climat de Crimée: votre lettre a réveillé en moi bien des souvenirs de tout genre. C'est le berceau de mon *Onegin*: et vous aurez sûrement reconnu certains personnages.[4]

Vous m'annoncez une traduction en vers de mon *Fountain of Bakhchisarai*. Je suis sûr qu'elle vous réussira comme tout ce qui sort de votre plume, quoique le genre de littérature auquel vous vous adonnez soit le plus difficile et le plus ingrat que je connaisse. A mon avis, rien n'est plus difficile que de traduire des vers russes en vers français,[5] car vu la concision de notre langue, on ne peut jamais être aussi bref. Honneur donc à celui qui s'en acquitte aussi bien que vous.

Adieu, je ne désespère pas de vous voir bientôt dans notre capitale, vu votre facilité de locomotion.

[1] Nikolai Borisovich Golitsin was a musician and a translator from Russian into French.

[2] Pushkin's poem 'To the slanderers of Russia'.
[3] At the time of the Polish rising (1830), when Pushkin was distressed by Mickiewicz's embittered views, see page 183.
[4] Probably the Raevskys.
[5] The same can be applied to English.

325. To Baron A. G. Barante[1]   *16 December 1836*
                                                         St Petersburg

Je m'empresse de faire parvenir à Votre Excellence les renseignements que vous avez désiré avoir touchant les règlements qui traitent de la propriété littéraire en Russie.

La littérature n'est devenue chez nous une branche considérable d'industrie que depuis une vingtaine d'années environ. Jusque là elle n'était regardée que comme une occupation élégante et aristocratique. Mme de Staël disait en 1811: *en Russie quelques gentilshommes se sont occupés de littérature (Dix Années d'exil).*[2] Personne ne songeant à retirer d'autre fruit de ses ouvrages que des triomphes de société, les auteurs encourageaient eux-mêmes la contrefaçon et en tiraient vanité, tandis que nos académies donnaient l'exemple du délit en toute conscience et sécurité. La première plainte en contrefaçon a été portée en 1824. Il se trouva que le cas n'avait pas été prévu par le législateur. La propriété littéraire a été reconnue en Russie par le souverain actuel.

La contrefaçon des livres étrangers n'est pas défendue et ne saurait l'être. Les libraires russes auront toujours beaucoup à gagner, en réimprimant les livres étrangers, dont le débit leur sera toujours assuré, même sans exportation; au lieu que l'étranger ne saurait réimprimer des ouvrages russes faute de lecteurs.

La prescription pour le délit de contrefaçon est fixé à deux ans.

La question de la propriété littéraire est très simplifiée en Russie où personne ne peut présenter son manuscrit à la censure sans en nommer l'auteur et sans le mettre par cela même sous la protection immédiate du gouvernement.

[1] Baron Amable Guillaume Barante, French historian, at the time Ambassador to Russia. Barante had written to Pushkin on 11 December 1836, asking him about copyright laws, as the person best qualified to speak on the subject.
[2] Chapter XVI: 'Quelques gentilshommes russes ont essayé de briller en littérature, et ont fait preuve de talent dans cette carrière; mais les lumières ne sont pas assez répandues pour qu'il y ait un jugement public formé par l'opinion de chacun.'

326. To Prince P. A. Vyazemsky

Second half 1835/1836
St Petersburg

. . . And in fact it wouldn't be a bad idea to embark on a dictionary or at least on a critical study of dictionaries.

327. To A. Tardif de Mello[1]

1836
St Petersburg

Vous m'avez fait trouver mes vers bien beaux, Monsieur. Vous les avez revêtus de ce noble vêtement,[2] sous lequel la poésie est vraiment déesse, *vera incessu patuit dea.* Je vous remercie de votre précieux envoi.

Vous êtes poète et vous enseignez la jeunesse; j'appelle deux bénédictions sur vous.

[1] Achille Tardif de Mello, French man of letters very interested in Pushkin's work.
[2] He had sent Pushkin his translation of *The Prisoner of the Caucasus.*

328. To Prince V. F. Odoevsky

December 1836
St Petersburg

Heavens above, your Excellency! Have some fear of God, there is absolutely no point of contact between me and Lvov, or Ochkin,[1] or children. Why should I collaborate in a children's newspaper? As it is, people are saying I'm falling into my second childhood. Except possibly for the money? Then it becomes a business and not a childish matter. However, let's talk about it.

[1] V. V. Lvov and A. N. Ochkin were editors of the periodical *Detskaya Biblioteka* (Children's Library) to which Pushkin refused to contribute.

Section VI

'DEATH OF A POET'

27 JANUARY 1837. Fate linked the name of a minor English poet with Pushkin's on the day he fought his fatal duel. Pushkin's last comment on literature, in fact the last words he ever wrote, concerned neither Voltaire, nor Byron, nor Shakespeare, nor Scott – but Barry Cornwall. On 26 January he had received an invitation to call on Mme A. O. Ishimov, whom he had approached about translating a few short plays by Cornwall for the fifth number of the *Sovremennik*. Pushkin had been interested in this genre since writing his own Little Tragedies and had selected the pieces he wanted to publish. It was arranged that he would drop in the volume (*The Poetical Works of Milman, Bowles, Wilson and Barry Cornwall* (Paris, 1829)) on the afternoon of the following day.

On 27 January there was a more pressing matter in hand. Pushkin, however, sat down and wrote a note of apology to Mme Ishimov, excusing himself from calling personally, and parcelled up the volume in question with the plays marked which he wanted translated. It is an extraordinary document: courteous and composed in style, firm in handwriting, with not a sign of stress to be seen. He then drove to Wolf's cake-shop to meet his second, Konstantin Danzas. Soon they were on their way to Chernaya Rechka where the assignation with d'Anthès was to take place. As they drove along the Neva they passed Natalia Pushkin in her carriage; she did not notice them and Pushkin averted his eyes.

They fought the duel in deep snow. D'Anthès fired first and Pushkin fell, wounded in the lower abdomen. Raising himself on his left elbow he managed to fire too and slightly injured d'Anthès in the ribs. Pushkin asked d'Archiac if he had killed his opponent. D'Archiac replied: 'No, but he is wounded in the arm and chest.' 'It's strange,' said Pushkin, 'I had thought it would give me pleasure to kill him but now I feel it would not. And yet it's all the same; if we both recover it will all start again.'

In *Evgeny Onegin* Pushkin had visualized the scene: the snow, the

479

measured paces, the signal to approach, the raised pistols, the death
of a poet:

> Onegin at the same
> Instant has fired. Thus fate disposes,
> And strikes the hour. The poet lets
> His pistol drop – his hand he sets
> Hard to his bosom, never saying
> One word, and falls – his clouded eye
> No pang, but death itself portraying.
> (Chapter VI, xxx-xxxi, trans. Oliver Elton.)

Unlike Lensky, Pushkin himself did not die straight away; he had
another forty-five hours of agony to live through.

In a memorable duel scene in *War and Peace*, Pierre Bezukhov staggers
away through the snow from his opponent whom he had wounded,
almost accidentally, sobbing out: 'Folly . . . folly!' It was all folly and
waste, and yet if Pushkin had survived would he and d'Anthès, as he
said, have started all over again?

As Pushkin was carried into his house by his valet one of the first
things he said was 'il faut que j'arrange ma maison.' He was brought
into the library and a bed was made up near his books. It seems fitting
that this should have been so: he had lived by them and would die
among them. At one point Zhukovsky, standing by his bedside, saw
him turn towards the shelves and say: 'Goodbye, my friends.'

The news of the gravity of his condition spread quickly and his
friends were soon at his bedside. Pletnev arrived first, then the Vyazemskys, Zhukovsky, A. I. Turgenev, Mme Karamzin, and finally the
distraught Elizaveta Khitrovo. Outside a crowd gathered and waited
for the doctor's bulletins.

Pushkin sent a message to the Tsar that he was dying and asked for
a pardon for himself and his second. The Tsar replied, begging Pushkin
to die a Christian and assuring him that he would care for his family.
Perhaps he felt a pang of remorse, for he was not above reproach
himself for the part he had played in encouraging the flirtatious atmosphere which had built up round the beautiful Natalia Pushkin, whom
he was so anxious to see gracing his court. At any rate he kept his
word: after Pushkin's death he paid off all his father's debts, published
his works at government expense, gave a handsome pension to his widow
and allowances to his children. Was this last move in the complex love-

hate relationship between the Tsar and Pushkin conscience-money for
the years of restrictions and censorship and humiliation?

All the friends who stood by him in those last hours bore witness to
Pushkin's astonishing composure and fortitude in the face of the agoniz-
ing pain as gangrene set in. He assured his wife that she was blameless
– 'it is a matter that concerns me only' he told her; and urged her to
leave the room when the pains were at their worst. He called her and
his children to come to him only when he was in control of himself.

The last rites were administered. At one point he turned to his
doctor, Dahl, and said that he had dreamt that they were flying together
up his bookshelves and that he had felt dizzy and had fallen. . . .

Zhukovsky and Turgenev were both at his side when the doctor
quietly said 'he is passing'. The blinds were drawn down at 2.45 p.m.
on 29 January and a very vulnerable man passed into legend. The
poet Anna Akhmatova has described this moment:

> Petersburg was witness of the fact that having heard the fatal news
> thousands of people thronged to the poet's house and with all of
> Russia they have remained there to this day.
>
> 'Il faut que j'arrange ma maison', said the dying Pushkin. In two
> days' time his house became a shrine for the whole of his native land.

Pushkin's body lay in state for three days at his house and 20,000
people filed past it. One of the Karamzin daughters, Princess Ekaterina
Meshchersky, described it to her sister-in-law:

> A crowd of all ages and of all conditions streamed by without a break,
> wave upon motley wave, moving past the foot of his bier: women,
> old men, children, schoolboys, peasants, some in sheepskin coats,
> some even in rags, had come to pay homage to the bodily remains
> of the nation's beloved poet.
>
> It was touching to see this plebeian homage, while our gilded
> salons and perfumed boudoirs did not spare a passing thought or
> regret for his short and brilliant career.

There were two nations in Russia. Pushkin had been made only too
aware of the hostility of court circles; his stricken friends now witnessed the homage of his humbler readers. Sophia Karamzin recounts
that Zhukovsky's eye was caught by an old man in tears. He asked his
name. 'Pushkin did not know me,' he replied, 'and I never saw him
alive but I grieve for the glory of Russia.' (Sophia Karamzin's letter of
2 February 1837.)

The Tsar feared that there would be a popular demonstration at the funeral and ordered it to be transferred from St Isaac's Cathedral to the Royal Stables Chapel. Admission was by ticket only and was largely confined to courtiers and the diplomatic corps; but a crowd stood outside.

The old family friend, A. I. Turgenev, was entrusted with the interment. He set off alone at midnight with Pushkin's coffin and passing Mikhailovskoe and Trigorskoe drove to the Svyatogorsky monastery. Twenty-six years had passed since he had driven with the eleven-year-old Pushkin to Tsarskoe Selo to place him at the Lycée. At daybreak on 6 February he threw a handful of earth into his grave.

Within a few days of Pushkin's burial his poetic mantle had fallen on an unknown lieutenant in the Hussars – Mikhail Lermontov. He wrote 'Death of a poet', an explosive indictment of the court circles, which he felt had hounded Pushkin to death, and of the man who had fired the shot: 'he could not understand in that blood-stained moment against what he was raising his hand.'

Lermontov's words rang out with passionate rhetoric and immediately the stifling machinery of authority went into action. He was arrested, court-martialled, and transferred to the Caucasus. Prince Odoevsky, who had managed to slip into the literary supplement of the *Russky Invalid* the only tribute to Pushkin allowed in the press, was refused permission to publish Lermontov's poem in the fifth number of the *Sovremennik* now planned as a memorial issue. The censors were busy again, but in spite of them Russian poetry was very much alive. That would have pleased Pushkin.

1837

———————

LETTERS

329. To A. O. Ishimov[1]
25 January 1837
St Petersburg

The other day I had the honour of calling on you and am extremely
sorry that I did not find you in. I wanted to speak to you on a business
matter: Peter Alexandrovich has given me reason to hope that you
would be willing to take part in the publication of the *Sovremennik*. I
agree to all your terms in advance and hasten to take advantage of
your goodwill. I want to introduce the works of Barry Cornwall[2] to
the Russian public. Would you be prepared to translate a few of his
dramatic sketches? If you would, I should be honoured to send you a
copy of his book.[3]

[1] Alexandra Osipovna Ishimov was a well-known children's author and
translator.
[2] The pseudonym of Bryan Waller Proctor, English poet and dramatist
(1787-1874).
[3] *The Poetical Works of Milman, Bowles, Wilson, and Barry Cornwall* (Paris, 1829).
Pushkin had been interested in the work of Wilson and Cornwall since
writing his own *Little Tragedies*. Mme Ishimov translated the five dramatic
scenes Pushkin had marked: 'Ludovico Sforza', 'Love cured by Kindness',
'The Way to Conquer', 'Amelia Wentworth' and 'The Falcon'. They were
published in the eighth issue of the *Sovremennik* (1837).

330. To A. O. Ishimov
27 January 1837
St Petersburg

. . . I am very sorry that I will not be able to accept your invitation for
today.[1] However, I have the honour of sending you the Barry Cornwall.
You will find at the end of the volume the plays marked with a pencil.
Translate them as well as you are able – I assure you that your translation will be unbeatable. Today I chanced to open your *History in Tales*,[2]
and was compelled to read on. That is how one should write![3] . . .

[1] Pushkin had a more urgent matter to attend to. His duel with d'Anthès
was fixed for 4.30 that afternoon.
[2] *History of Russia in Tales for Children*, Vol. I (December 1836).

[3] These were the last words that Pushkin wrote. On his death-bed he signed a list of his debts, but that signature written in 'a fairly firm hand' (A. I. Turgenev's words) did not survive.

When publishing Mme Ishimov's translations of Barry Cornwall's dramatic scenes in the eighth issue of *Sovremennik*, the editors wrote of this covering letter: 'The calm tone which prevails in this letter, the orderly pursuit of daily affairs unchanged to the last minute, the amazing precision over this matter in particular, even in the handwriting giving a total impression of inner quiet, all bear clear witness to the strength of the poet's soul.'

APPENDIX

SHORT-TITLE CATALOGUE OF
THE FOREIGN (NON-RUSSIAN) BOOKS
IN PUSHKIN'S LIBRARY

This catalogue is taken from that compiled by B. L. Modzalevsky and published in *Pushkin i evo sovremenniki*, issues IX-X (St Petersburg, 1910).

Pushkin treasured his library. He lived and, literally, died among his books. In the long years of his exile from the Russian capitals, the boxes of books he was regularly sent served as lifelines, tying him to the thought and culture of Europe to which he himself so richly contributed.

Much can be learnt of a man from his choice of books. His tastes, his enthusiasms, his obsessions, stand revealed on his shelves. The existence of this list is an invitation to browse in Pushkin's library while waiting for him to come into the room himself. What can one discover? What is one led to expect?

Of the 1,505 items Modzalevsky listed, numbers 1-444 were Russian books and numbers 530-1505 were foreign, so that it can be seen at a glance how preponderant was the role of the latter. On looking at the list of foreign books it becomes equally clear that throughout his life, for choice, Pushkin read mostly in French. The ancient classics, the Bible, Dante, Machiavelli, Luther, Shakespeare, Leibnitz, Byron, and countless other authors, history books and books on philosophy, cookery and medical books, books on literature and art: all are predominantly in French. But – and this shows his good intentions – when a work of literature is found in French translation, a copy of the original is nearly always at hand and there are plenty of dictionaries. Of English classics, only Bunyan's works and De Quincey's *Confessions of an English Opium Eater* (wrongly attributed to Maturin) are found exclusively in Russian.

Not only are the majority of the books actually in French, but many of those in other languages are in French editions, published either in Paris or Brussels. In between are found unusual imprints: Naples, Dublin, Perpignan, Chiswick, Philadelphia, Constantinople, and one book with the intriguing ex-libris: 'This book belongs to Sprang's Circulating Library, of the Post-Office, Tunbridge-Town, under the direction of Matthew Stidolph', which raises the intriguing question as to who travelled from Tunbridge to Russia and carelessly left his library book where Pushkin could pick it up.

The range of books is very wide and catholic in taste. It is a characteristic collection of a cultured gentleman of the late eighteenth and early nineteenth centuries. Similar libraries can be found in country houses in England. It faithfully reflects the impression we get of Pushkin from his letters: a man devoted to the study of literature and history; of liberal, even at times of radical, political views; fond of riding (there are several volumes on equitation) and of a bottle of wine; of amorous tendencies with a taste for risqué stories.

Two special collections, however, indicate a particular interest which Pushkin developed in periods of political unrest: one, of a dozen books on the Civil War in England, and another of nearly three dozen books on the French Revolution. These make one wonder whether, having devoted so much of his time as a dramatist, novelist and historian to the troubled times of the Pretender Dimitri and of the Pugachev rising, Pushkin planned to make later forays into English and French history. At any rate the fact that he read so much on the English Civil War helps to explain the extraordinary percipience of his short comment on Milton's character in his review of Chateaubriand's translation of *Paradise Lost*. Pushkin and Milton seem cultures apart and yet in a few words he had proved able to sum up the quality of the man. That was Pushkin all over: in appraising, he could cut through to essentials, and in writing, always find the *mot juste*.

As this list is taken direct from Modzalevsky's, which was printed in Russia in a foreign alphabet, with only occasional alterations of placing in order to preserve alphabetical order, and as it has not been possible to check all thousand entries, there will be some inconsistencies, for which the editor would like to apologize.

Foreign (non-Russian) books

AGOUB, J. *Mélanges de littérature orientale et française.* Paris, 1835.
Album littéraire. Choix d'articles extrait des meilleurs écrits périodiques publiés en France, sur la littérature, les arts et les sciences. Paris, 1832.
ALEMBERT, J. LE R. D'. *Esprit, maximes et principes de d'Alembert.* Genève, 1789.
ALFIERI, V. *Du Prince et des lettres.* Paris, 1818.
— *Tragedie scelte.* Parigi, 1825.
ALHOY, M. *Les Bagnes.* Paris, 1830.
Allgemeine deutsche Real-Encyklopädie für die gebildeten Stände (Conversations-Lexikon). Leipzig, 1830.
Almanach dédié aux dames. Pour l'an 1824. Paris.
AMPÈRE, J. J. *Littérature et voyages.* Bruxelles, 1834.
ANACREON. *Anacreontis reliquia.* Parisiis, 1823.
ANCELOT, J. A P. F. *Six Mois en Russie.* Bruxelles, 1827.
ANCILLON, F. *Pensées sur l'homme, ses rapports et ses intérêts.* Berlin, 1829.
Anecdotes et recueil de coutumes et de traits d'histoire naturelle particuliers aux différens peuples de la Russie. Londres, 1792.
The Annual Register, or a View of the history, politics, and literature of the
    year 1833. London, 1834.
    year 1834. London, 1835.
    year 1835. London, 1836.

Anthologia Graeca ad Palatina codicis fidem edita. Lipsiae, 1819.

Anthologie française, ou Choix d'épigrammes, madrigaux, portraits, épitaphes, inscriptions, moralités, couplets, anecdotes, bon-mots, reparties, histoirettes. Paris, 1816.

Antidote, ou Examen du mauvais livre superbement imprimé intitulé: 'Voyage en Sibérie, fait par ordre du Roi en 1761 . . . par M. l'Abbé d'Auteroche . . . 1768'. Amsterdam, 1771.

ANTOINE, A. *Histoire des émigrés français*, depuis 1789, jusqu'en 1828. Paris, 1828.

ANTOMMARCHI, F. *Derniers momens de Napoléon*. Paris, 1825.

ANVILLE, J. B. D'. *Géographie ancienne*. Paris, 1768.

APOLLODORE. *Bibliothèque d'Apollodore l'Athénien*. Paris, 1805.

APPERT, B. *Bagnes, prisons et criminels*. Paris, 1836.

ARIOSTO, L. *L'Orlando Furioso*. Parigi, 1825.

ARISTOPHANES. *Comédies grecques d'Aristophane*. Traduites en François . . . par madame Dacier. Altenbourg, 1762.

ARNAUD, F. T. M. DE B. *Épreuves du sentiment*. Paris, 1803.

ARNAULT, A. V. *Œuvres*. Théâtre. Paris, 1824.

— *Œuvres*. Fables et poésies diverses. Paris, 1825.

L'Art de donner à dîner, de découper les viandes, de servir les mets, de déguster les vins, de choisir les liqueurs, etc. Par un ancien Maître-d'Hôtel du Président de la Diète de Hongrie . . . Paris, 1828.

L'Art d'obtenir des places, ou la Clef des Ministères. Paris, 1817.

ATHÉNÉE. *Banquet des savans*. Traduit . . . par M. Lefebvre de Villebrune. Paris, 1789.

AUSTIN, SARAH. *Characteristics of Goethe*. From the German of Falk, Von Müller, etc. London, 1833.

B . . ., J. N. *Vie et aventures de Pigault-Lebrun*. Paris, 1836.

B., L. D. *Histoire civile, religieuse et littéraire de l'Abbaye de la Trappe*, et des autres monastères de la même observance . . . Paris, 1824.

BACH, S. *Il vivere*. Bruxelles, 1836.

BACMEISTER, H. L. C. *Russische Bibliothek*, zur Kenntniss des gegenwärtigen Zustandes der Literatur in Russland. Riga und Leipzig, 1773.

BAILLEUL, J. C. *Examen critique des Considérations de M-me la Baronne de Staël*, *sur les principaux événemens de la Révolution Française* . . . Paris, 1822.

BALLANCHE, P. S. *Œuvres*. Paris, 1830.

BALLANTYNES'S NOVELIST'S LIBRARY

Vol. I. *The Novels of Henry Fielding, Esq.* Viz. 1. Joseph Andrews, 2. Tom Jones, 3. Amelia, and 4. Jonathan Wild; complete in one volume. To which is prefixed, a memoir of the life of the author. London, 1821.

Vol. II. *The Novels of Tobias Smollett, M.D.* Viz. Roderick Random, Peregrine Pickle, and Humphrey Clinker. To which is prefixed a memoir of the life of the author. London, 1821.

Vol. III. *The Novels of Tobias Smollett, M.D.* Viz. Count Fathom, Sir Launcelot Greaves, and the translation of Cervantes's Don Quixote. London, 1821.

Vol. IV. *The Novels of Le Sage and Charles Johnstone.* Viz. Gil Blas, The devil on two sticks, and Vanillo Gonzales, by Le Sage; and The adventures of a guinea, by Johnstone. To which are prefixed, memoirs of the lives of the authors. London, 1822.

Vol. v. *The novels of Sterne, Goldsmith, Dr Johnson, Mackensie, Horace Walpole and Clara Reeve.* Viz. Tristram Shandy, Sentimental Journey, by Sterne. The Vicar of Wakefield, by Goldsmith. Rasselas, by Dr Johnson. The Man of Feeling, The Man of the World, by Mackensie. The Castle of Otranto, by Horace Walpole. The Old English Baron, by Clara Reeve. To which are prefixed, memoirs of the lives of the authors. London, 1823.

BALZAC, H. DE. *Le Médecin de campagne.* Bruxelles, 1833.

— *Le Centenaire*, ou les Deux Béringheld. Bruxelles, 1836.

— *Le Livre mystique.* Paris, 1836.

— *Le Lys dans la vallée.* Paris, 1836.

— *Scènes de la vie privée.* Bruxelles, 1836.

BARANTE, A. G. P. B. DE, BARON. *Histoire des Ducs de Bourgogne de la Maison de Valois, 1364-1477.* Paris, 1826.

— *Histoire des Ducs de Bourgogne.* Atlas.

— *Mélanges historiques et littéraires.* Bruxelles, 1835.

— *Tableau de la littérature française au dix-huitième siècle.* Paris, 1832.

BARBIER, A. *Il Pianto*, poëme. Paris, 1833.

— *Iambes.* Paris, 1832

BARETTI, J. *A Dictionary Spanish and English and English and Spanish.* London, 1778.

BARON, A. *Poésies militaires de l'antiquité*, ou Callinus et Tyrtée. Texte grec, traduction polyglotte, prolégomènes et commentaires. Bruxelles, 1835.

BARROW, J. *Voyage en Chine*, formant le complément du voyage de Lord Macartney. Paris, 1805.

BARTHÉLÉMY, A. M., ET MÉRY, J. *L'Insurrection.* Poème dédié aux Parisiens. Bruxelles, 1830.

BARTHÉLÉMY, J. J., ABBÉ. *Atlas des œuvres complètes.* Paris, 1822.

BAUDRY'S COLLECTION OF ANCIENT AND MODERN BRITISH NOVELS & ROMANCES

Vol. XV, XVI. HOPE, T. *Anastasius or Memoirs of a Greek*, written at the close of the eighteenth century. Paris, 1831.

Vol. XVIII. SCOTT, W. *Tales of my Landlord*, collected and arranged by Jedediah Cleishbotham . . . Fourth and last Series. Count Robert of Paris. Castle Dangerous. Paris, 1831.

Vol. XXXII. BULWER, E. L. *Pelham*, or the Adventures of a Gentleman. Paris, 1832.

Vol. XXXIII. BULWER, E. L. *Devereux*, a Tale. Paris, 1832.

Vol. XLI. MORIER, D. R. *Zohrab the Hostage.* Paris, 1833.

Vol. XLVII. BULWER, E. L. *The Disowned.* Paris, 1833.

Vol. L. COOPER, F. *The Headsman*, or the Abbaye des Vignerons. A Tale. Paris, 1833.

Vol. LIV. [SCOTT, M.] *Tom Cringle's Log.* Paris, 1834.

Vol. LVI. *Peter Simple.* Paris, 1834.

Vol. LVIII. MORIER, J. *Ayesha*, the Maid of Kars. Paris, 1834.

Vol. LIX. BECKFORD, W. *Italy, with sketches of Spain and Portugal*. Paris, 1834.

BAUDRY'S COLLECTION OF ANCIENT AND MODERN BRITISH AUTHORS

MACKINTOSH, SIR J. *History of the Revolution in England in 1688*. Paris, 1834.

Vol. XLVIII. BULWER, E. L. *England and the English*. Paris, 1833.

Vol. LXXII. HARRISON. *Passages from the Diary of a late Physician*. Paris, 1835.

Vols. LXXIII, LXXIV, LXXV. D'ISRAELI, I. *Curiosities of Literature*. Paris, 1835.

Vol. LXXIX. MOORE, T. *Memoirs of the life of the Right Honourable Richard Brinsley Sheridan*. Paris, 1835.

Vol. LXXX. MOORE, T. *Memoirs of Lord Edward Fitzgerald*. Paris, 1835.

Vol. LXXXII. MOORE, T. *Letters and Journals of Lord Byron:* with notices of his life, Vol. II. Paris, 1835.

Vol. LXXXIII. MOORE, T. *Travels of an Irish Gentleman in Search of a Religion*, with Notes and Illustrations. Paris, 1835.

Vol. LXXXVIII. LAMB, C. *Essays of Elia*, to which are added Letters, and Rosamund, a Tale. Paris, 1835.

Vol. LXXXIX. MORIER, J. *The Adventures of Hajji Baba of Ispahan*. Paris, 1835.

Vols. C, CI, CII, CIII, CIV, CV. *Selections from the 'Edinburgh Review'*. comprising the best articles in that Journal, from its Commencement to the present Time . . . Edited by Maurice Cross. Paris, 1835-6.

Vol. CXXXII. *The American in England*. Paris, 1836.

BAYLE, P. *Dictionnaire historique et critique*. Paris, 1820-4.

BAZIN DE RAUCOU, A. *L'Époque sans nom*. Esquisses de Paris, 1830-3. Paris, 1833.

BEAUMARCHAIS, P. A. C. DE. *Œuvres complètes*. Paris, 1828.

BEAUMONT, G. *Marie, ou l'Esclavage aux États-Unis*. Tableau de mœurs américaines. Paris, 1836.

BECKFORD, W.; WALPOLE, H., EARL OF ORFORD; LEWIS, M. G. *Standard Novels*. Vathek, by William Beckford, Esq.; The Castle of Otranto, by Horace Walpole, Earl of Orford; The Bravo of Venice, by M. G. Lewis, Esq. London, 1834.

BELL D'ANTERMONY, J. *Voyages depuis St-Pétersbourg en Russie dans diverses contrées de l'Asie* . . . Traduits de l'Anglois par M. . . . Paris, 1766.

Benson Powlet or Three French in Moscow in 1812. London, 1833.

BENTHAM, J. *Déontologie, ou Science de la morale* . . . Traduit . . . par Benjamin Laroche. Paris, 1834.

— *Œuvres*. Bruxelles, 1829-31.

— *Traités de législation civile et pénale*. Paris, 1830.

BENYOWSKY, M. A., COMTE. *Voyages et mémoires*. Paris, 1791.

BÉRANGER, P. J. DE. *Chansons inédites*. Paris, 1828.

— *Chansons nouvelles et dernières*. Paris, 1833.

BERBIGUIER, A. V. C. *Les Farfadets*, ou Tous les démons ne sont pas de l'autre monde. Paris, 1821.

BERGMANN, B. *Voyage de Benjamin Bergmann, chez les Kalmuks*. Traduit de l'allemand par M. Moris. Châtillon-sur-Seine, 1825.

BERNIS, F. J. DE PIERRES DE. *Œuvres*. Paris, 1825.

BERTRAND, A. *Lettres sur les révolutions du globe*. Bruxelles, 1833.

BIBLE. *La Sainte Bible*, contenant l'Ancien et le Nouveau Testament, traduite sur la Vulgate par M. Le Maistre de Saci. St-Pétersbourg, 1817.

— *La Bible*. Traduction nouvelle, avec l'Hébreu en regard . . . par S. Cohen. Paris, 1831-6.

— *Le Livre de Job*, traduit en vers français, avec le texte de la Vulgate en regard . . . par B. M. F. Levasseur. Paris, 1826.

— *Livres Apocryphes de l'Ancien Testament*, en François. Avec des notes, pour servir de suite à la Bible de Monsieur de Saci. Paris, 1742.

— *Le Nouveau Testament*, selon la Vulgate. Réimprimé sur la traduction française de Le Maistre de Sacy. St-Pétersbourg, 1815.

BIBLIOTHÈQUE LATINE-FRANÇAISE PUBLIÉE PAR JULES PIERROT

(1) CORNÉLIUS NÉPOS. *Les Vies*. Paris, 1827.

(2) FLORUS, L. A. *Abrégé de l'Histoire Romaine*. Traduit par F. Ragon. Paris, 1826.

(3) JUSTIN. *Histoire universelle*. Traduction nouvelle par Jules Pierrot. Paris, 1826-7.

(4) JUVÉNAL. *Satires*. Traduites par J. Dusaulx. Paris, 1826.

(5) PATERCULUS, C. V. *Histoire romaine*. Traduit par M. Després. Paris, 1825.

(6) QUINTE-CURCE. *Histoire d'Alexandre le Grand*. . . . Traduction nouvelle par MM. Aug. et Alph. Trognon. Paris, 1828-9.

(7) VALÈRE MAXIME. *Faits et paroles mémorables*. Traduction nouvelle par C. A. F. Frémion. Paris, 1827-8.

BIBLIOTHÈQUE LATINE-FRANÇAISE PUBLIÉE PAR C. L. F. PANCKOUCKE

(1) APULÉE. *Apulée*. Traduction nouvelle par M. V. Bétolaud. Paris, 1835.

(2) CÉSAR, J. *Mémoires*. Traduction nouvelle par M. Artaud. Paris, 1828.

(3) CICÉRON. *Œuvres complètes* . . . Traduction nouvelle par M. M. Andrieux, etc. Paris, 1829-35.

(4) CLAUDIEN. *Œuvres complètes* . . . Traduction nouvelle par M. M. Héguin de Guerle. Paris, 1830-3.

(5) HORACE. *Œuvres complètes*. Paris, 1831.

(6) LUCAIN, M. A. *Pharsale*. Paris, 1835.

(7) LUCRÈCE. *De la nature des choses*. Poëme; traduit en prose par de Pongerville. Paris, 1829-32.

(8) MARTIAL, M. VAL. *Épigrammes*. Paris, 1834-5.

(9) OVIDE. *Œuvres complètes*. Paris, 1834-5.

(10) PERSE. *Satires* . . . suivies d'un fragment de Turnus et de la satire de Sulpicia. Traduction nouvelle par A. Perreau. Paris, 1832.

(11) PÉTRONE, T. *Le Satyricon*. Paris, 1834-5.

(12) PHÈDRE. *Fables*. Traduction nouvelle par M. E. Panckoucke. Paris, 1834.

(13) PLAUTE. *Théâtre*. Traduction nouvelle . . . par J. Naudet. Paris, 1831-5.

(14) PLINE. *Histoire naturelle*. Traduction nouvelle par M. Ajasson de Grandsagne. Paris, 1829-33.

(15) PLINE LE JEUNE. *Lettres.* Traduites par De Sagy. Paris, 1826-9.

(16) PROPERCE. *Élégies.* Traduction nouvelle par J. Genouille. Paris, 1834.

(17) QUINTILIEN. *Institution oratoire.* Traduction nouvelle par C. V. Ouizille. Paris, 1829-35.

(18) SALLUSTE. *Œuvres.* Traduction nouvelle . . . par M. Ch. du Rozoir. Paris, 1829-33.

(19) SÉNÈQUE. *Œuvres complètes.* Paris, 1832-4.

(20) SÉNÈQUE, L. A. *Tragédies.* Traduction nouvelle par M. E. Greslou. Paris, 1834.

(21) STACE. *Œuvres complètes.* Paris, 1829-32.

(22) SUÉTONE. *Suétone.* Traduction nouvelle par M. de Golbéry. Paris, 1830-3.

(23) TACITE, C. C. *Œuvres.* Traduites par C. L. F. Panckoucke. Paris, 1830-5.

(24) TÉRENCE, P. *Les Comédies.* Traduction nouvelle par M. J. A. Amar. Paris, 1830-2.

(25) TITE-LIVE. *Histoire romaine.* Paris, 1830-5.

(26) VALÉRIUS FLACCUS. *L'Argonautique* ou Conquête de la Toison d'or. Poëme traduit pour la première fois en prose par J. J. A. Causin de Perceval. Paris, 1829.

(27) VIRGILE. *Œuvres complètes.* Traduction nouvelle par MM. Villenave et Charpentier. Paris, 1832-5.

BIBLIOTHÈQUE UNIVERSELLE DES ROMANS. Ouvrage périodique. Dans lequel on donne l'analyse raisonnée des Romans anciens & modernes, François, ou traduits dans notre langue . . . Paris, 1775; 1776; 1777; 1778; 1779; 1780; 1781; 1782; 1783; 1784; 1785; 1786; 1787; 1788; 1789.

BICHAT, X. *Recherches physiologiques sur la vie et la mort.* Paris, 1829.

BOCACE, J. *Contes et nouvelles.* La Haye, 1775.

BOCCACCIO, G. *Il Decamerone.* Firenze, 1820.

BOETTIGER, C. A. *Sabine* ou Matinée d'une dame romaine à sa toilette, à la fin du premier siècle de l'ère chrétienne. Paris, 1813.

BIGENICKI, F. *Obrana Casopisu pro Katolicke duchowenstwo.* Praze, 1835.

BOILEAU-DESPRÉAUX, N. *Œuvres.* Paris, 1816.

— *Œuvres.* Avec les commentaires revus, corrigés et augmentés, par M. Viollet-le-Duc. Paris, 1823.

BONJOUR, C. *Le Mari à bonnes fortunes,* ou la Leçon. Paris, 1824.

BONNET, C. *La Palingénésie philosophique,* ou Idées sur l'état passé et sur l'état futur des êtres vivans. Munster, 1770.

BONNEVAL, C. A. DE, COMTE. *Mémoires.* La Haye, 1741.

BORROW, G. *Targum,* or Metrical translations from thirty Languages and Dialects. St Petersburg, 1835.

BOSSUET, J. B. *Œuvres complètes.* Paris, 1836.

BOUFFLERS, S. J., CHEVALIER DE. *Œuvres.* Paris, 1813.

BOURDALOUE, L. *Œuvres.* Paris, 1834.

BOURDON, J. B. I. *La Physiognomonie* ou L'Art de connaître les hommes d'après les traits du visage et les manifestations extérieures . . . suivie des biographies physiognomoniques, portraits physiques et moraux de Napoléon, Benj. Constant, Lord Byron, Chateaubriand, baron Cuvier, Gall, Henri IV, Kleber, l'abbé de La Mennais, vicomte de Martignac, Mirabeau, Robespierre, Mad. de Staël, prince de Talleyrand, comte de Villèle, Wellington, etc. Paris, 1830.

BOUTOURLIN, D. P. *Histoire militaire de la Campagne de Russie en 1812.* Paris, 1824.

— *Relation historique et critique de la Campagne de 1799 des Austro-Russes en Italie.* St-Pétersbourg, 1812.

BRANTÔME, SEIGNEUR DE. *Œuvres.* Paris, 1787.

BRAUN, M. *Nouveau Dictionnaire de poche Français-Allemand et Allemand-Français.* Paris, 1821.

BRIAND, P. C. *Histoire d'Espagne,* depuis la découverte qui en a été faite par les Phéniciens, jusqu'à la mort de Charles III; traduite de l'anglais d'Adam. Paris, 1821.

BRILLAT-SAVARIN, J. A. *Physiologie du goût,* ou Méditations de gastronomie transcendante. Paris, 1834.

BROSSES, C. DE. *Lettres historiques et critiques sur l'Italie.* Paris, 1795.

BROUGHAM, H., LORD. *Discours sur la théologie naturelle,* indiquant la nature de son évidence et les avantages de son étude . . . Traduit de l'anglais . . . par J. C. Tarver. Bruxelles, 1836.

BRUMOY, P. *Théâtres des Grecs.* Paris, 1785-9.

BRUYN, C. DE. *Voyages de Corneille de Bruyn au Levant.* La Haye, 1732.

BRYGES, E. *The autobiography, times, opinions and contemporaries of Sir Egerton Bryges, Bart.* London, 1834.

BUCHON, J. A. *Chronique et procès de la Pucelle d'Orléans,* d'après un manuscrit inédit de la Bibliothèque d'Orléans. Paris, 1827.

BUFFON, G. L. DE, COMTE. *Histoire naturelle, générale et particulière.* Lausanne, 1791.

— *Histoire naturelle.* Paris, 1799.

— *Œuvres complètes.* Bruxelles, 1822.

BUHLE, J. G. *Histoire de la philosophie moderne,* depuis la Renaissance des Lettres jusqu'à Kant. Paris, 1816.

BULWER, E. L. *L'Angleterre et les Anglais* . . . traduit de l'anglais par Jean Cohen. Bruxelles, 1833.

— *Les Derniers Jours de Pompéi.* Paris, 1834.

— *Rienzi,* le dernier des Tribuns, traduit . . . par Melle A. Sobry. Bruxelles, 1836.

— *The Student.* Paris, 1835.

BULWER, H. *La France sociale, politique et littéraire.* Bruxelles, 1834.

BURDER, S. *Oriental Literature,* applied to the Illustration of the Sacred Scriptures especially with reference to antiquities, traditions, and manners. London, 1822.

BURKE, E. *Réflexions sur la Révolution de France.* Paris, 1823.

BURNS, R. *The Poetical Works.* Chiswick, 1829.

BUXTORFIUS, I. *Lexicon Hebraicum et Chaldaicum.* Glasguoe, 1824.

BYRON, G. G. N., LORD. *The Complete Works* of Lord Byron from the last

London edition. Now first collected and arranged, and illustrated with notes. Paris, 1835.

— *Conversations de Lord Byron avec la Comtesse de Blessington*. Paris, 1833.

— *Correspondance de Lord Byron avec un ami*, etc. Paris, 1825.

— *Mémoires de Lord Byron*, publiés par Thomas Moore; traduits de l'anglais par Mme Louise Sw.-Belloc. Paris, 1830.

— *The Works*. Complete in one volume. Francfort, 1826.

C . . ., V. *Tableau général de la Russie moderne*, et situation politique de cet Empire au commencement du XIXe siècle. Paris, 1802.

Le Cabinet satyrique, ou Recueil parfait des vers piquans et gaillards de ce temps. 1672.

CALDERÓN DE LA BARCA, D. PEDRO. *Las Comedias*. Leipsique, 1827-30.

CALMET, A. *Traité sur les apparitions des esprits, et sur les vampires*. Paris, 1751.

CAMPENON, F. N. V. *Essais de mémoires*, ou Lettres sur la vie, le caractère, et les écrits de J. F. Ducis. Paris, 1824.

CAMPISTRON, J. G. DE. *Œuvres*. Paris, 1750.

CANNING, G. *Œuvres poétiques* de George Canning, Premier Ministre de S.M. Britannique; traduites en vers français . . . par M. Benjamin Laroche. Paris, 1827.

CAPEFIGUE, J. B. H. R. *Histoire de la Réforme, de la Ligue, et du Règne de Henri IV*. Paris, 1834-5.

CASANOVA, J. *Mémoires de Jacques Casanova de Seingalt*. Bruxelles, 1833.

CASTÉRA, J. *Histoire de Catherine II*, Impératrice de Russie. Paris, 1809.

CASTI, G. *Gli animali parlanti*. Poema epico . . . Parigi, 1820.

— *Novelle*. Parigi, 1821.

— *Novelle galanti*. Berlino [cover missing].

— *Il poema Tartaro*. Filadelfia, 1803.

CATIFORO, A. *Vita di Pietro il Grande Imperador della Russia*. Venezia, 1748.

CATULLE. *Traduction complète des poésies* de Catulle, suivie des Poésies de Gallus et de la Veillée des Fêtes de Vénus . . . par François Noël. Paris, 1806.

CATULLUS, TIBULLUS, PROPERTIUS. *Ad optimorum librorum* fidem accurate editi. Lipsiae, 1812.

Causes criminelles célèbres du XIXe siècle. Rédigées par une société d'avocats. Paris, 1827-8.

CAZOTTE, J. *Œuvres badines et morales, historiques et philosophiques*. Paris, 1816-17.

CELLERIER FILS, J. E. *Introduction à la lecture des Livres Saints*, à l'usage des hommes religieux et éclairés. Genève, 1832.

CELLINI, BENVENUTO. *Vie de Benvenuto Cellini*, Orfèvre et sculpteur florentin, écrite par lui-même, et traduite par D. D. Farjasse. Paris, 1833.

Suivent les Cent Nouvelles, contenant les Cent Histoires Nouveaux qui sont moult plaisants à raconter en toutes bonnes compagnies, par manière de joyeuseté. La Haye, 1733.

CERVANTES SAAVEDRA, M. DE. *El ingenioso Hidalgo Don Quijote de la Mancha*. Paris, 1835.

— *Novelas exemplares*. Perpiñan, 1816.

— *Novelas ejemplares*. Paris, 1835.

CHABANON, M. P. G. DE. *Œuvres de théâtre*, et autres poésies . Paris, 1788.

CHAMFORT, N. S. R. *Œuvres complètes*. Paris, 1812.

Chansonnier français, ou Choix des meilleures chansons érotiques, libres, joyeuses, bachiques, poissardes, pastorales, villageoises, etc. Paris, 1829.

CHAPELLE, C. E., & BACHAUMONT, F. DE. *Voyage de Chapelle et de Bachaumont*, suivi de leurs poésies diverses . . . Paris, 1826.

CHAPPE D'AUTEROCHE, J. *Voyage en Sibérie*, fait par Ordre du Roi en 1761. Amsterdam, 1769.

CHARLEMAGNE, J. A. *Timon-Alceste*, ou le Misanthrope moderne. Roman philosophique. Bruxelles, 1834.

CHARLOTTE-ELIZABETH DE BAVIÈRE. *Fragmens de lettres originales*. Hambourg, 1788.

CHARPENTIER, J. P. *Essai sur l'histoire littéraire du Moyen Âge*. Paris, 1833.

CHATEAUBRIAND, F. R. DE, VICOMTE. *Œuvres complètes*. Bruxelles, 1826-1831.

— *Essai sur la littérature anglaise et considérations sur le génie des hommes, des temps et des révolutions*. Paris, 1836.

La Chaumière dans la grotte. Nouvelle égyptienne. Manuscrit échappé à l'incendie de la Bibliothèque des Ptolémées à Alexandrie. St-Pétersbourg, 1817.

CHAUSSARD, P. J. P. B. *Héliogabale*, ou Esquisse morale de la dissolution romaine sous les empereurs. Paris, 1802.

Chefs d'œuvre du théâtre indien. Traduit de l'original sanscrit en anglais par M. H. H. Wilson . . . et de l'anglais en français par M. A. Langlois. Paris, 1828.

CHÊNEDOLLÉ, C. J. DE. *Le Génie de l'homme*. Poëme. Paris, 1826.

CHÉNIER, A. *Œuvres complètes*. Paris, 1819.

Choix de discours de réception à l'Académie Française, depuis son établissement jusqu'à sa suppression. Paris, 1808.

CHOMPRE. *Dictionnaire abrégé de la Bible*. Paris, 1806.

CHOUDARD-DESFORGES, P. J. B. *Le Poète*, ou Mémoires d'un homme de lettres, écrit par lui-même. Hambourg, 1798.

CHRISTOPHE, M. *Dictionnaire pour servir à l'intelligence des auteurs classiques grecs et latins*. Paris, 1805.

Chroniques des tribunaux ou Choix des causes les plus intéressantes dans les divers pays de l'Europe. Bruxelles, 1835.

Chronique indiscrète du dix-neuvième siècle. [By Pierre La Halle and others.] Paris, 1825.

Chroniques pittoresques et critiques de l'Œil de Bœuf, des petits appartemens de la cour et des salons de Paris, sous Louis XIV, la Régence, Louis XV, et Louis XVI. Publiées par Mme la Comtesse Douairière de B. . . . Paris, 1830.

CLARK, H. *An Introduction to Heraldry*. London, 1834.

La Clef du cabinet des princes de l'Europe. 1704.

Supplément de la Clef, ou Journal historique sur les matières du tems. Verdun, 1713.

Suite de la Clef, ou Journal historique sur les matières du tems. Paris, 1717; 1723; 1765; 1766; 1767; 1769; 1772; 1773; 1775; 1776.

COCHRAN, J. D. *Narrative of a Pedestrian Journey through Russia and Siberian Tartary.* London, 1824.

COHEN, J. *Tutti Frutti.* Tiré des papiers d'un défunt, et traduit de l'ouvrage allemand du Prince Puckler Muskau par Jean Cohen. Bruxelles, 1834.

COLERIDGE, H. *Poems.* Vol. I. Leeds, 1833.

COLERIDGE, S. T. *Specimens of the Table Talk of the late Samuel Taylor Coleridge.* In two volumes. London, 1836.

COLERIDGE, SHELLEY & KEATS. *The Poetical Works of Coleridge, Shelley and Keats.* Complete in one volume. Paris, 1829.

COLLECTION DES MÉMOIRES RELATIFS À LA RÉVOLUTION D'ANGLE-TERRE. Accompagnée de notices et d'éclaircissements historiques, et précédée d'une introduction sur l'histoire de la Révolution d'Angleterre; par M. Guizot.

(1) MAY, T. *Histoire du Long-Parlement convoqué par Charles 1er en 1640.* Paris, 1823.

(2) WARWICK, P. *Mémoires de Sir Philippe Warwick sur le règne de Charles 1er,* et ce qui s'est passé depuis la mort de Charles 1er jusqu'à la Restauration des Stuart. Paris, 1823.

(3) PRICE, J. *Mémoires de John Price,* Chapelain de Monk, sur la Restauration des Stuart. Paris, 1823.

(4) LUDLOW, E. *Mémoires.* Paris, 1823.

(5) HUTCHINSON, MRS. *Mémoires.* Paris, 1823.

(6) JACQUES II. *Mémoires.* Paris, 1824-5. (Also: *Mémoires de Hollis. Mémoires de Huntington. Mémoires de Fairfax.* Paris, 1823.)

(7) HERBERT, T., AND BERKLEY, J. *Mémoires de Sir Thomas Herbert,* Valet de Chambre de Charles 1er, sur les deux dernières années du règne de ce prince. *Mémoires de Sir John Berkley,* sur les négociations de Charles 1er avec Cromwell et l'armée parlementaire. Paris, 1823.

(8) CLARENDON, H., LORD. *Journal* . . . sur les années 1687, 1688, 1689 et 1690. Paris, 1824.

(9) — *Mémoires.* Paris, 1823-4.

(10) BURNET, ÉVÊQUE. *Histoire de mon temps.* Paris, 1824.

(11) RERESBY, J.; BUCKINGHAM, DUC. *Mémoires de Sir John Reresby. Mémoires du Duc Buckingham.* Paris, 1824.

(12) *Procès de Charles 1er.* L'Eikon Basilike; Apologie attribuée à Charles 1er. Mémoires de Charles II, sur la fuite après la bataille de Worcester. Paris, 1823.

COLLECTION DES MÉMOIRES RELATIFS À LA RÉVOLUTION FRANÇAISE. Avec des notes sur leurs auteurs et des éclaircissements historiques par MM. Berville et Barrière.

(1) ROLAND. *Mémoires de Madame Roland.* Paris, 1821.

(2) FERRIÈRES, C. E., MARQUIS DE. *Mémoires.* Paris, 1822.

(3) LINGUET; DUSAULX. *Mémoires de Linguet, sur la Bastille, et de Dusaulx, sur le 14 juillet.* Paris, 1821.

(4) BOUILLÉ, F. C. DE, MARQUIS. *Mémoires.* Paris, 1823.

(5) BESENVAL, P. V. DE, BARON. *Mémoires.* Paris, 1821.

(6) BAILLY. *Mémoires.* Paris, 1821-2.

(7) WEBER. *Mémoires de Weber, concernant Marie-Antoinette* . . . Paris, 1822.

(8) CHOISEUL, DUC DE. *Relation du départ de Louis XVI, le 20 juin 1791,* écrite en août 1791, dans la prison de la Haute Cour Nationale d'Orléans. Paris, 1822.

(9) BARBAROUX, C. *Mémoires.* Paris, 1822.

(10) DUMOURIEZ, GÉNÉRAL. *La Vie et les mémoires.* Paris, 1822-3.

(11) GOGUELAT, BARON. *Mémoire.* Paris, 1823.

(12) CAMPAN, MME. *Mémoires sur la vie privée de Marie-Antoinette, Reine de France et de Navarre.* Suivis de souvenirs et anecdotes historiques sur les règnes de Louis XIV, de Louis XV et de Louis XVI. Par Mme Campan, Lectrice de Mesdames, et première Femme de Chambre de la Reine. Paris, 1823.

(13) *Mémoires sur les journées de septembre 1792,* par M. Jourgniac de Saint-Méard, Mme la Marquise de Fausse-Lendry, l'abbé Sicard, et M. Gabriel-Aimé Jourdan . . . Paris, 1823.

(14) *Mémoires sur l'affaire de Varennes,* comprenant le Mémoire inédit de M. le Marquis de Bouillé (comte Louis); Deux Relations également inédites de MM. les Comtes de Raigecourt et de Damas, celle de M. le Capitaine Deslon, et le Précis historique de M. le Comte de Valory. Paris, 1823.

(15) BONCHAMPS, MARQUISE DE. *Mémoires.* Paris, 1823.

(16) *Mémoires sur les prisons.* Tome premier et tome second. Paris, 1823.

(17) LOUVET DE COUVRAY, J. B. *Mémoires.* Paris, 1823.

(18) MEILLAN. *Mémoires.* Paris, 1823.

(19) *Mémoires sur la Vendée,* comprenant les mémoires inédits d'un ancien administrateur militaire des armées républicaines, et ceux de Madame de Sapinaud. Paris, 1823.

(20) TURREAU, GÉNÉRAL. *Mémoires pour servir à l'histoire de la guerre de la Vendée.* Paris, 1824.

(21) ORLÉANS. L. A. P. D'. *Mémoires de S.A.S. L. A. P. d'Orléans, Duc de Montpensier, Prince du Sang.* Paris, 1824.

(22) GUILLON DE MONTLÉON, A. *Mémoires pour servir à l'histoire de la ville de Lyon pendant la Révolution.* Paris, 1824.

(23) FRÉRON. *Mémoire historique sur la Réaction Royale, et sur les massacres du Midi.* Paris, 1824.

(24) DOPPET, GÉNÉRAL. *Mémoires politiques et militaires.* Paris, 1824.

(25) *Mémoires historiques et militaires sur Carnot.* Paris, 1824.

(26) RIVAROL, A., COMTE DE. *Mémoires.* Paris, 1824.

(27) HAUSSET, MME. *Mémoires de Madame du Hausset,* Femme de Chambre de Madame de Pompadour. Paris, 1824.

(28) MAILLANE, DURAND. *Histoire de la Convention Nationale* . . . suivie d'un fragment historique sur le 31 mai, par le Comte Lanjuinais. Paris, 1825.

(29) EDGEWORTH, H. E. *Journal de Cléry,* suivi des dernières heures de Louis Seize; du récit des événemens arrivés au Temple, par Madame Royale, fille du roi. Paris, 1825.

(30) ARGENSON, R. L. D', MARQUIS. *Mémoires,* Paris. 1825.

(31) *Le Vieux Cordelier,* journal politique. Paris, 1825.

(32) THIBAUDEAU, A. C. *Mémoires sur la Convention, et le Directoire.* Paris, 1824.

(33) *Guerres des Vendéens et des Chouans contre la République Française,* ou Annales des départemens de l'ouest pendant ces guerres. Paris, 1824-1825.

(34) *Mémoires sur le dix-huitième siècle et sur la Révolution Française.* Paris, 1822.

Collection des poètes français modernes. Bruxelles, 1829.

COLNET, C. *L'Hermite de Belleville* ou Choix d'opuscules politiques, littéraires et satiriques. Paris, 1833.

Les Consolations. Poésies. Paris, 1830.

CONSTANT DE REBECQUE, B. *Adolphe.* Paris, 1824.

— *Collection complète des ouvrages publiés sur le gouvernement représentatif et la constitution actuelle de la France,* formant une espèce de cours de politique constitutionnelle. Paris, 1818-20.

— *Commentaire sur l'ouvrage de Filangieri.* Paris, 1822.

— *Du polythéisme romain,* considéré dans ses rapports avec la philosophie grecque et la religion chrétienne; ouvrage posthume de Benjamin Constant. Paris, 1833.

Les Contes du gay sçavoir. Ballades, fabliaux et traditions du moyen âge, publiés par Ferd. Langlé . . . Paris, 1823.

Contes inédits des Mille et Une Nuits. Extraits de l'original arabe par M. J. de Hammer. Paris, 1828.

Contes inédits des Mille et Une Nuits. Traduits en français par M. G.-S. Trébutien . . . Tome second. Paris, 1828.

Conversations-Lexikon der neuesten Zeit in Literatur. Leipzig, 1832-4.

COOK, J. *Voyages and Travels through the Russian Empire, Tartary, and Part of the Kingdom of Persia.* Edinburgh, 1770.

COOPER, J. F. *L'Heidenmauer,* ou Le Camp des païens, légende des bords du Rhin. Paris, 1832.

— *Œuvres.* Traduction de M. Defauconpret. Paris, 1830-5.

COQUEREL, C. *Essai sur l'histoire générale du christianisme.* Paris, 1828.

CORDIER. *Traité raisonné d'équitation,* en harmonie avec l'Ordonnance de Cavalerie, d'après les principes mis en pratique à l'École d'Application de Cavalerie. Paris, 1824.

CORMON, B. J. L. *Dictionnaire portatif et de prononciation, Espagnol-Français et Français-Espagnol,* à l'usage des deux nations. Lyon, 1803.

CORNEILLE, P. *Œuvres complètes.* Paris, 1834.

COURIER DE MÉRÉ, P. L. *Œuvres complètes.* Paris, 1829.

Le Cousin de Mahomet. Avec figures. Constantinople, 1770.

CRABBE, G. *The Poetical Works.* Complete in one volume. Paris, 1829.

CRAPELET, G. A. *Cérémonies des gages de bataille selon les constitutions du bon Roi Philippe de France.* Représentées en onze figures . . . Paris, 1830.

CRÉBILLON, P. *Œuvres.* Paris, 1821.

— *Collection complète des œuvres.* Londres, 1777.

CRÉQUY, A. L., MARQUISE DE. *Souvenirs de la Marquise De Créquy*. 1710 à 1800. Bruxelles, 1834-6.

CROC DE CHABANNES, MARQUIS DU. *Cours élémentaire et analytique d'équitation*. Paris, 1827.

CRUICKSHANK, G. *Punch and Judy*. With illustrations drawn and engraved by George Cruickshank. Accompanied by the dialogue of the Puppet-Show . . . London, 1828.

La Cuisinière bourgeoise, suivie de l'office, à l'usage de tous ceux qui se mêlent de la dépense des maisons. [Title-page lost.]

CUNNINGHAM, A. *Notice biographique et littéraire sur Sir Walter Scott* . . . Traduite par A. J. B. Defauconpret. Paris, 1833.

CUVIER, G., BARON. *Discours sur les révolutions de la surface du globe*, et sur les changemens qu'elles ont produits dans le règne animal. Paris, 1828.

CUZEY, CHEVALIER DE. *Le Comte de Reding*. Tragédie. Paris, 1826.

CZERNICHEW, G., COMTE. *Théâtre de l'Arsenal de Gatchina*, ou Recueil de pièces de société. St-Pétersbourg, 1821.

DANGEAU, P., MARQUIS DE. *Mémoires et Journal*. Paris, 1830.

DANTE ALIGHIERI. *L'Enfer*. Traduit en français par M. Chevalier A. F. Artaud, Paris. 1828.

La Purgatoire. Traduit en français par M. Chevalier A. F. Artaud. Paris, 1830.

— *Le Paradis*. Traduit en français par M. Chevalier A. F. Artaud. Paris, 1830.

— *La Comédie de Dante*, de l'Enfer, du Purgatoire & Paradis, mise en ryme françoise et commentée par M. B. Grangier. Paris, 1596.

— *La Divine Comédie*. Traduite en vers français par M. Antoni Deschamps. Paris, 1829.

— *Opere poetiche* con note de diversi per diligenza e studio di Antonio Buttura. Tomo secundo. Parigi, 1823.

Débats de la Convention Nationale, ou Analyse complète des séances. Paris, 1828.

DEFOE, DANIEL. *The History of the Great Plague in London in the Year 1665*. London, [1832?].

— *Robinson Crusoé*. Traduction de Petrus Bobel. Enrichi de la vie de Daniel De Foë, par Philarète Chasles . . . Paris, 1836.

— *The Life and Adventures of Robinson Crusoe*. London, 1831.

DELANNEAU, P. A. *Dictionnaire de poche Latin-Français*. Paris, 1829.

DELAVIGNE, C. *Sept Messéniennes nouvelles*. Paris, 1827.

De l'esprit. Amsterdam, 1776.

DELILLE, J., ABBÉ. *Œuvres complètes*. Bruxelles, 1817-18.

DELORME, J. (pseud. of Sainte-Beuve). *Vie, poésies et pensées de Joseph Delorme*. Paris, 1829; Paris, 1830.

DEPPING, G. B. *Coleccion de los mas célebres romances antiguos españoles* históricos y caballerescos publicada por G. B. Depping y ahora considerablemente emméndada por un español refugiado (i.e. Vicente Salva). Londres, 1825.

Dernières Paroles. Poésies. Paris, 1835.

DÉSAUGIERS, M. A. *Chansons et poésies diverses*. Bruxelles, 1833.

Description du Pachalik de Bagdad, suivie d'une notice historique sur les

Wahabis, et de quelques autres pièces relatives à l'histoire et à la littérature de l'Orient. Par M. . . . Paris, 1809.

DES ESSARTS, N. T., LE MOINE. *Procès fameux.* Extraits de l'essai sur l'histoire générale des tribunaux des peuples tant anciens que modernes. Paris, 1786.

DESLANDES, L. *De l'onanisme* et des autres abus vénériens considérés dans leurs rapports avec la santé. Bruxelles, 1835.

DESPÉRIERS, B. *Cymbalum mundi,* ou Dialogues satyriques sur différens sujets. Amsterdam, 1753.

DEUTZ, S. *Arrestation de Madame.* Bruxelles, 1835.

DEZOBRY, L. C. *Rome au siècle d'Auguste,* ou Voyage d'un Gaulois à Rome à l'époque du règne d'Auguste et pendant une partie du règne de Tibère. Paris, 1835.

Dialoghetti sulle materie correnti dell'anno 1831. [Roma, 1833.]

Dictionnaire Anglais-Français, et Français-Anglais, abrégé de Boyer. Paris, 1831.

Dictionnaire critique et raisonné du langage vicieux ou réputé vicieux. Ouvrage pouvant servir de complément au Dictionnaire des difficultés de la langue française, par Laveaux; par un ancien professeur. Paris, 1835.

Dictionnaire d'anecdotes, de traits singuliers et caractéristiques, historiettes, bon mots, naïvetés, saillies, reparties ingénieuses, etc. etc. Riom, 1808.

Dictionnaire de l'Académie Française. Paris, 1835

Dictionnaire des proverbes français. Paris, 1821.

Dictionnaire historique des anecdotes de l'amour . . . Paris, 1832.

DIDEROT, D. *Œuvres.* Paris. 1821.

— *Œuvres inédites de Diderot.* Précédées d'un fragment sur les ouvrages de l'auteur, par Goethe . . . Paris, 1821.

DIDEROT, D. *Mémoires, correspondance et ouvrages inédits de Diderot.* Publiés d'après les manuscrits confiés, en mourant, par l'auteur à Grimm. Paris, 1830-1.

DIDIER, C. *Rome souterraine.* Bruxelles, 1834.

Dodécation ou le Livre des douze. Paris, 1837.

DOHNA, C., COMTE. *Mémoires originaux sur le règne et la cour de Frédéric I, Roi de Prusse.* Berlin, 1833.

DUCLOS, C. *Œuvres* Paris, 1820-1.

DUCOR, H. *Aventures d'un marin de la garde impériale,* prisonnier de guerre sur les pontons espagnols, dans l'Île de Cabréra et en Russie; pour faire suite à l'histoire de la campagne de 1812. Bruxelles, 1834.

DUFEY, P. J. S. *Histoire des Communes de France et Législation Municipale,* depuis la fin du XIe siècle jusqu'à nos jours. Paris, 1828.

DUFOUR, M. A. *Le Globe.* Atlas classique universel de géographie ancienne et moderne. Paris, 1830.

DUMAS, ADOLPHE. *Les Parisiennes.* Chant de la Révolution de 1830. Paris.

DUMAS, ALEXANDRE. *Don Juan de Marana ou la Chute d'un ange.* Mystère en cinq actes. Paris, 1836.

DUMESNIL, A. *Histoire de Philippe II, Roi d'Espagne.* Paris, 1824.

DUMONT, É. *Souvenirs sur Mirabeau et sur les deux premières assemblées législatives.* Bruxelles, 1832.

Du Pape. Par l'auteur des Considérations sur la France. Lyon, 1821.

DUQUESNEL, A. *Histoire des lettres avant le christianisme.* Cours de littérature. Paris, 1836.

E. A. *Vie d'Alexandre 1er, Empereur de Russie* . . . Paris, 1826.

ECKSTEIN, F. DE, BARON. *De l'Espagne.* Considérations sur son passé, son présent, son avenir. Paris, 1836.

EICHOFF, F. G. *Parallèle des langues de l'Europe et de l'Inde.* Paris, 1836.

Éloge historique de Catherine II, Impératrice de Russie. Londres, 1776.

Encyclopédie des gens du monde. Répertoire universel des sciences, des lettres et des arts. Paris, 1833-6.

ÉON DE BEAUMONT, CHEVALIER D'. *Les Loisirs du Chevalier D'Éon de Beaumont.* Amsterdam, 1774.

ÉPINAY, LOUISE F. P. DE LA LIVE D'. *Mémoires et correspondance* de Madame d'Épinay. Où elle donne des détails sur ses liaisons avec Duclos, J.-J. Rousseau, Grimm, Diderot, le baron d'Holbach, Saint-Lambert, Mme d'Houdetot, et autres personnages célèbres du dix-huitième siècle. Paris, 1818.

Errotika Biblion. Rome. De l'Imprimerie du Vatican, 1783.

ESCOUSSE, V. *Farruck le Maure.* Drame en trois actes et en vers. Paris, 1831.

L'Espion turc dans les cours des princes chrétiens, ou Lettres et mémoires d'un envoyé secret de la Porte dans les cours de l'Europe. Londres, 1742.

Essai historique sur le commerce et la navigation de la Mer-Noire . . . Paris, 1805.

Essais historiques sur la vie de Marie Antoinette, Reine de France, pour servir à l'histoire de cette Princesse. Londres, 1789.

FABRE D'OLIVET, A. *Les vers dorés de Pythagore.* Expliqués, et traduits pour la première fois en vers eumolpiques français; précédés d'un discours sur l'essence et la forme de la poésie, chez les principaux peuples de la terre. Paris, 1813.

Fairy Legends and Traditions of the South of Ireland. London, 1834.

FÉNELON, F. *Œuvres,* Paris, 1835.

FERLET, E., ABBÉ. *Observations littéraires, critiques, politiques, militaires, géographiques, etc., sur les Histoires de Tacite.* Paris, 1801.

Fêtes et courtisanes de la Grèce. Supplément aux Voyages d'Annacharsis et d'Antenor. Paris, 1821.

FICHTE, J. G. *Destination de l'homme.* Traduit de l'allemand par Barchou de Penhoën. Paris, 1832.

FLETCHER, J. *Histoire de Pologne.* Traduite de l'anglais, et continuée depuis la Révolution de Novembre 1830, jusqu'à la prise de Varsovie et la fin de la guerre. Paris, 1832.

FONTANIER, V. *Voyages en Orient, entrepris par ordre du Gouvernement Français,* de l'année 1821 à l'année 1829. Paris, 1829.

— *Voyages en Orient, entrepris par ordre du Gouvernement Français,* de 1830 à 1833 . . . Deuxième Voyage en Anatolie. Paris, 1834.

FONTENELLE, B. LE B. DE. *Œuvres.* Paris, 1761; 1766-7; 1767.

FONTENELLE, JULIA DE. *Recherches médico-légales sur l'incertitude des signes de la mort,* les dangers des inhumations précipitées, les moyens de constater les décès et de rappeler à la vie ceux qui sont en état de mort apparente. Paris, 1834.

FORGES DE PARNY, E. D. DE, VICOMTE. *Porte-Feuille volé*, contenant: 1. Le Paradis perdu, poème en quatre chants; 2. Les Déguisemens de Vénus, tableaux imités du grec; 3. Les Galanteries de la Bible, sermon en vers. Paris, 1805.

FORTIS, ABBÉ. *Voyage en Dalmatie*. Berne, 1778.

FOUGEROUX DE CAMPIGNEULLES. *Histoires des duels anciens et modernes*, contenant le tableau de l'origine, des progrès et de l'esprit du duel en France et dans toutes les parties du monde. Genève, 1835.

FOX, C. J. *Histoire des deux derniers rois de la Maison de Stuart*. Paris, 1809.

FRANKLAND, C. *Narrative of a Visit to the Courts of Russia and Sweden*, in the years 1830 and 1831. London, 1832.

FRANKLIN, B. *Mélanges de morale, d'économie, et de politique*. Extraits des ouvrages de Benjamin Franklin. Paris, 1826.

FRÉDÉRIC II, ROI DE PRUSSE. *Correspondance familière et amicale de Frédéric Second, Roi de Prusse, avec U. F. de Suhm*. Genève, 1787.

FROULLAI, M. J. B. R. DE, COMTE DE TESSÉ. *Mémoires et lettres du Maréchal de Tessé*, contenant des anecdotes et des faits historiques inconnus, sur partie des règnes de Louis XIV et de Louis XV. Paris, 1806.

GALIANI, F., ABBÉ. *Correspondance inédite*. Paris, 1818.

GALITZINE, PRINCESSE EUDOXIE. *De l'analyse de la force*. St-Pétersbourg, 1835.

GALT, J. *The Autobiography*. London, 1833.

GARAT, D. J. *Mémoires historiques sur la vie de M. Suard, sur ses écrits, et sur le XVIIIe siècle*. Paris, 1820.

GASTE, L. F. *Abrégé de l'histoire de la médecine considérée comme science et comme art dans ses progrès et son exercice*, depuis son origine jusqu'au dix-neuvième siècle. Paris, 1835.

GATTEL, ABATE. *Nuevo Diccionario portatil Español y Frances*. Paris, 1806.

GATTEL, CAPMANY, ET NUNEZ DE TABOADA. *Nouveau Dictionnaire de poche Français-Espagnol*. Paris, 1825.

GAUME, J., ABBÉ. *Du catholicisme dans l'éducation*, ou L'Unique Moyen de sauver la science et la société. Paris, 1835.

GÉRAUD, E. *Poésies diverses*. Paris, 1822.

Germanicus. Tragi-Comédie. Leyde.

Bound with the following other works:

Les Frayeurs de Crispin. Comédie par le S-r C. [Samuel Chappuzeau]. Leyde, 1682.

Le Mariage de la reine de Monomotapa. Comédie [par Belisle]. Leyde, 1682.

Arlequin, comédien aux Champs Élisées. Nouvelle historique, allégorique et comique. [Par Laurent Bordelon.] La Haye, 1694.

La Parisienne. Comédie de Mr [F. Carton] Dancourt. La Haye, 1694.

Le Muët. Par Mr [J.] Palaprat. La Haye, 1694.

Le Grondeur. Comédie par Mr Palaprat. La Haye, 1694.

L'Important de cour. Comédie par Mr de Palaprat. Paris, 1695.

GHERARDI, E. *Le Théâtre italien de Gherardi*, ou Le Recueil général de toutes les comédies et scènes françoises jouées par les comédiens italiens du roi pendant tout le temps qu'ils ont été au service. Paris, 1717.

GIBBON, E. *Histoire de la décadence et de la chute de l'Empire Romain.* Traduite de l'anglais . . . par M. F. Guizot. Paris, 1828.

— *Mémoires de Gibbon.* Suivis de quelques ouvrages posthumes et de quelques lettres du même auteur. Paris, 1793.

GILCHRIST, J. *Collection of Ancient and Modern Scottish Ballads, Tales, and Songs.* Edinburgh, 1815.

GINGUÉNÉ, P. L. *Histoire littéraire de l'Italie.* Paris, 1811-19.

GODWIN, W. *Les Choses comme elles sont,* ou Les Aventures de Caleb Williams. Lausanne, 1796.

— *Lives of the Necromancers,* or an account of the eminent persons in successive ages, who have claimed for themselves, or to whom has been imputed by others, the exercise of magical power. London, 1834.

GOETZ, P. VON, *Serbische Volkslieder.* St Petersburg, 1827.

GRAFIGNY, FRANÇOISE P. HUGUET DE. *Vie privée de Voltaire et de Mme du Châtelet,* pendant un séjour de six mois à Cirey. Paris, 1820.

GRAINVILLE, J. B. F. X. *Le Dernier Homme.* Paris, 1805.

Grammatyka dla szkol narodowych na klasse II. Krakowie, 1794.

GRANGERET DE LAGRANGE. *Anthologie arabe,* ou Choix de poésies arabes inédites. Paris, 1828.

GRATTAN, T. C. *The Heiress of Bruges.* A tale of the year sixteen hundred. London, 1831.

GRÉCOURT, J. B. J. W. DE. *Œuvres diverses.* Londres. [Berlin.]

GRESSET, J. B. L. *Œuvres complètes.* Paris, 1823.

GRIMM, F. M. VON, BARON. *Correspondance littéraire, philosophique et critique de Grimm et de Diderot,* depuis 1753 jusqu'en 1790. Paris, 1829-31.

— *Correspondance inédite de Grimm et de Diderot,* et recueil de lettres, poésies, morceaux et fragmens retranchés par la Censure Impériale en 1812 et 1813. Paris, 1829.

GUDIN DE LA BRENELLERIE, P. P. *Contes.* Précédés de recherches sur l'origine des contes. Paris, 1804.

GUIRAUD, A. *Flavien,* ou De Rome au désert. Paris, 1835.

GUIZOT, F. P. G. *Cours d'histoire moderne* . . . Histoire générale de la civilisation en Europe depuis la chute de l'Empire Romain jusqu'à la Révolution Française. Paris, 1828.

— *Cours d'histoire moderne* . . . Histoire de la civilisation en France depuis la chute de l'Empire Romain jusqu'en 1789. Paris, 1829-32.

Gulistan, ou Le Parterre-de-Fleurs du Cheikh Moslih-Eddin Sadi de Chiraz, traduit . . . par N. Semelet. Paris, 1834.

GUROWSKI, A., COMTE. *La Vérité sur la Russie et sur la révolte des Provinces Polonaises.* Paris, 1834.

GUTHRIE, M. *Dissertations sur les antiquités de Russie.* St-Pétersbourg, 1795.

HALÉVY, L. *Le Czar Démétrius.* Tragédie en cinq actes et en vers. Paris, 1829.

HALL, B. *Mémoires et voyages.* Bruxelles, 1834.

— *Schloss Hainfeld,* ou Un Hiver dans la Basse-Styrie. Paris, 1836.

HALLAM, H. *L'Europe au moyen âge.* Traduit de l'anglais . . . par M. M. P. Dudouit. Paris, 1828.

HAMILTON, COMTE. *Œuvres.* Paris, 1825.

HAMILTON, COLONEL. *Les Hommes et les mœurs aux États-Unis d'Amérique*. Paris, 1834.

HANKA, V. *Slovo o plku Igorevie*. Praze, 1821.

— *Prawopis Česky*. Praze. 1835.

HARRIS, T. M. *A Dictionary of the Natural History of the Bible*. London, 1833.

HARTSHORNE, C. H. *Ancient Metrical Tales Printed Chiefly from Original Sources*. London, 1829.

HAZLITT, W. *The Spirit of the Age; or Contemporary Portraits*. Paris, 1825.

— *Table-Talk; or Original Essays*. Paris, 1825.

HEEREN, A. H. L. *Manuel de l'histoire ancienne*, considérée sous le rapport des constitutions, du commerce et des colonies des divers états de l'antiquité. Paris, 1836.

HEINE, H. *Œuvres*. Paris, 1834-5.

— *De la France*. Paris, 1833.

HENNEQUIN, P. *Matinées d'un Dandy*. Imité de l'anglais. Paris, 1833.

HENRION, M. R. A. *Histoire de la Papauté*. Paris, 1832.

HÉRODOTE. *Histoire d'Hérodote*, suivie de la vie d'Homère. Nouvelle traduction, par A. F. Miot. Paris, 1822.

HERSCHEL, J. F. W. *Traité d'astronomie*. Traduit . . . par Augustin Cournot. Bruxelles, 1835.

— *Publication complète des nouvelles découvertes de Sir John Herschel dans le ciel austral et dans la lune*. Paris, 1836.

Les Heureux Orphelins. Histoire imitée de l'anglois.

HIPPOCRATE. *Nouvelle traduction des Aphorismes d'Hippocrate*, conférés sur l'édition grecque publiée en 1811 . . . par M. le chevalier De Mercy, Paris, 1817.

Histoire de Cicéron. Tirée de ses écrits et des monumens de son siècle. Amsterdam, 1784-5.

Histoire de l'assassinat de Gustave III, roi de Suède. Paris, 1797.

Histoire de la vie et des ouvrages de J.-J. Rousseau. Paris, 1821.

Histoire de Pierre I surnommé le Grand. [In two different editions.] Amsterdam et Leipzig, 1742.

Histoire des campagnes du Comte Alexandre Suworow Rymnickski. Londres, 1799.

L'Histoire des Grecs, ou de Ceux qui corrigent la fortune au jeu. Londres, 1758.

The History of the Bucaneers of America, being An Entertaining Narrative of the Exploits, Cruelties and Sufferings of the following noted Commanders Viz. Joseph Esquemeling, Pierre le Grand, Lolonois, Roche Brasiliano, Bat the Portuguese, Capt. Sharp, Capt. Walting, Cap. Cook &c Together with A Curious Description of the Manners, Customs, Dress and Ceremonies of the Indians inhabiting near Cape Gracias a Dios. Published for the Improvement and Entertainment of the British Youth of both Sexes. Glasgow, 1785.

The History and Lives of all the most Notorious Pirates and their Crews, from Captain Avery, who first settled at Madagascar to Captain John Grow and James Williams, his Lieutenant. . . . Giving a more full and true Account than any yet published of all their Murders, Piracies, Maroonings, Places of Refuge and Way of Living. To which is prefixed An Abstract of the Laws against Piracy. Glasgow, 1788.

HOBBES, T. *De la nature humaine*, ou Exposition des facultés, des actions & des passions de *l'Âme*, & de leurs causes déduites d'après des principes philosophiques qui ne sont communément ni reçus ni connus. Londres, 1772.

HOFFMANN, E. T. W. (Amédée). *Contes et fantaisies.* Bruxelles, 1834.

— *Œuvres complètes.* Paris, 1830-3.

HOMÈRE. *Œuvres complètes.* Traduites en français par Bitaubé. Paris, 1829.

— *Homeri Odyssea.* Glasguae, 1819.

HORACE. *Œuvres complètes.* Traduites en vers par P. Daru. Paris, 1816.

— *Traduction des Œuvres d'Horace.* Par M. René Binet. Paris, 1816.

HUGO, VICTOR. *Angelo*, Tyran de Padoue. Drame. Bruxelles, 1835.

— *Cromwell.* Drame. Paris, 1828.

— *Littérature et philosophie mêlées.* Bruxelles, 1834.

— *Marion de Lorme.* Drame. Paris, 1831.

— *Notre-Dame de Paris.* Tome premier. Bruxelles, 1832.

— *Odes.* Paris, 1827.

— *Œuvres complètes.* Poésie. V. Les Chants du crépuscule. Paris, 1835.

— *Œuvres.* Drames. V. Lucrèce Borgia. Paris, 1833.

— *Les Orientales.* Paris, 1829.

— *Le Roi s'amuse.* Drame. Bruxelles, 1833.

HUNT, J. H. L. *Lord Byron and some of his contemporaries.* With recollections of the author's life, and of his visit to Italy. London, 1828.

HURWITZ, H. *The Elements of the Hebrew Language.* London, 1829.

IMBERT, B. *Historiettes ou Nouvelles en vers.* Amsterdam, 1774.

IRVING, W. *Abbotsford and Newstead Abbey.* Paris, 1835.

— *Histoire des voyages et découvertes des compagnons de Christophe Colomb*, etc. Paris, 1833.

— *Esquisses morales et littéraires*, ou Observations sur les mœurs, les usages et la littérature des Anglois et des Américains. Paris, 1822.

— *Les Contes de l'Alhambra*, précédés d'un voyage dans la province de Grenade. Paris, 1832.

— *Histoire de la vie et des voyages de Christophe Colomb.* Paris, 1828.

— *Legends of the Conquest of Spain.* Paris, 1836.

ISOCRATE. *Œuvres complettes.* Paris, 1781.

ITESA MODEEN, M. *Shigurf Namah-i-velaët;* or Excellent Intelligence concerning Europe: being the Travels of Mirza Itesa Modeen in Great Britain and France. Translated from the original Persian Manuscript by James Edward Alexander, Esq. London, 1827.

[IZUARD DELISLE, J. B. C.] *La Bardinade* ou les Noces de la stupidité. Poème. 1765.

JACQUEMONT, V. *Correspondance de Victor Jacquemont avec sa famille et plusieurs de ses amis,* pendant son voyage dans l'Inde (1828-32). Paris, 1833.

JAL, A. *Scènes de la vie maritime.* Paris, 1832.

JAMERAY DUVAL, V. *Œuvres.* Londres, 1785.

JANIN, J. G. *L'Âne mort et la femme guillotinée.* Paris, 1829.

— *Paris depuis la Révolution de 1830.* Bruxelles, 1832.

JANIN, J. G. *Contes fantastiques et contes littéraires.* Tome I. Bruxelles, 1833.
— *Le Chemin de traverse.* Paris, 1836.
JOHNSON, S. *The Lives of the English poets.* London, 1826.
JOMINI, BARON. *Tableau analytique des principales combinaisons de la guerre et de leurs rapports avec la politique des états.* Bruxelles, 1831; St-Pétersbourg, 1836.
— *Histoire critique et militaire des guerres de la Révolution.* Paris, 1820.
JOSSE, A. L. *Nouvelle grammaire espagnole raisonnée* . . . Paris, 1809.
JULIEN, EMPEREUR. *Œuvres complètes de l'Empereur Julien.* Traduites pour la première fois du grec en français . . . par E. Tourlet. Paris, 1821.
JUNGER, J. F. *Marianne et Charlotte,* ou L'Apparence est trompeuse. Paris, 1795.
JUSSIEU, L. DE. *Simon de Nantua,* ou Le Marchand forain, suivi des œuvres posthumes de Simon de Nantua. Paris, 1832.
JUVÉNAL. D. J. *Satires.* Traduites en vers français . . . par V. Fabre de Narbonne. Paris, 1825.
— *Satires.* Traduites par J. Dusaulx. Paris, 1825.
KARADZIC, V. S. *Wolf Stephansohn's Serbisch-Deutsch-Lateinisches Wörterbuch.* Vienna, 1818.
— *Volkslieder der Serben Metrisch,* übersetzt und historisch eingeleitet von Talvj. Halle, 1825-6.
— *Chants populaires des Serviens* . . . Traduits, d'après Talvj, par Mme Élise Voiart. Paris, 1834.
KARR, A. *Le Chemin le plus court.* Paris, 1836.
— *Une Heure trop tard.* Bruxelles, 1833.
— *Vendredi Soir.* Paris, 1835.
KÉRALIO, L. F. *Histoire de la dernière guerre entre les Russes et les Turcs.* Paris, 1777.
KNICKERBOCKER, D. *Histoire de New-York,* depuis le commencement du monde jusqu'à la fin de la domination hollandaise, contenant, entre autres choses curieuses et surprenantes, les innombrables hésitations de Walter l'Indécis, les plans désastreux de William-le-Bourru, et les exploits chevaleresques de Pierre-Fort-Tête, les trois gouverneurs de New-Amsterdam. Paris, 1827.
KOBERSTEIN, A. *Manuel de l'histoire de la littérature nationale allemande.* Paris, 1834.
Koran. Traduit de l'arabe . . . par M. Savay. Paris, 1828.
KORDJAN. *Część pierwsza trilogji.* Spisek Koronacyjny. Paryż, 1834.
KOTZEBUE, A. *L'Année la plus remarquable de ma vie.* Suivie d'une Réfutation des mémoires secrets sur la Russie. Paris, 1802.
KOZLOFF, I. I. *Il Monaco.* Poema di Kozloff, tradotto dal Russo in Italiano da C. Boccella. Pisa, 1835.
[KRUEDENER, B. J. VON, BARONNE.] *Valérie,* ou Lettres de Gustave de Linar à Ernest de G. . . . Paris, 1804.
KUPFFER, A. T. *Voyage dans L'Oural,* entrepris en 1828 par A. The. Kupffer. Paris, 1733.
LA BEAUMELLE, L. DE. *Lettres de Monsieur De La Beaumelle à M. De Voltaire.* Londres, 1763.

LA BRUYÈRE, J. DE. *Œuvres*. Paris, 1820.

—; LA ROCHEFOUCAULD, F. DE; VAUVENARGUES, L. DE CLAPIERS, MARQUIS DE. *Œuvres de La Bruyère, de La Rochefoucauld et de Vauvenargues*. Paris, 1826.

LACENAIRE, P. F. *Mémoires, révélations et poésies de Lacenaire écrits par lui-même à la Conciergerie*. Paris, 1836.

LACROIX, S. F. *Traité élémentaire du calcul des probabilités*. Paris, 1822.

LA FONTAINE, J. DE. *Fables choisies mises en vers*. Paris, 1785.

— *Œuvres complètes*. Paris, 1826.

— *Œuvres*. Paris, 1826-7.

LA HARPE, J. F. DE. *Lycée ou cours de littérature ancienne et moderne*. Paris, 1834.

— *Œuvres diverses*. Paris, 1820-6.

— *Œuvres*. Paris, 1820.

LAMARTINE, A. DE. *Jocelyn*. Épisode. Journal trouvé chez un curé de village. Paris, 1836.

— *Souvenirs, impressions, pensées et paysages, pendant un voyage en Orient (1832-1833)*, ou Notes d'un voyageur. Paris, 1835.

LAMB, CAROLINE, LADY. *Glenarvon*. [A novel.] London, 1816. [Published anonymously.]

LAMB, C. *Tales from Shakespeare*. Designed for the use of young persons. London, 1831.

LAMENNAIS, H. F. DE. *Seconds Mélanges*. Paris, 1835.

LANDON, L. E. *The Poetical Works of L.E.L.* A new edition. London, [1830?].

LAPLACE, P. S., MARQUIS DE. *Essai philosophique sur les probabilités*. Paris, 1825.

LA ROCHEFOUCAULD, F. DE, DUC. *Maximes et réflexions morales*. Paris, 1802.

— *Mémoires*. Paris, 1804.

LAS CASES, M. J. E. A. D., COMTE DE. *Mémorial de Sainte-Hélène*, ou Journal où se trouve, consigné jour par jour, ce qu'a dit et fait Napoléon durant dix-huit mois. Bruxelles, 1823-4.

— *Suite au Mémorial de Sainte-Hélène*. Bruxelles, 1824-5.

LATOUCHE, H. DE. *Vallée aux loups*. Souvenirs et fantaisies. Paris, 1833.

LAVATER, J. G. *L'Art de connaître les hommes par la physionomie*. Paris, 1820.

LE BAILLY, A. F. *Fables*. Paris, 1823.

LEBASSU, JOSÉPHINE. *La Saint-Simonienne*. Paris, 1833.

LE BLANC, ABBÉ. *Lettres de monsieur l'Abbé Le Blanc*, historiographe des bâtimens du Roi. Lyon, 1758.

LE CLERC. *Histoire physique, morale, civile et politique de la Russie ancienne*. Paris, 1783. [2 copies.]

LEFÈVRE, J. *Sir Lionel D'Arquenay*. Paris, 1834.

LEFRANC, E. *Grammaire latine*. Paris, 1826.

LEGRAND D'AUSSY, P. J. B. *Fabliaux ou contes*. Fables et romans du XIIe et du XIIIe siècle, traduits ou extraits par Legrand D'Aussy. Paris, 1829.

LEIBNITZ, G. W. *Essais de Théodicée sur la bonté de Dieu, la liberté de l'homme, & l'origine du mal*. Lausanne, 1760.

— *Pensées de Leibniz sur la religion et la morale*. Paris, 1803.

LÉMONTEY, P. E. *Histoire de la régence et de la minorité de Louis XV jusqu'au ministère du Cardinal de Fleury.* Paris, 1832.

— *Essai sur l'établissement monarchique de Louis XIV,* et sur les altérations qu'il éprouva pendant la vie de ce prince. Morceau servant d'introduction à une Histoire critique de la France, depuis la mort de Louis XIV; précédé de nouveaux mémoires de Dangeau . . . Paris, 1818.

LEPRINCE DE BEAUMONT, MARIE. *Magasin des enfans,* ou Dialogues d'une sage gouvernante avec ses élèves. Paris, 1797.

LERMINIER, E. *Au-delà du Rhin.* Bruxelles, 1835.

— *De l'influence de la philosophie du XVIIIe siècle sur la législation et la sociabilité du XIXe.* Bruxelles, 1834.

— *Études d'histoire et de philosophie.* Paris, 1836.

— *Lettres philosophiques adressées à un Berlinois.* Paris, 1832.

LESUR, C. L. *Histoire des Kosaques,* précédée d'une introduction ou coup-d'œil sur les peuples qui ont habité le pays des kosaques, avant l'invasion des tartares. Paris, 1814.

Lettre au principal rédacteur du Journal des Débats, en réponse aux articles publiées par ce journal, sur le discours de l'Empereur de Russie à la députation de Varsovie. [Paris, 1835.]

LEURET, F. *Fragments psychologiques sur la folie.* Paris, 1834.

LEVESQUE, P. C. *Histoire des différents peuples soumis à la domination des Russes,* ou suite de l'Histoire de Russie. Paris, 1783.

LEWIS, M. G. *Journal of a West India Proprietor,* kept during a Residence in the Island of Jamaica. London, 1834.

LICQUET, TH. *Histoire de Normandie depuis les temps les plus reculés jusqu'à la conquête de l'Angleterre en 1066.* Rouen, 1835.

LIEMAN, AMALIE. *Amalien's von Lieman,* eines eilfjährigen Frauenzimmers Reisen durch einige russische Länder. Göttingen, 1794.

LIGNE, C. J., PRINCE DE. *Lettres et pensées du Maréchal Prince De Ligne,* publiées par Mad. la Baronne de Staël-Holstein. Paris, 1810.

— *Mémoires et mélanges historiques et littéraires.* Paris, 1827-8.

LIMES, J. M. *Les Halieutiques,* traduit du grec du Poème d'Oppien, où il traite de la pêche et des mœurs des habitans des eaux. Paris, 1817.

LINDE, M. S. B. *Słownik języka Polskiego.* Warszawa, 1807.

LINGUET, S. N. H. *Histoire du siècle d'Alexandre.* Amsterdam, 1769.

[LOEVE-VEIMARS, F. A., BARON.] *La Vie de E. T. A. Hoffmann.* Paris, 1833.

LOEVE-VEIMARS, F. A., BARON. *Résumé de l'histoire de la littérature allemande.* Paris, 1826.

LONGCHAMP ET WAGNIÈRE. *Mémoires sur Voltaire, et sur ses ouvrages,* par Longchamp et Wagnière, ses secrétaires. Paris, 1826.

LOUVET DE COUVRAY, J. B. *Vie du Chevalier de Faublas.* Paris, 1813.

LUC, J. A. *Éclaircissemens sur l'Apocalypse et sur l'Épître aux Hébreux,* ou Analyse de leur composition. Genève, 1832.

LUCIEN. *Lucien.* De la traduction de N. Perrot, S-r D'Ablancourt. Amsterdam, 1664.

LUDWIG VON BAYERN, KÖNIG. *Gedichte.* München, 1829.

LUTHER, M. *Mémoires de Luther écrits par lui-même.* Traduits et mis en ordre par M. Michelet. Paris, 1835.

MACCARTHY, J. *Nouveau Dictionnaire géographique universel.* Paris, 1824.

MACFARLANE, C. *Aventures et exploits des bandits et brigands de tous les pays du monde.* Paris, 1834.

MACHIAVEL, N. *Œuvres complètes de Machiavel.* Traduites par J. V. Périès. Paris, 1823-6.

— *Machiavel, ou Morceaux choisis et pensées de cet écrivain* sur la politique, la législation, la morale, l'histoire et l'art militaire; précédés d'un essai sur Machiavel. On y a joint une traduction nouvelle et complète du Prince. Par M-r Léon H. . . . Paris, 1823.

MACPHERSON, J. *The Poems of Ossian translated by James Macpherson Esq.* To which are prefixed a preliminary discourse, and dissertations on the œra and poems of Ossian. London, 1825.

Magazin des fées, ou Contes de fées de Perrault, de M-me Le-prince de Beaumont, de Fénelon, et de Madame d'Aulnoy. Paris, 1836.

MAISTRE, J. DE, COMTE. *Considérations sur la France.* Lyon, 1834.

— *Les Soirées de Saint-Pétersbourg,* ou Entretiens sur le gouvernement temporel de la providence; suivis d'un traité sur les sacrifices. Lyon, 1831.

MALCOLM, J. *Histoire de la Perse,* depuis les tems les plus anciens jusqu'à l'époque actuelle. Paris, 1821.

MALFILÂTRE, J. C. L. DE. *Poésies.* Paris, 1825.

MALTE-BRUN, V. A. *Précis de la géographie universelle.* Bruxelles, 1829.

— *Atlas universel de géographie ancienne et moderne.* Bruxelles, 1829.

MANGENOT, L., ABBÉ. *Poésies.* Maestricht, 1776.

MANSTEIN, LE GÉNÉRAL DE. *Mémoires historiques, politiques et militaires sur la Russie.* Lyon, 1772.

MANZONI, A. *Sulla morale Cattolica osservazioni di Alessandro Manzoni.* Parigi, 1834.

MARGERET, J. *Estat de l'Empire de Russie et Grand Duché de Moscovie.* Paris, 1679.

MARGUERITE DE VALOIS. *Contes et nouvelles* de Marguerite de Valois, Reine de Navarre. La Haye, 1775.

Marie. Roman. Paris, 1832.

MARLÈS, DE. *Pierre de Lara,* ou l'Espagne au XIe siècle. Paris, 1825.

MARMIER, X. *Études sur Goethe.* Paris, 1835.

MARMONTEL, J. F. *Œuvres complètes.* Paris, 1818-19.

— *Œuvres posthumes.* Paris, 1820.

MAROT, C. *Œuvres complètes.* Paris, 1824.

MARTIALIS, M. V. *Épigrammes de M. Val. Martial,* latines et françoises. Paphos.

MARTIGNAC, J. B. S., VICOMTE DE. *Le Couvent de Sainte-Marie au Bois.* Épisode. Précédé d'une notice sur la guerre d'Espagne en 1823. Paris, 1831.

MARTIN, L. A. *De l'éducation des mères de famille,* ou de la civilisation du genre humain par les femmes. Bruxelles, 1833.

MARTINEAU, HARRIET. *Contes de Miss Harriet Martineau sur l'économie politique.* Traduits . . . par M. B. Maurice. Bruxelles, 1834.

MARTINELLI, G. *Nuovo Dizionario portatile, Italiano-Francese.* Parigi, 1797.

Le Masque de fer, ou Les Aventures admirables du père et du fils. La Haye, 1785.

MATURIN, R. C. *Bertram, or the castle of St Aldobrand*. A tragedy in five acts. Paris, 1828.

— *Melmoth the Wanderer*. A tale. Edinburgh, 1820

Mazaniello, ou La Révolution de Naples. Tragédie en cinq actes et en vers.

MEDWIN, T. *The Shelley Papers*. Memoir of Percy Bysshe Shelley by T. Medwin, Esq. and Original Poems and Papers by Percy Bysshe Shelley. London, 1833.

— *Conversations of Lord Byron*. Noted during a residence with his lordship at Pisa in the years 1821 and 1822.

A Memoir of the Life of Peter the Great. (Family Library No XXXV.) London, 1832.

Mémoires d'un gentilhomme suédois, écrits par lui-même dans sa retraite. Berlin, 1788.

Mémoires secrets sur la Russie, et particulièrement sur la fin du règne de Catherine II et le commencement de celui de Paul I. Formant un tableau des mœurs de St-Pétersbourg à la fin du XVIIIe siècle. Amsterdam, 1800.

MERCIER, L. S. *Néologie*, ou Vocabulaire de mots nouveaux, à renouveler, ou pris dans des acceptations nouvelles. Paris, 1801.

[MÉRIMÉE, P.] *La Guzla*, ou Choix de poésies Illyriques. Paris, 1827.

MÉRIMÉE, P. *Mosaïque*. Recueil de contes et nouvelles. Paris, 1833.

— *Notes d'un voyage dans le Midi de la France*. Paris, 1835.

— *Théâtre de Clara Gazul*. Bruxelles, 1833.

MÉROVIR, PRINCE DES SUÈVES. *Le Palais de Scaurus*, ou Description d'une maison romaine. Paris, 1819.

MERSAN, D. F. MOREAU DE. *Pensées de Balzac* . . . Précédées d'observations sur cet écrivain, et sur le siècle où il a vécu. Paris, 1807.

MERTHGHEN. *Œuvres pastorales*. Traduites de l'allemand par M. le Baron de Nausell; suivies des Aulnayes de Voux, idylles françoises, par M. Le Boux de la Bapaumerie. Paris, 1783.

MÉZIÈRES, L. *Histoire critique de la littérature anglaise depuis Bacon jusqu'au commencement du dix-neuvième siècle*. Paris, 1834.

MICHELET, JULES. *Histoire de France*. Paris, 1833.

— *Histoire romaine*. Première partie: République. Paris, 1831.

— *Précis de l'histoire moderne*. Paris, 1832.

— *Précis de l'histoire moderne*. Bruxelles, 1834.

MICKIEWICZ, ADAM. *Konrad Wallenrod*. Petersburg, 1828.

— *Poezye*. Petersburg, 1829.

— *Poezye*. Paryż, 1828-32.

MIGNET, F. A. *Histoire de la Révolution Française depuis 1789 jusqu'en 1814*. Bruxelles, 1828.

Les Mille et Un Jours. Contes persans, traduits en françois par M. Petis de la Croix. Paris, 1766.

Les Mille et Une Nuits. Contes arabes, traduits en français par Galland. Paris, 1822-4.

MILLEVOYE, C. H. *Œuvres complètes*. Bruxelles, 1823.

MILLOT, C. F. X., ABBÉ. *Élémens de l'histoire de France, depuis Clovis jusqu'à Louis XV.* Paris, 1806.

MILTON, JOHN. *The Poetical Works of John Milton.* With explanatory notes and a life of the author by Rev. H. Stebbing. London.

— *Le Paradis perdu de Milton.* Traduction nouvelle, par M. de Chateaubriand. Paris, 1836.

— *The Poetical Works.* London, 1829.

— *The Works of John Milton.* With an introductory review by Robert Fletcher. London, 1835. [Bound with *The Poetical Works of John Milton.* London, 1824.]

MIRABEAU, V., MARQUIS DE. *L'Ami des hommes,* ou Traité de la population. La Haye, 1758.

MIRABEAU, G. H., COMTE DE. *Lettres du Comte de Mirabeau à un de ses amis en Allemagne.* Écrites durant les années 1786, 1787, 1788, 1789 et 1790. [Brunswick], 1792.

— *Mémoires biographiques, littéraires et politiques de Mirabeau,* écrits par lui-même, par son père, son oncle et son fils adoptif; et précédés d'une étude sur Mirabeau par Victor Hugo. Bruxelles, 1834.

— *Œuvres.* Paris, 1825-7.

MOHAMMED, BEN PIR ALI ELBERKEVI. *Exposition de la foi musulmane.* Traduite du turc... par M. Garcin de Tassy. Suivi du Pend-Nameh, poème de Saadi, traduit du persan, par le même; et du Borda, poème à la louange de Mahomet, traduit de l'arabe, par M. le baron Sylvestre de Sacy. Paris, 1828.

MOLIÈRE. *Œuvres de Molière.* Avec des notes de divers commentateurs. Paris, 1833.

— *Œuvres complètes.* Paris, 1826.

La Vie de M. de Molière. Paris, 1705.

MONTAIGNE, M. DE. *Essais.* Paris, 1828.

MONTANDON, C. H. *Guide du voyageur en Crimée.* Odessa, 1834.

MONTEMONT. *Lettres sur l'astronomie.* Paris, 1723. [Pushkin gave this book to his sister.]

MONTESQUIEU, C., BARON DE. *Œuvres complètes de Montesquieu,* précédés de son éloge, par d'Alembert. Paris, 1827.

MONTGOMERY, J. *A Poet's Portfolio;* or Minor Poems. London, 1835.

MOORE, THOMAS. *The Poetical Works.* . . . Complete in one volume. Paris, 1829.

— *Voyages d'un gentilhomme irlandais à la recherche d'une religion.* . . . Traduit de l'anglais par l'Abbé D. . . . Paris, 1833.

Moral Plays. Viz. 'Keep your Temper! or Know whom you marry', A Comedy; 'The Fate of Ivan', an historical Tragedy; And 'Miss Betsy Bull; or the Johnnies in Spain', a Melo-drama. By A Lady. London, 1832.

MORELLET, A., ABBÉ. *Mélanges de littérature et de philosophie du 18e siècle.* Paris, 1818.

MORGAN, S., LADY. *Mémoires sur la vie et le siècle de Salvator Rosa,* par Lady Morgan. Paris, 1824.

MORICE, É. *Essai sur la mise en scène depuis les Mystères jusqu'au Cid.* Paris, 1836.

MOSNERON, J. *Memnon ou le jeune Israélite*. Paris, 1806.

MULLER, G. P. *Voyages et découvertes faites par les Russes* le long des côtes de la *Mer Glaciale* & sur *l'Océan Oriental*, tant vers le *Japon* que vers *l'Amérique*. Amsterdam, 1766.

MULLER, J. *Histoire universelle*. Divisée en vingt-quatre livres . . . traduit de l'allemand par J. G. Hess. Liège, 1829.

MÜLLNER, A. *Dramatische Werke*. Braunschweig, 1828.

MURAVIEV, N. *Voyage en Turcomanie et à Khiva, fait en 1819 et 1820*. Paris, 1823.

MURKO, A. J. *Slovénsko-Némshki i Némshko-Slovénski Rózhni Besédnik*. Grádzi, 1833.

— *Deutsche-Slowenisches und Slowenisches-Deutsches Handwörterbuch*. Grätz, 1833.

— *Theoretisch-praktische Slowenische Sprachlehre für Deutsche*. Grätz, 1832.

MUSSET, A. DE. *La Confession d'un enfant du siècle*. Paris, 1836.

— *Contes d'Espagne et d'Italie*. Paris, 1830.

— *Poésies*. Bruxelles, 1835.

— *Un Spectacle dans un fauteuil*. Paris, 1833; 1834.

NAIGEON, J. A. *Mémoires historiques et philosophiques sur la vie et les ouvrages de D. Diderot*. Paris, 1821.

NAPOLÉON. *Précis des guerres de César* par Napoléon, écrit par M. Marchand à l'île de Ste-Hélène sous la dictée de l'Empereur et suivi de plusieurs fragmens inédits par Napoléon. Stouttgart, 1836.

NAVILLE, F. M. L. *De la charité légale*, de ses effets, de ses causes, et spéciale- ment des maisons de travail et de la proscription de la mendicité. Paris, 1836.

NEANDER, J. A. W. *Histoire de l'établissement et de la direction de l'église chrétienne par les Apôtres*. Traduite de l'allemand . . . par Ferdinand Fontanès. Paris, 1836.

NECKER, SUZANNE. *Mélanges*. Extrait des manuscrits de Mme Necker. Paris, 1798.

NEPOS, P. C. *Cornelii Nepotis Vitae excellentium Imperatorum*. Cum animadversi- onibus Ioh. Andreae Bosii. Lipsiae, 1806.

NICOLE, P. *Pensées* de Nicole de Port-Royal. Paris, 1815.

NIEBUHR, B. G. *Histoire romaine* . . . Traduit de l'allemand par M. P. A. de Golbéry. Paris, 1830-5.

NIELDON-GILBERT. *La Russie*, ou Coup d'œil sur la situation actuelle de cet empire. Paris, 1828.

NIEMEYER, A. H. *Grundsätze der Erziehung und des Unterrichts für Eltern, Hauslehrer und Schulmänner*. Halle, 1801.

NISARD, D. *Études de mœurs et de critique sur les poètes latins de la décadence*. Paris, 1834.

NODIER, C. *Examen critique des dictionnaires de la langue françoise*. Paris, 1829.

— *Mélanges de littérature et de critique*. Paris, 1820.

— *Mélanges tirés d'une petite bibliothèque*, ou Variétés littéraires et philosophiques. Paris, 1829.

— *Notions élémentaires de linguistique*, ou Histoire abrégée de la parole et de l'écriture. Paris, 1834.

NODIER, C. *Œuvres*. Bruxelles, 1832.

— *Questions de littérature légale*. Du plagiat, de la supposition d'auteurs, des supercheries qui ont rapport aux livres. Paris, 1828.

NOËL, F. J. M. *Dictionarium latino-gallicum*. Dictionnaire Latin-Français. Paris, 1825.

NOUGARET, P. J. B. *Histoire des prisons de Paris et des départemens*. Contenant des mémoires rares et précieux. Paris, 1797.

Nouvelle méthode, contenant en abrégé tous les principes de la langue espagnole, avec des dialogues familiers. Paris, 1764.

NUGENT, T. *Nouveau Dictionnaire de poche François-Anglois et Anglois-François*. Paris, 1823.

NUGENT, T., ET OUISEAU, J. *Nouveau Dictionnaire de poche Français-Anglais, et Anglais-Français*. Paris, 1828.

OLDECOP, A. *Nouveau Dictionnaire de poche Français-Russe et Russe-Français*. St-Pétersbourg, 1837.

O'MEARA, B. E. *Napoléon en exil*, ou‾L'Écho de Sainte-Hélène. Bruxelles, 1824.

ORLÉANS, DUCHESSE D'. *Mémoires, fragments historiques et correspondance de Madame la Duchesse d'Orléans*. Paris, 1832.

OSSIAN. *Ossian, fils de Fingal, barde du troisième siècle*. Poésies galliques, traduites sur l'anglais de M. Macpherson, par Le Tourneur. Paris, 1799.

OVERNAY, A., AND N. [Nézel], T. *Les Deux Réputations*. Comédie-vaudeville en un acte. Paris, 1825.

OVIDE. *Amours mythologiques*. Traduits des Métamorphoses d'Ovide par De Pongerville. Paris, 1827.

— *Œuvres complètes*.... Traduites en français ... par Le Franc de Pompignan. Paris, 1799.

— *Publii Ovidii Nasonis opera*. Parisiis, 1822.

OXENSTERN, A. G., COMTE D'. *Pensées de Monsieur le Comte d'Oxenstern sur divers sujets*, avec les réflexions morales du même auteur. Paris, 1756.

PAILLET-DE-WARCY, L. *Histoire de la vie et des ouvrages de Voltaire*. Paris, 1824.

PALAIOLOGUE, G. *Esquisses des mœurs turques au XIXe siècle*. Paris, 1827.

PALKOWITSCH, G. *Böhmisch-deutsch-lateinisches Wörterbuch*. Prag, 1820.

Panchatantra, ou Les Cinq Ruses, fables du Brahme Vichnou-Sarma ; aventures de Paramarta et autres contes. Le tout traduit pour la première fois sur les originaux indiens ; par l'Abbé J. A. Dubois. Paris, 1826.

PARIS, L. *Histoire de Russie d'après les chroniques nationales*. Paris, 1834.

PARNY, E. DE. *Œuvres complètes*. Bruxelles, 1827.

— *Mélanges*. Bruxelles, 1829.

— *Les Galanteries de la Bible*, suivies des Rosecroix, poëme en douze chants. Bruxelles, 1827.

— *Poésies érotiques*. Bruxelles, 1828.

— *Les Déguisements de Vénus et autres poëmes*. Bruxelles, 1828.

— *Œuvres inédites*. Bruxelles, 1827.

PASCAL, B. *Lettres écrites à un provincial*. Paris, 1829.

— *Pensées*. Paris, 1829.

PASSENANS, P. D. *La Russie et l'esclavage*, dans leur rapports avec la civilisation européenne. Paris, 1822.

PELLICO, S. *Des devoirs des hommes* . . . Traduit de l'italien . . . par Antoine De Latour. Paris, 1834.

— *Mes Prisons*. Mémoires de Silvio Pellico de Saluces, traduits de l'italien . . . par A. De Latour. Bruxelles, 1833.

— *Opere complete*. Parigi, 1835.

PELTIER, J. G. *The Trial of John Peltier, Esq.* for a libel against Napoleon Buonaparte, first consul of the French Republic at the Court of King's Bench, Middlesex on Monday, the 21st of February, 1803. London, 1803.

PERRAULT, C. *Contes*. Paris, 1836.

PERSE. *Satires*. Traduites en français par Sélis. Paris, 1822.

PESCHIER, A. *Histoire de la littérature allemande*, depuis les temps les plus reculés jusqu'à nos jours, précédée d'un parallèle entre la France et l'Allemagne. Paris, 1836.

PÉTRONE. *La Satyre*. Traduite en françois avec le texte latin. Cologne, 1694.

PHILIDOR, A. D. *Analyse du jeu des échecs*. Paris, 1820.

PICARD, L. B., ET MAZÈRES, E. J. E. *Les Trois Quartiers*. Comédie en trois actes et en prose. Paris, 1827.

PINDAR, P. [Pseud. of John Wolcot.] *The Works of Peter Pindar, Esq.*, with a copious index. London, 1826.

PIRCH, O. *Reise in Serbien im Spätherbst 1829*. Berlin, 1830.

Les Plaisirs de l'amour; ou Recueil de contes, histoires et poëmes galans. By La Fontaine, Doret, Gresset, etc. Tome premier. Paris, 1782.

PLANCHE, G. *Portraits littéraires*. Paris, 1836.

PLATON. *Œuvres*. Traduites par Victor Cousin. Paris, 1822-3.

POHL, K. *Theoretisch-praktische Grammatik der polnischen Sprache* mit Übungsaufgaben, Gesprächen, Titulaturen und den zum Sprechen nöthigsten Wörtern. Breslau, 1829.

POLIGNAC, J., PRINCE DE. *Considérations politiques sur l'époque actuelle*. Bruxelles, 1832.

POLLNITZ, K. L., BARON. *Lettres et mémoires*. Amsterdam, 1737.

POLLOCK, P. J. *Cours de langue anglaise*, ou Nouvelle Méthode pour apprendre promptement à parler et écrire correctement l'anglais. St-Pétersbourg, 1817.

POPE, A. *The Poetical Works*. With a Sketch of the Author's Life. London, 1825.

The Posthumous Works of a late Celebrated Genius, deceased. 'The Koran: or the life, character and Sentiments of Tria juncto in uno, M.N.A. or master of no arts.' [This has an ex-libris: 'This book belongs to Sprang's Circulating Library, of the Post Office, Tunbridge Town, under the direction of Matthew Stidolph.']

POTOCKI, A., COMTE. *Fragmens de l'histoire de Pologne*. Marina Mniszech. Paris, 1830.

[POTOCKI, J., COMTE.] *Avadoro*. Histoire espagnole. Paris, 1813.

— *Dix Journées de la vie d'Alphonse Van Worden*. Paris, 1814.

POTOCKI, J., COMTE. *Voyages dans les steps d'Astrakhan et du Caucase.* Paris, 1829.

POUJOULAT, J. F. *La Bédouine.* Paris, 1835.

Les Pourquoi et les parce que. Bruxelles, 1834.

POUSHKINE, A. *Il prigioniero del Caucaso.* Poemetto Russo di Alessandro Poushkine. Tradotto in Italiano da Antonio Rocchigiani. Napoli, 1834.

Précis des notions historiques sur la formation du corps des lois russes. St-Pétersbourg, 1833.

Précis historique de la destruction du Corps des Janissaires par le Sultan Mahmoud, en 1826. Traduit du turc par A. P. Caussin de Perceval. Paris, 1833.

Procès complet d'Émile-Clément De La Roncière, lieutenant au 1er régiment de lanciers, accusé d'une tentative nocturne de viol sur la personne de Marie de Morell. Paris, 1835.

Procès de Louis XVI, de Marie-Antoinette, de Marie-Elisabeth et de Philippe d'Orléans. Paris, 1821.

Procès fameux extraits de l'essai sur l'histoire générale des tribunaux des peuples tant anciens que modernes.

Procès Fieschi devant la Cour de Pairs. Paris, 1835.

La Promenade utile et recréative de deux Parisiens en cent soixante-cinq jours. Avignon, 1768.

PRUDHOMME, L. M. *Miroir historique, politique et critique de l'ancien et du nouveau Paris,* et du Département de la Seine. Paris, 1807.

PRZEZDZIECKI, A., COMTE. *Don Sébastien de Portugal.* Drame historique en prose en trois actes et cinq tableaux. St-Pétersbourg, 1836.

QUINET, E. *Ahasvérus.* Paris, 1834.

— *Napoléon.* Poème par Edgar Quinet. Paris, 1836.

R..., DE. *Don Manuel,* Anecdote espagnole. Par M. de R. Paris, 1821.

RABBE, A. *Résumé de l'histoire de Russie,* depuis l'établissement de Rourik et des Scandinaves, jusqu'à nos jours. Bruxelles, 1825.

RABELAIS, F. *Œuvres.* Paris, 1823.

RACINE, J. *Œuvres,* Paris, 1833.

RADCLIFFE, ANNE. *The novels.* Viz. 1. The Sicilian Romance, 2. Romance of the Forest, 3. The Mysteries of Udolpho, 4. The Italian, 5. Castles of Athlin and Dunbayne. Complete in one volume. To which is prefixed a memoir of the life of the author. London, 1824.

RAUMER, F. *L'Angleterre en 1835.* Lettres écrites à ses amis en Allemagne... Traduit de l'allemand par Jean Cohen. Paris, 1836.

REBOUL, J. *Poésies,* par Jean Reboul de Nîmes. Paris, 1836.

Recueil de pièces intéressantes concernant les antiquités, les beaux-arts, les belles-lettres et la philosophie. Paris, 1797.

Recueil de voyages au Nord. Contenant divers mémoires très utiles au commerce & à la navigation. Amsterdam, 1731-8.

RÉGNARD, J. F. *Œuvres.* Paris, 1802.

RÉGNIER, M. *Œuvres...* Précédées de l'histoire de la satire en France, pour servir de discours préliminaire, par M. Viollet-le-Duc. Paris, 1823.

[RÉGUINOT.] *Le Sergent isolé.* Histoire d'un soldat pendant la campagne de Russie en 1812. Ouvrage vendu au profit des Polonais. Paris, 1831.

REIFFENBERG, F., BARON. *Éclectisme, ou Premiers Principes de philosophie générale . . . Première partie. Section première.* Bruxelles, 1827.
— *Le Dimanche. Récits de Marsilius Brunck.* Bruxelles, 1834.
Relation des particularitez de la rébellion de Stenko-Razin contre le Grand Duc de Moscovie. La naissance, le progrez, & la fin de cette rebellion. . . . Traduit de l'anglois par C. Desmares. Paris, 1672.
Relation exacte et circonstanciée de la conduite de Tobie de Rocayrol, Lieutenant Colonel au service de S.M.I. & Colonel de S.M.B. Londres, 1753.
Religion Saint-Simonienne. Aux artistes du passé et de l'avenir des beaux-arts . . . Bruxelles, 1831.
Le Renard, ou Le Procès des animaux. Paris, 1803.
The Renowned History of the Seven Champions of Christendom, St George of England, St Denis of France, St James of Spain, St Anthony of Italy, St Andrew of Scotland, St Patrick of Ireland and David of Wales; and their sons. London.
La République de Platon, ou Dialogue sur la justice. Amsterdam, 1763.
Respublica Moscoviae et Urbes. Accedunt quaedam latine nunquam antehac edita. Lugduni Batavorum, 1630.
RICHARDSON, S. *The Novels. Viz. Pamela, Clarissa Harlowe, and Sir Charles Grandison. In three volumes. To which is prefixed a memoir of the life of the author.* London, 1824.
RICHTER, J. P. F. *Pensées de Jean-Paul. Extraites de tous ses ouvrages.* Paris, 1829.
RIGAULT DE ROCHEFORT. *Promenades à cheval, ou Manuel d'équitation à l'usage des gens du monde.* Paris, 1826.
RITCHIE, L. *The Library of Romance.* Edited by Leitch Ritchie. Vol. II: Schinderhannes, the Robber of the Rhine. By the Editor. London, 1833.
— *A Journey to St Petersburg and Moscow through Courland and Livonia.* London, 1836.
RIVAROL, A. DE. *Œuvres complètes.* Paris, 1808.
— *Esprit de Rivarol.* [Edited by F. J. M. Fayolle and C. de Chêndollé.] Paris, 1808.
ROBERTSON, W. *Histoire du règne de l'Empereur Charles-Quint,* précédée d'un tableau des progrès de la société en Europe depuis la destruction de l'Empire Romain jusqu'au commencement du seizième siècle. . . . Traduite de l'anglois par J. B. A. Suard. Paris, 1817.
RODD, T. *History of Charles the Great and Orlando,* ascribed to Archbishop Turpin. Translated from the Latin in Spanheim's lives of ecclesiastical writers; together with the most celebrated ancient Spanish Ballads relating to the twelve peers of France, mentioned in don Quixote; with English metrical versions, by Thomas Rodd. London, 1812.
ROGERS, [S.], CAMPBELL, [T.], MONTGOMERY, [J.], LAMB, [C.], AND WHITE, [H. K.]. *The Poetical Works of Rogers, Campbell, J. Montgomery, Lamb, and Kirke White.* Complete in one volume. Paris, 1829.
ROGERS, S. *Poems.* London, 1834.
Li Romans de Berte aus grans piés, précédé d'une dissertation sur les romans des douze pairs; par M. Paulin. Paris, 1832.

Le Roman du Renart, publié d'après les manuscrits de la Bibliothèque du Roi des XIIIe, XIVe et XVe siècles; par M. D. M. Méon. Paris, 1826.

Le Roman du Renart. Supplément, variantes et corrections. Paris, 1835.

RONSARD, P. DE. *Œuvres choisies.* Avec notice, notes et commentaires, par C. A. Sainte-Beuve. Paris, 1828.

ROSSET, F. *Les Histoires tragiques de nostre temps.* Lyon, 1666.

ROSSETTI, G. *Disquisitions on the antipapal spirit which produced the reformation;* its secret influence on the literature of Europe in general, and of Italy in particular. By Gabriele Rossetti, professor of Italian literature in King's College. Translated from the Italian by Miss Caroline Ward. London, 1834.

ROSSI, M. P. *Traité de droit pénal.* Bruxelles, 1829.

ROUSSEAU, J. B. *Œuvres.* Londres, 1749.

— *Œuvres.* Paris, 1820.

ROUSSEAU, J.-J. *Œuvres complètes* de J.-J. Rousseau, Citoyen de Genève. Paris, 1818-20.

— *Œuvres.* Correspondance. Lettres de J.-J. Rousseau et de Mme de la Tour de Franqueville. Paris, 1820.

— *Œuvres.* Correspondance. Lettres à M. du Peyrou. Paris, 1820.

RULHIÈRE, C. DE. *Histoire de l'anarchie de Pologne et du démembrement de cette république.* Paris, 1807.

— *Histoire ou anecdotes sur la révolution de Russie, en 1762.* Paris, 1797.

— *Œuvres posthumes.* Paris, 1792.

Sacontala, ou l'Anneau fatal. Drame traduit de la langue sanskrit en anglais, par Sir W-m Jones, et de l'anglais en français, par le Cit. A. Bruguière. Paris, 1803.

SAINT-FÉLIX, J. *Cléopâtre Reine d'Égypte.* Roman. Paris, 1836.

SAINT-FOIX, G. F. *Histoire de l'Ordre du S. Esprit.* Francfort, 1775.

SAINT-MARC-GIRARDIN. *Notices politiques et littéraires sur l'Allemagne.* Bruxelles, 1835-6.

SAINT-PIERRE, J. H. B. DE. *Œuvres complètes.* Bruxelles, 1820.

SAINT-RÉAL, C. DE, ABBÉ. *Œuvres choisies de l'Abbé de Saint-Réal.* Paris, 1819.

SAINT-SIMON, C. H., COMTE DE. *Doctrine de Saint-Simon.* Exposition. [By B. P. Enfantin and others.] Bruxelles, 1831.

SAINT-SIMON, L., DUC DE. *Mémoires.* Paris, 1826.

SAINTE-BEUVE, C. A. DE. *Critiques et portraits littéraires.* Paris, 1836.

— *Tableau historique et critique de la poésie française et du théâtre français au seizième siècle.* Paris, 1828.

— [See also under DELORME, Joseph.]

SALDERN, DE. *Histoire de la vie de Pierre III,* Empereur de toutes les Russies. Francfort-sur-le-Mein, 1802.

SALVANDY, N. A. *Histoire de Pologne avant et sous le Roi Jean Sobieski.* Paris, 1830.

SALVO, MARQUIS DE. *Lord Byron en Italie et en Grèce.* Londres, 1825.

SAVARY, A. J. M. R., DUC DE ROVIGO. *Extrait des mémoires de M. le Duc de Rovigo.* Concernant la catastrophe de M-r le Duc D'Enghien. Paris, 1823.

SAY, J. B. *Petit Volume contenant quelques aperçus des hommes et de la société.* Paris, 1818.

SCALIGER, J. J. *Scaligerana.* Coloniae Agrippinae, Apud Gerbrandum Scagen. 1677.

SCARRON, P. *Le Virgile Travesty en vers burlesques.* Lyon, 1728.

SCHABELSKI, A. *Voyage aux colonies russes de l'Amérique,* fait à bord du sloop de guerre l'Apollon, pendant les années 1821, 1822 et 1823. St-Pétersbourg, 1826.

SCHLEGEL, A. W. *Cours de littérature dramatique.* Paris, 1814.

SCHLEGEL, F. *Histoire de la littérature ancienne et moderne.* Traduite de l'allemand . . . par William Duckett. Paris, 1829.

SCHNITZLER, J. H. *La Pologne et la Russie.* Paris, 1831.

— *La Russie, la Pologne et la Finlande.* Paris, 1835.

SCHÖLL, M. S. F. *Histoire abrégée de la littérature romaine.* Paris, 1815.

SCHÖN, L. F. *Philosophie transcendantale,* ou Système d'Emmanuel Kant. Paris, 1831.

SCOTT, WALTER, SIR. *The Lady of the lake.* A poem. Edinburgh, 1810.

— *The Lay of the Last Minstrel.* A poem. London, 1811.

— *The Lord of the Isles.* A poem. Edinburgh, 1815.

— *Rokeby.* A poem. Edinburgh, 1815.

— *Œuvres complètes.* Romans historiques. Peveril du Pic, par Sir Walter Scott. Paris, 1824.

— *Chants populaires des frontières méridionales de l'Écosse,* recueillis et commentés par Sir Walter Scott, traduits de l'anglais par M. Artaud. Paris, 1826.

— *Œuvres complètes.* Traduction nouvelle. Woodstock, ou le Cavalier, Histoire du temps de Cromwell, année 1651; par Sir Walter Scott; traduit de l'anglais par A. J. B. Defauconpret. Paris, 1826.

— *The Prose Works.* Paris, 1827.

SCRIBE, A. E., AND MAZÈRES, E. J. E. *Le Charlatanisme.* Comédie-vaudeville en un acte. Paris, 1825.

SCRIBE, A. E., AND MELESVILLE, A. H. J. D. *Coraly, ou la Sœur et le Frère.* Comédie-vaudeville en un acte. Paris, 1824.

— *Le Confident.* Comédie-vaudeville en un acte. Paris, 1826.

— *La Demoiselle à marier,* ou la Première Entrevue. Comédie-vaudeville en un acte. Paris, 1826.

SÉDILLOT, L. A. *Manuel classique de chronologie.* Paris, 1834.

SÉGUR, L. P., COMTE DE. *Mémoires ou Souvenirs et anecdotes.* Paris, 1827; Bruxelles, 1826-7.

SÉGUR, P. P., COMTE DE. *Histoire de Napoléon et de la Grande-Armée pendant l'année 1812.* Bruxelles, 1825.

— *Histoire de Russie et de Pierre-le-Grand.* Bruxelles, 1829.

SEILER, A. *Kurzgefaszte Grammatik des Sorben-Wendischen Sprache nach dem Budissiner Dialekte von Andreas Seiler.* Budissin, 1830.

A Select Collection of Old Plays. In twelve volumes. A new edition with additional notes and corrections, by the late Isaac Reed, Octavius Gilchrist, and the Editor. London, 1825.

SENANCOUR, E. DE. *Isabelle.* Lettres. Paris, 1833.

SENANCOUR, E. DE. *Oberman*. Lettres. Paris, 1804.
— *Rêveries*. Paris, 1833.
SÉNECÉ, A. BAUDERON DE. *Œuvres diverses*. Paris, 1806.
SÉVIGNÉ, MARIE, MARQUISE DE. *Sevigniana, ou Recueil de pensées ingénieuses*, d'anecdotes littéraires, historiques & morales, tirées des lettres de Madame la Marquise de Sévigné. Auxerre, 1787.
SHAKESPEARE, W. *Œuvres complètes de Shakspeare*. Traduites de l'anglais par Letourneur. Nouvelle édition, revue et corrigée, par F. Guizot et A. P.
. . . précédée d'une notice biographique et littéraire sur Shakspeare; par F. Guizot. Paris, 1821.
— *The Dramatic Works of Shakespeare*. Printed from the text of Samuel Johnson, George Stevens and Isaac Reed. Complete in one volume. Leipsic, 1824.
SISMONDI, J. C. L. SIMONDE DE. *De la littérature du Midi de l'Europe*. Paris, 1829.
— *Histoire de la chute de l'Empire Romain et du déclin de la civilisation*, de l'an 220 à l'an 1000. Bruxelles, 1836.
— *Histoire des Républiques Italiennes du moyen âge*. Paris, 1826.
SMITH, [E.], AND DWIGHT, H. G. O. *Missionary Researches in Armenia*. London, 1834.
SMITH, HORACE. *Zillah*. Histoire juive, tirée des annales de Jérusalem . . . traduite de l'anglais par A. J. B. Defauconpret. Paris, 1829.
SMITT, F. *Suworow's Leben und Heerzüge*. Wilna, 1833.
SOLIGNAC, P. J. *Histoire générale de Pologne*. Amsterdam, 1751.
SOUTHEY, R. *Essays Moral and Political*. London, 1822.
— *The Poetical Works*. Complete in one volume. Paris, 1829.
— *Œuvres poétiques*. Traduites de l'anglais par M. B. de S. Roderick, Le Dernier des Goths, poème. Paris, 1820.
— *The Life of Nelson*. London, 1830.
SOUTZO, A. *Histoire de la Révolution Grecque*. Paris, 1829.
SOUVESTRE, E. *Les Derniers Bretons*. Paris, 1836.
SPINDLER, C. *L'Élixir du diable*. Histoire tirée des papiers du Frère Médard, Capucin. . . . Traduite de l'allemand par Jean Cohen. Paris, 1829.
STÄGEMANN, F. A. VON. *Historische Erinnerungen in lyrischen Gedichten*. Berlin, 1828.
STAËL-HOLSTEIN, A. L. G. DE, BARONNE. *Œuvres complètes* de Mme la Baronne de Staël, publiées par son fils. Paris, 1820.
STATIUS, P. P. *L'Achilléide et les Sylves de Stace*. Traduites en français par P. L. Cormilielle. Paris, 1802.
STENDHAL [pseud. M. H. Beyle]. *Le Rouge et le noir*. Chronique du XIXe siècle. Paris, 1831.
STERNE, L. *Œuvres complètes*. Paris, 1818.
— *Voyage sentimental*, suivi des Lettres d'Yorick à Éliza, par Laurent Sterne, en anglais et en français. Paris, 1799.
STRAHLENBERG, P. J. *Historie der Reisen in Russland, Siberien, und der Grossen Tartarey*. Leipzig.
STRUYS, J. *Voyages de Jean Struys, en Russie, en Perse et aux Indes*. Paris, 1827.

SUETONIUS, C. *Les Douze Césars*. Traduits du latin . . . avec des notes et des réflexions, par M. De La Harpe. Paris, 1805.

SWIFT, J. *The Works*. London, 1766.

SWIFT, J., BAGE, R., AND CUMBERLAND, *The novels of Swift, Bage, and Cumberland*. Viz. Gulliver's Travels, by Swift; Mount Henneth, Barham Downs, James Wallace, by Bage; Henry, by Cumberland. London, 1824.

Tableau de Paris. Amsterdam, 1782-9.

TACITUS, C. C. *Tacite*. Traduction nouvelle, avec le texte latin en regard; par Dureau de Lamalle. Paris, 1817-18.

TALLEMANT DES RÉAUX, G. *Les Historiettes de Tallemant Des Réaux*. Mémoires pour servir à l'histoire du XVIIe siècle. Bruxelles, 1834.

TANNER, J. *Mémoires de John Tanner, ou Trente Années dans les déserts de l'Amérique du Nord*, traduits sur l'édition originale, publiée à New York, par M. Ernest de Blosseville. Paris, 1835.

TAYLOR, J. *Unum Necessarium*. Or, The Doctrine and Practice of Repentance. Describing the Necessities and Measures of a Strict, a Holy, and a Christian Life. And Rescued from Popular Errors. London, 1655.

TAYLOR, T. *Memoirs of John Howard, Esq., F.R.S. the Christian Philanthropist:* with a Detail of his most extraordinary Labours in the Cause of Benevolence. London, 1836.

Tchao-Chi-Kou-Eul, ou L'Orphelin de la Chine. Drame en prose et en vers, accompagné des pièces historiques qui en ont fourni le sujet, de nouvelles et de poésies chinoises. Traduit du chinois par Stanislas Julien. Paris, 1834.

Théorie analytique des probabilités. [Paris, 1818?]

THÉRY, A. F. *De l'esprit et de la critique littéraires chez les peuples anciens et modernes*. Paris, 1832.

THIERRY, A. S. D. *Histoire des Gaulois,* depuis les temps les plus reculés jusqu'à l'entière soumission de la Gaule à la Domination Romaine. Paris, 1835.

THIERRY, J. N. A. *Dix Ans d'études historiques*. Paris, 1835.

— *Histoire de la conquête de l'Angleterre par les Normands,* de ses causes et de ses suites jusqu'à nos jours, en Angleterre, en Écosse, en Irlande et sur le Continent. Paris, 1830.

THIERS, L. A. *Histoire de la Révolution Française*. Liége, 1828.

THIESSÉ, L. *Résumé de l'histoire de Pologne*. Bruxelles, 1824.

THOMSON, J. *The Seasons*. Chiswick, 1820.

TIECK, L. *Le Sabbat des sorcières*. Chronique de 1459, traduit de l'allemand. Paris, 1833.

— *Œuvres complètes*. Contes d'artiste . . . Shakspeare et ses contemporains. Paris, 1832.

TILLY, J. P. A., COMTE DE. *Mémoires du Comte Alexandre Tilly* pour servir à l'histoire des mœurs de la fin du 18e siècle. Paris, 1828.

TOCQUEVILLE, A. C. H. M. CLÉREL DE. *De la démocratie en Amérique*. Paris, 1836.

TOLAND, J. *Le Nazaréen,* ou le Christianisme des Juifs, des Gentils et des Mahométans. Traduit de l'anglois. Londres, 1777.

TOLSTOY, J. *Essai biographique et historique sur le Feld-Maréchal Prince de Varsovie Comte Paskevitch d'Érivan*. Paris, 1835.

— *Lettre d'un Russe à un Russe*, simple réponse au pamphlet de Mme la duchesse d'Abrantès intitulé: Catherine II. Paris, 1835.

TOOKE, W. *The Life of Catherine II, Empress of Russia*. Dublin, 1800.

TOTT, F., BARON DE. *Mémoires du Baron de Tott, sur les Turcs et les Tartares*. Maestricht, 1786.

TOURNEMINE, P. *L'Oncle et le Neveu*, ou Les Noms supposés. Comédie-vaudeville en un acte. Paris, 1826.

TRENCK, F., BARON DE. *Mémoires de Frédéric Baron de Trenck*. Traduits par lui-même sur l'original allemand. Strasbourg, 1789.

Les Trente-Cinq Contes d'un perroquet. Contes persans, traduits sur la version anglaise. Par Madame Marie d'Heures. Paris, 1826.

TRESSAN, L. E. DE, COMTE, DUC DE LA VERGNE. *Œuvres*. Paris, 1822-3.

TROC, M. A. *Nowy Dykcyonarz to iest Mownik Polsko-Niemecko-Francuski*... Nouveau Dictionnaire Polonois, Allemand et François. Leipzig, 1764.

— *Nouveau Dictionnaire françois, allemand et polonois*. Leipzig, 1771.

— *Vollständiges deutsches und polnisches Wörterbuch*. Leipzig, 1772.

TROLLOPE, FRANCES, MRS. *Paris et les Parisiens en 1835*. Paris, 1836.

— *Domestic Manners of the Americans*. Paris, 1832.

ULLIAC-TRÉMADEURE, Sophie. *La Pierre de touche*. Paris, 1835.

VADÉ, J.-J. *Le Poirier*. Opéra-comique. La Haye, 1760.

— *Les Quatre Bouquets poissards*. ... Suite de la Pipe cassée. La Haye, 1760.

— *Il étoit tems*. Parodie de l'acte d'Ixion dans le ballet des élémens. La Haye, 1760.

— *La Nouvelle Bastienne*. Opéra-comique, en un acte, suivi du Divertissement de la Fontaine de Jouvence. La Haye, 1760.

— *Recueil noté de chansons de M. Vadé*. La Haye, 1760.

— *Les Troyennes en Champagne*. Opéra-comique en un acte. La Haye, 1759.

— *Le Confident heureux*. Opéra-comique en un acte. La Haye, 1759.

— *Jérosme et Fanchonette*. Pastorale de la Grenouillère, en un acte. La Haye, 1760.

— *Le Suffisant*. Opéra-comique. La Haye, 1758.

— *Le Bouquet du roi*. Opéra-comique en un acte. La Haye, 1760.

— *Lettres de la Grenouillère entre Mr Jérosme Dubois, Pêcheur du Gros Caillou, et Mlle Nanette Dubut, Blanchisseuse de linge fin*. Suite des 'Quatre Bouquets'. La Haye, 1760.

— *La Pipe cassée*. Poème épitragipoissardihéroïcomique. La Haye, 1760.

— *Le Rien*. Parodie des parodies de Titon et l'Aurore. La Haye, 1757.

— *Le Mauvais Plaisant*, ou le Drôle de corps. Opéra-comique en un acte. La Haye, 1759.

— *Airs choisis des troqueurs*. Opéra-comique.

— *La Fileuse*. Parodie d'Omphale. La Haye, 1760.

VALENTINI, G. W., BARON, *Traité sur la guerre contre les Turcs*. Traduit de l'allemand ... par L. Blesson. Berlin, 1830.

VALERIO, F. *Grammaire italienne*. Simplifiée et réduite à vingt-quatre leçons. Moscou, 1822.

VARIN, C. V., ET DE BIÉVILLE. *Phénomène ou l'Enfant du mystère.* Vaudeville en un acte.

VENDEL-HEYL, L. A. *Cours de thèmes grecs,* précédé d'une grammaire grecque. Paris, 1824-5.

VERA ET DE CUNNIGA, A. DE. *Le Parfait Ambassadeur.* Divisé en trois parties. Composé en espagnol par Don Antonio de Vera et de Cunniga. Leide, 1709.

Das veränderte Russland. Franckfurth und Leipzig, 1744; Hannover, 1739; Hannover, 1740.

VERGER, V. *Dictionnaire de la fable ou mythologie grecque,* etc. Paris, 1829.

VERGIER, J. *Œuvres.* Lausanne, 1752.

[VERRI, A.] *Les Nuits romaines au tombeau des Scipions.* Traduites de l'italien par M.F.G. Lausanne, 1796.

VICO, G. B. *Principes de la philosophie de l'histoire.* Traduits de la *Scienza nuova* de J. B. Vico. Paris, 1827.

VIDAILLAN, M. A. *Histoire politique de l'Église.* Paris, 1832.

Vie privée, politique et militaire des Romains, sous Auguste et sous Tibère. Dans une suite de lettres d'un patricien à son ami; traduites de l'anglais. Paris, 1801.

Vieux Contes. Pour l'amusement des grands et des petits enfans. Paris.

VIGÉE-LEBRUN, L. E. *Souvenirs de Madame Louise-Élisabeth Vigée-Lebrun.* Paris, 1835.

VILLEMAIN, A. F. *Cours de littérature française.* . . . Littérature du moyen âge, en France, en Italie, en Espagne et en Angleterre. Paris, 1830.

— *Cours de littérature française.* . . . Tableau du dix-huitième siècle. Paris, 1829.

— *Histoire de Cromwell,* d'après les mémoires du temps et les recueils parlementaires. Bruxelles, 1831.

VILLENEUVE-BARGEMONT, F. L., VICOMTE DE. *Histoire de René d'Anjou, Roi de Naples, Duc de Lorraine et C-te de Provence.* Paris, 1825.

Vision d'Hebal, Chef d'un clan écossais. Épisode tiré de la Ville des Expiations. Paris, 1831.

VOLNEY, C. F. *Œuvres.* Paris, 1825-6.

VOLTAIRE. *Correspondance inédite de Voltaire avec Frédéric II, le Président de Brosses et autres personnages.* Paris, 1836.

— *Œuvres complètes.* Paris, 1817-20.

— *Pensées, remarques et observations de Voltaire.* Ouvrage posthume. Paris, 1802.

— *Pièces inédites de Voltaire imprimées d'après les manuscrits originaux,* pour faire suite aux différentes éditions publiées jusqu'à ce jour. Paris, 1820.

— *Soirées de Ferney,* ou Confidences de Voltaire, recueillies par un ami de ce grand homme. Paris, 1802.

— *Tableau philosophique de l'esprit de M. de Voltaire.* Pour servir de suite à ses ouvrages, & de mémoires à l'histoire de sa vie. Genève, 1771.

VSÉVOLOJSKY, N. S. *Dictionnaire géographique-historique de l'Empire de Russie.* Moscou, 1823.

VULLIEMIN, L. *Essai historique sur l'Évangile.* Genève, 1828.

WALKER, J. *Walker's Pronouncing Dictionary, and Expositor of the English*

Language; in which the meaning of every word is clearly explained, and the sound of every syllable distinctly shown; exhibiting the principles of a pure and correct Pronounciation. To which are prefixed rules to be observed by the Natives of Ireland, Scotland, and London, for avoiding their respective peculiarities of speech. London, 1831.

WALPOLE, H., Earl of Orford. *Walpoliana.* Chiswick, 1830.

— *Reminiscences.* Written in 1788, for the amusement of Miss Mary and Miss Agnes B . . . y [Berry]; by Horace Walpole, late Earl of Orford. Chiswick, 1830.

WILKINSON, W. *Tableau historique, géographique et politique de la Moldavie et de la Valachie.* Paris, 1824.

WINKELMANN, J. *Histoire de l'art chez les anciens.* . . . Traduite de l'allemand. Paris, 1803.

XÉNOPHON. *L'Expédition de Cyrus,* ou la Retraite des Dix Mille. Ouvrage traduit du grec de Xénophon, par M.L.C.D.L.L., Maréchal des Camps & Armées du Roi. Paris, 1778.

YOUNG, E. *Les Nuits d'Young.* Traduites de l'anglais, par Le Tourneur. Paris, 1818.

ZSCHOKKE, J. H. D. *Histoire de la Suisse.* . . . Traduite de l'allemand . . . par J. L. Manget. Paris, 1828.

Foreign (non-Russian) reviews

BIBLIOTHÈQUE ACADÉMIQUE. Paris, 1810-11.

BULLETIN DU NORD. Journal scientifique et littéraire. Moscou, 1828.

THE ENGLISH REVIEW; or an abstract of English and Foreign Literature. Vols. I, II, III, IV, V, XV, XVI; for the years 1783, 1784, 1785 and 1790.

MONTHLY REVIEW. 1782.

LE PALAMÈDE. Revue mensuelle des échecs. Paris, 1836.

REVIEW BRITANNIQUE, ou Choix d'articles traduits des meilleurs périodiques de la Grande Bretagne . . . Bruxelles, 1830, 1831, 1833.

REVUE ÉTRANGÈRE de la Littérature, des Sciences et des Arts. Choix d'articles extraits des meilleurs ouvrages et recueils périodiques publiés en Europe. St-Pétersbourg, 1832, vols. I, II, III, IV. 1833, vols. V, VI, VII, VIII.

REVUE RÉTROSPECTIVE, ou Bibliothèque historique, contenant des mémoires et documens authentiques, inédits et originaux. . . . Paris, 1834-6.

SELECT BIBLIOGRAPHY

In preparing this edition no attempt was made to consult Pushkin's original manuscripts. All the translated material has been published in Russian in several editions, some of which are copiously annotated. Pushkin's letters have also been published in English, but the rest of the material in this volume is not available in full in any language other than Russian. Most of the books here cited are available at the British Library. (No place of publication is indicated for books published in the United Kingdom.)

I *Editions of Pushkin's works*

(A) COMPLETE

PUSHKIN, A. S. *Polnoe sobranie sochinenii.* Edited by M. A. Tsyavlovsky. 6 vols. 'Academia' edition: Moscow, Leningrad, 1936.
(This edition is fully annotated and well illustrated. It contains one or two items not included in the other Academy of Sciences editions listed below.)
— *Polnoe sobranie sochinenii.* Edited by M. Gorky, D. D. Blagoy, S. M. Bondi, B. V. Tomashevsky, etc. 16 vols. Academy of Sciences of the USSR: Moscow, Leningrad, 1937-49.
(Subsequent editions of Pushkin's works published by the Academy of Sciences are based on texts established in this edition. Volumes XIII–XVI which contain Pushkin's letters also include letters received by him. This edition is not annotated.)
— *Polnoe sobranie sochinenii.* General editor B. V. Tomashevsky. 10 vols. Academy of Sciences of the USSR: Moscow, Leningrad, 1949; 2nd edition 1956-8.
(The text of this edition is based on the Academy of Sciences edition of 1937-49. Volume VII contains Pushkin's critical writing; volume VIII his autobiographical prose, with notes by L. B. Modzalevsky; volume X his letters, with notes by L. B. Modzalevsky and I. M. Semenko. This is the most compact and fully annotated Soviet edition of Pushkin and is the basic text used by me for this edition.)
— *Biblioteka velikikh pisateley. Pushkin.* Edited by S. A. Vengerov. 5 vols. St Petersburg, 1907-11.
(Though outdated as a text, this edition provides some interesting illustrative material. It was one of the best-known editions in Russia before the Revolution.)

(B) SELECTIONS AND INDIVIDUAL WORKS

PUSHKIN, A. S. *Selected verse.* Introduced and edited by John Fennell. 1964.
(The 'Penguin' Pushkin, in Russian with a prose translation in English.)
— *Ruslan i Lyudmila.* 2nd edition. St Petersburg, 1828.
— *Kavkazsky Plennik.* St Petersburg, 1822, and St Petersburg, 1824.
(The latter contains a German translation of the poem.)
— *Evgeny Onegin.* Translated by Oliver Elton. New edition, revised by A. D. P.
Briggs. Everyman Russian Series, 1995.
(I have used this translation for quotations from this poem for, although by no
means perfect, it manages to preserve the flowing rhythm of the original.)
— *Eugene Onegin.* Translated and edited by Vladimir Nabokov. 4 vols. 1964;
revised edition, 1975.
(This translation is a labour of love but everything has been sacrificed to
verbal precision and the result is far from Pushkin's astonishing simplicity
and clarity of diction and from the limpid flow of his rhythm. The notes,
however, present an intriguing mosaic of Russian literary life in the nine-
teenth century and make good reading.)
— *The Complete Prose Tales.* Translated by G. L. Aitken, 1966; revised edition,
1978.
— *The Queen of Spades and Other Stories.* Translated by Rosemary Edmonds.
'Penguin Classics' edition. 1962.
— *Neizdanny Pushkin.* Edited by A. F. Onegin. St Petersburg, 1922.
— *Rukoyu Pushkina.* Edited by M. A. Tsyavlovsky, L. B. Modzalevsky,
T. G. Zenger. Academia, 1935.
— *Sovremennik.* Vols. 1-4 edited by A. S. Pushkin; Vols. 5-8 edited by V. A.
Zhukovsky, P. A. Vyazemsky, etc. St Petersburg, 1836-7.
(The B.L. has a bound photocopy of this publication.)

(C) PUSHKIN'S CRITICISM, DIARIES AND LETTERS

PUSHKIN, A. S. *Pushkin – Kritik.* Edited by N. V. Bogoslovsky. Moscow, 1950.
Reissued as *A. S. Pushkin o Literature,* Moscow, 1962.
(This is the nearest approximation to the present volume in Russian but
it deals more fully with Russian literature.)
— *Dnevnik (1833–1835).* Edited by B. L. Modzalevsky. Moscow, 1923.
— *Pisma.* 3 vols. Moscow, Leningrad, 1926-35.
(Volume I, 1815-25, and Volume II, 1826-30, edited and annotated by
B. L. Modzalevsky. Volume III, 1831-33, edited and annotated by L. B.
Modzalevsky. No more volumes published. This is the most com-
prehensively annotated edition of Pushkin's letters and is indispensable for
the following of his many personal allusions. The text and dating of the
letters have been revised in the later Academy editions.)
— *Pisma poslednikh let, 1834-1837.* Edited by N. V. Izmailov. Academy of Sci-
ences of the USSR: Leningrad, 1969.
(This supplements the edition of the letters by Modzalevsky listed above
and is fully annotated.)
— *The Letters.* Translated and edited by J. T. Shaw. 3 vols. Indiana Uni-

versity Press and University of Pennsylvania Press, 1963; new edition, University of Wisconsin Press, 1967-8.
(The notes in this edition are exceptionally good, telling one enough, but not too much.)
— *Pisma Pushkina i k Pushkinu* ne voshedshie v izdannuyu Rossiiskoy Akademiey Nauk perepisku Pushkina. Edited by M. A. Tsyavlovsky. Moscow, 1925.
— *Pisma k E. M. Khitrovo, 1827-32*. Edited by S. F. Platonov. Trudy Pushkinskovo Doma, no. 48. Leningrad, 1927.
— *Œuvres complètes*, publiées par André Meynieux. Préface de Henri Troyat. Tome I, Paris, 1953; tome III, Paris, 1958.
(Volume III. Letters and literary criticism.)
—*The Critical Prose of Alexander Pushkin*. Edited and translated by Carl R. Proffer. Bloomington, Indiana, 1970.
(This book reached the author when the 1971 edition was in the press.)

II *Biographical and critical works on Pushkin*

(A) BIBLIOGRAPHY

MEZHOV, V. I. *Pushkiniana*. St Petersburg, 1886.
BERKOV, P. N. AND LAVROV, V. M. (under the general editorship of B. V. Tomashevsky). *Bibliografiya proizvedenii A. S. Pushkina i literatury o nem, 1886-1899*. Academy of Sciences of the USSR: Moscow, Leningrad, 1949.
FOMIN, A. G. *Pushkiniana 1900-1910*. Leningrad, 1929.
— *Pushkiniana 1911-1917*. Leningrad, 1937.
DOBROVOLSKY, L. M., MORDOVCHENKO, N. I., and others. *Bibliografiya proizvedenii A. S. Pushkina i literatury o nem*. Pts. I-VII covering the years 1918-57. Academy of Sciences of the USSR: Moscow, Leningrad, 1952-60.
(This is a daunting record of the Pushkin industry in the Soviet Union.)

(B) COLLECTIONS OF ARTICLES, BOTH BIOGRAPHICAL AND CRITICAL

Pushkin i evo sovremenniki, materialy i issledovaniya, Issues I-XXXIX. Academy of Sciences of the USSR, 1903-30.
Pushkinskie mesta. Introduction by D. P. Yakubovich. Leningrad, 1936.
(Selections from Pushkin's works and from letters of his contemporaries.)
Vremennik Pushkinskoy Komissii. Edited by V. D. Bonch-Bruevich, etc. Issues I-VI. Academy of Sciences of the USSR: Moscow, Leningrad, 1936-41.
Pushkin v vospominaniyakh sovremennikov. Edited by A. L. Dymshits and D. I. Zolotnitsky. Leningrad, 1950.
(A very useful selection of contemporary reminiscences of Pushkin.)
A. S. Pushkin v Russkoy Kritike. Edited by V. Dorofeeva and G. Cheremina. Moscow, 1950.
(This includes a comprehensive selection of Belinsky's criticism of Pushkin.)
A. S. Pushkin 1799–1949. Materialy yubilaynykh torzhestv. Edited by S. I.

Vavilov, etc. Academy of Sciences of the USSR: Moscow, Leningrad, 1951.

Literaturnoe Nasledstvo. Issues 16-18 (on Pushkin), Moscow, 1934; issues 47-48 (on Griboedov), Moscow, 1946; issue 58 (on Pushkin, Lermontov and Gogol), Moscow, 1952; issue 59 (on Decembrist writers), Moscow, 1954; issue 91 (M. P. Alekseev on 'Russko-angliiskie svyazi'), Moscow, 1982. (These are invaluable collections of articles by leading Soviet scholars.)

(c) BOOKS ON PUSHKIN MOST FREQUENTLY CONSULTED

AKHMATOVA, ANNA. *Sochineniya.* Inter-language Literary Associates, 1968. (Vol. II contains articles on Pushkin's last tale – 'Of the golden cockerel'; on Benjamin Constant's *Adolphe* in Pushkin's work; on Pushkin's *Stone Guest*; and a short note on Pushkin's death. As with Marina Tsvetaeva's book listed below, it is particularly interesting to read of Pushkin's importance for a twentieth-century Russian poet.)

ANDRONIKOV, I. *Ya khochu rasskazat vam . . .,* Moscow, 1965. (This deals with the letters concerning Pushkin's last years written by the Karamzin family.)

ANNENKOV, P. V. *A. S. Pushkin. Materialy dlya evo biografii.* St Petersburg, 1873.
— *A. S. Pushkin v Aleksandrovskuyu Epokhu, 1799-1826.* St Petersburg, 1874.

ANTOKOLSKY, P. *Puti poetov.* Moscow, 1965. (Contains several essays on Pushkin.)

AVENARIUS, V. P. *Yunosheskie gody Pushkina.* St Petersburg, 1888.
— *Otrocheskie gody Pushkina.* Second edition. St Petersburg, 1891.

BACKÈS, J. L. *Pouchkine par lui-même.* Paris, 1966. (A very attractively illustrated, short book on Pushkin's life and work, which includes translations by the author into French of some of Pushkin's poems. The title is slightly misleading as the book is a biography not an autobiography.)

BALUKHATUY, S. D. (ed.) *Russkie pisateli o literature, XVIII-XX vekov.* Vol. I. Leningrad, 1939.

BARTENEV, P. I. *A. S. Pushkin. Materialy dlya evo biografii.* Moscow, 1855.
— *Pushkin v yuzhnoy Rossii.* Moscow, 1862. Republished *Russky Arkhiv* for 1913.
— *Rasskazy o Pushkine, zapisannye so slov evo druzey P. I. Bartenevym v 1851-60.* Edited by M. Tsyavlovsky. Leningrad, 1925.

BAYLEY, J. *Tolstoy and the Novel,* 1966. (Chapter I on Pushkin and Gogol.)
— 'Pushkin's Secret of Distance'. *Oxford Slavonic Papers,* New Series, Vol I (1968).

BEREZINA, V. G., etc. *Istoriya Russkoy zhurnalistiki XVIII-XIX vekov.* Edited by A. V. Zapadov. Moscow, 1966. (On Pushkin as a journalist.)

BLAGOY, D. D. *Tvorchesky put Pushkina, 1813–26.* Academy of Sciences of the USSR, 1950.
Tvorchesky put Pushkina, 1826–30. Moscow, 1967. (Monumentally detailed studies of Pushkin's work.)

BLAGOY, D. D. AND KIRPOTIN, V. Y. *Pushkin rodonachalnik novoy russkoy literatury*. Academy of Sciences of the USSR, 1941.

BLINOVA, E. M. *'Literaturnaya Gazeta' A. A. Delviga i A. S. Pushkina*. Moscow, 1966.

BLOK, A. 'O Naznachenii Poeta'. First published in *Vestnik Literatury*, No. 3 (1921).
(Speech made on the 84th Anniversary of the death of Pushkin, Petrograd, 11 February (29 January) 1921.)

COSTELLO, D. P. 'Pushkin and Roman Literature'. *Oxford Slavonic Papers*, Vol XI (1964).

EHRHARD, M. *V. A. Joukovski et le préromantisme russe*. Paris, 1938.

FRANK, S. L. *Etyudy o Pushkine*. Munich, 1957.

FREEBORN, R. *Turgenev: The Novelist's Novelist*. 1960.
(Deals with Pushkin's influence on later Russian novelists.)

GASTFREUND, N. A. *Tovarishchi Pushkina po Imperatorskomu Tsarskoselskomu Litseyu. Materialy dlya slovarya litseyistov pervovo kursa*, 1811-17. 3 vols. St Petersburg, 1912-13.

GESSEN, A. *Vse volnovalo nezhny um. Pushkin sredi knig i druzey*. Moscow, 1965.
— *. . . Moskva, ya dumal o tebe! Pushkin v Moskve*. Moscow, 1968.
(Among the weighty battalions of Russian' Pushkiniana, these two books stand out for exceptional sensitivity and lightness of touch.)

GESSEN, S. AND MODZALEVSKY, L. *Rasgovory Pushkina*. Moscow, 1929.

GIFFORD, H. *The Hero of his Time*. 1950.
(Chapter 2 on Griboedov's hero, Chatsky; chapter 3 on Evgeny Onegin.)
— *The Novel in Russia*. 1964.
(Chapter I on Pushkin.)

GINSBURG, L. *O lirike*. Moscow, Leningrad, 1964.

GROT, K. Y. *Pushkinsky Litsey (1811-1817)*. St Petersburg, 1911.

GROT, Y. K. *Pushkin, evo litseyskie tovarishchi i nastavniki*. Academy of Sciences, 1887.

IZMAILOV, N. V. *Pushkin v pismakh Karamzinykh, 1836-7*. Moscow, Leningrad, 1960.
(Very valuable documentation of the atmosphere which surrounded Pushkin's last years.)

KALAUSHIN, M. M. *Pushkin v portretakh i illyustratsiyakh*. Edited by D. D. Blagoy. Leningrad, 1951.

LEDNICKI, W. *Bits of Table Talk on Pushkin, Mickiewicz, Goethe, Turgenev and Sienkiewicz*. The Hague, 1956.

MAGARSHACK, D. *Pushkin*. 1967.

MAIKOV, L. N. *Pushkin, Biograficheskiye materialy*. St Petersburg, 1899.

MEYNIEUX, A. *Pouchkine homme de lettres et la littérature professionnelle en Russie*. Paris, 1966.
(A study which followed up A. Meynieux's French edition of Pushkin's letters and literary criticism.)

MITCHELL, S. 'The Digressions of *Yevgeny Onegin*: Apropos of some Essays by Ettore Lo Gatto.' *The Slavonic and East European Review*, Vol. XLIV, No. 102 (1966).

MODZALEVSKY, B. L. *Anna Petrovna Kern*. Leningrad, 1924.
(With special reference to Pushkin.)
— *Pushkin pod tainym nadzorom*. St Petersburg, 1922.
NOVIKOV, I. *Pushkin v izgnanii*. Moscow, 1951.
(A novel about Pushkin's southern exile.)
RAEVSKY, N. A. *Esli zagovoryat portrety*. Alma-Ata, 1965.
SHCHEGOLEV, P. E. *Duel i smert Pushkina*. Moscow, 1936.
(The best book on Pushkin's duel and death, combining a sensitive and balanced account of the events with the essential documentation.)
SIMMONS, E. J. *Pushkin*. 1937.
(An indispensable standard biography of Pushkin in English. It laid down the path which many have followed.)
SVYATOPOLK-MIRSKY, D. P., Prince. *Pushkin*. 1926.
(A short but characteristically perceptive account of Pushkin's life and work.)
TOMASHEVSKY, B. V. *Pushkin i Frantsiya*. Leningrad, 1960.
TROYAT, H. *Pushkin*. A Biography. Translated by Nancy Amphoux. New York, 1970. Original French version, *Pouchkine*, published in 2 vols., Paris, 1946.
(A very lively and readable standard life of Pushkin.)
TSVETAEVA, MARINA. *Moy Pushkin*. Moscow, 1967; reissued in England, 1977. Translated by J. Marin King in *A Captive Spirit: Selected Prose*. Ann Arbor, 1980; Virago, 1983.
(A touching personal account by a twentieth-century Russian poet of what Pushkin has meant to her.)
TSYAVLOVSKY, M. A. *Rasskazy o Pushkine*. Leningrad, 1925.
— *Kniga vospominanii o Pushkine*. Moscow, 1931.
TYNYANOV, YU. N. *Pushkin i evo sovremenniki*. Edited by V. V. Vinogradov. Moscow, 1969.
VEGNER, M. *Predki Pushkina*. Moscow, 1937.
VERESAEV, V. *Pushkin v zhizni*. 2 vols. Moscow, 1936; reprinted The Hague/ Paris, 1969.
— *Sputniki Pushkina*. 2 vols. Moscow, 1937; reprinted The Hague/Paris, 1969-70.
VICKERY. W. N. *Pushkin, Death of a Poet*. Indiana University Press, 1968.
WILSON, E. *The Triple Thinkers*. Twelve essays on literary subjects. 1952.
YATSEVICH, A. *Pushkinsky Peterburg*. Leningrad, 1935.
ZHIRMUNSKY, V. M. *Byron i Pushkin*. Leningrad, 1924; reissued Munich, 1970.
(A pioneer work, providing the fullest treatment of this subject.)
— 'On the Study of Comparative Literature.' *Oxford Slavonic Papers*, Vol. XIII (1967).

III *Original works by Pushkin's contemporaries, etc., referred to in the text*

ANGELOT, J. A. P. F. *Six Mois en Russie*. Paris, 1827.

BARATYNSKY, E. A. *Polnoe sobranie sochinenii*. Edited by I. N. Bozheryanov. 2 vols. St Petersburg, 1894.

BATYUSHKOV, K. N. *Sochineniya*. Edited by P. N. Batyushkov. St Petersburg, 1886.

BELINSKY, V. G. *Polnoe sobranie sochinenii*. Academy of Sciences of the USSR: Moscow, 1953.

— *Sochineniya Aleksandra Pushkina*. Edited by M. Polyakov. Moscow, Leningrad, 1949.

BESTUZHEV, A. A. *Sobranie stikhotvorenii*. Edited by G. V. Prokhorov with introduction and notes by N. I. Mordovchenko. Leningrad, 1948.

— *Polyarnaya Zvezda* (1822). Edited by A. Bestuzhev. St Petersburg, 1822.

BLAGOY, D. D. (Ed.) *Russkie Poety*. Antologiya v chetyrekh tomakh. Vols. I & II. Edited by D. D. Blagoy, etc. Moscow, 1965-6.
(This anthology has excellent short biographies of the poets included.)

BOWLES, W. L. *The Works of Alexander Pope*. Edited by the Rev. W. L. Bowles. 10 vols. 1806.

— *The Invariable Principles of Poetry*. 1819

BULWER-LYTTON, E. G. E., BARON LYTTON. *England and the English*. 2 vols. 1833.

BYRON, G. G. N., LORD. *Private Correspondence of Lord Byron*. 1824.

— *Correspondence of Lord Byron with a Friend*. Edited by the Rev. A. R. C. Dallas, 3 vols. Paris, 1825.

— *The Letters*. Everyman Library edition, 1936.

CATHERINE II OF RUSSIA. *Documents of Catherine the Great*. The correspondence with Voltaire, and the 'Instruction' of 1767 in the English text of 1768. Edited by W. F. Reddaway. 1931.

CHAADAEV, P. Y. *Œuvres choisies*. Publiées pour la première fois par le Prince Gagarin. Paris. 1862.

— *Sochineniya i pisma*. Edited by M. Gershenzon. 2 vols. Moscow, 1913-1914.

CHATEAUBRIAND, F. R. DE, VICOMTE. *Le Génie du christianisme*. 5 vols. Paris, 1802.

— *Sketches on English Literature*; with considerations on the spirit of the times, men and revolutions. 2 vols. 1836.

— *Essai sur la littérature anglaise* et considérations sur le génie des hommes, des temps et des révolutions. Standard French Works, vol. III. 1836.

CHÉNIER, A. M. DE. *Œuvres posthumes*. Paris, 1826.

CONSTANT DE REBECQUE, H. B. *Réflexions sur les constitutions, la distribution des pouvoirs et les garanties, dans une monarchie constitutionelle*. Paris, 1814.

— 'On the Liberty of the Press.' *The Pamphleteer*, Vol. 6 (1815).

CORNWALL, B. *The Poetical Works of Milman, Bowles, Wilson and B. Cornwall*. Paris, 1829.

DELVIG, A. A., BARON. *Stikhotvoreniya.* St Petersburg, 1829.
— *Stikhotvoreniya.* Leningrad, 1951.
DERZHAVIN, G. R. *Sochineniya.* 5 parts. St Petersburg, 1833-4.
DMITRIEV, I. I. *Sochineniya.* 3 parts. Moscow, 1818.
— *Vzglyad na moyu zhizn.* Moscow, 1866.
— *Pisma raznykh lits k I. I. Dmitrievu, 1816-1837.* Moscow, 1867.
— *Pisma I. I. Dmitrieva k knyazyu Vyazemskomu.* Edited by N. I. Barsukov. 2 vols. St Petersburg, 1897.
DOSTOEVSKY, F. M. *Rech o Pushkine proiznesennaya 8 iyunya 1880 goda v zasedanii Obshchestva Lyubiteley Rossyskoy Slovesnosti.* 1937.
FREDERICK II called the Great, King of Prussia. *Poésies diverses.* 1760.
GOGOL, N. V. *Pisma.* Edited by V. I. Shenrok. 4 vols. St Petersburg, 1902.
— *Sobranie sochinenii.* Introduction by N. L. Stepanov. 6 vols. Moscow, 1950.
— *Polnoe sobranie sochinenii.* Academy of Sciences of the USSR: Leningrad, 1951-2.
HAZLITT, W. *The Spirit of the Age.* 1825.
HERZEN, A. I. *Byloe i Dumy.* Leningrad, 1946.
— *My Past and Thoughts.* Translated by Constance Garnett, revised by H. Higgens. 4 vols. 1968.
HOBHOUSE, J. C., BARON BROUGHTON. *Recollections of a Long Life.* 6 vols. 1909-11.
HUGO, V. *Odes et ballades.* Paris, 1826.
— *Cromwell.* Paris, 1828.
HUME, D. *Essays and Treatises on Several Subjects.* 2 vols. 1825.
IRVING, W. *The Alhambra; or the New Sketch Book.* Paris, 1832.
KARAMZIN, N. M. *Istoriya Gosudarstva Rossyskovo.* 1st ed. 10 vols. St Petersburg, 1815-24. 2nd ed. 12 vols. St Petersburg, 1818-29.
KERN, ANNA. *Vospominaniya.* Edited by Yu. N. Verkhovsky. 'Academia.' Leningrad, 1929.
KÜCHELBECKER, V. K. *Lirika i poemy.* 2 vols. Leningrad, 1939.
— *Poeziya Dekabristov.* 1950.
LAMARTINE DE PRAT, M. L. A. DE. *Œuvres complètes.* 4 vols. Paris, 1834.
MILTON, J. *Le Paradis perdu.* Traduit en français . . . par le Vicomte de Chateaubriand. Paris, 1836.
MOORE, T. *Lalla Rookh.* An oriental romance. 1st ed. 1817.
— *Mémoires de Lord Byron.* Paris, 1830.
— *The Life of Lord Byron, with his letters and journals.* 1847.
MURAVIEV-APOSTOL, I. M. *Puteshestvie po Tavride v 1820 godu.* St Petersburg, 1823.
NEKRASOV, N. A. *Polnoe sobranie stikhotvorenii.* Moscow, Leningrad, 1931.
PÜCKLER-MUSKAU, H. L. H. VON, PRINCE. *A Regency Visitor.* The English tour of Prince Pückler-Muskau described in his letters, 1826-8. Edited by E. M. Butler. 1957.
PUSHCHIN, I. I. *Zapiski o Pushkine.* St Petersburg, 1907.
RADISHCHEV, A. N. *Puteshestvie iz St. Peterburga v Moskvu.* 1858.
— *A Journey from St Petersburg to Moscow.* Translated by Leo Wiener, edited by R. P. Thaler. Harvard University Press, 1958.

RAEVSKY, FAMILY OF. *Arkhiv Raevskikh*. Edited by B. L. Modzalevsky. 4 vols. St Petersburg, 1908-12.

ROUSSEAU, J.-J. *Émile, ou De l'éducation*. 6 vols. Paris, 1810.

RYLEEV, K. F. *Dumy, stikhotvoreniya*. Moscow, 1825.

SAINTE-BEUVE, C. A. DE. *Poésies complètes*. Paris, 1845.

SCOTT, WALTER, SIR. 'Character of Lord Byron.' *The Pamphleteer*, Vol. 24 (1813).

— *Woodstock;* or The Cavalier. 3 vols. 1826.

SCHLEGEL, A. W. VON. *Cours de littérature dramatique*. Traduit de l'allemand par A. A. Necker de Saussure. 3 vols. Paris and Geneva, 1814.

— *A Course of Lectures on Dramatic Art and Literature*. Translated by John Black. 2 vols. 1815.

SHAKESPEARE, W. *Œuvres de Shakespeare*. Traduites de l'anglais par Letourneur. 12 vols. Paris, 1822.

SIMONDE DE SISMONDI, J. C. L. *De la littérature du midi de l'Europe*. 4 vols. Paris, 1813.

— *Historical View of the Literature of the South of Europe*. Translated by T. Roscoe. 2 vols. 1846.

SOLLOGUB, V. A., COUNT. *Vospominaniya Grafa V. A. Solloguba*. Gogol, Pushkin i Lermontov. Moscow, 1866.

STAËL-HOLSTEIN, A. DE. *Considérations sur les principaux événements de la Révolution Française*. 3 vols. 1818.

— *Ten Years' Exile*. Translated from the French. 1821.

— *Mémoires de Madame de Staël* (*Dix Années d'exil*). Paris, Poitiers, 1843.

TANNER, J., called 'the Grey Hawk'. *Grey Hawk*. Life and adventures among the Red Indians. Retold by James Macaulay, 1883. Another edition, 1909.

— *An Indian Captivity, 1789-1822*. 2 pts. Sutro Branch California State Library Occasional Papers Reprint series, no. 20. San Francisco, 1940.

TOCQUEVILLE, A. C. H. M. CLÉREL DE, COMTE. *De la démocratie en Amérique*. 2 vols. Paris, 1835.

— *Democracy in America*. Translated by Henry Reeve. 4 vols. 1835-40.

TURGENEV, FAMILY OF. *Arkhiv brat'ev Turgenevykh*. 6 vols. Academy of Sciences, 1911-12.

(Vol. VI contains the correspondence of A. I. Turgenev with Prince P. A. Vyazemsky, edited by N. K. Kulman.)

VIGNY, A. V. DE, COMTE. *Cinq-Mars, ou une Conjuration sous Louis XIII*. Paris, 1855.

— *Cinq Mars*, or a Conspiracy under Louis XIII. Translated by W. Hazlitt. 1847.

VOLTAIRE, F. M. A. DE, *La Zayre*. Paris, 1733.

— *Voltaire's Correspondence*. Edited by T. Besterman. Geneva, 1953-65.

— *Correspondence inédite de Voltaire avec Frédéric II, le Président de Brosses et autres personnages*. Edited by T. Foisset. Paris, 1836.

— *Voltaire et le Président de Brosses*. Correspondance inédite suivie d'un supplément à la correspondance de Voltaire avec le roi de Prusse et d'autres personnages. Publiée par M. Th. Foisset. Paris, 1858.

VYAZEMSKY, FAMILY OF. *Ostafievsky Arkhiv Knyazey Vyazemskikh.* 4 vols. St Petersburg, 1899.
(This includes the correspondence of Prince P. A. Vyazemsky with A. I. Turgenev.)

VYAZEMSKY, P. A., PRINCE. *Polnoe sobranie sochinenii.* 9 vols. St Petersburg, 1878-84.

WORDSWORTH, W. *Poetical Works.* Paris, 1828; Paris, 1835.

YAKUSHKIN, I. D. *Zapiski, stat'i, pisma dekabrista I. D. Yakushkina.* Edited by S. Y. Shtreich. Academy of Sciences of the USSR: Moscow, 1951.

YAZYKOV, N. M. *Polnoe sobranie stikhotvorenii.* Edited by M. K. Azadovsky. Moscow, Leningrad, 1934.

ZHUKOVSKY, V. A. *Sochineniya.* Edited by A. D. Alferov. Moscow, 1902. Another edition, edited by P. V. Smirnovsky: Moscow, 1915. Another edition: Moscow, 1954.

IV *Books on the Romantic period in general and on Pushkin's contemporaries*

ALEKSEEV, M. P., AND MEILAKH, B. S. *Dekabristy i ikh Vremya.* Academy of Sciences of the USSR, 1951.

BABBITT, I. *Rousseau and Romanticism.* Boston and New York, 1919.

BADDELEY, J. F. *The Russian Conquest of the Caucasus.* 1908.

BAZANOV, V. G. *Ocherki Dekabristskoy Literatury.* Moscow, 1953.
(Part II deals with the work of Alexander Bestuzhev-Marlinsky.)

BOWRA, C. M. *The Romantic Imagination.* 1950.

BRUFORD, W. H. *Theatre, Drama and Audience in Goethe's Germany.* 1950.

CHASSÉ, C. *Napoléon par les écrivains.* Paris, 1921.

DAVIE, D. *The Heyday of Sir Walter Scott.* 1961.

DUBROVIN, N. T. *Istoria voyny i vladychestva Russkikh na Kavkaze.* 6 vols. St Petersburg, 1871-88.

GERSHENZON, M. O. *P. Ya. Chaadaev.* St Petersburg, 1908.

GROT, K. Y. *K biografii I. I. Dmitrieva.* Academy of Sciences of the USSR. 1902.

HERFORD, C. H. *The Post-War Mind of Germany, and other European studies.* 1927.

HEROLD, J. C. *Mistress to an Age.* A Life of Madame de Staël. 1959.

LANG, D. M. *The First Russian Radical.* Alexander Radishchev, 1749-1802. 1959.

LIRONDELLE, A. *Shakespeare en Russie, 1748-1840.* Paris, 1912.

MAZOUR, A. G. *The First Russian Revolution, 1825.* The Decembrist Movement: its origin, development and significance. University of California: Berkeley, 1937.
(An excellent account of the Decembrist movement.)

MERSEREAU, J. *Baron Delvig's 'Northern Flowers' 1825-32.* Literary Almanac of the Pushkin Pleiad. Southern Illinois University Press, 1967.

MOSKOV, E. A. *The Russian Philosopher Chaadayev, his Ideas and his Epoch.* New York, 1937.

OBOLENSKY, D. (ed.) *The Penguin Book of Russian Verse*. 1962.

PHILLIPS, W. A. *The War of Greek Independence, 1821-33*. 1897.

POTTO. V. A. (ed.) *Utverzhdenie russkovo vladychestva na Kavkaze*. Tiflis, 1901.

PRAZ, M. *The Romantic Agony*. Translated by A. Davidson. 1951.

RENNES, J. J. VAN. *Bowles, Byron and the Pope Controversy*. Amsterdam, 1927.

ROZANOV, I. N. *Pushkinskaya Pleiada*. Starshee pokolenie. Moscow, 1923. (On P. A. Pletnev and P. A. Katenin.)

SAKULIN, P. N. *Iz istorii russkovo idealizma*. Knyaz V. F. Odoevsky. 2 vols. Moscow, 1913.

SIMMONS, E. J. *English Literature and Culture in Russia, 1553-1840*. Harvard Studies in Comparative Literature, Vol. 12. Cambridge, Mass., 1935.

SIMMONS, J. S. G. 'Samuel Johnson "on the banks of the Wolga".' *Oxford Slavonic Papers*, Vol. XI (1964).

SMITH, L. PEARSALL. *Words and Idioms*: studies in the English Language. 1925.

STEINER, G. *The Death of Tragedy*. 1961. (Ch. 5 deals vividly with *Boris Godunov*.)

TALMON, J. L. *Romanticism and Revolt*. Europe 1815-1848. 1967.

TIEGHEM, P. VAN. *Le Mouvement romantique*. Paris, 1912.

— *L'Ère romantique*. Le romantisme dans la littérature européenne. (*L'Évolution de l'humanité*, no. 76, pt. 1.) Paris, 1948.

TURKEVICH, L. B. *Cervantes in Russia*. Princeton, 1950.

VENGEROV, S. A. *Kritiko-biografichesky slovar russkikh pisateley*. 6 vols. St Petersburg, 1886-1904.

VERKHOVSKY, Y. N. *Baron Delvig*. St Petersburg, 1922.

— *Poety-dekabristy*. Moscow, Leningrad, 1926.

VESELOVSKY, A. N. *V. A. Zhukovsky*. St Petersburg, 1904.

VILLEMAIN, A. F. *Cours de littérature française*. . . . Tableau du dix-huitième siècle. 4 pt. Paris, 1838.

VRANGEL, L. S., BARONESS. *Semya Raevskikh*. Paris, 1955.

WIMSATT, W. K. AND BROOKS, C. *Literary Criticism*. A short history. New York, 1957.

V *Short additional bibliography of books published since 1970*

ENGLISH TRANSLATIONS OF SELECTIONS AND OF INDIVIDUAL WORKS

PUSHKIN, A. S. *Collected Narrative and Lyrical Poetry*. Translated in the Prosodic Forms of the original by Walter Arndt. Ann Arbor, 1984. (This is an expanded version of the same translator's *Pushkin Threefold*, 1972.)

— *Selected Works* in two volumes. Translations by Irina Zheleznova and Avril Pyman. Moscow, 1974.

— *Eugene Onegin*. Translated by Charles Johnston. 1977. Penguin edition with an Introduction by John Bayley. 1979.

— *Mozart and Salieri*. The Little Tragedies. Translated by Antony Wood. 1982.

— *Narrative Poems by Alexander Pushkin and Michael Lermontov*. Translated by Charles Johnston. 1984.

— *Complete Prose Fiction*. Translated with an Introduction and Notes, by Paul Debreczeny. Stanford University Press, 1983.

— *Tales of Belkin*. Translated by Gillon R. Aitken and David Budgen. 1983.

LITERARY CRITICISM AND LETTERS

PUSHKIN, A. S. *Puskin–Kritik*. Edited by E. N. Lebedev and V. S. Lysenko. Moscow, 1978.

— *Perepiska A. S. Pushkina*. 2 vols. Edited by V. E. Vatsuro *et al*. Moscow, 1982. (This selection includes replies from Pushkin's correspondents.)

COLLECTIONS OF ARTICLES AND WORKS OF REFERENCE

ALEKSEEV, M. P. Editor. *Pushkin*. Sravnitelno-istoricheskie issledovaniya. Academy of Sciences, Leningrad, 1972 and 1984.

— *Vremennik Pushkinskoy Komissii*. Academy of Sciences, Leningrad, 1972.

CHEREYSKY, L. A. *Pushkin i evo okruzhenie*. Academy of Sciences, Leningrad, 1976. Second corrected and enlarged edition, 1988. (Biographical dictionary of 2500 of Pushkin's contemporaries.)

ISHCHUK, G. N. *et al*. *A. S. Pushkin i Russkaya Literatura*. Kalinin, 1983.

KUNINA, V. V. *Druzya Pushkina*. Perepiska; Vospominaniya; Dnevniki. 2 vols. Moscow, 1984.

MASHINSKY, S. I. Editor. *V mire Pushkina*. Moscow, 1974.

RICHARDS, D. J. and COCKERELL, C. R. S. Editors and translators. *Russian Views on Pushkin*. 1976.

VATSURO, V. E. *A. S. Pushkin z vospominaniyakh Sovremennikov*. 2 vols. Moscow, 1974.

BOOKS ON PUSHKIN, BOTH LIFE AND WORKS

ABRAMOVICH, S. L. *Pushkin v 1836 godu*. Academy of Sciences, Leningrad, 1984.

BAYLEY, J. *Pushkin*. A Comparative Commentary. 1971.

BRIGGS, A. D. P. *Alexander Pushkin*. A Critical Study. 1983.

DEBRECZENY, P. *The Other Pushkin*. A Study of Alexander Pushkin's Prose Fiction. Stanford University Press, 1983.

FEINBERG, I. *Chitaya tetradi Pushkina*. Moscow, 1981.

GESSEN, A. I. *Rifma, zvuchnaya podruga*. Etyudy o Pushkine. Moscow, 1973.

JAKOBSON, R. *Pushkin and his Sculptural Myth*. Translated and edited by John Burbank. The Hague/Paris, 1975.

LITVINENKO, N. *Pushkin i Teatr*. Formirovanie teatralnykh vozzreny. Moscow, 1974.

O'BELL, L. *Pushkin's Egyptian Nights*. The Biography of a Work. Ann Arbor, 1984.

RAEVSKY, N. *Portrety zagovorili*. Alma-Ata, 1974.

TERTS, A. (Andrey Sinyavsky) *Progulki s Pushkinym*. 1975.

VICKERY, W. N. *Alexander Pushkin*. New York, 1970.

INDEX

535